A

GENERAL INTRODUCTION

TO

𝔇𝔬𝔪𝔢𝔰𝔡𝔞𝔶 𝔅𝔬𝔬𝔨;

VOLUME II

A FACSIMILE REPRINT
PUBLISHED BY FREDERICK MULLER LTD.

A

GENERAL INTRODUCTION

TO

𝕯𝖔𝖒𝖊𝖘𝖉𝖆𝖞 𝕭𝖔𝖔𝖐;

ACCOMPANIED BY

INDEXES

OF THE

TENANTS IN CHIEF, AND UNDER TENANTS,

AT THE TIME OF THE SURVEY:

AS WELL AS OF

THE HOLDERS OF LANDS

MENTIONED IN DOMESDAY ANTERIOR TO THE FORMATION
OF THAT RECORD:

WITH

AN ABSTRACT OF THE POPULATION OF ENGLAND

AT THE CLOSE OF THE REIGN OF WILLIAM THE CONQUEROR,
SO FAR AS THE SAME IS ACTUALLY ENTERED.

ILLUSTRATED BY

NUMEROUS NOTES AND COMMENTS.

By Sir HENRY ELLIS, K.H. F.R.S. Sec. S.A.

PRINCIPAL LIBRARIAN OF THE BRITISH MUSEUM.

IN TWO VOLUMES.

VOL. II.

PRINTED BY COMMAND
OF
HIS MAJESTY KING WILLIAM IV.
UNDER THE DIRECTION OF
THE COMMISSIONERS ON THE PUBLIC RECORDS
OF THE KINGDOM.
1833.

Previously published by Command of
His Majesty King William IV
under the direction of
The Commissioners on the Public Records
of the Kingdom, 1833
This edition published by
Frederick Muller Ltd., Fleet St., London
1971

Reproduced and Printed by
Redwood Press Limited
Trowbridge & London

SBN 584 10926 1

INDEX

OF

PERSONS, MONASTERIES, &c.

ENTERED IN DOMESDAY BOOK,

AS HOLDING LANDS

IN THE TIME OF KING EDWARD THE CONFESSOR,

AND THROUGH LATER YEARS ANTERIOR TO THE
FORMATION OF THE SURVEY.

A.

A. *Norf.* 174.

A. [Ailmarus episcopus] *Norf.* 191 b. bis. 192, 192 b.
bis. 193, 194.

A. episcopus, *Norf.* 197, 198.

ABBATISSA [de Leofminstre], *Heref.* 180.[1]

ABEN, *Linc.* 341.

ABENDONE, Abbatia de, *Berks*, 58 b. *Oxf.* 154. 156 b.
Glouc. 166. *Warw.* 239.

ABET, 103 b.

---

[1] The Abbess continued to hold the land of this entry at
the time of the formation of the Survey. See the Index of
Tenants in Capite.

ABO, *Yorksh.* 371.

ABO, homo Heraldi Comitis, *Hertf.* 132 b.

ACCIPITRARIUS quidam, *Sussex*, 24.[1]

Accipitrarius, v. GODUINUS. SAUUINUS. WILLELMUS.

ACHEBRANNI S. Canonici,[2] *Cornw.* 121.

ACHESTANUS, *Norf.* 284 b.

ACHI, *Wilts*, 69 b. 73, 73 b. *Hertf.* 132. *Northampt.* 225 b. 228. *Warw.* 239. *Chesh.* 263 b. bis. *Clam. S. R. Linc.* 375 b. bis. *Suff.* 440.

ACHI unus liber homo, *Berks*, 62, 62 b.

ACHI homo Heraldi Comitis, *Cambr.* 196.

ACHI f. Siuuardi, *Linc.* 337.

ACHI huscarle Regis E. *Midd.* 130 b.

ACHI teignus Heraldi Comitis, *Hertf.* 138 bis, 142.

ACHI teignus Regis E. *Cambr.* 196. *Bedf.* 213, 213 b.

ACHIL., *Worc.* 177 b.

ACHIL liber homo, *Staff.* 248 b.

ACHIUS, *Suff.* 309, 438 b. 439 bis. 440.

ACHIUS liber homo, *Essex*, 91 b.

ACOLF tegnus, *Suff.* 354 b.   ⎫
ACOLFUS teinnus, *Suff.* 436 b. ⎬
  ⎭

ACULFUS liber homo Edrici commend. *Norf.* 154 bis.

ACUM, *Linc.* 344 bis.

ACUN, *Yorksh.* 307 b.

ADAM, *Hertf.* 134 b.[3]

ADELDREDA, Sancta, *Norf.* 159 b. *Suff.* 376 b. *v.* ÆDELDREDA. ÆLDREDA. ALDREDA.

ADELELMUS, *Kent*, 13.

ADELID, *Linc.* 368.

---

[1] He continued under-tenant of the same half hide when the Survey was made.

[2] The Canons of St. Keverne.

[3] He continued at the time of the Survey.

ADELINGI, *seu* ADELINGIA, Abbatia de, *Somers.* 91, 93,[1] 97.[1]

ADELIZ, *Bedf.* 217 b.

ADELO, *Yorksh.* 315 b.

ADELOLD, *Kent,* 1 b.

ADELOLDUS, *Kent,* 1 b.

ADELOLDUS teignus R. E. *Bedf.* 211.

ADELRIC, *Worc.* 177 b.

ADELRIC frater Brictrec [2] episcopi, *Heref.* 180 b.

ADELUUALDUS, *Somers.* 94.

ADELWOLDUS commendatus Edrici, *Suff.* 315 b.

ADEMAR, *Devon,* 104 b.

ADESTAN, *Somers.* 94. *Nottingh.* 286 b. 291. *Yorksh.* 326 b. *Linc.* 342, 347, 357 b. 360 b. 367 ter. 367 b. passim. 368. *Yorksh.* 374.

ADESTAN f. Godran, *Linc.* 337.

ADESTANUS commend. Vlsi, *Suff.* 282 b.

ADESTANUS teinnus, *Suff.* 298 b.

ADJUUAR', *Suff.* 396 b.

ADRET, *Dev.* 108.

ADSTAN, sub Heraldo, *Norf.* 148.

ADSTANUS, *Essex,* 25 b.

ADULF, *Heref.* 185 b.

ADULFUS, *Somers.* 92, 93, 94.

---

[1] In the two instances here noticed, the land had gone away from Athelney abbey before the Survey was made; in the first by exchange with the Earl of Moretaine, after the Conquest.

[2] Brictrec was Brihtegus, son to the sister of Wlstan archbishop of York. He was first abbat of Pershore; made bishop of Worcester in 1033; and died, according to Godwin, in 1038. He was a witness to the charter granted by Canute to Croyland Abbey.

Æchebrand, *Yorksh.* 301 b.

Ædelflete, *Dors.* 82.

Ædeldreda, Sancta, *Suff.* 413 bis. *v.* Adeldreda. Ældreda. Aldreda.

Ædgeua Comitissa, *Suff.* 300.

Ædi, *Suff.* 318 b.

Ædmær, *Devon,* 105.

Ædmundus presbyter, *Suff.* 431 b. bis.

Ædmundus S. [sc. de Bury] *Suff.* 321.

Ædricus, *Suff.* 284.

Ædricus grim. *Suff.* 293 b.

Ædricus liber homo commend. Edrici, *Suff.* 300.

Æduinus Comes, 241 b. *v.* Eduinus.

Ædwardus Rex, *v.* Edwardus.

Æduui, *Nottingh.* 284 b.

Ædwoldus, *Suff.* 424.

Ædwoldus liber homo Heroldi, et uxor ejus, commend. E. *Suff.* 347.

Ægeluuardus, *Suff.* 331.

Æileua, *Northampt.* 225.

Æilmar homo Leuuini Comitis, *Hertf.* 140.

Æilmarus de Ouu, *Bedf.* 213 b.

Æilmer, *Hants,* 41.

Æilmundus, *Leic.* 239.

Æilric, *Staff.* 249 b.

Æilric fil. Meriet, *Leic.* 234. *v.* Ælric, and Ailric, Marieti sune.

Æilricus, *Berks,* 60 b. *Staff.* 249 b.

Ælard, *Sussex,* 23.

Ældeua libera femina, *Berks,* 63 b.[1]

Ældid, *Shropsh.* 256 b.

Ældiet, *Worc.* 176.

,1 She held the same land when the Record of Domesday was made.

ÆLDIT, *Shropsh.* 255.

ÆLDRED, *Shropsh.* 260 b. bis.

ÆLDRED archiepiscopus,[1] *Glouc.* 167. *Yorksh.* 373 b. *v.* ÆLDREDUS. ÆLDRET.

ÆLDRED teignus R. E. *Hertf.* 133 b.

ÆLDREDA, Sancta, *Norf.* 162 bis. 162 b. *v.* ADELDREDA. ÆDELDREDA. ALDREDA.

ÆLDREDUS, *Hants,* 48 b.[2]

ÆLDREDUS archiepiscopus, *Worc.* 173. *Clam. in Chetst.* 376 b.

ÆLDRET, *Sussex,* 20. *Wilts,* 72 b.

ÆLDRET, archĭ. *Dev.* 103 b.[3]

ÆLFAG, *Nottingh.* 287 b. 292.

ÆLFEC, *Hants,* 41.

ÆLFECH, *Sussex,* 27. *Surrey,* 34.

ÆLFELMUS liber homo, *Oxf.* 157.

ÆLFER, *Suss.* 20. *Hants,* 41.

ÆLFERE, *Norf.* 244 b.

ÆLFETH, *Hants,* 40.

ÆLFLED, *Warw.* 239 b.

ÆLFLEDA, *Bedf.* 211.[4]

---

[1] See the former volume, p. 365. A purchase of land by him is recorded among the Clamores in Chetsteven :

" Archiepiscopus Ældredus adquisivit Lauintone et Schillintone cum berew. Harduic. de Vlf tope sune per pecuniam suam, quam ei dedit vidente Wapent. et postea viderunt sigillum Regis per quod resaisitus est de ipsis terris, quia Hilboldus eum dissaisierat de eis." Domesd. tom. i. fol. 376 b.

[2] He continued to hold his land when the Survey was formed.

[3] He is called, in the same folio, Eldred.

[4] She held the manor of Bolnhurst of King Edward. " Potuit dare cui voluit."

Ælfric, *Derb.* 273.

Ælgar, *Somers.* 88 b. *Shropsh.* 256 b. *Derb.* 274 b.
278 b. *Nottingh.* 280, 292 b. bis.

Ælger, *Clam. in Chetst.* 377.

Ælget, *Huntingd.* 206 b. 208.

Æli, *Shropsh.* 255.

Ælmær, *Shropsh.* 260. *Nottingh.* 287 b.

Ælmar, *Sussex,* 22 b. bis. *Surr.* 35, 35 b. *Heref.* 183 b.
Shropsh. 260. *Linc.* 339 b.

Ælmarus, *Surr.* 35 bis. *Berks,* 59 b. *Northampt.* 223.
Leic. 234 b. 235.

Ælmer, *Surr.* 31 b. *Hants,* 53. *Berks,* 57. *Somers.* 95 b.
Linc. 366, 368 b.

Ælmer homo Wluardi Wit, *Midd.* 130 b.

Ælmeri et fratres ejus, *Clam. in Chetst.* 377.

Ælmerus, *Dors.* 83.

Ælmerus episcopus, *Suff.* 379. *v.* A. Agelmarus. Ailm.
Ailmar. Ailmarus.

Ælmund, *Shropsh.* 258 bis.

Ælnod, *Hants,* 53. *Devon,* 106 b. *Worc.* 176. *Linc.*
346. *Clam. W. R. Linc.* 376.

Ælnodus, *Hants,* 40.

Ælric, *Shropsh.* 254, 259 b. *Nottingh.* 287 b. *Linc.*
347 b. *Clam. W. R. Linc.* 376. *Clam. in Chetst.*
377.

Ælric Meriete sune, *Clam. in Chetst.* 377.

Ælricus, *Heref.* 184 b.

Ælricus de burc, *Suff.* 347.

Ælsi, *Somers.* 88 b. *Worc.* 176 b. *Shropsh.* 256 b.
Nottingh. 284 b. 286 b. bis. *Linc.* 354.

Ælstanus, *Warw.* 243 b.

Æluert, *Somers.* 94 b.

Ælueua, *Sussex,* 23 b. *Oxf.* 157 b. *Shropsh.* 257.

ÆLUEUA Comitissa, *Nottingh.* 280 b.

ÆLUEUA mater Morcari Comitis, *Hertf.* } *v.* ALVEVA.
134 b. *Northampt.* 222.

ÆLUEUA libera femina, *Sussex,* 19.

ÆLUEUA quædam femina, *Worc.* 176.

ÆLUEUA homo Aschil, *Bedf.* 212.

ÆLUIN, *Nottingh.* 282 b.

ÆLURIC, *Heref.* 185 b. *Shropsh.* 257 b. *Derb.* 274 bis.

ÆLURICUS, *Heref.* 180 b.

ÆLUUACRE, *Hants,* 47. *Somers.* 95 ter.

ÆLUUARD, *Worc.* 174 b. 177. *Heref.* 181, 183. *Shropsh.*
255, 258 b. bis. *Chesh.* 266 b.

ÆLUUARD teinus Algari Comitis, *Worc.* 176.

ÆLUUARDUS, *Heref.* 184, 186 b. 187.

ÆLUUI, *Hants,* 49 b. *Glouc.* 170. *Worc.* 176 b. *Shropsh.*
257 b.

ÆLUUIN, *Yorksh.* 329.

ÆLUUINUS, *Somers.* 97 b. *Glouc.* 170. *Heref.* 180.
Shropsh. 256 b. *Yorksh.* 329 bis.

ÆLUUINUS cilt, *Worc.* 176.

ÆLWIUS, *Norf.* 177 b.

ÆLUUOLD, *Derb.* 277 b.

ÆLUUOLDUS, *Glouc.* 167 b.

ÆREFASTUS,[1] *Norf.* 197 b.

ÆRGRIM, *Shropsh.* 260 b.

ÆSTANUS canon. Heref. *Heref.* 182 b.

ÆTHELDREDA S. *Suff.* 414, 416 b. 417 b. 423 b. 424,
424 b. 427 b. 430, 431, 441 b. 442, 443, 443 b.
v. ÆLDREDA.

ÆTHERICUS, *Suff.* 314 b.

ÆTHESI commend. Guerti, *Suff.* 282 b.

---

[1] This was Arfastus who was made bishop of Elmham in
1070. He removed his see from Elmham to Thetford in
1075: and died in 1084.

ÆTMARUS teinnus Comitis Algari, *Suff.* 348 b.

ÆTNOD, liber homo commend. *Suff.* 420.

ÆTNODUS, *Essex*, 33.

AGELMARUS, *Essex*, 71 bis.

AGELMARUS episcopus, *Norf.* 193 b. *v.* A. ÆLMERUS.
AILM. AILMAR. AILMARUS.

AGELRED, *Kent*, 7.

AGELRICUS, *Dors.* 77 bis.

AGELUUARD, *Worc.* 174 b.

AGELUUARD et GODRIC, *Dors.* 82.

AGELUUARDUS, *Dors.* 83 b.

AGELUUARDUS prepositus Regis, *Suff.* 334 b.

AGEMUND, *Sussex*, 19, 19 b. 22.   *Hants*, 41 b. 48,
50 bis.[1] 50 b.[1] *Northampt.* 224. *Nottingh.* 284.[1]
Yorksh. 319.   *Linc.* 359 ter. 359 b. ter. 362, 371,
375, 376.

AGEMUND presbyter, *Linc.* 371 b.[2]

AGEMUNDUS, *Wilts*, 72. *Linc.* 341, 359 bis. 370 b.

AGEMUNDUS alter, *Hants*, 50.[2]

AGENULFI pater, *Wilts*, 68 b.

AGHEMUNDUS, *Hants*, 45.[2]

AGHETE, *Linc.* 361 b.

AIELUERT, *Dors.* 82 b.

AIFRIDE, *Yorksh.* 300 b.

AILAD, *Suff.* 413 b.

AILARDUS, *Dev.* 114 b.[3]

AILBERNUS liber homo, *Suff.* 375, 395.

AILBRIC, *Cornw.* 122 b.

---

[1] The lands of these entries were also held by Agemund
at the time of the Survey.

[2] The tenants of these three entries all continued to hold
their land when the Survey was made.

[3] He is called " Ailardus monacus" in the Exon. Domesday, p. 323.

AILBRIHT, *Cornw.* 122 b.

AILDEIG liber homo sub Guert, *Norf.* 271 b. bis.

AILET, *Northampt.* 220.

AILEUA, *Wilts*, 68. *Devon,* 109. *Warw.* 243 b.

AILEUA libera femina, *Berks*, 57.

AILEUA uidua, *Northampt.* 223 b.

AILHALLE, *Somers.* 94.

AILID, *Essex*, 71 bis. *Norf.* 232 b. 251 ter. 252 ter.

AILID libera femina, *Norf.* 250 b. bis.

AILID quædam femina, *Essex*, 69, 69 b.

AILID quædam libera femina, *Norf.* 252.

AILIDA, *Essex*, 30 b.

AILIET, *Derb.* 275. *Norf.* 263.

AILITH libera femina, *Suff.* 415 b.

AILM, *Cornw.* 121 b.

AILM' [episcopus] *Norf.* 192.

AILMAR, *Dors.* 82 b. bis. *Somers.* 94 b. *Dev.* 102 b.
    bis. 103, 106 b. 115 b. bis. 116 b. *Warw.* 242 b.[1]

AILMAR [episcopus] *Suff.* 379 b.

AILMARUS, *Surr.* 34. *Dors.* 82 b. *Devon,* 113. *Leic.*
    231. *Warw.* 241, 242 b. *Essex*, 71 b.[2] 72, 107.
    Suff. 356, 422.

AILMARUS commend. Edrico, *Suff.* 313.

AILMARUS Episcopus, *Norf.* 192, 192 b. 193 bis. 197
    bis. *Suff.* 331, 379, 379 b. 447. *v.* A. AILM. AILMAR.
    ÆLMERUS.

AILMARUS Episcopus Tedf. *Norf.* 191 passim. 191 b.

AILMARUS liber homo, *Essex*, 73 b. 76 b. 90 bis.

AILMARUS melc, *Essex*, 107.

AILMARUS presbyter, *Suff.* 284 b.

---

[1] The land of this entry was also held by Ailmar at the
formation of Domesday.

[2] In this instance the same person with Agelmarus.

AILMARUS teinnus regis E. *Essex,* 20, 72.

AILMARUS tennus, *Suff.* 302 b.

AILMER, *Dors.* 79 b. *Somers.* 96. *Devon,* 103, 110 b.
 114 b. 115 b. *Cornw.* 124, 125.

AILMUNDUS, *Warw.* 241.

AILOF, *Linc.* 365 b.

AILRED, *Warw.* 240 b.

AILRIC, *Somers.* 88, 94 b. bis. *Devon,* 106 b. bis. 109 b.
 Bucks, 148 b.[1] *Northampt.* 225. *Warw.* 242 b. bis.[2]
 Staff. 249 b. 250 b. *Linc.* 346.[3]

AILRIC f. Marsete, *Linc.* 337.

AILRICUS, *Glouc.* 164 b. *Worc.* 172 b.[4] 173, 173 b.
 Northampt. 226, 228 b. *Linc.* 370. *Essex,* 14 b.[5]
 Suff. 375, 441 b.

---

[1] Ailric also held the land noticed in this entry at the time of the Survey.

[2] In one of the two entries of Warwickshire, here referred to, Ailric likewise held when the Survey was taken.

[3] The Ailric of this entry is called " Alricus Marieti sune" in a charter of K. Will. Conq. confirming his gift of the manor of Dodinctone in Lincolnshire to the church of Westminster. MS. Cott. Faust. A. III. fol. 62. ÆLRIC Meriete sune occurs in the *Clam. in Chetst.* 377.

[4] He also held when the Survey was made.

[5] This entry is remarkable. " Keluedunam tenuit Ailricus T. R. E.—Hic supradictus Ailricus abiit in navale prelium contra Willielmum regem, et quando rediit cecidet in infirmitate. Tunc dedit Sancto Petro [Westmonast.] istud manerium, sed nullus hominum ex comitatu scit hoc nisi unus, et huc usque tenuit Sanctus Petrus tali modo hoc manerium, et neque brevem neque famulum Regis ex parte habuerunt postquam rex venit in istam terram." The Conqueror's own charter, however, confirming Kelvedon to Westminster, will be found in the Cottonian MS. Faust. A.

AILRICUS commend. Aschilli huscarli, *Suff.* 441 b.

AILRICUS commendatus Guerti, *Suff.* 282 b.

AILRICUS commendatus Saxo, *Suff.* 376 b.

AILRICUS deburc, *Suff.* 443.

AILRICUS liber homo Regis E., *Suff.* 376.

AILSI, *Devon*, 114 b.

AILUERD, *Staff.* 250.

AILUERT, *Dors.* 82 b. *Somers.* 94 b.

AILUEUA, *Dors.* 82 b.

AILUUARD, *Somers.* 94 b. bis. *Devon*, 107, 110 b. *Heref.* 185.

AILUUARDUS, *Somers.* 95 b. *Devon*, 103, 113 bis.

AILWARD, *Norf.* 247.

AILWI, *Suff.* 308.

AILWIUS de Tedforti, *v.* TEDFORTI.

AIMAR, *Devon*, 115 b.

AINAR et noverca ejus, *Linc.* 365 b.

AIOLF, *Devon*, 116.

AIRAF, *Hants*, 42.

AIRET, *Kent*, 1 b.

AISCHIL, *Nottingh.* 293.

AISIL, *Shropsh.* 257, 259 b.

AIULF, *Wilts*, 74. *Devon*, 115.

AIULF vicecomes, *Dors.* 83.

AIULFUS, *Somers.* 94. *Devon*, 109.[1]

AKI, *Suff.* 312.

AKIUS, *Suff.* 439 b.[2]

III. fol. 60. It recites, that Ailric's donation of the manor was confirmed by King Edward the Confessor, and so far refutes the traditional evidence recorded in the Domesday entry.

[1] He continued as an under-tenant of the land mentioned in this folio at the time of the Survey.

[2] The same person is also written Achius.

Ala liber homo commend. Mannio, *Suff.* 333.

Ala commend. Mannio, *Suff.* 336.

Alanus, *Suff.* 421.

Albani Sancti Ecclesia, *Hertf.* 135 b. *Bucks,* 145 b.[1]

Alberic, *Devon,* 109 b.

Albericus Comes, *Wilts,* 74. *Oxf.* 154, 156.

Albernus, *Suff.* 396 b.

Albertus dapifer abbatis de Ely, *Cambr.* 201 b.

Albertus homo abbatis de Ely, *Cambr.* 201 b.

Albertus Lothariensis,[2] *Bedf.* 216 b.[3]

Albrict, *Somers.* 98.

Albus, Aluuinus,

Albus, Oslac, *Northampt.* 220.

Albus, Vluuard,[4] *Hants,* 43 b. *v.* Uuit. Uuite.

Alcerl, *Devon,* 102 b. 103.

Alchel, *Yorksh.* 315 b.

Alchemont, *Yorksh.* 298.

Alchen, *Shropsh.* 258 b.

Alcher, *Devon,* 115 b. 116, 117.

Alcherio, *Devon,* 105 b.

---

1 Of nearly every manor belonging to St. Albans in these two counties it is said " *jacuit et jacet* in dominio Ecclesiæ." The manor of Henret in Berkshire, is mentioned as having been bestowed upon the Monastery by Nigel de Albingi or Albini. See Domesd. tom. i. fol. 59 b. This, of course, was in the time of the Conqueror. Nigel de Albini died in the third year of K. Stephen.

2 He is mentioned in a charter of Will. Conq. to the Abbey of Westminster. See the last edit. of Dugd. Mon. vol. i. p. 301.

3 He continued to hold Celgrave, the land here mentioned, with other property, in capite, when the Survey was formed.

4 He is called Wite in the Exon. Domesday, p. 116.

ALCHERL, *Devon*, 105 b. 106, 111.

ALCHETEL, *Yorksh.* 309 b.

ALCHIL, *Yorksh.* 324.

ALCOLM, *Yorksh.* 332.

ALCOLME, *Yorksh.* 332 bis.

ALCOT monachus, *Worc.* 174 b.

ALCUDE, *Linc.* 353 b.

ALDEBERTUS, *Dors.* 80.

ALDED, *Derb.* 275.

ALDEDA libera femina commend. E. de laxefella, *Suff.* 442.

ALDEN, *Northampt.* 226 b. ter. *Leic.* 231, 236. *Chesh.* 265 b. *Yorksh.* 301, 322 b. *Linc.* 344, 358. *Yorksh.* 373. *Suff.* 413.[1]

ALDEN homo Heraldi Comitis, *Bucks*, 150.

ALDENE, *Derb.* 276. *Nottingh.* 287 b. bis. *Yorksh.* 317 b. bis. 319, 319 b. bis. 321 b. 324 b. bis. *Linc.* 339 b. 340, 340 b. 341 b. 344, 344 b. ter. 348 b. 350 b. 356, 358, 358 b. bis. 369, 371. *Clam. in Chetst.* 377 b.

ALDENE et mater ejus, *Hertf.* 141 b.[2]

ALDENE et II. fratres ejus, *Linc.* 361.

ALDENE huscarl R. E. *Buck.* 152.

ALDENE presbyter, *Linc.* 336.[3]

ALDENE tope, *Linc.* 344.

ALDENUS, *Suff.* 412 b.

ALDEUUIF, *Yorksh.* 374 bis.

ALDGID uxor Grifin, *Warw.* 238 b.

---

[1] The Alden of this entry seems to have been the same person who in other of the Suffolk entries is termed Halden and Haldeinus.

[2] Aldene was still the under-tenant when Domesday Book was formed.

[3] He was one of the Lagemen of Lincoln T. R. E.

ALDI, *Shropsh.* 255.

ALDID libera femina, *Suff.* 446.

ALDIDA, *Somers.* 88 b.

ALDIET, *Shropsh.* 259.

ALDOLFUS, *Suff.* 340, 342 ter.

ALDRED, *Wilts,* 73 b. bis.[1] *Devon,* 117 b. *Yorksh.* 300, 320 b. bis.

ALDRED homo Morcari Comitis, *Buck.* 149 b.

ALDREDA libera femina, *Norf.* 174.

ALDREDA, Sancta, *Suff.* 381 b. 382, 382 b. 383, 383 b. 384, 384 b. 385, 385 b. 386, 386 b. 387, 387 b. 388, 388 b. *v.* ADELDREDA. ÆDELDREDA. ÆLDREDA.

ALDREDUS, *Somers.* 94. *Devon,* 117. *Glouc.* 165. *Essex,* 51.

ALDREDUS teignus R. E. *Hertf.* 139.

ALDREMAN, *Linc.* 342.

ALDRET, *Kent,* 14. *Hants,* 45. *Devon,* 108 b.

ALDVI, *Somers.* 99.[2]

ALDUIN, *Somers.* 92, 94.

ALDUINUS, *Hants,* 46. *Dors.* 83 b. 84 b. *Somers.* 98 b. *Oxf.* 160. *Glouc.* 167 b. *Suff.* 377.

ALDUINUS liber homo Stigandi, *Norf.* 259 b.

ALDULF, *Dev.* 108 b. *Yorksh.* 329. *Norf.* 229.

ALDULFUS, *Yorksh.* 298. *Suff.* 340, 342.

ALEBRIC, *Devon,* 108, 109 b. 110 passim.

ALEBRIX, *Devon,* 110 passim.

ALESTAN, *Sussex,* 18 b. *Hants,* 39, 47. *Berks,* 61. *Dors.* 80 b. *Somers.* 92 b. 94. *Dev.* 117 bis. 118 passim. *Cornw.* 121 b. bis. 138 b. *Glouc.* 166 b. bis. 167.

---

[1] In both instances Aldred continued to hold when the Survey was taken.

[2] He continued to hold this land at the time of the Survey.

Chesh. 266 b. *Yorksh.* 324. *Linc.* 365 b. bis. 368 passim. *Norf.* 146. *Suff.* 320.

ALESTAN liber homo commend. Vlueue, *Suff.* 323 b.

ALESTAN prepositus London, *Kent,* fol. 2 b.

ALESTAN teinnus Heroldi, *Heref.* 181 b.

ALESTANUS, *Dors.* 80 b. passim. *Bedf.* 214. *Essex,* 63 b. 67 b. 75, 84 b. 85 b. 155. *Norf.* 256 b. *Suff.* 441 b.

ALESTANUS liber homo, *Essex,* 64, 71 b. 72 b. 102.

ALESTANUS teinnus, *Suff.* 420 b. 421.

ALESTANUS teignus R. E., *Hertf.* 138 b.

ALEUESDEF, *Devon,* 112 b.

ALFA, *Nottingh.* 292 b.

ALFAC, *Suff.* 299 b.

ALFAG, *Nottingh.* 288.

ALFAH, *Buck.* 145 b.

ALFAH unus liber homo, *Buck.* 147.

ALFAHCUS, *Buck.* 144.

ALFEG, *Cornw.* 123 b. 125.

ALFEGA, *Essex,* 81.

ALFEIH, *Norf.* 190 b.

ALFER, *Kent,* 4. *Sussex,* 21 b. 22 b. *Dev.* 115. *Glouc.* 167.

ALFERD, *Yorksh.* 301.

ALFERD, Eduinus, *Leic.* 234 b.

ALFERE, *Norf.* 126.

ALFERE liber homo, *Norf.* 265 b. 269.

ALFERE tegnus Heroldi, *Norf.* 244.

ALFERUS, *Norf.* 120 b.

ALFGERUS liber homo, *Suff.* 288 b.

ALFHILLA, *Somers.* 90 b. *Devon,* 118 b.[1]

---

[1] She held the land mentioned in this folio in capite when the Survey was taken.

ALFIDIS vir, *Wilts,* 74.

ALFIT, Goduinus, homo Wigoti, *Midd.* 129.

ALFLED, *Surrey,* 31 b.

ALFLEDA, *Suff.* 321 b.

ALFLEDA libera femina commend. Heroldi, *Suff.* 348.

ALFLET, *Suff.* 321 b. *Devon,* 115. *Hertf.* 137 b. *Cambr.* 198.

ALFLET libera femina, *Norf.* 161. *Suff.* 309.

ALFLET commendata Haroldo, *Suff.* 351 bis.

ALFNOD, *Suff.* 432.

ALFRIC, *Worc.* 174 b. bis.

ALFRICUS, *Berks.* 58 b. *Norf.* 146 b.

ALFRIZ liber homo Stigandi, *Norf.* 246 b. bis.

ALFSI, *Suff.* 320.

ALFTRED quedam femina, *Essex,* 9 b.

ALFUUINUS frater Gode, *Suff.* 334 b.

ALGAR, *Sussex,* 19 b. 22. *Hants,* 46, 48, 51, 51 b. 53. *Berks,* 60. *Wilts,* 66, 72 b. bis. 73 b. 74 bis. *Dors.* 77, 80, 84. *Somers.* 88 ter. 90, 91 b. 92 b. ter. 93 bis. 94, 94 b. 95, 95 b. passim. 96 b. *Devon,* 102 b. bis. 103 passim. 106 ter. 106 b. 109 passim. 110, 110 b. bis. 111, 111 b. bis. 112 b. 113, 114, 118 b. bis.[1] *Cornw.* 121, 121 b. 122, 124. *Oxf.* 160. *Glouc.* 165 bis. *Worc.* 175. *Northampt.* 225, 226 b. 228. *Leic.* 236 b. *Shropsh.* 256, 257, 257 b. bis. 259 bis. *Derb.* 272 b. 273. *Nottingh.* 286. *Linc.* 342 b. bis. 343, 357, 367 b. bis. 371. *Clam. in Chetst.* 377 b. *Suff.* 355. *v.* ALGARUS.

ALGAR Comes,[2] *Oxf.* 154 bis. *Cambr.* 193 passim. 193 b.

---

[1] In both of these entries Algar appears also to have held at the time of the Survey.

[2] Algar Earl of Mercia, the son of Leofric and the Lady Godiva. He succeeded to the earldom of Mercia in 1057.

bis. *Northampt.* 222 passim. *Warw.* 241 b. 244 bis. *Staff.* 246 b. passim. 247 b. 248 ter. 248 b. 249 b. bis. *Derb.* 272 b. bis. 273. *Nottingh.* 281 b. 292. *Linc.* 338 passim. 348 b. bis. 351 b. *v.* ALGARUS Comes.

ALGAR homo Eddid Reginæ, *Bedf.* 216 b.

ALGAR homo Regis Edwardi, *Midd.* 130 b.

ALGAR homo Heraldi Comitis, *Midd.* 130 b.

ALGAR homo Stigandi archiepiscopi, *Cambr.* 198.

ALGAR homo Wigar, *Hertf.* 140 bis.

ALGARUS, *Wilts,* 69 b. 73. *Oxf.* 155 b. *Linc.* 368.[1] *Essex,* 40 b. 41, 74, 80 b. 102. *Norf.* 173. *Suff.* 289 b. 314, 342 b. 377 b. 386, 402.

ALGARUS Comes, *Midd.* 130 bis. *Buck.* 152 b. bis. *Cambr.* 189 b. 190 ter. 193, 196 bis. 109. *Hunt.* 203 b. *Northampt.* 220. *Staff.* 246 bis. 246 b. passim. *Essex,* 3 b. 4 bis. 21 b. bis. 36 b. 96 b. 98. *Norf.* 195. *Suff.* 421 b. 438 b.

ALGARUS commendatus Ailwardo preposito Regis, *Suff.* 333.

ALGARUS commend. Sc̃o Edmundo, *Suff.* 380.

ALGARUS commend. Edrici, *Suff.* 320 b.

He had previously succeeded Harold as Earl of the East Angles in 1053. He was banished by King Edward in 1055; and again after he became Earl of Mercia in 1058. By the help of Grifin Prince of Wales, and the Norwegian fleet, he re-obtained his earldom of Mercia, but died in 1059, leaving Edwin and Morcar his sons. See Sim. Dun. Script. x. Twysd. col. 189. Ingulphus, ed. Gale, p. 66. Dugd. Bar. tom. i. p. 10.

[1] He was here, sub-tenant of the same land, when Domesday was formed.

ALGARUS liber homo, *Essex*, 24, 64 b.

ALGARUS liber homo Heroldi, *Norf.* 129 b. 263.

ALGARUS liber homo sub Stigando, *Norf.* 177 b. *Suff.* 438.

ALGARUS tennus Regis E. *Suff.* 338 b.

ALGARUS teinnus Stigandi, *Norf.* 152 b.

ALGERUS, *Norf.* 263 b. *Suff.* 440.

ALGOD, *Nottingh.* 288.

ALGRIM, *Yorksh.* 298.

ALHAM, Edricus de, *Kent*, 11 b.

ALID libera femina, *Norf.* 250 b.

ALIET, *Warw.* 240.

ALLEF, *Linc.* 349 b.

ALLI, *Northampt.* 223. *Staff.* 250 b.

ALLI huscarl R. E. *Buck.* 152 b.

ALLI teignus R. E. *Buck.* 145 b. *Bedf.* 217, 218 b.

ALLIC, *Wilts*, 74. *Hunt.* 205 b.

ALLRIC et nepos ejus, *Hants*, 53 b.[1]

ALMÆR, *Somers.* 92 b. *Devon*, 106 b. 110 b. 114 b.

ALMÆR " antecessor Thomæ archiepiscopi."[2] *Yorksh.* 375 b. bis.

ALMÆR homo Alurici blac, *Hertf.* 133.

ALMÆRUS, *Surr.* 35. *Dors.* 83 b.

ALMÆRUS homo Aschil, *Bedf.* 213 b.

ALMAR, *Sussex*, 21 b. 23. *Surr.* 35 b. bis. *Hants*, 39 b. *Bucks*, 59, 61. *Dors.* 77 b. 79 b. 80 b. bis. 84, 84 b. *Somers.* 90, 93 b. 94, 94 b. 95 b. 96 b. 97 b. bis.

---

[1] " Tenuerunt in alod. de rege E." They held the same land as tenants in capite when the Survey was taken.

[2] That is, simply, the person who preceded the archbishop in the possession of the land. Thomas's predecessor in the *See* was archbishop Aldred, who has been noticed in p. 5.

Devon, 107 passim. 107 b. 108 bis. 111, 114,
114 b. 116 bis. 117 b. 118 bis. *Cornw*. 122 b.
124 b.[1] *Oxf*. 161. *Suff*. 297.

ALMAR homo Asgari stalre, *Hertf*. 134 b.

ALMAR homo Brictrici, *Buck*. 150 bis.

ALMAR homo Heraldi Comitis, *Buck*. 146 b.

ALMAR teignus R. E. *Cambr*. 201 b.

ALMARI pater, *Bedf*. 218.

ALMARUS, *Surr*. 35. *Wilts*, 71 b. bis. 73. *Dors*. 80,
83 b. *Somers*. 89, 93. *Cambr*. 194 passim.[2] 198 b.
Northampt. 220 bis. 223 b. *Warw*. 241 b. *Staff*.
248. *Essex*, 32. *Norf*. 196, 200, 211. *Suff*. 285 bis.
321, 340 ter. 341 b. bis. 343, 379 b. 426 b.

ALMARUS alter, *Suff*. 340.

ALMARUS commend. Eilrici de Burg, *Suff*. 413.

ALMARUS commendatus Abb. Ely, *Suff*. 375.

ALMARUS [episcopus], *Norf*. 194, 194 b. bis.

ALMARUS episcopus,[3] *Norf*. 159 bis. 175 b. 196, 198 b.
199. *Suff*. 379 b. *v*. AILMARUS. ÆLMARUS.

ALMARUS frater Stigandi, *Norf*. 195.

---

[1] He continued to hold under the Earl of Moretaine at
the time of the Survey.

[2] Once he is entered as continuing to hold at the time of
the Survey.

[3] Egelmar, Ethelmar, or Ailmar, brother of Stigand, succeeded him in the bishoprick of Elmham in 1047. He was
deprived by the synod held at Winchester in 1070. Her-
bert de Losinga, when at Rome, in 1093, is stated to have
obtained leave to remove the see of Thetford to Norwich :
but that Norwich was designed for the seat of the bishoprick at an earlier day, is evident from a passage in the
Domesday Survey, tom. ii. fol. 117, in which King William
the Conqueror is expressly said to have given fourteen
mansuræ to Ailmar " ad principalem sedem Episcopatus."

ALMARUS homo Alurici de Flicteuite, *Bedf.* 214 b.

ALMARUS homo Guert comitis, *Hertf.* 138.

ALMARUS homo Roberti f. Wim̃. *Cambr.* 197 b.

ALMARUS homo Tosti comitis, *Bedf.* 216 b.

ALMARUS homo Vlmari, *Bedf.* 218.

ALMARUS homo Wallef, *Cambr.* 197 b.

ALMARUS homo Wallef comitis, *Cambr.* 193, 193 b.

ALMARUS liber homo, *Ess.* 33 b. *Norf.* 159 b.

ALMARUS liber homo commend. Edrici, *Suff.* 388.

ALMARUS liber homo sub Stigando, *Norf.* 177 b.

ALMARUS teignus regis E. *Bedf.* 217.

ALMER, *Sussex,* 21 b. *Surr.* 35 b. *Somers.* 96 b. *Devon,*
      107 b. 108 ter. 108 b. 110 b. bis. 112 b.[1] 114, 114 b.
      115 b. 117. *Cornw.* 123, 123 b. 124 b. *Hertf.* 141.

ALMERUS homo Bundi stalri, *Buck.* 148 b.

ALMUND, *Staff.* 248. *Yorksh.* 332.

ALMUNDI S. Æcclesia, *Shropsh.* 258.

ALMUNDUS, *Staff.* 248 ter.

ALMUNDUS, Sanctus, Sciropesberie, *Shropsh.* 252, 253.

ALMUNT, *Yorksh.* 331 b. bis.

ALNOD, *Sussex,* 18, 18 b. 20 b. 21 b. bis. 22, 22 b. 24.
      Surr. 31 b. 34 b. ter. *Hants,* 41, 45, 46 b. 51, 53.
      Wilts, 70 b. bis. 71, 73 b. *Dors.* 80 passim. 83 b.
      85. *Somers.* 88, 90, 92, 92 b. 95, 96, 98, 99 (bis).
      Devon, 106, 106 b. bis. 107, 108, 112, 114, 116
      bis. *Cornw.* 122, 122 b. 123, 124, 124 b. bis.[2] 125
      bis. *Oxf.* 155 b. *Leic.* 234 b. 237. *Warw.* 241 b.
      Chesh. 267 b. *Linc.* 345 b. 359, 369. *Clam. S. R.*
      Linc. 375 b. bis. *Suff.* 376 b.

---

[1] In this instance also at the time of taking the Survey.

[2] In both these instances he continued to hold at the
Survey.

ALNOD abbas, *Kent*, 4.

ALNOD liber homo, commend. Edrico, *Suff.* 320 b.

ALNOD Cantuariensis, *Northampt.* 220.

ALNOD chentiscus teignus regis E. *Buck.* 145.

ALNOD cild, *Kent*, 2. *Sussex*, 17 b. *Surr.* 31. *Hants*,
46.

ALNOD cilt, *Kent*, 1, 6, 6 b. 7 bis. 7 b. 8, 8 b. 10 b. } [1]

ALNOD cit [cilt?], *Kent*, fol. 9 b.

ALNOD unus liber homo, *Sussex*, 25.

ALNOD homo Stigandi archiepiscopi, *Hertf.* 134 b.
bis.

ALNOD teignus Stig. archiep. *Hertf.* 142.

ALNOD Grud, homo Stigandi archiep. *Hertf.* 134 b. }

ALNOD Grutt, *Hertf.* 134.

ALNODUS, *Sussex*, 26, 26 b. *Hants*, 48. *Wilts*, 70 b.
Dors. 80, 82 b. *Somers.* 97 b. ter. *Devon*, 104 b.
ter. 112 b. bis. 114. *Oxf.* 157 b.

ALNODUS cilt, teignus R. E. *Buck.* 144 b.

---

[1] Kelham, from Hasted's History of Kent, says, " This
Alnod Cilt was Ulnoth, fourth son of Earl Godwin, and
younger brother to King Harold, who, from the royalty of
his kindred, had the addition of cilt; a similar denomination
to the Latin word *clito*, with which those of royal blood
were always honoured in those times. He was sent into
Normandy as a hostage upon Godwin's restoration from
banishment, where he continued the whole reign of King
Edward; after the Norman Conquest he was brought
back into England, and kept prisoner at Salisbury till his
death." Illustr. p. 174.

One of Alnod's manors in Sussex, Alsistone, consisting
of fifty hides of land, was bestowed by the Conqueror upon
Battle Abbey.

ALNODUS Lundoniensis, (temp. Haroldi Regis,)[1] *Surr.*
    32.

ALNODUS teignus R. E. *Buck.* 145.

ALNOHT liber homo Stigandi archiepiscopi, *Cornw.*
    123 b. ter.

ALNOLD liber homo, *Suff.* 378.

ALNOLDUS, *Hunt.* 206 bis.

ALNOT liber homo commendatus, *Suff.* 313 b.

ALNOT presbyter, *Clam. S. R. Linc.* 375.

ALNOTH, *Suff.* 334 b.

ALNOTH homo Normanni vicecomitis, *Suff.* 334 b.

ALNOTHUS homo Heroldi, *Suff.* 341 b.

ALNOTUS, *Suff.* 341 b.

ALODIARII duo, *Hants,* 51 b. *Berks,* 59 b. 60 b.

ALODIARII tres, *Berks,* 63 b.

ALOUS, *Dev.* 112 b.

ALREBOT, *Kent,* 14.

ALREDI pater, *Kent,* 1 b.

ALREFORDA, Aluric de, *Essex,* 101 b.

ALRET, *Kent,* 9, 10 b. 14.

ALRIC, *Sussex,* 24. *Surrey,* 35 b. bis. *Hants,* 39 b. 45 b.
    50 bis. 53 b. *Wilts,* 69, 69 b. bis. 72 b. 74 b. *Dors.*
    79 b. 83 b. *Somers.* 88, 92, 93 b. bis. 94, 95 b. bis.[2]
    96. *Devon,* 100 b. 103, 109 b. 110 b. 111 passim.
    114, 114 b. bis. 116 b. bis. 117 b. bis. 118 b.[3] *Cornw.*
    122 bis. 123 bis. 123 b. 124 bis. 124 b. bis.[4] *Glouc.*

---

[1] He is called Alwardus de London in one of the Conqueror's charters to Westminster Abbey.   MS. Cotton.
Faust. A. III. fol. 64.

[2] In both those instances, also when the Survey was
taken.

[3] Also when the Survey was made.

[4] In both these entries likewise.

170. *Worc.* 174 b. *Heref.* 184 b. *Bedf.* 212. *North-ampt.* 223 b. 224 bis.[1] *Staff.* 248, 249 b. 250 b. bis.[2] *Shropsh.* 254. *Nottingh.* 285. *Yorksh.* 301, 316 b. 317 bis. 317 b. passim. *Linc.* 352, 353 b. 354. *Essex,* 28.

ALRIC, in paragio, *Devon,* 115.

ALRIC bolest, *Buck.* 153.

ALRIC deburch, *Suff.* 413.

ALRIC f. Goding, *Buck.* 147 b. bis. 148.

ALRIC filius Goding, teignus R. E. } *v.* ALRICUS. *Buckingh.* 147 passim.

ALRIC homo Aluuini f. Goding, *Buck.* 146 b.

ALRIC homo Asgari stalri, *Hertf.* 140.

ALRIC homo et teignus regis E. *Buck.* 147 b.

ALRIC homo Heraldi Comitis, *Buck.* 150.

ALRIC homo Osulfi, *Buck.* 149.

ALRIC homo Stigandi archiep. *Hertf.* 137 bis.

ALRIC homo Wluui episcopi, *Buck.* 152 b.

ALRICI pater, *Hants,* 50 b.

ALRICUS, *Hants,* 40. *Berks,* 62. *Dors.* 83. *Buck.* 148. *Oxf.* 157 b. *Glouc.* 168 b. *Worc.* 172 b.[3] *Bedf.* 218,[4] 218 b.[5] *Northampt.* 223 b. bis. 226 b. *Warw.* 239 b. *Staff.* 249, 249 b. 250 b.[6] *Essex,* 59 b. 70 b. 83 b. 92, 97 b. *Suff.* 400 b. bis.

ALRICUS episcopus, *Sussex,* 18, 19.

ALRICUS filius Goding, *Buck.* 147 b. *v.* ALRIC.

ALRICUS gangemere, et soror ejus, *Buck.* 144 b.

---

[1] In one of these two, at the time the Survey was formed.

[2] Once, likewise at the Survey.

[3] Called " Ailricus " in another entry of the same page. He occurs as under-tenant at the time of the Survey, fol. 172 b.

[4] [5] [6] Also at the time of the Survey.

ALRICUS liber homo, *Suff.* 446 b.

ALRICUS liber homo Guerti, *Nottingh.* 283 b. bis.

ALRICUS monachus, *Cambr.* 196, 200.

ALRICUS presbyter, *Hertf.* 141 b. *Cambr.* 194.

ALRICUS teghus, *Buck.* 149 b.[1]

ALRICUS teinus, *Norf.* 246 b.

ALRICUS teignus Regis E. *Buck.* 147 b. bis. *Bedf.* 211. *Essex,* 42.

ALRICUS Wintremele, *Bedf.* 218 b.[2]

ALRIS, *Devon,* 109.

ALSELMUS, *Essex,* 83 b.

ALSI, *Kent,* 11. *Hants,* 43, 46, 49, 53 b.[3] *Berks,* 58. *Wilts,* 72. *Dors.* 79 b. 82. *Somers.* 98, 98 b. *Devon,* 105, 106 b. 112 passim. 115, 117 bis. 117 b. bis. *Cornw.* 123, 124 b. bis.[4] 125. *Cambr.* 195 b. 197. *Northampt.* 228 b. *Warw.* 239, 240, 240 b. 244 b.[5] *Shropsh.* 256 b. 257, 260. *Chesh.* 265 bis. *Yorksh.* 301, 315 b. 316, 319 b. bis. 320, 326. *Linc.* 354 passim. 357 ter. 357 b. 365 b. 369. *Yorksh.* 373 b. 375. *Norf.* 269.

ALSI abbas, *Surrey,* 36 b.[6] *Hants,* 41 b.

ALSI de Bruneham homo Eddid Reginæ, *Bedf.* 213 b. bis.

ALSI homo Alli fratris ejus, *Bedf.* 216 b.

ALSI homo Eddeuæ, *Hertf.* 137. *Cambr.* 195 b.

ALSI homo Reginæ Eddid, *Bedf.* 209 b.

ALSI liber homo, *Ess.* 24 b.

ALSI monachus, *Wilts,* 65 b.

[1 2 3] Likewise when the Survey was formed.

[4] In one of these two entries he continued to hold at the Survey.

[5] Also at the time of the Survey.

[6] If this was Alsi abbot of Bath, he died in 1087. Sim. Dunelm. 213.

ALSI pater, *Hants*, 42 b.

ALSI presbyter, *Hants*, 46. *Wilts*, 73.

ALSI teignus R. E. *Cambr*. 196. *Norf*. 130.

ALSICUS liber homo, *Norf*. 233.

ALSIDUS, *Essex*, 72 b.

ALSIUS, *Essex*, 34. *Suff*. 303, 444 b.

ALSIUS liber homo, *Norf*. 178 b. bis. *Suff*. 437

ALSIUS Bolla, liber homo, *Essex*, 80.

ALSTAN, *Cornw*. 125.

ALSTAN liber homo unus Edrici commend. *Norf*. 154 b.

ALSTANUS, *Dors*. 80, 83 b. *Norf*. 173 b. 266 b.

ALTEI, *Hants*, 45.

ALTET, *Kent*, 11.

ALTI, *Staff*. 248.

ALTIUS liber homo commend. *Suff*. 421 b.

ALTIUS liber homo teignus, *Suff*. 421.

ALTOR, *Yorksh*. 300 b. bis, 331.

ALTSTANUS, *Norf*. 144 b.

ALUARDUS, *Essex*, 66 b.

ALUED, *Suff*. 435 b.

ALUER, *Yorksh*. 300.

ALUERD, *Dors*. 77 b.

ALUERLE, *Yorksh*. 300 b.

ALUERON, *Dors*. 80.

ALUERT, *Dors*. 82 b.

ALUET, *Wilts*, 66.

ALUENE [1] quædam femina Siuuardi, *Buck*. 151.

ALUERD, *Somers*. 94 b. bis. 99.[2]

ALVEREDUS de Merleberg, *Worc*. 175.[3]

---

[1] Qu. Alueue.

[2] He also occurs as holding at the time of the Survey.

[3] This was at Stoche, where he had held twelve hides and a virgate T. R. E.; increased to fifteen hides at the time of the Survey.

ALUERON, *Devon,* 112 passim.

ALUERT, *Devon,* 108.

ALUEUA, *Berks,* 63 b. *Devon,* 106 b. 108, 112,[1] 112 b.
114, 115 b. bis. 118 b.[2] *Cornw.* 122. *Shropsh.*
257 bis. *Norf.* 161 b. 162, 167. *Suff.* 320 b. 385 b.

ALVEVA Comitissa, *Leic.* 231 b.

ALUEUA mater Morchari comitis, *Suff.* } *v.* ÆLVEVA.
373 b.

ALUEUA libera femina, *Devon,* 112 b. *Essex,* 80, 100.
Norf. 160 b. bis. *Suff.* 335.

ALUEUE, *Dors.* 85.

ALUIED, *Somers.* 87 b. 88 b.

ALUIED de Elesberie, *Buck.* 146.

ALUIET, *Sussex,* 20. *Hants,* 46. *Berks,* 58. *Somers.* 88 b.
95 b. 96. *Cornw.* 123 b. *Hertf.* 138 b. *Heref.* 185.
Staff. 248. *Shropsh.* 259. *Suff.* 377, 395.

ALUIET homo comitis Algari, *Cambr.* 194 b. 195.[3]

ALUIET commendatus Alsio nepti Comitis Radulfi, *Suff.*
322.

ALUIET homo Eddid Reginæ, *Buck.* 148.

ALUIET libera femina, *Suff.* 435.

ALUIET monachus de Evesham, filius Vluiet, *Worc.*
177 b.

ALUIET presbyter, *Cambr.* 191 b.[4]

ALUIN homo Stigand archiepiscopi, *Hertf.* 132 b.

ALUINUS, *Devon,* 109. *Worc.* 177 b. *Yorksh.* 329. *Suff.*
321, 333 b. 340, 419, 441 b.

ALUINUS liber homo, *Suff.* 414 b.

---

[1] Also when the Survey was taken.

[2] Alveva continued to hold the property of this entry in
capite when the Survey was formed.

[3] He likewise held when the Survey was formed.

[4] Also at the Survey.

Aluinus liber homo T. R. E. *Norf.* 120 b.

Aluinus liber homo commend. Esgaro stalre, *Suff.* 395.

Alvinus liber homo sub Stigando, *Norf.* 224 b.

Aluinus liber homo Stigandi, *Suff.* 426.

Aluinus presbyter, *Suff.* 376 b.

Aluinus teinnus, *Essex*, 53 b.

Aluiua libera femina, *Suff.* 334 b.

Alun, *Derb.* 278 b.

Alunold, *Somers.* 88 b.

Aluol presbyter, *Suff.* 375 b.

Aluoldus commend. Guerti, *Suff.* 445.

Aluort, *Suff.* 437.

Alured, *Surrey*, 36 b. *Hants*, 45, 51. *Berks*, 59 b. 60 b.
　　Dors. 79, 82. *Somers.* 88 b. *Devon*, 102, 108 b.
　　bis. *Warw.* 244 bis. *Staff.* 250. *Yorksh.* 301 b.
　　330 b.

Alured et ii. alii, *Dors.* 79 b.

Alured homo Asgari stalri, *Hertf.* 133 b. 138, 139 b.

Alured liber homo sub Stigando, *Buck.* 143.

Alured vicecomes, *Dors.* 83.

Aluredus, *Surrey*, 32 b. *Dors.* 79, 82. *Norf.* 278.
　　Suff. 411 b.

Aluredus biga, *Kent*, 9.

Aluredus marescal, *Cornw.* 121 b.

Aluredus presbyter, liber homo Stigandi, *Buck.* 143 b.

Aluret, *Kent*, 6. *Yorksh.* 300.

Aluret commendatus Scalpio, *Suff.* 420.

Aluric, *Kent*, 7, 9. *Sussex*, 21, 21 b. 24. *Surrey*, 31,
　　31 b. 35 b. *Hants*, 44 b. 45, 45 b. 47 b. bis. 48 b.
　　bis. 49 b. 51, 51 b. bis.[1] 53 b. passim. 54.[2] *Berks*,

---

[1] In these two entries, Aluric held at the time of the
Survey.

[2] Also when the Survey was formed.

61 b. 62 b. 63 b. *Wilts,* 69, 70, 70 b. 71 passin
71 b. 72, 73, 73 b.[1] 74 b. ter. *Dors.* 75 b. passim.
77 b. bis. 79 b. ter. 83, 83 b. bis. 84, 84 b. passim.[2]
Somers. 86, 88 bis. 88 b. ter. 89, 90, 92 bis. 92 b.
93 b. ter. 94 bis. 95 b. ter. 96, 97 b. 98 b. *Devon,*
102 b. bis. 104 b. 105 b. 107, 107 b. 108 b. 109
bis. 109 b. bis. 110 bis. 110 b. ter. 112 b. 113 ter.
113 b. 114 bis. 114 b. bis. 116 ter. 116 b. 117 b.
118 b. bis.[3] *Cornw.* 122 passim. 122 b. bis. 124 bis.
124 b. 125 passim. *Oxf.* 158 bis. 159. *Glouc.* 162 b.
167 bis. *Worc.* 174 b. 177 b. bis. *Heref.* 181, 184 b.
185 b. *Cambr.* 196 b. 197 b. bis. *Hunt.* 207 bis.
Northampt. 223 b. 224 b. 227. *Leic.* 233 b. bis.
Warw. 240 b. bis. 241 b. *Staff.* 249. *Shropsh.* 252 b.
254 bis. 256 passim. 256 b. bis. 257 b. 258 b. bis.
Chesh. 264 b. *Derb.* 274 b. 275 b. *Nottingh.* 283.
285, 285 b. 287, 291, 292, 292 b. passim. 293 ter,
Yorksh. 315 b. 317. *Linc.* 339 b. 340, 340 b. bis.
343, 354, 360 b. 367 b. passim. *Clam. S. R. Linc.*
375. *Clam. in Chetst.* 377 b. *Suff.* 320.

ALURIC de Alreforda, *Essex,* 101 b.

ALURIC blac, *Hertf.* 133.

ALURIC busch, *Hertf.* 140.

ALURIC camerarius R. E. *Buck.* 151.

ALURIC capus, *Cambr.* 196 b.

ALURIC cild, T. R. E. *Essex,* 64.

ALURIC commend. Guerti, *Suff.* 339.

ALURIC diaconus, *Suff.* 423 b.

ALURIC homo Ælmari Belintone, *Hertf.* 141.

ALURIC homo Aluric belinton, *Hertf.* 137 b.

---

[1] Also when the Survey was formed.
[2] In each entry of 84 b. he likewise held at the Survey.
[3] In both entries also T. R. W.

ALURIC homo Borred, *Bedf.* 210.

ALURIC homo Abbatis de Certesi, *Midd.* 129.

ALURIC homo Godric vicecomitis, *Buck.* 152.

ALURIC homo Goduini f. Vlestan, *Hertf.* 138.

ALURIC homo Stigandi, *Hertf.* 133.[1]

ALURIC homo Wluui Episcopi, *Buck.* 152 b.

ALURIC liber homo, *Chesh.* 265 b. bis.

ALURIC pic, *Devon,* 113.

ALURIC teignus R. E. *Buck.* 152.

ALURIC vicecomes, *Hunt.* 203.

ALURIC uuelp, *Oxf.* 160.

ALURICI pater, *Hants,* 51 b.[2]

ALURICUS, *Kent,* 8. *Surr.* 35. *Hants,* 41, 49, 51. *Berks,*
58 b. *Glouc.* 168, 169 b. *Bedf.* 218 b. *Northampt.*
223 b. *Warw.* 240 b. 242. *Shropsh.* 258 b. *Derb.*
274. *Essex,* 11, 11 b. 24 b. 29 b. 33, 63 b. 66, 83,
85, 91 b. 95 b. 155. *Norf.* 120 b. 245 b. 268 b.
Suff. 287, 297 b. 299, 303 b. 312 b. 315, 339 b.
341 b. 342, 342 b. 343, 346 b. 351, 375 b. 377,
377 b. 380 b. 386 b. 389 bis. 394 bis. 400, 410,
422 b. 423, 425, 441.

ALURICUS biga, *Essex,* 30.

ALURICUS camp, *Essex,* 67 b. 70 b. 83.

ALURICUS campa, *Suff.* 403 b.

ALURICUS capin, *Suff.* 378.

ALURICUS commendatus Brun, *Suff.* 338.

ALURICUS commendatus Edrici, *Suff.* 314 b. 320.

ALURICUS commendatus Heroldi, *Suff.* 292.

ALURICUS commendatus Saxo, *Suff.* 374 b. bis.

ALURICUS filius Brune, *Suff.* 374.

---

[1] The same person with " Aluric blac."

[2] " Alrici pater," probably the same person, occurs
fol. 50 b.

ALURICUS filius bundi, *Suff.* 334 b.

ALURICUS filius Fabri, *Suff.* 314 b.

ALURICUS filius Wisgari, *Suff.* 389 b.

ALURICUS filius Wluiet commend. Heroldi, *Suff.* 373 bis.

ALURICUS frater Alsi et Adestan, *Linc.* 357 b.

ALURICUS, occisus in bello apud Hastinges, *Hunt.* 208.

ALURICUS Godricsone, *Cambr.* 189.

ALURICUS homo Alurici parvi, *Bedf.* 214 b.

ALURICUS liber homo, *Essex*, 4 b. 12, 33, 69 b. 79, 93 bis. *Norf.* 120 b. bis. 126 b. 160, 201 b. 259. *Suff.* 295, 300, 353 b. 378 ter. 420, 420 b. 429 bis.

ALURICUS liber homo Edrici, *Suff.* 432 b. 438.

ALURICUS liber homo Guerti, *Suff.* 302.

ALURICUS liber homo Heroldi, *Suff.* 406 b. 428 b.

ALURICUS liber homo Stigandi, *Norf.* 153, 176 b.[1]

ALURICUS unus liber homo, *Berks*, 62, 62 b.

ALURICUS Mapesone, *Worc.* 176 b.

ALURICUS presbyter, *Cambr.* 196 b. *Suff.* 446 b.

ALURICUS presbyter commendatus Wisgaro, *Suff.* 394.

ALURICUS presbyter liber homo, *Essex*, 42 bis. 42 b. *Suff.* 376 b.

ALURICUS scoua, *Hertf.* 134 b.

ALURICUS sochemannus, *Essex*, 78.

ALURICUS Stari, commend. Guert, *Suff.* 395 bis.

ALURICUS Stikestare, *Suff.* 339 b. bis.

ALURICUS teinnus, *Suff.* 299, 353.

ALURICUS teignus R. E. *Buck.* 152. *Cambr.* 198 b. *Bedf.* 214. *Essex*, 12.

---

[1] " Iste Aluricus utlagav' et Prepositus Regis Ulketel saisivit terram in manu Regis, et Rogerus Bigot rogavit a Rege, et concessit ei."

ALURICUS parvus teignus Regis E. *Bedf.* 214.

ALURICUS tegnus Heroldi, *Norf.* 268.

ALURICUS teinnus Regis tempore Regis Edwardi, *Suff.* 296.

ALURICUS uuand, *Essex,* 51 b.

ALURICUS vicecomes, *Hunt.* 208.

ALURICUS de Weinhou, *Suff.* 430 b. bis.

ALURICUS de Wenhou, *Suff.* 425.

ALURIZ, *Hunt.* 206.

ALUUACRE, *Wilts,* 72.

ALUUALDUS, *Somers.* 92. *Devon,* 115 b.[1]

ALUUARD, *Kent,* 6 b. 10 b. *Sussex,* 21 b. 22, 22 b. 23. *Surrey,* 33, 36. *Hants,* 45, 47 b. 48 b. 49 b. *Berks,* 61. *Wilts,* 69, 69 b. 70, 73. *Dors.* 81 b. 82 b. 83 b. bis. 84 b. bis. *Somers.* 87.[2] 87 b. bis. 88, 90, 91 b. bis. 92 b. 93 bis. 93 b. 94 bis. 95. 96, 98 b. bis. 99. *Devon,* 102 b. 110 b. 112 b. 114, 115 b. 117 b. *Cornw.* 121 b. 124 b. bis.[3] 123, 124, 125. *Hertf.* 134, 137 b.[4] *Glouc.* 170. *Worc.* 175. *Heref.* 184, 187, 187 b. *Warw.* 241, 243 b. *Staff.* 249. *Yorksh.* 307 b. passim. 315, 315 b. 316, 317.

ALUUARD cilt teignus Regis E. *Buck.* 147 b.

ALUUARD homo Roberti f. Wim. *Cambr.* 201.

ALUUARD homo Ælmær de Belintone, *Hertf.* 142.

ALUUARD homo Algari Comitis, *Hertf.* 141 b.

ALUUARD homo Goding, *Buck.* 148 b.

---

[1] Also at the Survey. He is likewise written " Alwoldus."

[2] In this entry, also at the time of the Survey.

[3] In both of these entries he likewise held when the Survey was taken.

[4] Also at the time of the Survey.

ALUUARD homo comitis Heraldi, *Hertf.* 137 bis. 137 b. bis.

ALUUARD teignus Heraldi Comitis, *Hertf.* 137.

ALUUARD homo Stigandi archiepiscopi, *Hertf.* 134.

ALUUARD et Aluuin, *Dors.* 82.

ALWARDI aurifabri pater, *Berks*, 63 b.

ALWARDI et fratrum ejus pater, *Somers.* 99.[1]

ALUUARDUS, *Kent,* 6 b. 8. *Sussex,* 28 b. *Surrey,* 31. *Hants,* 43, 44 b. 48. *Berks,* 63 b. *Wilts,* 66 passim. 67, 70, 72 b. bis. *Dors.* 79 bis. 79 b. bis. 80 b. 81 b. 82, 82 b. bis. 83 passim. 84 passim.[2] 84 b. bis.[3] *Somers.* 87 b. bis. 90, 91 b. bis. 93 b. ter. [4] 94 b. 96, 97 b. 99. *Devon,* 102 bis. 103, 104 b.[5] 105 bis.[6] 109 bis. 109 b. 110 bis. 110 b. ter. 112 b. bis. 113, 113 b. 114, 115. *Hertf.* 134 b. *Buck.* 152. *Glouc.* 166 b. *Worc.* 173, 174 b. *Heref.* 184. *Warw.* 240 b. *Staff.* 248 b. 249. *Essex,* 11 b. 74, 95, 95 b.

ALUUARDUS belrap, homo Alrici, *Suss.* 25 b. ter. *Berks,* 61. *Devon,* 112 b. *Bedf.* 214 b.

ALUUARDUS liber homo, *Essex,* 24, 24 b.

ALUUARDUS Dore, *Essex,* 94.

ALUUARDUS presbyter, *Berks,* 58 b.

ALUUARDUS homo Alestan de Boscumbe, *Hertf.* 138 b.

---

[1] " Alward et fratres" continued to be the under-tenants at the Survey.

[2] In one of these entries he is mentioned as continuing to hold.

[3] In one entry, also at the Survey.

[4] In one of these entries, also at the time of the Survey.

[5] In this instance he continued to hold when the Survey was made.

[6] In both these instances also.

ALUUARDUS homo Algari comitis, *Hertf.* 141 b. 142.

ALUUARDUS homo Alrici filii Godingi, *Bedf.* 214 bis.

ALUUARDUS homo S. arch. *Hertf.* 133 b.

ALUUARDUS homo Wluui Episcopi, *Bedf.* 214 b.

ALUUARDUS teinus regis E. *Glouc.* 165.

ALUUARE, *Devon*, 101.

ALUUART, *Essex*, 70.

ALUUEN libera femina, *Essex*, 42.

ALUUEN quædam femina, *Buck.* 147.

ALUUI, *Kent*, 1 b. *Sussex*, 29. *Hants*, 46 b. 48, 48 b,
49 b. 50 b.[1] *Berks*, 63 b. *Wilts*, 72 b. bis. 73 bis.
74, 74 b. *Dors.* 82 b. 84, 84 b. 85. *Somers.* 93
passim. 94 b. 95 b. passim. 97 b. passim. 98 b.
Devon, 105, 112 b. 113 b. 115 b. bis. *Cornw.* 124.
Buck. 149 b. *Oxf.* 160 b. bis. *Glouc.* 167, 170.
Worc. 174 b. passim. 174 b. ter. 175 bis. 176 b. bis.
Warw. 238 b. 242 b. 243 bis. *Shropsh.* 255, 260 b.
Nottingh. 284 b. bis. *Linc.* 342, 352 b. *Norf.* 174,
185.

ALUUI alter, *Worc.* 175.

ALUUI blac, *Worc.* 174 b.

ALWI harparius, *Cambr.* 196.

ALUUI homo Algari Comitis, *Cambr.* 198.

ALUUI homo Brictric, *Buck.* 148 b.

ALUUI homo Heraldi Comitis, *Glouc.* 165 bis.

ALUUI pater, *Berks*, 59.

ALWI de Tetfordo, *Norf.* 174 b.

ALUUID puella, *Buck.* 149.

ALUUIN, *Kent*, 6 b. *Somers.* 88 b. *Devon*, 108 b. 113 b.
ter. 114 b. 118 b. *Cornw.* 122 bis. 122 b. bis. 123,
123 b. *Oxf.* 158, 160 b. *Glouc.* 167. *Worc.* 174 b.

---

[1] Also when the Survey was made.

Northampt. 223. *Nottingh.* 288. *Yorksh.* 316, 326 b.
passim. 329. *Linc.* 340, 342 b. 350 b. bis. 351
bis.

ALUUIN episcopus,[1] *Yorksh.* 304 b.

ALUUIN homo Ælmari de Belintone, *Hertf.* 141.

ALUUIN homo Wigot, *Midd.* 129.

ALUUIN presbyter, *Somers.* 90.

ALUUINE, *Glouc.* 170. *Hunt.* 207 b. *Nottingh.* 287 b.
Linc. 353 b. bis. *Yorksh.* 374.

ALUUINE cilt, *Hunt.* 206.

ALUUINUS, *Kent*, 6 b. 7, 7 b. 9 b. *Sussex*, 19, 19 b. 21,
21 b. 24 bis. 24 b. 28, 28 b. 31, 32 b. 34 b. 35 bis.
35 b. 36. *Hants*, 41 b. 43 b. 45, 45 b. bis. 46 b.
48 b. 49 bis. 50, 50 b. *Berks*, 58 b. 60 bis. 60 b.
63, 63 b. *Wilts*, 69 b. 70, 71, 72 passim. 72 b. ter.
73 b. 74, 74 b. ter. *Dors.* 75 b. bis. 79 bis. 82 b. 84.
Somers. 86 b. 92, 93, 93 b. bis. 94, 95 b. 97, 97 b.[2]
98 b. *Devon*, 102 passim. 102 b. bis. 103 passim.
103 b. 105, 105 b. 106, 107, 109 passim. 109 b.
passim. 110 bis. 111 passim. 111 b. bis. 113, 113 b.
passim. 114, 115, 116 bis. 118 b.[3] *Cornw.* 122,
122 b. ter. 123 bis. 123 b. 124, 124 b. *Midd.* 129.
Oxf. 155 b. 157 b. 159, 160, 160 b. *Glouc.* 163 b.
167 passim. 168, 171. *Worc.* 174 b. *Heref.* 179 b.
181, 183 b. 186 b. 187 b. *Hunt.* 203 b. *Bedf.*
218 bis.[4] 218 b. *Northampt.* 223, 223 b. bis. 224 b.
bis. *Leic.* 232 bis. 233, 234, 235 b. 236. *Warw.*

---

[1] Alwyn, or Egelwyn, bishop of Durham, who succeeded
his brother Egelric in 1056. He was expelled in 1070, and
died a prisoner in the Abbey of Abingdon in 1072.

[2] He continued to hold in this entry at the time of the
Survey.

[3] Also at the time of the Survey.

[4] In one of these instances Aluuinus continued to hold.

238 b. 240, 240 b. 241 b. passim. 242 b. bis. 243 b. *Staff.* 248 b. 250. *Shropsh.* 256 b. *Derb.* 274. *Nottingh.* 287 b. *Yorksh.* 298 bis. 308 b. 326 b. *Linc.* 339 b. 340, 350, 350 b. passim. 353, 353 b. 357 b. 369 b. *Yorksh.* 373 b. *Essex,* 30 b. 31, 40 b. 78, 81 b. 94. *Norf.* 112 b. 179, 277, 278. *Suff.* 321 b. 342 b. 346 b. 377, 378, 380, 396, 396 b. bis. 419, 422, 433 b.

ALUUINUS alter, *Staff.* 248 b. *Suff.* 321 b.

ALUUINUS abb. de Ramesy, *Hunt.* 208.[1]

ALUUINUS albus, *Hants,* 50 b.[2]

ALUUINUS albus, homo Comitis Leuuini, *Midd.* 130 b.

ALUUINUS blach, *Hunt.* 207.

ALUUINUS Boi, *Surrey,* 31.

ALUUINUS f. Brictmar, *Midd.* 127 b.[2]

ALUUINUS coc, bedellus, *Cambr.* 190.[2]

ALUUINUS commend. Ælmari [episcopi], *Suff.* 380.

ALUUINUS cubold, *Northampt.* 220 b.

ALUUINUS deule, *Hunt.* 206 b. 208.

ALUUINUS deule, homo Episcopi Lincoliensis, *Bedf.* 210 bis. 210 b. bis.

ALUUINUS dode homo Alurici parvi, *Hertf.* 141.

ALUUINUS abbas de Evesham, *Worc.* 177 b.[3]

---

[1] See the passage in which he occurs quoted, vol. i. p. 306.

[2] Also when the Survey was formed.

[3] Aluuinus, Æluuinus, or Eluui, was Abbat of Evesham from 1058 to 1077. He occurs in the entry above referred to, in the record of the Worcestershire possessions of Urso d'Abetot, who appears to have usurped, or at least obtained, various lands, which at an earlier day had belonged to Evesham Abbey.

Of three hides in Vptune, it is said, " Aluuinus Abbas de

ALUUINUS frater Wlui Episcopi, *Bedf.* 211 b.

ALUUINUS forst, *Hants*, 52 b.

ALUUINUS frater Lewini, *Warw.* 244 b.

ALUUINUS de Godtone, *Hertf.* 138 b.

ALUUINUS Godton, homo R. E. *Hertf.* 142 b.

ALUUINUS Godtuna, *Essex*, 36.

ALUUINUS Gotone, *Hertf.* 135 b.

ALUUINUS homo Ælmari de Belintone, *Hertf.* 141.

ALUUINUS homo Alestan de Boscumbe, *Bedf.* 212.

ALUUINUS homo Borred, *Bedf.* 210.

ALUUINUS homo Borret, *Bedf.* 210.

ALUUINUS homo Eddeuæ pulchræ, *Buck.* 152 bis.

ALUUINUS homo reginæ Eddid, *Buck.* 144, 148, 150 b.

ALUUINUS homo regis E. *Midd.* 130. *Bedf.* 217 b. bis.

ALUUINUS homo Eduuini, *Buck.* 145 b.

ALUUINUS homo Estan, *Buck.* 145.

Evesham tenuit, et in Abbatia recte deberet esse teste Comitatu."

There are two other entries of very curious detail; one relating to a half hide in Witune, the other to four hides of land in Hantune, under the same circumstances; but these entries have been already quoted in the former volume of the present work, pp. 338, 339.

Urso d'Abetot, it will be remembered, was the person concerning whom Aldred Archbishop of York is said to have composed the memorable couplet;

"Hatest thou Urse,
Have thou God's curse."

Under Sopeberie, in Gloucestershire, Urso's oppression upon the people of a salt-work on the King's land is strongly marked. "Ad hoc manerium pertinet una virgata in Wiche quæ reddebat xxv. sextaria Salis. VRSUS VICECOMES *ita vastavit homines quod modo reddere non possunt sal.*" Tom. i. fol. 163 b.

ALUUINUS homo Goduin de Benefella, *Hertf.* 134.

ALUUINUS homo Heraldi comitis, *Bedf.* 216.

ALUUINUS liber homo, *Sussex*, 25. *Berks*, 61 b. *Worc.* 175 bis.

ALUUINUS homo Stori, *Bedf.* 216 b.

ALUUINUS homo Syredi f. Sybi, *Buck.* 146.

ALUUINUS homo Wluui episcopi, *Bedf.* 215.

ALUUINUS liber homo, *Essex*, 3, 12, 12 b. 24 b. 43, 82 b. 97. *Norf.* 263, 263 b.

ALUUINUS liber homo commendatus Alurico antec. Roberti Grenonis, *Suff.* 420.

ALUUINUS liber homo commendatus Edrico, *Suff.* 309, 327 b.

ALUUINUS commendatus Gueit, *Suff.* 282.

ALUUINUS commendatus Guert, *Suff.* 446.

ALUUINUS frater Episcopi Wluui, *Buck.* 151 b.

ALUUINUS pater T. *Warw.* 241 b.

ALUUINUS pater Turchilli, *Warw.* 241.

ALUUINUS pater Turchilli de Warwic, *Warw.* 240 b.

ALUUINUS presbyter, *Bedf.* 218 b.[1] *Nottingh.* 282 b.

ALUUINUS sochemannus R. E. *Hertf.* 140.

ALUUINUS teignus R. E. *Hertf.* 135, 136 b. *Buck.* 148 passim. *Bedf.* 216. *Essex*, 42.

ALUUINUS teinus Edwini comitis, *Worc.* 172.

ALUUINUS teignus Heraldi Comitis, *Hertf.* 138 b.

ALUUINUS venator, *Northampt.* 229. *Essex*, 102 b.

ALUUINUS venator, homo Eddid reginæ, *Hertf.* 139 b.

ALUUINUS venator, homo Comitis Leuuini, *Hertf.* 134 b.

ALUUINUS vicecomes, *Glouc.* 162 b. 163, 167 bis. *Hunt.* 206 b. *Warw.* 238 b. 239 b.

---

[1] He continued to hold at the time of the Survey; see the Index of Tenants in capite, vol. i. p. 372.

ALUUINUS vicecomes, pater Turchil, *Warw.* 241.

ALUUIUS, *Wilts,* 69. *Norf.* 195. *Suff.* 355.

ALUUIUS commend. Edrici de Laxefella, *Suff.* 380 b.

ALUUOL, *Warw.* 241 b.

ALUUOLD, *Sussex,* 21 b. *Hants,* 51. *Wilts,* 74, 74 b.
 Dors. 80 b. 85. *Somers.* 88, 88 b. bis. 89, 90, 95 b.
 96 bis. 96 b. 97 b. passim. *Devon,* 108. *Cornw.*
 123 b. 125. *Glouc.* 170 b.[1] *Worc.* 176, 177 b. bis.
 Heref. 186. *Hunt.* 206. *Chesh.* 266 b. *Nottingh.*
 284 b. 285 b. *Linc.* 336.[2]

ALUUOLD et soror ejus, *Wilts,* 72.

ALUUOLD et v. fratres ejus sochemanni, *Hunt.* 206,
 208.

ALUUOLD teinus Eduini comitis, *Worc.* 172.

ALUUOLDUS, *Hants,* 39 b. *Devon,* 106 bis. 107, 108 b.
 109, 112 b. 116 b. *Cornw.* 123 b. *Glouc.* 169 b.
 Worc. 177, 177 b. *Hunt.* 208. *Leic.* 233 b. 235 b.
 Warw. 240, 250 b.[3] *Suff.* 448.

ALUUOLDUS abbas, *Norf.* 201.

ALUUOLDUS camerarius, (temp. Regis Haroldi,) *Berks,*
 58.

ALUUOLDUS homo Regis E. *Bedf.* 211.

ALUUOLDUS homo Wluui Episcopi, *Bedf.* 216.

ALUUOLDUS teignus R. E. *Bedf.* 211.

ALUURICUS, *Suff.* 389.

AMOD una libera mulier, *Suff.* 312 b.

AMUND, *Suff.* 433 bis.

AMUNDUS, *Suff.* 433, 433 b. bis. 441 b.

---

[1] He continued to hold at the Survey.

[2] He was one of the Lagemen of Lincoln T. R. E., and
continued such at the time of the Survey.

[3] Also at the time of the Survey.

ANAND huscarl R. E. *Hertf.* 140 b.

ANAND liber homo commend. S. Edmundi, *Suff.* 294.

ANANDUS, *Nottingh.* 282.

ANANT, *Suff.* 332 b. 434 bis.

ANANT liber homo, *Norf.* 195 b. 196. *Suff.* 291 b.

ANANT teinus, *Norf.* 259 b.

ANAUT liber homo, *Buck.* 152.

ANCHOLFUS, *Norf.* 205.

ANDRAC, *Hants,* 49.

ANDREÆ, S. Canonici, *Somers.* 89 b.[1]

ANDREAS S. *Suff.* 347.

ANGARUS, *Suff.* 411.

ANGARUS stalra, *Suff.* 440.

ANGERUS stalra, *Norf.* 248.

ANGLI duo, *Buck.* 147,[2] 152.[2]

ANGLI duo, unus homo Brictrici et alter homo Azoris, *Buck.* 144 b.

ANGLI duo, homines Haming, *Buck.* 150.[1]

ANGLI quinque, *Staff.* 248.

ANGLICUS, *Hertf.* 133,[1] 136.

ANGOT, *Hants,* 44.

ANSCHIL, *Kent,* 1 b. 6 b. bis. 7, 8 b. *Surrey,* 31, 34, 36. *Berks,* 60, 63 b. *Dors.* 84 b.

ANSCHIL homo Episcopi Hereford, *Heref.* 187.

ANSCHIL teignus regis E. *Bedf.* 212 b.

ANSCHIL presbyter, *Hants,* 52.

ANSCHILLUS, *Hants,* 46 b. *Bedf.* 218 ter. *Essex,* 37 b. *Suff.* 405 b. 448 b.

ANSCOT, *Worc.* 175.

---

[1] Also at the Survey.

[2] In both instances also, when the Survey was taken.

ANSCULFUS vicecomes,[1] *Surr.* 36. *Berks,* 148 b.

ANSFRIDUS, *Hants,* 48 b.

ANSFRIGUS, *Surrey,* 32.

ANSGARUS,[2] *Essex,* 58, 59, 60 b. 61 ter. 61 b. passim.
62, 63. *Suff.* 411, 412 b.

ANSGER, *Devon,* 112.

ANSGER liber homo Goduini, *Worc.* 175 bis.

ANSGERUS, *Suff.* 322 b.

ANSGERUS sub Angero Stalre, *Norf.* 248.

ANSGOT, *Sussex,* 25 b. bis. 31. *Devon,* 118.[3] *Heref.*
182 b. *Chesh.* 263 b. 266 b.

ANSGOT commend. Edeue faire, *Suff.* 295.

ANSGOT homo Stigandi archiepiscopi, *Hertf.*142. *Cambr.*
200 b.

ANSGOT liber homo, *Essex,* 93.

ANSKETILLUS presbyter, *Suff.* 334 b.

ANUNDUS presbyter, *Suff.* 441 b.

ANUNT dacus, *Essex,* 25 b.

APE, *Somers.* 88.

APPE, *Wilts,* 73.

ARCEBALDUS, *Suff.* 443.

ARCENBALDUS, *Suff.* 443.

ARCHEL, *Yorksh.* 300. *Linc.* 345 bis. 347, 353. *Clam.*
in Chetst. 377.

ARCHEL filius Vlf, *Yorksh.* 374.

ARCHEL filius Vlstan, *Yorksh.* 373 b.

---

[1] See WILLELMUS filius Ansculfi, in the Index of Tenants
in capite.

[2] He was the same person, in most of these entries, with
ASGAR stalre. See the entry in *Suff.* 411, which will be
hereafter quoted.

[3] Also at the taking of the Survey.

ARCHETEL, *Heref.* 185 bis. *Shropsh.* 256, 257 b.

ARCHIL, *Leic.* 230 b. bis. *Warw.* 241 b. *Chesh.* 266 b.
Nottingh. 286 b. *Yorksh.* 298, 298 b. 300 passim.
300 b. 301 ter. 301 b. bis. 306, 307, 308, 310 b.
ter. 311 ter. 312, 312 b. passim. 313, 315 b. passim. 316, 317 b. 318 passim. 319, 320, 320 b. bis.
321 b. bis. 322, 323, 327, 328 b. 329 bis. 330 ter.
331,[1] 331 b. passim. 332 passim. *Linc.* 340 b. 341,
342, 360 b. 361, 367, 370, 371 ter. *Clam. W. R.*
Linc. 376 b.

ARCHIL et frater ejus, *Yorksh.* 373 b.

ARCHIL homo Turchil, *Warw.* 241.

ARCHIL tanus Heraldi comitis, *Heref.* 184.

ARCHILBAR, *Linc.* 352 b.

ARCHILLUS commend. Edrici, *Suff.* 316.

ARCHISTI, *Norf.* 138.

ARDEGRIP, *Linc.* 342.

ARDUINUS, *Norf.* 223 b.

ARDUL, *Yorksh.* 323.

ARDULF, *Yorksh.* 301 bis.

AREGRI, *Shropsh.* 256.

AREGRIM, *Chesh.* 265 b.

ARET, *Devon,* 106 b.

ARFASTUS, *Norf.* 197.

ARFASTUS episcopus, *Suff.* 394. *v.* ÆREFASTUS.

ARIC, *Devon,* 107 b.

ARICH, *Linc.* 343.

ARLINGUS, *Essex,* 59.

ARNEBRAND, *Yorksh.* 332.

ARNEGRIM, *Yorksh.* 300 b.

ARNENGER, *Yorksh.* 300 b.

---

[1] Also when the Survey was formed.

ARNUI, *Leic.* 237. *Yorksh.* 324 b. *Linc.* 339 b. 348 b.

ARNUI presbyter, *Nottingh.* 292 b.

ARNUINUS presbyter, *Worc.* 172 b.

ARNUL, *Warw.* 241.

ARTOR, *Yorksh.* 308, 316, 329 b. *Linc.* 341.

ARTOR presbyter, *Yorksh.* 330 b.

ARULF, *Yorksh.* 308.

ASA, *Yorksh.* 322 b. ter. 331. *Linc.* 373 b.

ASA, uxor Bernulfi, *Linc.* 373.

ASCER, *Linc.* 366.

ASCHA, *Inter Ripam et Mersam,* 269 b.

ASCHI, *Warw.* 243.

ASCHIL, *Dors.* 79 b. *Hunt.* 205 b. 206. *Bedf.* 213,
213 b. *Northampt.* 224 b. ter. *Warw.* 240 b. 241 b.
Nottingh. 293 bis. *Yorksh.* 301, 311 b. 313 ter.
320 b. passim. *Linc.* 340 b. 342 ter. 343 passim.
345 b. bis. 346 ter. 347, 352 b. 357 ter. 357 b.
360, 363 b. 366. *Clam. N. R. Linc.* 375 b. passim.
376. *Clam. W.R. Linc.* 376 b. *Suff.* 393.

ASCHIL tainus Regis, *Clam. in Chetst.* 376 b.

ASCHIL teignus R. E. *Hertf.* 139. *Bedf.* 212 b. ter. 213
passim. 213 b.

ASCHILBAR, *Linc.* 347.

ASCHILLUS huscarlus, *Suff.* 441 b.

ASCI, *Shropsh.* 257 b.

ASCIUS presbyter, *Norf.* 273.

ASCORED, *Kent,* 11.

ASELOC, *Nottingh.* 285 b.

ASELOC (*interl.* Durand), *Nottingh.* 285 b.

ASFORD, *Nottingh.* 285. *Yorksh.* 327. *Linc.* 357 b. 366.

ASFORT, *Linc.* 342. *Clam. W.R. Linc.* 376.

ASGAR, *Devon,* 100 b. bis. 111 b. 112, 112 b. bis.
Cornw. 122. *Hertf.* 139 b. *Oxf.* 160. *Northampt.*
227 bis. 227 b. passim.

ASGAR stalre,[1] *Buck.* 149 b.   *Cambr.* 200 b.   *Warw.* 243 b.
ASGAR stalrus, *Midd.* 129 b.   *Hertf.* 140.

---

[1] The Harleian MS. 3776, one of those which relate to
Waltham Abbey, furnishes the pedigree of Asgar Stalre:

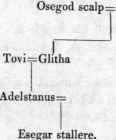

Osegod scalp=

Tovi=Glitha

Adelstanus=

Esegar stallere.

Geoffrey de Mandeville is said to have succeeded Asgar
in such lands as belonged officially to him, " non in totum
quidem possessionem quam possederat pater, sed in eam
tamen quæ pertinebat ad stallariam, quam nunc habet
comes Willielmus." This is corroborated by the entries in
Domesday, and explains them. Of the manor of Clapham
in Surrey we read, " Dicunt homines quod Goisfridus hoc
manerium injuste habet, *quia ad terram Asgari non pertinet;*"
tom. i. fol. 36. Again, in the same folio, under Weneberge,
" *non est de terra Asgar.*" In Berkshire, Middlesex, Hertfordshire, Oxfordshire, Northamptonshire, Warwickshire,
and Essex, Geoffrey de Mandeville's lands are marked uni-
formly as having been, in former time, the property of
Asgar or his homagers. Of Geoffrey's lands in Suffolk, in
contradistinction to the rest, it is more than once said, that
he did not hold them as of the honor or fee which had
been Ansgar's: as in tom. ii. fol. 411, under Cratinga,
" Gosfridus habet pro manerio *ex dono Regis,* et sub eo
Willielmus de Botevilla, *sed non pertinuit* AD FEUDUM Ansgari, antecessoris Gosfridi."

In the town of Hertford, Geoffrey de Mandeville possessed the tenement or mansion which had been Asgar's:
" Goisfridus de Magnavile habet occupatum quoddam qui
fuit Esgari stalri." *Hertf.* 132.

ASGAR stalrus R. E. *Midd.* 129 b. bis.

ASGARUS, *Norf.* 248.

ASGARUS stalre, *Buck.* 143 b.

ASGER, *Yorksh.* 373 b.

ASGOT, homo Heraldi Comitis, *Buck.* 144.

ASI, *Yorksh.* 308.

ASLAC, *Linc.* 341, 353, 357 b. 359 bis. 367.

ASLACUS commend. Burcardi, *Suff.* 407 b.

ASLI, *Linc.* 344 b.

ASSEMANNUS liber homo commend. *Suff.* 436.

ASSORINUS, *Essex*, 88, 91 b.

ASUL, *Yorksh.* 312 b. bis.

ASULF, *Yorksh.* 307.

ATHELWOLD presbyter commend. S. E.[1] *Suff.* 293 b.

ATILIC, *Worc.* 177 b.

ATSERUS, *Suff.* 443.

ATSUR commendatus Edrici de Laxefella, *Suff.* 444.

ATTILE, Edmer, *Hertf.* 136 b.

ATULES, Edmer, teignus R. E. *Midd.* 129 b.

AUDOENUS, Sanctus, *Essex*, 22.

AUDUID, *Yorksh.* 312, 331.

AUDULF, *Yorksh.* 301, 311 b.

AUEGRIN, *Warw.* 242 b.

AUELIN teignus R. E. *Buck.* 144.

AUELINUS teignus R. E. *Buck.* 144, 144 b.

AUEUE, *Heref.* 187 b.

AUGUSTINUS, *Staff.* 249.

AUIC, *Hunt.* 206, 207 b. *Derb.* 274 b. ter.

AVIGI, *Bedf.* 211 b.

AUITIUS, *Wilts,* 74 b.

AURED, *Dors.* 80.

Aurifaber, v. LEUUINUS.

AUSGARUS, *Suff.* 411 bis. 411 b.

---

[1] Sancti Edmundi.

Austin, *Shropsh.* 255.

Austin alter, *Shropsh.* 255.

Austinus, *Shropsh.* 258 b. 259 b.

Autbert, *Yorksh.* 330 b.[1]

Auti, *Sussex,* 29. *Hants,* 46, 49 b. *Glouc.* 168 b. 169 b. *Shropsh.* 256, 259 b. bis.[2] *Derb.* 278 b. *Linc.* 344 bis. 357 b. *Norf.* 262.

Auti huscarle Comitis Algari, *Bedf.* 213.

Autius teinus, *Suff.* 425 b.

Awart liber homo commendat. Edrico, *Suff.* 320 b. 321.

Azelinus homo comitis Tosti, *Bedf.* 217 b. bis.

Azer f. Burg, *Linc.* 337 bis.

Azer f. Sualeuæ, *Linc.* 337.

Azor, *Kent,* 1, 1 b. 6 b. 9. *Sussex,* 19 b. 21, 21 b. bis. 22 b. 23, 24 b. passim. 26 b. ter. 27 passim. 27 b. bis. 28 bis. 28 b. passim. *Surrey,* 34, 34 b. bis. 35 bis. 35 b. 36 bis. *Hants,* 45 b. 46. *Berks,* 57 b. *Wilts,* 64 b. 66 bis. 69 b. ter. *Dors.* 83 b. 84 b. passim. *Somers.* 89, 99. *Oxf.* 157 b. 160, 161. *Worc.* 173, 173 b. 174, 175 bis. *Heref.* 183 b. *Northampt.* 220 b. bis. 224, 225. *Warw.* 239 b. 240 b. 244. *Shropsh.* 254, 256 b. bis. 257 bis. 258 b. 259, 260 b. *Nottingh.* 288 bis. 291 b. 293. *Yorksh.* 324. *Linc.* 336 b. 342 b. bis. 357, 366 bis. 366 b. *Clam. in Chetst.* 376 b. 377, 377 b.

Azor et fratres ejus, *Linc.* 344 b.

Azor dispensator, *Berks,* 62.

Azor f. Lefsi, *Northampt.* 223 b.

Azor f. Saleuæ, *Nottingh.* 280 b.

Azor frater Siuuardi, *Linc.* 366.

---

[1] Also when the Survey was taken.

[2] In both these instances, also at the Survey.

Azor homo Ansgari, *Midd.* 129 b.

Azor filius Tored, teignus R. E. *Buck.* 143 b.

Azor Toti filius, *Buck.* 149 b. bis. 151 b. bis. ⎱
Azor Toti filius huscarle R. E. *Buck.* 152 b. ⎰ *v.* Azo-
Azor filius Toti teignus R. E. *Buck.* 152 b.　　RIUS.

Azor quidam liber homo, *Sussex,* 25, 25 b. bis.

Azor homo Bored, *Bedf.* 209 b.

Azor huscarle R. E. *Midd.* 130.

Azorius filius Toti homo Reginæ Eddid, *Buck.* 151 b·

Azur, *Oxf.* 159 b. *Northampt.* 227. *Warw.* 244.

B.

B. Abbas S. Eadmundi,[1] *Suff.* 372.

Baco, *Linc.* 340.

Bada, *Derb.* 278, 278 b.

Bade, Abb. de, *Glouc.* 164.

Bagatona, Leuuinus de, tenus[2] Regis E. *Suff.* 427.

Bain' vicecomes, *Essex,* 6.

Balchi, *Glouc.* 170 b.

Balchi commend' Aistan, *Suff.* 376.

Baldeuinus, *Warw.* 240 b. 242 passim.

Baldric, *Derb.* 274 b. 275. *Nottingh.* 290.

Balduinus, *Berks,* 61 ter. 61 b. bis. 62 b. *Wilts,* 69 b.
　　Buck. 148 b.[3] 149.[3] *Glouc.* 160 bis. *Northampt.*
　　224 b. passim. *Leic.* 232. *Warw.* 242 passim.

---

[1] Baldwin Abbat of St. Edmund's Bury. Simeon of Durham places his death 2 cal. Jan. 1097. The Saxon Chronicle and the Annales S. Edmundi de Burgo say, in 1098. He has been mentioned in the former volume, p. 304, as a monk of St. Denys, and King Edward the Confessor's physician. He became Abbat of St. Edmundsbury in 1065.

[2] Teinus.

[3] He continued to hold in these instances when the Survey was made.

BALDUINUS Comes, *Devon,* 100.

BALDUINUS f. Herluini, *Glouc.* 163.

BALDUINUS homo Stigandi archiepiscopi, *Buck.* 148 b. bis.

BAR, *Yorksh.* 373.

BAR liber homo commend. Radulfo stalra, *Suff.* 294 b.

BAR, Gameltorp, *Yorksh.* 332.

BAR, Seiar, *Norf.* 223 b.

BAR, Seiardus, *Midd.* 128. *Norf.* 223 b.

BARCH, *Yorksh.* 301, 327 b.

BARDI, *Northampt.* 221 passim. *Leic.* 231. *Linc.* 337, 344 b. passim.

BARED, *Yorksh.* 317 b.

BARET, *Yorksh.* 299 b. 301, 315 b. 316 passim. 316 b. bis. 329 b. 331 b. *Linc.* 362 b.

BARN, Siuuard, *Warw.* 242. *Nottingh.* 280 b. *Linc.* 337, 369.

BARNE, *Linc.* 344 b.

BASIN, *Yorksh.* 301, 304 b. 306, 320 b. bis. 331 b. 373 ter.

BASINE, *Yorksh.* 325 bis.

BATOC, Turchil, *Warw.* 243.

BATSUEN, *Shropsh.* 257 b.

BEDEFORD, Goduuinus burgensis de, *Bedf.* 218.[1]

BEDEFORD, Goduuidere de, *Bedf.* 218 b.[2]

Bedel, Brictmarus, *Suff.* 446.

BEDLING, *Sussex,* 28.

BELAM, *Chesh.* 266 b.

BELEHORNE, Bricmer, *Hunt.* 208.

BELINTONE, Ælmer de, *Hertf.* 141.

BELRAP, Aluuardus, homo Alrici, *Bedf.* 214 b.

---

[1] He continued to hold his land at the Survey.

[2] He also continued to hold his land when Domesday Book was formed.

BENEDICTUS, Sanctus, *Buck.* 148, 158 b. 159.

BENNE, Leuuinus, *Suff.* 419.

BENZ, Osmund, *Derb.* 278 b.

BEORUS liber homo, *Suff.* 373 bis.

BER, *Yorksh.* 322.

BERCHINGES, Ædcclesia de, *Midd.* 128 b. *Essex,* 57 b.[1]⎫

BERCHINGIS, S. Maria de, *Essex,* 17 b. 18, 18 b.⎬

BERCHINGIS, Abbatissa de, *Essex,* 107.⎭

BERCSI, *Heref.* 181.

BERE, *Devon,* 117 b.

BERENG' homo Sancti E. *Suff.* 449.

BERGULUER, *Yorksh.* 315.

BERLEA, Almarus de, *Essex,* 101 b.

BERN, *Dors.* 82 b. *Northampt.* 220. *Norf.* 222 b.

BERNAC, *Linc.* 351 b.

BERNARDUS, *Shropsh.* 258 b.

BERNARDUS presbyter R. E., *Hunt.* 208.

BERNE, *Yorksh.* 301 b.

BERNOLTUS, *Kent,* 11 b.

BERNULF, *Chesh.* 264, 266 b. *Inter Ripam et Mersam,* 269 b. *Yorksh.* 298, 311, 311 b. 312, 322, 322 b. bis. 323.

BERNULFUS, *Staff.* 248, 250 b. *Yorksh.* 298, 310 b. 311, 322, 323.

BERRUARIUS, *Suff.* 385 b.

BERS, *Chesh.* 265.

BERTOR, *Linc.* 351, 351 b. 356.

BERTUNT, *Shropsh.* 259.

BESI, *Oxf.* 159 b.

BESO, *Suff.* 322, 419.

BESY, *Rutl.* 293 b. *Linc.* 367.

---

[1] Land at Roinges, possessed by Geoffrey de Mandeville, which, according to the testimony of the Hundred, had belonged to the Abbey of Berking.

BETESLAU, Vlueua, *Hants*, 43.[1] *Wilts*, 74 b.

BETTICE, homo Wluini de Esteuuiche, *Hertf.* 140 b.

BEVRARIA, Drogo de, *Norf.* 198 b.[2]

BEVRELI, Canonici de,[3] *Yorksh.* 373. ⎫

BEVRELI, S. Joh. de, *Yorksh.* 304, 374. ⎭

BICHE, *Devon*, 112.

BIGA, *Surrey*, 31 b.

Biga, Esber, *v.* ESBER. SBERN.

BIL, *Glouc.* 169 b.

BISCOP, *Northampt.* 220, 223, 224, 226,[4] 229 bis.

BISI teignus R. E. *Buck.* 150 b. bis.

BITURICENSIS, Herveus, *Suff.* 352.

BLAC, *Sussex*, 18. *Yorksh.* 323.

BLAC, Aluric, *Hertf.* 133, 141 b.

BLAC, Brictricus, *Suff.* 440 b.

BLACH, Aluuinus, *Hunt.* 207.

BLACH homo Augi, *Bedf.* 211 b.

BLACHE, homo S. Albani, *Hertf.* 136.

BLACHEMAN, *Kent*, 13. *Hants*, 49, 53 b. bis. *Berks*, 59 bis. *Oxf.* 160. *Glouc.* 170. *Suff.* 376.

BLACHEMAN commendatus Edrico, *Suff.* 313.

BLACHEMAN homo Tosti Comitis, *Buck.* 145 b. bis.

BLACHEMAN presbyter, *Oxf.* 156 b.

BLACHEMANNUS, *Suff.* 342.

BLACHEMANUS, *Suff.* 315, 339 b. 342, 343.

BLACHEMER, *Shropsh.* 260 b.

---

[1] She had held her land from the Monastery of St. Peter, Winchester, " usque ad obitum. Post mortem ejus reddidit rex W. hoc manerium eidem Ecclesiæ pro sua anima et uxoris suæ."

[2] He is mentioned in the former volume, p. 382.

[3] Called " Clerici de Beurelei," *Yorksh.* fol. 304.

[4] He continued to hold his land at the time of the Survey.

BLACRE, *Yorksh.* 323 ter.

BLACSUNE, *Suff.* 345, 377.

BLACSUNUS, *Suff.* 377.

BLACUIN homo regis E. *Cambr.* 190.

BLACUINUS vicecomes R. E., *Cambr.* 201 bis. 201 b.
    Suff. 377, 396.

BLACUINUS commendatus Siwardo [de Meldona], *Suff.*
    416 b.

BLACUN, Herbertus, *Suff.* 447.

BLACUS, Brictricus, *Suff.* 396.

BLAKEMAN, *Suff.* 313.

BLAKEMANNUS, *Suff.* 334 b. 441 b.

BLAKEMANUS, *Suff.* 341 b.

BLANCAR, Robertus, *Norf.* 243.

BLUNDUS, Robertus, *Norf.* 276 b. 277 b. 278.

BOCHE, *Kent,* 11.

BODA, *Hants,* 46, 48 b.

BODDUS, *Essex,* 26 b.

BODE, *Wilts,* 72, 74 b.

BODIN, *Staff.* 249 b.

BODING constabularius, *Buck.* 151 bis.

BOI, Aluuinus, *Surrey,* 31.

BOIA, *Devon,* 101 b.

BOLE, *Linc.* 351 b.

BOLEST, Alric, *Buck.* 153.

BOLLA, *Hants,* 40, 52 b. 53 bis.

BOLLA, Alsius, liber homo, *Essex,* 80.

BOLLE, *Hants,* 46 b. *Wilts,* 72 ter. 74 b. *Dors.* 84.

BOLLO, *Somers.* 92.

BOLLO presbyter (cum aliis VII. liberis tainis T. R. E.)
    Dors. 84.[1]

BOLN, *Dors.* 84.

---

[1] He continued to hold at the Survey.

BOLNE, *Hants*, 50.

BONDE, *Kent*, 7. *Hants*, 48, 54. *Berks*, 60 b. 72 b. *Dors*. 85. *Yorksh*. 324.

BONDE liber homo, *Norf.* 197 b.

BONDI, *Glouc.* 166 b. *Northampt.* 227 b.[1] 228 ter. 228 b.

BONDI stalrus, *Bedf.* 218 b.

BONDIUS, *Essex*, 57 bis.

BONDO liber homo, *Cornw.* 121 b. *Suff.* 393 b.

BONDUS, *Essex*, 83 b. *Norf.* 233, 237 bis. 237 b. *Suff.* 343, 442.

BONDUS commend. Ailmari Episcopi, *Suff.* 380 b.

BONDUS liber homo, *Norf.* 261.

BONDUS liber homo commend. Edrici, *Suff.* 325.

BORDA, *Essex*, 67.

BORET presbyter, *Hunt.* 206.

BORGARET, *Devon*, 114.

BORGERED, *Cornw.* 125.

BORGERET, *Devon*, 108 b.

BORGERET et Vluric homo ejus, *Buck.* 145 b.

BORRED, *Hunt.* 203. *Bedf.* 210.

BORRET, *Buck.* 145 b.

BORRET et Vluric homo ejus, *Buck.* 145 b.

BOSCOMBE, Alestan de, *Glouc.* 169.

BOSCOME, Alestan, *Somers.* 96 b.

BOSCUMBE, Alestan de, *Wilts*, 71 b. *Hertf.* 138 b. ter. 139.

BOSCUMBE, Alestan de, teignus R.E. *Bedf.* 211 b. 212.

BOSCUMME, Alestan, *Wilts*, 71 b.

Boso liber homo, *Essex*, 100.

---

[1] He held the land of this entry at the time of the Survey.

BOSTEINNUS, *Suff.* 398 b.

BOT, Aldred, *Kent,* 13.

BOTI, *Suff.* 423.

BOTI homo regis E. *Suff.* 334.

BOTILD, *Linc.* 366.

BOTIUS, *Suff.* 419.

BOTIZ, *Sussex,* 19.

BOU, liber homo, *Norf.* 265 b.

BOUI, *Northampt.* 220, 223. *Leic.* 237. *Warw.* 240, 240 b. *Nottingh.* 287 b.

BRAND, *Clam. in Chetst.* 376 b.

BRAND huscarl regis E. *Hertf.* 138 b.

BRANDULF, *Yorksh.* 374.

BRANDUNA Vluric de, *Essex,* 101 b.

BRANTING, *Bedf.* 214.

BRANTINGUS homo regis E. *Bedf.* 218 b.

BRANUUINE, *Derb.* 277 b.

BREME, " liber homo Regis E. qui fuit occisus in bello Hastingensi," *Suff.* 409 b.

BRENFELDE, Ecclesia S. Mariæ de, *Shropsh.* 258.

BRESIBALT, *Kent,* 13.

BRETEL, T. R. E, *Cornw.* 124.

BRI. [*sc.* BRISMER], *Suff.* 423 b.

BRICFRID, *Dors.* 84 b.

BRICHTMARUS, T. R. E. *Suff.* 437.

BRICMAR, *Sussex,* 28 b.[1] *Leic.* 237.

BRICMÆR, *Sussex,* 26 b.

BRICMER Belehorne, *Hunt.* 208.

BRICNOD, *Wilts,* 73 b. *Dors.* 82 b.

BRICSI, *Dors.* 83. *Glouc.* 167.

BRICSI cild, *Surrey,* 35.

---

[1] " Bricmar tenuit de Azor, et Azor de Heraldo."

BRICSIC, *Somers.* 98 b.

BRICSIUS, *Essex,* 48.

BRICSMAR, *Hants,* 46, 49 b. *Worc.* 175. *Heref.* 183 b.

BRICSMAR teinus regis E. *Worc.* 177.

BRICSTAN, *Sussex,* 22.

BRICSTEC, *Berks,* 62 b.

BRICSTEG Episcopus Wirecest.,[1] *Worc.* 173.

BRICSTOUUARD, *Somers.* 99.

BRICSTUAL, *Shropsh.* 257 b.

BRICSTUARDUS, *Berks,* 58.

BRICSTUI, *Devon,* 108 b.

BRICSTUINUS, *Warw.* 238 b.

BRICTERE, liber homo Stigandi, *Suff.* 450 bis.

BRICTEUA, *Devon,* 118. *Linc.* 371.

BRICTICUS, *Essex,* 101 b.

BRICTMAR, *Worc.* 172 b. *Linc.* 368 b.[2]

BRICTMAR', *Suff.* 419.

BRICTMARUS, *Essex,* 31 bis. 63 b. 72, 72 b. 74 b. 97.
    Suff. 384 b. 411 b. 423 b. 424, 424 b.

BRICTMARUS bedel, *Suff.* 446.

BRICTMARUS commend. Edrici, *Suff.* 318 b.

BRICTMARUS commendatus Vlueue, *Suff.* 322.

BRICTMARUS liber homo, *Essex,* 27 b. 101. *Suff.* 295,
    423.

BRICTMARUS liber homo commendat. Edrico, *Suff.*
    320 b.

BRICTMARUS, liber homo Heroldi, *Suff.* 429.

BRICTMARUS teinus Regis Eaduuardi, *Essex,* 26.

BRICTMER, *Worc.* 174 b. bis.

---

1 Called also Brictrec and Brihtegus. See p. 3, note 2,
of the present volume.

2 Two manors in Cretune : " h'b'r Fredgist et Brictmar."
" Terra Brictmar, frigsoka sub Fredgist."

BRICTOLFUS, *Essex*, 102.[1]

BRICTREDUS teinus Eduini Comitis, *Worc.* 172.

BRICTRIC, *Sussex*, 26 b. *Surr.* 31 b. *Hants*, 39 b. 40,
47 b. 48 b. *Berks*, 61 b. 62, 63 passim. 63 b. *Wilts*,
66 b. 68 b. 69, 70 bis. 72 b. *Dors.* 77 b. 79 bis.
79 b. bis. 82 b. 83 bis. 85. *Somers.* 88 bis. 90,
91 ter. 93, 93 b. ter. 94, 95 b. 96,[2] 98 b. bis. 99.
Devon, 101 passim. 102, 102 b. passim. 104 bis.
105 b. passim. 106 bis. 107 b. bis. 108. 108 b.
bis. 109 b. 110, 110 b. 111, 112 b. bis. 113 bis.
115, 115 b. 116, 116 b. passim. 117 b. bis. 118.
118 b. bis. *Cornw.* 120, 122, 123 passim. 124 b.
bis.[2] *Buck.* 149. *Oxf.* 159 b. *Glouc.* 164, 167 b.
170 b. ter.[2] *Worc.* 174 b. ter. *Heref.* 180 b. ter.
185 b. bis. *Warw.* 241,[2] 243 b. bis. 244. *Shropsh.*
256. *Linc.* 341.

BRICTRIC fil. Algar,[3] *Glouc.* 163 b. passim. 166 b. *Worc.*
173 bis.

---

[1] He continued to hold at the Survey.

[2] Brictric continued to hold the land in fol. 96, and in
one of the entries in 98 b. at the time of the Survey: as
well as the lands entered in 124 b. bis. 170 b. ter. and
241.

[3] Kelham, from Rudder's Gloucestershire, p. 739, says,
" Brictric had the honor of Gloucester, which was a noble
seigniory, and many other great estates, by inheritance from
his grandfather Hailward Snow; but having incurred the
displeasure of Maud, queen to William the Conqueror, and
daughter to Baldwin Earl of Flanders, by refusing to marry
her when he was ambassador at her father's court, she
revenged the insult by procuring his imprisonment, and the
confiscation of all his possessions." Illustr. p. 165.

Of four manors in Cornwall, tom. i. fol. 120, it is certainly
said, " Infrascriptas terras Brictric tenebat, *et post* MA-

BRICTRIC homo Eddid reginæ, *Hertf.* 136 b.   *Buck.* 150
   bis. 150 b.

THILDIS REGINA." Mathilda's manors in Gloucestershire,
fol. 163 b., had also been Brictric's.

The anonymous continuator of Wace, who wrote in the
reign of Henry the Third, and who says he translated his
Poem at Amesbury in Wiltshire, is perhaps the oldest authority for the story of Matilda's disappointment. He states
Brictric to have died in prison at Winchester, without heir,
and that his property in consequence escheated, and was
disposed of by the Conqueror, in part to *his Queen* and in
part to Robert Fitz Haimon. But the honor of Gloucester,
which had been Brictric's, was really bestowed upon Robert
Fitz Haimon by King William Rufus: so that Wace's continuator is guilty of at least one anachronism.

The following is the passage from the continuator of
Wace. MS. Cotton. Vitellius A. x. fol. 129.

  " Willam bastard' de Normondie,
    Le fiz Rob't od la cher hardie,
    Englet're par force conquist,
    Rois e sires la einz remist.
    Le ior de Noel fu corune
    Od m'lt gᵃnt sollempnite,
    E a la pentecoste e leste
    Malde sa femme a reine leue;
    Ceste Malde de flandres fu nee,
    Meis de escoce fu appelee
    Pur sa mere, ke fu espuse
    Al roi de escoce ki lout roue;
    Laquele iadis qᵃnt fu pucele
    Ama un conte dengleterre,
    Brictrich Mau le oi nomer
    Apres le rois ki fu riche ber;
    A lui la pucele enuera messager
    Pur sa amur a lui procurer,
    Meis Brictrich Maude refusa

Brictriç liber homo, *Devon*, 112 b. *Essex*, 102.
Brictric teinus Eddid reginæ, *Worc.* 176 b.

---

f. 129 b.   Dunt ele m'lt se coruca,
　　　　　　Hastiuement mer passa
　　　　　　E a Willam bastard se maria:
　　　　　　Qⁿt Willam fu corune
　　　　　　E Malde sa feme a reine leue,
　　　　　　Icele Malde se purpensa
　　　　　　Coment vengier se purra
　　　　　　De Brictriche Mau kele ama,
　　　　　　Ki a femme p'ndre la refusa;
　　　　　　Tant enchanta son seignor,
　　　　　　Le rei Willam le Conqueror,
　　　　　　Ke de Brictrich Mau lad grante
　　　　　　De faire de lui la volente;
　　　　　　La reine par tot le fist guerreier
　　　　　　K' ele li uolt desheriter,
　　　　　　Pris fu a haneleye a son maner,
　　　　　　Le ior ke Saint Wlstan li ber
　　　　　　Sa chapele auoit dedie;
　　　　　　A Wyncestre fu amene,
　　　　　　Ilokes morut en prison
　　　　　　Brictrich Mau par treison;
　　　　　　Qⁿt il fu mort senz heir de sei
　　　　　　Son heritage seisit le Rei,
　　　　　　E cum escheit tint en sa main
　　　　　　Dekes il feoffa Rob't fiz haim,
　　　　　　Ki oueke lui de Normondie
　　　　　　Vint od m'lt grant cheualerie:
　　　　　　La t're ke Brictrich li leissa
　　　　　　Franchement a Robert dona.
　　　　　　Willam ki fu rois e sires
　　　　　　Par tot fist ses mestries,
　　　　　　Les contez, e les baronies,
　　　　　　Les sokages, e les serganties,
　　　　　　Dona al Bretons e a Normanz."

　　　　　　*   *   *   *

BRICTRIC teignus regis E. *Buck.* 149 b. 150 b. 151.
Glouc. 167 b.

BRICTRICI pater, *Wilts,* 73 b. passim.

BRICTRICIUS, *Devon,* 112 b.

BRICTRICUS, *Norf.* 224. *Suff.* 397 b. 426 b.

BRICTRICUS filius Doddi, *Worc.* 173 b.

BRICTRICUS liber homo Stigandi, *Norf.* 259.

BRICTRICUS blac,
BRICTRICUS blacus, } *v.* BLAC. BLACUS.

BRICTRICUS prepositus S. Eadmundi, *Suff.* 437 b.

BRICTSUINUS, *Berks,* 58 b.

BRICTUALDUS, *Devon,* 113.

BRICTUARDUS, *Berks,* 61.

BRICTUI, *Dors.* 80 b.

BRICTUID, *Somers.* 92 b.

BRICTUIN, *Dors.* 80 b. 84 bis.[1] 84 b.[1] *Somers.* 94, 96.
Devon, 112 b. *Northampt.* 226. *Leic.* 241 b.

BRICTUINUS, *Sussex,* 19, 22 bis. 28 b. *Hants,* 53. *Dors.*
79, 82. *Somers.* 91, 93. *Worc.* 173.

BRICTUINUS homo Heraldi Comitis, 146 b.

BRICTUOLD, *Devon,* 102 b. bis. 110 b. 117 b.

BRICTUOLDUS, *Dors.* 82. *Devon,* 102 b. 111 bis.

BRICTUOLT, *Suff.* 305, 377 b. 440 b.

BRICTUUARD, *Berks,* 60 ter.

BRICTUUOLDUS, *Somers.* 99.

BRICXTRIC teignus R. E. *Bedf.* 212.

BRIDEUUOLDUS, *Devon,* 115 b.

BRIFORD, *Linc.* 350 b.

BRIHFERD, *Cornw.* 123.

BRIHMARUS, *Suff.* 424, 424 b. ter.

BRIHT, *Suff.* 424.

---

[1] Brictuin continued to hold the lands mentioned in these
folios at the time of the Survey.

BRIHTMANUS, *Suff.* 346 b.

BRIHTMAR liber homo, *Suff.* 424 b.

BRIHTMARUS, *Suff.* 299, 321, 341, 342 b. 343.

BRIHTMARUS commend. Edrici, *Suff.* 326, 444.

BRIHTMARUS liber homo commendatus Edrici de Laxefel, *Suff.* 442.

BRIHTMARUS commend. Heroldi, *Suff.* 443.

BRIHTMARUS commend. S. *Suff.* 343 b.

BRIHTMERUS, *Suff.* 442 b.

BRIHTNOTHUS, *Suff.* 340 b. 346, 380 b.

BRIHTNOTUS commend. Edrici, *Suff.* 325 b.

BRIHTRICUS, *Suff.* 340, 340 b. 342 bis. 342 b. 442 bis.

BRIHTRICUS commend. Alric deburch, *Suff.* 413.

BRIHTRICUS commend. dim. Brihtmarus et dim. Stanmar, *Suff.* 424.

BRIHTRICUS liber homo S. *Suff.* 346.

BRIHTUOLDUS musla, *v.* MUSLA.

BRIHTWALDUS commendatus Reginæ, *Suff.* 433.

BRINOT, *Linc.* 352.

BRISID, *Devon,* 115 b.

BRISMAR, *Sussex,* 29 b. *Wilts,* 72 b. bis. 73 b. bis. *Dors.* 80 b. *Somers.* 89, 92, 93 b. bis. 94, 95, 96, 99.[1] *Devon,* 103, 105 b. 106 passim. 106 b. passim. 107 ter. 107 b. 108, 108 b. 111 b. ter. 113, 117 b. ter. 118. *Cornw.* 120 b. 121 b. bis. 122 passim. 122 b. bis. 123 bis. 125. *Heref.* 185 b.

BRISMER, *Devon,* 107 b. 110 b. 114 b. *Cornw.* 123 bis. 123 b. 125. *Glouc.* 169 b. *Heref.* 184, 184 b. *Chesh.* 264 b. *Suff.* 423 b.

BRISNOD, *Dors.* 83. *Somers.* 86, 92, 93.

BRISTEC, *Berks,* 61 b. ter.

---

[1] He continued to hold the land, mentioned in this folio, when the Survey was formed.

BRISTEI, *Berks*, 62.

BRISTEUUARD, *Berks*, 62 b.

BRISTOALDUS, *Devon*, 111.

BRISTOALDUS presbyter, *Heref.* 183 b.

BRISTOARDI presbyteri pater, *Wilts*, 65 b.

BRISTUALDUS, *Cornw.* 122.

BRISTUI, *Sussex*, 21 b.

BRISTUIN, *Somers.* 92.

BRISTUOLDUS, *Devon*, 109, 113.

BRISTUUARD, *Somers.* 92.

BRISTUUI, *Wilts*, 72.

BRISTUUOLDUS, *Somers.* 94 b.

BRITEUA, *Linc.* 359.

BRITFLEDA libera femina, *Suff.* 309 b.

BRITHEUE, *Hunt.* 207.

BRITHMARUS homo Heraldi Comitis, *Midd.* 130.

BRITHWOLDUS, *Suff.* 433.

BRITMAR, *Somers.* 96. *Warw.* 240 b.

BRITMARUS, *Suff.* 305.

BRITNOD, *Dors.* 79. *Cornw.* 122 b. *Warw.* 240.

BRITNODUS, *Somers.* 88, 94 b. *Warw.* 238 b. 240 b.

BRITRIC, *Linc.* 336.

BRIXE cilt, *Kent*, 6, 6 b.

BRIXI, *Sussex*, 20 b. 24 b. 29. *Surrey*, 36 bis.[1] *Wilts*,
    69 b. *Somers.* 95, 96 b. *Devon*, 102 b. *Cornw.*
    123 b. ter.

BRIXI cilt, *Kent*, 1 b. 6 b.

BRIXI, Godel de, *Kent*, 6 b.

BRIXIUS, *Suff.* 445 b.

---

[1] The Brixi of this entry, who held the manor of Hatcham
in Camberwell T. R. E., is supposed to have given name to
the hundred of Brixton, anciently called Brixistan. See
Lysons, Env. of Lond. edit. 1811, vol. i. p. 89.

BRIXTUIN teignus R. E. *Buck.* 146 b.

BROCLES, *Linc.* 348 b.

BRODE liber homo, *Glouc.* 164.

BRODER, *Staff.* 249.

BRODO, *Bedf.* 218.[1] *Norf.*[2] 277.

BRODOR, *Staff.* 249 bis.

BRODOS, *Linc.* 342 b.

BRODRE, *Devon*, 109. *Cornw.* 123.

BRUHISE, *Linc.* 359.

BRUMAGE, *Northampt.* 223.

BRUMAN homo S. archiepiscopi, *Buck.* 146 b.

BRUMANBEARD homo Normanni dimid. et dimid. Bri-
mari, *Suff.* 334 b.

BRUMANNUS, *Kent*, 2.

BRUMANUS, *Suff.* 342.

BRUMARUS, *Suff.* 342.

BRUN, *Chesh.* 264, 266, 266 b. ter. *Derb.* 274, 277 b.
Nottingh. 287 b. *Rotel.* 293. *Suff.* 337 b. ter. 378.

BRUN liber homo, *Essex*, 74 b.

BRUN presbyter, *Oxf.* 157.[3]

BRUN presbyter et mater ejus, *Yorksh.* 298.

BRUNARUS presbyter, *Suff.* 440.

BRUNE, *Derb.* 275. *Nottingh.* 287 b. *Yorksh.* 300 b.
301, 373 b.

BRUNEHAM, Alsi de, homo Eddid reginæ, *Bedf.* 213 b.
bis.

BRUNESUNE, *Kent*, 6.

---

[1] He remained under-tenant of the same property when
held in capite by Judith wife of Richard Tailgebosc.

[2] He still held the land of this entry at the formation of
the Survey.

[3] Brun also still continued to hold his land at the time of
the Survey.

BRUNGAR, T. R. E. *Dors.* 79. *Devon,* 103, 107 b. 111.
Suff. 377.

BRUNGAR liber homo Rotberti [patris Sueni de Excesse],
Suff. 401 b. bis.

BRUNGART, *Suff.* 322.

BRUNIER, *Linc.* 371.

BRUNIHT, *Shropsh.* 257 b.

BRUNING, *Kent,* 6. *Hants,* 52 b. 54.¹ *Wilts,* 71 b.
Somers. 93 b. *Heref.* 180 bis. 183, 184. *Warw.*
241.¹ 241 b. 244 b.

BRUNO, *Somers.* 99.

BRUNUS, *Essex,* 48. *Suff.* 441 b.

BRUNWINUS, *Suff.* 299 b. 375 b.

BRUNUUINUS commendatus Guerti, *Suff.* 442.

BU, *Yorksh.* 332.

BUBBA, Brictmarus, liber homo Haroldi, *Suff* 323 b.

BUCFESTRE, Æcclesia de, *Devon,* 103 b. 104.²

BUGE, *Nottingh.* 292 b.

BUGERED, *Devon,* 110 b.

BUGHERED, *Devon,* 107.

BUGO, *Nottingh.* 289 b. *Yorksh.* 307 b.

BULUI, *Hunt.* 205 b.

BUNDA, *Suff.* 334.

BUNDA faber, *Suff.* 334 b.

BUNDE, *Yorksh.* 373 b.

BUNDE, liber homo, *Norf.* 226.

BUNDI, *Hants,* 48 bis. 49, 60. *Dors.* 83 b. *Somers.*
92 b. *Oxf.* 157 b. *Cambr.* 198. *Northampt.* 225
bis. 226, 228. *Warw.* 240, 244 b.

---

¹ Bruning still held the lands of these entries when
Domesday was formed.

² See the former volume, in the Index to the Tenants in
Capite. It is called " Bulfestrensis Abbatia" in the Exon
Domesday.

BUNDI forestarius, *Oxf.* 154 b.

BUNDINUS, *Berks,* 60 b.

BUNDIUS, *Essex,* 57.

BUNDO, *Heref.* 184 b.   *Norf.* 237 b. 238 bis. 238 b. 239
  bis. *Suff.* 397.

BUNDO liber homo, *Norf.* 270 b.

BUNDUS, *Yorksh.* 298.   *Essex,* 59 b.   *Norf.* 237 bis.

BUNDUS commend. Guerti, *Suff.* 445.

BUNDUS liber homo Heroldi, *Norf.* 260 b.

BUNDUS unus teinus, *Norf.* 258.

BURC, Ailricus de, *Suff.* 443.

BURC, Ælfricus de, *Suff.* 347.

BURCARDUS, *Essex,* 63 b.   *Suff.* 407.

BURCARDUS de Fenelai, *Buck.* 143.

BURCARDUS huscarle regis E. *Buck.* 146 b.

BURCH, Brumanus de, *Suff.* 314 b.

BURCHARD, *Nottingh.* 285 b.   *Suff.* 301 ter. 301 b. 302.

BURCHARD', *Suff.* 299.

BURCHARDUS, *Suff.* 301 b. 322, 407 b. 408.

BURCHARDUS teignus regis E. *Buck.* 147.

BURCHART, *Nottingh.* 285 b.

BURCHERIC, *Suff.* 378.

BURCHRICUS, *Suff.* 339 b.

BURCKARDUS, *Suff.* 407, 407 b.

BURKART, teinnus, *Buck.* 152 b.

BURG, S. Edmundi de, Abbatia, *Cambr.* 192. *Bedf.*
  210 b. *Northampt.* 219, 222. *Linc.* 336 b. 337,
  345 b. passim. *Essex,* 19 b. *Norf.* 209, 275 b. *Suff.*
  356 b.

BURG, S. Petrus de, *Hunt.* 205, 208 b. 210 b. *Northampt.*
  221. *Leic.* 231. *Nottingh.* 284. *Linc.* 345 b.

BURGEL, *Wilts,* 71.

BURGENSES duo qui fuerunt Leuuini comitis, *Buck.*
  143.

BURGENSES duo de Colecestra, *Essex*, 106 b.

BURGENSES IIII. homines Alrici, *Buck*. 143.

BURGENSES quatuor, homines Azoris f. Toti, *Buck*. 143.

BURGENSES XVIII. in Hertforde habet rex W. qui fuerunt homines Heraldi et Leuuini comitum, *Hertf*. 132.

BURGENSES de Pevenesel, *Sussex*, 20 b.

BURGENSIS de Bochingeham qui fuit homo Burcardi de Fenelai, *Buck*. 143.[1]

BURGENSIS, homo Azor f. Toti, *Buck*. 143 bis.

BURGENSIS quidam de Oxeneford, *Buck*. 143 b.

BURGENSIS unus qui fuit Wilaf. *Buck*. 143.

BURGERED, *Devon*, 114, 117 b. *Cornw*. 124 b.

BURLI, Wihenoc de, *Norf*. 275.

BURNES, Godric, *Kent*, 1.

BURNES, Godricus, *Kent*, 13 b.

BURNOD, *Kent*, 10.

BURRED, *Bedf*. 210. *Northampt*. 220 b. passim.

BURREDI filius, *Northampt*. 221.

BURRER, *Shropsh*. 257.

BURRET, *Bedf*. 209 b. bis.

BURRICUS, *Suff*. 242, 441 b.

BURRICUS liber homo Radulfi Stalra, *Suff*. 431.

BURRO, *Cambr*. 197 b.

BUSCH, Aluric, *Hertf*. 140.

C.

CABE, *Cambr*. 191 b.

CADIAND, *Heref*. 181.

CADUUALENT, *Cornw*. 120 b.

---

[1] Also at the Survey.

CÆDD, Sanctus, Sciropesberie, *Shropsh.* 252, 253.

CAFLO, *Somers.* 94.[1]

CALPUS liber homo, *Norf.* 240.[1]

Camerarius, v. HUGO. WENESI. WINESIUS.

Camerarius R. E. *v.* HUGO. WANESI.

CAMP, Aluricus, *Essex,* 67 b. 70 b. 83 b.

CAMPA, Aluricus, *Suff.* 403 b.

CAMPO,[2] Aluricus, *Suff.* 421 b. 448.

CANA, *Sussex,* 19, 20 b. 21. *Surr.* 31 b.

Canceler, v. REMBALDUS.

CANDOVRE, Clerici de, *Hants,* 44 b.

CANE, *Sussex,* 19 b. 22.

CANISTRE, *Dev.* 113.

CANO, *Sussex,* 22 b. bis.

Canonici S. Achebranni, *Cornw.* 121.[3]

Canonici S. Berrione, *Cornw.* 121.[3]

Canonici de Bevreli, *Yorksh.* 304, 373, 374.

Canonici S. Carentoch, *Cornw.* 121.[3]

Canonici S. Probi,[3] *Cornw.* 121.

Canonici Ebor. *Yorksh.* 298.

Canonici duo Eccl. de Hereford, *Heref.* 181 b.

Canonici de Nistenestoch, *Dev.* 117.

Canonici de Oxenford, *Buck.* 146.

Canonici S. Pierani, *Cornw.* 121.[3]

CANTORBERIA, Sta Trinitas de, *Essex,* 8 b.

CANTUAR. S. Trin. *Suff.* 416 b.

---

[1] He continued to hold at the time of the Survey.

[2] Kelham translates this, " A. the champion." Illustr. p. 171. In both entries, however, here referred to, Aluricus campo held his land in the time of Edward the Confessor: and we have no mention of the office of a champion so early.

[3] These Cornish Canons all continued to hold their lands at the Survey. St. Burien's is still a College.

CANTUIN, *Warw.* 239 b. bis.

CANUD, Galterus, *Norf.* 280.

CANUS, *Sussex,* 18 b.

CANUT liber homo comitis Algari, *Suff.* 403.

Capellanus, v. ESMELLT.

CAPIN, Aluricus, *Suff.* 378.

CAPUS, Aluric, T. R. E. *Cambr.* 196 b.

CARENTOCH, S. *v. Canonici.*

CARI, *Leic.* 233 b.

CARLE, *Sussex,* 21 b. 28. *Hants,* 47 b. bis. *Somers.* 97.
   Shropsh. 257. *Chesh.* 263 b. 265 b. *Derb.* 278 b.
   Yorksh. 300, 301 passim. 307, 322 b. bis. 323 ter.
   326, 330 b. 332. *Linc.* 348 bis. 368 b. ter.[1] 371.
   Clam. in Chetst. 377 b.

CARLESONE, Godric, *Kent,* 1.

CARLEWUDA, Wihtricus de, *Suff.* 314 b.

CARLO, *Sussex,* 22 b. 36 b. *Berks,* 63. *Wilts,* 70 b.
   Shropsh. 254.

CARMAN, *Wilts,* 70 b.

CARON, pater Willelmi de, *Bedf.* 210.

CASCHIN, *Derb.* 273, 274. *Nottingh.* 285.

CASSA, Vluricus, *Essex,* 49 b.

CAUA prepositus, *Hants,* 42.

CAUUA, Vluricus, *Essex,* 60 b.

CECUS quidam, *Nottingh.* 293.

CEDD, Sanctus, *Staff.* 247 ter.

CEDDE, Sanctus, *Shropsh.* 259. *Chesh.* 263, } *v.* CÆDD.
   266 b. bis.

CELCOTT, *Suff.* 394 b.

CELEINUS, *Wilts,* 72 b.

CELESTAN, *Wilts,* 74 b.

---

1 Of two manors in Carlebi it is said, " h'b'r Dane et
Carle :" " Terra Carle frigsoca sub Dane."

CELLINC, *Derb.* 275.

CELMAR, *Worc.* 176 b.

CELRED, *Somers.* 92, 92 b. *Warw.* 240.

CELRIC, *Somers.* 91, 93, 97 b.

CERNEL, S. Petrus de, *Dors.* 77 b. 78.

CERRET homo Turchil, *Warw.* 241.

CERTESYG, Abb. S. Petri de, *Surr.* 32 b. *Hants,* 43 b. *Berks,* 59 b.

CESTRE, Ecclesia Cath. de, *Staff.* 247.

CESTRE, S. Wareburg de, *Staff.* 248 b.

CESTRE, Episcopus de, *Warw.* 238 b. *Staff.* 247. *Shropsh.* 252. *Chesh.* 263 passim. *Derb.* 273. *Nottingh.* 280 b.

CETERITH, Abbatia de, *Suff.* 389.

CETRIZ Ecclesia S. Mariæ de, *Hertf.* 132, 136. }[1]
Cambr. 193.

CHELBERTUS homo Edid reginæ, *Bedf.* 218 b.[2]

CHENEGAR, *Devon,* 111.

CHENESTAN, *Devon,* 108 b.

CHENEUE, *Somers,* 93.

CHENEUUARD, *Worc.* 177.

CHENIAS, *Devon,* 112, 113.

CHENICTE, *Yorksh.* 301.

CHENING, *Hants,* 48.

CHENISI, *Cornw.* 122 b.

CHENISTRE, *Devon,* 107 b. bis.

CHENNA, *Hants,* 50 b.

CHENP, Vluric, *Berks,* 58 b.

CHENRIC, *Northampt.* 225 b.

CHENTIS homo Leuenot f. Osmundi, *Buck.* 146 b.

CHENTISCUS, Alnod, teignus regis E. *Buck.* 145.

---

[1] Chateris, in Cambridgeshire.

[2] " De hac terra (*sc.* III. virg. et dim.) tenuit istemet I. virg. homo fuit Eddid reginæ."

CHENTUINUS, *Warw.* 240.

CHENUARD, *Warw.* 243 b.

CHENUI, *Wilts,* 70 b.

CHENUICELLE, *Glouc.* 169 b.

CHENVICHELLE teignus Regis E. *Glouc.* 164.

CHENVIN, *Wilts,* 69 b. *Staff.* 250 b.[1]

CHENUT, *Yorksh.* 301. *Linc.* 356 b. 357.

CHEPIN, *Chesh.* 263 b.

CHEPING, *Hants,* 39 b. 46 b. passim. 47 passim. 51.
52. *Berks,* 62 b. *Wilts,* 73 b.[2] *Somers.* 94 b. 96.
Devon, 104 b. 107.

CHEPINGUS, *Hants,* 41.

CHERICUS, *Suff.* 450.

CHETEBER, *Yorksh.* 319 b.

CHETEL, *Hants,* 44 b. bis. 47, 51 b. bis. 52, 52 b. bis.
53. *Wilts,* 68 b. 70 bis. *Somers.* 95, 97 b. bis.
Devon, 112 b. 114. *Buck.* 153.[3] *Glouc.* 167, 170 b.
bis.[3] *Heref.* 180. *Shropsh.* 256, 258 b. bis. 259.
Chesh. 267 b. *Inter Ripam et Mersam,* 269 b. *Derb.*
273, 274, 274 b. 275 b. ter. 276. *Yorksh.* 301,
301 b. bis. 309 b. 315 b. 317 b. 320 bis. 326 b.
passim. 328, 330 b. 331 b. 332. *Linc.* 342, 354
bis. 356 b. 361 b. bis. 367, 371. *Yorksh.* 373 b.
ter.

CHETELBAR, *Linc.* 366 b.

CHETELBER, *Hunt.* 205 b. *Yorksh.* 319 b. 330 b. *Linc.*
342. *Clam. N. R. Linc.* 375 b. bis.

---

[1] He continued to hold his land at the time of the Survey
in capite.

[2] He held the land of this entry, a single virgate, at the
time of the Survey.

[3] Chetel continued to hold his lands, in the folios 153 and
170 b., at the time of the Survey.

CHETELBERN, *Nottingh.* 290.[1] *Linc.* 370 b. bis.

CHETELBERN liber homo, *Norf.* 149 b.

CHETELBERNUS, *Warw.* 240 b.

CHETELBERT, *Hunt.* 207 b. *Yorksh.* 319 b.

CHETELBERTUS, *Worc.* 176 b. *Northampt.* 228 b.[2] 239.

CHETELBURN, *Linc.* 342.

CHILBERT, *Yorksh.* 301 passim. 307 passim. 307 b.
    326, 331 bis.

CHILBERT et frater ejus, *Yorksh.* 301.

CHILBERT Torfin, *Yorksh.* 307 b.

CHILBERTUS, *Yorksh.* 307.

CHILUERT, *Yorksh.* 300, 324 b. ter. *Linc.* 343.

CHINESI, *Somers.* 95 b.

CHINESTAN, *Devon,* 108 b. *Cornw.* 122 bis.

CHINIAS, *Devon,* 112 b.

CHIPINC, *Suff.* 322 b.

CHIT, Wluuinus, homo Haroldi Comitis. *Hunt.* 208 bis.

CHITEL, *Cornw.* 123 b.

CICESTRE, Episcopus, *Sussex,* 16 b. 20 b.

Cild, v. BRICSI. BRIXE. BRIXI. EDUUARD. GODUINUS.
    VLMAR. WLUUARD.

CILLE, *Yorksh.* 322 b.

CILLEHAM, Siret de, *Kent,* 1.

Cilt, v. BRIXE. BRIXI. EDUUARD. EDUUI. ELMER.
    GODUINUS. LEURIC. LEUUIN. LEUUINUS. SUAIN.
    SUAN. SUEN. VLFRIC. VLUUI.

CIRECESTRE, Ecclesia de, *Glouc.* 166 b.

---

[1] He continued under-tenant of the same land, to Roger
of Poictou, at the time of the Survey.

[2] The land of this entry, which Chetelbert had held
freely in the time of K. Edward the Confessor, he held at
the time of the Survey as an under-tenant of the Countess
Judith.

CLAC, *Linc.* 352, 356 b. 358, 360, 365 b. *Clam. S. R.*
    Linc. 375.

CLAMAN, *Yorksh.* 301 b.

CLAREBOLDUS, *Suff.* 428.

Clerici, v. CANDOVRE. ELINTONE. NEOTI S.

Clericus, v. EDUUARDUS.

CLIBER, *Yorksh.* 332.

CLIBERT, *Yorksh.* 303, 330 b. 331, 331 bis.

CLOCH, Godric, *Worc.* 174 b.

CNUD, *Yorksh.* 306 b. 324 b. 326 b.

CNUT, *Derb.* 278 b. *Nottingh.* 293. *Yorksh.* 298 b. 300
    bis. 300 b. passim. 301, 307, 310 b. 311, 312, 317,
    323, 324 b. 327 b. *Linc.* 347 b. *Yorksh.* 374
    ter.

COBBE, Leuricus, *Suff.* 334 b.

Coc, Aluuinus, bedellus, *Cambr.* 190.[1]

CODE, *Linc.* 350 bis. 357 b. 364 bis. *Clam. S. R. Linc.*
    375 b.

CODOLF, *Hants,* 46 b.

CODRICUS dimidius sub-commendatus, *Suff.* 430.

CODUIUS, *Suff.* 393 b.

COFSI, *Yorksh.* 310.

COL.[2] *Linc.* 356 b.

COLA, *Sussex,* 20 b. 22 b. 27, 27 b. bis. *Surrey,* 35 b.
    bis. 36 b. *Glouc.* 168 b. *Essex,* 54.

COLÆ pater, *Wilts,* 73 b.

COLÆ CASTRO, Godricus de, *Essex,* 30.

COLBEN, *Chesh.* 266, 267 b.

COLBERT, *Devon,* 109 b. *Chesh.* 264 b. 265. *Linc.* 368.

---

[1] His land was only half a virgate, which he continued
to hold at the Survey.

[2] A contraction for " Colsuan."

COLBERTUS, *Devon*, 104 b. 115 b. *Chesh.* 265 bis.

COLBRAND, *Devon*, 107, 115 b. bis. *Yorksh.* 331 b.
v. COLEBRAND.

COLE, *Sussex*, 19 b. *Wilts*, 69 b. *Devon*, 109, 112 b.
Derb. 274.

COLEBRAN, *Warw.* 244 b.

COLEBRAND, *Dors.* 80. *Yorksh.* 300 b. v. COLBRAND.

COLECESTRA, Aluui de, *Norf.* 217 b.

COLEG', *Linc.* 370 b.

COLEGRIM, *Heref.* 187 b. *Derb.* 275 b. *Nottingh.* 291 b.
Linc. 370 bis. 370 b. passim.[1] v. COLGRIM.

COLEMAN, *Surr.* 35. *Hants*, 47 b. *Berks*, 60. *Oxf.* 154,
161.

COLEMAN liber homo sub Stigando, *Norf.* 227 b.

COLEMANNUS liber homo Stigandi, *Norf.* 240.

COLEMANUS, *Essex*, 40 b. 102. *Suff.* 419, 339 b.
340.

COLEMANUS liber homo, *Norf.* 180 b.

COLGRIM, *Yorksh.* 306 b. ter. 407. v. COLEGRIM.

COLGRIN, *Hants*, 51. *Somers.* 93.

COLIBERTUS, *Hants*, 50 b.

COLLE, *Derb.* 275 b.

COLLINC, *Shropsh.* 256.

---

[3] Colegrim is a Lincolnshire name which occurs in all the
Indexes of the present volume. When Thorold of Bukenhale gave the lands of Spalding to Croyland Abbey in 1051,
among the " adscriptitii glebæ," who were transferred with
their families and chattels to the abbey, we find " Colgrinum
prepositum meum, et totam sequelam suam, cum omnibus
bonis et catallis quæ habet in dictâ villâ et in campis ejus
et mariscis, absque aliquo de omnibus retinemento." Gale,
Rerum Anglic. Script. tom. i. p. 86.

Colne, *Derb.* 275 b.

Colo, *Wilts,* 72 bis. *Somers.* 96 b. *Cornw.* 122 b. ter.
124 b.[1]

Colo liber homo, *Essex,* 26 b.

Colo liber homo Asgari stalre, *Norf.* 149 b.

Colocar, Modgeua de, *Suff.* 314 b.

Coloen, *Kent,* 11.

Cols', *Linc.* 356 b.

Colsege liber homo, *Essex,* 40.

Colsuan, *Cambr.* 194 b. passim.[2] *Linc.* 356 b. passim.
Clam. S. R. Linc. 375. *Clam. N. R. Linc.* 376.

Colsuen, *Wilts,* 70 b. *Clam. in Chetst.* 377, 377 b.

Coluin, *Devon,* 106.

Colvinus, *Devon,* 118 b. ter.[3]

Comes, v. Balduinus. Edduinus. Edgarvs. Eustachius. Goduinus. Guerd. Guert. Guertus.
Gurert. Gurt. Haroldus. Herold. Heroldus. Hugo. Leuric. Leuricus. Leuuinus.
Morcar. R. Comes. R. Comes vetus. Radulfus.
Siuuard. Siuuardus. Tosti. W. Comes. Wallef. Walleuus. Waltef.

Comitissa, v. Ghida. Gida. Goda. Gode. Godeva.
Godeue. Godiva. Gudeta. Gueda. Gueth.

Commend. Grimolfi, *Suff.* 347.

Commendati iii. Burckhardi, *Suff.* 407 b.

Commendati homines iii. Halden, *Suff.* 413.

---

[1] Colo continued to hold in this entry at the time of the
Survey.

[2] " Istemet tenuit sub Eddeva T. R. E." He continued
to hold at the time of the Survey, both here and in Lincolnshire.

[3] He continued to hold these, with additional lands, at
the time of the Survey.

CONSTANTIENSIS Ecclesiæ Canonici, *Dors.* 79.[1]

COOLF, *Hants*, 51, 52.

Constabularius, v. BODING.

COOLLE, *Wilts*, 72 b.

COPSI, *Yorksh.* 298 b. 327. *Linc.* 363 bis.[2]

CORBUN, Hugo de, *Norf.* 278.

COSTELIN, *Heref.* 181.

COVENTREU, Ecclesia sive Abbatia de, *Warw.* 238 b.[3]

COUTA, *Suff.* 332 b.

CRAC, Grimbold, *Linc.* 347 bis.

CRAUELAI, Monasterium S. Firmini de, *Buck.* 149.[4]

CRENEBURNENSIS Ecclesia, *Wilts*, 67 b. *Dors.* 77 b.
Devon, 104.

---

[1] The BISHOP OF COUTANCE held nothing, T. R. E.

[2] Copsi was vicegerent to Tosti Earl of Northumberland, and a considerable benefactor to the Church of Durham. He made his submission to the Conqueror at the same time with Edwin and Morcar, and was appointed by him procurator of that part of the province of Northumbria north of the Tyne. Ordericus Vitalis, who calls him Coxo, gives an account of his assassination by the people of his own province, in consequence of his attachment to William. See Simeon of Durham, col. 37 ; and William of Poictou, p. 212, in Duchesne's Normannici Scriptores.

[3] The time of King Edward the Confessor is unnoticed in the entries of lands in other counties, which belonged to the Church of Coventry.

[4] A half virgate, which the Monastery continued to hold at the Survey. Lysons, describing North Crawley in Buckinghamshire, says, " At this place was an ancient monastery, dedicated to St. Firmin, which is mentioned in the Survey of Domesday. It was destroyed or fell to decay so long before the general dissolution of monasteries, that no notice of it has been found in any records subsequent to the abovementioned Survey." Mag. Brit. *Buck.* p. 545.

CRIN, *Yorksh.* 311.

CROC, Leswinus, *Suff.* 350. ⎫
CROC, Leuuinus, *Essex*, 89. ⎭

CROILAND, Abb. de, *Linc.* 337.

CRUILAND, Abbatia de, *Hunt.* 204.

CRUILAND, S. Guthlacus de, *Cambr.* 192 b. *Hunt.*
  204. *Northampt.* 222 b. *Linc.* 346 b. passim.
  364 b. *Clam. in Chetst.* 377, 377 b.

CRUCAN, *Yorksh.* 330 b.

CUBOLD, Aluuinus, *Northampt.* 220 b.

CUDULF, *Wilts*, 72 b.

CUDULFUS, *Wilts*, 73 b.[1]

CUULF, *Glouc.* 165.

CUTBERTUS, Sanctus, *Yorksh.* 298. ⎫
CUTBERTUS S. Dunelm. *Yorksh.* 304 b. ⎭

D.

DACHELIN, *Dors.* 80 b.

DACUS, *v.* OINUS. PHIN. TOL.

DAGOBERTUS, *Glouc.* 162.

DAINZ, *Shropsh.* 255 b.

DANE, *Nottingh.* 285 b. *Linc.* 340 b. 353, 356 b. bis.
  368 b. passim.

DANEMUNDUS homo Asgari stalri, *Cambr.* 198 b.

DANUS, *v.* OSMUNDUS. SIMOND. STRANG. TURCHILLUS.

Dapifer Abbatis S. Eadmundi de Burg, *Norf.* 275 b.

DEDOL, *Chesh.* 263 b. 264 b. bis.

DEDOU, *Chesh.* 265.

DEINCORA, *Linc.* 353 b.

DELFIN, *Yorksh.* 317 b.

DENA teinus regis E. *Glouc.* 168.

---

[1] He continued to hold the same land in capite at the
Survey.

DENE, *Wilts*, 73.

DEPEKIN liber homo commend. Heroldi, *Suff.* 425 b.

DERCH, *Chesh.* 265 b. bis.

DERINC, *Surrey*, 31 b.

DERINC filius Sired, *Kent*, 1 b.

DERING, *Kent*, 6.

DERINGUS, *Suff.* 342 b.

DEROLFUS, *Essex*, 102. *Suff.* 384 b.

DERSTANUS, *Suff.* 342 b.

DE RULFUS, *Suff.* 450.

DEULE, Aluuinus, *Hunt.* 206 b. 208.

DEULE, Aluuinus, homo Episcopi Lincoliensis, *Bedf.* 210 bis. 210 b. ter.

Diaconus, v. EDRICUS. ELSI. GODRICUS. GODUINUS. LIURICUS. ODA. ODE. RAYNERIUS. SAXFORDUS. VLF. WLURICUS.

DIMIDII homines III. commend. Algari, *Suff.* 386.

DIM' lib. homo commend. *Norf.* 189.

Dispensator, v. AZOR.

DODA, *Sussex*, 21, *Hants*, 39.

DODA, Leuuinus, *Warw.* 244.

DODE monachus, *Dors.* 84 b.

DODE, Aluuinus, homo Alurici parui, *Hertf.* 141.

DODINC, *Essex*, 86 b.

DODINGUS, *Midd.* 127. *Essex*, 56 b.

DODING, homo Asgari stalri, *Buck.* 149 b.

DODO, *Wilts*, 71 b. *Dors.* 75 b. 83 bis. 84. *Somers.* 98 b. *Devon*, 102, 102 b. ter. 103, 105 b. 107 b. ter. 112 b. 115 b. *Cornw.* 123, 124 bis. 124 b.[1] *Glouc.* 167 b. *Worc.* 173. *Warw.* 243 b. *Shropsh.* 258 b. 259 ter. *Chesh.* 267.

---

[1] Dodo held the land of this entry at the time of the Survey, under the Earl of Moretaine.

Dodo alter, *Glouc.* 167 b.

Dolesuuif, *Devon,* 106 b.

Dolfin, *Derb.* 278 b. bis. *Yorksh.* 301 b.

Domne, *Wilts,* 72 b. *Somers.* 93 b.

Domniz, *Berks,* 60 b.

Domno, *Wilts,* 72 b. *Somers.* 94, 94 b. 95 b. 97.

Don, *Berks,* 62.

Done, *Devon,* 118.

Döne, *Wilts,* 73 b.

Donne, *Devon,* 118 bis.[1]

Donninc, *Devon,* 105.

Donning, *Worc.* 174 b. *Chesh.* 267 b.

Döno, *Wilts,* 72 b.

Donno, T. R. E. *Somers.* 98 bis. 99. *Devon,* 105 b. bis.

Donnus, *Hants,* 52 b.

Dons, *Glouc.* 170 b.[2]

Dore, Aluuardus, *Essex,* 94.

Dot, *Chesh.* 259 b. 263 b. 264 bis. 265, 265 b. passim. 266, 266 b. 267 passim. 267 b. bis. *Inter Ripam et Mersam,* 269 b. *Suff.* 297 b.

Dot liber homo, *Essex,* 43. *Suff.* 404.

Doth, *Essex,* 67.

Dotus, *Bedf.* 218 b.

Dotus homo Dei, *Buck.* 150 b.

Dovre, Canonici S. Martini de, *Kent,* 1 b. 2.

Dringhel, *Yorksh.* 329 b.

Dringlel, *Yorksh.* 329 b.

Drogo homo Roberti Malet, *Norf.* 276 b.

Drondus, *Northampt.* 227.

---

[1] He continued to hold the land of these two entries, at the time of the Survey, in capite.

[2] He held the same land in capite at the Survey.

DUGLEL, *Yorksh.* 301.

DUNELMENSIS Episcopus, *Yorksh.* 304 b. 373.[1]

DUNESTAN, *Yorksh.* 301.

DUNNE, *Somers.* 96 bis. *Glouc.* 168 b.

DUNNIHT, *Shropsh.* 257 b.

DUNNINC, *Hunt.* 206 b. *Derb.* 274 b. 275 b. 277 b. *Nottingh.* 293. *Yorksh.* 319.

DUNNING, *Glouc.* 163 b. 167 b. *Worc.* 174 b. bis. *Staff.* 249, 250 b.[2] *Shropsh.* 258 b. 259 bis. 260 b. *Chesh.* 266 b. 267 b. passim.[3] *Derb.* 275 b. *Nottingh.* 285 b.

DUNNO, *Somers.* 94 b.

DUNS, *Glouc.* 168 b.

DUNSTAN, *Somers.* 92. *Derb.* 276 b. 277 b. *Nottingh.* 285 b. *Yorksh.* 298, 315 b. 318 passim. 321 b.

DURAND, *Hants*, 51.

DURAND, Aseloc, *Nottingh.* 285 b.

DURANDUS, *Suff.* 340, 342, 342 b. 343, 442, 442 b. 446.

DURANDUS commendat. Edrico de Laxefelda, *Suff.* 275 b.

DURANDUS liber homo, *Suff.* 425.

DURILDA, *Suff.* 341 b.

DUSTAN, *Yorksh.* 317 b.

---

[1] Yorkshire was the only county, south of his palatinate, in which the Bishop of Durham held lands in the time of King Edward the Confessor. His Yorkshire land was much wasted in the Conqueror's ravage in 1070.

[2] He held the land of this entry in capite at the Survey.

[3] In one of the entries of this folio, Dunning continued to hold the same land of Earl Hugh when Domesday was formed.

Duuua, *Essex*, 102.

Duuua libera femina, *Essex*, 36.

Duuen, *Yorksh.* 302.

Dyonisii S. Parisii Ecclesia, *Oxf.* 157. *Glouc.* 166.

E.

E. regina,[1] *Essex*, 87 bis.

Eadmundi, S. Abbatia, *Cambr.* 192.[2] *Essex*, 19. *Norf.* 209, 209 b. 210, 210 b. 211, 211 b. 212. *Suff.* 356 b. 405.

Eadmundus, Sanctus, *Suff.* 413 b. bis. 435, 447, 448 b.

Eaduinus, *Norf.* 224.

Ealgarus liber homo sub Stigando, *Norf.* 259 b.

Earne, *Yorksh.* 328 b.

Ebbi homo Brictric f. Algar, *Glouc.* 165.

Eborac. archiepiscopus, *Nottingh.* 280 b. *Yorksh.* 298, 302, 302 b. *Clam. S. R. Linc.* 375 b.

Eboracenses Canonici, *Yorksh.* 298.

Eboraci, Christi Ædifecclesia juxta Civitatem, *Yorksh.* 327.

Eboraci, S. Petrus, *Yorksh.* 298 b. 302 b. 303 passim. 303 b. passim.

Ebrard homo Willelmi Colit, *Yorksh.* 301 b.

Ebrardus, *Linc.* 357 b.

Eburg, *Yorksh.* 316 b.

Eccha prepositus, *Devon*, 100.

Echebrand, *Nottingh.* 290 b.[3]

Echebrant, *Chesh.* 266.

Echefrid, *Yorksh.* 374.

---

[1] Eddeva.

[2] The lands belonging to the Abbey in Bedfordshire and Northamptonshire do not seem to have been among the possessions of the Monastery T. R. E.

[3] He continued to hold when the Survey was made.

ECULF, *Linc.* 347 b. bis.

EDDED Regina, *Linc.* 336 b.

EDDEDA, *Buck.* 147.

EDDEUA, *Kent,* 7 b. *Sussex,* 23 b. bis. 26 b. bis. 27 b.
    Hants, 39 b. *Wilts,* 68 b. *Devon,* 105, 111 b. 112 b.
    Cornw. 124. *Buck.* 145 ter. *Cambr.* 194 passim.
    195 passim. 195 b. passim. *Linc.* 362 ter. 362 b.
    363.

EDDEUA et II. sochemanni homines ejus, *Cambr.* 193 b.
    bis.

EDDEUA,[1] *Somers.* 86.

EDDEVA monialis, *Hertf.* 136 b. bis.

EDDEVA puella, homo S. archiepiscopi fuit, *Hertf.* 134 b.

EDDEUA pulchra,[2] *Hertf.* 134, 137 passim. *Buck.* 146 b.
    Cambr. 194 passim. 194 b. passim. 195, 195 b.
    passim. 199 b. 200. *v.* EDDEUE. EDEUA.

---

[1] Daughter of Earl Godwin, and the same person who is
called Eddeua, Eddid, Eddida, and Eddied Regina. The
land here referred to, probably belonged to her before her
marriage. The explanation of this will be given in the present Index when Gunnild is spoken of, who was her sister,
unnoticed by our historians.

The Harleian Manuscript, 3977, a Consuetudinarium of
St. Edmunds Bury, says, " Sicut spina rosam, genuit God-
wynus EDITHAM."

[2] Mr. Sharp, in his translation of William of Malmesbury,
p. 249, speaking of the personal beauty of Editha the Confessor's queen, says, " in Domesday Book, under Stortford
in Herts, she is styled ' the Fair.' But this is a mistake;
the property of Eddeva or Editha Regina, and the property
of Eddeva Pulchra or the Fair, being each distinguished
throughout the record with a care and accuracy evidently
not unintentional. The manor of Storteford, moreover,
never belonged at any time to Editha the Queen.

EDDEVA Regina, *Kent*, 2.
EDDEUA uxor Vluuardi, *Buck.* 147.

Turner, in his History of England, vol. i. p. 64, quoting
the circumstances which attended the search for Harold's
body on the field of Hastings, which was recognized only
by his favourite Editha, surnamed Swanneshals or Swans-
neck,[a] says, " this Editha is the Editha Pulchra so often
mentioned in Domesday." But this opinion seems to have
been taken up by Mr. Turner, merely because in a manuscript
note in the margin of the Narrative he quoted, he found
written, " Ista Editha nominatur EDITHA PULCHRA in Libro
Domesday." The Narrative here alluded to, of the two
monks who watched the battle, obtained William's permission to bring away the body of Harold, and afterwards
carried the mistress to aid their search, will be found, MS.
Cotton. Jul. D. VI. on vellum, of the fourteenth century;
whilst the marginal note, from which the additional information was obtained, is in a hand of a date near three cen-
turies later; and, unsupported by the manuscript itself, or
by collateral evidence, is no more than a surmise of some
possessor of the manuscript who is not known.

The present writer has another opinion to offer, as to
Eddeva pulchra. He believes her to have been Editha, the
sister of Edwin and Morcar, widow of Griffin Prince of the
Welsh, and the Queen of Harold.

William of Jumieges, in his account of Harold's victory
obtained in Wales in 1065, says, " Grithfridi quoque Regis
Wallorum, postquam hostilis illum gladius peremit *pulchram
conjugem* ALDITH, præclari Comitis Algari filiam, sibi uxorem junxit." Duchesne, Script. p. 285.

It is to be observed, that throughout the Domesday Survey, Harold is never mentioned as KING; his wife, therefore, would not be likely to be designated as a Queen: yet

---

[a] " Editha cognomento Swanneshals quod Gallicè sonat collum Cigni."

EDDEUA uxor Wluuardi, *Buck.* 145 bis.
EDDEUE, *Somers.* 94.

---

that he had two wives there can be no question : his children were by the first wife ; the second was Aldith, Editha, Algiva, or Eddeva, names which were all synonimes. That Aldith or Algytha was beautiful we have Norman authority : there is no known record of her death : and the time was, comparatively, so short, between the battle of Hastings and the Conqueror's distribution of forfeited lands, that we cannot but wonder to find every mention of a wife of Harold omitted in the Domesday returns.

Florence of Worcester, p. 634, says, that after the fate of the battle of Hastings was known, and Harold's death, Edwin and Morcar came to London, and sent off their sister Algitha to Chester. " Cujus morte audita Comites Eadwinus et Morcarus (qui se cum suis certamini subtraxere) Lundoniam venere et sororem suam Algitham reginam sumptam ad civitatem Legionum misere."

The lands which are entered in Domesday as possessions of EDDEVA PULCHRA, are of great if not of royal amount. She held in different counties more than two hundred and thirty hides, equal to twenty-seven thousand six hundred acres. Her fee in Cambridgeshire, amounting to more than a hundred and fifty-eight hides, was considered as fit to form a part of the reward of Alan Earl of Bretagne. Among the under-tenants of Eddeva Pulchra, too, we find a person allied to the royal family. Of the manor of Fulbourn in Cambridgeshire, it is said, " Comes Alanus tenet in Fuleborne VIII. hid. *Hoc manerium tenuit* GODUINUS *cilt* homo Eddeuæ pulchræ. Non potuit recedere." Upon her lands in Hertfordshire, too, which were granted to Earl Alan, her chaplain, occurs, " Leuing presbyter homo Eddeuæ."

Whether it would be likely that a mistress of Harold should hold such tracts of land, or that she should have had a person of such high rank for an under-tenant, unalienable

Eddeve quædam femina, *Worc.* 178.[1]

Eddeue femina Syred, *Buck.* 143.

Eddeue pulchra, *Cambr.* 193 b. *v.* Eddeua. Edeua.

Eddid, *Kent,* 8, 11. *Sussex,* 18 b. *Berks,* 58 b. *Worc.*
   172 b. *Heref.* 183 b. *Warw.* 244.[2] *Shropsh.* 259,
   260 bis. 260 b. ter. *Yorksh.* 306 b.

Eddid quædam femina, *Berks,* 63 b.

Eddid Regina, *Kent,* 14 b. *Sussex,* 18 b. 21 b. bis. 22.
   Surrey, 30, 30 b. ter. *Hants,* 38 ter. 38 b. 40, 43,

---

as he is recorded to have been from his service to Eddeva,
or that she should have had an ostensible chaplain, the
reader will judge.

Eddeua dives, probably alluding to the amount of property above enumerated, seems to have been only another
appellation for Eddeva pulchra.

A concubine of Harold has been already noticed in the
former volume, where, in the second folio of the Survey of
Kent, Ralph Curbespine, or Crookthorn, is entered as holding four masures in the city of Canterbury, which had
belonged to her. Here was a mistress residing at a short
distance from the field of Hastings.

Of Eddeva Swanneshals, mentioned in the monkish narrative, the present writer has found no other notice,[a] except
in the Chronicle of John of Oxnede, MS. Cotton. Nero, D.
ii. fol. 204, who names her, in four words, as a benefactress
to the Abbey of St. Benet Holm. " Edgyue Suanneshals
dedit Thurgarton." Domesday says of Thurgarton, only,
" semper tenuit Abbatia."

[1] She continued to hold at the time of the Survey.

[2] In this entry she is recorded to be still holding at the
time of the Survey.

---

[a] Another copy of the story occurs in the Harleian MS. 3776, headed,
" Quid accidit Walthammensibus circa patroni sui sepulturam pie solli-
citis, sed mulieris cujusdam errore delusis."

43 b. *Berks*, 56 b. 57 ter. 58, 60 b. 63 b. *Wilts*,
65 ter. 73. *Dors.* 77. *Somers.* 91, 97, 99. *Devon*,
100 b. passim. *Midd.* 129 b. *Buck.* 144 b. bis.
149 b. 151, 153 passim. *Oxf.* 157 b. 159 bis.
Glouc. 163. *Heref.* 180, 180 b. 184. *Northampt.*
219, 220. *Rutl.* 293 b. ter. *Linc.* 337 bis. *Suff.*
426 bis. 427. *v.* EDDIDA. EDDIED.

EDDIDA, *Somers.* 96. *Devon*, 110 b. *Cornw.* 121 b.

EDDIDA Regina, *Wilts*, 63 b. *Somers.* 97.

EDDIED, *Heref.* 183, 183 b.

EDDIED Regina, *Worc.* 176 b. *Heref.* 183 b.

EDDIED soror Odonis comitis, *Heref.* 186.

EDDIET, *Glouc.* 170 b.[1]

EDDIUA, *Sussex*, 23. *Yorksh.* 325 passim. 325 b. *Linc.*
353, 362, 363. *Yorksh.* 373.

EDDIUE, *Yorksh.* 325 passim. 325 b. bis. *Linc.* 357,
363.

EDDUINUS Borgreti filius teignus R. E. *Buck.* 145.

EDDUINUS Comes, *Staff.* 248 b.

EDDULF, *Devon*, 107. *Yorksh.* 307, 316.

EDDULFI pater, *Hants*, 50.

EDDULFUS, *Wilts*, 66 bis. *Devon*, 106 b. 107 b.

EDELDREDA, S. *Suff.* 413.

EDELMUNDUS, *Inter Ripam et Mersam*, 269 b.

EDELRIC, *Linc.* 348.

EDELUUALDUS, *Somers.* 93 b.

EDERICUS, *Kent*, 9 b. 13 b. *Bedf.* 217 b.[2]

EDERICUS homo Algari Comitis, *Hertf.* 140 b.

EDERICUS homo Alurici cilt, *Cambr.* 200.

EDERICUS homo Asgari stalre, *Buck.* 147 b.

EDESTAN, homo Alnodi Chentis, *Buck.* 149.

---

[1] She continued to hold when the Survey was made.
[2] Edricus still held the land of this entry.

EDEUA, *Essex*, 7 b. 12 b. bis. 31 b. 35 ter. 35 b. *Suff.* 295, 295 b.[1]

EDEUA faira, *Norf.* 285. *Suff.* 430 b. 431 bis.

EDEUA quædam femina, *Essex*, 36.

EDEUA pulchra, *Cambr.* 189 b. *v.* EDDEUA.

EDEUA Regina, *Essex*, 27, 54, 87 ter. *Suff.* 290, 448 b.

EDEULF, *Heref.* 185 b.

EDGAR, *Hunt.* 205 b. bis.

EDGARI pater, *Wilts*, 65.

EDGARUS Comes, T. R. E. *Essex*, 3 b.

EDGED, *Leic.* 235.

EDGIDA monialis, *Worc.* 173 b.

EDIC, *Shropsh.* 255 b.

EDID, *Kent*, 1 b.

EDID Regina, *Buck.* 145. *Leic.* 230 b. *Linc.* 337 b. ter. 338, 338 b. 339.

EDIED quædam libera femina, *Suff.* 286 b.

EDIET, *Heref.* 183 b. *Shropsh.* 252.

EDILT liber homo, *Suff.* 296 b.

EDIUA dives, *Suff.* 410.

EDLOUEDIEF, *Devon*, 112 b.

EDMÆR, *Devon*, 105 passim. 114. *Shropsh.* 259.

EDMÆRUS, *Surr.* 31 b.

EDMAR, *Wilts*, 70 b. *Dors.* 79 b. bis. *Somers.* 94, 99. *Devon*, 107, 110, 115 bis. 115 b. bis. 116, 116 b. 117 b. bis. *Northampt.* 223.

EDMARUS, *Devon*, 106. *Northampt.* 220, 223. *Essex*, 27 b.

EDMARUS teignus Heraldi Comitis, *Hertf.* 136 b.

EDMER, *Surrey*, 35 b. *Dors.* 79 b. ter. 80. *Somers.* 90 b. 92 b. bis. *Devon*, 102 b. passim. 104 b. 105 bis. 105 b. 107 b. 108 b. 109 b. 114 b. 115, 116 b.

---

[1] In the two last entries " Edeua" is the same person who is called Eddeua pulchra and Eddeua faira.

117 b. bis. *Cornw.* 122, 125 bis. *Glouc.* 163 b.
166. *Shropsh.* 256 b. bis.

EDMER atre, *Devon,* 104 b.[1]

EDMER Attile, *Hertf.* 136 b.

EDMER Atula, teignus Regis Edwardi, *Midd.* 129 b.
Buck. 146.

EDMER presbyter, *Sussex,* 18, 20 b.

EDMVND, *Shropsh.* 259 b.[2] *Yorksh.* 320 b. passim.

EDMUNDI S. Abbatia, *Bedf.* 210 b. *Essex,*⎫
     19 b. 20.   ⎬ *v.* EDMUN-

EDMUNDI de Burgo, Ecclesia S. *Cambr.* ⎭ DUS S.
     192.

EDMUNDI pater, *Hants,* 50.

EDMUNDUS, *Sussex,* 20 b. *Berks,* 59 b. 62 b. bis. *Glouc.*
166. *Staff.* 248 ter. *Shropsh.* 256 b. *Yorksh.* 320 b.
bis. *Suff.* 395.

---

[1] The lands of Edmer atre were given to the Earl of
Moretaine. In the folio above referred to, of certain lands
of the richer Saxons, it is said, " Has prædictas XVII. terras
tenet Comes Moriton' cum terra Edmer Atre quæ ei deli-
berata est; nam libere eas tenebant T. R. E. supradicti
Taini." The lands of Ordulf, another of the greater Saxons,
were given to the Earl of Moretaine at the same time. In
the next folio we read, " Has infrascriptas VII. terras tenet
Comes cum terra Ordulfi." Edmer Atre and Ordulf were
in all probability partizans of Githa, the mother of Harold,
when she instigated the people of Exeter, in 1068, to break
out into open rebellion.

Edmer atre is called Edmeratorius in the Exon Domesday, pp. 190, 191. At the end of one or two entries in the
latter page, we read, " Istam terram tenet Comes *cum
honore Edmeratorii:*" and again, " terram tenet Comes *cum
honore Ordulfi."* In the Exon Domesday, p. 487, Edmer.
atre is called AILMARUS ATER, *Ailmar the black.*

[2] He continued to hold when the Survey was made.

EDMUNDUS homo Heraldi Comitis, *Hertf.* 133, 134.

EDMUNDUS liber homo Roberti filii Wimarc, *Suff.* 295 b.

EDMUNDUS, Sanctus, *Nottingh.* 284 b. *Norf.* 234. *Suff.* 356 b. bis. 357, 357 b. ter. 358 b. bis. 359 bis. 359 b. bis. 360 ter. 360 b. 361 b. ter. 362 ter. 362 b. bis. 363 b. 364 ter. 364 b. ter. 365, 368 ter. 368 b. ter. 369 ter. 369 b. ter. 370, 370 b. 371 b. 381, 401 b. 425 b. 426.

EDMUNDUS teignus R. E. *Buck.* 149 b.

EDNOD, *Sussex,* 20. *Hants,* 41, 48 b. 50, 53 b. bis. *Berks,* 60.[1] *Wilts,* 72. *Dors.* 80 ter. 82. *Somers.* 91 b. bis. *Devon,* 101 b. 102 b. *Cornw.* 123 b. 124 b.[2] *Glouc.* 164. *Linc.* 370 b. *Essex,* 70 b. *Suff.* 377 b.

EDNOD dapifer, *Wilts,* 69.[3]

EDNOD liber homo, *Essex,* 85 b.

EDNOD stalre, *Berks,* 58 b.[4]

---

[1] Tempore Haroldi Regis.

[2] He still held the land of this entry when the Survey was taken.

[3] " Hæc v. man. tenuit Ednod dapifer T. R. E."

[4] Possibly the same person who is called Ednod dapifer in the entry above.

He had held the manor of Shippen in Berkshire in the time of Edward the Confessor, which was afterwards given to the Abbey of Abingdon. The Saxon Chronicle calls him Eadnoth stallere. He was Harold's master of the horse, but made his peace with the Conqueror, and apparently entered his service. He was killed in 1068, in opposing the sons of Harold when they came upon their expedition into Somersetshire. Florence of Worcester, p. 635, after mentioning the flight of Edgar Atheling and his sisters to Scotland, says, " Dum hæc agerentur Haraldi regis filii Godwinus, Eadmundus, Magnus, de Hybernia redeuntes in Su-

EDNODUS, *Wilts*, 72 b. *Devon*, 106, 111 b.

EDNOTH, *Suff.* 340.

EDRED, *Wilts*, 69 b. *Somers.* 97. *Devon*, 118.[1]

EDRED homo Asgari, *Hertf.* 139 b.

EDREDUS, *Devon*, 117.

EDREDUS liber homo commendatus Wisgaro, *Suff.* 351 b.

EDRIC, *Sussex*, 23 b. *Hants*, 39, 43 b. 45 b. ter. 46,
    47 b. 48 b. 51, 53 b.[2] *Berks*, 59, 61. *Wilts*, 70 b.
    bis. 71 b. 73, 74 b. bis. *Dors.* 80 b. bis. 84 b.
    Somers. 88 ter. 89, 93 b. 94 bis. 96 b. 97 bis. 98
    passim. 98 b. *Devon*, 102, 103 bis.[3] 103 b. bis. 104
    b. ter. 105, 105 b. 106 b. 108, 110 b. 112, 113 b.
    ter. 114, 116 bis. 116 b. 117, 118 bis. *Glouc.* 169,
    170. *Worc.* 176 bis. *Heref.* 183 b. passim.[4] 187 b.[5]
    Northampt. 223 bis. *Warw.* 238. *Staff.* 250 b.
    Shropsh. 254 b. 255 b. passim. 256 b. bis. 258 pas-
    sim. 258 b. ter. 259, 260. *Chesh.* 265, 265 b. bis.
    Derb. 274, 274 b. bis. 275, 276, 278 b. *Nottingh.*
    285 b. *Linc.* 341 b. 347 b. 348 b. 349 b. bis. 356 b.
    358 ter. 359, 362, 365 b. *Essex*, 30 bis. 43. *Norf.*
    241 b. *Suff.* 297, 342, 375 b.

---

mersetania applicuerunt. Quibus EADNOTHUS, qui fuit
Heraldi regis Stallarius, occurrit cum exercitu, et cum eis
prælio commisso, cum multis aliis occisus est : illi vero
potiti victoria. De Domnania et Cornubia præda rapta non
modica, in Hyberniam redierunt."

Several of the entries in the Survey under EDNOD simply,
certainly belong to Ednod Stalre.

[1] He continued to hold this land when the Survey was
taken.

[2] This land he still held when the Survey was made.

[3] In one of the entries of fol. 103 he still held at the time
of the Survey.

[4] The Edric of fol. 183 b. seems to be Edric salvage.

[5] He held the same land in capite at the Survey.

EDRIC cecus, *Wilts*, 74.[1]

EDRIC homo Algari comitis, *Hertf.* 141 b.

EDRIC frater Godrici, *Clam. S. R. Linc.* 375.

EDRIC grim, *v.* GRIM.

EDRIC lang, *v.* LANG.

EDRIC, liber homo, *Shropsh.* 255.

EDRIC liber homo Stigandi, *Norf.* 217.[2]

EDRIC mancus, *Devon*, 100 b.

EDRIC salvage,[3] *Heref.* 183 b. *Shropsh.* 256, 256 b. 258 b.

---

[1] He continued to hold when the Survey was made.

[2] " Tenuit I. car. terræ et dimid. [in Saisselingam] sub eo T. R. E. cum soca et saca postquam rex venit in Angliam. Ut autem se redimeret a captione Walerami invadavit eam idem Edricus pro I. marca auri et pro VII. lib. in Sancto Benedicto."

[3] *Edric* salvage, *the ferocious.* He was also called *sylvaticus*, the forester.

The three following passages from Simeon of Durham, give the chief points of his history with which we are acquainted :

A. D. 1067. " Eo tempore extitit quidam præpotens minister Edricus cognomento Silvaticus, filius Alfrici fratris Edrici Streone. Cujus terram quia dedere se regi dedignabatur, Herefordenses Castellani et Ricardus filius Scrob frequenter vastaverunt. Sed quotiescunque super eum irruerunt multos e suis militibus et scutariis perdiderunt. Iccirco ascitis sibi in auxilium regibus Wallanorum, Blethgerto videlicet et Ritwaldo, idem vir Edricus, circa assumptionem S. Mariæ, Herefordensem provinciam usque ad pontem amnis Lucge devastavit, ingentemque prædam reduxit." Sim. Dun. col. 197.

A. D. 1070. " Vir strenuissimus Edricus cognomento Silvaticus, cujus supra meminimus cum rege Willielmo pacificatur." Ibid. col. 202.

" Anno 1072. Post assumptionem Sanctæ Mariæ Rex

EDRIC spur, teignus R. E. *v.* SPUR.

EDRIC et EDRIC, *Chesh.* 265 b.

EDRICI frater, *Hants,* 45 b.

EDRICI pater, *Glouc.* 170 b.

EDRICUS, *Kent,* 11, 12. *Sussex,* 19 b. *Surrey,* 30 b.
    Hants, 40 b. 43, 46 b. 53 b. *Wilts,* 70 bis. 71 bis.
    73. *Dors.* 80. *Devon,* 102 b. 107, 113 b. *Cornw.*
    123 b. 124. *Glouc.* 167 b. 169 b. *Heref.* 180.
    Northampt. 223. *Warw.* 239, 239 b. 240 b. 243
    bis. 244 b. *Staff.* 249. *Shropsh.* 254 bis. 258 bis.
    258 b. ter. 259 b. 260 bis. *Essex,* 51, 52 b. *Norf.*
    131 b. 133 b. 144 b. 153 b. 154, 198, 219 b. 234,
    240 b. 243. *Suff.* 292, 305, 307 b. 310 b.[1] 312 b.
    313 b. 314, 319 b. 320, 329 bis. 336 b. 339 b. bis.
    342, 343, 348, 376 b. 378, 386 b. 394, 396 b.
    400, 403, 407 b.[2] 432 b. 438, 440 b. 441 b. 442,
    442 b. 443, 444.

EDRICUS homo Asgari stalre, *Hertf.* 133 b.

EDRICUS commendatus Edrico, *Suff.* 310 b. 441.

EDRICUS commendatus Edrici de Laxefella, *Suff.* 443 b.

Willielmus habens in comitatu suo Edricum cognomento
Silvaticum, cum navali et equestri exercitu, Scotiam pro-
fectus est ut eam suo subjugaret ditioni." Ibid. col. 203.

[1] " Hic Edricus commendatus fuit Edrico de Laxefelda
antecessori Rotberti Malet priusquam rex E. obiisset. Postea udlagavit Edricus. Rex E. saisivit totam suam terram.
Postea conciliatus est regi E. et concessit ei terram suam;
dedit etiam brevem et sigillum ut quicunque de suis liberis
commendatis hominibus ad eum vellent redire, suo concessu
redirent Hunc Edricum saisivit R. E. in sua manu. Postea
non vidit Hundret ut ad Edricum dominum suum rediret;
sed tunc ipse dicit et offert judicium quod rediit, et liberos
homines quos habet sub se commend. tenet; et ex eis revocat Robertum warant."

[2] The Edricus of this entry is Edricus de Laxefella.

EDRICUS commendatus Normanni, *Suff.* 341.

EDRICUS diaconus, *Suff.* 449.

EDRICUS filius Ingoldi, *Suff.* 299 b.

EDRICUS grim, *v.* GRIM.

EDRICUS homo comitis Alani, *Buck.* 150 b.

EDRICUS homo Edrici de Laxefelda, *Buck.* 148 b.

EDRICUS homo G. *Buck.* 148 b.

EDRICUS de Laxefel, *v.* LAXEFEL. LAXEFELDA. LAXE-
FELLA.

EDRICUS unus liber homo, *Oxf.* 155, 155 b. bis. *Worc.* 175.

EDRICUS liber homo, *Essex*, 23 b. 25, 30, 83. *Suff.* 399,
419, 421 b.

EDRICUS liber homo commendatus Edrico, *Suff.* 344 b.

EDRICUS liber homo Edrici de Laxefelda, *Norf.* 150.

EDRICUS liber homo, rector navis Regis Edwardi, *Norf.*
200.

EDRICUS pur, *Cambr.* 196 b.

EDRICUS saluage, *v.* EDRIC.

EDRICUS sochemannus sub Edrico. *Norf.* 154 b. bis.

EDRICUS spuda, *v.* SPUDA.

EDRICUS stirman, *Worc.* 173 b.[1]

---

1 Of five hides belonging to the Bishop of Worcester's
manor of Norwiche, situated at Hindelep and Alcrintun, it is
here said, " Edricus stirman tenuit, et deserviebat cum aliis
servitiis ad regem et Episcopum pertinentibus." This passage is explained, as well as Edric's office, in the Commemoratio Placiti inter W. Episcopum et Walterum Abbatem
de Eovesham, printed in Heming's Chartulary, tom. i. p. 80.
" Ibi affuerunt ex parte Episcopi probabiles personæ, paratæ
facere prædictum sacramentum : quarum unus fuit EDRICUS
qui fuit tempore Regis Eduuardi *stermannus navis Episcopi,*
et *ductor exercitus ejusdem Episcopi ad servitium Regis ;* et hic
erat homo Rodberti Herefordensis Episcopi, ea die qua
sacramentum optulit, et nichil de Episcopo W. tenebat."

EDRICUS tegnus, *Worc.* 178. *Norf.* 260 b.

EDUIN, *Devon,* 110, 114 b. bis. *Oxf.* 159 b. *Chesh.*
268 b. *Yorksh.* 312.

EDUINUS, *Kent,* 1 b. 9. *Sussex,* 23 b. *Surrey,* 35. *Hants,*
45, 49 b. *Berks,* 62 b. *Wilts,* 69 b. 70 b. bis. 71,
74,[1] 74 b. *Dors.* 87 b. 91, 92, 93, 94. *Devon,*
104 b. 106, 107, 112 b. 114, 114 b. 118 b.[2] bis.
Oxf. 160. *Heref.* 185 b. passim. 186 b. 187.
Northampt. 220 b. 223 bis. 223 b. 224 bis. 225 bis.
227. *Leic.* 236. *Warw.* 241 passim. 241 b. *Staff.*
249 b. *Shropsh.* 254 b. 257 b. 258 b. 259 bis.
Chesh. 264 b. 265, 267 bis. 267 b. 268 b. bis.[3]
Derb. 278. *Linc.* 365 bis. *Essex,* 58 b. *Norf.*
202 b. *Suff.* 395, 411 b.

EDUINUS in paragio, *Devon,* 115.

EDUINUS Alferd, *v.* ALFERD.

EDUINUS f. Burred, *Northampt.* 221 bis.

EDUINUS commendatus Ailwardo preposito Regis, *Suff.*
333.

EDUINUS commend. Edeuæ, *Suff.* 295 b.

EDUINUS Comes, *Oxf.* 154 b. bis. *Worc.* 172 bis. 172 b.
Heref. 180 b. *Warw.* 238 ter. 240 b. 241 b. 243 ter.
244. *Staff.* 249 b. *Shropsh.* 252 b. 253 b. passim.
254 bis. 256 bis. 257, 257 b. ter. *Chesh.* 263 b.
passim. 264 passim. 266 b. 267, 268, 268 b. ter.
269 bis. *Derb.* 274, 275. *Yorksh.* 298 b. 299, 309,
310 b. 313, 315, 319. *Linc.* 338.

---

[1] He held the land of this entry in capite at the time of
the Survey.

[2] He continued to hold the land of one of these entries
when the Survey was made.

[3] In one of these entries he continued to hold his land at
the time of the Survey, of Robert de Roelent, under Earl
Hugh Lupus.

EDUINUS Grut, *v.* GRUT.

EDUINUS homo Azorii, *Buck.* 146 b.

EDUINUS liber homo, *Berks,* 62. *Chesh.* 264 bis. 264 b. bis. *Suff.* 296, 355 b.

EDUINUS presbyter, *Essex,* 64 b. *Suff.* 353.

EDUINUS vicecomes, *Warw.* 238 b. 241.

EDUINUS liber homo Guerd, *Norf.* 225.

EDUIUS liber homo, *Essex,* 103. *Suff.* 378.

EDULF, *Yorksh.* 317.

EDUUALDUS, *Somers.* 93 b.

EDUUARD, *Kent,* 1 b. *Worc.* 174 b. bis.

EDUUARD, *Chesh.* 266 ter. 267 b. bis. *Derb.* 274 b. *Yorksh.* 316. *Linc.* 360 b. 367. *Suff.* 298 b.

EDUUARD cild, *Linc.* 336 b.

EDUUARD cilt, *Buck.* 146, 147 b. *Linc.* 366 b.

EDUUARD cilt homo Heraldi comitis, *Buck.* 146.

EDUUARD cilt teignus Regis E. *Buck.* 147 b. bis.

EDUUARD liber homo, *Chesh.* 267 b.

EDWARDI pater, *Wilts,* 74. *Bedf.* 218.

EDUUARDUS, *Kent,* 8 b. 11. *Sussex,* 19, 20, 20 b. 28 b. *Hants,* 44 b.[1] 47, 48 bis. 49 b. *Berks,* 59 b. 62, 63 passim. *Wilts,* 67 b. 70 b.[2] *Somers.* 88 b. 95 bis. *Devon,* 108, 109 b. 113 b. 117 b. *Cornw.* 122. *Worc.* 174 b. *Bedf.* 218 b. *Northampt.* 226, 228 b. ter. *Chesh.* 266 bis. 267 b. *Derb.* 278 b. *Essex,* 32 b. bis. 58, 58 b. *Suff.* 342.

EDUUARDUS clericus, *Dors.* 77 b.

---

[1] He continued to hold the land here mentioned as a sub-tenant to Earl Roger. He had held it of Earl Godwin T. R. E.

[2] He continued to hold other land in Wilts, mentioned in the same folio with this, under Alured de Merleberge, at the time of the Survey.

Eduuardus homo Abbatis S. Albani, *Bedf.* 217 b.

Eduuardus unus liber homo, *Essex*, 24 b.

Eduuardus filius Suani, *Essex*, 98 b. ⎫

Eduuardus f. Suani, homo Regis E. *Midd.* 130 b. ⎭

EDWARDUS Rex, *Surr.* 30 bis. 30 b. *Hants*, 38, 38 b. ter. 39, 39 b. ter. 52. *Berks*, 56, 56 b. passim. 57 ter. 57 b. passim. 58. *Wilts*, 64 b. passim. 65 bis. 75 passim. 86 passim. 86 b. passim. *Devon*, 100 bis. 100 b.[1] 104 b. 110, 110 b. 111 b. 112 b. 114 bis. *Cornw.* 121. *Midd.* 127. *Hertf.* 132. *Buck.* 143 b. *Glouc.* 162, 162 b. passim. 163 passim. 164, 166, 167 ter. 168 b. 169, 169 b. bis. *Worc.* 172 passim. 172 b. bis. 174 b. 176 b. bis. *Heref.* 179, 179 b. passim. 181 passim. 184 b. bis. 186. *Cambr.* 189 b. passim. *Hunt.* 203 b. passim. 207, 208. *Bedf.* 217 b. *Northampt.* 219, 219 b. *Leic.* 230, 230 b. *Warw.* 238 passim. *Staff.* 246 bis. *Shropsh.* 253 passim. 253 b. passim. 259 b. 260. *Chesh.* 268. *Inter Rip. et Mersam,* 269 b. bis. 270 passim. *Derb.* 272 bis. 272 b. ter. 273. *Nottingh.* 280 bis. 281 bis. 281 b. *Yorksh.* 298, 299 b. bis. 300, 304 b. *Norf.* 110, 110 b. 111 b. 112 b. 114 bis. 118, 119 b. 127. *Suff.* 281 b. bis. 282 bis. 289 b.[2]

Eduuardus teignus R. E. *Buck.* 147 b. 148.

---

[1] At the end of a long list of lands in this folio, it is said, " Hæc xix. Maneria fuerunt in dominio Regis Edwardi et pertin. ad Regnum."

[2] There are but few instances recorded in Domesday, of the Conqueror alienating lands or possessions which had belonged to King Edward the Confessor. One, however, occurs, *Dev.* 105. " Comes Moriton' habet in Execestre unam æcclesiam, et unam domum, et unum virgultum quæ fuerunt in dominio regis Eduuardi."

EDUUARDUS homo Tosti comitis, *Buck.* 148.

EDUUARDUS uuit. *v.* UUIT.

EDUUI, *Hants,* 50, 51, 53 b.[1] *Dors.* 80.   *Devon,* 102 b.
104 b. 106 b. 107, 108,[1] 111, 114 b. bis. *Cornw.*
122 b. bis. 123 bis. 123 b. passim. 124. *Glouc.*
168 b. 169. *Worc.* 176, 176 b. 177. *Heref.* 180,
184 bis. 184 b. 185 bis. 187. *Shropsh.* 259, 260 b.
Nottingh. 284 b.

EDUUI cilt, *Heref.* 182 b. 184 bis. 184 b. ter. 185 bis.

EDUUI homo abbatis de Ely, *Cambr.* 199.

EDUUI presbyter, *Kent,* 10 b.

EDUUIN, *Surrey,* 31 b.

EDUUINE, *Derb.* 272.

EDUUINUS, *Kent,* 8. *Sussex,* 21, 29. *Cornw.* 122 b.
Worc. 177. *Heref.* 180. *Derb.* 278. *Suff.* 385 b.

EDUUINUS Comes, *Worc.* 177. *Staff.* 248. *Yorksh.*
301 b. 307 b.

EDUUINUS faber, *Suff.* 314 b.

EDUUINUS filius Borret, *Buck.* 145 b.

EDUUINUS unus liber homo, *Berks,* 60.

EDUUINUS homo Asgari stalri, *Bedf.* 209 b.

EDUUINUS homo Regis Eduardi, *Midd.* 130 b.

EDWINUS presbyter, *Hants,* 49 b.

EDUUINUS teignus regis E. *Midd.* 130 b. *Buck.* 145.

EDUUINUS teinus, *Norw.* 204.

EDWINUS, *Norf.* 203, 204, 204 b.

EDWINUS teinus dominicus R. E. *Norf.* 203.

EDWINUS venator, *Hants,* 50 b.[2]

---

[1] He continued to hold the land mentioned in these folios
when the Survey was made.

[2] Edward the Confessor had given him his land, consisting of two hides. He continued to hold them " de firma
regis" at the time of the Survey.

EDUUIUS, *Devon,* 107 b.[1]

EDUUNUS, *Kent,* 8 b.

EDUUOLDUS, *Somers.* 95, 95 b. *Essex,* 11 b.

EDUUOLT, *Essex,* 11.

EDUUOLT prepositus Regis E. *Essex,* 23.

EDZI, *Cornw.* 123 b.

EDZI homo Goded, *Hertf.* 134.

EGBERT, *Yorksh.* 298.

EGBRAND, *Yorksh.* 311 b. 373.

EGELFRIDE, *Yorksh.* 300 b. 327 b.

EGFRIDE, *Yorksh.* 301 ter.

EGHEBRAND, *Yorksh.* 301 b.

EGLESHAM, Abbatia de, *Glouc.* 166.

EILAF, *Somers.* 93. *Devon,* 115. *Worc.* 176 b. *Hunt.*
    206. *Yorksh.* 300 b. 324 b. *Linc.* 365 b.

EILESBERIE, Aluied de, *Buck.* 146.

EILEUA, *Wilts,* 65.

EILEUA quædam libera femina, *Berks,* 62.

EILMER, *Glouc.* 164.

EILMERUS, *Glouc.* 170 b.

EILRIC, *Linc.* 363 ter. *Clam. in Chetst.* 377.

EINGAR homo Heraldi Comitis, *Buck.* 151 b.

EINULF, *Shropsh.* 256.

EINULFUS, *Yorksh.* 298.

EIRIC, *Linc.* 365 b. *Clam. W. R. Linc.* 376.

EIULF, *Cornw.* 121, 123 b.

ELAF, *Glouc.* 166 b. bis. *Yorksh.* 298, 301. *Linc.* 339 b.
    bis. 365 b. bis.

ELAF teignus R. E. *Hertf.* 140 b.

ELDED femina Osuuold, *Hants,* 40.

ELDEUA, *Somers.* 96 b.

ELDID, *Yorksh.* 373.

---

[1] He continued to hold at the time of the Survey.

ELDILDÆ vir, *Wilts*, 74.

ELDILLE, *Devon*, 110 b.

ELDIT quædam femina, *Berks*, 63 b.

ELDRED, *Wilts*, 71 b. *Dors*. 82 b. *Somers*. 89, 92 b. 99
    bis.[1] *Devon*, 108 b. 118 [1] bis. *Glouc*. 165. *Shropsh*.
    254 b. 256, 260. *Yorksh*. 310 b. 311 b. 320 b.
    329.

ELDRED arcĥ. *Devon*, 103 b.

ELDRED archiepiscopus, *Glouc*. 168. *Warw*. 238 b.
    Yorksh. 302 b. passim. 303, 303 b. passim. 304,
    373 b.

ELDRED frater Odonis, *Hants*, 42 b.

ELDRED homo Stigandi archiepiscopi, *Buck*. 151.

ELDRED teignus R. E. *Hertf*. 133 b.

ELDREDUS, *Devon*, 108. *Cambr*. 194 b.

ELDREDUS archiepiscopus, *Glouc*. 164 b. bis. *Worc*. 173.

ELDREDUS fr. Odonis, *Hants*, 50 b.[2]

ELDRET, *Hertf*. 141 b

ELDUIF, *Yorksh*. 306 b.

ELDVINUS, *Shropsh*. 259 b.[3]

ELEUA, *Worc*. 177.

ELFAC, *Shropsh*. 259.

ELFAG, *Derb*. 274 b. 276.

ELFEG, *Derb*. 274 b.

ELFELMUS, *Sussex*, 18. *Hants*, 50 b.

ELFELT, *Glouc*. 170.

ELFER, *Sussex*, 19 b. 20 b.

---

[1] In both instances of fol. 99, as well as in those of 118,
Eldred continued to hold in capite at the time of the
Survey.

[2] He held of the King both in Edward the Confessor's
time and at the Survey.

[3] He held the same land under Earl Roger at the
Survey.

ELFGIVA monialis, *Worc.* 173 b.

ELFIN, Sanctus, *Inter Rip. et Mers.* 269 b.

ELFLET, *Heref.* 184 b. bis. *Yorksh.* 301 b.

ELFLET, I. libera femina, *Midd.* 128.

ELFRIC, *Derb.* 275.

ELGAR, *Dors.* 83 b. *Heref.* 181, 184 b. *Shropsh.* 260 b.

ELGET, *Huntingd.* 208.

ELI, *Chesh.* 264 b.[1]

ELI, Abbas de, *Essex*, 36 b. *Suff.* 332 b. 435, 450.

ELI, S. Adeldreda de, *Essex*, 18 b. 19, 19 b.

ELIARD, *Shropsh.* 254 b.

ELIERT, filii, *Berks*, 59.

ELIET, *Worc.* 177 b. *Shropsh.* 258 b.

ELINTONE, Clerici villæ de, *Dev.* 100 b.

ELMÆR, *Sussex*, 22 b. *Shropsh.* 259 b. *Chesh.* 265 b.
  269 b. *Linc.* 339 b.

ELMÆR sochemannus Regis E. *Cambr.* 199 b.

ELMÆRUS homo Heraldi comitis, *Hertf.* 141.

ELMÆRUS unus liber homo, *Berks*, 62.

ELMÆRUS homo Aluric f. Goding, *Buck.* 146 b.

ELMAR, *Hants*, 50 b. *Wilts*, 71 b. *Somers.* 98, 98 b.
  Devon, 108. *Glouc.* 163. *Heref.* 183, 183 b. 185 b.
  Shropsh. 255 b. 258 bis. 259 b. 260. *Yorksh.* 319.
  Linc. 340 b.

ELMARUS, *Cambr.* 190.

ELMARUS teignus regis E. *Buck.* 151.

ELMER, *Kent*, 11. *Surrey*, 31 b. 35 b. *Hants*, 44, 46,
  53.[2] *Dors.* 81 b. *Somers.* 90, 98. *Devon*, 104 b.
  106, 107 b. ter. 108, 110 bis. 110 b. 111. *Cornw.*
  122. *Glouc.* 169 b. bis. *Heref.* 180 bis. 184 b. 187 b.

---

[1] He held the same land at the Survey, as of Earl
Hugh.

[2] " Tenuit de rege E. in alod."

bis.[1] *Shropsh.* 255 b. 256 b. 257 ter. 257 b.
259 b. *Chesh.* 268 b. *Derb.* 274 b. *Nottingh.* 285 b.
Linc. 339 b. 358, 366 b.

ELMER de Belintone, *v.* BELINTONE.

ELMER cilt, *Heref.* 185.

ELMER unus liber homo, *Berks,* 57.

ELMER, postea monachus Eccl. de Wirecestre, *Worc.* 173.

ELMER venator, *Surrey,* 31.

ELMUND, *Warw.* 239. *Shropsh.* 255 bis. 258, 258 b.
259 b. bis.[2]

ELMUNDUS, *Staff.* 248. *Shropsh.* 255 b. bis. 256, 256 b.
258 bis. 258 b.

ELNOC, *Glouc.* 168.

ELNOD, *Surrey,* 34 b. *Hants,* 54.[3] *Dors.* 80. *Somers.*
96. *Glouc.* 166 b. bis. *Heref.* 184, 184 b. 185.
Shropsh. 256 b. 259. *Derb.* 278. *Nottingh.* 286.
Linc. 340 b. bis. 342, 345 b. 346 bis. 348 b. 356 b.
357 passim. 366. *Clam. W. R. Linc.* 376.

ELNODUS, *Wilts,* 66. *Nottingh.* 283.

ELOUS, *Devon,* 110.

ELRIC, *Kent,* 1 b. *Wilts,* 69 b. *Devon,* 115. *Cornw.* 123.
Worc. 174 b. *Heref.* 184 b. *Hunt.* 207 b. *Shropsh.*
255, 255 b. 259, 260 b. *Chesh.* 265 b. *Derb.* 274,
274 b. ter. 275 b. 278. *Nottingh.* 292 b. *Yorksh.*
308, 308 b. 316 b. 317, 317 b. 331 b. *Linc.* 348 b.

---

[1] He held the land of this entry of the King, at the time
of the Survey, as he had done of King Edward.

[2] Elmund and his son Alward continued to hold the
land of one entry in fol. 259 b. at the time the Survey was
made.

[3] Of the land of this entry it is said, " Ipse tenuit in
paragio T. R. E." He continued to hold it, but in entirety,
at the time of the Survey.

ELRICUS, *Hants,* 40. *Glouc.* 169 passim. 169 b. *Worc.*
    177. *Heref.* 187. *Shropsh.* 254 b. *Essex,* 32.
ELRICUS filius Wluiat Heroldi, *Suff.* 444.
ELSI, *Hants,* 43 b. 48. *Somers.* 89, 95 passim. 95 b.
    Devon, 111 b. *Glouc.* 170 b.[1] *Heref.* 183 b. bis.
    Hunt. 206. *Shropsh.* 258 b. *Derb.* 274. *Nottingh.*
    282 b. 286, 289 b. *Yorksh.* 298, 300 b. 309, 315 b.
    ter. 316 bis. 316 b. 317, 319 ter. 321. *Linc.* 354.
ELSI abbas, *Berks,* 62 b.[2]
ELSI abbas de Ramesy, *Hants,* 43 b.[3]

---

[1] He continued to hold the land of this entry in capite
when the Survey was formed.

[2] Among the lands of Ralph de Mortemer. " Isdem
Radulfus tenet Borgefel, et quidam miles de eo. Elsi abbas
tenuit de veteri monasterio Wintoniensis Ecclesiæ, testimonio sciræ, T. R. E. et postea, donec Vtlage fuit."

[3] He does not occur in the entry here referred to as a
land-owner, but as a witness respecting the manor of He-
lingey, claimed by the monks of Jumieges from the bishoprick of Winchester.

This Elsi is a personage relating to whom a very curious
Narrative is preserved, in a poetical Work of the fourteenth
century, entitled " Cursor Mundi," written in the dialect of
the North of England : a poem hitherto scarcely noticed
by the English antiquaries ; but copies of which are extant,
of the period just named, in the Cottonian Collection, in
the library of the College of Physicians at Edinburgh, two
in the Bodleian, one in the College of Arms, one in the
Harleian Collection, and one, the most curious, in the library
of the University of Gottingen.

Elsi is represented in one of the fits or cantos of this
Poem to have been sent by William the Conqueror to Denmark, to appease Suein, who, upon the news of his nephew's
fate at Hastings, made preparations for a descent upon
England, to revenge Harold's death.

Elsi diaconus, *Clam. in Chetst.* 376 b.
Elsi f. Caschin, *Nottingh.* 280 b.

MS. Cott. Vesp. A. iii.

[The various readings are from the Edinburgh MS.]

[fol. 138 b.
col. 1.]

A king was hight William Basterd,
That warraid in Ingland ful hard,
Swa stalworth man he was of hand
That wit his forse he wan the land;
Selcuth keneli cuth he fight,
And slogh the king that Harald hight,
That born was o the Danis blod;
For qui he [1] him wit-stod.
Than bar Willam the senurre
Of Ingland and of Normundie.
The king o Danema[r]k onan
Herd that king Harald was slan:
O wiit almast he wald vte-wind
For luue of him that was his frend.
Scippes did he dight him thar
In til Ingland for to fare,
Apon the Normanz for to fight,
That wan the land wituten right;
For he swar be the king of heuen
Of Harald the slaghter suld he heuen.
To king William bodword was broght,
O this tithand he him for-thoght,
He scund him sar that werr suld ris,
And warnist him on mani wise.
He gadir sauders her and thar
To strenth his castels eueraiquar,
Als he that Conquerur was gode
And for to warrai vnderstode:

[col. 2.]

His consail badd him for to faind [2]
The king of Danemerk wit seand,[3]
For to spek abute sum pais
Bituix him and the Danais.
    This ilk time, that [ike] of-sai,
Was an abbot of Ramessai,

---

[1] " the land "   [2] " fand "   [3] " sand "

H 2

ELSI jllinge, *Nottingh.* 280 b.
ELSTAN, *Glouc.* 170.

The nam of him men cald Elsis,[1]
A hend man he was, and wise ;
A gret resun wel sceu he cuth
Wit vten ani mer in muth.
This abbot o this erand ber
Was chosin to be messager,
Vnto Danemerc for to fare,
A lerd man o mikel lare.
Wit triffor [2] son his scipp was tift,
O presaundes mani and riche gift :
O siluer and gold giftes to bede,
Mar than mister es to rede,
The sing o pes alsua to bring
Bituix Willam and that other king ;
And o thai scippes for to spir,
Quen thai aghteld for to stir.
Elsis to scipping son him did,
His bir bleu als he self wald bidd ;
He past the see that was sa bradd,
His presand to the king he mad ;
His presand welcum was, and he,
Als bringand wont was to be :
Til erls and baruns o that rike
Than gaf he sere-kin giftes rike ;
Thai that he had na giftes til
Wit hightes fair he wan thair will,
Sa wele in speche than cuth he spell,
That al that ost he did to duell.
  Quen all his nedis wele war dun
Thai dightid him his scipping son,
Thair sail thai sett up o thair scipp,
Sir Elsis and his felauscip.
His giftes gaf he noght in vain,
Bot fair presandes thai sent again.
Forth thai floted on that flod,
For al to will thair bir tham stode,

---

1 " Elis"   2 " trissor "

ELSUID monialis, *Linc.* 337 b.
ELTOR, *Yorksh.* 309 b.

At the last moght thai noght se
Bot heuen aboue tham and the see:
The weder, als in somer smeth,
Son began to rug and reth,

[fol. 139. col. 1.]

That ilke wau til other weft,
And bremli to tho barges beft.
The lift it blakend al to night,
On ilk side tham slaked sight,
The se for reuthnes wex al rede ;
To reuth was turnd al thair rede.
The wind ras ganis tham vnride,
The see tham sailed on ilk side ;
Thar bleu on thaim mani brem blast,
Thair mast it raf, and cordes brast :
Strangli strait than war thai stadd,
The mariners war selcuth radd ;
Sua rad war thai neuer ar,
For thai war neuer in parel mar,
Ful wansum war thai than o rede,
For drereli thai dred the ded.
Quen thai had striuen ai quils thai moght,
Again that storm al was for noght ;
Thai lete it wandir vp and dun,
Thair scip ai redi for to drun,
Thai wandred waful on that flod,
Criid and wep as thai war wod.
Thaa sori loked ai sua for-suonken,
Quen the scip suld quelm and drunken,
On Jhesu Crist thai cri and call,
And on Maria that helpes all.
" Leuedi," thai said, " that es sa mild,
Prai for us to thi suet child,
All mon we drun sa, wailawai !
Leuedi nu help, for well thou mai !"
Thai wrang thair hend and wep ful sar،
As men war carked al wit care,
Apon thair brestes fast thai beft,
Al in God self thai tham bileft :

H 3

ELUEUA, *Hants*, 49. *Devon*, 112. *Shropsh.* 257, 258 b.
bis.

Bot sco that euer es bot o bale
Til all that hope in hir has hale,
Her suicur son to ham sco sent,
That in sli murning on hir ment.
Dun be that scip an angel light,
In selcuth clething scene o sight;
This angel to thaa quakand kidd,
And thus to thaim his erand did :
" Elsis," he said, " lift vp thi chere,
Cum ner, spek wit this messagere."
All thai that in that ferrcost fard
War medd quen thai him sagh and herd.
[col. 2.] This angel thus he tald his tale,
" Elsis," he said, " if thou will hale,
Cum o this scipp to land fere,
Thou sal nu hete and wou me her
That thou sal don als I the sai,
Til al the kirkes that thou mai,
Quen thou cumis in til England,
For to do tham at vnderstand
For to halu thes ilk fest dai,
Wit al the wirscip that thai mai ;
In hali kirc rinnand bi yer,
Als geten was ur lauedi dere.
For geten bituix man and womman
Was sco, that neuer wem had nan;
Geten was sco to be born,
For to lech al that war forlorn.
This es the day that sco was geten,
Lok neuer mar it be for-geten ;
Qua halus it, witvten fail,
Bath liif and saul it sal tham wail,
Do wou, Elsis, and hald thi vou,
It sal the turn to mekel pru.
To that angel than spak Elsi,
" Sai me signe," he said, " quharbi
I, and all mi munikes, mai
And all cristen men knau [1] that dai."

[1] " halic "

Eluine, *Derb.* 275 b.
Eluinus, *Berks,* 61 b.

" To knau that dai it es ful eth ;
The aghtand dai o that moneth
That man clepes o the yeir
Decembre in the kalunder,
That es to dai that ic of men,
Quen geten was that leudi scene."
" Sai me," said Elsis, " qua-kin wise
Of hir we sal mak this seruis,
Sin thar es propre nan I knau."
" Gladli, Sir, I sal you scau ;
The seruis of hir birth you tak,
Thar of ye sal the seruis mak :
Of a word thar in es redd
To set another word in sted ;
Ai quar yee sai *Natiuite*
This word, *Concepciun,* sal be ;
For to change thar es na mar,
Of al the seruis that es thar."
Bot nu es said on other wise
Propre o this fest hali seruise

[fol. 139 b. col. 1.] Til ilk man that will it say
Redi has it hali that dai.
  O this bodword blit was Elsi,
And thanked Crist and me leuedi :
Gladli he hight, and wit god will,
The comandement al for to fill.
Quen the abbot had that vou al mad,
Vte of thair sight this angel glad ;
Als suith na langer can thai duell,
The lem can light the storm it fell,
Ful fair become that see to sight,
And thai bigan thair takel dight.
Thair wind to well god fare thai fand,
Til thai com in til Ingland,
Wit al thair farnet and thair fere
Thai com til land bath hale and fere.
  Elsis began this comandment
Son for to sceu his couent ;

H 4

Eluolt liber homo, *Glouc.* 170 b.
Eluret, *Kent,* 10 b.

>   Al the chance that him bitide
>   Al communli he it vn-did:
>   To wirscip hir concepciun,
>   That of vr plight us gat pardun.
>   This fest fra than folk forth held,
>   Thar of ilkan til other teld.
>   This ilk abbot at Ramesai
>   Asetnes set in his abbai,
>   Thar in this ai [1] all for to stand,
>   To quils that abbai bes lastand:
>   And sua men dos in stedes fele,
>   Sua aght al do that his hir lele.
>   The stori that wit for to sai,
>   Euer quen we will hald this dai;
>   Mai naman serue her in lede,
>   That sco ne yeldes tham thar mede:
>   Sco dos us her to serue hir sua,
>   That we be wit hir euer and a.

The miraculous conclusion of the story, relating to the origin of celebrating the Feast of the Conception, gives the whole the appearance of a fable. The historical portion, however, must have had some foundation in truth. It is remarkable, that the eighth of Wace's works, enumerated by Mr. George Ellis in the Notes to his Specimens of the early English Poets, vol. i. p. 54, is said to be " *A History of the Origin of the Feast of the Conception,* which is supposed to have been established by William the Conqueror, and was kept in Normandy with such magnificence that it was usually called in France the Feast of the Normans. It is to be found in the Royal Library at Paris."

In the Duke de la Valliere's library there was a MS. which seems to have contained the French text, that is, the original of the whole Canto relating to Elsi. See the Cat. La Vall. tom. ii. p. 247: and it contained the author's name,

>   " Gaces ot non icel qui fist
>   Ceste estoire et en romans mist."

[1] " servis "

Eluric, *Chesh.* 265 b. *Derb.* 274 bis. 276.
Eluricus, *Heref.* 180.

The editor of the Catalogue supposes this author to have been Gace Brulès, a French poet of the thirteenth century there can be no doubt, however, but that it was Wace.

Elsi, Ailsius, or Elsinus is usually stated to have been made abbat of Ramsey in 1080, and to have died in 1088 ; but we have the evidence of Charters in the Ramsey Register, Cotton. MS. Vesp. E. ii. fol. 9, that he was abbat in the time of Edward the Confessor, to whose charter of privileges he signs as a witness, " Ego Agelsius abbas hoc meum desiderium ad perfectum adduxi et a Rege hilariter suscepi :" he also witnesses a charter of the Conqueror in 1077, ibid. fol. 10 b. " Ego Ailsinus abbas hoc munificentiæ donum a Rege petii et gratanter accepi." These signatures are proofs that he was in communication and confidence with both sovereigns. The Historia Ramesiensis states him to have also aided Harold with his counsels, which might be a reason for the Conqueror selecting him for a mission to Denmark.

Elsi, or Elsinus, is evidently the same Abbat who, in a passage of Domesday quoted in a former page of the present work, vol. i. p. 306, is called Aluuinus, and who rendered some service to King Edward the Confessor, which is not explained, in his exile. There is another passage in the same folio of the Domesday Survey, tom. i. fol. 208, which alludes to *an absence of this Abbat in Denmark*, whether in the reign of Edward or William is not distinctly ascertainable, but probably early in the latter.

" De ii. hid. quas Radulfus filius Osmundi tenet in Emingeforde dicunt quod una ex his erat in die R. E. de dominio Æcclesiæ de Ramesy et contra voluntatem Abbatis tenere illum. De altera hida dicunt quod Godricus tenuit eam de Abbate : sed *cum Abbas esset in Danemarka*, Osmund pater Radulfi rapuit eam a Sauuino Accipitrario, cui Abbas eum dederat ob amorem Regis."

The English Poem appears to have detailed Elsi's own story as related to his Monks.

ELURILDE, S. Terra, *Yorksh.* 329.

ELUUACRE, *Somers.* 95 b. ter.

ELUUAR, *Worc.* 174 b.

ELUUARD, *Somers.* 88, 95. *Glouc.* 170. *Worc.* 175 b.
Heref. 181, 183, 186 b. *Shropsh.* 255 bis. 255 b.
bis. 256, 259 b. *Chesh.* 265, 265 b. passim. 268.
Nottingh. 285 b.

ELUUARDUS, *Wilts,* 69. *Devon,* 101, 104 b. 110 b. 112 b.
115. *Glouc.* 170. *Worc.* 174 b. *Heref.* 180 bis.
180 b. bis.

ELUUI, *Wilts,* 72. *Cornw.* 121. *Heref.* 185. *Shropsh.*
256, 259. *Nottingh.* 284 b. 285 b. *Linc.* 361.[1]

ELUUIN, *Devon,* 108 b. *Nottingh.* 288. *Yorksh.* 329.

ELUUINE, *Derb.* 276. *Nottingh.* 292 b.

ELUUINUS, *Hants,* 47. *Somers.* 96. *Glouc.* 169 b. bis.
Shropsh. 254, 256 b. *Nottingh.* 281 b. *Yorksh.*
301 b. *Essex,* 35 b.

ELUUINUS f. Vlf. *Northampt.* 226 b.

ELUUIUS, *Essex,* 19.

ELUUOLD, *Derb.* 274 b.

ELY, Abbas de, *Cambr.* 199, 200 passim. 200 b. 201
passim. *Hunt.* 203.

ELY, Abbatia Etheldredæ de, *Hants,* 40 b. *Hertf.* 135.
Cambr. 189 b. 190 b. 192, 199 b. 202 b. *Hunt.*
204. *Linc.* 336 b. *Essex,* 18 b. *Norf.* 212 b. 213,
213 b. 214, 214 b. 215, 267, 270. *Suff.* 381 b.
v. ALDREDA, S.

ENGELBRICUS canonicus Episc. Lond. *Midd.* 127 b.[2]

ENGELRI, *Hertf.* 137,[3] 142.

---

[1] He held the same land under Walter de Aincurt when
the Survey was formed.

[2] He was still sub-tenant to the Bishop when the Survey
was made.

[3] In this entry he is the same person with Engelricus,
who follows.

ENGELRICUS, *Hertf.* 137. *Essex*, 6 b. bis.

ENISAN, *Yorksh.* 310 b. bis. 311 b. bis. 312 b.

EPY homo Brictric, *Buck.* 151 b.

ERCHEBRAND, *Chesh.* 266.[1]

ERDING, *Surrey*, 34 b. 35 bis.

ERFASTUS [Episc.] *Suff.* 379, 379 b. bis.

ERGRIM, *Heref.* 185 bis.

ERIC frater Tosti de Saltrede, *Hunt.*[2] 208 b.

ERICH, *Rutl.* 293 b. *Linc.* 367.

ERLEBALD, *Wilts,* 72.

ERLEBALDUS, *Somers.* 94.

ERLECHIN, *Chesh.* 265.

ERLENC, *Hants,* 45 b.

ERNE, *Chesh.* 266 passim. 268 b. bis.

ERNEBER, *Yorksh.* 301. *Linc.* 353 passim. 358, 366,
366 b.

ERNEBOLDUS, *Somers.* 95.

ERNEBRAND, *Yorksh.* 332.

ERNEBURNE, *Clam. in Chetst.* 376 b.

ERNEGRIN, *Warw.* 238 b.

ERNEIS, *Cornw.* 122 b.

ERNESI, *Glouc.* 167, 168 b. 169 b. passim. *Heref.* 180, 185.

ERNET, *Suff.* 340.

ERNEUINUS et mater ejus, *Warw.* 243.

ERNEUUI, *Warw.* 243.

ERNI, *Chesh.* 263 b. 266.

---

[1] He held the same land, at the time of the Survey, of
William Fitz Nigel, which he had previously held " ut liber
homo."

[2] " De terra Tosti de Saltrede dicunt [homines qui jura-
verunt in Huntedune] quod Eric frater ejus denominavit
eam Ecclesiæ de Ramesy post mortem suam, et fratris et
sororis suæ."

ERNIET, *Worc.* 177 b. *Shropsh.* 257 b. ter. 260 b. *Chesh.* 265 ter. 266 b. 267. *Derb.* 274 b. *Suff.* 437.

ERNIET teinus Eduini Comitis, *Worc.* 172.

ERNOLD, *Kent,* 11.

ERNU, *Shropsh.* 254.

ERNUI, *Somers.* 96 b. *Heref.* 183, 184 b. 185 b. 186 bis. 187. *Northampt.* 225 b. *Warw.* 242 b. 243, 243 b. bis. *Staff.* 250 b. *Shropsh.* 255 b. bis. 256,[1] 258, 259. *Chesh.* 263 b. 266, 267 b. 268 b. *Derb.* 275, 276, 278 b.[2] *Nottingh.* 290 bis. *Yorksh.* 298, 306 b. 315 bis. 316 b. 321 b. *Linc.* 342, 352 passim. 365 b.

ERNUI alter, *Yorksh.* 298.

ERNUI fot, *Chesh.* 263 b.

ERNUI tainus Heraldi Comitis, *Heref.* 186 b.

ERNUIN, *Worc.* 177. *Heref.* 183. *Warw.* 243. *Chesh.* 265 bis. 267 b. bis. *Derb.* 278. *Yorksh.* 298, 317, 324, 329 bis. *Linc.* 352, 360, 374.

ERNUIN liber homo, *Chesh.* 264 b.

ERNUIN presbyter, *Nottingh.* 293. *Yorksh.* 331. *Linc.* 336 b. 347.

ERNUINUS, *Shropsh.* 255 b. *Chesh.* 264 b.

ERNUINUS presbyter, *Linc.* 371. *Clam. N. R. Linc.* 376.

ERNUIT, *Shropsh.* 256.

ERNULF, *Warw.* 238 b. *Yorksh.* 302.

ERNULFUS, *Suff.* 402.

ERNULFUS liber homo, *Essex,* 27.

---

1 The land of this entry was held by Ernui, at the time of the Survey, under Robert Fitz Corbet, who was the under-tenant of Earl Roger. Ernui is himself mentioned as the old possessor, " Ipse tenuit et liber homo fuit."

2 He continued to hold the land of this entry of the King when the Domesday Survey was made.

FADER, *Norf.* 222 b. 223, 226 b. *Suff.* 391.

Femina quædam, Devon, 114 b.

FALTENHAM, Leostanus de, *Suff.* 314 b.

FANCHEL, *Linc.* 341.

FARDAN, *Yorksh.* 329.

FARDEIN, *Yorksh.* 323.

FARGRIM, *Yorksh.* 322 b.

FASTOLF, *Linc.* 336 b.[1]

FECH, *Shropsh.* 257. *Yorksh.* 332.

FECHE, *Worc.* 176 b.

FEG, *Yorksh.* 332.

FEGARUS, *Suff.* 342.

FELAGA, *Essex,* 95, 102 b.

FENCHEL, *Clam. N. R. Linc.* 375 b. 376.

FENELAI, Burcardus de, *Buck.* 143.

FENISC, Vlf, *Hunt.* 203. *Derb.* 277 b. *Nottingh.* 280 b. *Linc.* 354 b. bis.

FERRARIIS, Hermerus de, *Norf.* 273.

FILII Elrici, *Hants,* 52.

FILII Godeuert, *Clam. S. R. Linc.* 375.

FIN, *Linc.* 362.

FIN danus, *Buck.* 153.

FINEGAL, *Yorksh.* 309.

FISC, liber homo, *Norf.* 258 b.

FISCANNENSIS Ecclesia, *Sussex,* 17.[2]

FITEL, *Somers.* 98.

FITHEUS, *Wilts,* 72 b.

FLOTEMAN, *Yorksh.* 301 b. 312 b. 313.

Forestarii tres, Somers. 98 b.

---

[1] " Habebat unam Ecclesiam [in Burgo Stanford] de Rege quietam, cum VIII. acris."

[2] One manor only; " tenet de Rege Rameslie, et tenuit de rege E."

Forestarius, v. Bundi. Leuuinus.[1]

Forn, *Yorksh.* 325.

Forne, *Glouc.* 167. *Yorksh.* 298, 301 b. 315 b. 322 b.
329 b. passim.

Forst, Aluuinus, *Hants,* 52 b.

Fot, Ernui, *Chesh.* 263 b.

Fot, Goduuinus, *Kent,* 7.[2]

Fradre, teinus Regis E. *Norf.* 226.

Frambolt, Goduinus, teignus regis E. *Bedf.* 216 b.

Fran, *Chesh.* 265 b. *Yorksh.* 324 b. bis.

Frana commendatus Edrici, *Suff.* 442 b.

Francig. quidam, Worc. 174 b.

Francones homines tres, *Warw.* 241.[3]

Frane, *Sussex,* 20 b. 22, 22 b. *Worc.* 173. *Nottingh.*
282 b. 283 b. 284 b. 286 bis. 289 b. *Yorksh.* 325.
Linc. 356 b. bis. 357.

Frane et frater ejus, *Yorksh.* 374.

Frane alter, *Yorksh.* 325.

Frane f. Tor, *Yorksh.* 374.

Frane teinus Eduini Comitis, *Worc.* 172.

Frano, *Sussex,* 21. *Northampt.* 221, 228.

---

[1] Kelham, Illustr. p. 216, says, " There was a forester
appointed by the King to take care of his forests in every
county." These foresters answered for such part of the
crown revenue as was under their care. See Madox, Hist.
Excheq. 4to edit. vol. i. p. 355.

[2] His land was a half solin, that is half a hide, at Crai in
Kent, still called, from Goduinus Fot, its owner in King
Edward's time, Foots-Cray.

[3] Of these *Francones homines,* in Berdingeberie, it is said,
" Ipsi tenuerunt libere T. R. E." At the time of the Survey,
however, Berdingeberie was held by Goslinus under Turchil
de Warwic: and the homines francones are entered as if
attached to the manor, with the villans and bordarii.

FRANPALT, Goduinus, *Bedf.* 215 b.

FRANPOLD, Goduinus, *Bedf.* 215.

FRATRES, *Berks*, 63. " II. man. v. fr'm." *Yorksh.* 306 b.

FRATRES duo, *Berks*, 62. *Dors.* 77, 83. *Devon*, 102 b.
   104 b. *Buck.* 152. *Glouc.* 163. *Northampt.* 223.
   Leic. 238.[1] *Warw.* 242 b. *Nottingh.* 288: *Yorksh.*
   316, 317 b. *Linc.* 360.

FRATRES duo homines Asgari stalri, *Hertf.* 133 b.

FRATRES duo homines Aluuardi cilt, *Buck.* 144 b.

FRATRES duo, unus homo Asgari stalri, alter Abbatis de
   Ely, *Hertf.* 133 b.

FRATRES duo, homines R. E. *Buck.* 153.

FRATRES duo, horum unus homo R. E. alter homo
   Tochi, *Hertf.* 139.

FRATRES duo, Godric et Edric, *Glouc.* 168 b.

FRATRES II. homines Comitis Leuuini, *Hertf.* 136 b.

FRATRES duo, homines Stig. archiepiscopi, *Hertf.* 141 b.

FRATRES duo, unus homo Stigandi archiepiscopi, alter
   homo Leuuini Comitis, *Midd.* 130 b.

FRATRES duo, unus homo Vlf et alter homo Eddevæ,
   Buck. 144.

FRATRES duo (in paragio,) *Hants*, 50 b.

FRATRES duo teigni regis E. *Buck.* 147.

FRATRES tres, *Hertf.* 142. *Buck.* 147. *Warw.* 242 b.
   Nottingh. 287 b. *Linc.* 341, 360.

FRATRES quatuor, *Warw.* 241.[2]

FRATRES quinque, *Glouc.* 168 b. *Staff.* 249 b.

FRAUUIN, *Sussex*, 23 b.

---

[1] " Hanc terram [Wimundewalle] tenuerunt II. fratres
pro II. ⵕ et postea emit alter ab altero partem suam, et
fecit unum Manerium de duobus, T. R. E."

[2] They continued to hold under Turchil de Warwic at
the Survey. Of their former tenure it is said, " Idem ipsi
tenuerunt et liberi fuerunt."

FRAUUINUS, *Devon*, 114 b. 117, 117 b.

FREBERTUS tainnus, *Essex*, 57 b.

FREDEBERNUS, *Suff.* 396.

FREDERIC, *Kent*, 13.

FREDGHIS, *Nottingh.* 288 passim.

FREDGIS, *Northampt.* 223, 226. *Nottingh.* 290.

FREDGIST, *Yorksh.* 300 b. ter. 381 bis. *Linc.* 366, 368 b.

FREDREGIS, liber homo, *Norf.* 165 b.

FREDRI, *Sussex*, 27, 28.

FREGIS, *Northampt.* 223 bis. 224.[1]

FREGIST, *Northampt.* 227.

FREOWINUS, *Suff.* 343.

FREUUINUS, *Essex*, 32 b.

FRIDEBERTUS, *Cambr.* 200.

FRIDEBERTUS homo Leuuini Comitis, *Buck.* 144 b.

FRIEBERNUS, *Essex*, 62, 63.

FRIEBERNUS teinnus Regis T. R. E. *Suff.* 411 b.

FRIEBERTUS, *Essex*, 5 bis. 25.

FRODO, *Suff.* 336 b.

FRODO frater Abbatis, *Essex*, 103 b.[2]

FROGERUS vicecomes, *Berks*, 57.

FUGLO homo Alrici filii Godingi, *Bedf.* 214.

FULBERTUS, *Norf.* 207 b.[3]

FULCARDUS, *Suff.* 419.

FULCARDUS dimid. commendat. Edrico, *Suff.* 320 b.

FULCHER, *Yorksh.* 327 b.

FULCHERI, *Linc.* 361 b. passim. 369, 369 b. bis.

FULCHERI et II. fratres ejus, *Linc.* 347.

---

1 Fregis, probably the same person with Fredghis, Fredgis, Fredgist, and Fregist, is particularly mentioned in Gaimar's Metrical History as one of the opponents of the Conqueror, with Copsi and Merlesuain.

2 See vol. i. p. 421.

3 He continued to hold at the Survey.

FULCHERICUS, *Linc.* 371.

FULCHERUS, *Norf.* 211 bis. 211 b.

FULCHI, *Sussex,* 22 b. *Hants,* 49 b.

FULCHRI, *Yorksh.* 328, 339 b.

FULCOIUS, *Sussex,* 24.[1]

FULCUI, *Sussex,* 29 b. *Surr.* 36.

FULGHEL, *Hants,* 52.

FURCARDUS, *Suff.* 419.

FURSA, *Hunt.* 206.

FYACH, *Linc.* 337.

G.

G.[2] avunculus Radulfi, *Norf.* 262.

GALTERUS [de Gadomo], *Norf.* 276 b.

GAM, *Yorksh.* 301, 328 passim. 373 b.

GAME, *Leic.* 233 b. *Yorksh.* 311 b. 320 b. 328 passim.
329 b. passim. 300 b. 331 bis.

GAMEBAR, *Yorksh.* 301 b. 322.

GAMEL, *Staff.* 250 b. *Shropsh.* 256 b. 257 b. 258 b.
Chesh. 267 b. *Derb.* 274 bis. 275 b. passim. 276 bis.
Rotel. 290, 294. *Yorksh.* 300, 300 bis. 300 b.
passim. 301 bis. 301 b. bis. 303, 306, 306 bis.
307 bis. 309 b. 310 b. 311 bis. 311 b. bis. 312,
314 passim. 314 b. ter. 315 b. 316 ter. 317, 317 b.
bis. 318 passim. 319 b. 320 b. 321, 321 b. passim.
323, 324 b. 325, 327, 327 b. passim. 328 b. 329 b.
bis. 331, 331 b. 332 passim. *Linc.* 342 bis. 343,
346 b. 350 passim. 350 b. bis. 351, 352, 352 b.
356, 362 bis. 365. *Yorksh.* 373 b.

---

[1] He had held Rachetone in Sussex of King Edward,
which at the time of the Survey was held by Iuo as under-
tenant to Earl Roger. Fulcoius, however, held half a hide,
at the time of the Survey, in Meredone.

[2] Goduinus.

GAMEL f. Osberti, *Yorksh.* 298 b.

GAMELI pater, *Chesh.* 267 b. bis.

GAMELBAR, *Yorksh.* 298, 301 b. passim. 321 b. bis.
322 passim. 326 b. passim. 327 ter. 332.

GAMELBER, *Yorksh.* 301 b.

GAMELCARLE, *Yorksh.* 298.

GAMELTORP bar, *Yorksh.* 332.

GAND, S. Petrus de, *Kent,* 12 b.[1]

GANGEMERE, Alricus et soror ejus, *Buck.* 144 b.

GARDULF, *Linc.* 361 b.

GARLE, *Yorksh.* 331.

GELLINGE, Aluricus de, occisus in bello apud Hastinges,
Hunt. 208.

GENUIS, *Essex,* 106 b.

GENRET, liber homo sub Stigando, *Norf.* 176.

GENUST, *Shropsh.* 258 b.

GENUT, *Shropsh.* 258 b.

GERINUS, *Hants,* 52.

GERLING, *Dors.* 83 b.

GERMUNDUS homo Walteri Gifart, *Norf.* 276 b.

GERNAN, *Yorksh.* 309 b. 312 b.

---

1 The manor of Lewisham, to which the entry here referred to relates, and to which Greenwich was an appen-
dage, was given by Elthruda, niece of King Alfred, about
the year 900, to the Abbey of St. Peter, Ghent, which continued in possession of it till the suppression of the Alien
Priories by King Henry V. Lysons mentions three con-
firmations of this grant among the Cartæ antiquæ at the
Tower; the first by King Edward the Confessor, but not in
1038 as he supposes, since King Edward the Confessor
did not succeed to the Crown till 1041. The other con-
firmations were from King Henry I. and King Henry II. See
Lysons, Env. of London. edit. 1811, vol. i. pt. ii. pp. 497,
559.

GERNEBER, *Yorksh.* 316 b. bis.[1] 317 bis. 317 b. passim. 376 b.

GERNEBERN, *Derb.* 276.

GERNEBERNE, *Yorksh.* 301.

GEROLDUS, *Suff.* 423 b.

GERT, *Norf.* 223 b. 242 b. 246 b.

GEST frater Sarici, *Wilts,* 74.

GETDA, *Leic.* 230 b.

GETHE uxor Radulfi Comitis,[2] *Buck.* 148.

GETHNE, *Shropsh.* 258 b.

GHERI, *Shropsh.* 254 b. 255 b.

GHIDA, *Wilts,* 65 passim. *Somers.* 86 b.
87 bis. *Cornw.* 123 b.

GHIDA comitissa, *Devon,* 104. } *v.* GIDA.[3]

GHIDA mater Heraldi Comitis, *Devon,* 100 b. passim.

GHIL, *Yorksh.* 301.

GHILANDER, *Yorksh.* 323.

GHILE, *Yorksh.* 309 b.

---

[1] Also at the time of the Survey.

[2] The wife of Ralph de Mant, first Earl of Hereford. See vol. i. p. 433, note [1].

[3] Gueda, Gida, or Githe, the mother of Harold, was sister to Sweyn king of Denmark.

The Annals of the Church of Winchester, under the year 1052, speak well of her: " Githa uxor Godwini, femina multas habens facultates, pro anima ejus multis Ecclesiis in elemosyna multa contulit, et Wintoniensi Ecclesiæ dedit duo maneria, scilicet Bleodonam et Craukumbam, et ornamenta diversi generis." She was in Exeter when William the Conqueror laid siege to that town, in 1068, but made her escape, and got over into Flanders. Ordericus Vitalis, speaking of those who fled at this time, says, " Inter hæc Gisa, Goduini uxor, Heraldi genitrix, ingentem gazam clan-

GHILEBRID, *Yorksh.* 331 b.

GHILEMICEL, *Yorksh.* 301, 332.

GHILEPATRIC, *Yorksh.* 309 b. 311, 311 b. ter.

GHILLE, *Yorksh.* 312, 312 b. bis.

GIDA, *Dors.* 78 b. *Warw.* 239 b. 306 b.

GIDA comitissa, *Sussex,* 23 ter. 24. *Berks,*
    59 b.   } *v.* GHIDA.
GIDA mater Heraldi, *Surr.* 34.   } GUEDA.[1]

GILEMICHEL, *Yorksh.* 302.

GILEPATRIC, *Yorksh.* 311.

GIRALDUS, Raimundus, *Essex,* 66.

GIRARDUS, *Glouc.* 163.

GIROLDUS, *Suff.* 423.

GISLEBERTUS, *Wilts,* 66. *Suff.* 408.

GISO episcopus,[2] *Somers.* 86,[3] 89 b.

GITDA, *Northampt.* 225 b. passim. 226 passim.

---

culum sumpsit, et pro timore Guillelmi Regis, in Galliam, non reditura transmeavit."

Kelham, Illustr. p. 225, says, she died by a stroke of lightning.

She held, in different counties of England, previous to the Survey, more than three hundred and thirty hides, or thirty-nine thousand six hundred acres of land.

[1] See p. 117.

[2] Giso, Gisa, or Gise Hasban, a native of Lorraine. He was consecrated Bishop of Wells in 1061. He died in 1088. The " Historia de Episcopis Bathon. et Wellensibus ad annum M.CCCC.XXIII. authore Canonico Wellensi," printed in Angl. Sacr. tom. i. p. 559, contains much relating to Harold's estates, which, after the confiscation of 1051, had been given to the Church of Wells by King Edward the Confessor, but of which Harold gained the re-possession, greatly to Bishop Giso's discomfort.

[3] Also at the Survey.

GLADEWINUS, *Suff.* 442.

GLADUIN, *Staff.* 250 b. *Derb.* 278 b. *Nottingh.* 287 b. 288.

GLADUINE, *Linc.* 343 b.

GLADUINUS, *Nottingh.* 286.

GLADUINUS homo abbatis S. Albani, *Buck.* 146.

GLASTINGBERIENSIS ABBATIA, *Hants*, 43 b. *Berks*, 59 b. 66 b. *Wilts*, 69 b. *Dors.* 77 b. *Somers.* 88, 90, 91 b. 92. *Devon*, 103 b. *Glouc.* 165.

GLEUUINUS, *Chesh.* 267.

GLOUUEC. S. Oswaldus, *Glouc.* 164 b. ter.

GLOUUECESTRE, S. Petrus de, *Glouc.* 164 b. bis. 165 b. passim.[1]

GLUNIER, *Yorksh.* 298, 301, 301 bis. 301 b. 311, 315 bis. 315 b. bis. 320, 332.

GOD, *Kent*, 9, 14. *Sussex*, 18 b. *Wilts*, 69 b.

GODA, *Sussex*, 18 b. 19 b. 21 b. ter. *Somers.* 94 b. *Devon*, 113 b. bis. 114 b. *Oxf.* 160 b. *Cambr.* 193 passim. 193 b. bis. 195. *Rutl.* 293 b. bis. *Essex*, 106 b. *Suff.* 340, 342 passim. 342 b.

GODA alter, *Suff.* 342.

GODA comitissa, *Sussex*, 17 bis. 18 b. 19, 19 b. 25. *Surr.* 36 b. *Dors.* 75 b. 76. *Midd.* 130. *Buck.* 151 b. bis. *Glouc.* 166 b. bis. 170 ter. *Nottingh.* 280 b.

GODA comitissa, soror R. E. *Surr.* 34.

GODA soror R. E. *Glouc.* 166 b.

} *v.* GODE.

GODA commendata Algari comitis, *Cambr.* 198.

GODA commend. Goduin filio Tuke, *Suff.* 333.

---

[1] There is no indication that the possessions of St. Peter Gloucester, in the counties of Worcester and Hereford, had belonged to it T. R. E.

GODA homo Eddid. reginæ, *Hertf.* 142.

GODA liber homo, *Suff.* 376 b.

GODA libera femina, *Suff.* 339, 396.

GODBOLD, *Buck.* 148.

GODDUA, *Suff.* 340 b.

GODE, *Wilts*, 74.[1] *Devon*, 109, 110, 114 b. 116 b. 117.
  Hertf. 137 b. *Hunt.* 206. *Nottingh.* 291 b. *Suff.*
  334 b.

GODE homo regis Edwardi, *Hertf.* 137.

GODE et filius ejus, *Hertf.* 140.

GODE comitissa, *Nottingh.* 287. *v.* GODA.

GODED, *Derb.* 273.

GODEFRIDI scutularii pater, *Dors.* 85.[2]

GODEL de Brixi, *Kent*, 6 b.

GODELENT, *Yorksh.* 298.

GODEMAN, *Somers.* 92 b. *Northampt.* 223 b. *Linc.*
  336.

GODEMANUS, *Suff.* 342 b.

GODERE, *Suff.* 346.

GODERE liber homo, *Essex*, 94 b.

GODERICUS vicecomes, *Buck.* 144.

GODERUS liber homo, *Essex*, 12 b.

GODESA, *Kent*, 11. *Hants*, 53 b.

GODESSA, *Kent*, 12 b.

GODESTANUS, *Suff.* 378.

GODET quidam liber homo, *Essex*, 42 b.

GODEUA, *Wilts*, 73. *Devon*, 116 b. *Cambr.* 202. *Northampt.*
  223 b. *Warw.* 241. *Staff.* 248, 248 b. bis. 249 bis.
  Derb. 278.

---

[1] She continued to hold the land of this entry in capite
at the time of the Survey.

[2] The son continued to hold at the time of the Survey.

GODEUA Comitissa, *Worc.* 177 b. *Leic.*
231 b. *Staff.* 247 b. 249 b. 250 bis.
Shropsh 254, 256, 257, 257 b. 258. } *v.* GODEUE.
Nottingh. 280 b. 283 b.   GODIVA.[1]
GODEUA uxor Leurici comitis, *Warw.* 244.

GODEVÆ vir, *Somers.* 90 b.

GODEUE, *Wilts*, 71. *Devon*, 112 b. *Hertf.* 139 b. *Cambr.*
194. *Inter Ripam et Mersam*, 269 b.

GODEUE comitissa, *Nottingh.* 284 bis.   *v.* GODEUA.
GODIVA.

GODEUERT, *Linc.* 365 b. *Clam. S. R. Linc.* 375.

GODGEUA libera femina, *Suff.* 443 b.

GODGEUA libera femina commendata, *Suff.* 354 b.

GODHIT, *Shropsh.* 259.

GODID, *Chesh.* 267 ter.[2]

GODID quædam femina, *Essex*, 13.

GODID homo Asgari stalri, *Hertf.* 137 bis. 137 b. bis.
139 b. 140.

GODIL, *Kent*, 8 b.

GODINC, *Suff.* 377.

GODINC liber homo, *Norf.* 127 b.

GODING, *Hants*, 45 b. *Staff.* 249.

GODING homo Edrici calvi, *Bedf.* 218.

GODING homo Osberni monachi, *Hertf.* 135 b.

GODINGUS, *Essex*, 155. *Suff.* 340 b. bis.

GODINGUS homo Eddeuæ pulchræ, *Cambr.* 198 b.

GODIUA, *Staff.* 249.

GODIVA comitissa, *Warw.* 239 b.

GODMAN, *Hants*, 39 b. 48 b. *Somers.* 97. *Devon*, 106 b.
107 b. 108 b. *Cambr.* 200.

GODMAN teinnus, *Suff.* 436 b.

---

[1] See an Account of her, vol. i. p. 426.

[2] At the time of the Survey, Godid continued as under-
tenant only of one of the three lands here entered.

GODMANNUS, *Suff.* 404, 404 b.

GODMANUS, *Suff.* 340 b. 351 b. 393 b. bis. 441.

GODMANUS commend. Edeue, *Suff.* 295.

GODMANUS liber homo, *Essex,* 98.

GODMANUS sochemannus Roberti, *Essex,* 47.

GODMARUS, *Suff.* 294 b.

GODMARUS homo Alestan, *Bedf.* 212.

GODMUND homo Wallef, *Cambr.* 202.

GODMUNDUS, *Dors.* 82. *Hertf.* 142 b.[1]   *Bedf.* 218.[1]
Norf. 238 b.

GODO, *Sussex,* 20. *Devon,* 115.

GODREDUS, *Linc.* 336 b.

GODRIC, *Kent,* 6, 7 bis. 8, 10 b. *Surrey,* 36 b. *Hants,*
44 b. 45 b. 48, 49, 49 b. 51, 52 b. 53 ter. 53 b.
54 bis.[2] *Berks,* 60 b. 61 b. *Wilts,* 71 bis. 72 ter.
72 b. 73 b. 74, 74 b. *Dors.* 79 b. 81 b. bis. 82 bis.
Somers. 91 b. 92, 92 b. bis. 93 bis. 93 b. ter. 94,
99. *Devon,* 107 bis. 110, 111 b. bis. 114 bis. 116
ter. 116 b. 117 b. 118 passim. *Cornw.* 121 bis.
122 b. bis. *Oxf.* 160, 160 b. *Glouc.* 169 b. *Worc.*
174, 174 b. passim. 175 bis. 176 b. 177 b. *Heref.*
183, 187 b. ter. *Cambr.* 200. *Hunt.* 204 b. *Nor-*
thampt. 222 b. 223 b. 224 b. *Leic.* 231 ter. *Warw.*
240 ter. 243 b. *Staff.* 249, 250 b. ter. *Shropsh.*
255 b. bis. 257 b. 258 b. 259 b. 260. *Chesh.* 263 b.
264, 264 b. 265, 265 b. 266 b. passim. 268. *Derb.*
273, 274 b. ter. 275, 275 b. 278 passim. 278 b. bis.
Nottingh. 284 b. 285, 285 b. 286 passim. 287 bis.

---

[1] Godmundus continued to hold the lands mentioned in
these two entries, of the King, at the time of the Survey.
Each consisted of no more than three virgates.

[2] Godric continued to hold this land in capite at the time
of the Survey. It was half a hide.

287 b. 288 ter. 290, 291, 292 bis, 292 b. *Yorksh.*
301 bis. 303 b. 315, 316 bis. 316 b. 317, 319 ter.
319 b. *Linc.* 337, 347, 349, 349 b. passim. 350,
352, 352 b. 354, 356 b. 357, 359, 360, 361, 362,
364 b. passim. 365, 366, 366 b. 368 b. *Clam. N.
R. Linc.* 376. *Clam. in Chetst.* 377. *Norf.* 166.
Suff. 297, 320, 320 b. 395, 413, 419 bis. 440.

GODRIC alter, *Derb.* 274 b.

GODRIC et II. fratres ejus, *Linc.* 341.[1]

GODRIC et alii VI. taini, *Nottingh.* 284 b.

GODRIC et BRUNO in paragio, *Dors.* 79.

GODRIC Carlesone, *Kent,* 1. ⎫
GODRIC fil. Carle, *Kent,* 6 b. ⎭

GODRIC f. Eddeue, *Linc.* 336.

GODRIC et EDRIC frater ejus, *Clam. S. R. Linc.* 375.

GODRIC liber homo, *Suff.* 376.

GODRIC tegnus regis E. *Essex,* 43.

GODRIC frater Wluui episcopi, *Buck.* 144.

GODRIC unus liber homo, *Berks,* 60 b.

GODRIC homo Almari de Benintone, *Hertf.* 138.

GODRIC homo Asgari stalre, *Buck.* 151.

GODRIC homo regis E. *Cambr.* 199 b.

GODRIC homo Osuui, *Buck.* 149.

GODRIC homo Stig. archiep. *Hertf.* 135 b.

GODRIC presbyter, *Hants,* 53 b.[2] *Cornw.* 124 .

GODRIC teinus Algari Comitis, *Worc.* 176.

GODRIC teinus R. E. *Glouc.* 168. *Bedf.* 210 bis.

GODRICI Mal filii, *Hants,* 50 b.

---

[1] " Duo serviebant tertio."

[2] At Melevsford. " Ipse tenuit in paragio de rege E."
He held in capite as one of the Thani Regis at the time of
the Survey. A hide and a half.

GODRICI pater, *Wilts,* 74.

GODRICUS, *Kent,* 8 b. 10 b. 11. *Sussex,* 27, 27 b. *Hants,*
52 b. *Berks,* 57 b. 60 b. 61. *Wilts,* 65, 69 bis.
Somers. 91, 94. *Cornw.* 120. *Glouc.* 166 b. bis.
169. *Worc.* 173 bis. 175. *Heref.* 186 b. *Hunt.*
203 b. 208. *Northampt.* 222, 224 b. *Warw.* 240 b.
Staff. 249 bis. *Derb.* 276, 278 b. *Linc.* 336. *Clam.*
S. R. Linc. 375, 375 b. bis. *Essex,* 12, 20 b. 23,
25 b. 46, 47 b. ter. 67, 104, 106 b. *Norf.* 133,
200 b. 220, 228 bis. 242 b. 245 b. 278 passim.
285 b. *Suff.* 317 b. 321, 324 b. 331 b. 333 b.
339 b. 340 bis. 340 b. 341 bis. 342, 342 b. bis.
343, 353, 356, 375 b. 377 b. 385 b. 393 b. 395,
395 b. 424, 424 b.

GODRICUS alter, *Suff.* 339 b.

GODRICUS commend. Vlsi, *Nottingh.* 282 b.

GODRICUS commendatus Heroldi, *Suff.* 336 b. 402 b.

GODRICUS commend. cujusdam commendati Heroldi,
Suff. 423 b.

GODRICUS diaconus, *Linc.* 371 bis.

GODRICUS faber, *Suff.* 339 b.

GODRICUS filius Gareuinæ, *Linc.* 336.

GODRICUS f. Toruort, *Linc.* 337.

GODRICUS liber homo, *Berks,* 62 b. *Essex,* 33 b. 46,
49, 94, 96. *Norf.* 278 b. *Suff.* 298 b. 441 b.

GODRICUS liber homo Heroldi, *Suff.* 346.

GODRICUS liber homo Kitel, *Norf.* 254.

GODRICUS liber homo commend. homo Godrici de Rossa,
Norf. 279.

GODRICUS homo Vicecomitis, *Bedf.* 211 b.

GODRICUS longus, *Suff.* 339 b.

GODRICUS presbyter, *Hants,* 46. *Hunt.* 206 b. 208.
Suff. 342 b.

GODRICUS presbyter commendatus Edrici de Lassefella, *Suff.* 316.

GODRICUS socheman Edrici, *Suff.* 318 b.

GODRICUS teignus regis E. *Worc.* 175, 177. *Essex,* 44 b.

GODRICUS Vicecomes,[1] *Berks,* 57 b. passim. 58, 60 b. ter.

GODRIDA, *Yorksh.* 331.

GODTON, Aluuinus homo R. E. *Hertf.* 142 b.

GODTONE, Aluuinus de, *Hertf.* 138 b.

GODTOVI, *Surrey,* 35 b. bis.

GODUIN, *Sussex,* 18 b. 21 b. 24. *Hants,* 38, 45, 45 b. 49 b. *Wilts,* 72 b. 74 b. *Somers.* 92. *Devon,* 107, 109 b. 115 b. 118 ter.[2] *Cornw.* 123 bis. *Midd.* 127 b. *Cambr.* 197. *Staff.* 250 b. *Chesh.* 265 b. 266 b. 267. *Derb.* 274 bis. 274 b. bis. 275 b. *Nottingh.* 287 b. 291 bis. *Rutl.* 293 b. *Yorksh.* 317 b. ter. 329 ter. *Linc.* 340 b. 342 b. 354, 357, 359 b. bis. 360 bis. 368. *Clam. N. R. Linc.* 376.

GODUIN alter, *Yorksh.* 329.

GODUIN commend. Stigandi, *Linc.* 336.

GODUIN filius Dudeman, *Kent,* 9.

GODUIN homo Alestan teigni Regis, *Bedf.* 212.

GODUIN homo Almari de Benintone, *Hertf.* 137 b.

GODUIN homo Aschil, *Bedf.* 213.

GODUIN homo Engelrici, *Hertf.* 136 b.

---

[1] He was under-tenant of Fifield, in Berkshire, to the Abbat of Abingdon T. R. E. The Abingdon Register, Claud. C. IX. fol. 133, says, that he held this estate of the Abbat for three lives, but was killed in the battle of Hastings. Henry de Ferrariis, it is added, " hanc villam cum altera (*sc.* Kingestun) suæ ditioni adjecit."

[2] The same Godwin is entered as holding both these and other lands in capite, in the same page, at the time of taking the Survey.

GODUIN homo Heraldi Comitis, *Hertf.* 133. *Bedf.* 217.

GODUIN homo Leuuini Comitis, *Buck.* 144.

GODUIN homo episcopi Wluui, *Buck.* 148..

GODUINE, *Hunt.* 206 b. *Linc.* 341, 368.

GODUINE filius Edric, *Yorksh.* 374.

GODUINUS, *Kent,* 7, 8 b. 9, 11 b. *Sussex,* 21 b. bis. 22 b.
  23. *Hants,* 39 b. bis. 40, 40 b. 41, 45 ter. 46, 47 b.
  passim. 49, 51, 52. *Berks,* 61 b. 62, 62 b. *Wilts,* 68 b.
  ter. 69 b. 72 b. 73 b. bis. *Dors.* 79 b. 81 b. 82, 83,
  83 b. *Somers.* 88 b. 89, 92, 93 b. 94 bis. 94 b. 99.
  Devon, 102, 104 b.[1] 105 b. 106, 107 b. bis. 108 b.
  109 b. *Cornw.* 123 b. *Hertf.* 136 b. 140 b.[2] *Oxf.*
  161. *Glouc.* 169. *Worc.* 173 bis. *Heref.* 187, 187 b.
  Hunt. 203 b. 205. *Northampt.* 222 b. ter. 223,
  223 b. 224, 228 b. *Leic.* 234. *Warw.* 241,[3] 244 b.[3]
  Staff. 248 ter. 248 b. bis. 249 bis. 249 b. 250, 250 b.
  ter. *Shropsh.* 254 b. 255, 256 b. ter. 257 bis. 267
  ter. *Derb.* 275 b. ter. *Nottingh.* 283 b. 284, 293.
  Yorksh. 301 bis. 313, 317 b. bis. *Linc.* 339 b. 350
  bis. 368, 369 bis. *Clam. S. R. Linc.* 375 b. *Essex,*
  11 b. 28, 66, 67, 83. *Norf.* 132 b. bis. 134, 144 b.
  222, 224, 234, 259, 262, 274. *Suff.* 305 b. 318 b.
  320, 328 b. 340 b. 394.

GODUINUS alter, *Norf.* 246 b.

GODVINUS et mater ejus,[4] *Somers.* 99.

---

[1] Goduinus continued to hold this land in capite at the
Survey.

[2] In the time of Edward the Confessor he must have been
the freeholder of this land. " Istemet tenuit T. R. E. et
vendere potuit." He held it at the time of the Survey as
under-tenant to Geoffrey de Mandeville.

[3] Goduinus continued to hold these lands in capite at
the Survey.

[4] The son continued to hold when the Survey was taken.

Goduinus accipitrarius, *Hants,* 50 b.[1]

Goduinus Alferi filius, *Suff.* 304 bis. 314 b.

Goduinus Alsies sone, tennus Edeue Reginæ, *Suff.* 306 ter.

Goduinus avunculus Rad. Comitis, *Norf.* 131.

Goduinus burgensis de Bedeford, *Bedf.* 218.[2]

Goduinus cild, *Cambr.* 195 b.

Goduinus cilt, abbas Westmon.[3] *Buck.* 146.

Goduinus cilt, homo Edeuæ pulchræ, *Cambr.* 193 b.

Goduinus Comes, *Kent,* 1, 4 b. 7 b. 8, 8 b. 9, 9 b. 11, 12, 13, 14. *Sussex,* 22, 22 b. 23, 23 b. 24, 24 b. 25, 26, 27, 29. *Surrey,* 32, 36. *Hants,* 38 bis. 44 b. bis. 45, 49, 53.

Goduinus diaconus, *Essex,* 58 b. 98 b.[4]

Goduinus filius Herald.[5] *Somers.* 86 b. bis.

---

[1] He continued to hold of the King at the Survey.

[2] He continued, at the time of the Survey, to hold the same land in capite; increased in point of quantity.

[3] Eadwinus, here called Goduinus, succeeded Wulnoth as Abbat of Westminster, A.D. 1049. In the entry above referred to, the word *cilt* is written over Goduinus. Sporley assures us that Eadwine, as he calls him, was of English descent. In one of the Conqueror's charters this same abbat is called Aglwi. It was in the time of Godwine that the Church of Westminster was pulled down, and re-built in a more splendid form by King Edward the Confessor. Godwine, or Eadwine, died in or before 1072.

[4] He continued to hold the land of this entry in capite at the Survey.

[5] This was the son of King Harold. The entry is among the lands which had belonged to Earl Godwin's children.

According to Capgrave, Harold had a daughter, Gunnild, who was cured of blindness by St. Wlstan. Snorro men-

Goduinus filius Leuuini, *Bedf.* 214.

Goduinus homo Borret, *Bedf.* 218.

Goduinus homo Eddeue, *Cambr.* 193 b.

Goduinus homo regis E. *Bedf.* 217 b.

Goduinus homo abbatis de Ely, *Cambr.* 199, 199 b.

Goduinus homo Guert comitis, *Bedf.* 217 b.

Goduinus homo Leuuini comitis, *Buck.* 144 b.

Goduinus homo Tosti comitis, *Bedf.* 216 b.

Goduinus homo Vlf, *Buck.* 149.

Goduinus homo Wallef comitis, *Cambr.* 202 b. bis.

Goduinus liber homo, *Sussex*, 25 passim. 25 b. *Dors.*
        79. *Chesh.* 263 b. *Essex*, 12, 80, 88 bis. 88 b. 101,
        102. *Norf.* 126, 153 b. *Suff.* 296, 378, 405, 425 b.

Goduinus liber homo Edrici de Laxefelda, *Norf.* 148 b.

Goduinus liber homo dimidius Edrici, *Norf.* 246 b.

Goduinus liber homo Gert, *Norf.* 246.

Goduinus liber homo Reginæ, *Suff.* 332.

Goduinus, sub Stigando, *Norf.* 143.

Goduinus liber homo Stigandi, *Norf.* 230.

Goduinus liber homo, qui postea utlagavit, *Norf.* 274.

Godvinus prepositus, *Dors.* 84.[1]

Goduinus presbyter, *Sussex*, 17 b. 27 bis. *Hants*, 43.
        Buck. 153.[2] *Nottingh.* 288. *Essex*, 95 b.

Goduinus presbyter, liber homo, *Suff.* 422 b.

Goduinus presbyter S. arch.[3] *Buck.* 146.

---

tions Githa as the name of another daughter who married
Waldemar Prince of Holgard, son of Jarislaus. See Snorro,
Peringskiold's edit. vol. ii. p. 178.

[1] He continued to hold the same hide of land at Winter-
borne in capite, when the Survey was taken.

[2] He continued to hold the land of this entry, at the
Survey, as an under-tenant of Lewinus de Niweham.

[3] Presbyter Stigandi archiepiscopi.

GODUINUS teinnus Regis, *Essex*, 49 b.

GODUINUS teignus R. E. *Hertf.* 140 b. *Bedf.* 215.

GODUINUS Tokesone, *Norf.* 246 b.[1]

GODUIUS commendatus Saxo, *Suff.* 376 b. bis.

GODUIUS liber homo commend. *Suff.* 375 b.

GODUS, *Wilts*, 70, 71.

GODUUI, *Cambr.* 194 b.

GODUUIDERE de Bedeford, *Bedf.* 218 b.[2]

GODUUIN filius Carli, *Kent*, 9.

GODUUINUS, *Heref.* 186 b. *Nottingh.* 284 b. *Norf.* 199, 231 b. 234 bis. 284.   *Suff.* 340, 341, 387, 396, 396 b. 419, 440, 441 b. bis. 442.

GODWINUS Comes, *Sussex*, 16, 17 b. 18, 19 b. 20, 21, 21 b. bis. *Glouc.* 164. *Worc.* 176 b. *Heref.* 181.

GODWINUS commendatus, *Suff.* 292.

GODWINUS commend. Gerti, *Norf.* 269.

GODWINUS commendatus Stigandi, *Suff.* 446 b.

GODWINUS filius Tuka, *Suff.* 335 b.

GODUUINUS homo Wluui, *Buck.* 148.

GODUUINUS liber homo, *Norf.* 151 b. 157.   *Suff.* 422 b.

GODUUINUS liber homo commend. Guerti, *Nottingh.* 284.

GODUUINUS liber homo Stigandi, *Suff.* 377.

GODUUINUS presbyter, homo Heroldi, *Suff.* 343.

GODWINUS teinnus, *Suff.* 414.

GODWINUS teinus regis E. *Suff.* 402 b.

GOERTH, *Norf.* 257.

GOGAN homo Edeue, *Cambr.* 194 b.

GOLA, *Essex*, 71.

---

[1] The same with Godwinus filius Tuka, *Suff.* 335 b.

[2] He continued to hold his land at the time of the Survey.

GOLDE, et Vluric filius ejus, *Hunt.* 207 b.

GOLDERON homo Leuenot, *Bedf.* 214 b.

GOLDINUS homo comitis Heraldi, *Midd.* 128 b.

GOLDSTAN, *Kent,* 1 b.

GOLDUINUS, *Sussex,* 18 b. 21.

GOLDUS, *Cambr.* 201.

GOLEGRIM, *Derb.* 275 b.

GOLLEUE, *Hants,* 50 b.

GOLNIL huscarle Regis E. *Buck.* 146 b.

GOLSTAN, *Essex,* 101 b.

GOLTOUI, *Surrey,* 36 b.

GOLUINUS, *Sussex,* 21.

GONCHEL, *Linc.* 357.

GONCHETEL, *Linc.* 366.

GONDREDE, *Sussex,* 25.

GONHARD, *Devon,* 112.

GONNAR, *Devon,* 112 b.

GONNEUUATE, *Linc.* 347, 359 b. passim. 360 bis. 370 b.

GONNI homo Aluric filii Goding, *Buck.* 153.

GONNIL, *Somers.* 88.

GONUERD, *Somers.* 99.

GORT, *Sussex,* 25 b.

GOS, *Hunt.* 203, 208.

GOSFRIDUS, *Norf.* 196.

GOSP', *Yorksh.* 301 b. 330 passim.

GOSPAT', *Yorksh.* 332 bis.

GOSPATRIC,[1] *Yorksh.* 298 passim. 300 passim. 300 b.

---

[1] See the former volume, p. 428, in the Index of Tenants in capite. Ordericus Vitalis, noticing the death of Goisfridus Abbat of Croyland, A.D. 1124, says, " Cui Gallevus, angligena, Crulandensis cœnobii monachus, *frater Gospatricii* de magnâ nobilitate Anglorum, successit."

passim. 301 b. bis. 305 b. bis. 309 b.[1] 310 ter. 310 b.[1]
311 bis.[1] 312 bis.[1] 312 b.[1] 328 b. passim. 330 passim.[1] 331, 331 b. 332.

GOTIL, *Essex*, 56 bis.

GOTILD, *Essex*, 56.

GOTIUS, *Essex*, 54 b. 55 b. bis.

GOTIUS liber homo, *Essex*, 20.

GOTLAC, *Chesh.* 263 b.

GOTONE, Aluuinus, *Hertf.* 135 b.

GOTRA, *Essex*, 68 b.

GOTRA liber homo, *Essex*, 64 b.

GOUTI, huscarle Heraldi comitis, *Midd.* 129.

GOUTI liber homo, *Suff.* 294 b.

GOUTI teignus Heraldi comitis, *Hertf.* 137 b.

GOZELINUS, *Nottingh.* 288.

GOZELINUS filius Lanberti, *Clam. S. R. Linc.* 375.

GRENE, *Sussex*, 29.

GRESLET, Albertus, *Inter Rip. et Mersam*, 270.

GREUE, *Linc.* 348 bis.

GRIBOL, *Linc.* 371.

GRICHETEL, *Shropsh.* 257.

GRICHITEL, *Nottingh.* 288.

GRIFIN, *Cornw.* 123 b.

GRIFIN Rex, *Chesh.* 263,[2] 269.

---

[1] In all the folios here referred to, Gospatric continued
to hold lands, either in capite or as sub-tenant of Earl Alan,
at the time of the Survey.

[2] " Rex E. dedit regi Grifino totam terram quæ jacebat
trans aquam quæ DE vocatur. Sed postquam ipse Grifin
forisfecit ei, abstulit ab eo hanc terram et reddidit Episcopo de Cestre et omnibus suis hominibus qui antea ipsam
tenebant."

GRIKETEL, liber homo, *Norf.* 171.[1]

GRIM, *Devon,* 108 b. bis.   *Cornw.* 122 bis. 122 b. 123.
  Worc. 176. *Heref.* 181, 187. *Warw.* 243 b. *Chesh.*
  263 b. 266, 267. *Nottingh.* 285 b. bis. 286 b. 287 b.
  Yorksh. 298 bis. 300 b. ter. 301 ter. 308, 309 b. bis.
  322 bis. 328 b. bis. *Linc.* 362 passim. 373 b.

GRIM homo Eddeue, *Cambr.* 195 b.

GRIM, Edricus, *Suff.* 293, 293 b. 294, 296 b. 297,
  417 b. 431, 443.

GRIM, homo R. E. *Midd.* 129 b.

GRIMBALD homo Bisi, *Buck.* 148 b.

GRIMBALDUS, *Linc.* 350.

GRIMBALDUS homo Eddeuæ, *Cambr.* 195 b.

GRIMBALDUS homo regis E. *Bedf.* 216.

GRIMBER, *Linc.* 366 b.

GRIMBERT, *Linc.* 366 b.

GRIMBOLD, *Linc.* 364, 365 b.

GRIMBOLD Crac, *Linc.* 347 bis.

GRIMBOLDUS, *Linc.* 350 passim.

GRIMCHEL, *Linc.* 361 b.

GRIMCHIL, *Yorksh.* 315.

GRIMMUS commendat. Guert. *Suff.* 420.

GRIMOLFUS, *Suff.* 298 b.

GRIMOLFUS liber homo commend. Reginæ, *Suff.* 433 b.

GRIMULF, *Warw.* 242 b.

GRIMUS, *Essex,* 69, 98. *Suff.* 299 b. bis. 340 b. bis. 420.

GRIMUS liber homo, *Essex,* 84, 101 b. *Suff.* 336 b.

GRIMUS prepositus, *Essex,* 4 b.

GRINCHEI, *Chesh.* 267 b.

GRINCHEL, *Nottingh.* 287 b. bis. 288. *Yorksh.* 301, 324,
  324 b. *Linc.* 340 b. 341, 342 b. 350,354 bis. 356

---

[1] He continued to hold at the Survey.

passim. 357 b. 360, 362 b. 363, 365 b. *Yorksh.*
374. *Clam. N. R. Linc.* 376 bis.

GRINCHELLUS, *Essex,* 68 bis.

GRINCHET, *Warw.* 242.

GRINCHETEL, *Heref.* 183 b. *Yorksh.* 298.

GRINCHIL, *Nottingh.* 286 b. *Linc.* 352, 352 b. 353 b.
357 b. 361 b.

GRINO, Robertus, *Essex,* 5 b.

GROSSUS, Willielmus, *Norf.* 276 b.

GRUD, Alnod, homo Stigandi archiepiscopi, *Hertf.* 134 b.

GRUNULFUS, *Suff.* 452.

GRUT, Eduinus, *Essex,* 67, 95.

GRUTT, Alnod, 134.

GUDA comitissa, *Sussex,* 28 b.

GUDDA, *Cornw.* 123 b.

GUDETA comitissa, *Linc.* 362.

GUDHEN, Goduinus, *Essex,* 99.

GUDMUND, *Wilts,* 73. *Dors.* 84.[1]

GUDMUNDUS, *Essex,* 53 bis. 53 b. bis. 54. *Suff.* 406 b.
410 b.

GUDMUNDUS liber homo, *Essex,* 32.

GUDMUNT, *Linc.* 343.

GUDMUNT homo regis Edw. *Hunt.* 210.

GUDRET, *Clam. N. R. Linc.* 376.

GUEDA comitissa, *Sussex,* 27. *Hants,* 38 b. ⎫ *v.* GHIDA.
    39 b. ⎪   GIDA.
GUEDA mater Heraldi comitis, *Glouc.* 164. ⎭

GUEDE, *Linc.* 369.

GUERD, *Norf.* 190 b.

GUERD comes, *Sussex,* 28. *Cambr.* 197 b. ter. *v.* GUERT.
    GUERTUS. GURERT. GURT.

---

[1] Also when the Survey was taken.

GUERT, *Sussex*, 28 b. *Hants*, 47 b. *Berks*, 59 b. 61.
   Essex, 10 b. *Norf.* 115 b.[1] 132, 144 b. 193 b. *Suff.*
   377, 380 b. 420, 422 b. bis. 442.

GUERT comes, *Cambr.* 202 bis. *Bedf.* 217.
   Norf. 274 b. 287.

GUERTUS comes, *Norf.* 283 bis. 283 b.
   Suff. 290.

v. GUERD.
   GURERT.
   GURT.[2]

GUERT iste, *Norf.* 272.

GUERTUS, *Suff.* 407, 407 b. 432.

---

[1] The Guert of this entry is Guert comes.

[2] The fate of Leuuine and Guerth, the brothers of Harold, at the battle of Hastings, is one of the settled events of history: recorded both in the English and the Danish Chronicles. " Hic ceciderunt Leuuine et Gurd, fratres Haroldi Regis," is the inscription over the subject of their deaths in the Baieux Tapestry.

There is a tale, however, of the twelfth century, which represents Guerth to have escaped alive. He is said to have been seen in extreme age by Henry the Second himself, to have spoken mysteriously respecting Harold, and to have declared that the body of that Prince was not at Waltham. The whole was, probably, the fabrication of one of the secular canons, who were ejected at the re-foundation of Waltham Abbey in 1177.

The Legend alluded to is preserved in the Harleian Manuscript 3776, fol. 21 b.

" *Quid frater Haroldi, Gurta nomine, Abbati Waltero vel aliis responderit super fratris sui, requisitus, cineribus vel sepultura.*

" In diebus vero Regis Henrici Secundi visus est tam ab ipso Rege quem a magnatibus terræ et populo Gurta frater Haroldi, quam in libro suo jam dictus historiographus, tempore adventus Normannorum aliquid plus puero ætatis habuisse refert, prudentia vero animi et probitate nil distare

GUETH comitissa, *Buck.* 148 bis.[1]
GUIOLFUS, *Suff.* 351 b.
GULBERTUS, *Yorksh.* 373 b.
GULUERT, *Glouc.* 170.
GUN' unus liber homo Radstarte, *Norf.* 146 b.
GUNCHIL, *Linc.* 365 b.
GUNDULF, *Glouc.* 164 b.[2]
GUNDULFUS, *Sussex*, 21 b.

---

a viro. Erat autem jam tunc grandævus valde, et sicut ea tempestate a multis accepimus qui eum viderant, venustus aspectu, facie decorus, proceritate corporis admodum longus; hunc vidit etiam piæ recordationis canonicorum regularium quod Waltham abbas primus, dompnus Walterus, a quo, una cum fratribus sibi adherentibus, in curia Regis apud Wodestocam diligenter sciscitari studuit utrum re vera cineres germani sui in suo ut credebatur Monasterio servarentur. Quibus ille Anglicè respondit, Rusticum ait quemlibet habere potestis Haroldum, non habetis. Ad locum tamen per seipsum venit Crucem Sanctam adoraturus: ostensoque sibi sarcophago fratris, ut dicebatur, oblique illud intuitus, non ait homo scit, sic enim jurabat, Non hic jacet Haroldus. Vivat in longum, et vigeat in Christo. Dominus Michael canonicus, probatæ religionis, camerarius Ecclesiæ Walthamensis qui, multis astantibus, quorum nonnulli adhuc supersunt, hæc ab ore viri se audivisse constanter asseverat."

Among the forgotten fables of the day, a story was undoubtedly prevalent, that Harold had escaped from Hastings. Giraldus Cambrensis asserts that it was believed he had fled from the battle pierced with wounds, and with the loss of his left eye, and that he ended his days holily and virtuously as an anchoret at Chester. Itin. edit. Franc. 1603, p. 874. Brompton and Knighton quote the story.

[1] She is elsewhere called " Gethe uxor Radulfi Comitis."
[2] He continued to hold at the time of the Survey.

GUNEUUARE, *Yorksh.* 307 bis.

GUNNAR, *Wilts,* 73.

GUNNER, *Heref.* 186 b. bis. *Chesh.* 264 b. *Yorksh.* 315.

GUNNERE, *Berks,* 62 b. *Suff.* 342 b.

GUNNERUS, *Essex,* 48 b.[1]

GUNNEUARE, *Yorksh.* 305 b.

GUNNEUUATE, *Linc.* 341, 347, 354.

GUNNI, *Somers.* 96 b.

GUNNILD, *Sussex,* 28 b. *Somers.* 86 b. 87.[2]

---

[1] He continued to hold the same land under Suein of Essex.

[2] For these, and the other lands which are comprised in the second column of fol. 86 b. and the five first entries of the first column of fol. 87, the Exeter Domesday has a distinct title : " Terre Regis quas tenuit Godwinus Comes et filii ejus in Sumerseta." Gunnild is called "Gunnila filia Comitis Godwini." The other personages of the entries are the Countess Ghida, Harold, Tosti, Eddeua, and Godwin the son of Harold. In the entry in *Sussex,* 28 b. at Chingestune, Gunnild is said to have held seven hides " de Heraldo." The land here referred to was also among the old possessions of Godwin and Earl Harold.

By the kindness of John Bidwell Esq., of the Foreign Office, F. S. A. and of Mr. Moke of Bruges, the compiler of the present Index is enabled to lay before the reader a copy of an Inscription upon an ancient leaden plate, which was found by some workmen, in 1786, while repairing a wall in the Church of St. Donat at Bruges, where Gunnilda was interred, and which supplies in few words the story of her life. This inscription is at present preserved at Bruges, in the Church of St. Sauveur.

✠ " Pater noster : Credo in D'm patrē, & cetera que in Simbolo ap'lor' sunt scripta.

" Gunildis nobilissimis orta parentibus, genere Angla, patre Goduuino Comite sub cujus dominio maxima pars

GUNNINC, *Chesh.* 265 b.
GUNNOR, *Chesh.* 266 b.

---

militabat Angliæ, matre Githa illustri prosapia Dacor' ori-
unda. *Hæc* dū voveret adhuc puella virginalē castitatē,
desiderans sp'uale conjugiū, sprevit connubia nonnullor'
nobiliū principū, *hæcque* dum jam ad nubilem ætat' p'veniss&,
Anglia devicta a Wuillelmo Normannorum Comite, et ab
eodem interfecto fratre suo rege Anglorum Haroldo; Re-
licta patria apud *S'ctu'* Audomarū aliquot annos exulans in
Flandria, Xp'm quē pie amabat in pectore *Scc'* semp'
colebat inop'e *circa* sibi fāmulantes hilaris et modesta, erga
extraneos benivola & justa, pauperibus larga, suo corpori
admodum parca; quid dicā, adeo ut omnibus illecebris se
abstinendo, p' multos annos ante sui diem obitus non ves-
ceretur carnibus, neq' quidq' q'd sibi dulce visum est gus-
tando, sed vix necessaria vite capiendo, cilicio induta, ut
nec etiā q'busdā pateret familiaribus confl'ctando cū viciis
vicit in virtutibus. Dehinc transiens Bruggas, et ibi trans-
volutis q'busdā annis & īde *pertransiens* in Dacia, huc
reversa, virgo transmigravit in Domino, Anno incarnationis
d'm Mᴵ.LXXXVII. non' k'l' Sept'b', luna XXII."

The words in italics in this copy are conjectural upon
obliterations.

The same letter which brought this Inscription, brought
another from the same church, in honour of another Gunnilda, the half-sister of Edward the Confessor, who is mentioned in our Chronicles, and who married the Emperor,
Henry the Black.

" Nobilissimæ dominæ Gunildæ, Canuti Angliæ, Daniæ-
marcæ, Norvegræ, et Sueciæ Regis filiæ, Imperatoris Au-
gusti Henrici nigri laudatissimæ conjugi, post acceptam
gravissimam a marito injuriam hoc in Castello (Burgum
nempe Brugense) religiose viventi, et Anno Domini MXLII.
XII. kal. Sept. defunctæ, hoc monumentum Ecclesia, cui
perquam erat munifica, erexit."

A short notice of this second Gunnilda occurs, among
some historical entries in the Consuetudinarium of the

GUNNULFUS, *Suff.* 335.

GUNRE, *Yorksh.* 301 b. bis. 311 b. bis.

GUNUER, *Heref.* 184, 186 b. *Shropsh.* 260..

GUNUERT, *Heref.* 183. *Shropsh.* 256.

GUNUUAR, *Shropsh.* 260 b.

GUNWARDUS, *Shropsh.* 255, 258.

GURERT comes, *Suff.* 294. *v.* GURT.

GURET, *Linc.* 336.

GURT comes, *Norf.* 210. *v.* GUERD. GUERT. GUERTUS.
      GURERT.

GUTHLACI, S. Ecclesia, *Heref.* 182 b. 183.

GUT MUNDUS, *Suff.* 408 b. 427.

GUTMUNDUS, *Suff.* 406, 406 b. 408, 408 b. 409.

GUTMUNDUS frater Ulurici abbatis de Eli, *Suff.* 410 b.

GUTMUNDUS teinnus, *Suff.* 408.

H.

HACHE, *Devon,* 111 bis.

HACO, Turkil, *Norf.* 223 b.

HACON, *Hants,* 38 b. *Oxf.* 159. *Chesh.* 265 b. bis.
      266 b. *Derb.* 274 b. 277 b. bis. 278 b.

Abbey of St. Edmunds Bury, Harl. MS. 3977: a volume of
the fourteenth century: " Anno gratiæ M.XL. Harde-
cnutus filius Cnuti et Emmæ Reginæ frater Sancti Edwardi
qui regnavit annis tribus. *Huic erat soror, nomine Gunnilda,*
PULCHERRIMA FEMINARUM, quam Henricus Romanorum
imperator duxit uxorem, *de qua celebris fama usque ad
presens habetur.*" The particulars of the cruelty alluded to
in the Inscription may be found in Brompton. Script. x.
col. 933.

The Gunnilda mentioned in the Saxon Chronicle under
the year 1045, " who resided at Bruges a long while, and
then went to Denmark," Ingr. p. 216, is a distinct personage from either of the Gunnildas who have been just
mentioned.

HACONUS, *Essex*, 68 b.

HACUN, *Wilts*, 71. *Oxf*. 160. *Essex*, 79.

HACUN liber homo R. E. *Nottingh*. 282 b.

HACUNUS commend. Guerti, *Nottingh*. 283 b.

HADEMAR, *Devon*, 105 b.

HADEUUI, *Heref*. 185 b.

HADIMARUS, *Devon*, 104 b.

HADUIC, *Heref*. 185.

HADULFUS, *Warw*. 241 b.[1]

HADUUINUS, *Heref*. 183.

HAEMAR, *Cornw*. 124 b.

HAGANA, *Norf*. 205.

HAGANA liber homo, *Norf*. 121 b.

HAGANA, Vlricus, *Suff*. 434 b.

HAGANE, *Norf*. 173.

HAGANE, tegnus Regis E. et Stigandi commendatus, *Norf*. 130 b.

HAGANUS, *Norf*. 152.

HAGENE, *Heref*. 186.

HAGRIS commend. Vlueue, *Suff*. 323 b.

HAIMERUS, *Devon*, 104 b.

HAIMINC, *Sussex*, 20 b.[2] *v.* HAMINC.

HAIRAUDUS, *Sussex*, 28.

HAKENA, *Norf*. 122.

HAKENE, *Norf*. 121, 121 b.

HALDANUS liber homo, *Essex*, 78 b.

HALDEINUS liber homo, commend. Heroldi, *Suff*. 411 b. 412 ter.

HALDEN, *Chesh*. 265 b. bis. *Nottingh*. 291 b. *Yorksh*. 298. *Berks*, 61 b. bis. *Suff*. 318.

HALDEN liber homo, *Suff*. 412 b. 413 bis.

---

[1] He also held at the time of the Survey.

[2] He held the same land, under the Earl of Moretaine, at the Survey.

HALDENE, *Yorksh.* 317, 318, 327.

HALDENUS, *Suff.* 399 b.

HALTOR, *Yorksh.* 306.

HAMBE, *Linc.* 352 b.

HAMINC, *Sussex,* 21 bis.[1] 26 b. *Glouc.* 169 b. *Nottingh.*
  289. *Linc.* 337, 361 bis. *v.* HAIMINC.

HAMINC homo regis E. *Cambr.* 194 b.

HAMINGUS teignus R. E. *Buck.* 150 bis.

HANDONE, clerici de, *Staff.* 247 b.

HANUART, *Yorksh.* 331.

HAPRA, Vluuinus, *Essex,* 94.

HAR, *Essex,* 6 bis.

HARD', *Cambr.* 198.

HARDECHINUS, *Suff.* 393 b.

HARDECNOT, *Suff.* 340.

HARDECNUT, *Linc.* 336.[2]

HARDEWINUS, *Norf.* 224 b.

HARDINC, *Suff.* 404 b.

HARDING, *Wilts,* 67 b. 68 b. 74 ter.[3] *Dors.* 82 b. *Somers.*
  90 b.[4] *Leic.* 231 b. passim. *Warw.* 239 b. ter.

HARDINGUS, *Wilts,* 69. *Suff.* 333 b.

HARDUINUS, *Essex,* 90 b. *Norf.* 224, 225 b. *Suff.* 353 b.
  383.

HARDUINUS frater Comitis [de Moretaine], *Suff.* 291 b.

HARDUL, *Yorksh.* 331 b.

HARDULF, *Devon,* 103. *Nottingh.* 284 b.

HARDWINUS, *Norf.* 245. *Suff.* 424.

HAREGRIM liber homo, *Chesh.* 265.

---

1 " Haminc ten. de com. [de Moretaine] et ipse tenuit
de rege E.

2 He was one of the Lagemen of Lincoln : Suardine, his
son, had succeeded him at the time of the Survey.

3 In these three entries Harding also occurs as the tenant
at the time of the Survey.

4 Also when the Survey was formed.

HAREGRIN, *Yorksh.* 331.

HAROLD, *Nottingh.* 282 b. bis. 286. *Yorksh.* 317 b. 325, 340.

HAROLD stalre, *Linc.* 337.

HAROLDUS, *Yorksh.* 323 b. *Linc.* 340 b. 350 b. *Essex,* 1 b. bis. 2, 2 b. 4 b. 7. 14 b. 15, 15 b. 26 b. bis. 27 bis. 31, 32 b. 59, 61, 84, 85, 90 b. 95. *Suff.* 289 b. 378, 394, 420, 420 b. 423.

HAROLDUS comes, *Cambr.* 193, 196. *Hunt.* 205 b. 208. *Rutl.* 298 b. *Yorksh.* 298 b. 305 bis. 321. *Linc.* 337, 349 ter. 349 b. ter. 351 b. *Essex,* 106 b. *v.* HERALDUS Comes. HEROLD Comes. HEROLDUS Comes.

HAROLDUS filius Radulfi comitis,[1] *Warw.* 244.[2] *v.* HE-RALDUS.

Harparius, Aluui, *Cambr.* 196.

HASTEN, *Chesh.* 266.

HAUUARD, *Yorksh.* 300 ter. 300 b. bis.

HAUUART, *Yorksh.* 300 b. bis.

HECHE, *Devon,* 109 ter. 109 b. bis. 110, 111 bis. 111 b.

HEDNED, *Yorksh.* 298.

HEDUL, *Derb.* 275.

HELEWIS neptis Eruasti episcopi, *Norf.* 200 b.

HELGA, *Nottingh.* 286.

HELGE, *Nottingh.* 286 b.

HELGHI, *Sussex,* 22 bis. 24.

HELGHINUS, *Sussex,* 25 b.

HELINS, *Norf.* 200.

HELMELEA, Leuericus de, *Suff.* 314 b.

HELTOR, *Yorksh.* 329 b.

---

[1] Son of Ralph Earl of Hereford before the Conquest. See the present work, vol. i. p. 471.

[2] He was tenant in capite for the same property at the Survey; see vol. i. p. 433.

HENRICUS, *Norf.* 254 b.

HER, *Dors.* 82 b. *Essex*, 5.

HERALDUS, *Sussex*, 21, 28. *Surr.* 32, 34, 36 b. *Berks*, 57 b. passim. 58 ter. 63 b. *Wilts*, 71 bis. *Norf.* 113.

HERALDUS [*sc.* Comes], *Kent*, 6, 6 b. *Sussex*, 17. *Surr.* 34. *Norf.* 172 b.

HERALDUS Comes,[1] *Kent*, 9. *Sussex*, 18 b. 19, 21 b. bis. 22, 25 b. 26 bis. *Surr.* 30 bis. 30 b. 31, 32. *Hants*, 38 ter. 39, 39 b. bis. 44 b. 46 b. 47. *Berks*, 57, 59 b. 60, 62 b. *Wilts*, 64 b. 65 passim. 69 bis. 71, 71 b. 72, 72 b. 74 b. *Dors.* 75 b. 78 b. ter. 82 b. 83. *Somers.* 86 b. passim. 87 bis. 88 b. 89 b. 92, 97. *Devon*, 101 passim. 102, 104 bis. *Cornw.* 120, 120 b. passim. 121 b. 122, 123, 128 b. *Hertf.* 132, 132 b. passim. 133 passim. 138. *Buck.* 143 b. bis. 144, 148 b. *Oxf.* 154 b. bis. 157 bis. 160 b. *Glouc.* 162 b. 163, 164, 166 b. 167 b. 168, 168 b. 169. *Worc.* 174. *Heref.* 179, 179 b. bis. 180, 181 passim. 181 b. bis. 182 passim. 182 b. bis. 183 bis. 184 bis. 184 b. bis. 185 b. passim. 186 passim. 186 b. passim. 187 ter. 187 b. bis. *Cambr.* 190, 200, 202 bis. *Leic.* 237 ter. *Staff.* 246. *Shropsh.* 257. *Chesh.* 265 b. bis. *v.* HAROLDUS Comes.

---

1 In various entries, some of which have been enumerated in the former volume, p. 313, Domesday continually complains of what are called the " Invasiones," the usurpations of HAROLD, and of his alleged violations of the property of the church. It must be allowed, however, both for the Saxon and the Norman times, that these usurpations, or forcible entries upon lands or other possessions, were often made by the ministers or bailiffs of the great allodial tenants, in the name, but without the knowledge of their masters. William himself, in the charter which he granted to West-

HERALDUS filius Radulfi comitis, *Midd.* 129 b. *v.* HA-
ROLDUS.

---

minster Abbey in 1067, charges Hamo his steward with
unjustly seizing on the church of St. Clement Danes in the
Strand, " violenter et injuste sibi usurpavit," and which he
had himself caused to be restored.

There is a very curious document in the Cottonian Collection in the British Museum, Augustus II. n. 90, which has
not hitherto been sufficiently noticed. It is an original Narrative in Saxon, upon a strip of vellum, not of the time of
Harold the Second, but of Harold Harefoot, written in all
probability by Ælfgar, who is mentioned in it, or some
fellow-monk, by order of Archbishop Eadsy, concerning
Sandwich, as belonging to Christ Church, Canterbury; the
toll of the port of which had been forcibly entered upon
in the King's name by Ælfstan abbat of St. Augustine.
Ælfgar, a monk of Christ Church, after an interval of near
a year, was sent by the archbishop to make his complaint
to Harold, who lay sick at Oxford, and in imminent
danger. Livingus bishop of Crediton, and Thancred the
monk, were at that time with the King, and these, with
Ælfgar and one Osward, went to his bed-side, and re-
proached him with the usurpation; when Harold unhesi-
tatingly swore by Almighty God and by his angels, that it
was "neither his rede nor his deed" that man should ever
deprive Christ Church of Sandwich. It was soon seen,
says the writer, that the taking of it was other man's
thought, not the King's, and that it had been seized by
the direction of Abbat Ælfstan. The King sent Ælfgar
back to the Archbishop, with the fullest confirmation in
words of the possession of Sandwich as he and his monks
had at any time held it. Ælfstan, who had received the
third penny in toll at Sandwich, offered ten pounds as a fine
to retain it. The acquisition of it for his monastery had
been the sole object of the usurpation. He afterwards, as
the document informs us, attempted to establish a rival

HERBERTUS camerarius Rogeri Bigot, *Norf.* 278.
HERCH homo Brictrici, *Buck.* 150.

---

port at " Hyppesfleote." It finishes, " This is all truth.
Believe who will. In no other way did Abbat Ælfstan
command the payment of the third penny at Sandwich.
God's blessing be with us all, and for ever. Amen."

" Her kẏþ on þison gewrite þ Harold king. let beridan
Sandwic of xp'es cẏrcean him sylfan to handa. & hæfde hit
him wel neh twelf monað. & twegen hærunge timan swa
þeah fullice. eall ongean Godes willan. & agen ealra halgena
þe restað innon xp'es cyrcean swa swa hit him syððan
sorhlice þær æfter agiode. & amanc þisan siþan siðe wearð
Ælfstan abb' æt S'c'e A. & begeat mid his smeh-wrencan.
& mid his golde. & seolfre eall dyrnunga æt Steorran þa þe
wæs þæs kinges rædes-mann þ hī gewearð se þridda penig
of þære tolne on Sandwic þa gerædde Eadsige arce b' þa he
þis wiste. & eall se hired æt xp'es cẏrc' betweonan heom
þ man sende Ælfgar munuc of xp'es cẏrc' to Harolde
kingce. & wæs se king þa binnan Oxana-forde swẏþe
geseocled. swa þ he læg orwene his lifes. þa wæs Lyfinge
b' of Defenan-scire. mid þam kincge. & Ðancred munuc
mid him. þa com Cristes cẏrc' sand to þā b'. & he forð þa
to þam kincge. & Ælfgar munuc mid hī. & Oswcrd æt
Hergerdes-hā. & Ðancred. & sædon þā kinge. þ he hæfde
swẏðe agẏlt wið Crist þ he æfre sceolde niman ænig þing. of
xp'es cẏrc' þe his fora-gengceon dẏdon þider-inn. sædon þā
kinge þa embe Sandwic þ hit wæs hī to handa geriden. þa
læg se king & asweortode eall. mid þare sage. & swor
syððan under God ælmihtine & under ealle halgan þar to
þ hit næfre næs. na his ræd na his dæd. þ man sceolde æfre
Sandwic don ut of xp'es cẏrc'. þa wæs soðlice gesẏne þ hit
wæs oðra manna g'þeaht næs na Haroldes kinges. & soðlice
Ælfstanes abbodes ræd wæs mid þā mannan þe hit of xp'es
cẏrc' ut geræddon. þa sende Harold king Ælfgar munuc
agen to þā arce b' Eadsige. & to eallon xp'es cẏrc' munecan.
& grette hig ealle Godes gretincge & his. & het þ hig

HERCUS, *Hants*, 40 b.
HEREFORD, Ecclesia de, *Heref.* 181 b.

---

sceoldan habban Sandwic into xp'es cẏrc'. swa full. & swa
forð swa hig hit æfre hæfdon on ænies kinges dæge. ge on
gafole. ge on streame. ge on witun. ge on eallon þā þingan
þe hit æfre ænig king fẏrmest hæfde ætforan hī. þa Ælfstan
abb'. þis of-axode þa com he to Eadsige arceb'. & bæd hine
fultumes to þā hirede embe þone þriddan penig. & hi begen
þa to eallon gebroþran & bædon þone hired þ Ælfstan abb'
moste beon þæs þriddan peniges wurðe of þære tolne. &
gyfan þā hirede. x. p'd. ac hy for-wẏrndon heom ealle
togædere endemes. þ he hit na sceolde næfre gebidan.
& wæs þeah Eadsige arceb' swiðor his fultum þon' þæs
hiredes. & þa he ne mihte na forð her mid þa gyrnde he þ
he moste macian fornan gen Mildrẏþe æker ænne hwerf wið
þone wodan to werianne. ac eall se hired him forwyrnde þæs
forð ut mid ealle. & se arceb' Eadsige let hit eall to heora
agene ræde. þa gewearð se abb. Ælfstan æt. mid micelan
fultume. & let delfon æt Hyppeles-fleote an mẏcel gedelf.
& wolde þ scip ryne sceolde þær inne licgean eall swa hig
dydon on Sandwic. ac hī na speow nan þinge þær on. for
þam þe he swingð eall on idel þe swincð ongean x'pes
willan. & se abb' let hit eall þus. & se hired fenge to heora
agenan. on Godes gewitnesse. & s'c'a Marian & ealra þara
halgena þe restað innan x'pes cẏrcean. & æt s'c'e Augustine.
þis is eall soð gelyfe se þe wylle. na gebad Ælfstan abb'
næfre on nanan oþre wisan þone þriddan penig on Sandwic.
Godes bletsung si mid us eallon a on ecnẏsse. Amen."

The date of this Narrative is closely ascertainable. Eadsige, according to the Saxon Chronicle, was made Archbishop in November 1038. Harold Harefoot died at Oxford,
on the 16th before the kalends of April 1040. The third
penny had been detained for near a year. This will bring
the date of the present writing to the year 1039.

No detailed mention of the port of Sandwich occurs in
Domesday; but in allusion to it, in the account of the

HEREFORD, Ecclesia S. Guthlaci de, *Worc.* 176. *Heref.*
    182 b. 183.
HEREFORD, Episcopus de, *Glouc.* 165. *Worc.* 174.
    Shropsh. 252. *Essex,* 26.
HEREMANNUS, *Suff.* 341 b.
HEREUUARD,[1] *Linc.* 364 b. *Clam. in Chetst.* 376 b.
HEREUUARDUS, *Warw.* 240, 240 b. bis.[2] 241. *Clam. in*
    Chetst. 377.

---

town, it is said, " Hoc Burgum tenet Archiepiscopus et est
de vestitu Monachorum, *et reddit simile servitium Regi sicut*
DOVERE."

Various instances may be cited from different parts of
Domesday, of the arbitrary disposition of property by
bailiffs. Under Etwelle in Surrey, fol. 30, it is said, " Tes-
tantur homines de Hundredo quod in hoc Manerio sub-
tractæ sunt duæ hidæ et una virgata quæ ibi fuerunt
T. R. E. sed PRÆPOSITI *accommodaverunt eas suis amicis.*"
See another instance under the lands of the Abbey of
Westminster, fol. 32.   Among the lands of Robert Fitz
Hugh in Cheshire, tom. i. fol. 264 b. under Burwardeslei,
we read, " Ibi III. hidæ. De hac terra I. hida fuit ablata
ab Ecclesia S. Werburgæ. *Hanc vendiderunt* PRÆPOSITI
Comitum Edwini et Morcar cuidam Ravenchil."

[1] " 1072. Hoc tempore fuit Hereward qui cum sociis suis
per paludes latitavit." Annales S. Edm. de Burg. MS. Harl.
447.

This was Hereward, or Herward, the younger son of
Leofric Earl of Mercia, who was chosen, by the prelates
and nobility who retired to the Isle of Ely after the Conqueror's invasion, to be the general of their forces. His
heroic character has been already alluded to, vol. i. p. 308.

He was lord of Brune in Lincolnshire, and the marshes
adjoining. He left Turfrida, his only daughter and heir,
married to Hugh de Evermont lord of Deeping.

[2] Also when the Survey was formed.

HEREUUOLDUS, *Suff.* 314.

HERFASTUS Episcopus, *Suff.* 447. *v.* ÆREFASTUS. AR-
FASTUS.

HERFRIDUS, *Surr.* 30.

HERFRINDUS, *Norf.* 246.

HERLENG, *Berks,* 63. *Dors.* 77 b. *Glouc.* 163 b.

HERMANNUS Episcopus [Sarisb.], *Berks,* 58.

HERNETOC, *Heref.* 180.

HEROLD, *Suff.* 313.

HEROLD, et GODEUERT, et ALURIC, fratres, *Clam. S. R.*
Linc. 375.

HEROLD Comes, *Norf.* 144.

HEROLD', *Norf.* 109 b. bis.

HEROLDUS, *Nottingh.* 287.

HEROLDUS [*sc.* Comes], *Essex,* 5 ter. 6, 54 b. 55 bis.
63, 75. *Norf.* 111, 114 b. bis. 115, 151, 185,
196 b. bis. 197 b. 227, 232, 235, 235 b. 236, 236 b.
252 b. *Suff.* 428, 428 b. 442.

HEROLDUS Comes, *Kent,* 6 b. *Linc.* 336. *Clam. in*
Chetst. 377.

HEROLDUS homo Eluui hiles, *Glouc.* 170.

HEROLDUS liber homo in commendatione Abbatis de
Eli, *Suff.* 375.

HEROLFUS, *Norf.* 275 b.

HEROULDUS, *Hants,* 39 b.

HERUEUS, *Oxf.* 154 b. *Suff.* 408, 408 b.

HERUEUS de berũ, *Suff.* 413.

HERULFUS, *Surr.* 32. *Cambr.* 196.

HERULFUS homo Eddeuæ, *Cambr.* 195.

HERULFUS teignus R. E. *Cambr.* 196.

HILDEUERT, *Suff.* 342 b.

HOBBESUNE, Leuricus, *Suff.* 404 b. *v.* OBBESUNE.

HOCH, *Cambr.* 201 b. *Linc.* 358.

HOFWARDUS liber homo, *Norf.* 264.

Hoga, *Nottingh.* 286.

Holundus, *Worc.* 177.

Holchetel, *Linc.* 348 b.

Holefest liber homo, *Essex*, 36.

Holangar, *Hants*, 51.

Holmo S. Benedictus de, *Norf.* 216, 216 b. 217, 217 b. 218, 218 b. 219, 219 b. 220, 220 b. 221.

Holt liber homo, *Essex*, 102.

Homdai homo Heraldi comitis, *Bedf.* 216 b.

Homo Abbatis S. Albani, *Hertf.* 133.

Homo unus Algari comitis, *Cambr.* 201 b. 202 bis.

Homo Alrici, *Buck.* 145 b.

Homo unus Alrici filii Goding, *Buck.* 146 b. 148.

Homo Alueradi de Withunga, *Buck.* 146.

Homo Aluuini uari, *Buck.* 149 b.

Homo unus Asgari stalre, *Cambr.* 198, 200 b. 201 bis.

Homo Azor fil. Toti, *Buck.* 144 b.

Homo Bondi stalre, *Buck.* 146 b.

Homo Borret, *Buck.* 145 b.

Homo Brixtrici, *Bedf.* 212.

Homo unus Regis E. *Cambr.* 200 b. 201 b. *Northampt.* 219 b.

Homo Elmer de Belintone, *Hertf.* 141.

Homo reginæ Eddid, *Hertf.* 139 b.

Homo unus Guerd Comitis, *Cambr.* 198.

Homo Goduini abbatis Westmonasterii, *Buck.* 146.

Homo Guert Comitis, *Cambr.* 202.

Homo quidam Heraldi Comitis, *Buck.* 151 b. *Bedf.* 212 b.

Homo Leuuini Comitis, *Midd.* 129 b. 134 b. *Buck.* 144 b. 146.

Homo abbatis de Ramesyg, *Hertf.* 137. *Cambr.* 201.

Homo unus Roberti f. Wimarc, *Cambr.* 200 b.

Homo Stig. archiepiscopi, *Hertf.* 133 b. *Buck.* 144 b.

HOMO Aluuoldi de Stiuetone, *Bedf.* 209 b.

HOMO unus Tosti Comitis, *Buck.* 144.

HOMO unus Wallef, *Cambr.* 197, 202.

HOMO unus Wallef Comitis, *Cambr.* 201 b. 202 b.

HOMO Wluui episcopi, *Buck.* 148.

HOMINES Borred, *Bedf.* 210.

HOMINES Eddeuæ feminæ Syred, *Buck.* 143.

HOMINES Goduini cilt, *Cambr.* 196 b. 201 b.

HOMINES teigni unius R. E. *Cambr.* 201.

HOMINES II. Asgari stalre, *Hertf.* 139 b.

HOMINES duo Alric f. Godingi, *Buck.* 146 b.

HOMINES duo Abbatis de S. Albano, *Buck.* 146.

HOMINES duo, *Oxf.* 159.

HOMINES duo Algari Comitis, *Staff.* 249 b.

HOMINES duo Brictric, *Buck.* 148 b. 150 b.

HOMINES duo, unus homo Brictric alter homo Azoris,
   Buck. 150.[1]

HOMINES duo Burredi, *Northampt.* 229.

HOMINES II. R. E. *Bedf.* 212, 212 b. 215.

HOMINES duo R. E. Goduinus et Torchillus, *Buck.*
   152.

HOMINES II. Godrici vicecomitis, *Buck.* 144.

HOMINES II. Goduini de Benefelle, *Hertf.* 137 b.

HOMINES duo Goduini cilt, *Cambr.* 201 b.

HOMINES duo Heraldi Comitis, *Cambr.* 202.

HOMINES duo Leuuini Comitis, *Buck.* 144.

HOMINES II. Ordulfi, *Devon,* 155.

HOMINES duo Sired, *Buck.* 147.

HOMINES duo Vlf, *Buck.* 148 b.

HOMINES tres, *Sussex,* 20. *Buck.* 153.[2]

---

[1] Also tenant at the Survey.

[2] The same " Homines " continued to hold at the time of
the Survey.

HOMINES III. Algari Comitis, *Hertf.* 133.

HOMINES tres Brictrici fil. Algar, 170.

HOMINES tres Leurici Comitis, *Warw.* 243 b.

HOMINES III. S. archiepiscopi, *Buck.* 146 b.

HOMINES tres Stigandi archiepiscopi, *Hertf.* 134, 134 b.

HOMINES quatuor, *Northampt.* 227.

HOMINES quatuor Anschil, *Hertf.* 138 b.

HOMINES quatuor Wallef com. *Cambr.* 202.

HOMINES quinque, *Heref.* 183 b.

HOMINES Eddeue v. *Cambr.* 193 b.

HOMINES x. Aluuini de Godtone, *Hertf.* 138 b.

HOMINES XII. sequentes faldam Edrici, *Norf.* 124.

HOMINES XXIII. *Essex,* 37.

HONEUAINUS, *Wilts,* 73.

HOPEWELLA, Aluricus de, *Suff.* 314 b.

HORIM, Aluuinus, teignus R. E. *Bedf.* 215 b.

HORLING, *Berks,* 60 b. 61.

HORNE, Aluuinus, *Midd.* 128 b.

HORNE, Aluuinus, teignus R. E. *Hertf.* 142 ter.

HOROLFUS, *Essex,* 3 b. 20 b.

HORTONE, Ecclesia de, *Devon,* 104. ⎫
HORTUNENSIS Abbatia, *Dors.* 78 b. ⎭

HOSMUNDUS, *Suff.* 334 b.

HOUDEN, *Clam. in Chetst.* 376 b.

HVECHE, *Cornw.* 125.[1]

HUGO, *Linc.* 371 bis.

HUGO camerarius, *Berks,* 63. *Warw.* 239. ⎫
HUGO camerarius Regis Edwardi, *Hunt.* 208. ⎭

HUGO filius Huberti, *Kent,* 10 b.

HUMMAN homo Alli, *Buck.* 152 b.

HUNA, *Suff.* 342 b.

---

[1] He was likewise tenant at the time of the Survey.

Huna liber homo Edrici, *Suff.* 324 b.

Hunchil, *Yorksh.* 315 b.

Hundic, *Yorksh.* 301.

Hundin, *Chesh.* 264 b.

Hundinc, *Derb.* 276. *Yorksh.* 308.

Hunding, *Chesh.* 267 b.

Hundulf, *Chesh.* 264 b. *Derb.* 272, 276.

Hune, *Yorksh.* 324 b.

Hune liber homo commend. Radulfi stalra, *Suff.* 297 b.

Hunef, *Kent,* 9. *Hunt.* 203, 208.

Hunepot, *Suff.* 297.

Huni, *Shropsh.* 260.

Huninc, *Shropsh.* 255 b.

Huning, *Shropsh.* 255 b.

Hunneue, *Hunt.* 206 b.

Hunni, *Shropsh.* 255, 258,[1] 259 b.

Hunnic, *Shropsh.* 259.

Hunnit, *Shropsh.* 258.[2]

Hunnit cum fratre suo, *Shropsh.* 258.[3]

Hunnith, *Shropsh.* 258 bis.

Hunta, *Hants,* 51 b. *Staff.* 249.

Hunta et Pagen, *Hants,* 51 b.

Hunus, *Suff.* 395.

Huscarl, *Somers.* 95 b. *v.* Ingulfus. Leuric. Leuricus.

Huscarl, homo regis E. *Cambr.* 195.[4]

---

[1] Also tenant at the Survey.

[2] Also at the time of the Survey.

[3] Also when the Survey was formed.

[4] Huscarles have been usually considered as domestic servants; but they were also military retainers. ꝥ Toꞃꞇꞁꝺeꞃ eopleꞃ huꞃcaꞁlaꞃ þaꞁ oꝼꞁoꝺon ealle þe þe hꞁꝷ ꝷeaxꞁan mꞁhꞇon. Sax. Chron. Ingr. p. 253.

HUSCARLE, *Surr.* 36 bis. *Somers.* 99.[1] *Glouc.* 167.
HUSTEMANUS, *Suff.* 341 b.
HUTHTRADUS, *Suff.* 428.
HUTHTRET, *Suff.* 428.

I. & J.

IADULFUS, *Somers.* 98 b. bis.
JALF, *Linc.* 364 passim.
JAUL, *Cornw.* 125.
ILBERTUS vicecomes, *Hertf.* 132 b. bis. 133, 142,[2] 179 b.
INEUUAR, *Devon,* 106, 111, 116 bis.
INEUUARUS, *Devon,* 105 b.
IN GALTLUS tennus, T. R. E. *Norf.* 264 b.
INGARUS teinnus, *Essex,* 22 b.
INGEFRID, *Yorksh.* 301.
INGELRI, *Oxf.* 159 b.
INGELRICUS, *Hertf.* 136 b. ter. *Essex,* 26 b. 27 b. bis.[3]
    30 b. bis. 34, 34 b. *Suff.* 303 bis.
INGELRICUS de Sancto Paulo Londoniæ, *Essex,* 32 b.
INGEMUND, *Linc.* 352.
INGEMUNDUS, *Linc.* 347 b. bis. 361 b.
INGEUUAR, *Hunt.* 207.
INGOLF, *Nottingh.* 290 b.
INGREDE, *Yorksh.* 301, 330 b.
INGUARE teignus R. E. *Cambr.* 201 b.
INGUARUS, *Essex,* 33.
INGUARUS liber homo, *Essex,* 80.

---

1 Also when the Survey was formed.
2 From this entry it appears that Ilbertus was sheriff, sometime in the reign of the Conqueror.
3 Also when the Survey was formed.

INGULF, *Somers.* 99. *Linc.* 370.

INGULFUS, *Essex,* 53 b. 68.

INGULFUS huscarl, *Suff.* 442.

INGUUARA, *Essex,* 81.

INGUUARUS, *Essex,* 80 b. bis. 81.

JOHANNES, *Dors.* 82 bis. 98. *Devon,* 109 bis. *Norf.* 265 b.[1]

JOHANNES danus, *Somers.* 89 b.

JOSEPH, *Oxf.* 154 b.

JOUIN, *Cornw.* 123 b.[2]

IRIC, *Devon,* 104 b.

IRICUS I. liber homo commend. *Suff.* 298 b.

JUDICHEL venator, *Cambr.* 193 ter.

JUIN, *Devon,* 108 b.

JUING, *Somers.* 98.

JULIANA, S. Sciropesberie, *Shropsh.* 252, 253.

IUO, *Linc.* 350 b.

JUSTAN, *Nottingh.* 285 b. 286. *Linc.* 371.

JUSTANUS, *Hants,* 41 b.

JUSTINUS, *Hants,* 51 b.

Juvenis Ricardus, *Worc.* 177 b.

K.

KEE, *Norf.* 242 b.

KENEUUARD, *Glouc.* 168 b. 174.

KENEUUARDUS, *Glouc.* 172 b. 173.

KENUUARDUS teinus regis E. *Glouc.* 167 b.

KENOLDUS, *Suff.* 441 b.

KENRIC' liber homo, *Suff.* 294 b.

KENRICUS, *Suff.* 299 b. bis. 341 b.

---

[1] He held the land of this entry in capite at the time of the Survey.

[2] He held the same land at the Survey.

Kerinc liber homo, *Suff.* 434 b.

Ketel, *Hants*, 43. *Cornw.* 122 b. *Oxf.* 159 b. *Heref.*
    184 b. *Northampt.* 224 b. *Essex*, 75 b. *Norf.* 201,
    206 b. 223, 243 b. 254 b. bis. 264 b. bis. 271.
    Suff. 335 b.

Ketel liber homo, *Norf.* 233, 233 b. 234. *Suff.* 440.

Ketel liber homo Edrici, *Hertf.* 131.

Ketel presbyter, *Nottingh.* 298.

Ketel liber homo Stigandi, *Norf.* 264 b. 266.

Ketel liber homo teignus, *Suff.* 421.

Ketel tegnus Regis Edwardi, *Suff.* 416 b.

Ketel teinnus Stigandi, *Norf.* 254.

Ketelber, *Clam. S. R. Linc.* 375 bis.

Ketelbern, *Worc.* 174 b.

Ketelbert, *Worc.* 174 b.

Ketellus, *Suff.* 436

Ketelus, *Suff.* 445.

Keteluua, *Suff.* 341 b.

Keueua i. libera femina, *Suff.* 387.

Kochaga, *Heref.* 179.

Kochagana, *Heref.* 179.

Kyluertestuna, Thuri de, *Suff.* 314 b.

L.

Ladulf, *Devon*, 107 b.

Lag, Turgod, *Yorksh.* 298 b. *Linc.* 352 b. 353 ter.

Laghemannus, *Essex*, 95 b.

Lagman, *Yorksh.* 301 bis.

Lambe, *Linc.* 351.

Lambecarl, *Linc.* 349 b. ter.

Lanbecarle, *Linc.* 339 b.

Lanbertur, *Clam. S. R. Linc.* 375.

Lanc, *Berks*, 58, 63.

LANCFER, *Hunt.* 206.

LANCH, *Surr.* 35 b. *Hants*, 38. *Wilts*, 74.

LANCHEI, Ecclesia de, *Surr.* 34.

LANG, *Hants*, 39 b.

LANG, Edric, teinus Heraldi Comitis, *Glouc.* 164.

LANGABEINUS, *Suff.* 333 b.

LANGE, *Wilts*, 74.

LANGFER, *Northampt.* 220. *Suff.* 342 bis.

LANGFERE, *Suff.* 411.

LANT, *Bedf.* 218 b.

LANT homo Leuenot teigni R. E. *Bedf.* 215 b.

LASCIUUS, Robertus, *Essex*, 66 b.

LAXAFELDA, Edricus de, *Suff.* 325,
    325 b.

LAXAFELLA, Edricus de, *Suff.* 316 b.
    328 bis. 328 b. bis.

LAXEFEL, Edricus de, *Suff.* 442.

LAXEFELDA, Edricus de, 135. *Norf.*
    179 b. bis. *Suff.* 310 b. 317.

LAXEFELLA, Edricus de, *Suff.* 407, 442.
    443 b. 444.

> *v.* LESEFELDA.
> LESSEFELLA.

LEDI, *Shropsh.* 260 b.

LEDMANUS, *Suff.* 332 b.

LEDMAR, *Devon*, 114. *Essex*, 34.

LEDMARUS, *Cambr.* 198.

LEDMARUS homo comitis Tosti, *Bedf.* 213 b.[1]

LEDMARUS liber homo, *Essex*, 28 b. bis. *Suff.* 303 b.

LEDMARUS presbyter, *Essex*, 39.

LEDMER, *Derb.* 274 b. 275 b.

LEDMERUS. *Suff.* 377 b.

LEDRIC, *Oxf.* 160.

---

[1] He continued at the Survey.

LEDUINUS, *Devon*, 114. *Yorksh.* 322. *Linc.* 352, 357 b.
358, 369 bis.

LEDUUI, *Shropsh.* 258 b.

LEDUUINUS, *Yorksh.* 308 b.

LEFCHIL, *Yorksh.* 308.

LEFCILT, *Suff.* 337 b.

LEFELM, *Surr.* 35.

LEFFCILT, *Suff.* 404.

LEFFCILT commendatus Stigandi, *Suff.* 337.

LEFFLET quædam libera femina, *Suff.* 290 b.

LEFLED, *Heref.* 183.

LEFLEDA libera femina, *Suff.* 433.

LEFLET, *Berks*, 57. *Hertf.* 134 b. *Hertf.* 183 passim.
187 passim. *Cambr.* 195 b. *Shropsh.* 260 b. bis.

LEFMER, *Somers.* 89. *Devon*, 111 b.

LEFMERUS, *Somers.* 94.

LEFOLT, liber homo Heroldi, *Norf.* 258 b.

LEFQUENA, *Suff.* 419.

LEFRIC prepositus, *Worc.* 173 b.

LEFRICUS, *Suff.* 299 b.

LEFRIZ filius Bose tegnus Regis, *Norf.* 228 b.

LEFSI, *Hants*, 41 b. 45 b. *Northampt.* 227, 228. *Linc.*
359 b. 368 b.

LEFSI homo Wallef, *Cambr.* 197 bis.

LEFSIDA, *Wilts*, 66.

LEFSINUS, *Sussex*, 20. *Somers.* 99.

LEFSIUS, *Essex*, 31, 82. *Suff.* 320 b.

LEFSIUS liber homo, *Essex*, 34.

LEFSIUS unus liber homo, *Norf.* 164 b.

LEFSTAN, *Kent*, 10 b. *Heref.* 185 b.

LEFSTAN liber homo, *Heref.* 179.

LEFSTANUS, *Northampt.* 223 b. *Essex*, 31 b. bis. *Suff.*
417.

LEFSTANUS abbas S. Eadmundi,[1] *Suff.* 444 b. *v.* LEUE-
STANUS.

LEFSTANUS liber homo, *Essex,* 42 ter.

LEFSTANUS prepositus, T. R. E. *Essex,* 91.

LEFSUNE, commendatus Leurico Hobbesune, *Suff.* 337.

LEFTANUS, *Essex,* 68.

LEFTANUS liber homo, *Essex,* 46, 64 b.

LEFWINUS, *Suff.* 398 b.

LEIMAR, *Devon,* 114. *Shropsh.* 255 b.

LEISINI, *Yorksh.* 320 b.

LEISING, *Yorksh.* 300.

LEIT teignus R. E. *Buck.* 144.

LEMAN, *Hants,* 38 ter.

LEMAR, *Sussex,* 22.

LEMAR homo Brictric, *Buck.* 150.

LEMAR homo Stigandi archiepiscopi, *Hertf.* 138.

LEMARUS, *Surr.* 35 b. *Hertf.* 141. *Bedf.* 218 b. *Essex,*
102.

LEMARUS homo Stigandi archiep. *Hertf.* 135, 138.

LEMARUS teignus R. E. *Bedf.* 215.

LEMER, *Shropsh.* 259 b.

LEODMAR, *Dors.* 80.

LEOFLEDA, *Suff.* 342 b.

LEOFRICUS, *Suff.* 342 b.

LEOFSI, *Suff.* 312 b. 442.

LEOFSIUS, *Suff.* 442.

LEOFSTANUS, *Suff.* 339 b. 340 b. bis. 341, 343.

LEOFSTANUS liber homo Edrici, *Suff.* 317 b.

LEOFSUNA, *Suff.* 340 b.

LEOMER, *Dors.* 83 b.

---

[1] He was chosen abbat of St. Edmundsbury in 1044, and
died on the kalends of August 1065. See Mon. Angl., last
edit. vol. iii. p. 100.

Leouestanus, *Suff.* 342.

Lepsi, *Sussex,* 24. *Heref.* 185 bis. *Cambr.* 196 b. *Derb.*
274 b. bis. *Yorksh.* 308 bis. *Linc.* 342 b. 347,
356 b. *Clam. in Chetst.* 376 b.

Lepsi homo Brictrici, *Buck.* 150 bis. 150 b.

Lepsi homo Tosti Comitis, *Bedf.* 217.

Lepsi, sochemannus R. E. *Hertf.* 138 b. 139.

Lesefelda, Edricus de, *Suff.* 311 b. ⎫ *v.* Laxafelda.
Lesfelda, Edricus de, *Suff.* 311 bis. ⎭ Lessefella, &c.

Lesinc, *Yorksh.* 320 b. *Linc.* 359 b.

Lesing, *Yorksh.* 300 passim. 301 b.

Lesius, *Norf.* 239 b.

Lessefella, Edricus de, *Suff.* 316. *v.* Laxafelda.
Lessefella.

Lestan, *Kent,* 6.[1] *Suff.* 321, 337 b.

Lestan commendatus Abbati de Eli, *Suff.* 351 b.

Lestanus, *Essex,* 33. *Suff.* 417 b. 419.

Lestanus liber homo, *Norf.* 261 b. bis.

Leswinus croc, *Suff.* 350.

Let, *Glouc.* 163 b.

Letfled, *Linc.* 357 b.

Letflede, *Heref.* 180.

Leua i. soc. femina, *Suff.* 325.

Leuardus liber homo, *Essex,* 4.

Leue, *Hunt.* 207.

Leuecild, *Essex,* 92.

Leuecilt, *Essex,* 43, 102.[2]

Leueclai, *Wilts,* 72.

Leuecol, *Yorksh.* 315 b.

Leuedai, *Somers.* 88 b. 97. *Essex,* 57 b.

Leuefa, *Hertf.* 142 b.

---

1 " Lestan tenuit de rege E. et post mortem ejus vertit
se ad Alnod Cilt, et modo est in calumpnia."

2 Also at the time of the Survey.

LEUEGAR, *Surr.* 32.[1] *Dors.* 85. *Somers.* 93 b. 95. *Devon,*
102 b. 105 b. 107 b. 108, 111 b. 114, 114 b. 115 b.
116 b. 117.

LEUEGARUS homo regis Edwardi, *Bedf.* 217 b.[2]

LEUEGET, *Warw.* 239 b.

LEUENO, *Northampt.* 226 b.

LEUENOD, *Wilts,* 71. *Glouc.* 166 b. *Heref.* 180, 187.
Shropsh. 256 b.

LEUENOT, *Kent,* 1 b. 8. *Sussex,* 18, 19, 22 b. 26 b.[3]
Wilts, 66, 70 b. bis. 71 passim. *Devon,* 106 b.
Cornw. 124 b.[4] *Oxf.* 159 b. *Glouc.* 166 b. 168 b.
Worc. 176. *Heref.* 180, 186 b. *Northampt.* 222 b.
223 b. bis. 224, 226 b. passim. 227 b. *Leic.* 231,
233 b. *Warw.* 240 ter. *Shropsh.* 254 b. 255 b. bis.
256, 257 b. 260. *Chesh.* 264, 264 b. passim. 265
bis. 265 b. 266 bis. 267 bis. 267 b. 268 b. ter.
Derb. 273, 274 b. ter. 275 bis. 276, 277 passim.
277 b. bis. 278 b. *Nottingh.* 289 b. ter. *Rutl.* 293 b.
Yorksh. 300, 318.

LEUENOT homo Regis E. *Buck.* 151 b. *Chesh.* 264 b.

LEUENOT sterre, *Derb.* 275.

LEUENOT teignus regis Edwardi, *Worc.* 177. *Bedf.*
215 b. passim. 216 bis.

LEUERICUS, *Suff.* 441 b.

LEUERON, *Dors.* 84 b. *Cornw.* 122, 124 b.

LEUERON homo Stig. archiepisc. *Hertf.* 140 b.

LEUERONE, *Dors.* 83.

LEUESTANUS, *Suff.* 314 b. 395.

---

[1] " Leuegar tenuit de Heraldo et serviebat ei sed quo
voluisset cum terra ire potuisset. Quando obiit hanc terram tribus filiis suis dispertuit, T. R. E."

[2] Also at the Survey.

[3] He continued to hold at the Survey.

[4] He continued at the Survey as under-tenant to the Earl
of Moretaine.

LEUESTANUS abbas, *Suff.* 389 b. *v.* LEFSTANUS.

LEUESTANUS commendat. fin. *Suff.* 395.

LEUESTANUS liber homo commendat. cuidam commendato, *Suff.* 376.

LEUESTINUS, *Suff.* 341.

LEUESUNA liber homo Gutmundi, *Suff.* 403, 404.

LEUESUNUS, *Essex*, 51, 59, 59 b.

LEUESUNUS commend. Stigandi, *Suff.* 423.

LEUET, Wluuardus, *Bedf.* 212.

LEUETUNA, Glemanus de, *Suff.* 314 b.

LEUEUA, *Kent*, 8 b. *Dors.* 82 b. *Hertf.* 132 b. bis. 133, 140. *Linc.* 371 b.[1] *Essex*, 24, 56, 69.

LEUEUA, abbatissa,[2] *Berks*, 60.

LEUEUA commendata Wallef comitis, *Bedf.* 213.

LEUEUA homo regis E. *Bedf.* 217.

LEUEUA libera femina, *Essex*, 40 b.

LEUEUA libera femina, *Suff.* 372 b. 375.

LEUEUA quædam libera femina, *Berks*, 62.

LEUEUA lib. femina commend. Haldeini, *Suff*, 411 b.

---

[1] Also at the time of the Survey.

[2] This is among the possessions of the Abbat of Battle in Berkshire. " Ipse abbas tenet in Reddinges æccl'am cum VIII. hidis ibi pertin. Leueua abbatissa tenuit de rege E."

Mann, in his History of Reading, p. 121, says, the Church spoken of in this entry " was no doubt St. Mary's, being the oldest Church in the town." Leueua seems to have been the last Abbess of the Nunnery here, which was virtually ruined by the Danes in the middle of the ninth century: and the eight hides were probably all the property which remained to the found ation after the Conquest.

In Somersetshire, in the notice of Combe, a manor belonging to Shaftsbury Abbey, the Exon Domesday, p. 176, notices an Abbess of the name of LEUEUA, who had held that manor T. R. E., who is not noticed in the Exchequer Domesday, tom. i. fol. 91, although in other respects the Entries correspond.

LEUEUE, *Cambr.* 194, 194 b.

LEUID quædam femina, *Essex,* 62.

LEUIET, *Sussex,* 16 b. *Dors.* 82. *Oxf.* 161. *Worc.*
177 b. *Heref.* 183 b. 187. *Warw.* 243. *Shropsh.*
255 b. 257 b. *Chesh.* 266. *Nottingh.* 282 b. 285.
Suff. 391 b. 396.

LEUIET et GODUINUS, *Warw.* 241.[1]

LEUIET presbyter, *Bedf.* 211.[2]

LEVIETÆ vir, *Wilts,* 74.

LEUIETUS, *Suff.* 339 b.

LEUIGET, *Northampt.* 221.

LEUILD, *Essex,* 57 b.

LEUINC, *Kent,* 9. *Yorksh.* 317 b.

LEUINCUS, *Essex,* 85.

LEUING, *Hants,* 51, 51 b. 53 b. *Wilts,* 72. *Somers.* 91,
92 b. 93 b. 94, 96, 98 b. bis. *Heref.* 186, 186 b.
Leic. 233. *Chesh.* 265. *Derb.* 274, 275 b. 276.
Nottingh. 285 b.

LEUING homo abbatis S. Albani, *Buck.* 146 b.

LEUING homo R. E. *Buck.* 148 b.

LEUING presbyter homo Eddeuæ, *Hertf.* 137.

LEUINGUS, *Inter Ripam et Mersam,* 269 b. *Nottingh.*
291.

LEUINGUS presbyter, *Yorksh.* 298.

LEUINUS, *Suff.* 320, 332 b. 339 b. 426 b.

---

[1] He continued to hold when the Survey was taken.

[2] He occurs in the entry of the land at Bideham (now
Biddenham), belonging to the church of St. Paul Bedford.
" Hanc terram tenuit Leuiet presbyter in elemosina de
rege E. et postea de rege W. Qui presbyter moriens concessit æcclesiæ S. Pauli I. virg. de hac terra, Radulfus vero
Tallgebosc. alias duas virgatas addidit eidem æcclesiæ in
elemosina."

LEUINUS liber homo, *Norf.* 227, 227 b.

LEUINUS tennus regis E. *Suff.* 348.

LEUOLT teinnus, *Norf.* 208.

LEUREDUS, *Essex*, 64. *Suff.* 423.

LEURET, *Kent*, 13 b. *Sussex*, 19 b. 28 b. *Devon*, 112.

LEURIC, *Kent*, 1 b. 7 b. *Sussex*, 20. *Surr.* 31 b. *Wilts*,
70 b. 73. *Somers.* 90, 94, 96 bis. *Devon*, 106,
106 b. ter. 111, 114 b. 116, 118 b.[1] *Cornw.* 123,
124 b. bis. *Oxf.* 159, 160. *Worc.* 177 b. *Heref.*
185 b. 186. *Hunt.* 203, 203 b. 208 b. *Northampt.*
223 bis. 223 b. passim. 224, 224 b. 226 b. 227
passim. 227 b. 228, 228 b.[1] *Leic.* 233 b. bis. 234,
237. *Warw.* 243,[1] 243 b. 244. *Staff.* 250 b. bis.
Shropsh. 254, 255, 256, 258 bis.[1] 259 b. *Chesh.*
263 b. 265. *Derb.* 274 bis. 275 b. 276 bis. 277
passim. 277 b. *Nottingh.* 284, 285 b. 286 b. 289 b.
ter. 292, 293. *Rutl.* 293 b. *Linc.* 342 b. 361,
363 b. bis. *Clam. in Chetst.* 377. *Suff.* 297 bis.
344, 355, 386 b. 419.

LEURIC abb. S. Petri de Burg.[2] *Linc.* 366 b.

LEURIC cilt,[3] *Linc.* 369. *Clam. in Chetst.* 377 b.

LEURIC Comes, *Warw.* 238 b. 239. *Shropsh.* 252 b.
    v. LEURICUS.

---

[1] Leuric, in the four entries here referred from, held the
same land at the time of the Survey.

[2] He is said to have been related to the royal family;
nephew to Leofric Earl of Mercia. He became abbat of
Peterborough in 1057. In 1066 he was in the English
army, where sickening he returned to his monastery. The
Saxon Chronicle gives him a high character.

[3] Kelham, Illustr. p. 175, interprets " Leuric cilt" to be
Leofric Duke of Mercia. His authority for this does not
appear.

LEURIC Episcopus Execestriæ,[1] *Cornw.* 120 b. *Oxf.*
155.

LEURIC f. Leuuini, *Leic.* 235 b. bis.

LEURIC filius Osmundi teignus R. E. *Bedf.* 212 b.

LEURIC homo Azor, *Buck.* 151 b.

LEURIC homo Borgred, *Bedf.* 215.

LEURIC homo Brixtrici, *Bedf.* 212.[2]

LEURIC homo Edrici Comitis, *Buck.* 148 b.

LEURIC homo Episcopi Lincoliensis, *Bedf.* 212.

LEURIC homo Leuuini Comitis, *Midd.* 130 b.

LEURIC huscarl Com. Leuuini, *Hertf.* 140.

LEURIC liber homo, *Chesh.* 266.

LEURICUS, *Glouc.* 166 b. 167 b. 169, 169 b. *Worc.*
174 b. *Hunt.* 208 b. *Northampt.* 223. *Leic.* 234,
235 bis. *Warw.* 240 b. bis. 244. *Derb.* 275 b. 276,
278 b. *Nottingh.* 284, 291. *Linc.* 353, 368 b. 369,
371. *Essex,* 23 b. 84 b. bis. *Norf.* 253. *Suff.* 315,
323 b. 336 b. 340 ter. 340 b. 341 bis. 341 b. 342
bis. 342 b. bis. 344 b. 351 b. bis. 395, 397, 442.

LEURICUS abbas de Bertone, *Derb.* 273.[3]

LEURICUS coccus, *Suff.* 314.

LEURICUS Comes, *Shropsh.* 259 b. *v.* LEURIC.

LEURICUS commendatus Algaro Comiti, *Suff.* 395 b.

LEURICUS commendatus Bristrico preposito Sancti Eadmundi, *Suff.* 437 b.

---

[1] Leofric, or Leuric, the last bishop of Crediton. He
obtained permission from King Edward the Confessor to
transfer the seat of his diocese to Exeter, A. D. 1050. See
Chron. Exon. Eccl. MS. Laud. Bibl. Bodl. 627, fol. 93 b.
Mon. Angl. last Edit. vol. ii. pp. 514, 526. Leofric died
Feb. 10th, 1073.

[2] Also at the time of the Survey.

[3] He died in 1085.

LEURICUS commend. Edrici, *Suff.* 309 b.

LEURICUS Hobbesune, *Suff.* 404 b.

LEURICUS homo Regis E. *Bedf.* 211.

LEURICUS homo Eduuini, *Buck.* 145.

LEURICUS homo Heraldi Comitis, *Buck.* 144 bis.

LEURICUS homo Osulfi, *Hertf.* 136 b.

LEURICUS homo Abbatis de Ramesy, *Bedf.* 216.

LEURICUS liber homo, *Suff.* 417, 437 b.

LEURICUS monachus, *Berks,* 61 b.

LEURICUS Obbesune, *Suff.* 405 b.

LEURICUS tennus, *Suff.* 303.

LEUSTAN liber homo Ulfi, *Norf.* 259.

LEUSTANNUS presbyter commendatus Guerti, *Suff.* 335.

LEUSTANUS, *Suff.* 416 b.

LEUUARD, *Kent,* 10. *Sussex,* 22.

LEUUARE, *Hertf.* 133 b.

LEWESTANUS commendatus, *Suff.* 292.

LEUUI, *Oxf.* 159 b. *Glouc.* 168 b. *Worc.* 176. *Shropsh.* 254 b. 256.

LEUUI homo Asgari, *Cambr.* 194 b.

LEUUI homo Eduui, *Buck.* 150 b.

LEUUI homo Stigandi archiepiscopi, *Oxf.* 159.

LEUUIN, *Hants,* 44 b. *Shropsh.* 257 bis. *Nottingh.* 282 b. 283 b. 286.

LEUUIN f. Aluuin, *Nottingh.* 280 b.

LEUUIN Chaua prefectus regis, *Buck.* 153.[1]

LEUUIN çilt, *Bedf.* 211, 214 b. 216 b. *v.* LEUUINUS.

LEUUINE, *Hunt.* 206. *Derb.* 272, 276. *Nottingh.* 287.

LEUUINE f. Alwine, *Linc.* 337.

LEUUINE homo Wallef Comitis, *Bedf.* 216.

---

1 He continued to hold at the Survey.

LEUUINE presbyter,[1] 336.

LEUUINI duo, *Glouc.* 169 b.

LEUUINI de Niuueham mater, *Warw.* 244.

LEUUINUS, *Kent,* 1 b. 7, 7 b. 11, 13 b. *Sussex,* 18 b.
19, 21 b. 22 b. 23 b. 24, 24 b. 27, 27 b. 28 b. ter.
29 ter. *Surr.* 36. *Hants,* 40 b. 41, 49 b. 50 b. bis.[2]
Berks, 58 b. 60, 60 b. bis. *Wilts,* 69 b. 74 b. bis.
Dors. 77, 79 b. 80 bis. 85. *Somers.* 91 b. bis. 92,
93 b. 95, 96 bis. *Devon,* 111 b. 117 b. *Cornw.* 125.
Hertf. 136 b.[3] 139. *Buck.* 153. *Oxf.* 160 b. ter.
Glouc. 165 b. 166, 166 b. ter. 168 b. 169 b. 170 b.
Worc. 173.[4] *Heref.* 185. *Bedf.* 210 b.[5] *Northampt.*
223 b. bis. 224, 225. *Leic.* 230 b. 231 b. 232, 234,
235 b. 237. *Warw.* 238 b. 239 b. bis. 240 ter.
240 b. 243 b. passim. *Shropsh.* 257. *Chesh.* 265 b.
bis. 266, 266 b. ter. 267. *Derb.* 274 b. bis. 276,
278, 278 b. *Yorksh.* 316, 317. *Linc.* 336 b.
356 b. 364 b. *Clam. W. R. Linc.* 376. *Essex,* 30 b.
31, 35 b. 52, 54, 70, 76, 86 b. bis. 89, 102, 103 b.
Suff. 321, 336, 352, 374 b. 375 b. 377, 377 b.
397.

LEUUINUS aurifaber, *Berks,* 58 b.

LEUUINUS calvus, *Suff.* 436.

---

[1] He was one of the Lagemen of Lincoln, T. R. E.
Leuuine afterwards became a monk, and his place as Lageman, at the time of the Survey, was filled by Buruolt his
son.

[2] In one entry he continued at the Survey.

[3] The land which Leuuinus held in this entry "de Rege,"
he tenanted at the time of the Survey under the Earl of
Moretaine.

[4] " II. hid. ad Nortvne. Leuuinus tenuit et inde radman
Episcopi fuit."

[5] Also at the Survey.

Leuuinus cilt, *Hertf.* 136. *Bedf.* 211.[1]
   Shropsh. 253 b. *Derb.* 274 b. 278.
   Essex, 82, 86 b. } *v.* Leuuin.
Leuuinus cilt liber homo, *Suff.* 376 b.
Leuuinus cilt teignus R. E. *Bedf.* 216 b.
Leuuinus Comes, *Kent,* 7, 7 b. 8, 9. *Sussex,* 18 b.
   Surr. 31 b. bis. *Somers.* 87 b. *Devon,* 101 passim.
   Midd. 127.[2] *Hertf.* 134. *Buck.* 143 b. 144 ter.
   144 b. bis.
Leuuinus commendatus Edrico de Laxefella, *Suff.*
   374 b.
Leuuinus Episcopus,[3] *Staff.* 248 b.
Leuuinus filius Brun, *Suff.* 314 b.
Leuuinus filius Ringulfi, *Suff.* 322.
Leuuinus forestarius, *Hants,* 38.
Leuuinus frater Alsi, *Buck.* 148 b.
Leuuinus homo Burgeredi, *Buck.* 151 b.
Leuuinus homo Godrici, *Buck.* 146.
Leuuinus homo Goduini de benefelle, *Hertf.* 138.
Leuuinus homo Heraldi Comitis, *Hertf.* 139, 141,
   142 b.

---

[1] He had possessed the manor of Cadendone in Bedford-shire, which at the Survey belonged to the Canons of St. Paul's. The Record adds, " Canonici habent brevem Regis in quo habetur quod ipse hoc Manerium dedit Ecclesiæ S. Pauli."

[2] Earl Lewin was the under-tenant only in this entry. He had the occupation. The manor of Harrow, to which it relates, had been purchased for his Church by Arch-bishop Wilfred, A D. 822. See the Chartulary of the See of Canterbury. MS. Bibl. Bodl. p. 22.

[3] Leofwine Bishop of Litchfield. He presided from 1053 to 1066. His successor, Peter, removed the See to Chester. See vol. i. p. 395.

Leuuinus liber homo, *Oxf.* 156 b. bis. *Essex,* 3, 91 b. *Suff.* 427 b.

Leuuinus liber homo Edrici, *Suff.* 304.

Leuuinus liber homo Heroldi, *Suff.* 426 b.

Leuuinus unus liber homo, *Sussex,* 19, 20, 25.

Leuuinus teinnus, *Suff.* 427 b.

Leuunus teignus R. E. *Hertf.* 139, 139 b. 142. *Buck.* 148. *Bedf.* 215 bis.

Leuuold, *Kent,* 10.

Leuuord, *Nottingh.* 292 b.

Leuuric, *Suff.* 375 b.

Leuuricus, *Suff.* 385 b.

Libera femina de qua habuit Normannus commenda- tionem, *Suff.* 332.

Libera femina una, *Essex,* 10, 22, 27, 29, 36 b. 69 b. bis. 82, 103. *Norf.* 126 b. 136, 188, 196, 203 b. 262 b. *Suff.* 292, 379 b.

Libera femina una sub Stigando, *Norf.* 125.

Libera femina i. commend. Sce Æ. *Suff.* 386 b. 448 b.

Libera femina commend. Edrici, *Norf.* 277 b.

Liber homo unus, *Essex,* 23 b. bis. 27 b. 28, 28 b. bis. 29 ter. 29 b. bis. 30, 31, 34 b. 37, 38 bis. 43 b. bis. 44 b. passim. 45, 45 b. 46 b. ter. 55, 55 b. 61, 61 b. bis. 62, 62 b. 64, 64 b. bis. 65 passim. 65 b. 69 b. 71, 71 b. 73 b. bis. 75 b. 78, 78 b. bis. 80 b. 81, 82, 83 b. bis. 84 bis. 85 b. 86 bis. 89 b. 90, 90 b. 92 b. 95, 95 b. 96, 96 b. 97, 99, 99 b. 100 b. 101 ter. 102 b. bis. 103, 103 b. *Norf.* 120, 123 b. bis. 124, 125, 126, 126 b. 128, 129 b. bis. 146 b. 148, 150, 154 b. 156 b. 161 b. 164, 164 b. bis. 167 b. bis. 169 b. 173, 173 b. 182 ter. 183 passim. 183 b. passim. 184 bis. 187 passim. 188, 189 b. bis. 190 passim. 190 b. 197 b. bis. 202, 204, 205 b. bis.

226, 257, 266 b. 268, 268 b. 274. *Suff.* 284 b.
285, 285 b. bis. 300 b. 312 b. 397, 436.

LIBER homo unus dimid. *Norf.* 124 b. 130 b. 171 b.

LIBER homo unus et dim. *Norf.* 188.

LIBER homo I. commend. *Suff.* 379 b. ter. 432 b.[1]

LIBER homo I. commend. Ælmari, *Suff.* 380 bis.

LIBER homo I. commend. S. Ætheldredæ, *Suff.* 325 b.

LIBER homo I. Ailmari episcopi, *Norf.* 197, 201.

LIBER homo I. S. Aldredæ, *Norf.* 186. *Suff.* 336.

LIBER homo I. Algari, *Norf.* 275 b.

LIBER homo I. Allmari episcopi, *Norf.* 199 b.

LIBER homo I. Almari, *Norf.* 199.

LIBER homo I. episcopi Almari, *Norf.* 198 b. 200 bis.
200 b. 201 passim. 273.

LIBER homo unus Alnoht, *Norf.* 124.

LIBER homo unus et duo dim. Alnoth commend. *Norf.*
124.

LIBER homo I. Alsi, *Norf.* 199.

LIBER homo unus Alwi, *Norf.* 174 b.

LIBER homo I. commend. S'c'i Æ. *Suff.* 387.

LIBER homo I. et dim. commend. S. Æ. *Suff.* 387.

LIBER homo I. commend. Ailrici, *Suff.* 400 b. bis.

LIBER homo I. S. Aldredæ commend. *Suff.* 303.

LIBER homo I. commendatus cujusdam commendati Almari episcopi, *Suff.* 381.

LIBER homo I. commend. Almari episcopi, *Suff.* 380.

LIBER homo I. commendatus Alsci nepoti Comitis R.
Suff. 324.

LIBER homo commend. Alurici, *Suff.* 335 b.

LIBER homo commend. Aluuini, *Suff.* 423 b.

LIBER homo unus Ansgot commend. *Norf.* 185 b.

---

[1] " Pater ejus antea saisitus."

LIBER homo unus Bondo, *Norf.* 182 b.

LIBER homo I. commendatus, Brictredo, *Suff.* 450.

LIBER homo commend. Brihtwaldi, *Suff.* 433.

LIBER homo I. commend. dim. Burchardi et dimid.
Vlsi, *Suff.* 407 b.

LIBER homo I. commend. Burckardi, *Suff.* 407.

LIBER homo I. Canuti, *Suff.* 403.

LIBER homo I. commend. Durandi, *Suff.* 442 b. 443.

LIBER homo I. commend. E. *Suff.* 324 b. ter.

LIBER homo I. commend. e. et uxor ejus commend.
Halden, *Suff.* 413.

LIBER homo I. Ediue divitis, *Suff.* 410.

LIBER homo unus Edrici, *Norf.* 124 b. 124 b. bis. 186,
187. *Suff.* 315, 315 b.

LIBER homo Edrici commend. *Norf.* 125, 125 b. 154
bis. 155, 247. *Suff.* 304 b. 310, 315 b. 316 b. 317
bis. 317 b. 318, 319 bis. 324 b. passim. 325 ter.
325 b. ter. 326 bis. 443.

LIBER homo I. commend. Edrici de Laxafella, *Suff.*
326 b. ter. 327 passim. 407.

LIBER homo integer unus Edrici, *Norf.* 130.

LIBER homo unus Eduini commendat. *Norf.* 175 b.
278.

LIBER homo I. Regis Edwardi, *Norf.* 190, 276 b. 282 b.

LIBER homo I. Edwini, *Norf.* 203, 203 b. 204.

LIBER homo I. Elmari commend. *Norf.* 201 b.

LIBER homo unus Elwini, *Norf.* 184.

LIBER homo unus Gert, *Norf.* 185 b.

LIBER homo unus sub Gert, *Norf.* 186.

LIBER homo I. Gerti, *Norf.* 200 b.

LIBER homo Gerti commend. *Norf.* 200.

LIBER homo unus Goduini, *Norf.* 186 b. *Suff.* 315 b.

LIBER homo I. et dim. commend. Goduini, *Suff.* 318 b.

LIBER homo Goduini sub Gert, *Norf.* 186 b.

LIBER homo nomine Goduinus, *Essex*, 28.

LIBER homo unus Godwini, *Norf.* 175 bis.

LIBER homo unus Guerd, *Norf.* 187.

LIBER homo unus Guert, *Norf.* 133 bis. 158 b. 173, 210.

LIBER homo unus Guerti, *Norf.* 129. *Suff.* 347 b.

LIBER homo commendat. I. Guerti, *Suff.* 407 b. bis.

LIBER homo I. commend. Haldeini, *Suff.* 411 b. 412.

LIBER homo Heraldi commend. *Norf.* 125, 167, 250, 258 b.

LIBER homo unus Heroldi, *Norf.* 115 b. 150 b. 162 b. 163, 186 b. bis. 257 b. 268. *Suff.* 292, 300, 441.

LIBER homo I. Heroldi quem tenuit Edricus diaconus qui fuit mortuus cum eo in bello, *Suff.* 449.

LIBER homo I. occisus ad bellum Hastingis, *Norf.* 275.

LIBER homo I. Sancti Benedicti de Holmo commend. *Norf.* 200 b.

LIBER homo unus Hosmart, *Norf.* 160.

LIBER homo unus Ketelli, *Norf.* 171, 172.

LIBER homo Lefrici de Torendana, *Norf.* 155.

LIBER homo unus R. stalre, *Norf.* 123.

LIBER homo commend. I. R. stalra, *Suff.* 293 bis.

LIBER homo I. Saxonis, *Suff.* 374.

LIBER homo commend. Stanuino sub Heroldo, *Suff.* 305 b.

LIBER homo sub Stigando, *Norf.* 127, 140, 143, 171, 174 b. 176 b. 186, 186 b. bis. 189, 190 bis. 202, 250 b. 265. *Suff.* 379 b.

LIBER homo I. commend. Stigandi, *Suff.* 412, 412 b.

LIBER homo I. integer et II. dim. homines Godwini sub Stigando, *Norf.* 176 b.

LIBER homo I. Suartingus, *Suff.* 443.

LIBER homo unus Tohli vicecomitis, *Norf.* 264.

LIBER homo I. Toredi, *Suff.* 415 b.

LIBER homo I. sub Toret, *Norf.* 253 b.

LIBER homo unus dimid. Ulchetel, *Norf.* 176.

LIBER homo unus Ulfi commend. 185 b. bis.

LIBER homo unus Ulketelli, *Norf.* 176, 177.

LIBER homo unus Ulketelli, et. dim. lib. sub eo, *Norf.* 176.

LIBER homo unus Withri, *Norf.* 179 b.

LIBER homo I. sub-commend. Vlueue, *Suff.* 323 b.

LIBER homo unus Wisgari, *Suff.* 428 b.

LIBER homo commend. Wulmari, *Suff.* 348.

LIBERI homines duo, *Berks,* 60 bis.[1] 62 b. *Essex,* 10, 23 bis. 24, 36 b. 50 b. 52, 79 b. 80 b. 81, 81 b. 92 b. 93 b. 94, 95 b. *Norf.* 120, 123 b. 125 b. 131. 142. 146 b. bis. 150. 160, 160 b. 161. 165 b. 168 b. 182 b. 183 b. 184. 188 b. 189 b. bis. 190. 199. *Suff.* 284 b. 285. 396 b. 397, 398.

LIBERI homines commend. Edrici, *Suff.* 315 b.

LIBERI homines commend. Edrici Grim, *Suff.* 294.

LIBERI homines commend. II. *Suff.* 324 b. 379 b.

LIBERI homines dimidii II. *Nottingh.* 285 b.

LIBERI homines II. commend. Achi, *Suff.* 440.

LIBERI homines II. commend. S. Æ. *Suff.* 347.

LIBERI homines II. Algari commend. *Norf.* 130.

LIBERI homines II. Almari commend. *Norf.* 199 b.

LIBERI homines II. Almari episcopi, *Norf.* 199 b.

LIBERI homines II. Alsi, *Suff.* 350.

LIBERI homines II. Alsi commendatione, *Suff.* 374.

LIBERI homines duo Alnoth commend. *Norf.* 124.

LIBERI homines duo Altnoth commend. *Norf.* 124.

LIBERI homines duo, I. et dimid. Altnoth et dim. Aluredi commend. *Norf.* 124.

---

[1] In one of these entries it is said, " Tenuerunt de rege E. in alod ;" in the other, " Tenuerunt T. R. E."

LIBERI homines II. Anant, *Suff.* 434.

LIBERI homines II. Aslac et Lefrici commend. *Norf.* 203 b.

LIBERI homines II. I. commend. Brihtwoldi et alter commend. Brihtmari, *Suff.* 326.

LIBERI homines II. commend. Brictuoldi, *Suff.* 433 b.

LIBERI homines II. Burckardi, *Suff.* 407 b. bis. 408.

LIBERI homines II. Ediuæ commend. *Norf.* 285.

LIBERI homines duo, unus fuit homo Edrici et alter homo Ed. et S. Bened. *Norf.* 148 b.

LIBERI homines duo, unus Edrici alter Almarus, *Norf.* 171 b.

LIBERI homines II. unus homo Edrici de Laxefelda, alter Radulfi stalra, *Norf.* 134 b.

LIBERI homines duo Edrici, *Norf.* 154 b. 171, 284. *Suff.* 315 b.

LIBERI homines II. commend. Edrici, *Suff.* 317, 317 b. bis. 318, 324 b. 326 b.

LIBERI homines II. Edrici gri', *Suff.* 294.

LIBERI homines II. sub-commend. Edrici, *Suff.* 320 b.

LIBERI homines duo, I. commend. Edwardi Regis et alter Guerti, *Suff.* 347.

LIBERI homines II. Edwini commend. *Norf.* 203 bis.

LIBERI homines II. integri Edwini, *Norf.* 203.

LIBERI homines II. Gerti. *Norf.* 184, 199, 270 b.

LIBERI homines II. commend. Gerti, *Suff.* 319.

LIBERI homines II. Godwini, *Norf.* 264.

LIBERI homines II. Gued.[1] *Norf.* 158 b.

LIBERI homines II. Guerd, *Norf.* 116,

LIBERI homines II. commend. Haldeini, *Suff.* 412 bis.

LIBERI homines II. Harduini, *Norf.* 284 b.

LIBERI homines II. Heroldi, *Norf.* 187. *Suff.* 435 b.

---

[1] *f.* Guerd.

LIBERI homines II. Heroldi et Almari episcopi, *Norf.* 187.

LIBERI homines II. Sancti Benedicti de Hulmo, *Norf.* 200 b.

LIBERI homines duo, Houardus et Vlsi, *Essex*, 13.

LIBERI homines II. commend. Osmundi. *Suff.* 319 b. bis.

LIBERI homines II. commendati Paxo, *Suff.* 375 b.

LIBERI homines II. R. stalre, *Norf.* 123.

LIBERI homines II. Stigandi, *Norf.* 263 b.

LIBERI homines duo Ulchetel, *Norf.* 176.

LIBERI homines II. Vlueue, *Suff.* 323 b.

LIBERI homines III. *Berks,* 57, 62 b. bis. *Dors.* 85.[1]
Oxf. 160 bis.[2] *Staff.* 248 b. 249 b. ter. 250. *Essex,* 35, 37 b. bis. 52 b. 58 b. 63 b. 78, 87, 97 b. 101 b. 103 bis. *Norf.* 131 b. 132, 168, 183 b. 184, 187, 188, 189 bis. 189 b. bis. 190, 190 b. 200 b. 202, 205. *Suff.* 285. 387, 421, 422 b. 436, 444, 445.

LIBERI homines III. commendati, *Suff.* 321.

LIBERI homines III. unus integer, duo dim. Stigandi commend. *Norf.* 175 b.

LIBERI homines III. Almari, *Norf.* 199 b.

LIBERI homines III. Alnoht, *Norf.* 124.

LIBERI homines tres Aluuard, Saulf, et Eluuard, *Norf.* 175.

LIBERI homines III. S. Benedicti, *Norf.* 205.

LIBERI homines III. commend. Edrici, *Suff.* 318 b. 321 b. 325, 348.

LIBERI homines commend. III. Edrici Grim, *Suff.* 294.

LIBERI homines III. de quibus habuit Edricus commend. et dimid. socam, *Buck.* 148 b.

---

1 " Qui has terras tenebant T. R. E. poterant ire quo volebant."

2 " Tres liberi homines libere tenuerunt."

LIBERI homines III. II. Edwini I. Gert commend. *Norf.*
203 b.

LIBERI homines III. et dim. commend. Godrici antec.
Sueni, *Suff.* 318 b.

LIBERI homines III. commend. Goduini, *Suff.* 318.

LIBERI homines tres sub Guerd, *Norf.* 147 b.

LIBERI homines III. commendati Gudmundi, *Suff.* 406 b.

LIBERI homines III. Gudmund. comm. tantum, *Suff.*
409.

LIBERI homines III. II. commend. Halden, et tertius
commend. S. Edeld, *Suff.* 413.

LIBERI homines tres, unus Heroldi, alter Radulfi stalre,
tercius Ketelli, *Norf.* 171.

LIBERI homines III. commend. Regi, *Suff.* 335 b.

LIBERI homines III. commend. Stigando, *Suff.* 310.

LIBERI homines III. commend. Turmodi de Perham,
Suff. 286 b.

LIBERI homines III. Ulchetel, *Norf.* 176 ter.

LIBERI homines III. Ulfi, *Norf.* 185 b.

LIBERI homines III. et dim. commend. *Suff.* 327.

LIBERI III. et II. dim. homines, *Norf.* 176 b.

LIBERI homines quatuor, *Berks,* 60, 60 b. *Dors.* 85.
Worc. 173.[1] *Essex,* 4 b. 32, 65 b. 88. *Norf.* 123 b.
183, 183 b. 185 b. 187, 188, 188 b. 189, 189 b.
bis. 201 b. 203, 205, 250. *Suff.* 320 b. 334, 406.

LIBERI homines IIII. Achi, *Suff.* 440.

LIBERI homines Algari quatuor, *Norf.* 130.

LIBERI homines IIII. Edwini, *Norf.* 203 b.

---

[1] " Quatuor liberi homines tenebant de Episcopo [de
Wirecestre] T. R. E. reddentes omnem socam et sacam, et
circset, et sepultura, et expeditiones, et navigia, et placita,
ad predictum hundredum [quod vocatur Oswaldeslav]; et
nunc faciunt similiter qui tenent."

LIBERI homines IIII. Godduini, *Norf.* 264.

LIBERI homines IIII. Godrici, *Norf.* 264, 279.

LIBERI homines Heroldi IIII. *Norf.* 198 b. 279.

LIBERI homines commend. IIII. *Suff.* 299.

LIBERI homines commend. IIII. Athestani, *Suff.* 300.

LIBERI homines IIII. commend. Edrici, *Suff.* 316 b. 319, 324 b. 326, 327.

LIBERI homines IIII. commend. Goduini fil. Alferi, *Suff.* 315.

LIBERI homines IIII. commend. Halden, *Suff.* 412 b.

LIBERI homines IIII. commend. Ringulfo, *Suff.* 322.

LIBERI homines quatuor Ulchetel, *Norf.* 176, 177.

LIBERI homines integri IIII. *Norf.* 203.

LIBERI homines quinque, *Berks,* 61 b. 63 b.[1] *Essex,* 23, 66 b. 87 b. 94. *Norf.* 131. 157 b. 183 b. 187 b. bis. 188 b. bis. 228, 228 b. *Suff.* 423, 436.

LIBERI homines v. commend. *Suff.* 346.

LIBERI homines v. Ailmari commendati, *Suff.* 379 b.

LIBERI homines commend. v. Anandi, *Suff.* 294.

LIBERI homines v. Brihmari, *Suff.* 424 b.

LIBERI homines v. Brihtmari, *Suff.* 442 b.

LIBERI homines v. commendati Burchardi, *Suff.* 335 b.

LIBERI homines v. Edeuæ faire, *Suff.* 285.

LIBERI homines commend. v. Edrici, *Suff.* 316 b. 318 b. 320 b.

LIBERI homines v. integri et VII. dim. lib. homines commend. Edrici Grim, *Suff.* 293 b.

LIBERI homines v. II. erant commendati Edrici de Laxafella et III. commend. Vlurici, *Suff.* 348.

LIBERI homines v. et dim. Eduini com. *Norf.* 203 b.

LIBERI homines v. et dim. commend. Guerti, *Suff.* 407.

LIBERI homines v. Witgari commend. tantum, *Suff.* 411.

---

[1] " In alod. de rege E."

LIBERI homines sex, *Essex*, 59 b. 87 b. *Norf.* 164, 170, 187 b. 189 b. 190. *Suff.* 295, 323, 397, 397 b.

LIBERI homines VI. commend. *Norf.* 189.

LIBERI homines integri VI. *Norf.* 203.

LIBERI homines VI. et dim. *Norf.* 189 b.

LIBERI homines VI. Sanctæ Aldredæ, *Suff.* 355.

LIBERI homines VI. Aluiet. *Suff.* 322.

LIBERI homines VI. commendati Leuuini de Bachetuna, *Suff.* 321 b.

LIBERI homines VI. commend. Brihtuuoldi, *Suff.* 433.

LIBERI homines VI. commendati Burcardo, *Suff.* 407.

LIBERI homines VI commendati Durandi, *Suff.* 442 b.

LIBERI homines VI. Ediuæ divitis, *Nottingh.* 285.

LIBERI homines commend. VI. Edrici grim, *Suff.* 293, 293 b.

LIBERI homines VI. Eduini, *Norf.* 197 b.

LIBERI homines VI. unus eorum Osgot vocatus, *North-ampt.* 226 b.

LIBERI homines sex R. Stalre, *Norf.* 123.

LIBERI homines sex commend. Radulfi stalra, *Suff.* 295.

LIBERI homines commendati sex, Turmodi de Perham, *Suff.* 286.

LIBERI homines VI. et II. dimid. commend. Vlchetel, *Suff.* 326 b.

LIBERI homines VI. integri ; tres Ulketel, tercius Alwi de Tetfordo, quartus Genred, quintus Alured commend. *Norf.* 175 b.

LIBERI homines septem, *Berks*, 60. *Norf.* 129 b.

LIBERI homines Alsi septem, *Norf.* 130 b. 140, 189 b. 205 bis. 292 b. 388 b.

LIBERI homines VII. commend. *Suff.* 379 b.

LIBERI homines VII. et dimid. commend. Æduoldi, *Suff.* 347.

LIBERI homines VII. commend. S. Æ. *Suff.* 346.

LIBERI homines VII. quinque fuerunt Alflet commend. tantum, II. commend. Regis, *Suff.* 350.

LIBERI homines VII. commendati Algaro, *Suff.* 338 b.

LIBERI homines VII. Almari commend. *Norf.* 199 b.

LIBERI homines septem; quatuor Sancti Benedicti, duo Alwi, unus Almari episcopi, *Norf.* 174 b.

LIBERI homines VII. commendati Edrici, *Suff.* 327.

LIBERI homines VII. et dim. commend. Edrici grim, *Suff.* 294.

LIBERI homines integri VII. Ulchetel, *Norf.* 176.

LIBERI homines VII. commend. Vlueue, *Suff.* 323.

LIBERI homines VII. commend. Wisgari, *Suff.* 392.

LIBERI homines VIII. *Essex*, 38, 74 b. *Norf.* 188, 189 b. *Suff.* 323 b. 375 b. 397.

LIBERI homines VIII. et dim. commend. S. Æ. *Suff.* 347.

LIBERI homines VIII. commendat. Sanctæ Æ. *Suff.* 386 b.

LIBERI homines Algari octo, *Norf.* 130.

LIBERI homines VIII. Almari commend. *Norf.* 200 b.

LIBERI homines VIII. Almari episcopi, *Norf.* 199 b.

LIBERI homines octo, II. Alwoldi abbatis, v. Rathon. de Giming, I. Osberti, *Norf.* 171 b.

LIBERI homines commend. Edrici VIII. *Suff.* 316.

LIBERI homines VIII. commend. Halden. *Suff.* 412 b.

LIBERI homines VIII. commendati Leustani, *Suff.* 335.

LIBERI homines VIII. commend. Stanuini, *Suff.* 318 b.

LIBERI homines octo Ulketelli, *Norf.* 177.

LIBERI homines VIII. commend. Vlueue, *Suff.* 322 b.

LIBERI homines novem, *Norf.* 166 b. 174 b. 178 b. 183, 187 b. 189, 204 b.

LIBERI homines IX. commend. *Norf.* 204 b.

LIBERI homines IX. Godewini tokesone *Norf.* 246 b.

LIBERI homines IX. Heroldi, *Heref.* 187.

LIBERI homines novem Stigandi, *Norf.* 181 b.

LIBERI homines novem, et quatuor dim. Stigandi, *Norf.* 152 b.

LIBERI homines x. *Norf.* 139, 166 b. 397 bis.

LIBERI homines x. commendati, dim. Brihmari et dim. Quengeuet mater ejus, *Suff.* 424 b.

LIBERI homines x. commendati Edrici, *Suff.* 324 b. 406 b.

LIBERI homines x. et II. dim. commendati Edrici Grim. *Suff.* 293 b.

LIBERI homines x. Gut mundi, *Suff.* 409.

LIBERI homines x. Ketelli, *Suff.* 436.

LIBERI homines XI. *Essex*, 99. *Norf.* 189. *Suff.* 436.

LIBERI homines XI. commend. *Suff.* 414, 433 b.

LIBERI homines XI. Alsi, *Norf.* 130 b.

LIBERI homines XI. commendati Durandi, *Suff.* 442 b.

LIBERI homines commend. XI. Guerti, *Suff.* 293.

LIBERI homines XI. Stigandi, *Norf.* 151 b.

LIBERI homines XII. *Essex*, 37. *Norf.* 189 b. 197. 251 b. *Suff.* 335, 422.

LIBERI homines XII. commend. *Suff.* 338.

LIBERI homines integri XII. *Suff.* 325 b.

LIBERI homines XII. commendati Burrici, *Suff.* 431.

LIBERI homines commend. XII. Edrici, *Suff.* 316 b. 324, 326 b.

LIBERI homines XII. et dim. commendati Edrico, *Suff.* 317 b.

LIBERI homines XII. et IX. dim. commend. Edrici, *Suff.* 325 b. 326.

LIBERI homines XII. et dim. commend. Edrici Grim. *Suff.* 293 b.

LIBERI homines XII. commendati Guerti, *Norf.* 283.

LIBERI homines XII. novem Rade commend. et unus Wastret, et unus Ulmari, et unus communis Abbati de Sancto Edmundo et de Eli, *Norf.* 125 b.

LIBERI homines XII Stigandi, *Norf.* 175.

LIBERI homines XII. Ulketelli commend. *Norf.* 175.

LIBERI homines XIII. *Suff.* 397.

LIBERI homines XIII. commendati, *Suff.* 442 b.

LIBERI homines XIII. commend. Edrici de Laxafelda, *Suff.* 325.

LIBERI homines XIV. *Norf.* 188 b. *Suff.* 353.

LIBERI homines XIIII. commend. Godrici, *Suff.* 354.

LIBERI homines integri Ulketel XIIII. *Norf.* 175.

LIBERI homines XV. *Essex,* 87 b. *Norf.* 197 b. *Suff.* 334.

LIBERI homines commend. XV. *Suff.* 316 b.

LIBERI homines XV. Almari Episcopi commend. *Norf.* 199.

LIBERI homines XV. commend. Burcardi, *Suff.* 407.

LIBERI homines XV. sub Olfo, *Norf.* 187 b.

LIBERI homines XV. Rade et Ulmari commend. *Norf.* 125 b.

LIBERI homines commendati XV. Stigandi, *Suff.* 288 b.

LIBERI homines XVI. *Norf.* 244 b. *Suff.* 397, 409.

LIBERI homines XVI. commendati, *Suff.* 293 b.

LIBERI homines XVI. et dimid. *Norf.* 189.

LIBERI homines XVI. commend. S. Æ. *Suff.* 348.

LIBERI homines Alsi XVI. *Norf.* 123.

LIBERI homines XVI. com. Brictmari et Quengeuet, *Suff.* 424 b.

LIBERI homines XVI. commend. Edrici, *Suff.* 319 b.

LIBERI homines XVII. commend. Edrici. *Suff.* 317 b.

LIBERI homines XVII. Gutmundi, *Suff.* 409.

LIBERI homines XVIII. *Norf.* 204 b. *Suff.* 394.

LIBERI homines Almar' commend. XVIII. *Norf.* 200 b.

LIBERI homines XVIII. commendati Guthmundi, *Suff.* 406.

LIBERI homines XX. *Norf.* 147 b.

LIBERI homines XX. commend. Edrici, *Suff.* 375 b.

Liberi homines xx. Rade commend. *Norf.* 125 b.

Liberi homines xx. duo Stigandi commend. et xviii.
Sancti Edmundi commend. *Norf.* 139.

Liberi homines xxi. *Suff.* 377, 397.

Liberi homines commendati xxi. *Suff.* 298 b.

Liberi homines commend. xxi. Edrici, *Suff.* 316.

Liberi homines xxi. commendati Suartingi, *Suff.* 442 b.

Liberi homines xxii. xx. commend. Edrici, et ii.
Sanctæ Æ. *Suff.* 317.

Liberi homines xxiii. ad socam S. Bened. *Norf.* 160.

Liberi homines xxiv. *Norf.* 167.

Liberi homines xxiv. commend. Edrici, *Suff.* 319.

Liberi homines xxv. *Suff.* 355 b. 380 b.

Liberi homines commend. xxv. Edrici de Laxafella,
Suff. 316.

Liberi homines xxvi. commendati Saxo, *Suff.* 375 b.

Liberi homines commendat. xxvii. Alurici, *Suff.* 300 b.

Liberi homines xxvii. et dim. sub Olfo, *Norf.* 187 b.

Liberi homines xxviii. quinque Stigandi, et xxiii.
Sancti Edmundi. *Norf.* 139.

Liberi homines xxx. *Essex*, 37.

Liberi homines xxx. Ulketel, *Norf.* 175.

Liberi homines commendati Heroldi xxx. *Suff.* 292.

Liberi homines xxxi. commendati Edrici, *Suff.* 317 b.

Liberi homines xxxii. *Norf.* 167.

Liberi homines xxxiii. sub Stigando, *Norf.* 166.

Liberi homines xxxiiii. commend. Turmodo, *Suff.*
388 b.

Liberi homines xxxvi. Almari commend. *Norf.* 200 b.

Liberi homines xxxvi. Ediuæ divitis, *Norf.* 284 b.

Liberi homines xl. *Suff.* 381.

Liberi homines xl. commend. Leuuino, *Suff.* 426 b.

Liberi homines xlvii. *Norf.* 166.

Liberi homines lxxx. *Norf.* 134.

LIGUL, *Yorksh.* 301 bis. 327 b.

LIGULF, *Derb.* 273 bis. 274. *Yorksh.* 300 bis. 300 b. passim. 301 bis. 306 passim. 307 ter. 307 b. 308, 308 b. 315 b. 316, 317, 317 b. 321 b. bis. 323, 324, 327, 330, 330 b. 331 bis. *Linc.* 373 b. 374.

LIGULFI duo, *Derb.* 275. *Yorksh.* 300 b.

LIGULFUS, *Derb.* 278. *Yorksh.* 298, 301, 307 b.

LIHTWINUS, *Suff.* 346.

LINBALDUS monachus, *Berks.* 59.

LINCOL. Ecclesia S. Mariæ, *Oxf.* 155.

LINCOLNIENSIS Ecclesia, *Northampt.* 222.

LINCOLNIENSIS Episcopus, *Buck.* 143 b. *Oxf.* 155. *Cambr.* 190. *Hunt.* 203, 203 b. *Bedf.* 210. *Linc.* 336, 337, 344.[1]

LINXI, *Hants,* 49.[2]

LISEMAN, *Wilts,* 74.[3]

LISIUS *Norf.* 239 b. 240.

LIUING, *Somers.* 94, 98 b.

LIURICUS diaconus, *Suff.* 334.

LIUUARA, *Somers.* 97.

LIUUARD abbas [de Micelenie], *Somers.* 91.[4]

LIUUINUS, *Essex,* 53 b.

LOCHI, *Northampt.* 224.

LOCRE, *Nottingh.* 285.

LODRIC, *Warw.* 244.

LODRIC quidam liber homo, *Berks,* 62 b.

---

[1] The Bishopric of Lincoln possessed lands in more counties than are here referred to at the time of the Survey; but Domesday does not designate them as the property of the See, T. R. E.

[2] " Tenuit de rege E. in paragio."

[3] Also at the formation of the Survey.

[4] This is the only mention of him any where.

LOFF, *Dev.* 115.

LONDONIENSIS Episcopus, *v.* LUNDONIENSIS.

LONGUS, Godricus, *Suff.* 339 b.

LORD, *Norf.* 147.

Loripes quidam, *Buck.* 153.[1]

LOTEN, *Chesh.* 265.

LUDI, *Heref.* 187 b.

LUDRI teinus comitis Algari, *Heref.* 185.

LUFCHEL, *Nottingh.* 285.

LUNDON, Canonici S. Pauli de, *Midd.* 127 b. 128. *Hertf.* 136. *Essex,* 12 b.

LUNDONIENSIS Episcopus, *Midd.* 127. *Hertf.* 133 b. *Essex,* 9 b. 11, 26 b.

LURC commend. *Suff.* 406 b.

LUSTUINUS, *Suff.* 336 b. 352.

LUSTWINUS commendatus Edrici, *Suff.* 315, 433.

LUTTINUS, *Essex,* 102 b.

LUUARE, *Staff.* 250.

LUUEDE, *Chesh.* 265.

LUUET, *Staff.* 249 b.

LUUETOTE, *Yorksh.* 374.

M.

MABAN, *Yorksh.* 315.

MACHEL, *Yorksh.* 332.

MACHERN, *Yorksh.* 332.

MACHUS, *Cornw.* 121.[2] *Linc.* 358.

MACUS, *Yorksh.* 325, 330 b. *Linc.* 358 bis.

MADOCH, *Glouc.* 170 b.[3]

---

[1] Also at the formation of the Survey.

[2] Also at the taking of the Survey.

[3] He held the same land in capite at the Survey.

MAGBANEC, *Yorksh.* 300 bis.

MAGNE, *Hunt.* 207.

MAGNO Suert, *Surr.* 36 b. *v.* MANNIUS.

MAINARD, *Wilts,* 74 b.

MAINARDUS, *Hants,* 48 b. *Norf.* 276.

MAINO quidam, *Oxf.* 155 b.

MAL, Godrici, filii, *Hants,* 50 b.

MALET, Robertus, *Norf.* 276 b.

MALET, Willielmus,[1] *Linc.* 350 b. *Clam. Ebor.* 373, 373 b. 374.

MALF, Godricus, *Hants,* 51 b. passim.[2]

MALGRIM, *Yorksh.* 309.

MALGRIN, *Yorksh.* 300 b. passim.

MALMESBURIENSIS quidam Abbas Anglicus, *Wilts,* 67.[3]

MAN, *Yorksh.* 324 b.

MANCUS, Edric, *Dev.* 100 b.

MANEGOT, *Warw.* 242.

MANESUNA, *Suff.* 340 b.

MANNA, *Norf.* 257.

MANNICUS liber homo, *Essex,* 24 b.

MANNIG, *Suff.* 429 b.

MANNIG liber homo, *Suff.* 429 b.

MANNIUS Swert, teinnus, *Suff.* 292 b. bis. *v.* MAGNO.

MANNO, *Hants,* 41, 48. *Somers.* 96.

MANSTANUS, liber homo commend. abbati de Eli, *Suff.* 336 b.

---

[1] Of whom sèe Vol. i, p. 449.

[2] His sons continued to hold all their father's lands at the Survey.

[3] " Abstulit II. hid. terræ in Breme de dominio æcclesiæ et dedit cuidam preposito et postea uni taino, qui nullo modo separari poterat ab æcclesia."

MANSUNA, *Suff.* 334, 339 b. 340.

MAPESONE, Aluricus, *Worc.* 176 b.

MARCULF, commend. Edrici, *Suff.* 373 b.

MARCULFUS, commendatus Edrici antecess. R. Malet,
   Suff. 450.

MARIÆ, S. Ecclesia, [Sciropesberie,] *Shropsh.* 252.

MARTINI, S. London, Ecclesia,[1] *Essex*, 20 b.

MARTINUS, *Northampt.* 224.

MARUAEN quædam libera femina, *Norf.* 247 b.

MARUUEN, *Bedf.* 211.

MATER Comitis Heraldi, *Dors.* 75 b. *v.* GHIDA. GIDA.

MATER Morchari Comitis, *Suff.* 286 b. 287. *v.* ÆLVEVA.
   ALVEVA.

MATER Leuuini de Niuueham, *Warw.* 244.

MATHELD, *Dev.* 116.

MATHILA, *Dev.* 118.

MATHILD, *Dev.* 112.

MAUUA liber homo, *Suff.* 419 b.

MELC, Ailmarus, T. R. E. *Essex*, 107.

MELDONA, Sewardus de, teinnus, *Suff.* 416.

MELDUNA, Sewardus de, *Suff.* 416.

MELLESSAM, Alwinus de, *Suff.* 409 b.

MELMIDOC, *Yorksh.* 300 b.

MEMBREFELDE, Ecclesia S. Gregorii de, *Shropsh.* 253.

MENLEUA, libera femina, *Suff.* 419.

MERDE, Aluuinus de, *Hertf.* 142 b.[2]

MERDO, *Linc.* 356.

MERE, *Linc.* 353 b.

MEREFIN, *Northampt.* 223 b.

MERESUUET, *Somers.* 93 b.

---

[1] It had been founded.
[2] Also at the formation of the Survey.

MEREUIN, teinus Odonis comitis, *Heref.* 184 b.[1]

MEREUINUS, *Warw.* 240.

MEREUUIN, *Heref.* 181. *Warw.* 240. *Yorksh.* 322 b.

MERKEN, *Cornw.* 125.

MERLESUAIN, *Somers.* 86, 95 passim. 96 b. *Dev.* 113 b. passim. *Cornw.* 121 b. ter. 122, 122 b. ter. 124 b. ter. *Yorksh.* 298, 313.

MERLESUAINE, *Somers.* 86.

MERLESUAN, *Yorksh.* 325 b. passim. 326 bis.

MERLESUEN, *Yorksh.* 298 b. 325 b. ter. *Linc.* 337, 362 b. 363. *Yorksh.* 374. *Clam in Chetst.* 376 b. bis.

MERLOSUEN, *Linc.* 372 b. passim.

MERLOSUEN uicecomes T. R. E. *Clam. W. R. Linc.* 376.

}[2]

MERUEN, *Hants,* 45 b.

MERUENA libera femina, *Essex,* 95.

MERUIN, *Surr.* 35 b. *Warw.* 244.

---

[1] Odo received the Earldoms of Devon, Somerset, and Dorset from King Edward the Confessor, upon the revolt of Godwin and Harold in 1052. See the Script. post Bedam, Hen. Hunt. fol. 209 b.

[2] The Black Book of Peterborough, now in the Library of the Society of Antiquaries, preserves several charters, both of Edward the Confessor and King William the Conqueror, attested by Merleswein: one, of the date of 1060. In charters of both reigns he signs *Merlesuein vicecomes.*

It is probably in this official character, that Wace speaks of Merlesuain as one of those who had engaged to forward forces to the South in aid of Harold, when he marched after the battle of Stanford Bridge against the Conqueror.

The Saxon Chronicle, Ingram's edit. p. 266, says, he accompanied Edgar Atheling to the Court of Scotland in 1067.

MERUINUS, *Cambr.* 194 b.

MEURDOCH, *Yorksh.* 298.

MICELENIE, Ecclesia de, *Somers.* 91.

MICHAELIS, S. Ecclesia, *Cornw.* 120 b.

MICHAHEL, Sanctus, in Flixtuna, *Suff.* 381.

MIDDELTUN, abbas de, *Dors.* 82.

MIDDELTUNENSIS Abbatia, *Hants,* 43 b. *Dors.* 78.

MILBURG, S. Ecclesia, Sciropesberie, *Shropsh.* 252, 252 b. 254.

MILDA libera femina, *Suff.* 419.

MILEGRIM, *Yorksh.* 306 b. bis.

MILNEGRIM, *Yorksh.* 301, 307 b. 373.

MODEPHEFE libera femina Algari, *Norf.* 149 b.

MODEVA, *Yorksh.* 298.[1]

MODGEVA libera femina commendatus Sancto E. *Suff.* 354 b.

MODINC, *Essex,* 49 b. bis.

MODINGUS homo reginæ Eddid, *Bedf.* 213 b.

MODUINUS, *Essex,* 96.

MOITHAR liber homo Edrici, *Norf.* 154 b.

MOLLEVE, *Kent,* 11, 11 b. 13 b.

Monacha, v. QUENDRUD.

Monachus, v. LEURICUS.   LINBALDUS.   OSBERNUS. VLGAR.   VLUUINUS.

MONACHUS UNUS de Monast. de Bade, *Somers.* 89 b.

Monialis, v. ELFGIVA.   ELSUID.

MONTFORT, Hugo de, *Norf.* 212 b.

MONULFUS presbyter, *Suff.* 398.

MORCAR, *Buck.* 152 b. bis.[2] *Leic.* 234 b. *Shropsh.* 259 b.

---

1 " Nigellus Fossart habet II. mans. Modeuæ et tenet de Rege."

2 In both these instances he also held at the Survey, under the Countess Judith.

Derb. 278. *Nottingh.* 285 b. 286 b. 287 b. *Yorksh.*
298, 298 b. bis. 304 b. bis. 308 ter. 313 passim.
316 bis. 323 b. passim. 330 b. *Linc.* 341, 357 b. bis.
358 b. 360 b. ter. 366 b. *Yorksh.* 373. *Clam. S. R.*
Linc. 375 b. bis. *Clam. W. R. Linc.* 376 b. *Clam. in*
Chetst. 377 b.

MORCAR Comes, *Heref.* 179 b. *Northampt.* 219 b. 225 b.
Leic. 230. *Staff.* 248 b. *Shropsh.* 253 b. ter. 254 b.
255 b. bis. 256 b. bis. 259. *Chesh.* 265 b. 267.
Nottingh. 281 b. *Yorksh.* 298 b. 299 ter. 299 b.
passim. *Linc.* 336, 337 bis. 337 b. passim. 338,
338 b. 340, 360, 360 b. passim. 362 b. 364 b. *Clam.*
in Chetst. 377 bis.

MORCAR homo Heraldi Comitis, *Buck.* 152.

MORCAR presbyter de Lintone, *Bedf.* 216 bis.

MORCARUS presbyter, *Bedf.* 209.

MOREGRIM, *Suff.* 340.

MOREGRIMUS, *Suff.* 340 b.

MOREWINUS, *Suff.* 324 b. 388.

MORFAR, *Chesh.* 267 b. *Yorksh.* 317 b.

MORFARE, *Yorksh.* 315 bis. 318.

MORGANAU, *Glouc.* 167 b.

MORUANT, *Suff.* 434.

MORULFUS, *Yorksh.* 298.

MULE, *Yorksh.* 307, 320 b. 373.

MULIER una, soror Stigandi, *Norf.* 116.

MULO, *Yorksh.* 304 b.

MUNDINGUS, *Suff.* 336 b.

MUNDRET, *Chesh.* 262 b.

MUNULFUS, *Suff.* 299 b.

MURDAC, *Yorksh.* 323 b.

MURDOC, *Yorksh.* 324 b. 325.

MUSCHAM, *Clam. in Chetst.* 376 b.

MUSLA, Brihtuoldus, *Suff.* 413.

N.

Neoti S. Clerici, *Cornw.* 121.[1]

Neuham, Leuuinus de, *Buck.* 151 b.[2] 153 passim.

Neuueham, Leuuinus de, *Buck.* 143.[3]

Nicholaus aurifaber Comitis Hugonis, *Norf.* 279.

Nigellus, *Buck.* 150. *Yorksh.* 273 b.

Nigellus quidam serviens Roberti Comitis, *Suff.* 291 b.

Nistenestoch, Canonici de, *Dev.* 117.

Niuelig, *Yorksh.* 315.

Niuelin, *Yorksh.* 315.

Noriolt, *Suff.* 413 b.

Norman, *Kent*, 1, 8 b. 13 b. 14. *Suss.* 18, 18 b. 21, 28.
    Surr. 36 b. *Hants*, 45, 48 b. 49 b. *Berks*, 58 b.
    passim. 59 b. *Wilts*, 72.

Norman, *Somers.* 93. *Dev.* 104 b. 105 b. bis. 106, 107,
    115 b. 116 b. *Hunt.* 206 b. *Northampt.* 223, 256 b.
    Leic. 234. *Yorksh.* 298, 300 bis. 300 b. bis. 301,
    305 b. passim. 306 bis. 306 b. 307 ter. 310 b. 311 b.
    312, 315 b. 316 b. 320 b. 321 b. passim. 322 b.
    passim. 326 b. 329 b. 331 ter. *Linc.* 361. *Yorksh.*
    373 bis. 373 b. bis. 374.

---

[1] How much later than the Domesday Survey the College
of Neotstow continued as a monastic foundation is unknown.
Tanner says, the Church of St. Neot afterwards belonged to
Montacute Priory in Somersetshire. The Canons were
under-tenants to Richard Fitzgilbert, for two hides and a
half virgate of land at Wiboldestono in Bedfordshire. See
Bedf. 216.

St. Neot, in honour of whom the College was founded,
was long reputed to have been the brother of King Alfred;
but his Legend, lately published by Mr. Davies Gilbert, is
inconsistent with the story of royal birth.

[2] In all these entries he continued to hold at the Survey.

[3] Also at the Survey.

NORMAN filius Malcolumbe, *Linc.* 371 b.

NORMAN filius Vlf, *Yorksh.* 373.

NORMAN liber homo, *Norf.* 253.

NORMAN, Merewine sune, *Clam. in Chetst.* 377.

NORMANNUS, *Cambr.* 202. *Bedf.* 212 b.[1] *Clam. N. R.*
   Linc. 375 b. *Clam. in Chetst.* 377. *Essex,* 29, 34,
   49 b. 70 b. *Suff.* 130 b. 331 b. 332 ter. 335, 338 b.
   339 b. 340 passim. 340 b. passim. 341 passim. 341 b.
   passim. 428, 438.

NORMANNUS commendatus, *Suff.* 333.

NORMANNUS filius Tanredi, *Suff.* 350 b.

NORMANUS filius Tanri, *Suff.* 349 b.

NORMANNUS filius Tauredi, *Suff.* 348 b.

NORMANNUS teinus, *Suff.* 333.

NORMANNUS vicecomes, *Suff.* 312 b.

NORMANUS, *Northampt.* 225 b. bis. 228, 229.

NORMANUS filius Tanre, *Suff.* 350.

NORMANUS, liber homo, *Norf.* 252 b.

NORWIC, Sanctus Michaelis de, *Norf.* 201 b.

NOVI, *Heref.* 181.[2]

O.

OBBESUNE, Leuricus, *Suff.* 405 b. *v.* HOBBESUNE.

OCSEN, *Hants,* 48 b. bis.

ODA, *Hants,* 39 b. bis. 45 b. *Berks,* 57 b.

ODA diaconus, *Yorksh.* 374.

ODE, *Dors.* 75 b. *Staff.* 249. *Yorksh.* 315 ter. 324 bis.
   374.

---

[1] Also at the time of the Survey.

[2] He sub-tenanted the same land at the time of the
Survey.

ODE diaconus, *Yorksh.* 329.

ODE presbyter, *Yorksh.* 374.

ODEMAN, *Hants,* 39 b. *Dev.* 112.

ODERUS, *Norf.* 229.

ODEUA, *Dev.* 118.

ODFRID, *Yorksh.* 331 b.

ODIL, *Yorksh.* 309 b.

ODINCAR, *Derb.* 277 b. *Nottingh.* 286 passim. 286 b. *Linc.* 365 b.

ODINCARL, *Linc.* 355 b.

ODINCARLE, *Nottingh.* 285 b. *Yorksh.* 343.

ODO, *Hants,* 48 b. *Wilts,* 73 b. *Cornw.* 121. *Worc.* 176. *Warw.* 242 b. *Yorksh.* 329 b. passim. *Norf.* 244 b. *Suff.* 443.

ODO homo Brictrici, *Buck.* 150 b.

ODO de Wincestre, *Hants,* 52.

ODULFUS, *Yorksh.* 298. *Suff.* 356.

OFCHETEL, *Norf.* 165.

OFFA, *Sussex,* 23.

OFFA liber homo commend. Stigandi, *Suff.* 434 b.

OFFELS, *Cornw.* 124.[1]

OFFERD, *Linc.* 358 b.

OFFERD, *Dev.* 115. *Cornw.* 124 bis.[2]

OFFERS, *Dev.* 106 bis. 106 b. 107, 107 b. bis. 108, 108 b. 111 b. *Cornw.* 124 passim.[3]

OFFO teinus Stigandi, *Norf.* 186.[4]

OFFRAM, *Linc.* 367, 368 bis. 370 b. 371 bis. 377 b.

OFFRAM, *Linc.* 358 b. bis.

OFL liber homo, *Norf.* 178 b.

---

1 He also held at the time of the Survey.
2 In both of these entries he continued to hold.
3 In all these entries he continued to hold at the Survey.
4 He continued at the Survey.

OGHE, *Nottingh.* 290.

OINUS dacus, *Essex*, 25.

OIRANTI pater, *Hants*, 53 b.

OLBOLT, *Sussex*, 17 b.

OLF, *Suff.* 348 b. 411 b.[1]

OLFUS, *Norf.* 135 b. 229.

OLFUS liber homo, *Norf.* 252 b. *Suff.* 296 b. 298.

OLFUS teinnus, *Norf.* 180, 180 b. bis. *Suff.* 429, 429 b.

OLFUS teinnus R. E. *Norf.* 150.

OLGRIM *Clam. S. R. Linc.* 375.

OLKETEL liber homo Edrici, *Norf.* 260.

OLOVA quædam femina, *Norf.* 232 b.

OLVIET, *Linc.* 358.

OLUIUS, *Ess.* 75.

OLUUARDUS, *Hants*, 45.

OLUUINUS, *Worc.* 176. *Warw.* 239.

ONOUUINUS, *Dors.* 83 b.

ORDE, *Somers.* 92.

ORDEC, *Warw.* 242 b.

ORDGAR, *Somers.* 93.

ORDIN, *Chesh.* 263 b.

ORDINC, *Kent*, 1 b.

ORDINC tegnus, *Norf.* 229 9.

ORDING, *Kent*, 6 b.

ORDMÆR homo Brictric, *Buck.* 146.

ORDMÆRUS homo Eddeuæ, *Cambr.* 195 b. bis.

ORDMAR, *Leic.* 235 b.

ORDMER, *Staff.* 249 b.

ORDMER homo abbatis de Ramsey, *Hertf.* 141 b.

ORDOLF, *Berks*, 62 bis.

---

[1] He continued to hold at the Survey.

ORDRIC, *Kent,* 9. *Somers.* 98 b. *Dev.* 105 b. 111 b.
117 passim. *Buck.* 148. *Glouc.* 170, 170 b. *Warw.*
240, 241 bis. 241 b. passim. 243. *Shropsh.* 257 b.
Nottingh. 284 b. *Suff.* 321.

ORDRIC homo Leuenot, *Bedf.* 215 b.

ORDRIC tainus, *Somers.* 87.[1]

ORDRICUS, *Cornw.* 123. *Essex,* 78. *Suff.* 340 b. 410, 419.

ORDUI, *Surr.* 36. *Bedf.* 218 b. bis.[1] *Warw.* 243 b.
Shropsh. 257, 259.

ORDULF, *Somers.* 92. *Dev.* 101 b. 104 b. passim. 105
passim. 113 b. 114 b. 115. *Cornw.* 121 b. bis.

ORDULF tainus, *Somers.* 87.[1]

ORDULFUS, *Wilts,* 70 b. *Devon,* 101.

ORDUUI, *Hunt.* 206. *Shropsh.* 257 b.

ORDUUI burgensis de Bedeford, *Bedf.* 218.[1]

ORDUUI homo Wigot, *Buck.* 150 b.

ORDUUOLD, *Hants,* 48.

ORDUUOLDUS, *Wilts,* 74, 74 b.

ORGAR, *Somers.* 94, 98 b. *Dev.* 104 b. *Cambr.* 193, 200.

ORGAR, *Northampt.* 223 b. passim.

ORGARUS, *Essex,* 92, 92 b. 103. *Suff.* 314 b.

ORGARUS liber homo, *Essex,* 20. *Norf.* 151 bis. 151 b.
262.

ORGARUS vicecomes Regis E. qui postea fuit homo
Asgari stalri, *Cambr.* 197 bis. 199.

ORGRIM, *Shropsh.* 257.

ORM, *Yorksh.* 298, 300 b. ter. 301 bis. 301 b. passim.
305 b. 306, 306 b. ter. 307 passim. 311 b.[1] 312 b.
315 b. 317, 320 b. 325 b. bis. 327, 327 b. passim.
328 passim. 329, 329 b. passim. 330 b. bis. 332 bis.
Linc. 347. *Yorksh.* 373, 373 b.

---

[1] Also at the time of the Survey.

ORMAR, *Berks,* 63 b. *Northampt.* 228. *Staff.* 249, 249 b.

ORMARUS, *Northampt.* 224. *Staff.* 248 b.

ORMARUS liber homo, *Essex,* 83.

ORMCHETEL, *Linc.* 348 b.

ORME, *Chesh.* 266. *Yorksh.* 298, 301 b. *Yorksh.* 373.

ORMER, *Derb.* 274 b. *Suff.* 355.

ORMER, presbyter, *Sussex,* 20 b.

ORNOD, homo Roberti filii Wimarch, *Cambr.* 199 b. bis.[1]

ORTHI teinus Heroldi, *Suff.* 381.

ORUENOT, *Heref.* 187 b.

ORULFUS, *Cambr.* 200.

OSBER, *Yorksh.* 306 b. 322 b.

OSBER alter, *Yorksh.* 322 b.

OSBERN, *Somers.* 94. *Nottingh.* 285, 285 b. 286 b.

OSBERNUS, *Norf.* 185.

OSBERNUS avunculus Aluredi de Marleberge, *Heref.* 186.

OSBERNUS episcopus, *Wilts,* 64 b. } [2]
OSBERNUS episcopus Execestriæ, *Cornw.* 121 b. }

OSBERNUS f. Ricardi,[3] *Heref.* 180.[4] 186 b. passim. *Shropsh.* 260 bis.[5]

OSBERNUS liber homo, *Suff.* 297.

OSBERNUS liber homo Alurici, *Suff.* 394 b. bis. 395.

OSBERNUS monachus S. Albani, *Hertf.* 135 b.

OSBERNUS teinnus, *Norf.* 267 b. bis.

---

[1] In one of these, also when the Survey was taken.

[2] See vol. i. p. 460.

[3] See the Note under " Siuuardus liber homo."

[4] Also at the time of the Survey.

[5] The lands which Osbern Fitz Richard held in the Confessor's time, recorded in folios 186 b. and 260, he also held in capite at the time of the Survey.

Osbertus, *Essex,* 89 b. *Suff.* 343.

Osbertus masculus, *Suff.* 417.

Oschetel, *Shropsh.* 259 bis.

Oschetel prepositus Regis [T. R. E.], *Norf.* 280.

Oschil, *Shropsh.* 259.

Osfertus, *Suff.* 314, 340, 340 b.

Osfordus, *Norf.* 168.

Osfort unus liber homo Heroldi, *Norf.* 186 b.

Osgarus burgensis de Bedeford, *Bedf.* 218.[1]

Osgod, *Glouc.* 169. *Heref.* 184 b. *Nottingh.* 292 b. bis.

Osgot, *Hants,* 53 bis. *Berks,* 61 bis. *Dev.* 105 b. 106.
       Glouc. 167 b. passim. *Northampt.* 226 b. 229. *Leic.*
       230. *Chesh.* 264 b. bis. *Linc.* 341, 357. *Suff.* 377 b.

Osgot liber homo, *Suff.* 374 b.

Osgot quidam liber homo, *Berks,* 61.

Osgot homo Eddeue, *Hertf.* 137.

Osgotus, *Norf.* 152. *Suff.* 342.

Osiar, *Kent,* 13 b.

Osier, *Kent,* 11.

Osiet, *Bedf.* 218 b.[2]

---

[1] Also at the time of the Survey.

[2] He continued to hold this land at the time of the
Survey, together with a half hide of land in another place,
the tenure of which occurs but once in Domesday. " In
eodem [Wilge] hund. tenet Osiet regis prefectus dimid.
hidam de Rege. Hanc terram tenuit ı. sochemannus tempore Regis Edwardi *quem Rex. W. cum terra hac prædicto
Prefecto commendavit, ut, quamdiu viveret, victum et vestitum
ei preberet.*"

William the Conqueror occasionally provided for old
soldiers in this manner. The Abingdon Register, MS.
Cotton. Claudius, C. ix. fol. 134, contains some particulars
which are here transcribed, not merely as illustrating the
Conqueror's practice, but because they afford at the same

OSIET homo R. E. *Bedf.* 214.
OSKETEL, *Suff.* 334 b.

---

time some little contribution toward a picture of the times.
A common soldier, unfit for further service, addresses himself personally to the King to obtain support for the rest
of his life from those by whom he had been immediately
employed in war.

The chapter is, " De militibus istius Ecclesiæ." Adelelm
mentioned in it became abbat of Abingdon in 1071, upon
the deposition and imprisonment of his predecessor.

" In primordio autem sui adventus in Abbatiam non nisi
armatorum septus manu militum alicubi procedebat. Et
quidem necessario id fieri oportebat. Multæ enim novi-
tates conjuratorum indies passim contra regem et regnum
ejus ebullientes universos in Anglia se tueri cogebant.
Tunc Walingaforde et Oxeneforde et Wildesore, ceterisque
locis, castella pro regno servando compacta. Unde huic
abbatiæ militum excubias apud ipsum Wildesore oppidum
habendas regio imperio jussum; quare tali in articulo
hujus fortunæ milites transmarini in Angliam venientes,
favore colebantur præcipuo. Taliter itaque regni tumultu-
antibus causis dominus Adellelmus abbas locum sibi com-
missum munita manu militum secure protegebat: et primo
quidem stipendiariis in hoc utebatur. At his sopitis incur-
sibus, cum jam regis edicto in annalibus annotaretur quot
de episcopiis quotve de abbatiis ad publicam rem tuendam
milites, si forte hinc quid causæ propellendæ contingeret
exigerentur; eisdem donativis prius retentis abbas mansiones
possessionum ecclesiæ pertinentibus inde delegavit edicto
cuique tenore parendi de suæ portionis mansione. Quæ
possessiones ab eis habitæ fuerant quos tainos[1] dicunt et in
bello Hastingis occubuerant. A quibus vero eædem possessiones primo usui ipsorum distributæ sint tainorum vel
cujus rei necessariæ gratia supervacaneum est perscru-

---

[1] tahinos, MS. Claud. B. VI.

OSKETEL liber homo, *Suff.* 299 b.
OSKETELLUS commend. Stigandi, *Suff.* 380.

---

tari; quandoquidem jam plurima quod divino judicio as-
sistant tempora preterierint, qui solus qua intentione fiant
singulorum actus liquido perpendit et quid inde recte
judicari debeat novit. Quare mortuis his quicquam ca-
lumpniarum opponere desinimus. Unum tantummodo pro
vero edicere possumus, quia perparum illarum fuerit possessionum quod in solo proprioque servorum Dei usu et pere-
grinorum susceptione ac obsequio ab his qui illas ecclesiæ
distribuerunt non fuerit delegatum. Porro qui vel parentelæ
vel secularis alicujus respectu gratiæ donativo eo abusus
fuerit, is videat an sua consideratio rectior ante dominum
quam donantis ecclesiæ quod sibi proprium constat habeatur; Nam benefacta meliorum causa sæpe commutari
solent. Itaque de his sat dictum, quare stilus ad historiam
inchoatam vertatur.

Tunc temporis milites quidam Abbendonenses, Regis pro
negotio Normanniam missi, dum maris in medio remigarent
a piratis capiuntur, spoliantur, quibus etiam manus trun-
cantur; talique infortunio vix vivi abire permissi dumum [1]
revertuntur. *Quorum unus,* HERMERUS *nomine,* necdum alicujus terræ portionem adeptus dum pro diffactionem suam
ab abbate sibi minus inde intenderetur *Regem adiit,* quid
perpessus sit ostendit, unde in futurum victitet omnino
sumptus sibi deesse conquestus est; *Cui* REX *compatiens,*
Abbati mandavit debere se hujusmodi homini tantum terræ
aliquorsum providere, qua quamdiu vixerit possit sustentari.
Paruit abbas imperatis, et possessionem de victualio monachorum quæ Denceswrht [2] dicitur, curiæ Offentunæ sub-
jectam, illi delegavit. Ita vir ille privatus domi sua tantum
procurabat, de militiæ procinctu quoad vixit nil exercens.
Hoc itaque eventu apud Offentunam dominium abbatiæ

---

[1] Domum, Ib.
[2] Denchworth, nine miles to the S. W. of Abingdon.

OSKETELUS, *Suff.* 342.

OSLAC, *Northampt.* 224 b. *Leic.* 230 b. 234. *Shropsh.* 254. *Essex,* 79 b.

OSLAC albus, *Northampt.* 220.

OSLAC teinnus, *Suff.* 405 b.

OSLACUS, *Norf.* 242.

OSLACUS commendatus Edrici de Lassefelda, *Suff.* 315.

OSLACUS liber homo, *Essex,* 25 b. 82.

OSMAR, *Leic.* 237.

OSMER, *Dev.* 107 b. 109. *Chesh.* 265 passim. 265 b. ter. 268 b. *Derb.* 274.

OSMERI pater, *Somers.* 99.[1]

OSMUND, *Somers.* 92 b. *Leic.* 230 b. 233 b. *Derb.* 277 b. 278 b. *Nottingh.* 284 b. 289 b. *Linc.* 368 b. ter.

OSMUND benz, *Derb.* 278 b.

OSMUND Stramun. *v.* STRAMUN.

OSMUNDUS, *Surr.* 34 b. ter. *Hants,* 44 b. bis. 50. *Somers.* 88. *Oxf.* 160 b. *Northampt.* 223 bis. 224, 226 bis. 227. *Derb.* 275 b. bis. 278 b. *Nottingh.* 290. *Yorksh.* 315 b. *Linc.* 360 b. 368 b. *Norf.* 120, 153, 160, 167 b. ter.

OSMUNDUS danus, *Northampt.* 227.

OSMUNDUS f. Leuric, *Northampt.* 223.

OSMUNDUS liber homo, *Suff.* 297 b. 354.

OSMUNDUS unus liber homo, *Berks,* 63.

OSMUNDUS liber homo commend. E. *Suff.* 324.

OSMUNDUS pater Rad'. *Hunt.* 208.

OSMUNDUS tainus, *Wilts,* 68 b.

OSTEBRAND, *Chesh.* 267.

---

diminutum. Item in Wichtham de terra villanorum Curiæ Cumenore obsequi solitorum, illo *ab abbate cuidam militi nomine* HUBERTO v hidarum portio distributa est."

[1] " Osmerus ipse," was the tenant at the Survey.

OSTULA liber homo, *Suff.* 297 b.

OSUL, *Yorksh.* 319, 319 b. bis.

OSULF, *Hants,* 46 b. *Wilts,* 72. *Dev.* 102, .109 b. bis.
Cornw. 121 b. 124, 124 b. passim. *Buck.* 150.
Northampt. 223 b. 233 b. *Yorksh.* 316, 316 b.[1] 317,
319 b. 320, 321 b. *Linc.* 362, 366.

OSULF filius Frane teignus R. E. *Hertf.* 138 bis. *Buck.*
149. *Bedf.* 215 ter.

OSULF homo Brictrici, *Buck.* 150.

OSULF homo regis E. *Buck.* 145 b.

OSULF teignus R. E. *Buck.* 149.

OSULFUS, *Northampt.* 225 ter. *Suff.* 339 b. 384 b.

OSULFUS homo Eddeuæ, *Cambr.* 195.

OSUUALD, *Somers.* 90.

OSWAR, *Dors.* 77.

OSUUARD, *Kent,* 1 b. 9, 13 b. *Suss.* 19 b. *Surr.* 36 b.
Glouc. 170 b.[1] *Yorksh.* 301, 331. *Norf.* 247.

OSUUARD vicecomes, *Kent,* 2 b.

OSUUARDI pater, *Wilts,* 74.

OSUUARDUS, *Kent,* 7 b. 8, 8 b. 9, 10. *Suss.* 18, 20, 21,
22, 22 b. 26 b. bis.[1] 27, 29. *Surr.* 33, 34. *Wilts,*
69 b. 73 bis. 74 b. *Somers.* 98 b. bis. *Nottingh.*
284 b. *Ess.* 23 b.

OSUUI homo Alrici, *Buck.* 151.

OSUUI homo Alrici f. Goding, *Buck.* 148 bis.

OSUUI homo Asgari stalri, *Hertf.* 139 b.

OSUUI homo Brictrici, *Buck.* 148 b.

OSUUI homo comitis Tosti, *Bedf.* 218 b.

OSUUID, *Glouc.* 167.

OSUUOL, *Surr.* 34 b.

OSWOLDUS, *Surr.* 36 b.

---

[1] Also at the Survey.

Otbertus, *Yorksh.* 298.

Otburuilla, Rogerus de, *Suff.* 383 b.

Ote, *Yorksh.* 325.

Othemus, *Suff.* 381.

Otho, *Surr.* 35.

Othonis pater, *Wilts,* 74.

Otre, *Dev.* 105, 109, 109 b. 110 bis. *Yorksh.* 301
  ter.

Otro, *Shropsh.* 254.

Otti, *Suff.* 340.

Oualet, *Sussex,* 29 b.

Oudenecar, *Nottingh.* 284 b.

Oudfride, *Yorksh.* 305 b.

Oudgrim, *Nottingh.* 284 b.

Oudon, *Linc.* 352.

Oudulf, *Yorksh.* 300 b.

Ouen, *Heref.* 187 b.

Ouiet, *Shropsh.* 257 b.

Ouiet homo Aschil, *Bedf.* 213, 216.

Ouiet homo regis E. *Bedf.* 217.

Ouiet teignus R. E. *Bedf.* 215.

Oune, *Linc.* 347 b.

Outbert, *Linc.* 343.

Outi, *Leic.* 237. *Warw.* 239. *Chesh.* 265. *Linc.* 336,
  344 b. 357, 357 b. bis. *Clam. W. R. Linc.* 376 b.
  Clam. in Chetst. 377 b.

Outi f. Azer, *Linc.* 337.

Ouu, Æilmarus de, *Bedf.* 213 b.

Ouuin, *Chesh.* 265 b.

Ouuine, *Derb.* 276.

Ouuinus, *Chesh.* 265 b.

Oxeneford, Canonici de, *Buck.* 146. *Oxf.* 157.

P.

PADDA, *Suff.* 331 b.

PAGANUS, *Norf.* 264.

PAGEN, *Glouc.* 170.

PALLINUS, *Warw.* 242.

PARISII, Ecclesia S. Dyonisii, *Oxf.* 157. *Glouc.* 166.

PAT, *Chesh.* 268.

PATER Alredi, *Kent,* 1 b.

PATER Alrici, *Hants,* 50 b.

PATER Alsi, *Hants,* 42 b.

PATER Alurici, *Hants,* 51 b.

PATER Alwardi aurifabri, *Berks,* 63 b.

PATER cujusdam bedelli Regis W. *Bedf.* 218 b.

PATER Ernvini presb. homo regis E. *Bedf.* 211.

PATER Gameli, *Chesh.* 267 b. bis.

PATER Willielmi de Caron, *Bedf.* 210.

PAULINUS, *Somers.* 96.

PAULI S. Ecclesia Lond. *Surr.* 34. *Hertf.* 136. *Essex,*
    9 b. 12 b.

PBOCHESTAN, Aluuinus, *Leic.* 232.

PERCI, Willielmus, *Yorksh.* 332.

PERLO, *Somers.* 93 b.

PERSORE, Ecclesia S. Mariæ de, *Glouc.* 166. *Worc.* 175.

PETROCUS, Sanctus, *Cornw.* 120 b. 121.

PETRUS S. in Sciropesberie, *Shropsh.* 254 b. 260.

PEUREL Willelmus, *Northampt.* 220.

PHIN, *Suff.* 395 b.

PHIN dacus, *Essex,* 41.

PHIN liber homo, *Essex,* 98 b.

PIC, Aluric, *Dev.* 113.

PILEUUIN, *Nottingh.* 283 b. 291.

PIN, *Glouc.* 164 b.

PINCHENGI, Ansculfus de, *Buck.* 148 b.[1]

PINSTAN, *Suff.* 320 b.

POINC, Godricus, *Essex*, 37 b.

POINTEL, Tedricus, *Essex*, 4, 6, 6 b.

Porcarius unus, T. R. E. *Heref.* 179 b.

PR' unus, *Norf.* 133.[2]

PREBENDARIA una R. E. *Cambr.* 201.

PREFECTUS de Stanes, *Midd.* 129.

Prefectus, v. CHAUUA.

Prepositi duo Haroldi Comitis, *Yorksh.* 298.

Prepositi Comitis Eduini et Morcar, *Chesh.* 264 b.

Prepositus, v. ECCHA. GODUINUS. GRIMUS. LEFRIC. LEFSTANUS. RADBODA. TOSTII. TOUI.

Prepositus Regis E. *v.* EDUUOLT.

Presbyter, v. BERNARDUS. BLACHEMAN. BOLLO. BORET. BRISTOALDUS. BRUN. BRUNARUS. EDMER. EDUUI. EDUUINUS. ERNUIN. ERNUINUS. ESMELD. GODRIC. GODRICUS. GODUINUS. GODUUINUS. KETEL. LEDMARUS. LEUIET. LEUING. LEUINGUS. LEUSTANUS. LEUUINE. MONULFUS. MORCAR. MORCARUS. ODE. RAINBALDUS. REINBOLD. ROBERTUS. SAMARUS. SAUINUS. SEMAR. SIUUARD. SONULFUS. SPIRITES. SPIRTES. SUARINUS. TORCHIL. TUERBERNUS. TURBERTUS. TURCHIL. VITALIS. VLGAR. VLMARUS. VLMERUS. VLSI. VLSTAN. VLUARDUS. VLUIET. VLURICUS. VLUUARD. WIHTREDUS. WLUUINUS.

---

[1] " Hoc manerium [Esenberge] tenuit Heraldus Comes, et ipsum excambiavit Ansculfus de Pinchengi pro dim. Bisenberge, contra Radulfum Talgebosch jussu regis Willielmi."

[2] " In Wittuna I. pr' (unus presbyter) xxx. acr. in Elemosina."

PRESBYTER quidam, *Hertf.* 142 bis.[1]

PRESBYTER quidam et soror ejus, *Hertf.* 142.[1]

PRESBYTER unus, *Ess.* 96.

PRESBYTER R. E. *v.* WLMARUS.

PRESBYTER I. liber homo, *Ess.* 22 b.

PRESBYTERI duo, *Worc.* 173, 200 b.

PRESBYTERI de Bomine, *Dev.* 117 b.[1]

PRESBYTERI de Wrehantune, *Worc.* 176.[1]

PUR, Edricus, *Cambr.* 196 b.

Q.

QUENDRUD monacha. *Linc.* 370 b.

QUENGEVET mater Brihmari, *Suff.* 424 b. bis.

R.

R. Comes, *Warw.* 244 b. *Norf.* 128 b. 129, 144.

R. Comes vetus,[2] *Norf.* 128 b.

R. filius Corbucini, *Norf.* 250.

R. Stabra,[3] *Suff.* 293.

R. Stalara,[4] *Norf.* 269 b. } *v.* RADULFUS stalre.

R. Stalre t. r. E. *Norf.* 122 b.

RACHENILD, *Bucks,* 62 b.

RADA liber homo Heroldi, *Suff.* 432 bis.

RADBODA prepositus Rad. Stalra, *Norf.* 229 b.

Radchenistri id est liberi homines, *Glouc.* 166.

---

[1] Also at the time of the Survey.

[2] " Old Earl Ralph, the father of Ralph de Guader Earl of Norfolk." Kelh. p. 307.

[3] A clerical error for R. stalre.   [4] R. stalre.

Radchenistri duo, *Glouc.* 163 b.

Radchenistri tres, *Glouc.* 163 b.

Radmanni duo, Aluuard et Vlfricus, *Worc.* 175.

Radmans duo, *Worc.* 175 b. *Heref.* 185 b.

Radmans quatuor, *Inter Rip. et Mers.* 269 b.

Radmans VIII. Ageluuard, Eduuard, Brictmer, Saulfus, Aluuinus, Godric, Aluui, Ketelbert, *Worc.* 174 b.

RADOLF, *Linc.* 347.

RADULFUS, *Wilts,* 73. *Essex,* 47. *Norf.* 262. *Suff.* 408 b.

RADULFUS Comes, *Bucks,* 61. *Northampt.* 226 b. *Leic.* 231, 232 bis. 234, 236. *Warw.* 243, 244. *Linc.* 337. *Norf.* 115, 119 b. 126 b. 127, 147, 149, 150 b. 166, 194.

RADULFUS stalra, *Norf.* 122 b. 158, 158 b. 217 b. 218 b. 229 b. 265. *Suff.* 293, 297, 409 b. 411 b. 431.

RADULFUS stalre, *Cornw.* 121 b. *Linc.* 337 b. 347, 347 b. bis. 348 ter. 348 b. *Clam. in Chetst.* 377. } *v.* R. stalre.

RADULFUS stalrel. *Linc.* 337.

RÆNOLDUS, *Norf.* 200.

RAFRIDUS, *Norf.* 222 b.

RAFUUIN, *Staff.* 249.

RAGENAL, *Chesh.* 264. *Yorksh.* 319.

RAGENALD, *Nottingh.* 286 b. *Yorksh.* 308, 330 b. *Linc.* 366, 370 b. 371.

RAGENALT, *Nottingh.* 290 b.

RAGENILD, *Yorksh.* 315.

RAGENOT, *Yorksh.* 329.

RAINALD, *Nottingh.* 289 b. *Yorksh.* 308.

RAINALDUS, *Yorksh.* 308.

RAINBALDUS presbyter, *Dors.* 79.[1]

RAINERUS, *Norf.* 280.

RAM, *Yorksh.* 301 b.

RAMECHIL, *Yorksh.* 330 b. 331 b.

RAMESEIA, Ramesig, Rameseio, *seu* Ramesy, Sanctus
    Benedictus de, *Hertf.* 136. *Cambr.* 192 b. 201.
    Hunt. 203, 204, 204 b. 208. *Bedf.* 210 b. *Nor-
    thampt.* 222, 228. *Linc.* 346 b. 348. *Clam. in
    Chetst.* 377. *Norf.* 215, 215 b. *Suff.* 378 b. 419 b.

RANCHIL, *Yorksh.* 301 b. 328.

RANNULFUS frater Ilgerii, T. R. E. *Bedf.* 215. *Suff.*
    424.

RANULFUS, *Suff.* 443.

RASRIDUS, *Norf.* 221 b.

RATHO, *Norf.* 240.

RATHO liber homo, *Norf.* 268 b.

RAUAN homo Vlmari de Etone, *Bedf.* 212 b.

RAUECATE, *Chesh.* 266.

RAUECHEL, *Chesh.* 268 b.

RAUECHET, *Chesh.* 268 b.

RAUECHETEL, *Heref.* 180, 180 b. *Staff.* 249 b.

RAUECHIL, *Chesh.* 264 b. *Yorksh.* 298, 322.

RAVELIN, *Hants,* 50 b.[1]

RAVEN, *Chesh.* 264 b. *Derb.* 274, 275 b. *Yorksh.* 309 b.
    Suff. 320 b.

RAUENCHEL, *Chesh.* 264 b. *Derb.* 275 b. *Yorksh.* 298.

RAUENCHIL, *Yorksh.* 301 b. 318 bis. 324 b. bis. 325,
    330 b. 331 b. 374 bis.

RAUENE, *Chesh.* 267 b. bis.

RAUENGARIUS, *Essex,* 23 bis. 59 b.

RAUENSUAR, *Yorksh.* 301 b.

---

[1] He continued to hold at the time of the Survey.

RAUENSUARD, *Yorksh.* 301 b.

RAUENUS, *Suff.* 341 b. bis.

RAUESUA, *Chesh.* 268.

RAUESUAR, *Chesh.* 266.

RAUESUARD, *Shropsh.* 257.

RAUESUARDUS, *Chesh.* 268 b.

RAUESUE, *Chesh.* 267 b.

RAULFUS, *Suff.* 423 b.

RAUUEN homo Wluui Episcopi, 150.

RAYNERIUS pater Roberti Episcopi de Cestre, *Hertf.* 135.

RAYNERUS diaconus, *Clam. N. R. Linc.* 375 b. passim. 376.

REDER, *Yorksh.* 319 b. 324 b.

REDULF, *Linc.* 340 b.

REES, *Chesh.* 267 b.

REGIFERUS, *Suff.* 342.

REIDER, *Yorksh.* 319 b.

REIMBALDUS de Cirecestre, *Berks,* 63.

REINBALD, *Worc.* 174 b.

REINBALDUS, *Somers.* 86 b. *Worc.* 174 b.

REINBOLD presbyter, *Somers.* 99.

REMBALDUS canceler, *Heref.* 180 b.

REMIGII S. Ecclesia, *Northampt.* 222 b. *Staff.* 247 b. *Shropsh.* 252.

RENOLDUS, *Norf.* 196.

RESTEF, *Clam. N. R. Linc.* 376.

RESTELF, *Linc.* 342.

REUENESUARD, *Shropsh.* 260 b.

REUENSUARD, *Shropsh.* 258 b.

REUER, *Heref.* 186, 186 b.

RICARD, *Nottingh.* 282 b. 286.

RICARDUS, *Worc.* 172 b.

RICARDUS filius Comitis Gisleberti, *Essex,* 3 b.[1]

RICARDUS juvenis, T. R. E. *Worc.* 177 b.

RICARDUS pater Osberni, *Shropsh.* 260.

RICARDUS pater Osberni fil. Ric. *Worc.* 176 b. passim.

RINGUL, liber homo, *Norf.* 267.

RINGULFUS, *Norf.* 174 b.

ROBERTUS arhal',[2] *Norf.* 244.

ROBERTUS presbyter, *Linc.* 345.[3]

ROBERTUS Wimarc, *Essex,* 106 b.

ROBERTUS fil. Wimarc,[4] *Somers.* 92 b. *Hertf.* 137 b.
Heref. 186 b. 187. *Cambr.* 200 b. *Hunt.* 205 b.
207. *Essex,* 42, 48. *Suff.* 395 b. 436 b.

ROBERTUS filius Wimarcæ (post mortem Regis E.),
Essex, 44, 44 b. 45 bis. 46 b. bis.

Roc, *Suff.* 396 b.

ROCHES, Johannes de, *Bedf.* 210 b. 214.

ROGERUS filius Rainardi, *Norf.* 245.

ROLD, *Linc.* 370 b.

---

1 He was one of the witnesses to the Conqueror's charter
of 1077 to Westminster Abbey: as was " Baldewinus frater
ejus."

2 *Sc.* arbal', for arbalistarius.

3 At the time of the Survey he had become a monk of
St. Mary, Stow.

4 " Roberd Wymarche sune, stallere," occurs in one of
Edward the Confessor's charters to Westminster Abbey, as
one of his thains of Kent. See the Monast. Anglic. last
edit. vol. i. p. 298. He was the father of Suein of Essex.
In *Essex,* 101, we read " hanc terram invasit Robertus filius
Wimarc t. r. Willielmi, et adhuc tenet Suenus." In Suffolk,
as will be seen by the references in the page 207, he is
called " ROTBERTUS pater Sueni."

ROLF, *Nottingh.* 291 b. *Linc.* 342 b. ter. 343 b. 344 bis.
  347, 357 b. 358 bis. 360 bis. 360 b. 365 passim.
  Suff. 446.

ROLF f. Sceldeware, *Linc.* 337.

ROLFT, *Linc.* 345 b. 346 bis.

ROMESYG, *seu* ROMESEIENSIS Ecclesia, *Hants*, 43 b.
  Wilts, 68.

ROSCHEL, *Yorksh.* 301 bis.

ROSCHET, *Nottingh.* 286.

ROSCHIL, *Yorksh.* 301, 312 b. bis. 315 b.

ROT, Azor, *Kent*, 13.

ROTBERTUS, *Suff.* 401.

ROTBERTUS pater Sueni, *Suff.* 401 bis. 401 b.[1] 402
  passim.

ROTLESC huscarle, R. E. *Glouc.* 164.

ROTOMAGO, Ecclesia S. Mariæ de, *Dev.* 104.

ROVECESTRE, Episcopus de, *Kent*, 5 b.

ROULF, *Leic.* 233 b. 236.

ROZO, *Wilts*, 69 b.

RUFUS, Siuuardus, *Clam. in Chetst.* 376 b.

RUILLIC, *Heref.* 183 b.

RUSCHIL, *Yorksh.* 322.

S.

S. A. (Stigandus archiepiscopus), *Norf.* 145 b.

SAC, Aluuinus, *Bedf.* 210.

SÆMAR, *Dev.* 114 b.

SAGAR, *Dev.* 114 b.

SAGAR homo Wallef Comitis, *Cambr.* 202.

---

[1] " Super hanc habuit Sanctus E. soc. et sacam T. R. E.
et Rodbertus filius Wimarce et pater Sueni commendatione
tantum."

SAGEVA, *Cambr.* 196 b.

SAGRIM, *Northampt.* 224.[1] *Staff.* 250 b. *Linc.* 347.

SAIARDUS, *Suff.* 425 b.

SAIED, *Warw.* 239 b.

SAIET, *Bedf.* 218 b.[1]

SAIET unus tainus, *Oxf.* 154 b.

SAILT homo Leuuini Comitis, *Hertf.* 134 b.

SAISI, *Heref.* 186 b.

SAISIL, *Heref.* 186 b.

SALECOE, *Linc.* 354.

SALOMON, *Yorksh.* 327.

SALPUS, *Suff.* 377.

SALTREDE, Tosti de, *Hunt.* 208 b.

SALVAGE, Edric, *Heref.* 183 b. *Shropsh.* 253 b. ter. 254 b. 255 bis. 256, 256 b. 258 b. *v.* EDRIC.

SAMAR, *Somers.* 98 b.

SAMARUS liber homo, *Essex,* 49.

SAMARUS homo Alnod, *Hertf.* 134.

SAMARUS homo Leuuini, *Bedf.* 214 b.

SAMARUS presbyter homo Godæ comitissæ, *Bedf.* 212 b.

SANCTO GERMANO, Rogerus de, *Suff.* 448.

SAOLF, *Hants,* 51, 51 b.

SARED, *Somers.* 98.

SARED et frater ejus, *Dors.* 79 b.

SARIC, *Somers.* 86 b. 95, 98 b. *Dev.* 114 b.

SARISBERIENSIS Episcopus, *Berks,* 58. *Wilts,* 66. *Dors.* 75 b. *Oxf.* 155.

SARPO, *Somers.* 95 b.

SASFORD, *Yorksh.* 303 b. passim. 331.

SASFORD, unus liber homo, *Berks,* 61 b.

SAUARDUS, *Somers.* 96 b.

SAUINUS presbyter, *Essex,* 59.

---

[1] Also at the time of taking the Survey.

SAUL, *Wilts,* 71. *Dors.* 75 b. *Shropsh.* 260 b.

SAULF, *Hants,* 44 b. 50, 50 b. 51 b. *Berks,* 61 b. bis.
Wilts, 69 b. 72 b. *Somers.* 90 b.[1] 94, 96 b. *Dev.*
105, 109 b. 116, 118 ter.[1] *Cornw.* 122, 123 b.
124 b. *Worc.* 174 b. 175. *Northampt.* 220, 223.
Warw. 243 bis. *Shropsh.* 256 b. *Derb.* 275.

SAULFI pater, *Wilts,* 74.

SAULFUS, *Hants,* 45. *Worc.* 174 b. *Northampt.* 223 b.
Essex, 58 b.

SAUORD, *Hants,* 39 b.

SAUUARD, *Dors.* 83 b. *Warw.* 242 b.

SAUUARD homo Azor filii Toti, *Buck.* 147 b.

SAUUARDUS, *Wilts,* 71, 83, 84 b.[1] *Dev.* 111 b. 113.
Worc. 176 b. *Shropsh.* 254, 260.

SAUUARDUS homo comitis Heraldi, *Buck.* 146.

SAUUATA, *Northampt.* 224.

SAUUIN, *Hants,* 50 b. *Somers.* 86, 92. *Dev.* 108 b. 115
passim. 115 b. 116 b. *Cornw.* 123, 124.

SAUUINUS, *Hants,* 39 b. 41, 50,[1] 51 b. *Berks,* 62 b.
Wilts, 70 b. *Dors.* 82, 84. *Somers.* 94 b. *Dev.* 102 b.
103, 103 b. 104 b. bis. 106, 107 b. 108 b. 115 b.
116 b. *Cornw.* 124. *Glouc.* 167. *Worc.* 172 b.
Northampt. 220. *Shropsh.* 259.

SAUUINUS accipitrarius, *Hunt.* 208.

SAUUINUS unus liber homo, *Berks,* 62, 63 b.

SAUUOLD, *Oxf.* 160 b. *Worc.* 176 b. bis.

SAUUOLDUS, *Wilts,* 71. *Oxf.* 160. *Warw.* 243.

SAUUOLDUS homo Wluuardi cilt, *Buck.* 149.

SAXA, *Suff.* 423 b. 450.

SAXFORDUS diac. *Yorksh.* 298 b. bis.

---

[1] Also at the time of the Survey.

SAXI, *Hants,* 38 b. 49 bis. *Hunt.* 205 b. 207 bis. *Leic.*
  231 b. bis. 237 bis. *Warw.* 239 b. bis. 240. *Shropsh.*
  260 b.

SAXI teignus R. E. *Bucks,* 151.

SAXO, *Suff.* 305, 376 bis. 376 b. 417 b. bis. 418.

SAXULF, *Yorksh.* 330.

SAXULFUS, *Yorksh.* 315 b.

SAXWINUS commendatus Burchardi, *Suff.* 408.

SBERN, *Kent,* 7. *Sussex,* 24. *Cornw.* 122, 124. *Leic.*
  233 b. *Linc.* 347 bis. 365 b. 367.

SBERN biga, *Kent,* 2, 7, 7 b. 8, 12.

SBERN croc, *Nottingh.* 291 b. bis.

SBERN unus liber homo, *Leic.* 236.

SBERN Vlmer, *Nottingh.* 293.

SBERNE, *Hants,* 49 b. *Warw.* 238 b. *Chesh.* 268 b.
  Derb. 278 b. *Linc.* 354, 356 b. 365 b.

SCALDEFORT liber homo, *Essex,* 95.

SCALPIUS, *Suff.* 420.

SCALPIUS [teinus Haroldi], *Suff.* 419 b.

SCANCHEL, *Yorksh.* 306.

SCAPIUS, *Essex,* 67 b. *Suff.* 420 b.

SCAPIUS teinnus Haroldi, *Suff.* 419 b. bis.

SCELFRIDE, *Yorksh.* 328.

SCEMUND, *Linc.* 360 b.

SCEPTESBERIENSIS Abbatia, *Wilts,* 67 b. *Dors.* 78 b.

SCET liber homo, *Norf.* 257 b.

SCEUA, *Hants,* 54.

SCHEIT, *Norf.* 234 b.

SCHETT, *Norf.* 245 b.

SCIPTI, Godricus, *Essex,* 37 b.

SCIREBURNE, Monachi Episcopi Sarisberiensis in, *Dors.*
  77.

SCIREUOLD, *Glouc.* 167.

Scireuold et Vluuard in paragio, *Dors.* 79.

Scireuuoldus, *Dev.* 117 b.

Scirold, *Wilts,* 69 b.

Sciropesberie, Ecclesia S. Almundi, *Shropsh.* 252, 253, 258.

Sciropesberie, Ecclesia S. Ceddæ, *Shropsh.* 252, 253.

Sciropesberie, Ecclesia S. Julianæ, *Shropsh.* 252, 253.

Sciropesberie, Ecclesia S. Mariæ, *Shropsh.* 252, 252 b.

Sciropesberie, Ecclesia S. Milburgæ, *Shropsh.* 252, 252 b. 254.

Sciropesberie, Ecclesia S. Michaelis, *Shropsh.* 252 b.

Sciropesberie, S. Petrus in, *Shropsh.* 254 b.

Sclula, *Norf.* 232 b.

Scohies, Willielmus de, *Norf.* 276.

Scotcol, *Yorksh.* 315 b.

Scotecol, *Yorksh.* 307 b.

Scotel, *Northampt.* 224.

Scoua, Aluricus, *Hertf.* 134 b.

Scroti, *Warw.* 240.

Scrotin, *Warw.* 240, 244.

Scula, *Norf.* 245 b.

Scula liber homo, *Norf.* 221 b.

Scula teinnus regis E. *Suff.* 299.

Scule, *Linc.* 359.

Sech, Goduinus, *Essex,* 100 b.

Seduin, *Dev.* 109 b.

Seduinus, *Dev.* 114 b.

Seduuinus, *Dev.* 107.

Segarus, *Essex,* 25 b.

Segrida, *Yorksh.* 322 b.

Seiar bar, *Norf.* 223 b.

Seiardus bar, *Norf.* 128, 223 b. } *v.* Siuuard bar.

Selecolf, *Yorksh.* 298.

Seleuuinus, *Wilts,* 72.

SELUA, *Essex*, 67.

SEMÆR, *Shropsh.* 254 b.

SEMAN, *Surr.* 36 b.[1]

SEMAR, *Somers.* 95, 98 b.   *Dev.* 105 b. 110 b.   *Heref.*
    185, 187 bis.

SEMAR presbyter, *Hertf.* 142.

SEMARUS, *Hunt.* 204.[2]

SEMER, *Dev.* 104 b. 112.

SENDI, *Linc.* 352.

SERCAR, *Essex*, 86.

SERIC, *Somers.* 94 b.   *Dev.* 110, 114 b.   *Bucks*, 150.[3]
        Heref. 180, 184 b. bis. 186 b. bis.   *Leic.* 234 b.
        Nottingh. 290.

SERIC Alueue filius,[4] *Buck.* 147.

SERIC pater Godmundi, *Heref.* 185.

SERIC homo Leuuini Comitis, *Hertf.* 136 b.

SERIC homo Sired, *Buck.* 151 b.

SERICUS, *Nottingh.* 293.

SERLO, *Essex*, 73.[3]

SERUIENTES duo Wisgari, *Essex*, 41 b.

SESSI, *Shropsh.* 255.

SEUBAR, *Linc.* 353 b.

---

[1] In Copthorne Hundred in Surrey, " Ten. SEMAN unam
v. terræ quam tenuit de rege E. sed ex quo ven' W. rex in
Angliam servivit Osuuoldo. redd. ei xx. den. Hic se potuit
vertere quo voluit T. R. E." This entry is deserving of
notice. The owner became under-tenant of his land, " ex
quo Will. venit," upon payment of a rent : but he had no
longer the right of transferring himself as a " commendatus," which he possessed in the Confessor's time.

[2] He likewise held at the time of the Survey.

[3] Seric continued to hold in this entry at the Survey.

[4] He is the same person with " Sired fil. Alueue teignus
R. E."

SEUEN, *Linc.* 371.

SEULF, *Somers.* 94 b.

SEULF homo Com. Leuuini et Siuuardus frater, *Buck.* 152 b.

SEULF homo Radulfi Comitis, *Buck.* 152 b.

SEUUAR, *Shropsh.* 254 bis.

SEUUARD, *Berks*, 60 b. *Shropsh.* 254, 255, 256 bis. 257 b. 259 b. bis.[1] 260. *Derb.* 276. *Yorksh.* 319 ter. *Linc.* 350 b.

SEUUARDUS, *Kent*, 10. *Sussex*, 18. *Berks*, 62. *Dors.* 81. *Dev.* 107. *Shropsh.* 254 b. passim. 255 passim. 256, 258 b. 259 b. bis. 260 b. *Chesh.* 265 b. bis.

SEWARDUS antecessor Ranulfi Peverelli, *Suff.* 416, 416 b.

SEWARDUS de Meldona, teinus, *Suff.* 416.

SEWARDUS de Melduna, *Suff.* 416.

SEUUARDUS liber homo, *Shropsh.* 255, 255 b.

SEUUARDUS venator, *Hants*, 42 b.[2]

SEUUART, *Kent*, 6.

SEUUEN, *Linc.* 351 b.

SEUUI, *Wilts*, 70.

SEUUINUS, *Dev.* 106. *Glouc.* 170. *Suff.* 341 b. 342.

SEXI, *Hants*, 48 b. *Berks*, 57 bis. *Cambr.* 201. *Warw.* 240 b. 244 b.

SEXI, huscarle R. E. *Hertf.* 138.

SEXI teignus regis E. *Cambr.* 197 b.

SEXIUS, *Essex*, 88 b. 91, 93.

SIBE, *Somers.* 88.

---

[1] Seuuard continued to hold, in one of these entries, at the time of the Survey.

[2] He held his land as an under-tenant T. R. E., and at the Survey.

SICHET, *Linc.* 359.

SIDGAR, *Kent,* 14 b.

SIGAR, *Kent,* 1 b. *Wilts,* 70 b. *Cambr.* 197 passim.[1] 201 b. *Linc.* 342 b. bis.

SIGAR homo Asgari stalri, *Cambr.* 197.

SIGAR homo Wallef Comitis, *Cambr.* 202.

SIGARI pater, *Kent,* 1 b.

SIGARUS, *Essex,* 11 b.

SIGARUS liber homo, *Norf.* 227 b.

SIGHET, *Linc.* 359.

SIGREDA, *Yorksh.* 312.

SIMON teinus Eduini Comitis, *Worc.* 176 b.

SIMOND danus, *Warw.* 242 b.

SIMUNDUS, *Worc.* 174.

SINDI, *Yorksh.* 318.

SINOD, homo S. Mariæ de Cetriz, *Hertf.* 139, 141 b.

SIRED, *Kent,* 1 b. bis. 9 b. 10, 11 b. *Hants,* 44 b.[2] 45 b. *Somers.* 93. *Midd.* 127.

SIRED homo Algari Comitis, *Cambr.* 198 b.

SIRED f. Alueue teignus R. E. *Buck.* 147.

SIRED teignus regis Eduardi, *Buck.* 147.

SIRED homo Heraldi Comitis, *Hertf.* 141 b. *Buck.* 148 b.

SIREDUS, *Essex,* 83 b.

SIRET, *Sussex,* 25 b.

SIRET de Cilleham, *Kent,* 1.

SIRET homo Heraldi Comitis, *Hertf.* 141 b. *Buck.* 148 b.

SIREUUALD, *Dors.* 79 b. *Somers.* 95 b.

---

[1] In four instances in this folio he continued when the Survey was made.

[2] He continued to hold at the Survey.

SIREUUALDUS, *Dev.* 116 b.

SIREUUOLDUS, *Somers.* 91 b. *Cornw.* 124 b.[1]

SIRIC, *Linc.* 370 b. ter.

SIRIC homo Leuuini Comitis, *Buck.* 145 bis.

SIRICUS, *Nottingh.* 284. *Essex,* 24, 79 b. *Suff.* 343, 378, 434, 434 b.

SIRICUS commend. Edw. Regis, *Suff.* 319.

SIRICUS homo Edwardi Regis, *Suff.* 346.

SIRICUS liber homo, *Norf.* 269 b. *Suff.* 423, 437 b.

SIRICUS liber homo commend. Stigando, *Suff.* 322 b. ter.

SIROF, *Worc.* 173.

SISTAIN, *Shropsh.* 254 b.

SISTRIC, *Dev.* 103 b. *Cornw.* 121 b. bis.

SISTRIC abbas de Tavistoche, *Dev.* 103 b. ⎫
SITRIC abbas, *Cornw.* 121 b. ⎬ 2
 ⎭

SIUARDUS venator, *Oxf.* 160 b.[1]

SIUARGENT, *Yorksh.* 324 b.

SIUERD, *Northampt.* 220 b.

SIUERDUS, *Northampt.* 226 b.

SIUERT, *Linc.* 348 b.

SIUERTUS, *Suff.* 339 b.

SIULFUS, *Sussex,* 19 b.

SIUUARD, *Kent,* 6. *Hants,* 49. *Somers.* 93 b. *Dev.* 108 ter. 116. *Cornw.* 123. *Oxf.* 159. *Heref.* 186.

---

[1] He continued at the time of the Survey.

[2] Sihricus or Sihtricus, abbat of Tavistock, occurs as a witness in 1050 to the charter of King Edward the Confessor, in virtue of which the bishoprics of Cornwall and Devon became united at Exeter. In the Exeter Domesday he is frequently mentioned, and his name variously written. He is called Sihtricius, Sitricius, Sistricus, and Suetricus. He died on the 8th of the ides of April 1082. See Hearne, Notæ ad Guil. Neubrig. ex cod. antiq. tom. iii. p. 709.

Northampt. 227 bis. 228. *Warw.* 242 bis. 255 b.
bis. 258 b. 259 b. passim.[1] 260, 260 b. bis. *Derb.*
274 ter. 275 ter. 275 b. ter. *Nottingh.* 291 b. bis.
292 b.[2] *Rutl.* 293 b. *Yorksh.* 300, 300 b. 301 bis.
305, 306 bis. 306 b. bis. 309 b. 310, 316 b. 324
bis. 331 bis. 331 b. *Linc.* 336, 337 b. 340 b. 341 b.
343 b. 347 b. 348 b. 350 bis. 351, 352 b. 355 b.
bis. 356 bis. 358 bis. 358 b. ter. 360, 361 bis. 362,
363 b. ter. 365, 366 bis. 368 b. *Yorksh.* 374. *Clam.*
N. R. Linc. 375 b.

SIUUARD bar,[3] *Glouc.* 169. *v.* SEIAR. SEIARDUS.

---

[1] In two of these instances also when the Survey was
made.

[2] Also at the time of the Survey.

[3] Siward Bar, or Barn, is mentioned in the Saxon Chronicle, under the year 1071:

" This year Earl Edwin and Earl Morcar fled away, and
roamed in woods and fields. Then went Earl Morcar to
Ely by ship; but Earl Edwin was treacherously slain by his
own men. Then came Bishop Aylwine and SIWARD BARN,
and many hundred men with them, into Ely. When King
William heard that, then ordered he out a naval force and
land force, and beset the land all about, and wrought a
bridge, and went in, and the naval force at the same time,
on the sea-side. And the outlaws then all surrendered;
that was, Bishop Aylwine and Earl Morcar, and all that
were with them, except Hereward alone, and all those that
would join him, whom he led out triumphantly. And the
King took their ships and weapons, and many treasures;
and all the men he disposed of as he thought proper.
Bishop Aylwine he sent to Abingdon, where he died in the
beginning of the winter." Sax. Chron. Ingr. pp. 276, 277.

Siward Barn is also mentioned in the metrical History of
England, by Geoffrey Gaimar, MS. Reg. Brit. Mus. 4 C. XI.

SIUUARDBAR, *Yorksh.* 326. *Clam. W. R.*
    Linc. 376 b.

SIUUARD barn, *Warw.* 242. *Nottingh.* 280 b.
    Linc. 337, 369.

      v. SEIAR.
      SEIARDUS.

SIUUARD Comes, *Derb.* 273 b.

SIUUARD homo Aldeue, *Buck.* 146.

SIUUARD homo Aluuini de Godtone, *Hertf.* 142 b.

SIUUARD homo Comitis Heraldi, *Buck.* 152 b.

SIUUARD homo Wallef Comitis, *Cambr.* 202 b.

SIUUARD presbyter, *Linc.* 336 ter.[1]

SIUUARD Welle, *Derb.* 275 b.

SIUUARDUS, *Hants,* 50 b. *Berks,* 60 b. bis. 61 b. *Wilts,*
    71. *Somers.* 93, 99.[2] *Dev.* 106 b. 108, 115 b. *Oxf.*
    156 b. *Glouc.* 168. *Cambr.* 190. *Northampt.* 224
    bis. 227. *Leic.* 236 b. *Shropsh.* 260.[2] *Yorksh.*
    316 b. *Linc.* 350 b. bis. 353 b. 356, 357 b. 358,
    358 b. *Yorksh.* 373 b. bis. *Clam. S. R. Linc.* 375.
    Clam. in Chetst. 377. *Essex,* 35 b. 56 b. 66 b. 73
    passim. 74, 74 b. bis. 75 bis. 75 b. bis.

SIUUARDUS Comes, *Hunt.* 203,[3] 208.[4] *Yorksh.* 305 ter.

SIUUARDUS homo Heraldi Comitis, *Buck.* 146. *Cambr.*
    190 b.

---

[1] He was one of the Lagemen of Lincoln, T. R. E. At
the time of the Survey, he had been succeeded in that
office by Leduuin the son of Reuene.

[2] Also at the time of forming the Survey.

[3] Earl Siward's house in Huntingdon is mentioned here.
" Siwardus habuit I. mansionem cum domo, cum saca et
soca, quieta ab omni consuetudine, quam modo habet Judita
comitissa."

[4] " Testantur homines de Comitatu quod rex Edwardus
dedit Suineshefet Siuuardo comiti, soccam et sacam, et sic
habuit Haroldus comes, præter quod geldabant in Hund.
et in hostem cum eis ibant."

Siuuardus liber homo, *Shropsh.* 260 b.[1] *Essex,* 28.
  Suff. 377 b.

Siuuardus rufus, *Clam. W. R. Linc.* 376 b.

Siuuardus sochemannus R. E. *Hertf.* 136 b.

Siuuardus tegnus Regis, *Essex,* 72 b.

Siuuardus teinus et cognatus regis E. *Heref.* 180 b.

Siuuart, *Nottingh.* 287 b.

Siuuat, *Linc.* 359 b.

Siuuate, *Oxf.* 159. *Linc.* 355 b. *Clam. N. R. Linc.*
  375 b. bis. 376.

Siuuinus, *Clam. N. R. Linc.* 376.

Siuuoldus, *Somers.* 99. *Suff.* 340 b. 342 b.

Siuuradus homo S. arch. *Hertf.* 133 b.

Smail, *Wilts,* 72 b.

Smalo, *Wilts,* 72 b.

Smerius, *Suff.* 378.

Smert, *Suff.* 320 b.

Smeuuin, *Somers.* 94 bis.

Snellinc, *Cambr.* 191.

Snerri homo Eddeuæ pulchræ, *Hertf.* 137.

Snoch, Eduuardus, *Kent,* 10.

Snode, *Dev.* 113.

---

[1] There is a passage in the " Commemoratio Placiti
inter Wlstanum Episcopum Wigorn. et Walterum Abbatem
de Evvesham," a proceeding of the Conqueror's time,
printed in Heming's Chartulary of the Church of Worcester, tom. i. p. 80, in which this Siuuard of Shropshire
seems to be alluded to. " Affuit etiam *Siwardus dives
homo de Scropscyre,* et Osbernus filius Ricardi, et Turchil
de Warewicscyre, et multi alii seniores et nobiles, quorum
major pars jam dormiunt. Multi autem adhuc superstites
sunt qui illos audierunt, et adhuc multi de tempore regis
Willelmi idem testificantes."

SNOT, *Dev.* 109 b.

SOARTIN, *Hants,* 53.

SOARTINUS, *Hants,* 54.[1]

SOCHEMANNUS quidam, *Hertf.* 135 b. *Cambr.* 202.

SOCHEMANNUS unus, homo Anschil de Waras, *Hertf.* 138 b.

SOCHEMANNUS homo Gueræ comitis, *Hertf.* 138 b.

SOCHEMANNUS unus, *Hertf.* 133 bis.[1] 140.[1] *Cambr.* 194 b. 195 b. 196 b. *Bedf.* 218 b. *Essex,* 23 b. 35, 39 b. *Norf.* 129, 129 b. bis. 178 b.

SOCHEMANNUS unus Comitis Algari, *Cambr.* 198 b.

SOCHEMANNUS unus sub Edeua, *Cambr.* 194.

SOCHEMANNUS unus Edrici commend. *Norf.* 124 b. bis.

SOCHEMANNUS commend. I. Edrici, *Suff.* 326, 326 b.

SOCHEMANNUS unus Edrici de Laxsefelda, *Norf.* 182.

SOCHEMANNUS unus Guert, *Norf.* 145, 145 b.

SOCHEMANNUS unus, homo Heraldi, *Norf.* 146, 158 b.

SOCHEMANNUS unus Horoldi,[2] *Norf.* 236 b.

SOCHEMANNUS unus Regis, *Hertf.* 142 b.[1] *Cambr.* 199 b. 200 b. 201.

SOCHEMANNUS I. Rad. Stalra, *Norf.* 229 b.

SOCHEMANNUS unus Stigandi archiepiscopi, *Norf.* 124 b.

SOCHEMANNUS I. Vlnotus nomine, *Suff.* 315 b.

SOCHEMANNUS homo Abbatis S. Albani, *Hertf.* 140.

SOCHEMANNUS homo Aluuini uari, *Buck.* 144.

SOCHEMANNUS homo Asgari, *Hertf.* 139 b.

SOCHEMANNUS homo Eddeuæ pulchræ, *Hertf.* 140 b.

SOCHEMANNUS homo Leuuini Com. *Buck.* 144.

SOCHEMANNUS unus homo S. archiepiscopi, *Buck.* 146.

SOCHEMANNUS R. E. *v.* LEPSI. VLURIC.

---

[1] Also at the taking of the Survey.
[2] *Sc.* Heroldi.

SOCHEMANNI homines duo, *Midd.* 129 b. *Hertf.* 132
  bis. *Cambr.* 194 b. 195,[1] 195 b. bis. 198 bis. *Bedf.*
  213 b. bis. 214, 215 b. 216 b. 217 b. bis. 218.

SOCHEMANNI duo, *Essex*, 39, 39 b. 77. *Norf.* 158 b.

SOCHEMANNI duo, homines Alberti Lothariensis, *Midd.*
  129.

SOCHEMANNI homines duo Algari Comitis, *Hertf.* 141 b.
  Cambr. 198 b. bis. 201 b.

SOCHEMANNI duo; horum unus homo Algari Comitis,
  alter homo Eldret, *Hertf.* 141 b.

SOCHEMANNI duo; unus homo Algari comitis, alter de
  soca Regis, *Hertf.* 133 b.

SOCHEMANNI duo Anschilli, *Bedf.* 218.

SOCHEMANNI duo, homines Asgari Stalre, *Hertf.* 140,
  142.

SOCHEMANNI duo; unus homo Avelini et alter Alueue
  sororis Heraldi Comitis, *Buck.* 144 b.

SOCHEMANNI duo, homines Azoris, *Midd.* 130.

SOCHEMANNI homines II. de Brictric, *Bedf.* 215 b.

SOCHEMANNI homines duo Eddeue, *Hertf.* 137. *Cambr.*
  193 b.

SOCHEMANNI duo sub Eddeua, *Cambr.* 198 b. *Suff.* 397.

SOCHEMANNI duo Edrici, *Norf.* 124 b. *Suff.* 315 b.

SOCHEMANNI homines duo R. E. *Hertf.* 140 b. 141 b.
  Cambr. 195 b. 199 bis. 200, 202. *Bedf.* 213 b.
  218 b.

SOCHEMANNI duo; unus huscarl R. E. et alter homo
  Leuuini Comitis, *Hertf.* 136 b.

SOCHEMANNI duo abbatis de Ely, *Cambr.* 199, 200.

SOCHEMANNI duo; unus horum homo abbatis de Ely,
  alter homo regis E. *Cambr.* 201.

---

[1] Also at the Survey.

Soc. ii. Goduuini, *Suff.* 315.

Sochemanni homines ii. Godwini benefelle, *Hertf.* 138.

Sochemanni duo Guert, *Norf.* 145 b.

Sochemanni duo Comitis Heroldi, *Cambr.* 197 b.

Sochemanni homines duo homines Comitis Leuuini, *Hertf.* 134.

Sochemanni duo; unus homo Leuuini Comitis alter homo Heraldi Comitis, *Buck.* 144.

Sochemanni ii. Rob. fil. Wimarc, *Cambr.* 197 b.

Sochemanni duo Stigandi, *Norf.* 144 b.

Sochemanni homines duo Stigandi archiep. *Hertf.* 134 b. 141 b. bis. 142.

Sochemanni duo; unus homo Stigandi archiepiscopi, alter homo Algari Comitis, *Cambr.* 198 b.

Sochemanni duo; unus homo S. archiepiscopi, alter homo Wallef, *Cambr.* 200 b.

Sochemanni duo; unus homo Wallef, alter homo Regis, *Cambr.* 198 b.

Sochemanni duo; unus homo Wallef et alter homo Roberti filii Wimarc, *Cambr.* 198 b.

Sochemanni tres, *Hertf.* 134 b. 140 b. *Cambr.* 193 b. 196, 198, 200. *Bedf.* 211 b.[1] 213 b. bis. 214 b. 216, 216 b. 217 b. bis. *Essex,* 39 b. *Norf.* 129, 129 b.

Sochemanni tres; horum unus homo Algari, alter homo Rob. f. Wimarch, tercius homo R. E. *Cambr.* 200 b.

Sochemanni tres; horum duo homines Anschil de Wares, tertius homo Aluric Blac, *Hertf.* 141 b.

Sochemanni tres; duo eorum homines Asgari stalri, et tertius homo S. Albani, *Hertf.* 139 b.

---

[1] They continued in this entry at the Survey.

SOCHEMANNI tres, homines Azoris, *Midd.* 130.

SOCHEMANNI tres; unus homo S. Edildredæ, alter homo abbatis [de Ely] tercius homo Wallef, *Cambr.* 201 b.

SOCHEMANNI tres; horum unus homo Eddeuæ pulchræ, alter homo Algari, tercius homo Guerd, *Hertf.* 141 b.

SOCHEMANNI tres, homines R. E. *Hertf.* 140. *Cambr.* 199, 201. *Bedf.* 213 b.

SOCHEMANNI tres; unus horum homo R. E. fuit, alter homo Leuuini, tertius homo Azoris, *Midd.* 130.

SOCHEMANNI tres; horum unus homo Regis, alter homo S. archiepiscopi, tercius homo Wallef. *Cambr.* 202 b.

SOCHEMANNI tres abbatis de Ely, *Cambr.* 201.

SOCHEMANNI homines III. Engelrici, *Hertf.* 137.

SOCHEMANNI tres Heroldi, *Norf.* 158 b.

SOCHEMANNI tres Comitis Heraldi, *Cambr.* 202.

SOCHEMANNI tres; horum duo homines Heraldi Comitis, et tertius homo Ingoldi, *Buck.* 146.

SOCHEMANNI tres Stigandi archiep. *Hertf.* 134 b. bis. 201.

SOCHEMANNI tres; horum unus homo Stig. arch., alter homo Rob. f. Wimarc, tertius sochemannus R. E. *Hertf.* 133 b.

SOCHEMANNI III; unus homo S. arch. alter homo Leuuini Com. tertius homo Avelini, *Buck.* 144.

SOCHEMANNI homines III. Vlmari de Etone, *Bedf.* 212.

SOCHEMANNI tres; unus eorum homo Willelmi Episcopi, alter homo Asgari stalre, et tertius homo Eddeuæ pulchræ, *Hertf.* 134.

SOCHEMANNI homines quatuor, *Hertf.* 134 b. bis. 141. *Cambr.* 194, 198, 200. *Bedf.* 214, 216, 218. *Norf.* 110.

SOCHEMANNI quatuor, homines Aelmeri de Belintone, *Hertf.* 141.

SOCHEMANNI quatuor; tres homines Algari Comitis, et quartus homo Wallef, *Cambr.* 202.

SOCHEMANNI quatuor; horum unus homo Algari Comitis, alii homines Wallef Comitis, *Cambr.* 202.

SOCHEMANNI quatuor de soca Asgari stalri, *Hertf.* 139 b.

SOCHEMANNI quatuor; duo eorum homines Asgari stalri, tertius homo Heraldi Comitis, et quartus homo Aluuini de Godtone, *Hertf.* 140.

SOCHEMANNI quatuor; tres homines Brictrici, quartus homo Wige, *Buck.* 148 b.

SOCHEMANNI quatuor, homines R. E. *Hertf.* 140 b. *Cambr.* 201 b. *Bedf.* 213 b. 217.

SOCHEMANNI quatuor; tres homines R. E. quartus homo Edeuæ pulchræ, *Cambr.* 201 b.

SOCHEMANNI quatuor Abbatis de Ely, *Cambr.* 199.

SOCHEMANNI quatuor Stigandi, *Norf.* 159, 165 b.

SOCHEMANNI quatuor, homines Stigandi archiepiscopi, *Bedf.* 211 b.

SOCHEMANNI quatuor; unus horum homo Stigandi archiep. et alii tres Abbatis de Ramsey. *Cambr.* 198 b.

SOCHEMANNI homines quatuor Wallef Comitis, *Cambr.* 201 b.

SOCHEMANNI quinque, *Hertf.* 137 b.

SOCHEMANNI quinque; horum III. homines Algari Comitis, quartus homo Guert Comitis, quintus homo Heraldi Comitis, *Hertf.* 141 b.

SOCHEMANNI quinque; unus horum homo Algari
Comitis, et alii homines Regis E. *Cambr.*
198 b.

SOCHEMANNI quinque sub Eddeva, *Cambr.* 195.[1]

SOCHEMANNI homines v. regis E. *Cambr.* 200. *Bedf.*
218 b.

SOCHEMANNI quinque Abbatis de Ely, *Hunt.* 203.

SOCHEMANNI homines v. Vlmari, *Bedf.* 218.

SOCHEMANNI sex, *Cambr.* 193 b. bis. 194 bis. 195,
197 b. bis.[2] *Bedf.* 214 b. 215, 216 b. 217 b. 218 b.
Norf. 125, 129.

SOCHEMANNI vi. Aldredæ, *Suff.* 403.

SOCHEMANNI sex; horum iiii. homines Almer de Ba-
linton, quintus homo Stigandi archiep. sextus homo
R. E. *Hertf.* 141 b.

SOCHEMANNI sex; horum unus homo Asgari, alii v.
homines R. E. *Cambr.* 200 b.

SOCHEMANNI homines vi. Borret, *Bedf.* 210.

SOCHEMANNI sex; horum unus homo Eddeue, alii
homines abbatis de Ely, *Cambr.* 201.

SOCHEMANNI vii. *Cambr.* 195 b. 198 b.[1] *Bedf.* 214 ter.
Norf. 129.

SOCHEMANNI septem Regis E. *Cambr.* 200 b.

SOCHEMANNI septem Stigandi, *Norf.* 163 b.

SOCHEMANNI viii. *Bedf.* 214 b. 215, 217. *Northampt.*
326. *Essex*, 39 bis.

SOCHEMANNI viii. abbatis de Ely, *Cambr.* 200.

SOCHEMANNI octo; horum sex homines Regis fuerunt,
septimus homo R. fil. Wimarc, et octavus homo
Algari Comitis, *Cambr.* 198 b.

---

[1] Also at the time of the Survey.
[2] In one of the two, also at the Survey.

SOCHEMANNI octo; horum tres homines Stig. archiepiscopi, *Cambr.* 200.

SOCHEMANNI octo; horum duo homines R. E.; tres
homines S. archiepiscopi; unus homo Guerd
Comitis; unus homo Rob. f. Wimarc; et unus
homo Vlmari de Ettone, *Cambr.* 200 b.

SOCHEMANNI IX. Comitis Algari, *Essex,* 98 b.

SOCHEMANNI IX. Asgari stalri, *Hertf.* 137 b.

SOCHEMANNI homines X. *Cambr.* 190 b. 199. *Bedf.*
214 b. *Norf.* 129 b.

SOCHEMANNI X. Ex his VII. homines R. E., duo homines
Eddeue, decimus autem homo abbatis de Ely,
Cambr. 201.

SOCHEMANNI XI. *Buck.* 148 b. *Bedf.* 214 b. 218 b.[1]

SOCHEMANNI XI. Stigandi, *Norf.* 163 b.

SOCHEMANNI XII. *Bedf.* 214 b. 215.

SOCHEMANNI XII. Stigandi, *Norf.* 165.

SOCHEMANNI XII. horum VII. homines regis E. alii V.
homines Abbatis de Ely, *Cambr.* 201.

SOCHEMANNI XIII. *Cambr.* 195. *Norf.* 141 b.

SOCHEMANNI XIIII. *Cambr.* 200 b. *Bedf.* 218 b.

SOCHEMANNI XV; horum XI. homines regis E. alii tres
sub abbate de Ely, unus homo Sexi, *Cambr.* 201.

SOCHEMANNI XVI. *Cambr.* 200. *Bedf.* 215.

SOCHEMANNI XVI. Heroldi, *Norf.* 235 b.

SOCHEMANNI XVI. Stigandi, *Norf.* 158.

SOCHEMANNI XIX.; sex horum homines R. E. alii quatuor
homines Eddeuæ, et alii V. homines abbatis de Ely,
Cambr. 199.

SOCHEMANNI XX. *Bedf.* 215. *Norf.* 147.

SOCHEMANNI XX.; unus homo Algari Comitis, alii
homines R. E. *Cambr.* 200.

---

[1] The same Sochemen continued at the Survey.

SOCHEMANNI XXI. *Bedf.* 214.

SOCHEMANNI XXIII.; duo horum homines Stigandi archiepiscopi, septem homines Algari Comitis, et unus
homo Edeuæ, alii XIIII. homines R. E. *Cambr.*
200.

SOCHEMANNI XXIIII. *Cambr.* 200.

SOCHEMANNI XXVII. *Norf.* 129.

SOL, *Heref.* 181.

SONNEUA, *Yorksh.* 298.

SONULF, *Yorksh.* 301, 307 bis.

SONULFUS, *Yorksh.* 373.

SONULFUS presbyter, *Yorksh.* 298.

SORCHES, *Suff.* 322.

SORCHOUED, *Yorksh.* 306.

SOROR Stigandi, *Norf.* 116.

SORT, *Yorksh.* 298.

SORTCOL, *Yorksh.* 300 b.

SORTCOLF, *Yorksh.* 300 b. bis.

SORTE, *Nottingh.* 285 b.

SORTEBRAND, *Nottingh.* 293. *Linc.* 370 b. ter.

SOTA, *Linc.* 366.

SOTEMAN, *Dev.* 112 b.

SOTINZ, homo Tosti Comitis, *Buck.* 152.

SOUBERIE, Goduinus de, teignus R. E. *Hertf.* 138.

SPARHAUOC, *Suff.* 297.

SPARHAUOC liber homo commendatus Edrico, *Suff.* 308.

SPERAUOC, *Nottingh.* 286 b.

SPERHAUOC, *Nottingh.* 286 b. bis.

SPERRI, *Linc.* 352, 365.

SPERUN, commendatus Burcardo, *Suff.* 374 b.

SPIETA liber homo commend. *Suff.* 420 b.

SPILLE, *Linc.* 347.

SPIRITES, *Kent*, 1 b. *Hants*, 49.

SPIRITES presbyter, *Heref.* 183.

SPIRTES, *Wilts*, 73. *Heref.* 183 ter. *Shropsh.* 260 b.

SPIRTES presbyter, *Somers.* 91. *Shropsh.* 260 b.

SPORT, *Yorksh.* 310.[1]

SPRETMANUS, *Suff.* 340 b.

SPROT, *Derb.* 276. *Yorksh.* 301 bis. 306 b. 309 b. 310, 313 bis. 323, 327 b. 331 b. 373. *Essex,* 66 b.

SPROTTULFUS, *Nottingh.* 282 b. 284 b.

SPUDA, Edricus, *Suff.* 395 b.

SPUR, Edric, teignus R. E. *Cambr.* 200.

STAIGRIM, *Linc.* 347.

STAINULF, *Inter Rip. et Mers.* 269 b. *Yorksh.* 315, 317 b. bis. 318 bis.

STAINULFUS, *Yorksh.* 318 bis.

Stalra, Angerus, *Norf.* 248. *Suff.* 440.

Stalra seu *Stalre,* Radulfus, *Cornw.* 121 b. *Linc.* 337 b. 347, 347 b. bis. 348 ter. 348 b. *Clam. in Chetst.* 377. *Norf.* 122 b. 158, 158 b. 217 b. 218 b. 229 b. 265. *Suff.* 293, 297, 409 b. 411 b. 431.

Stalre, Ednod, *Berks,* 58 b.

Stalre, Harold, *Linc.* 337.

Stalrel, Radulfus, *Linc.* 337.

Stalrus, Bondi, *Bedf.* 218 b.

Stalrus, Esgar, *Hertf.* 132.

STAM *Yorksh.* 332.

STANARDUS, *Essex,* 98 b. *Suff.* 441 b.

STANART, *Suff.* 320 b. 419.

STANCHIL,[2] *Berks,* 60 b. 224. *Linc.* 352 bis. 371.

---

[1] The same person with Sprot.

[2] He had held Chingestune (Kingston Bagpuze) in the time of King Edward the Confessor. His land at the Survey belonged to Henry de Ferrariis. The Abingdon Register, evidently alluding to the same land and person, calls him

STANFLEDA, *Suff.* 341.

STANGRIM, *Linc.* 359. *Clam. W. R. Linc.* 376.

STANHARDUS, *Essex*, 20.

STANHART liber homo commend. Edrici, *Suff.* 320 b.

STANKER, *Suff.* 425 b.

STANMAR, *Suff.* 424.

STANMARUS, *Suff.* 339 b. 340 b.

STANNECHETEL, *Warw.* 243.[1]

STANUINUS commend. Edrici, *Suff.* 318 b.

STANUINUS commendatus Edrico, et postea homo Haroldi, *Suff.* 313, 313 b.

STANUINUS liber homo, *Suff.* 295.

STANUINUS liber homo commendatus Haroldo, *Suff.* 332.

STAPLEUIN, *Nottingh.* 287 b.

STAPLEUINE, *Derb.* 273.

STAPLEUUINUS, *Nottingh.* 287.

STARI, Aluricus, *Suff.* 395.

Turkillus, makes him in the interim of time to have transferred the superiority over his land at Chingestune to the Abbey of Abingdon, and adds that he died in the battle of Hastings.

" Nam quidam dives, Turkillus nomine, sub Heraldo, comitis testimonio et consultu de se, cum sua terra quæ KINGESTUN dicitur Ecclesiæ Abbendonensi et abbati Ordrico homaguim fecit, (licitum quippe libero cuique illo in tempore sic agere erat,) quatinus prædictæ villæ dominatio sub hujus Ecclesiæ perpetuo jure penderet. Hic cum in bello memorato occubuisset terram cujus dominationis investituram multo ante tempore quam bellum foret Ecclesia in manus habebat, Henricus de Ferrariis sibi usurpavit, abbate invalido obstare." MS. Cotton. Claud. C. IX. fol. 133.

[1] Also at the taking of the Survey.

STARLINC, *Suff.* 430 bis.

STARLINGUS, *Suff.* 297.

STATFORD, Canonici de, *Staff.* 247 b.

STAUHART, *Suff.* 332 b.

STEIN, *Chesh.* 263 b. bis.

STEINCHETEL, *Chesh.* 266 b.

STEINULF, *Heref.* 185 b. *Derb.* 273 b. passim. 278.

STEN, *Shropsh.* 254.

STENESNOC, *Hants*, 45 b.

STENULF, *Shropsh.* 254. *Chesh.* 266 b. 267 b. *Nottingh.* 285 b.

STENULFUS, *Chesh.* 264 b. *Yorksh.* 312.

STEPI, *Nottingh.* 290. *Linc.* 358 b.

STEPIOT, *Linc.* 340 b.

STER, *Linc.* 361 b.

STERCHER, *Essex*, 85 b.

STERCHERUS teignus R. E. *Hunt.* 209.

STERGAR huscarla Regis E. *Norf.* 266.

STERR, *Yorksh.* 298.

STERRE, *Hants*, 45 b. *Yorksh.* 298.

STICHEHARE, Aluuinus, *Midd.* 130 b.

STIGAND archiepiscopus, *Bedf.* 216 bis. 217 ter.

STIGANDI soror, *Norf.* 116.

STIGANDI archiepiscopi homines, *Bedf.* 211 b.

STIGANDUS, *Norf.* 136, 136 b. ter. 137 b. bis. 138 b. bis. 140 b. 141 ter. 142 bis. 143, 143 b. 191, 195, 197 b. 201, 210 b. 221 b. 222 b. 227 b. 228 b. 229 b. 230, 232 b. 244, 248 b. 251 b. 256, 256 b. 271, 274 b. *Suff.* 288 b. 289 passim. 322 b. 323, 331, 337, 412 b. 423, 426, 438, 447 b. 450 bis.

STIGANDUS, [*sc.* Archiep.] *Buck.* 143 b. *Norf.* 173, 173 b. ter. 176, 176 b. 177, 177 b. 180 b. 181 b. *Suff.* 372 b.

STIGANDUS Archiepiscopus, *Kent,* 1 b. 9 b.   *Surr.* 30.
　　Hants, 38, 40 b. bis. 43 b.   *Berks,* 58 bis.   *Dors.*
　　80.   *Somers.* 87 b. bis.   *Midd.* 127.   *Hertf.* 135,
　　135 b. 138, 142 b. bis.   *Bucks,* 142 b. bis.   *Oxf.*
　　155, 157.   *Glouc.* 164, 164 b. passim. 167 b. 169.
　　Norf. 175 b. bis.   *Cambr.* 189 b. 190 bis. 196,
　　199 b.   *Northampt.* 223.

STIGANDUS Episcopus, *Suff.* 412, 445.

STIKESTAC, Aluricus, *Suff.* 339 b. bis.

STILLA, Aluuinus, *Hants,* 40.

STILLE, Aluuinus liber homo, *Essex,* 71.

STINGANDUS, *Norf.* 140.   *Suff.* 288.

Stirman, Edricus, *Worc.* 173 b.

Stirman Regis E. v. TURCHIL. VLFECH.

STORI, *Warw.* 238 b.   *Derb.* 275.   *Nottingh.* 282 b. pas-
　　sim.   *Yorksh.* 326, 336, 337, 350 b. 351.

STORI homo Tosti Comitis, *Bedf.* 216 b.

STORIUS, *Suff.* 435.

STOU, S. Mar. *Linc.* 344.

STRAMI, *Wilts,* 74 b.

STRAMUN, Osmond, *Somers.* 94 b.

STRANG danus, *Glouc.* 170.

STRANGULFUS, *Suff.* 395.

STREMIUS, *Wilts,* 69 b.

STRIC, *Hunt.* 206.   *Northampt.* 228 b. 229.

STRUI, *Linc.* 352 b.

STRUOSTUNA, Goda de, *Suff.* 314 b.

STUBART, commend. Edrici, *Suff.* 320 b.

STUR, *Linc.* 361 b.

SUAIN, *Surr.* 32. *Wilts,* 69 b. 71.   *Dors.* 79 b.   *Somers.*
　　92 b. 99.   *Oxf.* 157 b.   *Northampt.* 227 b. passim.
　　Leic. 233.   *Warw.* 242, 243 bis.   *Staff.* 248 bis.
　　249.   *Shropsh.* 259 b.   *Derb.* 274, 276, 276 b. *Not-*

tingh. 288 b. bis. 289, 290 bis. 291 passim. *v.* SUEIN. SUEN. SUUEN.

SUAIN cilt, *Derb.* 276 b. bis.

SUAIN liber homo, *Staff.* 248.

SUAINI pater, *Wilts*, 74. *Dors.* 84,[1] 84 b.[1]

SUAN cilt, *Derb.* 276 b. bis.[2]

SUAN f. Suaue, *Linc.* 337. *v.* SUEN.

SUANUS, *Essex*, 84 b.

SUANUS vicecomes, *Essex*, 19 b.

SUARDCOL, *Yorksh.* 301.

SUARINUS presbyter, *Suff.* 377.

SUART, *Norf.* 243 b.

SUART hoga, *Suff.* 314.

SUART lingus, *Suff.* 334 b.

SUART, Suenus, *Essex*, 78 b. 91.

SUARTCOL, *Yorksh.* 329, 332 bis.

SUARTIN, *Hants*, 39 b.

SUARTIN f. Griboldi, *Linc.* 336.[3]

SUARTINC, *Linc.* 336.

SUARTINC liber homo, *Norf.* 206 b.

SUARTING, *Hants*, 51.

SUARTING homo Asgari stalre, *Buck.* 149 b.

SUARTINGIUS, *Suff.* 443.

SUARTINGUS, *Suff.* 314, 442 b. 443 b.

SUARTINUS homo Asgari stalre, *Buck.* 147 b.

SUARTLINUS, *Northampt.* 227.

SUARTRIC commend. Heraldo, *Suff.* 449.

---

[1] " Filius ejus," tempore Descriptionis.

[2] The same person with Suain cilt above.

[3] He was one of the Lagemen of Lincoln, and the same person who is called Suartinc in the next entry of the Index.

SUARTRICUS liber homo commendat. Haroldi, *Suff.*
320.

SUATRICUS abbas, *Dev.* 105 b.

SUAUE, *Linc.* 348 b.

SUDAN, *Yorksh.* 313.

SUDWELLE, S. Mariá de, *Nottingh.* 283.

SUEIN, *Surr.* 34. *Hants*, 49 b. *Glouc.* 164. *Shropsh.*
258 bis. *v.* SUAIN. SUEN. SUUEN.

SUEN, *Surr.* 36. *Shropsh.* 258 ter. *Nottingh.* 285, 287 b.
289, 291 b. *Yorksh.* 315 b. *Linc.* 337, 348 b. 350,
357, 357 b. 365, 371, 373 b. 376 bis. *v.* SUAIN.
SUEIN. SUUEN.

SUEN cilt, *Nottingh.* 288 b.

SUEN homo Asgari stalre, *Buck.* 149 b. ter.

SUEN liber homo, *Shropsh.* 254 b.

SUEN f. Suaue, *Nottingh.* 280 b. *Linc.* 336. *v.* SUAN.

SUEN Suert homo Eduuini comitis, *Buck.* 147 b.

SUEN homo Heraldi comitis, *Hertf.* 134 b. *Buck.* 151.

SUEN teignus R. E. *Buck.* 152 b.

SUENI pater, *Essex*, 43 b.[1] *v.* SUEINI pater.

SUENINC homo Heraldi comitis, *Buck.* 151.

SUENUS homo Aluuini uari, *Buck.* 144.

SUENUS Suart, *Essex*, 78 b. 91. *Suff.* 445 b.

SUENUS Vicecomes, *Essex*, 2 b. 7.

SUERT, Magno, *Surr.* 36 b. *v.* SWERT.

SUERTINGUS, *Suff.* 403.

SUET, *Dev.* 105.

SUETEMAN homo Vlmeri de Etone, *Bedf.* 218.

SUETINGUS, *Suff.* 341.

SUETINGUS liber homo, 36.

SUETMAN liber homo, *Norf.* 177.

" Suenus ipse successor," T. R. W.

Suetmanus, *Suff.* 340.

Suetth, *Somers.* 94.

Suga, *Chesh.* 268.

Suglo homo Alrici filii Godingi, *Bedf.* 214.

Sumersul, *Yorksh.* 327 b.

Summerde, *Linc.* 341.

Summerdus, *Clam. S. R. Linc.* 375.

Summerled, *Hunt.* 206 b. *Linc.* 340 b. 351 b. 356 b.

Summerlede, *Yorksh.* 300 b. *Linc.* 371.

Suneman, *Yorksh.* 301 b. *Suff.* 340 b.

Sunwinus, *Suff.* 422 b.

Super Dive, Ecclesia, *Berks,* 59.

Suuain, *Derb.* 278.

Suuarger, *Yorksh.* 325.

Suwart, *Suff.* 295 b. 296.

Suuen, *Yorksh.* 305 passim. 316, 316 b. 317 bis. 317 b. passim. 319 b. passim. 320, 324 b. passim. 325 bis. 329 b. bis. 330 b. *Linc.* 340,[1] 341, 343, 343 b. 352 bis. 352 b. *v.* Suain. Suein. Suen.

Suuen, homo Heraldi Comitis, *Hertf.* 140, 140 b. bis.

Swert, Mannius, teinnus, *Suff.* 292 b. bis. *v.* Suert.

Syric homo Eddid reginæ, *Buck.* 147 b.

T.

T. abb.[2] *Linc.* 345 b.

Taini, Teini, *seu* Teigni; in Wich vocato Norwich, *Chesh.* 268.

---

[1] The sons of Suen held the land of this entry at the time of the Survey.

[2] Turoldus, or Thorold, a Norman, Abbot of Peterborough from 1069 to 1098. See the Saxon Chronicle.

TAINI duo, *Berks*, 63 b. *Wilts*, 70, 71 bis. 71 b. 74 b.
bis. *Dors.* 75 b. bis. 79, 79 b. bis. 80, 80 b. 82 bis.
82 b. bis. 83 b. 84, 84 b. *Somers.* 87 b. 89 bis. 89 b.
90, 90 b. 92 ter. 92 b. passim. 93, 93 b. 94, 94 b.
passim. 95 bis. 95 b. 96 passim. 98 b. ter. *Dev.*
102 b. 104 b. 105, 105 b. 110, 111, 112, 112 b. bis.
114 b. 115, 116. *Hertf.* 133 b. bis. *Buck.* 145 b.
Glouc. 169, 169 b. *Bedf.* 211 b. 214. *Northampt.*
227 b. 229. *Staff.* 250. *Inter Rip. et Mers.* 269 b.
bis. *Yorksh.* 299 b. 300, 302 b. 305 b. bis.
315.

TAINI duo in paragio, *Dors.* 79, 79 b. 80, 84, 84 b.
Dev. 115 bis. 116 b. 117, 117 b.

TAINI duo, Aluuard et Aluui homo ejus, *Buck.* 147 b.

TAINI duo, Borret et Vluric homo ejus, *Buck.* 145 b.

TAINI duo, homines Brictric, *Buck.* 150.

TAINI duo, Regis E. *Hertf.* 140 b.

TAINI duo, homines R. E. *Hertf.* 137 b.

TAINI duo, horum unus homo R. E. et alter homo
Asgari stalri, *Hertf.* 713 b.

TAINI duo, unus horum homo Regis Edwardi, et alter
homo Heraldi comitis, *Midd.* 129.

TAINI duo, Godricus et Wilaus, *Buck.* 144 b.

TAINI duo, Heraldus et Aluui, *Buck.* 149.

TAINI duo, unus homo Heraldi comitis alter Leurici,
Glouc. 169 b.

TAINI duo, Leuric et Oluiet, *Buck.* 150 b.

TAINI duo, Rauaius et Vluuardus, *Buck.* 153.

TAINI duo, Sibi et Goduin homines Alrici filii Goding,
Buck. 150 b.

TAINI duo, homines Tosti Comitis, *Bedf.* 214.

TAINI duo, unus homo Wallef Comitis, *Buck.* 145 b.

TAINI tres, *Berks*, 59 b. 63, 63 b. *Wilts*, 72 b. 73 b.
74 b. *Dors.* 77, 79, 79 b. ter. 83, 83 b. 85. *Somers.*

87, 88 b. 89 bis. 92, 92 b. 93, 93 b. 94, 94 b. 95 b.
98 bis. 99 bis. *Dev.* 115, 116.[1] *Buck.* 145 b. 150 b.
Oxf. 158, 161. *Northampt.* 224 b. *Leic.* 234, 236.
Warw. 239 b. 240. *Staff.* 249 b. ter. *Shropsh.* 254
bis. 260. *Inter Rip. et Mers.* 269 b. passim. *Yorksh.*
300 b. passim. 301 bis. 329 b. 330 b. bis.[2]

TAINI tres in paragio, *Wilts,* 70 b. *Dors.* 79 b. 80 bis.
80 b. 81 b. 83 b. *Dev.* 114.

TAINI tres, *Dors.* 75 b.

TAINI tres cum uno clerico, *Somers.* 92 b.

TAINI tres Reginæ Eddid, *Hertf.* 135.

TAINI tres Regis E. *Bedf.* 217.

TAINI tres, Godric, Elric, et Ernui, *Glouc.* 167 b.

TAINI tres, horum unus Goduinus homo Heraldi comitis, alter Tori huscarle R. E., tertius Aluric homo
Eddid reginæ, *Buck.* 152.

TAINI tres, horum unus homo Leuuini Comitis, alter
homo Goduini cilt abbatis Westmon., tertius homo
Aluredi de Withunga, *Buck.* 146.

TAINI tres, duo homines Burgeret, tertius homo Alrici,
Buck. 146 b.

TAINI quatuor, *Dors.* 77 b. 82 b. 83, 84. *Somers.* 87 b.
88, 89 bis. 93 bis. 98. *Dev.* 105, 107, 108 b. *Bedf.*
214, 217, 218 b. *Northampt.* 223 b. 227 b.
Warw. 240 b. 242, 244 b. *Staff.* 249 ter. 249 b.
Shropsh. 259 b. *Inter Rip. et Mers.* 269 b.
Nottingh. 293. *Yorksh.* 300 b. 301 bis. 301 b. bis.
329 b. 331.

TAINI quatuor in paragio, *Dors.* 83 b. *Dev.* 115 b.
116 b.

TAINI quatuor pariter, *Wilts,* 73 b.

---

[1] Also at the time of the Survey.

[2] In one of these entries they continued at the Survey.

Taini quatuor, Aluuinus, Eduuinus, Almarus, et Thori, *Buck.* 147 b.

Taini quatuor, horum unus homo Aluuini, et alter homo Aluuini de Neuham, et tertius homo Aluuardi, et quartus homo Azori, *Buck.* 146.

Taini quatuor R. E. *Cambr.* 202.

Taini quatuor, unus homo Leuuini Comitis, alter homo Wluuen, tertius homo Leuuini de Mentmore, et quartus homo Brictrici, *Bucks*, 152.

Taini quatuor, Osulf, Osmund, Roulf, et Leuric, *Leic.* 233 b.

Taini quinque, *Wilts*, 73. *Dors.* 77, 79 b. 80 b. 82, 82 b. 83 b. *Somers.* 92, 92 b. 93. *Dev.* 114 b. *Buck.* 147 b. *Oxf.* 160 b. *Heref.* 180 b. *Bedf.* 214. *Northampt.* 223 b. *Leic.* 236 b. 237. *Staff.* 249 b. *Inter Rip. et Mers.* 269 b. bis. *Nottingh.* 286 b. bis. *Yorksh.* 301, 329 bis. 329 b. bis.

Taini quinque in paragio, *Dev.* 111 b. 116.

Taini quinque Eduini Comitis, Erniet, Aluuinus, Brictredus, Frane, Aluuold, *Worc.* 172.

Taini quinque, Heroldus unus eorum, Goduinus presbyter, Estanus, Godric homo Heroldi, Alueua uxor Heroldi, *Buck.* 149.

Taini quinque, Justan, Aseloc Durand, Eluuard, Vlman, Aseloc, *Nottingh.* 285 b.

Taini sex, *Dors.* 79 b. bis. *Somers.* 95 b. *Buck.* 147. *Staff.* 248, 249. *Shropsh.* 256. *Yorksh.* 329.

Taini sex in paragio, *Dors.* 79, 83.

Taini septem, *Dors.* 80 b. bis. *Somers.* 93. *Nottingh.* 286 b. 287. *Yorksh.* 315, 329.

Taini septem homines R. E. *Buck.* 151 b.

Taini octo, *Wilts*, 72. *Dors.* 79, 83. *Buck.* 146 b. 152. *Derb.* 276.

Taini octo habentes sub rege E. sacam et socam, *Hunt.* 206 b.

TAINI octo, unus eorum Alli homo regis E. senior aliorum fuit, *Buck.* 145 b.

TAINI octo, Aluunius, Vlf homo Asgari stalre, Algar homo Edwardi cilt, Elsi, Turchil, Lodi, Osulf, et Elricus, *Buck.* 148.

TAINI novem, *Dors.* 79, 82 b. 83 b. *Buck.* 149. *Bedf.* 214. *Staff.* 250 b.

TAINI novem tenentes in paragio, *Dors.* 83 b. *Dev.* 116 b.

TAINI decem, *Dors.* 84 b.[1] *Nottingh.* 284 b.

TAINI decem in paragio, *Dors.* 79.

TAINI decem Burgret, *Buck.* 145 b.

TAINI duodecim, *Dors.* 82.

TAINI XIV. *Oxf.* 158 b.

TAINI XVII. *Cornw.* 120.

TAINI viginti et unus, *Dors.* 81 b.

TAINI homines Alrici filii Goding, *Buck.* 152 b.

TAINUS unus, *Wilts,* 73. *Dors.* 79, 79 b. bis. 80, 82 bis. 82 b. 83 ter. *Somers.* 87 b. 89 b. bis. 90 b. ter. 92 b. ter. *Dev.* 100 b. 111, 117. *Cornw.* 121 passim. *Glouc.* 163 b. ter. 169. *Cambr.* 200 b. *Northampt.* 224.[2]

TAINUS unus liber, *Dors.* 83.

TAINUS quidam Edmær, *Glouc.* 162 b.

TAINUS Regis, *Essex,* 49.

TAINUS unus Regis E. *Cambr.* 199.

TAINUS Reginæ, *Linc.* 371.[2]

TAINUS Stigandi, *Norf.* 151 b.

TAINUS unus Stigandi, Osmundus, *Norf.* 155.

TALDUS, *Heref.* 181.

---

[1] They continued to hold at the time of the Survey.
[2] Also at the time of the Survey.

TALLGEBOSC, *seu* Tallebosc, Rad. *Bedf.* 211 bis.[1]

TARMOHT liber homo Regis E. *Norf.* 246.

TAVESTOCH, Abbatia de, *Dors.* 78 b. *Dev.* 103 b. passim. *Cornw.* 121.

TEDFORT, Aluuinus de, *Norf.* 181 b. ⎱
TEDFORTI, Aluuinus de, *Suff.* 330 b. ⎰ *v.* TETFORDO.

TEDGAR, *Hants*, 38. *Northampt.* 223 b.

TEDNCUS, *Suff.* 351 b.

TEDRIC, *Somers.* 93 b.

TEDRIC (tempore Haroldi Regis), *Surr.* 36 b.

TEDRICUS, *Essex*, 86.

TEIT commendatus dimidius Edrico prepositi Regis, *Suff.* 322 b.

TELA libera femina commend. *Suff.* 420.

TENUS[2] unus, *Norf.* 260.

TEODDRICUS, *Suff.* 342 b.

TEODERICUS, *Suff.* 427.

TEODRIC, *Somers.* 92 b. *Derb.* 275 b.

TEOLF, *Somers.* 96 b.

TEOS, *Inter Rip. et Mers.* 269 b.

TEPECHINUS commend. Heroldo, *Suff.* 404 b.

TEPEKIN, *Suff.* 405.

TETFORDIENSIS Episcopus, *Norf.* 191. *Suff.* 379, 379 b.

TETFORDO, Alwi de, *Norf.* 174 b. 175. *v.* TEDFORT.

TERUS, *Suff.* 427.

THOL, *Hants*, 47.

THOLE, *Yorksh.* 301 b.

THOLI, *Dors.* 80 b.

THOR, *Northampt.* 229 bis.

THORET, *Shropsh.* 254 b. *Chesh.* 268.

---

[1] He bestowed some small endowments of land upon the church of St. Paul at Bedford.

[2] *sc.* Teinus.

Thori, *Northampt.* 225 b. *Clam. in Chetst.* 377 b.

Thori homo regis E. *Buck.* 151 b.

Thori homo Leuuini Comitis, *Hertf.* 136 b.

Thori teignus R. E. *Buck.* 152.

Thouus teinnus, *Suff.* 405.

Thuinam, Canonici de, *Hants,* 44.

Thurbernus, *Essex,* 106.

Thure, *Suff.* 376 b.

Thuri, *Somers.* 91 b.

Thurmerus, *Suff.* 374 b.

Thurmot, *Nottingh.* 285, 285 b.

Tidulf, *Somers.* 88.

Tihellus, *Suff.* 373.

Tiselinus, *Essex,* 96.

Toc, *Yorksh.* 315 b.

Tocha, *Norf.* 169. *Suff.* 399. 418 b. *v.* Toka.

Tochæ, *Norf.* 161 b.

Toche, *Norf.* 163.

Toche liber homo, *Norf.* 160, 160 b.

Tochi, *Kent,* 6 b. 11 b. *Sussex,* 22. *Surr.* 34 b. *Wilts,*
    71, 73. *Somers.* 94 b. *Cambr.* 196 b. passim. 198.
    Northampt. 227. *Leic.* 235 b. *Warw.* 241. *Staff.*
    249. *Chesh.* 263 b. bis. 264 b. 265 bis. 266. *Derb.*
    274 b. 276 b. passim. *Nottingh.* 280 b. 289 passim.
    289 b. *Yorksh.* 306 b. 319, 326 bis. *Linc.* 360,
    361 b. 369 b. bis. 370, 371. *Yorksh.* 373 bis.

Tochi huscarle Regis E. *Midd.* 129.

Tochi f. Otta, *Yorksh.* 298 b.

Tochi filius Outi, *Linc.* 336, 337.

Tochi teignus R. E. *Buck.* 149. *Cambr.* 196.

Tochil teignus regis E. *Cambr.* 196 b.

Tocho, *Norf.* 258.

Tof, *Yorksh.* 301.

Toiswald, *Cornw.* 122 b.

TOKA, *Norf.* 122, 168 bis. 168 b. bis. 169 bis. 169 b.
170, 242 b.

TOKA liber homo, *Norf.* 257 b.

TOKA liber homo Heroldi commend. *Norf.* 186 b.

TOKA liber homo Stigandi, francigena, *Norf.* 250.

TOKA teinnus, *Suff.* 398 b.

TOKE liber homo, *Norf.* 165, 165 b.

TOKESONE, *v.* GODRICUS.

TOL, *Dors.* 80 b. bis. *Staff.* 248 b.

TOL dacus, *Hants,* 47.

TOLF, *Derb.* 278 b. bis.

TOLI, *Kent,* 6 b. *Wilts,* 71 b. bis. *Somers.* 92 b. *Dev.*
111 b. *Oxf.* 159 b. *Warw.* 242 bis. *Derb.* 278 b.
bis. *Linc.* 358 b. 364 b. *Norf.* 232. *Suff.* 334 b.
402.

TOLI f. Alsi, *Linc.* 337.

TOLI liber homo, *Worc.* 175.

TOLI vicecomes, *Suff.* 409 b.

TOLIUS, *Essex,* 59.

TOLIUS vicecomes, *Suff.* 338.

TONA, *Linc.* 354 bis.

TONE, *Yorksh.* 329.

TONNA, *Oxf.* 159 b. *Northampt.* 227 b. *Warw.* 238 b.
Clam. S. R. Linc. 375, 375 b. passim.

TONNE, *Linc.* 354 b. 355, 355 b. *Clam. S. R. Linc.*
375 b. bis.

TONS, *Wilts,* 70.

TOPE, *Linc.* 356.

TOPE, Aldene, *Linc.* 344.

TOPI homo Almari, *Hertf.* 141.

TOPIC, *Dev.* 108.

TOPIUS, *Essex,* 67.

TOR, *Yorksh.* 300 bis. 301 ter. 309 passim. 309 b. passim. 310 b. bis. 311 ter. 311 b. bis. 312 b. bis. 313,

324 bis. 324 b. bis. 325 bis. 327, 329 bis. 330 b.
Linc. 342, 351, 357. Norf. 222 b.

TORADRE, Norf. 267.

TORBER, Yorksh. 298 b. 325, 331.

TORBERN, Surr. 34 b. Yorksh. 331 b.

TORBERNUS, Essex, 32.

TORBERTUS, Wilts, 74 b.

TORBERTUS liber homo Stigandi, Norf. 176 b.

TORBRAND, Yorksh. 300 passim. 314, 314 b. bis. 329.

TORBRANT, Yorksh. 314 passim.

TORCHEL, Yorksh. 374 b.

TORCHETEL, Nottingh. 284 b. Linc. 357 b.

TORCHIL, Somers. 98. Hertf. 139. Nottingh. 205 b.
Yorksh. 298 b. 300, 300 b. ter. 301 bis. 301 b. bis.
306 passim. 306 b. ter. 308, 310, 310 b. 311 b. bis.
312 bis. 312 b. bis. 313 bis. 322, 324 ter. 324 b.
ter. 326 b. 327 b. 328, 329 b. 330 b. 331 b. 373 b.
Clam. in Chetst. 377.

TORCHIL homo Asgari, Hertf. 139 b.[1]

TORCHIL presbyter Tosti Comitis, Cambr. 202.

TORCHILLUS, Buck. 152 b.[1]

TORD, Norf. 247 b. 254.

TORED, Northampt. 223 b. Nottingh. 289 b. Yorksh.
320 b. 331. Suff. 415, 415 b. v. TORET.

TORET, Wilts, 68. Shropsh. 254 b. passim.[2] 255 b.[3]
Chesh. 265, 267, 267 b. 268 b. Nottingh. 286.
Yorksh. 328. Norf. 253. Suff. 414, 414 b. bis. 415.

TORETH, Chesh. 266.

TORETH tenn,[4] Norf. 250.

TORFIN, Yorksh. 298 b. 301, 301 b. 305 b. bis. 306 bis.

---

[1] Also at the time of the Survey.

[2] In two of these entries also at the Survey.

[3] He continued at the Survey.   [4] sc. Teinus.

307, 309 bis. 309 b. 310 passim. 310 b. ter. 311
passim. 332 passim. 379.

Tori, *Derb.* 274 b. *Nottingh.* 288 b. passim. *Yorksh.*
312, 326. *Linc.* 341 b. 345, 353, 361 passim.

Tori pater, *Berks*, 58.

Torif, Rold, *Linc.* 337.

Tormord, *Yorksh.* 306.

Torn, *Yorksh.* 306, 323. *Norf.* 248 b. 249 ter.

Torni, Tornyg, Abbatia de, *Cambr.* 192 b. *Hunt.* 205.
Northampt. 222 b.

Toroi homo Leuuini Comitis, *Buck.* 147.

Torol, *Linc.* 351 b.

Torolf, *Yorksh.* 300.

Torolf liber homo Stigandi, *Norf.* 202.

Torp, *Norf.* 251 b.

Torsus, *Dev.* 111 b.

Tort, *Norf.* 251 b. 256.

Toruerd, *Yorksh.* 324.

Toruert, *Norf.* 256 b.

Toruet, *Nottingh.* 289 b. *Linc.* 342 b.

Torulf, *Rotel.* 301.

Tosti, *Sussex*, 28 b. *Hants*, 47. *Heref.* 184. *Hunt.*
205 b. 206. *Warw.* 244. *Nottingh.* 281 b. 286.
Yorksh. 299 bis. *Linc.* 342, 343.

Tosti et Eric frater ejus, *Hunt.* 208 b.

Tosti Comes, *Hants*, 39 bis. 39 b. 48, 50 b. 52 passim.
53 b. *Berks*, 60. *Wilts*, 65, 71 b. *Somers.* 86 b.
Hertf. 133. *Buck.* 143 b. 147 b. *Oxf.* 157 b. *Glouc.*
166 b. 168 b. *Cambr.* 202. *Hunt.* 206 b. 208. *Bedf.*
217 b. passim. *Northampt.* 225, 228. *Nottingh.*
281. *Yorksh.* 301 b. passim. 307 b. 323 b. 332 bis.

Tostii quidam prepositus, *Hants*, 53 b.

Tostillus, *Hants*, 52.

Tostius, *Norf.* 200 b. *Suff.* 435 b.

TOSTIUS liber homo, *Essex*, 84 b.

TOTI, *Sussex*, 22. *Berks*, 61 ter. *Wilts*, 72. *Nottingh.* 284.

TOTIUS, *Essex*, 38 b.

TOU, *Dors.* 80 b.

TOUE liber homo, *Norf.* 183, 225.

TOUET liber homo, *Norf.* 173 b.

TOUI, *Surr.* 34 b. 36 b. *Hants*, 40 b. 45 b. 46, 46 b.
 passim. 49, 53 ter. *Berks*, 61 bis. 63 b. *Wilts*, 71,
 72 b. *Dors.* 80 b. *Somers.* 88, 88 b. 91 b. 94 b.
 98 b. passim. 99. *Dev.* 109 b. passim. 114 bis.
 Glouc. 165 b. 166 b. bis. 169 b. *Linc.* 359.

TOUI unus liber homo, *Berks*, 60 b.

TOUI huscarle Regis E. *Bedf.* 216 b. 217.

TOUI liber homo Gerti, *Norf.* 269.

TOUI prepositus villæ de Gildeford, *Surr.* 30.

TOUI teignus R. E. *Buck.* 152, 152 b.

TOUILLDA, *Essex*, 102 b.

TOUIUS, *Suff.* 404 b.

TOUIUS liber homo, *Essex*, 96.

TOUL, *Dors.* 82 bis.

TOULF, *Staff.* 250 b.

TOUUI, Alrici homo, filii Godingi, *Buck.* 147 b.

TOXUS, *Dors.* 80 b.

TRASEMUNDUS, *Wilts*, 72 b.

TRASMUNDUS, *Dors.* 82, 82 b.

TRAUUINUS, *Dors.* 79 b.

TREC, Algarus, *Norf.* 176 b.

TRINITAS, Sancta, *Suff.* 372 b. 373.

TROARZ, Ecclesia de, *Glouc.* 166 b.

TRUMUINUS, *Suff.* 405 b. 420.

TUBE, *Buck.* 148 b. *Warw.* 240 b.

TUFFA homo comitis Wallef, *Bedf.* 217 b.

TUINI tainus regis E. *Worc.* 177 b.

TUMI, *Worc.* 177, 177 b.

TUMME, *Yorksh.* 298.

TUNBI, *Hants*, 44 b.

TUNEMAN commend. Heroldi, *Suff.* 377 b.

TUNNA, *Berks*, 62.

TUNNE, *Linc.* 355, 355 b.

TURBER, *Nottingh.* 287. *Yorksh.* 298 b. 317, 322 bis. 324. *Essex*, 56 b.

TURBER liber homo, *Norf.* 146.

TURBERN, *Glouc.* 170. *Northampt.* 223, 223 b. passim. 224. *Warw.* 239 b. 240, 242. *Yorksh.* 301 bis. 301 b. bis. 331 b. bis. *Norf.* 147 b.

TURBERNUS, *Surr.* 36. *Cambr.* 194 b. 198 b. *Northampt.* 223 b. 224 b. *Essex*, 54 b. 55 b. *Suff.* 306, 341 b.

TURBERNUS homo Eddeue, *Heref.* 187.

TURBERNUS homo R. E. *Hertf.* 138 b.

TURBERNUS presbyter, *Suff.* 422 b.

TURBERNUS tainus regis E. *Worc.* 177 b.

TURBERTUS, *Dev.* 104. *Norf.* 147 b. *Suff.* 441 b:

TURBERTUS homo Algari Comitis, *Buck.* 151 b.

TURBERTUS homo Eddeuæ pulchræ, *Cambr.* 198 b.

TURBERTUS homo regis E. *Bedf.* 210.

TURBERTUS homo Godæ Comitissæ, *Buck.* 152 b. bis.

TURBERTUS homo Leuuini Comitis, *Midd.* 127, 130.

TURBERTUS presbyter Stig. archiep. *Hertf.* 141 b.

TURBERTUS teinus Heraldi Comitis, *Glouc.* 164.

TURBRAN, *Yorksh.* 301 b.

TURBRANT, *Yorksh.* 314 b. passim. 327.

TURCH homo abbatis de Ramesy, *Cambr.* 197 b.

TURCHEL, *Yorksh.* 306.

TURCHETEL, *Norf.* 205 b. bis. 206 passim. 207 passim. 207 b. bis. 208, 233, 266 b. *Suff.* 325 b.

TURCHETEL commend. Vlueuæ, *Suff.* 323.

TURCHIL, *Sussex*, 23 b.[1] 25 b. *Hants*, 52 b. *Berks*, 61, *Wilts*, 74.[1] *Somers*. 88 ter. *Oxf.* 159. *Glouc.* 167 b.

---

[1] Also at the time of the Survey.

169. *Worc.* 173 b. 175. *Heref.* 184, 184 b. passim.
185 b. ter. 187 ter. *Hunt.* 203, 206 b. *Northampt.*
225 b. 228 bis. 229. *Leic.* 236 b. *Warw.* 241 b. bis.
243, 244 b. *Shropsh.* 257 b. *Nottingh.* 285 b. bis.
290, 291 bis. *Yorksh.* 298 bis. 300, 300 b. 301,
303 b. 306 b. passim. 307 passim. 311, 311 b.
321 b. bis. 328, 329 b. 330 b. bis. *Linc.* 340 bis.
348 b. 357 bis. 358, 358 b. bis. *Yorksh.* 373 b.
379.

TURCHIL batoc, *Staff.* 243.

TURCHIL unus liber homo, *Berks,* 60 b.

TURCHIL homo Asgari stalri, *Hertf.* 139 b.

TURCHIL homo R. E. *Buck.* 151 b.

TURCHIL presbyter, *Hunt.* 206.

TURCHIL stirman Regis E. *Worc.* 174 b.

TURCHIL teignus R. E. *Bedf.* 213 b.

TURCHIL uuit, *Heref.* 187 ter.

TURCHILLI pater, *Wilts,* 74.[1]

TURCHILLUS, *Hunt.* 206 b. 208 b. *Bedf.* 218 b.[2]
   Northampt. 228 b. *Warw.* 239. *Essex,* 21 passim.
   25, 47 b. *Norf.* 223 b. 231 bis. 245, 267, 315,
   384, 386 b. bis. 399.

TURCHILLUS danus, *Hunt.* 203 b.

TURCHILLUS liber homo, *Essex,* 52, 94 b. *Norf.* 222 ter.

TURCHILLUS teinus, *Suff.* 417.

TUREUERT, *Yorksh.* 324 b.

TURFIN, *Yorksh.* 298.

TURGAR, *Worc.* 177. *Heref.* 186. *Shropsh.* 256. *Derb.*
   277 b. bis.

TURGAR homo Algari Comitis, *Cambr.* 198.

TURGAR teignus regis Edwardi, *Cambr.* 198.

TURGARUS commend. Guerti, *Nottingh.* 284.

---

[1] The son held at the Survey. .
[2] Also at the time of the Survey.

TURGIS, *Kent*, 1, 7, 8, 10, 13. *Derb.* 274 b. *Linc.* 350 b. bis. *Norf.* 239 b.

TURGIS teinus R. E. *Bedf.* 213.

TURGISLE, *Derb.* 278 b. *Linc.* 350 bis. 350 b. bis.

TURGISUS, *Kent*, 13. *Surr.* 31 b. 33. *Suff.* 418 b.

TURGISUS homo Balduini filii Herluini, *Buck.* 144 b.

TURGOD, *Kent*, 10. *Sussex*, 29. *Shropsh.* 259 bis. *Yorksh.* 374.

TURGOD lag, *Yorksh.* 298 b. *v.* TURGOT.

TURGOT, *Kent*, 10 b. *Sussex*, 24 b. *Wilts*, 70. *Oxf.* 159 bis. 160. *Warw.* 244 b. 250. *Shropsh.* 255, 257, 259 b. *Nottingh.* 291 b. *Yorksh.* 314 bis. 324 bis. 328 b. *Linc.* 337, 347, 351, 352 b.[1] 353 b.

TURGOT, homo Leuuini Comitis, *Buck.* 151.

TURGOT lag, *Yorksh.* 352 b. *v.* TURGOD.

TURGOT teignus R. E. *Buck.* 151.

TURGOTI pater, *Bedf.* 218 b.

TURGRIM, *Yorksh.* 301 b. *Norf.* 170.

TURI, *Hants*, 49. *Oxf.* 159. *Northampt.* 224. *Warw.* 241 b.

TURIUS, *Suff.* 445 b.

TURIUS liber homo Guert, *Suff.* 395.

TURIUS teinnus, *Suff.* 394.

TURKETEL, *Norf.* 258. *Suff.* 334 b.

TURKIL Haco, *Norf.* 223 b.

TURKIL de Uuereteham, *Suff.* 400.

TURLOGA, *Yorksh.* 300 b.

TURMOD, *Heref.* 182.

TURMODUS, *Suff.* 388 b.

TURMUND, *Dors.* 77. *Somers.* 89.

TUROLD, *Linc.* 351.

TUROLDUS, *Wilts*, 74 b. *Essex*, 73 b. *Norf.* 159, 229 b. *Suff.* 408 b.

---

[1] In this entry Turgot is the same person with Turgot lag.

TUROLDUS homo liber Estgari, *Norf.* 159.

TUROLDUS vicecomes,[1] *Linc.* 346 b.

TUROLF, *Yorksh.* 300 b. *Linc.* 361 b. *Clam. S. R. Linc.*
   375.

TUROLFUS, *Hunt.* 208.

TURORNE, *Yorksh.* 320 b.

TUROT, *Yorksh.* 311.

TURSTAN, *Glouç.* 168 b. 169. *Staff.* 250. *Nottingh.* 285,
   285 b. 286. *Yorksh.* 300 b. 318, 320 b. 324 b.

TURSTANE, *Yorksh.* 374.

TURSTANUS, *Suff.* 287, 450.

TURSTINI pater, *Somers.* 91 b.

TURSTINUS, *Hunt.* 203 b. *Staff.* 249 b. *Shropsh.* 259 b.
   Nottingh. 284 b. *Rotel.* 295 b. ter. *Norf.* 274. *Suff.*
   426 b.

TURSTINUS liber homo, *Essex,* 80. *Norf.* 178, 274.

TURSTINUS ruffus, *Essex,* 13.

TURSTINUS teignus Regis Edwardi, *Midd.* 130 b.

TURTIN. *Shropsh.* 257.

TURUED f. Vlued, *Linc.* 338.

TURUER, *Linc.* 352 b. 354, 364.

TURUERD, *Nottingh.* 285 b. *Linc.* 366 b. 370.

TURUERT, *Nottingh.* 286 b. 293. *Yorksh.* 325. *Linc.*
   341, 343 b. ter. 348, 358 b. 366, 366 b. passim.
   368 b. bis. 369, 370. *Yorksh.* 374.

---

[1] This was Thorold of Bukenhale, which manor he
bestowed upon Croyland Abbey. " ⅏ in Buchehale.—
Hanc terram," says the Record, " dedit Turoldus vice-
comes S. Guthlaco pro anima sua." Thorold's grant of
Spalding to Croyland Abbey is preserved in Ingulphus's
History; it is dated in 1051, fifteen years before the
Norman Invasion. See Gale's Rerum Anglic. Scriptores,
tom. i. p. 86.

TURUERT alius, *Linc.* 366 b.

TURUET, *Yorksh.* 330 b. *Linc.* 342.

TURULF, *Northampt.* 229. *Yorksh.* 302. *Linc.* 343, 356 b. 357.

TURULFUS, *Hunt.* 208.

V.

VBE, *Derb.* 274 b.

VCTEBRAND, *Derb.* 275 b. *Rotel.* 292. *Linc.* 368 b.

VCTRED, *Dev.* 106 b. 109, 116 b. *Cornw.* 122. *Hertf.* 141 b. *Chesh.* 266. *Inter Rip. et Mers.* 269 b. passim. *Derb.* 274 bis. 278 b. *Yorksh.* 298 bis. 300 b. 301, 305 bis. 305 b. passim. 306 passim. 306 b. 307 bis. 309, 310 b. ter. 315, 331, 332 bis.

VCTREDUS, *Dev.* 110, 110 b. *Chesh.* 264 b. *Inter Rip. et Mers.* 269 b. ter.

VDEBRUN commendat. Edrici, *Suff.* 326.

VDEMAN, *Chesh.* 264 b. 268.

Venator, v. EDWINUS. ELMER. JUDICHEL. SIUARDUS. VLUIET. VLURICUS. WLWI.

Venator Regis E. v. WIGOT. WLUUINUS.

VETULA quædam, *Derb.* 274 b.

VGELBERT, *Yorksh.* 301.

VGHETA, *Linc.* 361 b.

VGLEBERT, *Yorksh.* 301.

Vicecomes, v. ANSCULFUS. BLACUINUS. EDUINUS. EUSTACHIUS. EZI. GODERICUS. GODRICUS. NORMANNUS. OSUUARD. SUANAS. SUENUS. TOLI. TOLIUS. TUROLDUS. VRSUS.

Vicecomes R. E. *v.* ORGARUS.

VIDUA de Brictric, *Buck.* 146.

VILLANI duo, Godric et Vluric, *Buck.* 145 b.[1]

---

[1] They continued to hold at the Survey.

VILLANI quatuor, *Glouc.* 163 b.

VILLARIS, Monast. S. Mariæ, *Dors.* 79.

VITALIS, *Dev.* 115 b. 116 b. bis.

VITALIS, presbyter E. R. *Hunt.* 208.

VITEL, *Wilts,* 72 b. bis.

VIULFUS liber homo Edrici, *Norf.* 171 b.

VLBALDUS, *Sussex,* 18 b. 19 b.

VLBERT, *Chesh.* 268 b. *Inter Rip. et Mers.* 269 b.

VLBERT, frater Vlf. *Linc.* 336.[1]

VLBOLDUS, *Suff.* 337 b.

VLCHEL, *Chesh.* 264 b. *Derb.* 274, 274 b. bis. 275, 275 b. *Nottingh.* 293 bis. *Yorksh.* 298, 300 bis. 300 b. 301 ter. 301 b. 305 b. 306 b. 316 ter. 319 bis. 330 b. *Linc.* 350, 356 b. *Yorksh.* 373 b. 374.

VLCHEL abbas S. Guthlaci,[2] *Clam. in Chetst.* 377.

---

[1] He was a Lageman of Lincoln, both in K. Edward's time and at the Survey.

[2] Terram S. Guthlaci quam tenet Ogerus in Repingale dicunt fuisse dominicam firmam Monachorum, et Vlchel abbatem commendasse eam ad firmam Hereuuardo sicut inter eos conveniret unoquoque anno, sed abbas resaisivit eam antequam Hereuuardus de patria fugeret, eo quod conventionem non tenuisset.

Vlchel, called also Vlchetel and Wulketul, was appointed abbot of St. Guthlac Croyland by King Edward the Confessor in 1052. He was the immediate predecessor of Ingulphus the historian. He gave so great offence to Ivo Tailbois lord of Hoyland or Holand, by publishing the miracles performed at Earl Waltheof's tomb in the Chapter-house of Croyland, that he was summoned in 1075 to a Council at London, accused of idolatry, deprived of his abbey, and committed to prison at Glastonbury " sub cruentissimo tum abbate Thurstano procul a notis et a sua patria:" the treasure of his Abbey being at the same time confiscated to the King.

VLCHET, *Worc.* 177. *Heref.* 183 b. *Northampt.* 222 b.
225 b. bis. 229. *Nottingh.* 285 b. 290 bis. 292 b.
passim.

VLCHETE, *Worc.* 177. *Heref.* 183. *Shropsh.* 259.
Nottingh. 293.

VLCHETEL, *Glouc.* 164 b. *Worc.* 176. *Heref.* 187 b.
Northampt. 223. *Leic.* 237 bis. *Warw.* 241. *Shropsh.*
255 b. 257 b. 258 b. *Chesh.* 264 b. 265 b. *Derb.*
274 b. bis. *Nottingh.* 290. *Norf.* 149 b. 279.

VLCHETEL commend. Edrici de Laxafella, *Suff.* 326.

VLCHETEL liber homo, *Norf.* 182 b. bis. *Suff.* 300 b.

VLCHETEL liber homo Algar Comitis, *Worc.* 176.

VLCHETELL, *Norf.* 270 b.

VLCHIL, *Derb.* 275 bis. *Nottingh.* 287. *Yorksh.* 300
passim. 301, 301 b. 305 b. 306, 307 b. bis. 308
ter. 309 b. 310 bis. 312 b. bis. 315 bis. 315 b. 319,
322 bis. 322 b. bis. 324 b. 326 b. bis. 330 b. passim.
331, 331 b. bis. 332. *Linc.* 342 bis. 342 b. 347,
352, 356, 361 b. *Yorksh.* 373 b. bis. 374. *Clam.*
W. R. *Linc.* 376.

VLCHIL suabrodre, *Yorksh.* 374.

VLESTAN, *Kent,* 1 b. *Devon,* 113. *Derb.* 275 b.

VLESTANUS liber homo Edeuæ, *Suff.* 296.

VLF, *Surr.* 33, 36 b. *Dors.* 82 b. *Somers.* 93 b. bis. 96.
99.[1] *Dev.* 102 b. bis. 106, 106 b. bis. 108, 108 b.
109 ter. 110 b. 114, 115 bis. 116, 117, 118 b.[1] *Oxf.*
159 b. *Worc.* 175. *Hunt.* 205 ter. 207. *Northampt.*
222 b. ter. 223, 228 b.[1] 229 bis. *Leic.* 232, 235 b.
236 bis. 237. *Warw.* 240 b. *Shropsh.* 257. *Chesh.*
264 b. *Derb.* 274 b. 275 b. *Nottingh.* 290 b. passim.
Rutl. 293 b. *Yorksh.* 300 ter. 300 b. 301 passim.
301 b. bis. 303 passim. 306, 307, 309 bis. 316 b.

---

[1] In these entries Vlf also held at the time of the Survey.

320 b. 322, 324 passim. 324 b. passim. 331, 332
ter. *Linc.* 336 bis. 337, 340, 342 b. 343 b. 354 b.
passim. 355, 355 b. bis. 356,[1] 360 ter. 360 b. bis.
361 b. 362, 369. *Yorksh.* 373, 373 b. *Clam. in
Chetst.* 377, 377 b. *Norf.* 131 b. 226, 247.

VLF quidam homo, *Buck.* 149 b.

VLF et frater ejus, *Yorksh.* 374.

VLF cilt, *Linc.* 366.

VLF diaconus, *Yorksh.* 373, 374.

VLF fenisc, *Hunt.* 203. *Derb.* 277 b. *Nottingh.* 280 b.
Linc. 354 b. bis. *v.* VLFENISC. VLFFENISC.

VLF fil. Azor, *Northampt.* 220 bis.

VLF fil. Borgerete, *Buck.* 146 b.

VLF filius Suertebrand, *Linc.* 336.[2]

VLF homo Asgari stalre, *Buck.* 149 b.

VLF homo Heraldi Comitis, *Buck.* 146.

VLF homo Wallef Comitis, *Northampt.* 228.

VLF huscarle Regis E. *Midd.* 129. *Buck.* 149.

VLF pater Sortebrand, *Clam. in Chetst.* 377.

VLF tope sune,[3] *Clam. in Chetst.* 376 b.

VLF teignus R. E. *Midd.* 129. *Buck.* 148 b. bis. 149,
149 b. *Cambr.* 196 b. 197, 197 b. bis. *Essex,* 27.

VLFAC, *Worc.* 176 b. *Heref.* 181, 183. *Staff.* 250 b.
Shropsh. 254. *Chesh.* 265, 265 b. 266 b. 268 b.
Nottingh. 286, 286 b. *Yorksh.* 316 b. 319 passim.

---

[1] In the four last of the folios here referred to, Vlf is
the same person with Vlf fenisc.

[2] He was one of the Lagemen of Lincoln T. R. E. and
the same person who is called Vlf pater Sortebrand, a few
lines on. Sortebrand his son had succeeded him as Lageman when the Domesday Survey was formed.

[3] *Vlf filius Topi* was one of the witnesses to William the
Conqueror's Charter to the Abbey of Peterborough. See
Mon. Angl. last edit. vol. i. p. 383.

VLFACUS liber homo, *Chesh.* 263 b.

VLFAH, *Suff.* 339 b.

VLFAH alter, *Suff.* 339 b.

VLFAH pater Wlbald, *Suff.* 340.

VLFAR, *Derb.* 278.

VLFCHETEL, *Nottingh.* 287 b. *Linc.* 353 b. 368 b.

VLFECH, *Hunt.* 205 b.

VLFECH stirman Regis E. *Bedf.* 217 b.

VLFEG, *Glouc.* 167 ter.

VLFEGH, *Glouc.* 167 b.

VLFEIH liber homo, *Essex,* 62 b.

VLFEL, *Glouc.* 167 b. 170.

VLFELM, *Staff.* 250 b.

VLFELMUS, *Glouc.* 167.

VLFENISC, *Linc.* 364 b. bis. *Clam. in Chetst.* 376 b. *v.*
   VLF fenisc.

VLFER, *Sussex,* 20 b. 22.

VLFERT, *Dev.* 102 b.

VLFFEN, *Clam. in Chetst.* 377.

VLFFENISC, *Yorksh.* 298 b. 317. *v.* VLF FENISC.
   VLFENISC.

VLFIET, *Leic.* 231. *Nottingh.* 285 b. *Yorksh.* 320 b.

ULFKETEL, *Suff.* 334.

VLFLET, *Hants,* 39 b. *Berks,* 57. *Clam. in Chetst.* 376 b.
   Suff. 395 b.

ULFLET una libera femina sub Stigando Episcopo, *Norf.*
   175 b.

VLFMER, *Yorksh.* 373 b.

VLFON, *Sussex,* 21.

VLFRED, *Oxf.* 160.

VLFRET, *Dors.* 80.

VLFRIC, *Dev.* 100 b. *Staff.* 250.

VLFRIC cilt, *Derb.* 280 b.

ULFRIZ, *Norf.* 244 b.

VLFSTAN, *Derb.* 275.

VLFUS, *Nottingh.* 284 b. *Norf.* 121 b. 128. *Suff.* 332 b. 349 b.

VLFUS commendatus Guerti, *Nottingh.* 282 b. 284.

VLFUS teinnus, *Suff.* 379 b.

VLFWINUS commend. Ingulfi huscarli, *Suff.* 442.

VLGAR, *Sussex,* 19 b. *Hants,* 51 b.[1] *Berks,* 60. *Wilts,* 71, 71 b. bis. 72 b. bis. *Dors.* 83 b. *Somers.* 93 b. bis. *Glouc.* 167 b. *Staff.* 248. *Shropsh.* 256, 257 b. bis. 258, 259. *Linc.* 350 b. *Suff.* 396 b.

VLGAR monachus, *Somers.* 90 b. bis.

VLGAR presbyter, *Chesh.* 266 b.

VLGRIM, *Yorksh.* 323. *Linc.* 342 b. 343.

VLGRIM homo Comitis Leuuini, *Buck.* 150 b.

VLKETEL, *Norf.* 234.

VLKETEL, unus liber homo Edrici commend. *Norf.* 155.

ULKETEL liber homo Edrici, *Norf.* 174 b.

ULKETEL homo Heroldi, *Norf.* 228 b.

VLKETILUS, *Nottingh.* 284.

VLMÆR, *Nottingh.* 284 b. *Linc.* 342.

VLMÆRUS, *Surr.* 30 b.

VLMAR, *Sussex,* 21. *Wilts,* 70 b. 74 b. *Somers.* 87. *Dev.* 108 bis. 111, 111 b. 115 b. *Worc.* 176, 177 bis. *Northampt.* 225 b. *Shropsh.* 258. *Nottingh.* 282 b. 285, 285 b. *Yorksh.* 315. *Linc.* 343, 344 bis. 360. *Suff.* 297, 377, 419.

VLMAR cild, *Sussex,* 21 b.

VLMAR de Ettone teignus Regis E. *Cambr.* 202 b.

VLMAR liber homo, *Staff.* 248.

VLMARUS, *Wilts,* 70, 70 b.[2] 72 b. *Worc.* 176. *Northampt.* 223, 224.[2] *Warw.* 244. *Staff.* 248 b. 250 b. *Essex,*

---

[1] He held in this entry also when the Survey was taken.
[2] Also at the Survey.

12, 25 b. 38 bis. 41. *Norf.* 231 b. 232, 249 b. *Suff.*
297, 321 b. 333, 339 b. bis. 340, 340 b. 356, 386,
394, 396 b. 419, 442.

VLMARUS burgensis de Bedeford, *Bedf.* 218.[1]

VLMARUS commend. Edrici, *Suff.* 310.

VLMARUS homo Haldeni, *Suff.* 441 b.

VLMARUS homo Ordui, *Bedf.* 217 b.

VLMARUS liber homo, *Essex,* 49. *Suff.* 291 b.

VLMARUS liber homo S. Æ. *Suff.* 347 b. bis.

VLMARUS liber homo commendatus Edrici, *Suff.*
440 b.

VLMARUS presbyter, *Bedf.* 218 b.

VLMARUS presbyter Regis E. *Bedf.* 210 b.

ULMARUS teinus, *Suff.* 349 b. 351.

VLMARUS teignus R. E. *Bedf.* 218.

VLMARUS de Etone teignus R. E. *Bedf.* 212 bis. 212 b.
bis. 216 b. 218.

VLMER, *Sussex,* 18 b. 19 b. 23 b. *Wilts,* 69. *Somers.* 90.
Devon, 102 b. bis. 103 b. 107, 113. *Worc.* 176.
Staff. 248 b. *Derb.* 274 b. bis. *Nottingh.* 284 b. 285,
286 b. 288, 292 b. 293. *Linc.* 342. *Clam. W. R.
Linc.* 376.

VLMER Sbern, *Nottingh.* 293.

VLMER teignus regis E. 176.

VLMER homo Turchil, *Heref.* 185 b.

VLMERUS, *Hants,* 50 b. passim. *Essex,* 89.

VLMERUS quidam, liber homo, *Sussex,* 19.

ULMERUS teinus sub Heroldo, *Suff.* 350.

VLMERUS de Etone, *Cambr.* 197. *v.* VLMARUS.

VLMERUS presbyter, *Sussex,* 19. *v.* VLMARUS.

VLNOD, *Kent,* 10, 10 b. 11, 13, 13 b. 14. *Sussex,* 21 b.
23 b. *Surr.* 34 b. *Hants,* 39 b. 45, 49, 53, 53 b.

---

[1] He continued to hold at the Survey.

54 bis.[1] *Dors.* 83 b. *Somers.* 91 b. 95. *Devon,* 103 passim. 106 bis. 109 b. 111, 113 b. 114 b. 116, 117. *Cornw.* 122 b. 123, 123 b. *Glouc.* 165, 166 b. *Leic.* 235. *Warw.* 241. *Nottingh.* 287. *Linc.* 342 b.

VLNOD unus liber homo, *Berks,* 61 b.

VLNOD liber homo, *Suff.* 291 b. bis.

VLNOD presbyter, *Sussex,* 20 b.

VLNODI pater, *Wilts,* 74. *Hants,* 39 b. 48 b.

VLNODUS, *Devon,* 110 b. 111 b. *Heref.* 185. *Chesh.* 266 b.

VLNODUS homo Vlsi filii Borgret, *Bedf.* 214 b.

VLNOTH, *Norf.* 143 b. 262 b.

VLNOTH liber homo, *Suff.* 291.

VLNOTH liber homo Regis E. *Suff.* 291 b.

VLNOLT liber homo Stigandi commend. *Norf.* 247.

VLNOTUS, *Suff.* 339 b.

ULRICUS, *Norf.* 255. *Suff.* 429 b.

VLRICUS Hagana, *Suff.* 434 b.

ULRICUS teinus Regis E. *Suff.* 349 b.

ULSI, *Hants,* 54.[2] *Cornw.* 124 b. bis.[3] *Warw.* 241 b. *Chesh.* 267. *Derb.* 274 b. 275 b. bis. 276, 277 b. 278 bis. *Nottingh.* 282 b. 283, 284 b. 285 bis. 285 b. bis. 287 b. bis. 293. *Yorksh.* 308 bis. 330 b. 331 b. *Linc.* 358 b. 370 b. *Suff.* 336, 407 b.

VLSI alter, *Derb.* 274 b.

VLSI cilt, *Nottingh.* 287, 287 b. bis.

VLSI liber homo commend. Guerti, *Suff.* 432.

VLSI presbyter, *Kent,* 13.

VLSIET, *Yorksh.* 322 b.

---

[1] He continued in both instances to hold at the Survey.
[2] Also at the time of the Survey.
[3] In both entries, also at the Survey.

Vlsius, *Essex,* 54 b. 85 b. 96 b. *Suff.* 332, 420.

Vlsius liber homo, *Essex,* 96 b. bis.

Vlstan, *Kent,* 7 b. *Sussex,* 21 b. 24. *Hants,* 34 b. 46 b. 48 b. *Northampt.* 223 b. *Staff.* 250. *Nottingh.* 285, 285 b. *Yorksh.* 301, 306 b. 315, 319 b. 321, 321 b. 329, 373 b. *Norf.* 179 b. 184.

Vlstan presbyter, *Yorksh.* 374.

Vlstanus, *Warw.* 241 b. 244 b.

Vlstanus Episcopus, *Warw.* 243 b.[1]

Vlstanus liber homo, *Norf.* 171 b.

Vlstanus teignus, *Buck.* 145 b.

Vlsuin, *Linc.* 368 b.

Vlsy, *Nottingh.* 287 b.

Vltainus, *Hants,* 40.

Vltan, *Staff.* 249 b. bis.

Vltanus, *Kent,* 6.

Vluara, *Suff.* 419.

Vluardus presbyter, *Essex,* 76.

Vluer, *Yorksh.* 315.

Vlueron, *Kent,* 10 b. *Dev.* 112.

Vlueron libera femina, *Dev.* 113.

Vluert, *Somers.* 90.

Vluerun libera femina, *Norf.* 267 b. *Suff.* 303 b.

Vlueua, *Kent,* 10. *Sussex,* 22 b. 27 b. *Hants,* 47 b. 50 bis. 51 b. *Berks,* 62 b.[2] 63.[2] *Wilts,* 67, 69. *Dors.* 85 b. *Somers.* 91 b. bis. *Devon,* 102 bis. 103 bis. 104, 107, 111, 113 b. *Bedf.* 210. *Chesh.* 266 bis. *Essex,* 98. *Suff.* 321 b. bis. 322 bis. 323 b. bis. 330 b.

---

[1] Wulstan, the second of the name, bishop of Worcester. He was consecrated Sept. 8th, 1062. Godwin says he died Jan. 19th, 1095.

[2] " Tenuit in alod. de rege E."

VLUEUA beteslau, *Hants*, 43.[1]

VLUEUA commendata, *Suff.* 298.

VLUEUA commendata Stigando, *Suff.* 321 b. 323 passim.

VLUEUA quædam libera femina, *Sussex*, 24 b.

VLUEUA libera femina commend. Bric. *Suff.* 424.

VLUEUE, *Sussex*, 22 b. *Hants*, 38, 39, 45. *Chesh.* 264 b.
Linc. 368 b.

VLVI, *Chesh.* 264 b.

VLUIED, *Sussex*, 21 b.

VLUIET, *Kent*, 8, 10 b. *Hants*, 50 ter. 52 b, *Wilts*, 70 b.
Dors. 75 b. 77 b. 79 b. bis. 80 b. 83, 84,[2] 84 b.[2]
Somers. 92. *Dev.* 112 b. bis. *Cornw.* 124. *Glouc.*
167. *Worc.* 177 b. *Northampt.* 227 b. *Warw.* 244.
Staff. 248 b. bis. 249 ter. 250 b. bis. *Shropsh.* 254
bis. 254 b. bis. 255 b. 257, 257 b. 258, 258 b. bis.
259 passim. *Chesh.* 265, 267 passim. 268. *Derb.*
274, 274 b. ter. 275 b. 276. *Nottingh.* 283 b. bis.
285 b. 286 ter. 286 b. 288 bis. 291, 292 b. bis.
Yorksh. 304. *Linc.* 358, 365 ter. 268 b. *Clam.*
W. R. Linc. 376 b. *Clam. in Chetst.* 377 b. *Norf.*
122, 135. *Suff.* 377, 385 b.

VLUIET liber homo, *Chesh.* 265 b. *Norf.* 149.

VLUIET liber homo Guert, *Suff.* 315 b.

VLUIET pater Alwini, *Hants*, 50 b.

VLUIET pater Colæ venatoris, *Hants*, 50 b.

VLUIET presbyter, *Surr.* 33 b.

VLUIET homo Wluui episcopi, *Buck.* 150 b. bis.[3]

VLUIET venator, *Hants*, 50 b.[4] 52, 52 b.

---

[1] She continued to hold at the time of the Survey.

[2] In these two entries Vluiet continued to hold when the
Survey was formed.

[3] In both instances also at the Survey.

[4] He continued to hold when the Survey was taken.

VLUINUS, *Suff.* 321 b.

VLUOI, *Chesh.* 264 b.

VLURET, *Hants,* 49. *Suff.* 351.

VLURIC, *Kent,* 7, 7 b. *Sussex,* 21, 23. *Surr.* 36. *Hants,* 50 b. *Wilts,* 70 b. *Somers.* 94 b. 96. *Dev.* 105 b. 106, 106 b. 111 b. *Cornw.* 123, 123 b. *Oxf.* 159. *Glouc.* 165 b. *Heref.* 184 b. bis. *Hunt.* 207 b. *Northampt.* 223 b. *Warw.* 241, 241 b. *Staff.* 249, 250 b. *Shropsh.* 254 bis. 255, 255 b. 256, 257 passim. 257 b. ter. 258 passim. 258 b. 259 b. 260. *Chesh.* 264 b. 265,[1] 265 b. 266 b. bis. 267 b. bis.[2] *Derb.* 274 b. passim. 275, 276. *Nottingh.* 282 b. 283 b. 284, 288 bis. 288 b. 289, 289 b. ter. 290 bis. *Yorksh.* 301 b. 330 b. *Linc.* 370, 370 b.

VLURIC de Branduna, *Essex,* 101 b.

VLURIC liber homo, *Shropsh.* 257 b. *Chesh.* 264, 264 b.

VLURIC sochemannus Regis E. *Bedf.* 218.

VLURIC et Coleman homines Brictric, *Buck.* 150.

VLURIC homo Wallef Comitis, *Buck.* 152 b.

VLURICI Pater, *Hants,* 50. *Wilts,* 74 ter. *Dors.* 84 bis.

ULURICI venatoris Pater, *Hants,* 50 b. *Dors.* 84.

VLURICI duo, *Warw.* 241.

VLURICUS, *Sussex,* 24 b. *Hants,* 45 bis. 52 b. *Berks,* 58 b. 62 b. *Wilts,* 70. *Worc.* 173 b. *Hunt.* 206. *Northampt.* 224 b. *Warw.* 241. *Staff.* 249 bis. 249 b. bis. *Shropsh.* 256, 259. *Nottingh.* 284, 288. *Essex,* 29, 32, 57 b. 60 b. 69, 102 b. 103. *Norf.* 181, 255 b. 259, 292, 320, 321 b. 336 b. 339 b. 340 b. 341 b. 346 b. 372 b. 375, 391, 394, 403, 405, 410, 441 b.

VLURICUS alter, *Suff.* 341 b.

---

[1] In this entry he continued at the Survey.

[2] In both instances also at the Survey.

VLURICUS antecessor Eudonis filii Spiruit, *Suff.* 321.

VLURICUS cassa, *Essex,* 49 b.

VLURICUS cauuā, *Essex,* 60 b.

VLURICUS commendat. Edrico, *Suff.* 320.

VLURICUS commendat. Heroldo, *Suff.* 339.

VLURICUS filius Brictrici, *Suff.* 435 b.

VLURICUS frater Gutmundi abbat de Eli, *Suff.* 410 b.

VLURICUS unus liber homo, *Berks,* 57.

VLURICUS liber homo, *Essex,* 26, 36, 61, 79, 99 b. *Suff.*
  375 b. 427.

VLURICUS homo Alrici filii Goding, *Buck.* 147 b.

VLURICUS homo regis E. *Bedf.* 217 b.

VLURICUS liber homo Guerd, *Norf.* 255.

VLURICUS liber homo sub Guert, *Norf.* 255 b.

VLURICUS liber homo Haroldi, *Suff.* 345.

VLURICUS homo Stigandi archiepiscopi, *Buck.* 151.

VLURICUS presbyter, *Essex,* 75.

VLURICUS sochemannus Edrici, *Suff.* 316.

VLURICUS teinnus, *Suff.* 349 bis. 350 b.

ULURICUS teinnus regis E. *Suff.* 425, 429 b.

VLURICUS Wilde, *Linc.* 341, 370.

ULWAR, liber homo sub Stigando, *Suff.* 350.

VLUUARD, *Sussex,* 22 b. 24 b. *Surr.* 34 b. 35. *Hants,*
  38, 43 b. 47 b. 53 b.[1] *Berks,* 63. *Wilts,* 74 b.
  Somers. 94 b. 97, 98. *Devon,* 106 b. 112. *Glouc.*
  162 b. 169 b. *Northampt.* 221 bis. *Shropsh.* 260 b.
  Yorksh. 312.

VLUUARD albus, *Hants,* 43 b. *Somers.* 87. ⎫
VLUUARD Wit, *Dors.* 82.   ⎬
                                               ⎭

VLUUARD presbyter, *Heref.* 185.

VLUUARDUS, *Sussex,* 22 b. 26 b. 27 b. 28, 28 b. *Surr.*
  32 b. 33. *Hants,* 41, 44 bis. 45. *Berks,* 62 b.

---

[1] In this entry he continued at the Survey.

Wilts, 72 bis. 73. *Dors.* 77 b. 80 b. 84 b. *Somers.*
97, 98 b.[1] *Dev.* 104 b. 111, 113 ter. 114 b. *Glouc.*
167. *Heref.* 180. *Northampt.* 221 bis. *Warw.*
239 b.

VLUUARDUS abbas [Æccl. de Bade], *Somers.* 89 b.[2]

VLUUARDUS commend. Godrici, *Suff.* 424.

VLUUARDUS homo Eddid reginæ, *Buck.* 147.

ULWARDUS liber homo Stigandi, *Suff.* 427 b.

VLUUARDUS uuit, *Glouc.* 169. *v.* VLUUARD albus.
VLUUARD Wit.

VLUUARDI homines, *sc.* duo sochemanni, *Midd.* 129.

VLUUEN, *Berks,* 63 b. *Wilts,* 69 b. *Dors.* 80 b. *Somers.*
98.

VLUUENE, *Dev.* 103, 116 b.

VLUUI, *Surr.* 34. *Hants,* 51. *Wilts,* 69 b. 70. *Somers.*
88, 92. *Devon,* 112. *Glouc.* 169 b. *Warw.* 241 b.

VLUUI cilt, *Heref.* 187.

VLUUIC, *Kent,* 11 b.

VLUUID, *Wilts,* 70.

VLUUIET, *Staff.* 249. *Suff.* 419.

VLUUIET liber homo commend. Guert, *Suff.* 305 b.

VLUUILE Wilde, *Kent,* 13. *v.* VLURICUS Wilde.

VLUUIN, *Surr.* 34. *Warw.* 241 b.

VLUUINCHIT, *Chesh.* 266.

VLUUINE, *Yorksh.* 322. *Linc.* 369.

VLUUINUS, *Kent,* 7, 7 b. 9, 13 b. *Sussex,* 20. *Hants,*
48 b. *Berks,* 59 b. 60. *Wilts,* 70 b. *Somers.* 93 b.
94 bis. 94 b. *Devon,* 117 b. 118. *Cornw.* 124 b.
Glouc. 169 b. *Worc.* 172 b. 177 ter. *Heref.* 187.

---

1 Also at the Survey.

2 The Exeter Domesday supplies the name of another
abbat of Bath, p. 171. Sewaldus abbas. Seuoldus, p. 172.
Also p. 173. Wluuoldus.

Hunt. 207. *Northampt.* 226. *Warw.* 239 bis. 240 b. 241, 242 b. 243, 244. *Staff.* 249, 250 b. *Shropsh.* 254, 256 b. 259. *Essex,* 24 b. bis. 58, 60 b. 65 b. 66, 68, 76 bis. 76 b. bis. 77 bis. 77 b. passim. 79, 92, 107. *Suff.* 323 b. 397, 418 b. 419 bis.

Vluuinus et sorores ejus, *Essex,* 40 b.

Vluuinus canon, *Berks,* 58.

Vluuinus hapra, *Essex,* 94.

Vluuinus homo Asgari stalre, *Hertf.* 142.

Vluuinus liber homo, *Essex,* 11 b. bis. 74. *Suff.* 351, 418 b.

Vluuinus libomo,[1] *Suff.* 437 b.

Vluuinus teinnus Regis E. *Suff.* 418.

Vluuinus Linc. Episcopus,[2] *Hunt.* 203 b.

Vluuinus monachus, *Warw.* 239.

Vluuinus pater Vlstani, *Kent,* 1 b.[3]

Vluuinus teinus Eduini Comitis, *Worc.* 172.

Vluuoldus, *Somers.* 96.

Vluuredus, *Buck.* 153.

Vnban, *Derb.* 274 b.

Vnfac, *Nottingh.* 286.

Vnlof, Hants, 53. *Nottingh.* 287 b. *Linc.* 350 b.

Vnlot, *Kent,* 10 b.

Vnspac, *Nottingh.* 282 b. 286. *Norf.* 113 b.

Vntain, *Warw.* 241.

Vntan, *Staff.* 250.

Vntonius, *Warw.* 241 b.

Vrleuuine, *Berks,* 62.

Vrsus vicecomes, *Glouc.* 163 b.

---

[1] *Sc.* liber homo.

[2] Wlui bishop of Lincoln died in 1067.

[3] Vlstan the son held the land of this entry when the Survey was taken.

Vstredus liber homo commendatus Ailmaro Episcopo, *Suff.* 297.

Uthtret, *Suff.* 428 b.

Uxor Bolle, *Somers.* 98 b.

Vxor Lane, *Berks*, 56 b.

Uxor Teodrici aurifabri, *Oxf.* 160 b.[1]

Uxor Walterii de Laci,[2] *Glouc.* 165 b.

W.

W. Comes, *Oxf.* 154.

Wacra sub-commendatus, *Suff.* 298 b.

Wada et Egelric, *Dors.* 80 b.

Wade, *Dors.* 84. *Heref.* 185 b. *Derb.* 276 b. *Nottingh.* 285 b. 290 b.

Wadel, *Kent,* 9. *Dev.* 106, 115 b. *Cornw.* 125.

Wadelo, *Dev.* 113 bis.

Wadels, *Dev.* 114.

Wadhel, *Cornw.* 121 b.

Wado, *Wilts,* 74.[3] *Somers.* 92. *Dev.* 105 bis. 105 b. ter. 106 b. ter.

Waga, *Warw.* 242 b. passim. 250.

Waih, *Yorksh.* 324 b.

Wailoffus, *Suff.* 338.

Wailoffus liber homo commend. Abb. de Eli, *Suff.* 298 b.

Walduinus, *Suff.* 394.

---

[1] Her husband held the land in capite when the Survey was taken.

[2] She had held the manor of Duntesborne, but previous to the formation of Domesday Book had given it " pro anima viri sui" to St. Peter, Gloucester.

[3] He continued to hold T. R. W.

WALLE, *Somers.* 95 b.

WALLEF, *Wilts,* 70. *Warw.* 240 ter. 240 b.[1] *Derb.* 275.
Yorksh. 308 b. 320.

WALLEF Comes, *Surr.* 32. *Midd.* 130 b. *Cambr.* 189 b.
201 b. 202. *Hunt.* 203 b. 207. *Bedf.* 210 b.[2]
Northampt. 228 [3] passim. 228 b. bis. *Leic.* 233,
236. *Derb.* 274 b. *Rutl.* 293 b. ter. *Linc.* 367 bis.
Essex, 92. *v.* WALLEUUS. WALTEF.

---

[1] Wallef held this land, consisting of two hides, as an
under-tenant to the Earl of Mellent, when Domesday was
formed. The record says, " Idem Wallef libere tenuit
T. R. E."

[2] " Hanc terram [*sc.* Chenmondewiche] dedit S. Edmundo Wallef Comes et uxor ejus in elemosina T. R.
Willielmi."

[3] Among the lands entered in this folio, which had
belonged to Earl Waltheof, are those of " Riehale "
and " Belmestorp :" of these the following memorandum
occurs in the curious Register, in the library of the
Society of Antiquaries, called the Black Book of Peterborough, in a hand of a very early date.

These lands had been given to Peterborough Abbey by
Godgiva, a widow, who afterwards married Siward, Earl
Waltheof's father. Siward was allowed to retain possession
of the lands for his life, and a similar concession, under a
convention agreed to in King Edward the Confessor's pre-
sence, was made to Waltheof; the forfeiture of whose lands
was probably the reason why the property became ulti-
mately alienated from the Abbey.

The excommunication threatened at the end seems to
indicate that this memorandum was written while Earl
Waltheof was alive. The Countess Judith, Waltheof's
widow, retained possession of the lands.

" Godgive vidua dedit Sancto Petro in loco qui dicitur
Burch duas villas Righale et Beolmesthorp pro redemp-

WALLEUUS Comes, *Hunt.* 208. *v.* WALLEF comes.

WALLO, *Cornw.* 122.

WALRAUE homo Eddid reginæ, *Bedf.* 209 b.

WALRAUEN, *Linc.* 336.[1]

WALRAUENE, *Linc.* 362.

WALT', *Suff.* 413 b.

WALTEF, *Yorksh.* 298, 305 b. passim. 306 passim,

WALTEF Comes, *Linc.* 337, 366 b. *v.* WALLEF. WAL-
LEUUS.

WALTEIF, *Yorksh.* 306.

---

tione animæ suæ per consensum regis Ædwardi ; postea
accepit eam Siuuardus Comes in conjugio ; post tempus non
multum mortua est, et deprecatus est Siwardus Comes
abbatem Leofricum et fratres ut quamdiu viveret posset
habere supradictas villas, et post illius decessum reverte-
rentur ad Monasterium ; mortuoque Siwardo Comite, facta
est conventio ante Regem Ædwardum inter Waltheof filium
supradicti Comitis et Leofricum Abbatem, et accepit ipse
Waltheof v. marcas auri tali tenore ut ipse Waltheof haberet
Righale in vita sua, et Beolmesthorp quietam remansit in
Monasterio Sancti Petri per jussionem Regis Ædwardi,
Hoc actum est ante Regem publicè, sed post mortem Regis
fracta est Conventio ab ipso Waltheofo, Sed postea peni-
tentia ductus, veniente ipso ad Monasterium prefatum, concessit ambas terras Sancto Petro, eo tenore, ut ipse quamdiu viveret teneret, et post obitum illius ambas simul in
Monasterio dimitteret. Nec ipse aliquo modo istam Conventionem frangere, nec terras proprio reatu perdere
potest. Sed si quis istud instinctu diabolico evertere cupit,
sciat se excommunicatum cum ipso diabolo, in inferno mer-
cedem accipere. Fiat, Fiat." Reg. Abb. Peterb. ut supr.
fol. 23 b.

[1] He was one of the Lagemen of Lincoln T. R. E. Agemund, his son, had succeeded him at the time of the
Survey.

WALTERUS abbas de Evesham, *Worc.* 175 b. 177 b.[1]

WALTERUS Episcopus Hereford.[2] *Worc.* 173, 174 bis. *Heref.* 181 b. bis. 182 b.

WALTEU, *Yorksh.* 307 ter.

WALTHAM, Canonici de, *Surr.* 34 bis. *Bedf.* 210 b. } *Essex,* 15 b. 16, 16 b.

WALTHAM, Abbatia de, *Hertf.* 136.

WANA, *Kent,* 10 b.

WAND, Aluricus, *Essex,* 51 b.

WANTS, Aluricus, *Essex,* 51 b.

WARDHAM, Goduinus, *Hants,* 54.

WAREBURG, S. Cestr.[3] *Chesh.* 263 passim.

WARENNA, Will. de, *Norf.* 212 b.

WASO, *Cornw.* 123 b.

WATEMAN, *Dors.* 83.

WDEBRUN liber homo commendatus Edrico, *Suff.* 374.

WEGE, *Yorksh.* 316, 362 b.

WEGHE, *Linc.* 369.

WEINHOU, Aluricus de, *Suff.* 430 b.

WELERET, *Yorksh.* 298.

WELGRIM, *Linc.* 347.

WELLAND, *Dev.* 103.

WELLE, Siuuard, *Derb.* 275 b.

WELLENSIS Episcopus, *Somers.* 89 passim. 89 b. passim.

WELP, *Yorksh.* 324.

UUELP, Aluric, *Oxf.* 160.

WELRAUEN, *Linc.* 344 b.

---

[1] He became abbat of Evesham in 1077. Simeon of Durham places his death as late as 1104.

[2] He was consecrated bishop of Hereford A.D. 1060: and was succeeded by Robert de Lozinga, Dec. 29, 1079.

[3] St. Werburgh, Chester.

WENESI, *Surr.* 36 b. *Hants,* 46, 47.[1] *Wilts,* 73. *Shropsh.* 254 b.

WENESI camerarius R. E. *Buck.* 151. *Bedf.* 209.

WENESIUS, *Wilts,* 74.

WENESTAN, *Sussex,* 18 b. 20.

WENHOU, Aluricus de, *Suff.* 425.

WENIET, *Shropsh.* 255 b.

WENNINGUS commend. dim. S. Æ. *Suff.* 443 b.

VUENOT, homo Godrici vicecomitis, *Bedf.* 213.

WENRIC, *Glouc.* 167. *Heref.* 185.

UUERDEN, Wluric, *Hertf.* 142.

WESTER liber homo Guert, *Norf.* 267, 270 bis.

WESTMONAST. Abbatia S. Petri de, *Hertf.* 135. *Glouc.* 166. *Worc.* 172. *Bedf.* 211. *Northampt.* 222. *Essex,* 14.

WESTRE, *Yorksh.* 318 bis.

WETMAN, *Heref.* 181.

WGULAFRA, *Suff.* 326.

WHITA, *Suff.* 342 b.

WIBER, *Yorksh.* 322 bis.

WIBERT, *Yorksh.* 322.

WIBERTUS, *Inter Rip. et Mers.* 269 b.

WICHIGUS, *Warw.* 244 b.

WICHIN, *Devon,* 110 bis. 110 b. ter. 111, 114 ter. 114 b. bis.

WICHINCUS, *Suff.* 376.

WICHING, *Warw.* 243, 244 b.

WICHINGUS, *Suff.* 375 b.

WICHINUS, *Buck.* 150.[2]

WICNOD, *Dors.* 82.

---

1 " Wenesi tenuit (dim. hidam in Neteham hund.) de rege E. ad consuetudinem sicut ejus antecessor tenuit, qui fuit mediator caprarum."

2 He also held at the time of the Survey.

WICOLFUS, *Suff.* 338.

WICSTRICUS, *Berks,* 61 b. *Staff.* 248 b.

WICTRIC, *Shropsh.* 259. *Derb.* 274.

WIDARDUS, *Heref.* 186 b.

WIDEGRIP, *Staff.* 249.

WIDENESCI, Tovi, huscarle Heraldi Comitis, *Glouc.* 164.

WIDER, *Linc.* 348 bis.

WIDIUS, *Essex,* 55.

VUIET, *Chesh.* 263 b.

WIFARE, *Staff.* 249.

WIFLE, *Yorksh.* 301 bis.

WIFLET, *Wilts,* 72 b. *Glouc.* 162 b.

WIG teignus R. E. *Bedf.* 216 bis.

WIGA, *Glouc.* 170. *Shropsh.* 257. *Yorksh.* 330 b.

WIGA, homo R. E. *Buck.* 146.

WIGA homo Osulfi filii Frane, *Hertf.* 136 b.

WIGA teignus regis E. *Buck.* 147.

WIGAR, *Worc.* 177 bis. *Cambr.* 198.

WIGE, *Yorksh.* 330 b.

WIGHA, *Shropsh.* 257.

WIGHE, *Shropsh.* 257 bis. 257 b. *Chesh.* 266.

WIGLAC, *Linc.* 363 bis. *Clam. S. R. Linc.* 375 b. bis.

WIGOD, *Dev.* 102.

WIGOT, *Sussex,* 23 b. 26 b. 28 b. *Berks,* 62 b. *Wilts,* 71 bis. *Midd.* 129 bis. *Buck.* 150. *Oxf.* 159, 159 b. bis. *Glouc.* 169 b. *Warw.* 239.[1]

WIGOT venator regis E. *Bedf.* 217.

WIGOT de Walingford,[2] *Berks,* 62. *Buck.* 150 bis.

---

[1] The Wigot of several of these entries is Wigot de Walingford.

[2] Bishop Kennett, in his Parochial Antiquities, edit. 1695, p. 55, from William of Poictou, says, " After the decisive

WIGOTUS, *Hants,* 50 b.

WIHENOC, *Norf.* 231, 231 b.

WIHTGARUS, *Suff.* 343.

WIHTMARUS, *Suff.* 340, 342.

WIHTREDUS presbyter, *Nottingh.* 284.

WIHTRIC, *Suff.* 340.

WIHTRICUS, *Suff.* 339 b.

WIHTRICUS homo Heraldi, *Suff.* 342 b.

WIKINGUS, *Suff.* 342.

WILAC frater Achi, *Linc.* 337.

WILAF, *Buck.* 143.

WILAF homo Leuuini Comitis, *Buck.* 144 b. bis.

WILAF teignus Leuuini Comitis, *Buck.* 145.

WILDE, Vluricus, *Linc.* 341, 370.

WILEGRIP, *Staff.* 249 b. *Shropsh.* 254.

WILLA, *Northampt.* 224 b. bis.

WILLEGRIP, *Shropsh.* 258 b.

---

battle near Hastings, the Conqueror carried his forces into
Kent, and marching back from thence passed by London,
possesst by the party of Edgar Atheling, and came to
Walingford, where the lord of that town, WIGOD DE WA-
LINGFORD, went out to meet him, delivered the town to
him, and entertained him there, till Archbishop Stigand
and many of the grandees of Edgar's faction came and
offered their submission. For which service and merit of
the lord of that place, the victorious Prince, in policy to
ingratiate with the Saxons, and to reward his Normans,
gave Aldith, only daughter of the said Wigod, in marriage
to Robert de Oily, who, after her father's death, which
happened nigh the same time, in right of her, became
possesst of that great estate, wherein Burcester was in the
honor of Walingford, and Ambrosden in that honor which
was after called St. Walery."

WILLELMUS, *Dors.* 77 b.

WILLELMUS accipitrarius, *Kent*, 14.

WILLELMUS Episcopus Lond. *Midd.* 127 b. passim.
Hertf. 140. *Essex*, 9 b. 10, 10 b. bis.[1]

WILLIELMUS, *Nottingh.* 293. *Yorksh.* 301 b. ter. *Linc.*
352, 357 b. bis.

WILLIELMUS filius Sceluuard, *Nottingh.* 282 b.

WILLIELMUS filius Stur, *Hants*, 52 b.[2]

WILTUNIA Abbatia de, *Sussex*, 26.

WIMARC, *Somers.* 96 b.

WIMARC, Rob. fil. *Hunt.* 205 b. 207. *Essex*, 48,
106 b.

WIMARCÆ, Robertus fil. post mortem regis E. *Essex*,
44, 44 b. 45 bis. 45 b. bis. 46 b. bis.

WIMERUS, *Suff.* 398 b.[2]

WINCELCUMBE, Ecclesia de, *Glouc.* 165 b. passim.

WINCESTRE, Abbas de, *Hants*, 53.

WINCESTRE, Odo de, *Hants*, 52.

WINE, *Cornw.* 123.

WINEGOD, *Wilts*, 69 b. *Somers.* 90.

WINEMAR, *Dev.* 112 b.

WINESTAN, *Inter Rip. et Mers.* 269 b.

WINGE, *Essex*, 93.

WINTERLED, *Cambr.* 198.

WINTON. Abbatissa S. Mariæ, *Hants*, 48.

WINTONIENSIS Episcopatus, *Buck.* 143 b.

WINTON. Ecclesia S. Petri de, *Cambr.* 190.

---

[1] William Bishop of London was consecrated in Sept.
1051. Godwin and Stow say he died in 1070; but Wharton
proves him to have been living in 1075. See Le Neve's
Fasti Eccl. Anglic. p. 176.

[2] He also held when the Survey was taken.

WINTON. Æccl. S. Suuithuni, *Somers.* 91 b.

WINTRELET, *Chesh.* 265.

WINTREMELC, Alricus, *Bedf.* 218 b.[1]

WIRECESTRE, Episcopus de, *Worc.* 173 b. 174.

WIRECESTRE, S. Maria de, *Glouc.* 164 b. passim.

WIRELMUS, *Kent,* 13.

WISCAR, *Suff.* 390.

WISG'. *Essex,* 41 b. *Suff.* 391 b. 392.

WISGAR, *Suff.* 345 b.

WISGARUS, *Essex,* 35, 38 b. bis. 39, 40 b. bis. 41 bis.
    102. *Suff.* 352, 389 b. 391 bis. 391 b. bis. 392 b.
    393, 393 b. 395 b. 397, 428 b. 448 bis.

WISGARUS filius Alurici, *Suff.* 389 b.

WISLAC, *Hants,* 46, 51, 54.[2]

WISTAN liber homo Rad. Stalra, *Norf.* 134 b.

WISTRICUS, *Nottingh.* 287. *Suff.* 337 bis. 375.

WIT, Aluuinus, *Hants,* 50 b.[3] *v.* ALUUINUS ALBUS.

UUIT, Edwardus, *Bedf.* 212.

UUIT, Turchil, *Heref.* 187 bis.

UUIT, Vluuardus, *Kent,* 1 b. 9. *Dors.* 82. *Oxf.* 160.

UUIT, Wluuardus, teignus R. E. *Midd.* 129, 129 b.
    130.

UUITE, Wluuard, *Linc.* 337.

WITG'. *Suff.* 391 b. bis. 392.

WITGAR'. *Suff.* 391 b.

WITGARUS, *Suff.* 391 b. 392, 411, 440 b.

---

[1] Coldentone. " Tenuit T. R. E. Homo regis E. fuit, et
potuit dare cui voluit. Quam postea canonicis S. Pauli sub
W. rege dedit, et ut post mortem suam haberent omnino
concessit."

[2] In this instance he also held at the time of the Survey.

[3] Also at the Survey.

WITHER, *Oxf.* 157 b.

WITHER, liber homo, *Oxf.* 157.

WITHGARUS, *Suff.* 391 bis.

WITHMERUS, *Suff.* 291.

WITHRI, *Heref.* 184 bis. 184 b. bis. *Norf.* 228 b.

WITLAC, *Clam. S. R. Linc.* 375.

WITRIC, *Shropsh.* 254 b.

WIUAR, *Shropsh.* 257 b.

WIUARA, *Staff.* 250.

WIUELAC, *Linc.* 363 b.

WIULFUS, *Norf.* 198 b.

WLBALDUS, *Suff.* 339 b. 342 b.

WLF, *Northampt.* 227 b. *Linc.* 360 b.

WLFAH, *Suff.* 341 b.

WLFAHUS, *Suff.* 341 b.

WLFRIC, *Staff.* 250 b.

WLFRICUS, *Hants,* 40.

WLGAR, *Warw.* 240.

WLMAER, *Yorksh.* 317.

WLMAR, *Somers.* 88 b. *Linc.* 343.

WLMARUS, *Worc.* 178. *Suff.* 341.

WLMARUS liber homo Edrici de Laxafelda, *Suff.* 314.

WLMARUS presbyter R. E.[1] *Buck.* 151.

WLMER, *Heref.* 186 b.

WLMER homo Roberti filii Wimarc, *Cambr.* 198 b.

WLMERUS, *Suff.* 333 b.

WLNODUS, *Somers.* 91 b.

WLSI, *Yorksh.* 315 b.

---

[1] Wulnarus, probably the same person, chaplain to Wlfin Bishop of Dorchester, occurs as a witness to Thorold of Buckenhale's grant of Spalding to Croyland Abbey, in 1051. Wlmarus had held land in Buckinghamshire, which was then in the diocese of Dorchester.

Wlsi tainus regis E. *Worc.* 177 b.

Wlsinus, *Northampt.* 223. *Suff.* 333 b.

Wlstan, *Yorksh.* 315 b.

Wlstanus, *Oxf.* 159 b. bis. *Warw.* 241.

Wlstanus teignus R. E. *Buck.* 150 b.

Wluard, *Glouc.* 169 ter.

Wluardus, *Suff.* 341, 343.

Wluarus, *Suff.* 342.

Wlueua commend. *Suff.* 321 b.

Wlui, *Glouc.* 167.

Wluinus teignus regis E. *Cambr.* 199 b. passim.

Wluius, *Suff.* 343.

Wluredus, *Oxf.* 160.

Wluric, *Glouc.* 167 b. 170 b.

Wluric homo Asgari stalri, *Hertf.* 139 b.

Wluric uuerder, *Hertf.* 142.

Wluricus, *Suff.* 340, 342, 342 b. 399.

Wluricus diaconus, *Suff.* 334 b.

Wluricus liber homo, *Suff.* 311, 354.

Wluuar homo Anschil de Wares, *Hertf.* 141 b.

Wluuara vidua, *Northampt.* 220 b.

Wluuard, *Kent*, 11 b. *Hants*, 51. *Glouc.* 166 b. *Heref.*
　187.

Wluuard cild teignus regis E. *Buck.* 145.

Wluuard filius Eddeuæ, *Buck.* 143.

Wluuard homo Asgari stalri, *Hertf.* 137 b. 138 b.

Wluuard teignus R. E. *Buck.* 151 b.

Wluuard Uuit, *v.* Uuit. Uuite.

Wluuardus, *Wilts*, 66. *Dors.* 77 b. *Glouc.* 164, 168 b.
　Linc. 367 b. *Essex*, 93 b.

Wluuardus albus, *Wilts*, 66. *v.* Uuit. Uuite.

Wluuardus homo Asgari stalri, *Hertf.* 142.

Wluuardus homo reginæ Eddid. *Buck.* 153.

Wluuardus Leuet. *Bedf.* 212 bis.

WLUUARDUS uuit, teignus R. E. *v.* UUIT.

WLUUEN, *Wilts,* 69 b. bis. *Dors.* 80 b.

WLUUEN quædam femina, *Buck.* 150 b.

WLUUEN homo regis E. *Buck.* 150 b.

WLUUENE homo regis E. *Midd.* 130 b.

WLUUI, *Glouc.* 166, 167. *Clam. in Chetst.* 377 b.

WLUUI Episcopus Lincoliensis,[1] *Buck.* 143, 143 b. 144.
      Hunt. 209. *Linc.* 348.

WLUUI homo Asgari stalre, *Hertf.* 134.

WLUUI homo Eddeuæ, *Cambr.* 195 b.

WLUUI, homo Goduini de Benedfelle, *Hertf.* 134.

WLWI venator, *Surr.* 36 b.[2]

WLUUINE, *Hunt.* 208.

WLUUINUS, *Worc.* 177,[3] *Cambr.* 187, 190. *Suff.* 340 b.
      441 b.

WLUUINUS homo dim. *Buck.* 145 b.

WLUUINUS homo regis E. *Bedf.* 217 b.

WLUUINUS homo abbatis de Ely, *Cambr.* 190 b. 196.

WLUUINUS chit de Westone homo Heroldi Comitis,
      Hunt. 208 ter.

WLUUINUS venator regis E. *Cambr.* 190 b.

WLUUINUS homo Heraldi Comitis, *Hertf.* 140.

WLUUINUS teignus Heraldi Comitis, *Hertf.* 140 b.

WLUUINUS presbyter, commendatus Edrici, *Suff.* 315 b.

WNULFUS, *Somers.* 93.

WORDROU, *Devon,* 112.

WREHANTUNE, Presbyteri de, *Worc.* 176.[4]

---

[1] Ulf, or Wulfin, who died in 1067. He had succeeded
Eadnoth II. in 1049.

[2] He continued to hold at the time of the Survey.

[3] His name is written, in the same page, Vluuinus.

[4] They also continued at the Survey.

INDEX

OF THE

UNDER-TENANTS OF LANDS

AT

THE FORMATION

OF

THE DOMESDAY SURVEY.

INDEX

OF

UNDER-TENANTS OF LANDS

AT

THE FORMATION

OF

THE DOMESDAY SURVEY.

A.

A. [Ascelinus]. *Essex,* 45.

ABA, *Northampt.* 224 b.

ABBA, *Norf.* 117.

ABBAS [de Eli], *Suff.* 305, 305 b. 306.

ABBAS quidam de S. Gemano [1] de Salebi, *Linc.* 369 b.

ABEL, *Kent,* 4 b.

ABENDONE Abb. de, *Warw.* 241 b. bis.

ABERNON, Rogerius de, *Surr.* 35.

ABETOT, Vrso de, *Heref.* 180.

ABRAHAM presbyter, *Glouc.* 162.

ACARDUS, *Sussex,* 25 b. *Buck.* 148 b. *Worc.* 177 bis.

ACARDUS presbyter, *Sussex,* 25.

ACCIPITRARIUS quidam,[2] *Sussex,* 24.

ACHET, Walterus, *Buck.* 148.

ACUN homo Rogeri Pictavensis, *Linc.* 352.

---

[1] *sc.* S. Germano.

[2] " Ipsemet tenuit eam [I. hid.] pro ☉ in alodium."

T 3

ADAM, *Kent*, 7, 8 b. bis. 9 ter. 10 ter. 10 b. 11, 12, 14.
    Hertf. 134 passim. 134 b. ter. *Oxf.* 155 b. 156 bis.
    156 b. bis.

ADAM unus homo, *Kent*, 8.

ADAM filius Huberti, *Kent*, 6, 6 b. bis. 8 passim. 8 b.
    9 b. bis. 14 b. *Surr.* 31 b. bis.

ADAM homo Episcopi Lincoliensis, *Linc.* 344 b. bis.

ADELARDUS, *Inter Ripam et Mersam*, 269 b.

ADELDREDÆ S. Monachi, *Essex*, 2.

ADELEDMUS, *Norf.* 275.

ADELELMUS, *Berks*, 61. *Wilts*, 69 b. bis. *Heref.* 186 b.
    bis. *Leic.* 236. *Essex*, 77, 77 b. *Norf.* 208. *Suff.*
    419 bis.

ADELELMUS homo Colsuan, *Linc.* 357.

ADELINA joculatrix, *Hants*, 38 b.

ADELOLD, *Kent*, 7 b.

ADELOLDUS, *Kent*, 1 b.[1] 7 b. 8 b. bis. 9 b. 10 b. *Surr.*
    32.

ADELOLDUS camerarius, *Kent*, 7 b.

ADELOLFUS de Merc, *Essex*, 28 b.

ADELULFUS, *Kent*, 11 b. *Cambr.* 198, 199. *Essex*, 27,
    28, 28 b. 29, 31 b. 32 bis. 33 bis.

ADELWINUS, *Suff.* 352.

ADELUUOLDUS, *Kent*, 11.

ADESTAN, *Linc.* 348 b.

ADESTANUS, *Cambr.* 195.

ADOLFUS, *Dev.* 101 b.

ADOLOFUS, *Essex*, 34.

ADRET, *Somers.* 90 b.

ÆILRICUS archidiaconus, *Worc.* 173.

ÆLDEUA libera femina, *Berks*, 63 b.

ÆLDRED, *Shropsh.* 260 b.

---

[1] " Istemet tenuit T. R. E."

Ældred presbyter, *Sussex*, 17.

Ældredus frater Ode, *Hants*, 48 b.

Ælfelmus, *Staff.* 247.

Ælgotus, *Staff.* 249.

Ælmer presbyter, *Berks*, 56 b.

Aelons, *Suff.* 360 bis.

Ælueue fem. Wateman de Lond. *Midd.* 130 b. bis.

Æluuardus, *Heref.* 180.

Ærnoldus, *Suff.* 347.

Agemund,[1] *Nottingh.* 284.

Agemundus, *Northampt.* 228.

Agenetus, *Suff.* 358.

Agenulfus, *Wilts*, 68 b.

Aghemundus, *Hants*, 45.[2]

Agnes filia Aluredi [de Merleberge] uxor Turstini de
  Wigemore, *Heref.* 186.

Ailboldus pr. *Suff.* 360 b.

Ailmarus, *Warw.* 243.

Ailmarus filius Goduini, *Norf.* 272 b. 273 bis.

Ailric, *Buck.* 148 b. *Oxf.* 154. *Warw.* 242 b. bis.
  Nottingh. 287 b. bis.

Ailricus, *Glouc.* 164 b. *Warw.* 241. *Suff.* 360 b.

Ailuardus filius Belli, *Suff.* 391.

Ailuuacre, *Somers.* 90.

Ailuuardus, *Somers.* 97.

Aincurt, Walterus de, *Linc.* 340.

Airardus, *Dors.* 83.

Aistan, *Suff.* 446 b.

Aitard, *Chesh.* 266.

Aitardus, *Norf.* 124 b. bis. 125, 175, 180 b. 186 bis.
  188 b. 277 b. *Suff.* 331.

---

[1] " ħb." He had been the previous predecessor.

[2] He had been tenant before the Survey.

---

[1] " Idem tenebat T. R. E."   [2] *sc.* Alanus.

[3] " Predicti burgenses dim. hid. habent."

ALCHERUS, *Shropsh.* 255 bis. *Derb.* 274 b. passim. 275. *Essex*, 53 b.

ALDE, *Warw.* 241.

ALDED libera femina, *Suff.* 446.

ALDELIN homo Willielmi de Warena, *Linc.* 351 b.

ALDEN, *Nottingh.* 282 b.

ALDENE, *Hertf.* 141, 141 b.

ALDI quædam femina, *Surr.* 30 b.

ALDREDUS, *Glouc.* 165.

ALDRIE, Willielmus de, *Wilts*, 71 b. bis.

ALELMUS, *Worc.* 177. *Yorksh.* 324.

ALENCUN, Bernardus de, *Suff.* 443 b.

ALESTAN, *Som.* 90. *Buck.* 146 b. *Suff.* 320.

ALESTAN anglus, *Norf.* 178.

ALFLET, *Hertf.* 134.

ALFREDUS, *Sussex*, 27 b.

ALFRIC, *Somers.* 90 b. 91.

ALFRIDUS, *Leic.* 235 b.

ALGAR, *Berks*, 56 b. *Dors.* 77. *Dev.* 105 b. *Cornw.* 124 b. passim. *Northampt.* 220 b. bis. *Warw.* 241 b. *Linc.* 367 b.[1] 368.[2]

ALGARUS, *Northampt.* 220. *Essex*, 40 b. 73 b. 102. *Suff.* 352, 402.

ALGERUS, *Essex*, 92.

ALICH, *Hunt.* 205 b.

ALLIC, *Hunt.* 205 b.

ALMÆR, *Berks*, 61 b. 63.

ALMÆRUS, *Buck.* 146.

ALMANESCHES, Abbatia de, *Sussex*, 24 b. 25.[3]

---

[1] He had been the holder of the land before Wido, who was now tenant in capite, had received it.

[2] " ħɓ Algarus. — Idem Algar habet de Widone [de Credun]."

[3] The Benedictine Abbey of Almanesches, in the diocese

ALMAR, *Som.* 94 bis. *Cornw.* 124 b.[1] *Buck.* 146. *Warw.* 241.

ALMARUS, *Buck.* 146, 146 b. 150. *Cambr.* 194 bis. 194 b. 195 passim. 195 b. bis. *Bedf.* 218. *Leic.* 231 b. *Warw.* 241 bis. 241 b. bis. *Staff.* 250, 250 b. *Essex,* 32, 45 b. *Norf.* 272. *Suff.* 352, 426 b.

ALMARUS prepositus Regis, *Suff.* 352.

ALMER, *Dev.* 112 b.[2] 116 b.

ALMFRIDUS, *Essex,* 32 b.

ALMODUS homo Episcopi Dunelmensis, *Linc.* 341 bis.

ALNO, Willielmus de, *Suff.* 419 b. ter. 420 b.

ALNOD, *Kent,* 13 b. bis. *Cornw.* 124 b. passim.[3] *Warw.* 241.

ALNODUS, *Midd.* 129.

ALNODUS monachus, *Som.* 90.

ALNULFUS presbyter [in Gepeswiz], *Suff.* 290.

ALODIARII duo, *Berks,* 60 b.

ALRED, *Kent,* 1 b.

ALRIC, *Som.* 93 b. passim.[4] 94 ter. *Dev.* 112 bis. *Cornw.* 124 b. bis.[5] *Northampt.* 224 bis.[6] *Yorksh.* 316 b.[7] 317.[7]

ALRIC presbyter, *Staff.* 247 b.

---

of Seez, was originally founded about the year 700. It was destroyed in the Norman wars soon after A. D. 770; and refounded by Roger de Montgomery, A. D. 1060. See Neustria Pia, p. 364. Al. Priories, vol. i. p. 101.

[1] " Idem tenebat T. R. E."

[2] " Ipse tenebat T. R. E."

[3] Of one of four separate manors, it is said, " Idem tenebat T. R. E."

[4] In two instances, he had held T. R. E.

[5] " Idem tenebat T. R. E."

[6] In one entry, "Idem ipse tenuit."

[7] In these two instances, Alric held of Ilbert de Laci the land which had been previously his own.

ALRICUS, *Buck.* 149 b. *Worc.* 172 b. *Bedf.* 215 b. 218,
218 b. *Staff.* 247. *Derb.* 274 b.

ALRICUS commendatus Guerti,[1] *Suff.* 283 b.

ALRICUS archidiaconus, *Worc.* 173, 173 b.

ALSELIN, G. *Derb.* 274 b.

ALSELIN, Goisfridus, *Derb.* 275 b.

ALSI, *Hants,* 42 b. bis. 49, 52 b. 57 b. 58. *Cornw.*
124 b.[2] *Buck.* 153 bis. *Leic.* 234. *Staff.* 249. *Derb.*
275.

ALSI filius Brixi, *Hants,* 42.

ALSI de Ferend, *Oxf.* 154 b.

ALSI monacus, *Wilts,* 65 b.

ALTET quidam, *Kent,* 11.[3]

ALUERADUS, *Buck.* 146 b. *Cambr.* 198.

ALUEREDUS, *Buck.* 146 b. *Cambr.* 200 b.

ALUEUA, *Dev.* 112. *Oxf.* 154.

ALUID quædam Anglica, *Essex,* 45 b.

ALUIET, *Suss.* 29. *Berks,* 58. *Sussex,* 29.

ALUIET presbyter, *Cambr.* 191 b.[4]

ALULFUS, *Yorksh.* 322 b.

ALULFUS homo Willielmi de Perci, *Linc.* 354.

ALURED, *Berks,* 63 b.

ALUREDUS, *Kent,* 9 b. 11 b. *Sussex,* 17 b. 18, 20 b. bis.
22. *Berks,* 61 b. *Dors.* 77 b. 78 b. 80. *Somers.* 87,
87 b. 90, 91 b. bis. 92, 92 b. passim. 93 bis. *Dev.*
104 b. ter. 105 bis. 105 b. bis. *Dev.* 114 b. *Cornw.*
124 passim.

ALUREDUS, *Midd.* 129. *Oxf.* 155 b. 159 b. bis. *Worc.*
173. *Cambr.* 198. *Hunt.* 206. *Northampt.* 223 b.
224, 226, 228 bis. *Nottingh.* 281 b. 289 b. *Yorksh.*
308 b. 315 b. *Essex,* 44 b. 80.

---

[1] Tenuit.   [2] He had also held T. R. E.

[3] Also T. R. E.   [4] He had likewise held T. R. E.

ALUREDUS Anglus, *Norf.* 178 b.

ALUREDUS clericus, *Oxf.* 159.

ALUREDUS dapifer, *Kent,* 9 b.

ALUREDUS Hispan. *Glouc.* 162.

ALUREDUS homo Colsuan, *Linc.* 357.

ALUREDUS homo Durandi Malet, *Linc.* 365.

ALUREDUS [de Merleberg], *Somers.* 91 b.

ALUREDUS homo Comitis Moritoniæ, *Nottingh.* 282 b. bis.

ALUREDUS homo Odonis arbalistarii, *Linc.* 365 b.

ALUREDUS homo Osberni de Arcis, *Linc.* 364.

ALUREDUS homo Widonis de Credun, *Linc.* 367 passim.

ALUREDUS et socius ejus, *Oxf.* 155 b.

ALURIC, *Hants,* 51 b. bis. 54. *Berks,* 56 b. bis. 63. *Wilts,* 73 b. *Dors.* 84 b. *Somers.* 87, 87 b. *Dev.* 113 b. 118 b. bis. *Oxf.* 155 b. 158. *Warw.* 242 b. *Shropsh.* 252 b. *Suff.* 320, 446 b.

ALURIC alter, *Berks,* 56 b.

ALURIC, Estrat, *Suff.* 446 b.

ALURIC parvus, *Somers.* 87.[1] *v.* ALURICUS parvus.

ALURIC presbyter, *Hants,* 41 bis.

ALURICUS, *Sussex,* 19 b. *Berks,* 60 b. 62, 63 b. *Somers.* 89 b. *Northampt.* 221. *Essex,* 30 b. 70 b. *Suff.* 295 b. 360 b. 383, 400, 425, 446 b.

ALURICUS Chacepol, *Midd.* 127 b.

ALURICUS filius Rolf burgensis de Gipeswiz, *Suff.* 446.

ALURICUS frater Edrici, *Suff.* 447 b.

ALURICUS medicus, *Hants,* 51 b.

ALURICUS parvus, *Hants,* 51 b. *v.* ALURIC.

ALURICUS presbyter, *Bedf.* 213. *Suff.* 295, 295 b. bis. 446 b.

ALURICUS sochemannus, *Suff.* 361.

---

[1] He is called " Alfricus parvus de Hamtansyra " in the Exeter Domesd. p. 780.

ALURICUS teinnus, *Essex,* 26 b.

ALURICUS, Leuuinus, *Suff.* 446 b.

ALUUARD, *Wilts,* 68 b.[1] *Somers.* 87,[2] 93 b.[3] *Dev.* 104 b.[4]
105 b.[4] *Cornw.* 120, 124 b. bis.[5] *Hertf.* 137, 137 b.[6]
Shropsh. 259 b.

ALWARD filius Elmund, *Shropsh.* 259 b. passim.[7]

ALUUARD tainus, *Somers.* 87.[8]

ALUUARDUS, *Sussex,* 24 b. bis. *Wilts,* 66 bis. 68 b. 72.
Somers. 87 b. bis. 89, 97 b.[9] *Dev.* 104 b. bis. 105.[10]
Hertf. 141. *Oxf.* 154, 158. *Essex,* 102 b.

ALUUARDUS (clericus), *Sussex,* 16 b.

ALUUARDUS presbyter, *Wilts,* 65 b. 68 b.

ALWART, *Suff.* 321.

ALWEWE, *Suff.* 435 b.

ALUUI, *Kent,* 1 b.[11] *Dev.* 116 b. bis. *Oxf.* 154.

ALUUIN, *Berks,* 62. *Cornw.* 120. *Staff.* 247.

ALUUIN ret, *Hants,* 50.

ALUUINUS, *Sussex,* 19, 20, 21, 24,[12] 27. *Hants,* 40.[13]
Berks, 56 b. 59 b. *Dors.* 80. *Somers.* 97 b.[14] *Dev.*
118 b. *Oxf.* 154 ter. *Worc.* 175 bis. *Heref.* 185.[15]
Cambr. 193 b. *Bedf.* 212, 217 b. *Leic.* 232 b. 233,

---

[1] " Qui tenebat T. R. E."   [2] He had held T. R. E.

[3] " Ipse tenuit T. R. E."

[4] " Ipse tenebat T. R. E."

[5] " Ipse tenebat T. R. E."

[6] " Isdem qui tenet tenuit T. R. E. et vendere potuit."
He was now under-tenant to Robert Gernon.

[7] In two of the entries it is said, " Elmund tenuit."

[8] He was also the holder T. R. E.

[9] " Idem tenuit T. R. E."

[10] " Ipse tenebat T. R. E."

[11] " Iste idem tenuit in prebenda."

[12] " Istemet tenuit T. R. E."   [13] " Ipse tenuit T. R. E."

[14] " Ipse tenebat T. R. E."

[15] " Eduui cilt pater ejus tenuit."

---

[1] He had held T. R. E.

[2] In the second of these entries it is said, " Idem Alwaldus tenebat T. R. E."

[3] " Ipsi tenebant T. R. E."

ANGLI, *Wilts,* 68 bis.

ANGLI duo, *Wilts,* 66. *Midd.* 129 b. *Hertf.* 137 b. *Buck.* 144 b. 147.[1] 150.[2] *Northampt.* 221 b.

ANGLI quatuor, *Hants,* 50.[3]

ANGLI sex, *Bedf.* 210.

ANGLI liberi homines, *Oxf.* 155.

ANGLICI duo, *Nottingh.* 283.

ANGLICI III. *Yorksh.* 318.[4]

ANGLICUS quidam, *Buck.* 145 b. 148 b. *Essex,* 78. *Norf.* 209 b.

ANGLICUS unus, *Hants,* 40. *Wilts,* 65 b. 70 b. 71 b. *Devon,* 111 ter. *Hertf.* 133.[5] *Heref.* 184 b.

ANSCHETELLUS prepositus, *Norf.* 198.

ANSCHETIL presbyter, *Bedf.* 213 b.

ANSCHETILLUS, *Oxf.* 156 b. *Essex,* 9 b. 11 b. 24 b. 63 b. 64 b. 67, 83, 102. *Suff.* 332, 422 b.

ANSCHETILLUS homo Episcopi Londoniæ, *Essex,* 90.

ANSCHIL, *Berks,* 58 b. bis. 59. *Cambr.* 200 b.

ANSCHITIL, *Kent,* 7, 12. *Sussex,* 18, 20 bis. *Hants,* 45. *Berks,* 63. *Wilts,* 65 b. 67. *Somers.* 93 ter. 93 b. passim. *Devon,* 108, 110 ter. *Oxf.* 160. *Glouc.* 165, 168 b. 170. *Heref.* 179 b. *Shropsh.* 252, 259 b. *Yorksh.* 310 bis.

ANSCHITIL archidiaconus, *Kent,* 1 b.

ANSCHITIL f. Ameline, *Dors.* 83.

---

[1] " Istimet qui ten. tenuerunt T. R. E. et vendere potuerunt."

[2] " Istimet tenuerunt T. R. E. homines Haming fuerunt et vendere potuerunt."

[3] " Pater eorum tenuit in alodium T. R. E."

[4] " Nunc habent de Ilberto III. Anglici."

[5] " I. Anglicus ten. [de Archiep. Cantuar.] II[as]. acras terræ. Isdem tenuit T. R. E. in uadimonio. Potuit vendere."

ANSGERUS, *Dors.* 79 bis. 79 b. *Somers.* 86 b. 91 b. bis.
    Dev. 104 b. passim. *Oxf.* 156. *Glouc.* 164 b. *Staff.*
    249 b. *Chesh.* 268 b. *Nottingh.* 291 b.

ANSGERUS cocus,[1] *Somers.* 87.

ANSGOT, *Worc.* 173. *Yorksh.* 316.

ANSGOT homo Comitis W. *Heref.* 180 b.

ANSGOT, presbyter, *Warw.* 243 b.

ANSGOTUS, *Kent,* 2 b. 4, 6 b. *Sussex,* 20 b. 21, 22. *Surr.*
    31, 31 b. ter. *Wilts,* 65 b. *Midd.* 129 b. *Essex,* 47.

ANSGOTUS de Rouecestre, *v.* ROUECESTRE.

ANSLEPE, Winemarus de, *Northampt.* 229. *v.* HAN-
    SLEPE. WINEMARUS.

ANSLEUILE, Willielmus, *Hants,* 44 b.

ANSLEUILLE, Hunfridus, *Hertf.* 132.

APPEUILE, Walterus de, *Kent,* 9 b.

Arbalistarius, Bernerus, *Norf.* 110.

———————— Galterus, *Suff.* 320.

———————— Gislebertus, *Norf.* 117.

———————— Hugo, *Sussex,* 18 b.

———————— Robertus, *Norf.* 118.

———————— Walterus, *Suff.* 324 bis.

ARBERNUM, Rogerus de, *Suff.* 395 b.

ARCH', *Nottingh.* 283.

Archidiaconus, v. ÆLRICUS. ALRICUS. ANSCHITIL.
    GONFRIDUS.

ARCHIL, *Yorksh.* 322.[2]

ARCHIS, Willielmus de, *Suff.* 320.

---

[1] See Vol. i. p. 373.

[2] Archil was one of the Northumbrian lords who in 1068
joined in revolt, but afterwards made his peace with the
Conqueror. Dugdale gives an account of him in the
Baronage, tom. i. p. 3. chiefly from Simeon of Durham,
col. 80. He is also mentioned by Ordericus Vitalis. Numerous references to his former lands will be found in the
Index which precedes this.

ARCIS, Willielmus de, *Kent*, 3 b. 9 b. bis. *Suff.* 407.

ARDA, Ernulfus de, *Cambr*. 196. }
ARDE, Ernulfus de, *Bedf.* 211 passim. }

ARDULFUS, *Leic.* 233 b.

ARLINGUS, *Essex*, 59.

ARMENTERES, Robertus, *Berks*, 56 b.

ARNALDUS, *Sussex*, 25 b.

ARNEGRIM, *Nottingh.* 283 b. 291 bis.

ARNI, *Staff.* 249 b.

ARNULF presbyter, *Glouc.* 162.

ARNULFUS, *Warw.* 240 bis. *Suff.* 359 b. 369 b.

ARTUR quidam francig. *Worc.* 174 b.

ARTURUS, *Essex*, 50 b. bis.

ARUNDEL, Rogerius, *Dors.* 77 b.

Asc' [Ascelinus], *Essex*, 45.

ASCELINUS, *Essex*, 45, 63 b. 74 b.

ASCHIL presbyter, *Linc.* 367 b.

ASCOLF anglicus, *Norf.* 117.

ASELINUS, *Norf.* 189 b.

ASFORD, *Linc.* 346.

ASFORT, *Linc.* 346.[1]

ASLAC, *Linc.* 346.

ASLEN, *Staff.* 249.

ASNE, Hugo,[2] *Heref.* 180, 183.

ASSO, *Essex*, 67.

ASUERT homo Turoldi abbatis S. Petri de Burg. *Linc.* 346.

AUDOENO, S. Bernardus de, *Kent*, 9 b.

AVENEL, *Shropsh.* 259 b.

AUESGOT, *Cambr.* 202.

AUGUSTINI S. Abbas, *Kent*, 1 b. 6 b. 7 b.

AUGUSTINUS, *Sussex*, 25 b.

---

[1] Asford, Asfort, and Asuert homo Turoldi abbatis S. Petri de Burg, are apparently the same person.

[2] See the Index of Tenants in Capite, under LASNE.

Avigi, *Bedf.* 211 b.

Auigi homo Aschil antecessoris Hugonis Belcamp, *Bedf.*
211 b.

Aurifaber, Otho, *Cambr.* 190.

——————— Otto, *Essex*, 3 b.

——————— Rainbaldus, *Norf.* 273.

Auti, *Glouc.* 166. *Shropsh.* 259 b. bis.[1]

Auti unus homo, *Shropsh.* 260 b.

Azelin, *Somers.* 88 passim. 88 b. ter. 89 ter.

Azelinus, *Sussex*, 20 b. 21. *Berks*, 59. *Wilts*, 69 b.
bis. 72 bis. *Dors.* 82. *Sussex*, 89, 90 b. bis. 94 b.
Northampt. 221 b. 222. *Staff.* 248 bis. *Shropsh.*
260 b. *Chesh.* 268 b. *Derb.* 276 b. bis.

Azelinus homo Gisleberti de Gand, *Linc.* 355 b.

Azelinus homo Comitis Hugonis, *Linc.* 349.

Azo, *Sussex*, 24, 25. *Dors.* 83 b. *Northampt.* 222.
Leic. 236 b. *Shropsh.* 254, 254 b. ter. 255 bis.

Azo presbyter, *Nottingh.* 285.

Azor, *Hants*, 53 bis. *Midd.* 130.

Azor homo Ivonis Taillgebosc, *Linc.* 351 b.

B.

B. abb. [S. Edm.] *Suff.* 379.

B. abbas S. Eadmundi, *Suff.* 359 b.

B. Vicecomes, *Devon*, 100.

Baderon, Willielmus, *Glouc.* 162. *Heref.* 179 b.

Bagod, *Staff.* 249.

Baignar', Rad. *Essex*, 8 b.   ⎫
Baignard, Radulfus, *Norf.* 109 b. ⎬

Baignardus, *Essex*, 4 b. 6. *Norf.* 252 b. 275 bis.

Baignardus, Radulfus, *Essex*, 2, 13 b. 14 b. 31. ⎫
Baignart, Rad. *Essex*, 6 b.   ⎬
Bainard, *Norf.* 249.

---

[1] In both of these entries it is said, " Ipsemet tenuit."

BAINARD, Gaosfridus, *Norf.* 247 b.

BAINARDUS, *Norf.* 249. *Suff.* 415 bis.

BAINARDUS, Gaosfridus, *Norf.* 248 ter.

BAINARDUS, Willielmus,[1] *Suff.* 415.

BAINGIARDUS, *Surr.* 31 b.

BAINIARD, *Sussex,* 16.

BAINIARDUS, *Surr.* 31. *Midd.* 128.

BAIOCENSES Canonici, *Surr.* 31 b. ter.

BAIOCENSIS Episcopus,[2] *Kent,* 12. *Hants,* 50 b. *Hertf.*
    139. *Bucks,* 145. *Glouc.* 163 bis. 164. *Essex,* 6 b.

BALDEUINUS, *Norf.* 117.

BALDRICUS, *Kent,* 9 b. *Hertf.* 138. *Bedf.* 215. *Leic.*
    234. *Chesh.* 266 b.

BALDRICUS homo Episcopi Baiocensis, *Linc.* 343-b.

BALDRICUS homo Gozelini, *Linc.* 359.

BALDRICUS homo Gozelini filii Lanberti, *Linc.* 359 b.

BALDRICUS homo Comitis Hugonis, *Linc.* 349 b. bis.

BALDUINUS, *Kent,* 1 b. *Sussex,* 17. *Surr.* 36 bis. *Berks,*
    62 b. *Dev.* 113 bis. *Hertf.* 133 b. *Bucks,* 148 b.[3]
    149 bis.[3] *Glouc.* 164. *Worc.* 172, 174, 177 bis.
    Northampt. 222 b. 227 b. *Staff.* 250 bis. *Yorksh.*
    324, 324 b. *Linc.* 364. *Norf.* 195.

BALDUINUS homo Drogonis de Bevrere, *Yorksh.* 325.

BALDUINUS homo Raynerii de Brimou, *Linc.* 364.

BALDUINUS prepositus Episcopi [de Tedfort], *Norf.* 199.

BALDUINUS Vicecomes,[4] *Dev.* 100.

BALDUINUS et Guntardus, *Yorksh.* 324.

Balistarius, Bernerus, *Suff.* 381 b.

———————— Walterus, *Glouc.* 162.

BALT, Willielmus, *Essex,* 11 b.

BARB, Bernardus, *Heref.* 180.

---

[1] " Nepos Radulfi Bainardi."   [2] See Vol. i. p. 376.
[3] In both these entries it is said, " Istemet tenuit T. R. E.
et vendere potuit."   [4] See Vol. i. p. 377.

BARBES, Rotbertus de, *Kent,* 11.

BARET, *Yorksh.* 316 b. bis.[1]

BARO, Robertus, *Norf.* 117.

BASSET, Radulfus, *Hertf.* 137 b. *Buck.* 149 b.

BASSET, Ricardus, *Bedf.* 215.

BASSET, Willielmus, *Bedf.* 213.

BASUIN homo Roberti de Statford, *Linc.* 368 b. bis.

BEATRIX, *Somers.* 96 b. *Dev.* 110 b. 111, 114 b.

BEC, Walterus, *Buck.* 147 b.

BECH, Goisfridus de, *Hertf.* 132 b. 133, 135 b. 136 bis.

BECH, S. Maria de,[2] *Surr.* 34 b. bis. ⎫
BECH, Monachi de, *Oxf.* 159 b.   ⎭

BEDEFORD, Ecclesia de, *Bedf.* 210 b.

BEDEFORD, Ordui de, *Bedf.* 210 b.

BEDEFORD, Osgarus de, *Bedf.* 218.

Bedellus, v. Coc.

BEDEFORDE, Canonici de, *Bedf.* 217 b.

BELCAMP, Hugo de,[3] *Hertf.* 142 b. 210, 211 b. bis. 212,
    212 b. 215, 217 b. 218.

BELENCUN', Bernardus de, *Suff.* 442 b.

BELET, Willielmus, *Berks,* 56 b. *Dors.* 75 b.

BELFAGO, Radulfus de, *Norf.* 138, 229 b. *v.* BELLAFAGO.

BELFOU, Willielmus, *Berks,* 56 b. *Wilts,* 65 b.

BELLAFAGO, Rad. de, *Norf.* 110 b. 118, 137 b. 214,
    265, 265 b. 279. *v.* BELFAGO.[4]

BELUARD unus de Caruen, *Glouc.* 162.

BENEDICTUS, *Staff.* 248, 254 b.

BENEDICTUS abbas, *Northampt.* 226 b. *Leic.* 235 ter.

BENTHELMUS, *Som.* 89 b.

BENZELINUS, *Wilts,* 70.

---

[1] He had been the possessor before Ilbert de Laci, to
whom he was now under-tenant.

[2] See Vol. i. p. 378.   [3] See Vol. i. p. 379.

[4] See Vol. i. p. 380.

Bernulf, *Yorksh.* 311 bis.[1] 311 b. 312.[2]

Bernulfus, *Yorksh.* 312, 323 bis.

Beroldus, *Dors.* 83 b.

Berruarius, *Suff.* 385 b.

Berruarius, Herueu de, *Suff.* 386 b. 387 b.

Bertran, *Somers.* 93 b. 94.

Bertrannus, *Kent,* 13.

Beruoldus, *Norf.* 245 b.

Beuerde, Hugo de, *Suff.* 408.

Beulfus, *Dors.* 82.

Bevreli, Clerici de, *Yorksh.* 304.

Big', *Chesh.* 266 b. passim.

Bigot, *Chesh.* 266 b. passim. 268.

Bigot, Rogerus, *Norf.* 109 b. 110, 115, 117 b. 118, 118 b. 119, 137 b. 143, 143 b. bis. 150 b. 152 b. 153, 210, 214, 215 b. 236, 277, 277 b. *Suff.* 294 b. 299, 302, 310 b. 373 bis. 373 b. 374 b. 375, 375 b. 376, 377, 377 b. 378 b. ter. 385, 385 b. ter. 449.

Bigotus, Rogerus, *Suff.* 374, 374 b. 383.

Biscop, *Northampt.* 226, 228 b.

Bituricensis, Herueus de, *Suff.* 388 b.

Blach, Willielmus, homo Episcopi Baioc', *Hertf.* 142 b.

Blacheman, *Wilts,* 70 b.

Blancard homo Rogeri Pictavensis, *Linc.* 352 b.
Blancardus homo Rogeri Pictaviensis, *Linc.* 352 bis.

Blancus, Dimidius, *Essex,* 77, 78.

Blechu, *Cornw.* 120.

Bleio prepositus, *Glouc.* 162.

---

1 In both instances he had been the possessor before the manors belonged to Earl Alan.

2 " Ibi ħħ Bernulf maner. nunc idem ipse habet de Comite."

Blideburc, Rob. de, *Suff.* 415.

Blize quidam, *Kent*, 5.

Blohin, *Cornw.* 125 passim.[1]

Bloiet, Radulfus, *Hants*, 47.

Blon, Gislebertus,[2] *Suff.* 316.

Blon, Rodbertus,[3] *Suff.* 367 b. bis.

Blondus, Gislebertus,[4] *Suff.* 325. *v.* Blundus.

Blondus, Robertus, *Suff.* 370.

Blosseuile, Gislebertus de, *Buck.* 152 b. *Bedf.* 217.

Blundus, Gislebertus, *Suff.* 312 ter. 314. *v.* Blondus.

Blundus, Robertus, *Essex*, 76 b. *Norf.* 118. *Suff.* 367, 391, 447.

Boc uilla, Willielmus de, *Suff.* 411 bis. 412 b.

Bodin, *Yorksh.* 309 bis. 309 b. 310 passim. 310 b. 311 passim. 312, 312 b.

Bodin et Herueus, *Yorksh.* 309.

Bolebec, Hugo,[5] *Berks*, 56 b. *Bedf.* 211.

---

[1] Blohin's manors, five in number, are stated to have been an usurpation of the Earl of Moretaine from the church of St. Michael.

In this name, says Lysons, Mag. Brit. Cornw. p. lii. we recognize the ancestors of the ancient family of Bloyhon or Bloyowe, which became extinct (at least in its elder branch) in the fourteenth century, when the heiress married Tinten.

[2] An interlineation shows this to be Gislebertus Blundus.

[3] *f.* Robertus Blundus.

[4] Gilbert Blund founded the Priory of Ixworth in Suffolk, Taylor, in his Index Monasticus, says, about the year 1100. See Dugdale's extracts from the Collections of St. Lo Kniveton, "de fundatione ejusdem et Progenie Fundatoris," Monast. Anglic. last edit. vol. vi. p. 311. Gilbert Blund's great-grandson, William le Blonde, the last of the name, was killed at the battle of Lewes, 48th Hen. III. leaving no issue. See the Jermyn MS. Collections for Suffolk, vol. xxxvi. fol. 99.

[5] See Vol. i. p. 383.

Bollo, *Dors.* 78 b. 84.

Bollo presbyter, *Dors.* 79 bis. 84.[1]

Bondi, *Northampt.* 226 b. 227 b.[2]

Bono, *Somers.* 89 b.

Bonuaslet, Willielmus, *Buck.* 145.

Borci, Serlo, *Somers.* 96 b.

Bordinus, *Norf.* 206 bis. 274.

Borel, *Wilts,* 69 b. bis.

Boret et Turchil presbyteri, *Hunt.* 206.[3]

Borghillus, *Hants,* 43.

Bosc, Willielmus de, *Essex,* 81.

Boscroard, Willielmus de, et frater ejus, *Buck.* 149.

Boselin, *Sussex,* 16.

Boselinus, *Sussex,* 20 b.

Boso homo Aluredi de Lincole, *Linc.* 358.

Botericus, *Norf.* 232 b.

Botericus et Heroldus, *Norf.* 233.

Boterus, *Norf.* 234.

Boti liber homo, *Suff.* 291 b.

Botild, *Nottingh.* 283 b.

Botilt quædam femina, *Suff.* 448 b.

Braiboue, Hugo de, *Kent,* 8 b.

Braiose, Willelmus de,[4] *Sussex,* 16 b. bis. 26 b. 27, 27 b. *Wilts,* 65 b. *Dors.* 78 b.

Brant, Willielmus, *Norf.* 159 b.

Bretel, *Dors.* 79 bis. 79 b. passim. 80 bis. *Somers.* 86, 86 b. 92 passim. 92 b. passim. 93, 98 b. *Dev.* 104 b. bis. 105 b.

---

[1] He held the land of this entry T. R. E.

[2] " Idem Bondi libere tenuit."

[3] They had held the church of Botulvesbrige (which they now held) before the Survey.

[4] See Vol. i. p. 386.

Breteuile, Gislebertus de, *Hants*, 52. *Wilts*, 74 b.

Breteuille, Gislebertus de, *Oxf.* 161 bis.

Bretuile, Gislebertus de, *Hants*, 43 b.

Bricmær, *Sussex*, 26 b.

Brictmarus, *Suff.* 352, 384 b.

Brictmerus, *Suff.* 446 b.

Brictolfus, *Essex*, 102.[1]

Brictred et Derman, *Oxf.* 154.

Brictric, *Som.* 96, 98 b. *Cornw.* 120, 124 b. passim.
        Glouc. 166, 170 b. ter. *Warw.* 241. *Chesh.* 266.

Brictulfus, *Essex*, 33 b.

Brictuin, *Dors.* 77, 84 ter.

Brictuinus, *Dors.* 77 b. 84.

Brictuuardus, *Wilts*, 66.

Brien, *Cambr.* 194.

Brien, homo Roberti de Statford, *Linc.* 368 b. bis.

Briend, *Cornw.* 124 passim. *Staff.* 248 b. bis. 249 b.

Brienz, *Buck.* 148.

Brion, *Warw.* 242 b.

Brisard homo Comitis Hugonis, *Linc.* 349 b.

Brismer, *Heref.* 180.

Bristeua, *Oxf.* 155 b.

Bristist, *Berks*, 56 b.

Bristoaldus presbyter, *Heref.* 183 b.

Bristoardus presbyter, *Wilts*, 65 b.

Brito, Gozelinus, *Glouc.* 162.

Brito, Rogerus, *Somers.* 91.

Brito, Willielmus, *Hunt.* 207.

Brixi, *Cornw.* 120.

Brodo, *Bedf.* 218.

Broilg, Osbernus de, *Bedf.* 213 b.

Broilg, Osbertus de, *Bedf.* 213.

---

[1] He had held T. R. E.

BRUMAN, *Berks,* 56 b.

BRUMAN quidam sochemannus, *Cambr.* 189 b.

BRUN presbyter, *Oxf.* 157.

BRUN, W. de, *Suff.* 377.

BRUN prepositus de Gypeswiz, *Suff.* 337 b.

BRUNARDUS, *Norf.* 222 b.

BRUNEL homo Colsuan, *Linc.* 357 bis.

BRUNGAR, *Somers.* 88.

BRUNING, *Warw.* 241.[1]

BRUNNUINUS sochemannus, *Suff.* 418 b.

BRUNO, *Warw.* 243 b.

BUCARDUS, *Suff.* 367.

BUCI, Robertus de, *Leic.* 232 ter. 232 b. 236 passim. 236 b. *Staff.* 250 b. bis.

BUERED, *Staff.* 249 b.

BUERET, *Staff.* 249 b.

BUISSEL, Rogerus, *Som.* 94 b.

BUNDO, *Linc.* 341.

BURCI, Serlo de, *Som.* 87.

BURDET, Hugo, *Leic.* 236 ter. 236 b.

BURDET, Robertus, *v.* FILIUS. UXOR.

BURGENSES villæ S. Albani, *Hertf.* 135 b.

BURGENSES villæ de Herteford, *Hertf.* 132.

BURGHARD, *Norf.* 117.

BURNARDUS, *Bedf.* 212.

BURNART, *Essex,* 102.

BURNEUILLA, Willielmus de, *Norf.* 183 b. ⎫
BURNOLUILLA, Willielmus de, *Suff.* 337, 438. ⎬
BURNOUILLA, Willielmus de, *Suff.* 282, 336 b. passim. 342 b.[2] 343. ⎭

BURSIGNI, Willielmus de, *Essex,* 18 b.

---

[1] He had held T. R. E.

[2] This entry relates to Leuetuna, now Livington. The

Busch, Aluric, *Hertf.* 140.[1]

Busli, Rogerius de,[2] *Glouc.* 163 b.   *Leic.* 237.   *Inter Rip. et Mersam,* 270.

Buterus, *Leic.* 235 b.

C.

Cada',[3] W. de, *Suff.* 324 b. 325 b. ter. ⎤
Cada', Walterus de, *Suff.* 317.   ⎦

Cada', Willielmus de, *Suff.* 310.

Cadio, *Dev.* 106. *Staff.* 248 b. bis.

Cadomi, S. Stefanus, *Wilts,* 65.

Cadomo, Galterus, *seu* Walterus de, *Norf.* 154. *Suff.* 304 b. bis. 312 b. 313, 313 b. bis. 314, 318 passim. 320, 327 b. 329 b. 394 b.

Caflo, *Somers.* 94.[4]

Cahainges, Willelmus de, *Sussex,* 16 b. 20 b. ter. *Bucks,* 149 b.

Caisned, Radulfus de, *Sussex,* 17.

Calpus liber homo, *Norf.* 240,[5] 262.

Caluus, R. *Cambr.* 198 b.

Caluus, Robertus, *Cambr.* 198 b.

Calvus, Willielmus, *Glouc.* 162.

Jermyn MSS. for Suffolk, vol. xxxvii. fol. 186, say, " This most ancient family of Burnaville was seated at Livington, in Colnes Hundred, and very early extinct; for Sir William Burnaville died without issue male in the reign of Edward I, and left Margaret his sole daughter and heir: married to Jo. Weylond."

[1] " Istemet tenuit T. R. E. homo Suuen fuit de soca regis E. de consuetudine. i. obolum reddeb. vicecomiti per annum."

[2] See Vol. i. p. 389.   [3] *f.* W. de Cadamo.

[4] He had held T. R. E.

[5] Calpus had held the land of this entry, T. R. E.

Camerarius, Adeloldus, *Kent*, 7 b.

——————— Aiulfus, *Hants*, 52.

——————— Girardus, *Glouc.* 166.

——————— Goisfridus, *Hants*, 39.

——————— Herbertus, *Hants*, 42 b. 45 b.

——————— Hunfridus, *Surr.* 30. *Leic.* 230 b.

——————— Turstinus, *Hants*, 52.

——————— Willielmus, *Surr.* 35 b. *Midd.* 127, 127 b.
    Cambr. 190.

CANDORSO, Rogerus de, *Suff.* 406 b.

CANDOS, Rogerus de, *Suff.* 409 b. 410, 410 b.

Canonici manerii de Plintone, *Dev.* 100 b.

Canonici S. Pauli Lond. *Midd.* 127 b. bis. 128 passim.

Canonicus. v. ANSFRIDUS. DURANDUS. ENGELBRICUS.
    GODRIC. GOISFRIDUS. GUERI.

CANTUAR. Archiepisc. *Kent*, 11.

CANTUAR. Monachi, *Kent*, 3, 4, 5.

CAP¹, Willielmus, *Dev.* 103 b. *v.* CHEVRE.

Capellani Comitis Rogerii, *Shropsh.* 253.

Capellani Episcopi de Hereford, *Heref.* 182 b.

Capellanus, v. RADULFUS.

CARDON, Willielmus, *Essex*, 62 b.   }
CARDON, Willielmus, homo G. de Magnauitt, *Essex*, 19 b. }

CARDUN, Willielmus, *Essex*, 33 b. 100 b.

CARNOT', Radulfus, *Leic.* 232 ter.

CARON, Willielmus de, *Bedf.* 210 ter.¹ 210 b. bis. 212,
    212 b. bis. 214 b.

CARUN, Willielmus de, *Bedf.* 212.

---

¹ In one entry under the Bishop of Lincoln's land, to whom he was under-tenant, in this folio, it is said, " In hac terra [Estone] Episcopatus reclamet Willielmus de Caron LX. acr. inter planum et silvam super Hugonem de Belcamp. unde Radulfus Taillebosc desaisivit patrem ejusdem Willielmi, qui ipsam terram tenebat T. R. E. ut homines de Hundredo dicunt."

---

1 The Abbey of St. Peter at Castellion, or Conches, in the diocese of Evreux, was here an under-tenant to Ralph de Todeni, by whose father, Roger de Todeni, or Toeni, it had been founded, A.D. 1050.

2 " Ipse tenuit T. R. E."   3 " Ipsemet tenuit."

4 " Terram ad I. car. Hanc concessit ei W. rex."

5 " Ipse tenuit T. R. E."

6 In this entry, "ħb." He had been the previous possessor.

7 See Vol. i. p. 397.

CLARENBOLDO, Robertus, *Buck.* 149.

CLARON, *Nottingh.* 284 b. 285.

CLAUILE, Walterus de,[1] *Cornw.* 120 b.

CLAUILLA, R. de, *Suff.* 314 b.

CLAVILLA, Walterus de, *Suff.* 308.

Clerici duo, Berks, 56 b. *Yorksh.* 302.

Clerici duo alii, Berks, 56 b.

Clerici tres, Heref. 182. *Nottingh.* 283.

Clerici quatuor communiter tenentes, *Sussex,* 17.

Clericus, v. ALAN. ALBERTUS. ALBOLDUS. ALUREDUS.
EUSTACHIUS. GODEFRIDUS. HUGO. OSBERNUS.
PETRUS. RAIMAR. RANNULFUS. RICHERIUS. RO-
BERTUS. ROGERUS.

Clericus quidam, Sussex, 17.

Clericus unus, Som. 89. *Heref.* 182. *Nottingh.* 283.
Yorksh. 304.

Clericus Comitis E. *Essex,* 7.

Clericus Hugonis de Grentemaisnil, *Glouc.* 169.

CLODOAN, *Staff.* 249 b.

CLUNIACO abb. de, *Cambr.* 196. ⎫
CLUNIACO, Monachi de, *Hunt.* 205 b. ⎬ [2]
⎭

COC, Aluuinus, bedellus, *Cambr.* 190.

COCI, Albericus de, *Berks,* 58.

Cocus, Alboldus, *Hants,* 38 bis.

—— Ansgerus, *Som.* 87.

—— Garinus, *Norf.* 156.

—— Goscelmus, *Dors.* 77 b.

---

[1] See Vol. i. p. 398.

[2] The Abbey of Clugny in Burgundy was founded
A. D. 910, by William the first, Duke of Aquitaine and
Auvergne. Montacute in Somersetshire, and Lenton in
Nottinghamshire, were Cells to this house. Roger Earl of
Shrewsbury's charter, granting the manor of Chelton to
this abbey in the time of King William Rufus, is in the
Monasticon, last edit. vol. vi. p. 1109.

Cocus, Rotbertus, *Kent*, 13 b.

COLA, *Derb.* 274 b.

COLA anglicus, *Berks*, 62.

COLA homo Henrici de Ferieres, *Derb.* 274.

COLAUILLA, Gislebertus de, *Suff.* 315 b. 319, 324, 326.

COLBERTUS, *Devon*, 109. *Chesh.* 265.[1]

COLEGRIM, *Linc.* 341, 345 b. 346 b. bis. 347 b. 360 b.

COLEGRIM homo Comitis Alani, *Linc.* 348 bis. 348 b.

COLEGRIM homo Drogonis de Bevrere, *Linc.* 360 b. bis.

COLEGRIM homo Odonis arbalistarii, *Linc.* 366.

COLEGRIM homo Roberti de Statford, *Linc.* 368 b.

COLEVIL, Willielmus de, *Yorksh.* 322 b. ⎤
COLEVILE, Willielmus, *Yorksh.* 322 b. ⎦

COLGRIM, *Somers.* 89 b.

COLLE, *Derb.* 273 b. 277.

COLO, *Cornw.* 124 b.

COLSUAIN, *Som.* 88 b. bis.

COLSUAN, *Cambr.* 194 b. passim. *Linc.* 345 b.

COLSUAN homo Drogonis de Bevrere, *Linc.* 360 b.

COLSUAN homo Episcopi Dunelmensis, *Linc.* 341.

COLSUAN homo Gisleberti de Gand, *Linc.* 354 b.

COLSUAN homo Gozelini filii Lanberti, *Linc.* 359.

COLSUAN homo Comitis Hugonis, *Linc.* 349 b.

COLSUAN homo Rainerii de Brimov, *Linc.* 364.

COLSUEN, *Dev.* 112 b.

COLUIN, *Dev.* 106, 106 b. 116 b.

COLVINUS, *Dev.* 118 b. ter.

COLUMBANUS monachus,[2] *Surr.* 155 ter.

COLUMBELS, Rannulfus de, *Kent*, 7, 8 b. bis. 9.

COLUMBERS, Radulfus de, *Kent*, 11 b. 12 b.

Comes, v. ALANUS. E. EBROICENSIS. EUSTACHIUS. HUGO.

CONAN, *Oxf.* 155.

Concubina quædam Nigelli de Albingi, *Bedf.* 214.

---

[1] " Qui et tenuit."

[2] He was abbat of Eynsham in Oxfordshire.

CONDED homo Colsuan, *Linc.* 357 ter.

CONSTANT' Episcopus, *Wilts*, 66 b.

CONSTANTIENSIS Episcopus,[1] *Som.* 86 b. 87.   *Dev.* 100.
   Glouc. 162.

CONSTANTINUS, *Glouc.* 164 b.

Consul, v. EUSTACHIUS.

COQUUS quidam Regis W. *Glouc.* 162 b.

Coquus, Hugo, *Berks,* 58 b.

CORBELIN, *Surr.* 36 b.

CORBELINUS, *Sussex,* 23 b. 24. *Surr.* 32 b. *Northampt.* 229.

CORBET, Rogerus, *Shropsh.* 253 b. 254.

CORBIN, *Warw.* 238 b.

CORBINUS, *Kent,* 7 b.

CORBUN, Hugo de, *Norf.* 176 b. 278.   *Suff.* 333, 339.

CORBUN, W. *Essex,* 64 b.

CORCEL, Rogerius de, *Som.* 91 bis.

CORCELLE, Rogerus de,[2] *Somers.* 91, 96 b. *v.* CURCELLE.

CORMELIES, Abbatia de, *Hants,* 49.

CORMELIENSIS Abb. *Hants,* 52.

CORMELIIS, Abb. de, *Glouc.* 163, 164.   } [3]

CORMELIIS, Sancta Maria de, *Heref.* 179 b. passim·
   180, 180 b. 184 b.

CORMELIIS, Ansfridus de, *Glouc.* 164.   *Heref.* 179 b.

CO'RP, *Essex,* 67.

CREDUN, Wido de, *Linc.* 340, 355 b.

CRENEBURNE, Radulfus de, *Dors.* 83.

CRICHELADE, unus burgensis in, *Wilts,* 67.

CRISPIN, Milo,[4] *Wilts,* 71 b. 74 b. *Glouc.* 162 b. *Bedf.* 217.

CROC, *Wilts,* 67, 69.

CROC, Rainaldus, *Hants,* 52.

CRUEL, Robertus, *Sussex,* 18 bis.

---

[1] See Vol. i. p. 400.   [2] See Vol. i. p. 401.
[3] See Vol. i. p. 401. note 3.   [4] See Vol. i. p. 402

CUDHEN, Goduinus, *Essex*, 17 b. *v.* GUDHEN.

CUELAI, Humfridus de, *Norf.* 173, 179.

CULLINGUS quidam, burgensis [de Gepeswiz], *Suff.* 290.

CULTURÆ, S. Petri, Monachi, *Buck.* 147 b.

CURBESPINE, Radulfus de, *Kent*, 7 b. bis. 8 bis. 9 b. bis.
    10 b. ter. 11 ter. 11 b. passim. 12 b. *Suff.* 374.

CURBUN, Hugo de, *Suff.* 335.

CURCELLE, Rogerius de, *Som.* 86. *Shropsh.* 256 passim.
    v. CORCELLE.

CURCI, Ricardus de, *Oxf.* 154 b.

CURCON, Robertus de, *Norf.* 187.

CURCUN, Robertus de, *Norf.* 175 b. bis. 181 b. *Suff.*
    299 b. 331 b. ter. 336.

CUS, *Suff.* 334 b.

CUSTODES Castelli [*sc.* de Hastinges], *Sussex*, 20 b. 21.

D.

DANIEL, Rogerus, *Sussex*, 18 b.

Dapifer, *v.* ALUREDUS. EUDO. G. GODEFRIDUS. GODRI-
    CUS. HAMO. HELTUS. HENRICUS. IUO. ODO. RA-
    DULFUS.

Dapifer Henrici de Ferrariis, *Essex*, 57.

Dapifer Juditæ Comitissæ, Alanus, *Hunt.* 206 b. 207.

DAUID, *Dors.* 82. *Chesh.* 266. *Essex*, 31.

DAVID interpres, *Dors.* 83.

DE BEE UILLA, Willielmus, *Suff.* 374.

DEBERRUARIU', Herueu, *Suff.* 386 b. *v.* BERRUARIUS.

DEBU UILLA, W. de, *Suff.* 388.

DENOIERS, W. *Norf.* 195 b. *v.* DENUERS.

DENOMORE, Willielmus, *Suff.* 424.

DENUERS, Willielmus, *Norf.* 194, 198, 198 b.

DEPEIZ, Guerno,[1] *Suff.* 363 b.

DERAMIS, Rogerus, *Suff.* 449 b. *sc.* Rogerus de Ramis.

---

[1] *sc.* Guerno de Peiz.

Dereman, *Oxf.* 154.

Dereuuen, *Oxf.* 154.

Derinc, *Linc.* 347 b. 356.

Derisbou, Walter, *Suff.* 327.

Derman, *Oxf.* 154.

Deuais, Robertus, *Norf.* 176 b.

Deuals, Robertus de, *Norf.* 177 bis.

Deuernu', Huardus,[1] *Suff.* 353 b.

Deus saluæt dominas, Rogerus,[2] *Essex,* 21 b.

Diaconus, v. Galterus.

Diaconus quidam, Essex, 93 b.

Dirsi, *Suff.* 446 b.

Dispensator, Robertus, *Worc.* 172 b. 173, 173 b. bis. 174, 175.

———————— Willielmus, *Kent,* 3.

Doda, *Berks,* 56 b.

Doddus, *Worc.* 173 b.

Dodeman, *Dors.* 79, 79 b. ter. *Somers.* 91, 92, 93, 96 bis.

Dodemund et Warmund, *Somers.* 94 b.

Dodesone, Aluuinus, *Hertf.* 142.

Dodin, *Northampt.* 219, 227 b. 229.

Dodin homo Aluredi de Lincole, *Linc.* 358 b.

Dodinus, *Northampt.* 226 b. bis. 229.

Dodinus homo Aluredi de Lincole, *Linc.* 358 b.

Dodo, *Cornw.* 120, 124 b.

Dodo homo Aluredi de Lincole, *Linc.* 358 b.

Dolfin, *Derb.* 278 b.

Domnicus, *Bedf.* 212 b.

Donecan, *Somers.* 93.

Doneuuald, *Yorksh.* 312.

Donno, *Dev.* 105 b.

---

[1] *sc.* Huardus de Vernun.

[2] He occurs among the Tenants in Capite, in the former Volume, p. 404.

DORECESTRE unus burgensis in, cum x. acris, *Dors.* 75 b.

DOUENOLDUS, *Hants,* 53 b.

DOUUAI, Walscinus de, *Som.* 98 b.

DOUUAI, Walterius de, *Kent,* 6 b.

DREUUES, Amalricus de, *Wilts,* 70 b. 71.

DROGO, *Berks,* 56 b. 60, 62 b. *Dors.* 79, 80. *Somers.*
87 b. 88, 91 b. 92 ter. 92 b. passim. 93 passim.
94 b. *Dev.* 102, 103, 104, 104 b. passim. 105,
105 b. *Buck.* 148. *Oxf.* 157, 158 bis. *Glouc.* 165,
168. *Heref.* 180, 182 b. 183, 186 b. *Northampt.*
226 ter.

DROGO, *Warw.* 242 b. 243. *Staff.* 249 b. 250 ter. *Chesh.*
264 bis. 264 b. ter. *Derb.* 276. *Essex,* 90. *Suff.* 380.

DROGO quidam, *Linc.* 369 b.

DROGO f. Ponzii,[1] *Worc.* 174 b.

DROGO homo Radulfi nepotis Goisfridi Alselin, *Linc.*
369 b.

DUDEMAN, *Som.* 96 passim.

DUNNING, *Glouc.* 162. *Chesh.* 267 b.

DUNSTAN, *Yorksh.* 317 b.

DUR', Willielmus, *Wilts,* 70 b.

DURANDUS, *Sussex,* 17 b. 20 b. 21 b. 24. *Surr.* 36 b.
Hants, 40, 40 b. 47 b. 51 ter. *Wilts,* 65 b. 73.
Dors. 84. *Somers.* 95 b. 96 ter. *Glouc.* 164 b. 165,
166. *Heref.* 181. *Cambr.* 198 passim. 198 b. ter.
Leic. 234. *Chesh.* 265. *Norf.* 189 b. *Suff.* 316,
365, 446.

DURANDUS canonicus S. Pauli Lond. *Midd.* 127 b.

DURANDUS de Glouuecestre, *Hants,* 52.

DURANDUS prepositus, *Northampt.* 219.

DURANDUS uicecomes, *Glouc.* 162 ter. 162 b. 164 b.
165, 167.

DYNECHAIE, *Suff.* 320.

---

[1] See Vol. i. p. 405.

E.

E. Comes, *Essex*, 6 b.

EADVUUNUS, *Norf.* 184.

EBOR. Canonici S. Petri, *Yorksh.* 302 b. passim.

EBORACENSIS abbas, *Yorksh.* 305 bis. 314 passim.[1]

EBRARDUS, *Wilts*, 66, 67. *Yorksh.* 321 b. 322 bis.

EBRARDUS homo Willielmi Perci, *Yorksh.* 301 b.

EBROICENSIS Comes,[2] *Hants*, 52. *Oxf.* 156 b.

EBROIS, Rogerus de, *Norf.* 222 b. 225 b.

EBRULFI S. Abbatia, *Cambr.* 193 b. bis. *Warw.* 242. ⎫
EBRULFI S. Æcclesia, *Staff.* 248 ter.	⎬ 3
	⎭

ECHEBRAND,[4] *Nottingh.* 290 b.

EDDESHAM, Willielmus de, *Kent*, 4 b.

EDDEUA, *Buck.* 145.[5]

EDDID, *Oxf.* 154.

EDDIET, *Shropsh.* 259 b.

EDDILLE, *Dev.* 103 b.

EDDULFUS, *Dev.* 111. *Buck.* 150 b. *Warw.* 241. *Staff.* 247 b.

EDIED, *Suff.* 446 b.

EDELO homo Roberti de Statford, *Linc.* 368 b.

EDERICUS, *Bedf.* 217 b.

EDGAR, *Wilts*, 65.

EDMARUS, *Hunt.* 206. *Essex*, 46 b.

EDMER, *Som.* 87 b. 88. *Dev.* 103.

EDMUND, *Shropsh.* 259 b.[6]

---

1 In these entries as under-tenant to Berenger de Todeni.

2 See Vol. i. p. 408.

3 See an account of this Abbey, Vol. i. p. 408.

4 " ħɓ." He had been the previous possessor.

5 At Linforde; "tenet Eddeua de Episcopo" Constantiensi. "Hoc Manerium tenuit eadem Eddeva T. R. E."

6 "Ipsemet tenuit."

---

[1] " Et ipse T. R. E. tenuit."

[2] " Ipsemet tenuit de rege E."

[3] " Ipse tenebat T. R. E."

[4] " Ipse tenuit T. R·E."

[5] " Ipsemet tenuit T. R. E."

[6] " Roebertus de Roelent ten. [de Comite Hugone] Coleselt, et Eduinus de eo qui et tenuit ut liber homo."

[7] " Pater ejus tenuit T. R. E."

EDUUARDUS filius Edrici, *Dev.* 100 b.

EDWARDUS liber homo, *Sussex,* 20.

EDUUARDUS Vicecomes,[1] *Hants,* 43 b. *Wilts,* 64 b. 67 b.
69, 74, 74 b. bis.

EDUUI, *Hants,* 53 b.[2] *Berks,* 56 b. *Dev.* 108.[3] *Glouc.*
166 bis.

EDUUINE, *Kent,* 1 b.

EDUUIUS, *Dev.* 107 b.[4]

EGBERTUS homo Gisleberti de Gand, *Linc.* 354 b. ⎫
EGBRIHTUS homo Gisleberti de Gand, *Linc.* 355 b. ⎭

EHELO homo Roberti de Statford, *Linc.* 368 b.

EIDEUA, *Midd.* 130 b.

EILEUA, *Som.* 94. *Warw.* 243.

EILUUARD, *Shropsh.* 254.

EINBOLDUS, *Norf.* 253.

ELBERTUS, *Wilts,* 70 b.

ELDEID, *Sussex,* 26 b.

ELDRED, *Hants,* 40.[5] *Somers.* 93 b. *Shropsh.* 259 b. bis.
Yorksh. 310 b.[6] 311 b.[7] 322 bis.

ELDREDUS, *Hants,* 44. *Hertf.* 134. *Yorksh.* 329 bis.

---

[1] Edward of Salisbury, of whom see the former volume,
p. 411, among the Tenants in Capite.

[2] " Ipsemet tenuit de Rege E."

[3] " Idem tenebat T. R. E."

[4] " Ipse tenebat T. R. E."

[5] " Femina sua tenuit T. R. E.—Non potuit ire quo
voluit." The land was held under the Bishop of Winchester.

[6] This Eldred held under Earl Alan the manor which
had previously belonged to himself. " Ibi habebat Eldred I.
maner. Nunc idem habet de Comite."

[7] Of VI. Carrucates at Malmerbi. " Ibi habebat Eldred
man. nunc idem habet de comite et wast. est."

---

[1] " Uxor ejus tenuit in dote T. R. E."

[2] "Ipse tenuit de Rege E."

[3] " Ipsemet tenuit et liber homo fuit."

[4] " Ipsemet tenuit et liber homo fuit."

[5] " Ipsemet tenuit."

[6] In one instance, the land which he held under Ilbert de Laci had previously been his own.

[7] He had been the possessor before the time of the Survey.

[8] He held, in this instance, under Ilbert de Laci the land which Siuuard and he had previously held in capite.

Eluui, *Somers.* 89 b. *Glouc.* 166. *Linc.* 361.

Eluui homo Walterii de Aincurt, *Linc.* 361.

Eluuinus, *Heref.* 184.

Eluuius, *Essex,* 19 b.

Engelbricus canonicus, *Midd.* 127 b.[1]

Engeler, *Sussex,* 16, 24. *Somers.* 98. *Bedf.* 218.

Engenoldus, *Wilts,* 72.

Engenulfus, *Wilts,* 72 bis.

Enisan, *Yorksh.* 309 ter. 309 b. passim. 310 b. bis.
311 bis. 312 b.

Enisant, *Cambr.* 195. *Essex,* 77.

Er. [Ermenhaldus], *Cornw.* 121.

Erchebrand, *Chesh.* 266.[2]

Erchenbaldus, *Dev.* 104 b. 105 ter. *Cornw.* 124 ter.
Oxf. 159 b.

Erchenold homo Episcopi Lincoliensis, *Linc.* 344 b.

Erenbaldus, *Yorksh.* 324 b.

Erenburgis, *Wilts,* 72.

Erfastus, *Bedf.* 214 bis. 214 b. bis.

Erfastus homo Nigelli Albiniensis, *Bedf.* 211 b.

Erluinus, *Hunt.* 206.

Erm. [Ermenhaldus], *Cornw.* 121 b.

Ermenald, *Dev.* 103 b.

Ermenfridus, *Warw.* 239, 241, 241 b. bis. 244 b. *v.*
Hermenfridus.

Ermenfridus homo Osberni de Archeo, *Yorksh.*
329.

Ermenhaldus, *Cornw.* 121 bis.

Erm'iot, *Suff.* 295.

---

[1] " Isdem canonicus tenuit de Episcopo W. T. R. E.   Non potuit vendere."

[2] " Qui et tenuit ut liber homo."

ERNALDUS, *Sussex*, 23 b. 25. *Dev.* 111 b. *Bedf.* 217 b. *Northampt.* 227 b. bis. *Leic.* 232 b. ter. 233 ter. *Staff.* 248 b. *Essex*, 39 bis. 39 b. 101 b. bis. *Norf.* 232. *Suff.* 423.

ERNEGIS, *Yorksh.* 312.

ERNEGIS homo Episcopi Baiocensis, *Linc.* 342.

ERNEIS, *Somers.* 89, 89 b. 90 b. 94. *Leic.* 232 b.

ERNEIS homo Comitis Hugonis, *Linc.* 349.

ERNEISUS, *Leic.* 232 b.

ERNOLD, *Worc.* 176 b.

ERNOLFUS, *Suff.* 347.

ERNUCION, *Sussex*, 24 b. 25. *Shropsh.* 259.

ERNUI, *Shropsh.* 256. *Derb.* 278 b. bis. *Yorksh.* 315 b.

ERNUI homo Rogeri Pictavensis, *Linc.* 352. *v.* ERNUIN.

ERNUIN, *Derb.* 278.

ERNUIN homo Rogeri Pictavensis, *Linc.* 352, 352 b.

ERNUINUS, *Shropsh.* 255 b.

ERNUINUS presbyter, *Bedf.* 210.

ERNULFUS, *Wilts*, 70. *Midd.* 129 b. *Buck.* 147. *Bedf.* 212. *Yorksh.* 316. *Linc.* 360 b. *Essex*, 72. *Suff.* 360, 363, 402.

ERNULFUS quidam, *Hants*, 49 b.

ERNULFUS homo Rogeri de Busli, *Nottingh.* 286.

ERNUZON, *Berks*, 59 b.

ERTEIN, *Shropsh.* 259 b.

ESCALERS, Harduinus de, *Cambr.* 190 b.

ETTARD,[1] *Suff.* 331.

EUDO, *Kent*, 9 b. *Buck.* 152 b. *Glouc.* 164 b. *Linc.* 348 b. *Essex*, 19. *Norf.* 240, 246.

---

[1] He was the same person with Aitardus who occurs in the same folio.

Eudo dapifer,[1] *Berks,* 56 b. *Bedf.* 210 b. bis. 215. *Essex,* 6 b. 13 b. *Suff.* 404 b.

Eudo filius Clama, *Norf.* 110 b.

Eudo filius Nigelli, *Suff.* 292 bis.

Eudo homo Comitis Alani, *Linc.* 347 b. 348 b. ter.

Euen, *Suff.* 440 b.

Euerwinus burgensis [Norwicensis], *Norf.* 117.

Euesham, Abb. de, *Worc.* 174 bis.

Eurardus, *Som.* 90 b. 91 b. *Cambr.* 199 b. bis. *Hunt.* 204 b. *Essex,* 63.

Eurardus homo Willielmi de Perci, *Linc.* 354.

Euroldus homo Gozelini filii Lanberti, *Linc.* 359 b.

Euruinus, *Oxf.* 158, 158 b.

Eustachius, *Sussex,* 26 b. *Hunt.* 204 bis. 204 b. 208 bis. *Northampt.* 221 b. 222 bis. 226, 228 b. *Essex,* 27 b.

Eustachius clericus, *Sussex,* 19.

Eustachius Comes, *Som.* 87. *Essex,* 9 b. 104, 106 b. } [2]
Eustachius Consul, *Essex,* 20 b.

Eustachius Vicecomes, *Hunt.* 206 b. bis.

Eustacius, *Hunt.* 203 b. 205 b. *Northampt.* 222 bis.

F.

Fabri, *Berks,* 56 b.

Faderlin, *Hants,* 45, 45 b. 46 b. 48 b.

Fadrelin, *Hants,* 45.

Faeicon, *Norf.* 145 b.

Faeto, Radulfus, *Norf.* 257.

Falcus, *Suff.* 363.

Farman, *Kent,* 3.

Farmannus, *Suff.* 387.

Farmannus commendatus Wicolfi, *Suff.* 338.

---

[1] See Vol. i. p. 415.

[2] Eustace Earl of Boulogne. See Vol. i. p. 416.

FASTRADUS, *Somers.* 89 passim.

FATATUS, Radulfus, *Essex,* 79, 79 b.

FECH, *Shropsh.* 257.

FEGGO, *Leic.* 236 b.

FELCHERUS, *Northampt.* 224 ter.

FELGERES, Rad. de, *Berks,* 63 b.

FELGERIS, Rad. de, *Norf.* 278.

Femina quædam, Kent, 13 b. *Dors.* 79.

Feminæ II. *Norf.* 117.

FEREND. Alsi de, *Oxf.* 154 b.

FERENDONE, Elsi de, *Glouc.* 164, 165 b.

FEREIRES, Henricus de,[1] *Oxf.* 154 b.

FERERES, Henricus de, *Berks,* 58.

FERERIIS, Henricus de, *Glouc.* 166 b.

FERMEUS, *Suff.* 418 b.

FERRARIIS, Henricus de, *Derb.* 272 b. 276 b.

FERRERES, Henricus de, *Berks,* 57 b. passim. *Wilts,* 64 b. *Staff.* 248.

FERRON, *Northampt.* 222.

FILIA Rogeri [de Ramis], *Suff.* 422 b. bis.

FILII Arfasti Episcopi, *Norf.* 118 b.

FILII Gamel, *Yorksh.* 311 b.[2]

FILII quatuor Osfort, *Norf.* 186 b.[3]

FILIUS Boselin, *Sussex,* 16.

FILIUS Roberti Burdel,[4] *Leic.* 232 b.

FILIUS Roberti Burdet, *Leic.* 232 b. bis.

FILIUS Cole de Basinge, *Hants,* 50.

FILIUS Costelini, *Heref.* 181.

FILIUS Eurebold, *Dors.* 83 bis.

---

1 See Vol. i. p. 418.

2 In Danebi. " Ibi habebat Gamel maner.   Nunc habent filii ejus de Com. [Alano.]"

3 Osfort had held the manor " sub Heroldo."

4 *sc.* Burdet.

FILIUS Alsi de Ferendone, *Berks,* 56.

FILIUS Leuuini, *Derb.* 278 b.

FILIUS Odonis camerarii, *Dors.* 81 b.

FILIUS Willelmi Tahum, *Kent,* 8 b.

FILIUS Turaldi, *Kent,* 6 b.

FILIUS Turoldi, *Essex,* 22 b. ter. 23 bis. 25.

FILIUS Wadardi, *Oxf.* 159.

FILIUS Wasuuic, *Glouc.* 162.

FIRMATUS, *Cambr.* 199 b. bis.

FISCA'NO, Willielmus, *Hants,* 41.

FLA'BARD, Ranulfus,[1] *Wilts,* 67 bis. *Somers.* 89 b.

FLA'MART, Ranulfus, *Berks,* 58.

FLA'MENS, Walterus, *Bedf.* 210 b.

FLANBARD, Rannulfus, *Surr.* 30 b. ter. *Oxf.* 157.

FLANDR' Walt',[2] *Bedf.* 215 b. bis.

FLAVUS, Robertus, *Wilts,* 73.

FLINT, Aluuinus, *Suff.* 446 b.

FLOC, Goisfridus de, *Sussex,* 19 b.

FOLCHERAN, *Somers.* 88.

FOLCRAN, *Somers.* 88 b.

FOLET, Willelmus, *Kent,* 4 b. bis. 5.

FONTENED, Æcc̄ta S. Stefani de, *Wilts,* 72 b.

FORIST, Willielmus, *Hants,* 53 b.

Forestarius, Herbertus, *Hants,* 39.

Fossator, Hereberd, *Norf.* 117.

FRAGRIN, *Staff.* 247.

FRANE, *Staff.* 247.

FRANCI duo, *Bedf.* 215. *Essex,* 42.

FRANCI duo, Godeboldus et Odo, *Essex,* 43 b.

FRANCI duo, Giroldus et Ih̄os, *Essex,* 44 b.

FRANCI Homines, *Essex,* 4 b.

FRANCIG' quidam, *Hertf.* 140 b.

FRANCIG' unus, *Heref.* 182. *Leic.* 233 b.

---

[1] See Vol. i. p. 420.   [2] See Vol. i. ut supr.

FRANCIG' duo, *Staff.* 247.

FRANCIG' duo, et sex Angli, *Bedf.* 210.

FRANCIG' quatuor, *Sussex,* 23 b.

FRANCIG' milites quatuor, *Kent,* 12.

FRANCIGENA quidam, *Kent,* 3 b.

FRANCO, *Dev.* 113.

FRANCO quidam, *Shropsh.* 252.

FRANCO homo Drogonis de Bevrere, *Yorksh.* 324 b. ter.
325.

FRANCUS, *Suff.* 432.

FRANCUS homo unus, *Shropsh.* 254 b.

FRANKUS, *Norf.* 250.

FRANO, *Leic.* 234.

FRATER Reinbaldi, *Glouc.* 165 b.

FRATRES IIII. *Warw.* 241.

FRAUUINUS, *Wilts,* 74 b. *Cornw.* 125.

FREDGIS, *Nottingh.* 282 b. 288.

FREDGIS homo Colegrim, *Linc.* 370 b.

FREDGIS et VLUIET[1], *Nottingh.* 288.

FREDO,[2] *Suff.* 363 b.

FRODO, *Norf.* 210 b. bis. 211 b. 212 b.   *Suff.* 359 b.
360, 366 b. 368.

FRODO frater Abbatis,[3] *Suff.* 359 b. 363 b. 396.

FRODRO, *Suff.* 181 b.

---

[1] " ħƀ Fredgis."

[2] *sc.* Frodo frater abbatis Balduini.

[3] Frodo has been already noticed in the former Volume,
p. 421. There are two short passages, however, in the
account of his lands in Suffolk, which the editor had not
the means of commenting upon when the former page was
printed.

Under Lavenham, *Suff.* 355, it is said, " Lavenham tenuit
Alwius sub Sancto Edmundo cum soca T.R.E.; modo tenet
Frodo de rege W. et *reclamat ad feudum suum,* dicens quod
liberata fuit ei." And again, in the next folio, " In Bukes-

FROGERIUS, *Berks*, 58.

FROISSART, Willielmus, *Bedf.* 213 bis.

FROMA, Æcclesia S. Johannis de, *Som.* 86 b.

FRUMOND, homo Drogonis de Bevrere, *Yorksh.* 324 b.

FULBERTUS, *Kent*, 9 b. 10, 10 b. bis.[1] *Bedf.* 212. *Leic.*
232 b. *Norf.* 206 b.

FULBERTUS quidam sacerdos Herm. *Norf.* 117.

FULBERTUS homo Gisleberti de Gand, *Linc.* 355 b.

FULBRIC, *Warw.* 243 b.

FULCARDUS, *Cornw.* 120 b. *Suff.* 320 b.

---

salla tenuerunt xxv. liberi homines III. car. terræ et dim.
in soca Regis qui fuerunt *liberati* Frodoni."

The circumstance, as in Lavenham, of the brother of the
abbat of St. Edmundsbury holding lands in fee, which in
the Confessor's time had been a part of the endowment of
his brother's Monastery, seems explained by a passage in
the Consuetudinarium of that foundation, MS. Harl. 3977,
fol. 18, relating to some other manors : " Willelmus primus
Rex dedit Sancto Edmundo, prima vice qua ejus requisivit
suffragium, Brok et omnia appentitia ejus. Item alia vice
totum feodum Brichtulfi fil. Leomari, *unde feodatus est Frodo*
frater Abbatis Baldwini. Nam ad opus Ecclesiæ et FRATRIS
SUI *ipse Abbas impetravit omnes terras prædicti viri a Rege,*
sc. hæc Maneria, Cheuenton, Saxham, Dunham, Tostoke et
Sumerleston."

Abbat Baldwin's influence at Court will be explained by
a reference to the passages in the former volume, p. 304,
and in the present volume, p. 46. He was a royal physician.

The pedigree of Frodo's descendants will be found in the
Jermyn Collections for Suffolk, MSS. Brit. Mus. vol. xlix.
fol. 95.

[1] The Fulbert, or Fulbertus, of the Kentish entries is
called, by Hasted, Fulbert de Dover. After the seizure
of the Bishop of Baieux's possessions, he had the ward of
Dover Castle. Hasted's Hist. of Kent, vol. ii. p. 752.

FULCHEIUS, *Cambr.* 194.

FULCHER, *Shropsh.* 254, 259.

FULCHER', *Suff.* 366 b. 367 b.

FULCHEREDUS, *Hants*, 43. *Midd.* 127 b.

FULCHERUS, *Bedf.* 217 b. bis. *Northampt.* 226 b. ter.
228 b. *Shropsh.* 252, 254 b. *Yorksh.* 323. *Norf.*
164 b. 209 b. 211 passim. *Suff.* 357 b. 359, 365 b.
bis. *v.* PARISIACENSIS.

FULCHERUS homo abbatis [S. Trin. Norw.], *Norf.* 118.

FULCHO, *Yorksh.* 323. *Suff.* 405, 405 b.

FULCHREDUS, *Suff.* 313.

FULCO, *Dev.* 109 passim. 115 b. *Hertf.* 140 b. *Buck.*
151 b. bis. *Oxf.* 158 b. bis. *Leic.* 232 b. 236, 237.
Warw. 240, 240 b. *Shropsh.* 255, 258, 258 b. bis.
Chesh. 264 b. *Yorksh.* 320, 321 b.

FULCO homo Drogonis de Bevrere, *Yorksh.* 325.

FULCO homo Willielmi de Perci, *Linc.* 354 bis.

FULCO homo Osberni de Arches, *Yorksh.* 329, 329 b. bis.

FULCO homo Rogerii de Busli, *Nottingh.* 284 b. bis.
285, 285 b. bis. 286 b. bis.

FULCO homo Gisleberti Tison, *Yorksh.* 326 b.

FULCOINUS, *Hants*, 51.

FULCOLDUS, *Hants*, 47 b. *Dev.* 110 b. *Hertf.* 136 b.
Buck. 146.

FULCRAN, *Somers.* 88, 88 bis.

FULCREDUS, *Wilts*, 67. *Dors.* 83 bis.

FULCUINUS, *Hants*, 51 bis. *Somers.* 95 bis. *Buck.* 151.

FULCUIUS, *Cambr.* 194 b. bis.

FULCVIVS, *Shropsh.* 259 bis.

FULKEREDUS, *Suff.* 390 b.

FULO [1] homo Rogeri de Busli, *Nottingh.* 285 b.

FURIC, *Suff.* 295 bis.

---

[1] *sc.* Fulco.

G.

G. *Essex*, 102.

G. [Goisbertus], *Dev.* 115 passim.

G. dapifer, *Suff.* 331 b.

G. Episcopus, *Hants*, 52. *Glouc.* 163.

GADINC, *Suff.* 446 b.

GADIO, *Oxf.* 158.

GADOMO, Galterus de, *Norf.* 277 b.

GALICERUS, *Essex*, 70.

GALT', *Essex*, 11 b. 36 b. 44 b. 46, 79 b. 81, 86, 88, 91, 95.

GALT' filius Alberi, *Suff.* 304.

GALT' filius Guiberti, *Essex*, 3 b. 4.

GALTERIUS, *Norf.* 243.[1]

GALTERUS, *Essex*, 58, 58 b. 59 b. 60, 67 b. *Norf.* 154, 154 b. bis. 155, 162 b. 170 b. 202 b. 241 b. *Suff.* 305 b. 308, 318 b. 320, 321 ter. 328 b. 329 b. 359, 366 b.

GALTERUS arbalistarius, *Suff.* 320.

GALTERUS diaconus,[2] *Norf.* 193.

GALTERUS filius Alberici, *Suff.* 306 b. bis.

GALTERUS filius Grip, *Suff.* 329 b.

GALTERUS filius Grippi, *Suff.* 329 bis.

GALTERUS filius Richerii, *Suff.* 313.

GAMAS, *Suff.* 369.

GAME, *Yorksh.* 300.

GAMEL, *Chesh.* 267 b. bis. *Yorksh.* 315 b. 316 b. bis. 317 b.

GAMEL tainus, *Inter Rip. et Mersam*, 270 bis.

---

[1] The Galterius of this entry seems to be Walter Gifard.
[2] See Vol. i. p. 421.

GAMEL et CHETELBER, *Yorksh.* 317.

GAMEL et ELRIC, *Yorksh.* 316 b. 317 b.

GAMELINUS homo Normanni de Adreci, *Linc.* 361 b. bis.

GAND Gislebertus de,[1] *Linc.* 353, 364 b. *Derb.* 278. }
GANT, Gislebertus de, *Linc.* 345 b.

GAOSFRIDUS [Bainardus], *Norf.* 248 ter. 249, 250, 251 b. 253.

GAR', *Suff.* 374 b. 375.

GAR', Willielmus de, *Essex,* 37, 38. *Norf.* 213 b.[2]

GARENGERUS, *Essex,* 83, 87 b. *Suff.* 298 b. 338 passim.[3] 423.

GARINUS, *Essex,* 72 b. 76 b. *Norf.* 254 bis. 254 b. ter. 278 b. *Suff.* 328 b. 416 b.

GARINUS cocus, *Norf.* 156.

GARMUND, *Somers.* 95 b.

GARNERUS, *Essex,* 26, 44, 46, 46 b. *Suff.* 441 bis.

GARNERUS homo Ricardi filius Comitis Gisleberti, *Essex,* 103.

GATELEA, Radulfus, *Norf.* 239.

GAUFRIDUS, *Kent,* 12 b. *Buck.* 150. *Cambr.* 195 b. *Linc.* 368 b. *Norf.* 245 b. bis.

GAUFRIDUS homo Rogerii de Busli, *Nottingh.* 286 b.

GAURINCUS, *Suff.* 363 b.

GAUSFRIDUS, *Norf.* 146, 149.

GEMETICENSIS Abb.[4] *Wilts,* 65.

GEMETICO, Abb. de, *Som.* 87.

GERALDUS, *Heref.* 184 bis. 185 b.

GERARDUS, *Som.* 91 b. 95. *Leic.* 234 b. bis. *Shropsh.* 258 b. passim. 259 passim.

GERARDUS vigil, *Norf.* 117.

---

1 See Vol. i. p. 422.   2 William de Warenna.
3 Also called Warengerus.   4 See Vol. i. p. 423.

GERBODO, *Yorksh.* 316, 317, 324 b.

GERELMUS, *Shropsh.* 259.

GERMANI, S. Ecclesia,[1] *Cornw.* 120 b. bis.

GERMANUS, *Hants,* 41, 45.

GERMUNDUS, *Hertf.* 139 b. bis. *Buck.* 149 b. *Bedf.* 211 b. *Essex,* 39 b. 62 b. 70 bis. 70 b. 101 b. *Suff.* 393 b. bis.

GERN', Robertus, *Norf.* 279.

GERNEBER, *Yorksh.* 316 b. bis.[2] 317 b.

GERNON, Robertus,[3] *Essex,* 10 b.

GEROLD, *Warw.* 238 b.

GEROLDUS, *Sussex,* 21 b. *Warw.* 238 b. *Essex,* 83 bis.

GERON, *Dev.* 115 b.

GHERUI, *Hants,* 39.

GIFARD, Osbernus, *Hants,* 52. *Glouc.* 164 b.

GIFARD, Walterus,[4] *Hants,* 50. *Bucks,* 57, 59. *Norf.* 112, 114, 242 b.

GIFARDUS, *Suff.* 426.

GIFART, *Norf.* 258 b. 260.

GIFART, Galterus,[5] *Norf.* 114 b. 115.

GIFART, Osbernus, *Wilts,* 66 b.

---

[1] A collegiate church appears to have been endowed at St. German's at a very early period : the secular canons of which are said to have been exchanged for regulars by Bishop Leofric, who united the Sees of Cornwall and Crediton at Exeter A.D. 1050. In the first of the entries above referred to, these canons are noticed as holding twelve out of twenty-four hides at St. German's, belonging to the Cornish lands of the See of Exeter.

[2] In both instances he held, under Ilbert de Laci, the land which had been previously his own.

[3] See Vol. i. p. 423. [4] See Vol. i. p. 424.

[5] *sc.* Walterus Gifard.

268 bis. *Inter Ripam et Mersam,* 269 b. *Yorksh.*
315, 316. *Essex,* 9 b. *Norf.* 165 b. *Suff.* 305 b.
306, 306 b. 307, 309, 311 b. 313, 313 b. 324 b.
326 b. 327 bis. 390 b. 395 b. 404 b.

GISLEBERTUS arbalistarius, *Norf.* 117.

GISLEBERTUS Episcopus Lisiacensis,[1] *Buck.* 144.

GISLEBERTUS filius Garini, *Essex,* 4.

GISLEBERTUS filius Salomonis, *Bedf.* 215.

GISLEBERTUS f. Turoldi, *Som.* 87. *Glouc.* 164 b. 166.
Worc. 173 b. 174 b. 175 bis. 176. *Heref.* 181.

GISLEBERTUS frater Roberti clerici, *Hants,* 40.

GISLEBERTUS homo episcopi Baiocensis, *Essex,* 90.

GISLEBERTUS homo Hugonis filii Baldrici, *Linc.* 356 b.

GISLEBERTUS homo abbatis S. Petri de Burg, *Linc.*
345 b. 346.

GISLEBERTUS homo Rogerii de Busli, *Nottingh.* 285.

GISLEBERTUS homo Archiepiscopi Eboracensis, *Linc.*
339 b. bis.

GISLEBERTUS presbyter, *Surr.* 32. *Bucks,* 143 b. *Hunt.*
206 b. *Suff.* 411 b.

GISLEBERTUS venator, *Chesh.* 267.

GISLEBERTUS vicecomes, *Sussex,* 20 b. *Heref.* 183.

GISLOLDUS, *Shropsh.* 258.

GISO Episcopus, *Somers.* 86,[2] 87.

GLAM UILLA, R. de, *Suff.* 400 b.

GLANVILL, Robertus de, *Suff.* 304, 304 b. 309, 329.

GLANVILLA, Rotbertus de,[3] *Suff.* 308 b. 315 b. 317 b.
bis. 319, 327.

---

[1] See Vol. i. p. 424.

[2] " De hoc manerio [Alseburge] tenet Giso Episcopus
unum membrum Wetmore quod ipse tenuit de rege E.
Pro eo computat Willielmus vicecomes in firma regis XII. lib.
unoquoque anno."

[3] He was the ancestor of Ralph de Glanville, chief justice

GLAUILL, Robertus de, *Norf.* 219 b.

GLEDUINUS, *Leic.* 233 b.

GLEU, *Bedf.* 215 b.

GLEU homo Godefridi de Cambra, *Linc.* 366.

GLEU homo Aluredi de Lincole, *Linc.* 357 b. bis. 358 b. bis.

GLODOEN. *Staff.* 249.

GLOUUEC. S. Oswaldus, *Glouc.* 164 b. bis.

GLOUUECESTRE, Durandus de, *Hants,* 52. *Wilts,* 70 b.

GODARDUS homo Gozelini filii Lanberti, *Linc.* 359.

GODARTUS, *Suff.* 396 b.

GODEBOLD, *Berks,* 63 b.

GODEBOLDUS, *Berks,* 61. *Shropsh.* 259 b. *Essex,* 43 b. 46, 47.

GODEBOLDUS presbyter, *Shropsh.* 253 passim.

GODEFRIDUS, *Kent,* 3 b. 4 b. *Sussex,* 16, 20 b. 22, 25 b. 26, 26 b. ter. 27. *Surr.* 31. *Berks,* 58 b. 61. *Wilts,* 69, 69 b. *Dors.* 77 bis. *Devon,* 106 b. bis. 110 b. 112 b. ter. *Cornw.* 120 b. *Hertf.* 141. *Buck.* 151 b. *Oxf.* 158 b. 159, 160. *Worc.* 173, 173 b. *Heref.* 180, 186. *Bedf.* 210 bis. *Northampt.* 221. *Linc.* 231, 234. *Yorksh.* 321 b. bis. 322 bis. 346. *Essex,* 456.

GODEFRIDUS clericus, *Sussex,* 22.

GODEFRIDUS dapifer, *Kent,* 4 b. bis.

GODEFRIDUS [miles], *Dors.* 77.

GODEFRIDUS presbyter, *Sussex,* 21.

GODEFRIDUS et EURARDUS, *Essex,* 63.

GODEFRIDUS homo Abbatis S. Petri de Burg, *Linc.* 346.

---

of England in the time of Henry the Second. The Glanvilles had large possessions in Butley, Bushale, Shertham, and Shottisham. Their chief seat was at Butley, where they founded a Priory, and an Abbey at Leiston.

GODERET, *Essex*, 82.

GODERUN, *Oxf.* 154.

GODESCAL, *Wilts*, 72. *Som.* 90.

GODEUE, *Somers.* 90 b.

GODID, *Chesh.* 267.[1] *Essex*, 13.

GODINCUS, *Suff.* 295 b.

GODINGUS, *Essex*, 41.

GODMAN, *Suff.* 249.

GODMANNUS, *Suff.* 404, 404 b.[2]

GODMANUS, *Essex*, 47.

GODMUND, *Heref.* 184 b. bis.

GODMUNDUS, *Hertf.* 142 b.[3] *Heref.* 180, 180 b. 185.
   Bedf. 218.[3] *Warw.* 243.

GODRIC, *Hants*, 54 bis.[4] *Berks*, 56 b. bis. *Wilts*, 70.
   Som. 98. *Oxf.* 154. *Glouc.* 166. *Worc.* 176 b.
   Warw. 240 bis. 241. *Staff.* 249 b. *Linc.* 370 b.
   Norf. 136. *Suff.* 320, 446 b.

GODRIC, canonicus S. Martini, *Kent*, 2.

GODRICUS, *Kent*, 1 b. *Surr.* 34 b. *Berks*, 60 b. *Oxf.*
   156 b. *Heref.* 182. *Northampt.* 222. *Leic.* 233.
   237 bis. *Warw.* 240 b. *Staff.* 247 b. 249. *Derb.*
   274. *Linc.* 368. *Essex.* 45, 47 b. bis. 73 b.

GODRICUS, *Norf.* 115 bis. 119 b. 120 b. 121, 133 bis.
   147, 196 b. 204 b. 205, 276 b. 277 b. *Suff.* 290 b.
   bis. 393 b.

GODRICUS commend. Gisleberti balastarii, *Suff.* 444 b.

---

1 " Ipsa tenuit et libera fuit."   She was now the tenant
of Ralph, the tenant of Earl Hugh.

2 " Tenuit T. R. E. et adhuc tenet."

3 " Istemet tenuit de rege E."

4 He continued to hold this land, a single hide, in capite
at the time of the Survey.   See Vol. i. p. 426.

Godricus dapifer, *Yorksh.* 309 bis. *Essex,* 7 b. *Norf.* 215.

Godricus filius Herebold, *Suff.* 314.

Godricus homo Comitis Alani, *Linc.* 348 bis.

Godricus quidam tainus, *Heref.* 186.

Goduin, *Cornw.* 120. *Warw.* 241.

Goduinus, *Sussex,* 18 b. 22 b. *Surr.* 35 b. *Berks,* 56 b. 62. *Somers.* 87 b. 90, 90 b. *Dev.* 104 b. 106 b. *Cornw.* 124 b. *Hertf.* 130, 136 b. 140 b. 142 bis. *Oxf.* 154. *Heref.* 180, 180 b. *Bedf.* 217 b. *Northampt.* 220, 226 b. 227. *Leic.* 230 b. 234, 236 b. *Warw.* 241. *Nottingh.* 288, 291 b. *Yorksh.* 302 b. *Essex,* 51. *Norf.* 186 passim. 186 b. *Suff.* 296,[1] 320, 328 b. 335 b. 352.

Goduinus quidam anglicus, *Essex,* 37.

Goduinus homo Waldini Britonis, *Linc.* 365.

Goduinus homo Widonis de Credun, *Linc.* 367 b. 368.

Goduinus homo Roberti de Statford, *Linc.* 368 b.

Goduinus liber homo, *Essex,* 101.

Goduinus presbyter, *Buck.* 153.[2] *Nottingh.* 287 b.

Godan, *Essex,* 76 b.

Goduui, unus Anglicus, *Bedf.* 211.

Goduuinus, *Norf.* 157, 231 b.[3] *Suff.* 284, 371.

Godwinus burgensis [Norwic.], *Norf.* 117.

Godwinus filius Tuka, *Suff.* 335 b.[4]

Goduuinus, Godric, *Suff.* 446 b.

---

[1] The Goduinus of this entry held a manor as under-tenant to Earl Alan, which he had himself held T. R. E.

[2] " Istemet tenuit T. R. E."

[3] He had held T. R. E.

[4] " Tenuit et tenet."

GODZELINUS, *Somers.* 97.

GOISBERTUS, *Dev.* 115 ter. 115 b. *Oxf.* 158 bis. *Staff.* 248.

GOISFRIDUS, *Kent,* 3. *Sussex,* 16 b. 17, 17 b. bis. 18 b. 20 bis. 23 b. 24 b. *Surr.* 31 b. *Hants,* 40 bis. 40 b. bis. 41, 46 bis. 47 b. 53 b. passim. *Berks,* 61. *Dors.* 81 b. 82. *Somers.* 87 b. 88 b. 93 ter. 94 passim. 96, 97 b. bis. 98. *Dev.* 103, 103 b. passim. 114 b. *Hertf.* 135, 135 b. 140 b. *Bucks,* 147. *Oxf.* 153 b. bis. *Glouc.* 167, 167 b. bis. 169 b. *Heref.* 183, 185 b. *Cambr.* 195, 195 b. *Northampt.* 220 b. bis. 221 b. bis. 227 passim. *Leic.* 234. *Warw.* 243. *Staff.* 248, 249, 249 b. *Shropsh.* 254 b. 255 b. 260. *Chesh.* 266. *Inter Rip. et Mers.* 269 b. bis. *Derb.* 276 b. 277. *Nottingh.* 289 b. *Yorksh.* 310 b. bis. 311 bis. 322 b. passim. *Essex,* 27 b. 44, 59, 68 b. 71, 89 b. *Suff.* 393 b.

GOISFRIDUS quidam, *Rutl.* 293 b.

GOISFRIDUS camerarius, *Hants,* 39.

GOISFRIDUS canonicus, *Sussex,* 20.

GOISFRIDUS clericus, *Sussex,* 18.

GOISFRIDUS Episcopus, *Wilts,* 66. *Northampt.* 229.

GOISFRIDUS filius Hamonis, *Suff.* 396 b.

GOISFRIDUS filius Malæ, *Kent,* 9 b.

GOISFRIDUS homo Normanni de Adreci, *Linc.* 361 b. ter.

GOISFRIDUS homo Hugonis filii Baldrici, *Yorksh.* 328.

GOISFRIDUS homo Drogonis de Bevrere, *Linc.* 360 b. passim.

GOISFRIDUS homo Rogeri de Busli, *Nottingh.* 284 b. 285 bis. 286 b. bis.

GOISFRIDUS homo Archiepiscopi Eborac. *Yorksh.* 302 bis.

GOSELINUS, *Norf.* 211 b.

GOSFRIDUS, *Norf.* 196. *Suff.* 434 b. bis.

GOSLINUS, *Warw.* 241.

GOSPATRIC,[1] *Yorksh.* 310 b. passim.[2] 311[3] passim. 311 b. bis. 312 bis. 312 b.[4] passim.

GOTWINUS, *Suff.* 384 b. 422 b.

GOZE, *Sussex,* 26 b.

GOZET, *Chesh.* 267.

GOZEL homo Radulfi, *Nottingh.* 290.

GOZEL homo Ivonis Taillgebosc, *Linc.* 350.

GOZELINUS, *Sussex,* 21 ter. 27 b. *Surr.* 32 b. *Hants,* 48, 52. *Berks,* 61 bis. 61 b. *Wilts,* 71, 72 b. *Somers.* 86 b. *Devon,* 107 b. 108, 115 b. *Hunt.* 206. *Northampt.* 224 b. *Chesh.* 263 b. 267 ter. *Derb.* 273 b.

GOZELINUS et GRICHEL, *Nottingh.* 288.

GOZELINUS filius Lanberti, *Linc.* 355.[5]

GOZELINUS homo Drogonis de Bevrere, *Linc.* 360.

GOZELINUS homo Aluredi de Lincole, *Linc.* 358 ter. passim. 358 b. ter.

GOZELINUS homo Hugonis comitis, *Rutl.* 293 b. *Linc.* 349 b. 350 b.

GRAI, Anchitillus de, *Oxf.* 161.

---

[1] See Vol. i. p. 428.

[2] In two entries he held what had been Archil's. "Nunc habet quod habuit."

Gospatric seems to have been placed under the surveillance of Earl Alan.

[3] In one, "Hanc habuit Gospatric et nunc habet iterum de comite."

[4] In all or most of these latter entries he had been the previous possessor of the land.

[5] "Habet unam Ecclesiam in Haberdingham."

Grando, Hugo, de Scoca, *Berks,* 56 b.

Grantcurt, Walterus de, *Cambr.* 196.

Grantham, Ecclesia S. Wlfranni de, *Linc.* 343 b.

Grapinel, *Essex,* 44.

Greistan, Æccl. S. Mariæ de, *Som.* 92 b *v.* Grestain.
    Gresten.

Greno, Robertus, *Essex,* 90 b.

Grentemaisnil, Hugo de,[1] *Hants,* 52. *Hertf.* 134 b.
    Worc. 176. *Bedf.* 215. *Leic.* 236 passim. 236 b.

Grento, *Devon,* 103 b. *Shropsh.* 255 b.

Greslet, Albertus, *Inter Rip. et Mersam,* 270.

Grestain, Abbas de, *Sussex,* 20 b. 21 b. ⎫
    passim. *Cambr.* 193.   ⎪
Grestain, S. Maria de, *Wilts,* 68 b.   ⎬ *v.* Greistan.[2]
Grestain, Monachi de, *Buck.* 146 b.   ⎪
Gresten, S. Maria de, *Suff.* 291 b.   ⎭

Grichel, *Nottingh.* 288.

Grichetel, *Heref.* 181.

Grifin, *Cornw.* 120. *Heref.* 184 b.

Grifin filius Mariadoc Regis, *Heref.* 187.

Griketel, *Norf.* 171.[3]

Grim, *Warw.* 242 b. *Essex,* 69.

Grimbaldus, *Northampt.* 228 b. passim. *Leic.* 236 b.
    bis.

Grinon, Robertus, *Essex,* 17 b.

Gros, Willielmus, *Bedf.* 215.

Gualterus, *Norf.* 180 b.

Guarinus, *Suff.* 310 bis.

Gudhen, Goduinus, *Essex,* 99. *v.* Cudhen.

---

[1] See Vol. i. p. 429.   [2] Ibid. ut supr.
[3] " Tenuit et adhuc tenet."

Gudmundus, *Essex,* 55.

Gudmundus frater Turchilli de Warwic, *Warw.* 241.

Gueri canonicus S. Pauli Lond. *Midd.* 127 b.

Gvericus, *Norf.* 261 b.

Guerlinus, *Wilts,* 67.

Guert homo Comitis Alani, *Linc.* 348 b.

Guibertus, *Essex,* 36 b.

Gvihu'marus, *Norf.* 148.

Gulaffra, Willielmus, *Suff.* 305.

Gulafra, Willielmus, *Suff.* 305 bis. 305 b. 306, 310 bis. 316 b. bis.

Gulbertus, *Midd.* 129 b. *Hunt.* 206. *Leic.* 232 b. *Derb.* 275 b. 277 b. *Essex,* 37.

Gulbertus homo Hugonis filii Baldrici, *Yorksh.* 327 b.

Gulfer homo Roberti de Statford, *Linc.* 368 b.

Gulferedus homo Roberti de Statford, *Linc.* 368 b.

Gummar, *Yorksh.* 329.

Gunduinus, *Wilts,* 72 b. *Leic.* 236 b.

Gundulf, *Glouc.* 164 b.[1]

Gunequata, *Suff.* 446 b.

Gunfridus, *Surr.* 32 b. *Wilts,* 67, 67 b. bis. 70 b. *Worc.* 177 b. bis. *Northampt.* 225. *Norf.* 258 b. 259 bis.

Gunfridus homo Roberti de Todeni, *Linc.* 353 bis.

Gvnhar, *Cornw.* 124 b.

Gunnerus, *Essex,* 48 b.[2]

Guntardus, *Som.* 98. *Yorksh.* 324.

Gunter, *Wilts,* 70 b.

Gutbertus, *Essex,* 60 b.

---

[1] " Tenuit et tenet."

[2] " Totham tenuit Gunnerus T. R. E. et adhuc tenet sub Sueno."

H.

HACUN homo Radulfi Paganel, *Linc.* 362 b.

HADEUUINUS, *Glouc.* 152.

HADULFUS, *Warw.* 241 b.

HAGEBERTUS, *Essex*, 6 b.

HAGHEBERTUS, *Essex*, 96 b.

HAIMARDUS, *Buck.* 151 b.

HAIMERUS, *Norf.* 147 b.

HAIMINC, *Sussex*, 20 b.[1]

HAIMO, *Kent*, 8 b. *Wilts*, 68 b. bis. 69. *Dors.* 79, 79 b. *Dev.* 110 b. ter. *Chesh.* 266 b.

HAIMO Vicecomes,[2] *Kent*, 3 b. 4, 6 b. 7, 9 b. bis. *Surr.* 32 b. 33 passim.

HALANANT, *Suff.* 294 b.

HALSARD, *Surr.* 35 b.

HAME, *Cornw.* 120 b.

HAMELIN, *Dev.* 105. *Cornw.* 120, 123 passim.[3] *Yorksh.* 316.

HAMELIN homo Hugonis filii Baldrici, *Linc.* 356 bis.

HAMELINUS, *Sussex*, 23 b. bis. *Dev.* 104 b.

HAMELINUS homo Hugonis filii Baldrici, *Linc.* 356.

HAMINC, *Sussex*, 21 bis.[4] 21 b.[5]

---

1 " Haiminc tenet de Comite [de Moretaine] Clotintone et ipse tenuit de Rege E. et potuit ire quo voluit."

2 See Vol. i. p. 432.

3 Whether Hamelin of Devonshire and Hamelin of Cornwall were the same person, does not appear. In the latter county Hamelin held twenty-two manors under the Earl of Moretaine. He is supposed to have been the ancestor of the Trelawny family, and to have resided at Treloen, one of the manors described in the Survey as his property.

4 In both instances it is said, "Ipse tenuit de rege E."

5 " Ipse tenuit de Goduino Comite."

HAMO, *Chesh.* 263 b. 264, 266 b. passim. 268, 268 b.
    bis. *Suff.* 296, 296 b. bis. 297, 297 b.

HAMON, *Dev.* 110 b.

HANTONE, burgenses de, *Northampt.* 219.

HANTONE, presbyteri de, *Staff.* 249 b. bis.

HARD', *Hertf.* 137.

HARDEUUINUS homo Walchel, *Northampt.* 220 b.

HARDING, *Wilts,* 74 ter.[1] *Somers.* 90 b.[2] *Oxf.* 154. *Warw.*
    241.

HARDUUINUS, *Cambr.* 190 b. ter. 191 passim. 191 b.
    194, 196 b. *Chesh.* 266 bis.

HAROLDUS, *Suff.* 419 b. bis. 420 bis. 420 b. 423, 425.

HASTINGS, Rad. de, *Essex,* 83 b.

HASTINGES, Robertus de, *Sussex,* 17.

HATO, *Essex,* 32 b.

HECHAM, Godricus de, *Norf.* 272 b.

HELDEREDUS, *Hants,* 45.

HELDREDUS, *Hants,* 45 b. 46 b. 47.

HELDRET, *Suff.* 303.

HELDRICUS, *Cornw.* 125.

HELDUINUS, *Leic.* 234.

HELGOD, *Shropsh.* 256 b.

HELGOT, *Dev.* 114. *Buck.* 152 bis. *Staff.* 248, 249 bis.
    Shropsh. 257, 258 b. passim. 260 b. ter.

HELIO, *Staff.* 249 bis.

HELIUS, *Norf.* 191 b. 195, 199 b.

HELMERUS, *Norf.* 206 b.

HELTO, *Kent,* 6, 8 b. 9. *Buck.* 144 ter. 144 b.

HELTUS dapifer et nepos ejus, *Kent,* 2 b.

HENGEBALDUS, *Shropsh.* 253 b.

---

[1] In each entry it is said, " Ipse tenuit T. R. E."

[2] " Harding ten. de abbate [Glastingb.] Ipse tenuit
similiter T. R. E."

HENRICUS, *Berks,* 60, 60 b. *Derb.* 275 bis. 275 b. 276.
    Yorksh. 324. *Suff.* 358.

HENRICUS alter, *Berks,* 60 b. ter.

HENRICUS dapifer, *Berks,* 60 b.

HERALDUS, *Kent,* 14. *Sussex,* 16 b. *Wilts,* 65 b. 73 bis.
    Heref. 182 b. *Norf.* 172 b.

HERALDUS (miles), *Sussex,* 16 b.

HERBERTUS, *Kent,* 10, 11 bis. *Sussex,* 17. *Surr.* 36 b.
    Hants, 46, 48 b. bis. *Wilts,* 66, 72. *Somers.* 93 b.
    94 b. 96 b. 97 ter. *Dev.* 111 b. *Oxf.* 158 b. *Glouc.*
    166 b. 167. *Worc.* 176 b. bis. *Heref.* 180, 184 bis.
    Hunt. 206 bis. *Leic.* 230 b. *Shropsh.* 255, 256 b.
    ter. 258 b. *Chesh.* 264, 264 b. 275. *Rutl.* 293 b.
    Suff. 319 b.

HERBERTUS camerarius, *Hants,* 42 b. 45 b.

HERBERTUS filius Juonis, *Kent,* 7 b. 9 b. 13 b. *Hertf.*
    135 b. *Bedf.* 209 b. passim.

HERBERTUS forestarius, *Hants,* 39.

HERBERTUS homo Normanni de Adreci, *Linc.* 361 b.
    bis. 362.

HERBERTUS homo Eustachii, *Hunt.* 206.

HERBERTUS homo Odonis arbalistarii, *Linc.* 365 b. bis.

HERBERTUS homo Archiepiscopi Ebor, *Linc.* 339 b. ter.

HERBERTUS homo Juditæ Comitissæ, *Linc.* 367.

HERBRANDUS, *Buck.* 147. *Worc.* 175, 177 b.

HERDING, *Hants,* 43.

HEREBERD fossator, *Norf.* 117.

HEREFORD, Episcopus de, *Worc.* 173.[1]

HEREFORD, S. Petrus de, *Shropsh.* 260 b.

HEREUUARDUS, *Worc.* 173. *Warw.* 240, 240 b.

HERFRIDUS, *Kent,* 10, 10 b. 11, 13 b. *Surr.* 30 b. 32.

---

[1] " Walterus episcopus tenuit T.R.E. ad omne servitium
Episcopi de Wirecestre."

HERION, Tihellus de, *Essex*, 24.

HERLEBALDUS, *Hants*, 45. *Worc.* 173 b. 177 b. passim.

HERLEBOLDUS, *Worc.* 177 b.

HERLEUINUS, *Warw.* 240.

HERLUIN, *Som.* 88, 88 bis.

HERLUINUS, *Somers.* 88. *Northampt.* 221. *Norf.* 234.

HERLUUINUS, *Norf.* 234 b.

HERMAN, *Wilts*, 66, 71 b. *Worc.* 176 b. 181. *Staff.* 249 b.

HERMAN homo Gozelini filii Lanberti, *Linc.* 359, 359 b.

HERMANNI Episcopi nepos, *Wilts*, 66.

HERMENFRIDUS, *Warw.* 241.

HERM'FRIDUS homo Osberni de Arches, *Yorksh.* 329.

HERMER, *Dev.* 112 b.

HERMERUS, *Berks*, 59. *Dev.* 111 b. 113. *Norf.* 118, 274, 275.

HERMERUS homo Ivonis Taillgebosc, *Linc.* 350.

HERNOLDUS, *Heref.* 186.

HEROLDUS, *Sussex*, 16 b. *Norf.* 196 b.

HEROLFUS, *Sussex*, 18 b.

HERPUL, *Hants*, 52 b.

HERTALDUS S. Trinitatis, *Midd.* 128 b. bis.

HERUEU [de Berruarius], *Suff.* 386 b. 387 b.

HERUEUS, *Kent*, 13, 13 b. 14. *Berks*, 57. *Wilts*, 64 b. 65, 68, 74 b. *Dors.* 78. *Buck.* 149. *Oxf.* 155 b. bis. 156, 156 b. *Cambr.* 200. *Warw.* 242 b. *Staff.* 249 b. passim. *Yorksh.* 309 bis. 310 bis. 316. *Linc.* 348. *Essex*, 35 bis. *Norf.* 149 b. *Suff.* 387 b. 388, 408 b.

HERUEUS homo Comitis Alani, *Nottingh.* 282 b. *Linc.* 348.

HERUEUS de Ispania, *Essex*, 35 b. ter.

HERUIUS deb. *Norf.* 117.

HESDINC, Ernulfus de,[1] *Hants*, 43.

HESDING, Arnulfus, Ernulfus, *seu* Hernulfus de, *Kent*, 6, 6 b. 9 bis. *Wilts*, 66, 67 b. 71 b. *Buck*. 144 b. 145. *Staff*. 249.

HEZELINUS, *Berks*, 59.

HILDEBRAND lorimarius, *Norf.* 117.

HISPANIA, Aluredus de, *Wilts*, 64 b. *Somers*. 86. *Glouc*. 162.

HOMO unus archiepiscopi Cantuar. *Kent*, 4 b.

HOMO unus Gisleberti de Gand, *Linc*. 354 b.

HOMO unus Rogeri de Jurei,[2] *Glouc*. 164 b.

HOMO unus Hugonis de Port, *Hants*, 45 b.

HOMO Gisleberti Rauemer, *Linc*. 355 b.

HOMO Roberti fil. Wimarc. *Hertf*. 133 b.

HOMINES Drogonis de Bevrere, *Yorksh*. 323 b.

HOMINES Eustachii Comitis, *Hertf*. 138 b.

HOMINES Comitis Moritonensis, *Dev*. 100 b.

HOMINES Episcopi Thetfordiensis, *Norf.* 117.

HOMINES Willielmi de Warenna, *Norf*. 277.

HOMINES duo, *Dors*. 81 b. *Hertf*. 141 b. *Buck*. 150 ter. *Cambr*. 194 b. 202.

HOMINES II. Goisfridi Alselin, *Linc*. 369 b. 370.

HOMINES II. Osberni de Arcis, *Yorksh*. 329 bis.

HOMINES II. Rogeri de Busli, *Nottingh*. 284 b. 285, 285 b.

HOMINES II. Godefridi de Cambrai, *Linc*. 366 ter.

HOMINES II. S. Remigii Remis, *Northampt*. 222 b.

HOMINES tres,[3] *Sussex*, 20. *Hertf*. 141 b.

HOMINES archiepiscopi III. *Kent*, 4.

HOMINES v. *Sussex*, 20.

HOMINES archiepiscopi quinque, *Kent*, 3 b. bis.

---

[1] See Vol. i. p. 434.   [2] *sc*. Ivri.
[3] " Qui et T. R. E. tenuerunt."

Hosdena, Hugo de, *Suff.* 341 b. bis.

Hosdenc, *Suff.* 330.

Hosdenc, Hugo de,[1] *Essex,* 88. *Norf.* 187. *Suff.* 337 bis.

Hosed, Walterus, *Wilts,* 64 b.

Hotot, Hugo de, *Rutl.* 293 b.

Houardus, *Essex,* 13.

Huardus, *Wilts,* 69. *Hertf.* 139 b. *Leic.* 232 b. ter. 233.

Hubald, Hugo, *Bedf.* 216 b. bis.

Hubaldus, Hugo, *Bedf.* 216 b. bis.

Hubb', *Suff.* 310.

Hubertus, *Sussex,* 20 b. *Berks,* 58 b. 60 b. *Dors.* 79 b. ter. *Somers.* 92, 95. *Dev.* 112, 116 b. *Warw.* 242. *Staff.* 248 b. *Essex,* 58, 88 bis. *Norf.* 154 b. bis. *Suff.* 304, 306 b. 309 b. 314, 324, 324 b. 325, 326 b. 327 b. 328.

Hubertus homo Radulfi Pagenel, *Yorksh.* 325 b.

Huboldus, *Wilts,* 70.

Hveche, *Cornw.* 125.

Hugo, *Kent,* 11. *Sussex,* 16 b. 18, 18 b. passim. 19, 19 b. bis. 20, 20 b. bis. 21, 22 b. 24 passim. 25, 25 b. 26, 27 b. ter. *Surr.* 31 b. bis. 36. *Hants,* 40, 46 ter. 46 b. 47 b. bis. 48 b. *Berks,* 56 b. 61 b. *Wilts,* 66, 69, 70 b. 71, 71 b. ter. 72 b. 73. *Dors.* 80 b. ter. 82 bis. 82 b. 83 b. passim. 84. *Somers.* 87 b. 89 b. 92 b. 93 b. 94 b. bis. 95 b. 96 bis. 96 b. 97 passim. 97 b. *Dev.* 103 b. 105, 105 b. 107 b. bis. 108, 111. *Hertf.* 139 b. *Buck.* 146 b. 147 ter. 147 b. passim. 148 passim. *Oxf.* 156, 158 b. 159, 160. *Glouc.* 167, 167 b. 168. *Worc.* 176 b. 177 bis. *Heref.* 184 bis. 185 passim. *Cambr.* 190, 196, 197 b. 198 b. *Hunt.* 207. *Bedf.* 214 b.

---

[1] See Vol. i. p. 438.

215, 215 b. passim. 216, 217 passim. 217 b. passim.
Northampt. 220 b. 222 b. bis. 224 b. passim. 225,
225 b. ter. 226 b. ter. 227 bis. 228 b. passim. 230 b.
231, 232 b. bis. 233 passim. 233 b. 234 ter. 234 b.
bis. *Leic.* 237 bis. *Warw.* 240 b. 242 b. bis. 243 b.
244 ter. *Staff.* 249 ter. *Shropsh.* 259. *Chesh.* 263 b.
266 b. passim. 268 bis. *Derb.* 274 b. *Rutl.* 293 b.
Essex, 11 bis. 12 b. 19 b. 24 b. passim. 25, 30 bis.
45 b. 60, 62, 63 b. 64 65, 84 b. *Norf.* 160, 189,
190, 192 b. 224, 224 b. bis. 227 b. 228 b. 230 b.
237, 237 b. *Suff.* 310, 399.

Hugo arbalist. *Sussex,* 18 b.

Hugo (clericus), *Sussex,* 16 b.

Hugo Comes, *Berks,* 58 b. *Glouc.* 164 b. *Shropsh.*
254.[1]

Hugo coquus, *Berks,* 58 b.

Hugo f. Baldrici,[2] *Northampt.* 219 b.

Hugo f. Constantii, *Warw.* 242.

Hugo filius Goldæ, *Suff.* 398 b.

Hugo [*sc.* f. Grip], *Dors.* 78, 78 b.

Hugo f. Grip, *Dors.* 79, 84 b.

Hugo filius Malgeri,[3] *Essex,* 54 b.

Hugo filius Malgi, *Essex,* 54 bis.

Hugo f. Norman, *Chesh.* 268 b. 269 bis. *Yorksh.* 305
bis. *Suff.* 299, 301, 302.

Hugo f. Osberni, *Chesh.* 266 b. passim. 268 b. ter.

Hugo filius Rannulfi, *Sussex,* 27.

Hugo filius Rogeri Comitis, *Staff.* 246.

Hugo *f.* Turgisi, *Shropsh.* 258 b.

---

[1] " Hugo Comes tenet de Rogerio Comite in Walis
terram de Gal." See Vol. i. p. 437.

[2] See Vol. i. p. 436.

[3] " Quidam miles Hugonis de Monteforti nomine Hugo
filius Malgeri."

Hugo filius Willelmi, *Kent*, 9 b.

Hugo homo Osberni de Arches, *Yorksh*. 329.

Hugo homo Archiepiscopi Eboracensis, *Linc*. 340.

Hugo homo Hugonis filii Baldrici, *Yorksh*. 328.

Hugo homo Juditæ Comitissæ, *Linc*. 367 bis.

Hugo homo Episcopi Lincoliensis, *Linc*. 345.

Hugo homo W. de Scoies, *Norf*. 117.

Hugo homo Roberti de Statford, *Linc*. 368 b.

Hugo homo Ivonis Taillgebosc, *Linc*. 350.

Hugo interpres, *Somers*. 87.

Hugo miles Abbatis de Ramesyg, *Hunt*. 204.

Hugo nepos Herberti, *Kent*, 7, 7 b. passim. 8 passim.
    10, 11.

Hugo nepos Herberti, homo Episcopi Baioc. *Nottingh*.
    284.

Hugo [nepos Herberti] et Adeloldus, *Kent*, 7 b.

Hugo uicecomes, *Hants*, 47.

Hugol', *Berks*, 63.

Hugolinus, *Wilts*, 66 b. *Essex*, 12 bis.

Hunaldus, *Essex*, 96.

Hunfridus, seu Humfridus, *Sussex*, 22 b. *Hants*, 52 b.
    53. *Wilts*, 66 b. 71 bis. *Dors*. 79, 79 b. 82. *Somers*.
    89, 92 b. 98. *Cornw*. 125. *Hertf*. 133 b. bis. 134,
    136 b. 139 bis. *Buck*. 146 b. bis. *Oxf*. 155 b. 156.
    Glouc. 162 b. 163 b. passim. *Cambr*. 197 b. passim.
    200 bis. *Hunt*. 205 b. *Bedf*. 210. *Northampt*. 223
    passim. 223 b. *Linc*. 236. *Warw*. 244 ter. *Staff*.
    248 b. *Chesh*. 264 b. bis. 266. *Yorksh*. 315 b. 316,
    317. *Essex*, 10 b. 11 b. 54 b. 72, 75 b. 79 b. *Norf*.
    254, 258, 259, 259 b. bis. 260, 260 b. ter. 261,
    262 b. 279 b. *Suff*. 294 b. 295, 305 b. 315 b. 325,
    325 b. 327 b. 329 b. bis. 330, 369, 398, 398 b.

Hunfridus camerarius, *Surr*. 30 b. *Leic*. 230 b.

Hunfridus filius Alberici, *Suff*. 417.

I. & J.

---

[1] " Ipse tenuit et liber fuit."

INGELBALD, *Dev.* 102 b.

INGELBERTUS, *Dors.* 77.

INGELRAMNUS, *Dors.* 82. *Somers.* 98.

INGELRAN, *Linc.* 360.

INGELRANNUS, *Sussex,* 17 b. 18 bis. 18 b. ter. *Heref.*
184 bis. *Hunt.* 204 b. 206. *Northampt.* 224, 227.
Shropsh. 257, 260 ter. 260 b.

INGELRANNUS filius Widonis de Reinbuedcurt, *Linc.*
363 b.

INGELRANUS, *Shropsh.* 257.

INGELRICUS, *Essex,* 14, 26, 28, 28 b. 29, 29 b. bis.
30 b. ter. 31, 31 b. 32 b. 33 passim. 34 passim.
102.

INGENULF, *Leic.* 237.

INGENULFUS, *Warw.* 240 bis.

INGRANNUS homo Rogerii de Busli, *Nottingh.* 285.

INGULF, *Som.* 91.

INGULFUS, *Hants,* 46 b. *Norf.* 193 b.

INGULFUS monachus, *Surr.* 34.[1]

Interpres, David, *Dors.* 83.

Joculator Regis, Bardic, *Glouc.* 162.

Joculatrix, Adelina, *Hants,* 38 b.

JOHAIS, *Warw.* 243 bis.

JOH'S, *Essex,* 45 b.

JOHANNES, *Surr.* 34 b. bis. 35 ter. *Dors.* 77 b. bis.
Somers. 87 b. 89, 90 b. 93 b. *Hunt.* 203 b. *Leic.*
233 b. *Northampt.* 227 b. *Derb.* 275. *Norf.* 265 b.
Suff. 363.

JOHANNES filius Ernuc'un, *Essex,* 84.

JOHANNES filius Galerami, *Essex,* 3.

JOHANNES homo Ernegis de Baryn, *Yorksh.* 328 b.
Linc. 362 b.

---

[1] See Vol. i. p. 439.

JOHANNES homo Eustachii, *Hunt.* 206.

JOHANNES nepos Walerami, *Norf.* 214 bis. 217.

JOUIN, *Cornw.* 123 b. ter.[1]

JOVINUS, *Cornw.* 123 b. passim.

JOUUINUS, *Cornw.* 120.

IRICUS, *Suff.* 383.

ISAC,[2] *Norf.* 118. *Suff.* 352 b.

ISELDIS, *Dors.* 84.

ISENBARD, *Northampt.* 221 b.

ISENBARDUS, *Hertf.* 140 b.

ISEUUARDUS, *Oxf.* 155, 155 b.

ISPANIA, Herueus de, *Essex*, 35 b. ter.

JUDHELBUS, *Dev.* 101.

JUDICHEL, *Wilts*, 70. *Bedf.* 218.

JUHELLUS, *Warw.* 243.

JUNAINUS, *Essex*, 27.

JUNANUS, *Essex*, 31.

JUNEN, *Hunt.* 204 b.

IUO, *Sussex*, 23, 24, 24 b. *Buck.* 146 b. 147 b. *Nor-*
   thampt. 224 b. bis. *Leic.* 232 b. ter. 233, 233 b.
   Linc. 368. *Suff.* 425.

IUO dapifer Hugonis de Grent', *Bedf.* 218.

IUO homo Gisleberti, *Linc.* 355 b.

IUO homo Eudonis fil. Spirewic, *Linc.* 360.

IVO homo Roberti de Todeni, *Linc.* 353 bis. 353 b.

JURAN, *Hants*, 52 b.

IUREI, Rogerus de,[3] *Berks*, 58. *Glouc.* 162 b. bis. 164.

---

[1] In each, " Ipse tenebat T. R. E."

[2] This was not a common name in the eleventh century.
The Exeter Domesday, p. 71, in the enumeration of the Hun-
dreds of Somerset, mentions "Isaac prepositus canonicorum
Sancti Andreæ," as an under-tenant.

[3] Rogerus de Ivri.

Iuri, Acardus de,   *Bedf.* 213.

Juri, Rogerus de,[1] *Buck.* 144 b.

Ivri, Rogerus de, *Oxf.* 155 b. 156 b. 161.   *Glouc.* 168 b.

Iwardus, *Shropsh.* 259 b.

Iuuein, *Warw.* 242 b.

K.

Keresburg, Osbernus de, *Glouc.* 170.

L.

Labatailge, Abbas de, *Sussex,* 17 b. *Dev.* 100 b. 101. }

Labatailge, Monachi de, *Dev.* 100.

Lacei, Ilbertus de, *Buck.* 145.

Lachelinus, *Dev.* 117.

Laci, Ilbertus de,[2] *Oxf.* 154 b. 155 b. *Linc.* 364.

Laci, Rogerus de,[3] *Wilts,* 72 b. *Oxf.* 161 ter. *Glouc.*
    162 bis. 166, 166 b. *Worc.* 172 b. 173 bis. 173 b.
    174, 174 b. *Heref.* 179 b. bis. 180 ter. 181 b. 182 b.
    186 b. 187 b. *Northampt.* 224 b. bis. *Shropsh.* 252,
    256 bis. 256 b. passim.

Laci, Walterus de, *Berks,* 59 b. *Glouc.* 164, 170.
    Heref. 179 b. 182 b. bis.

Lambertus, *Essex,* 31, 31 b. ter. 61. *Norf.* 168 b.
    169 b.

Lanbertus, *Dors.* 77. *Somers.* 97 b. 98. *Cambr.* 196 b.
    bis. *Leic.* 234. *Chesh.* 264 b.

Lanbertus homo Drogonis de Bevrere, *Yorksh.* 324 b.

Lanbertus homo Gozelini filii Lanberti, *Linc.* 359 b.

Lanbertus presbyter, *Berks,* 56 b.

Lancavetone, Canonici S. Stefani de,[4] *Cornw.* 120.

---

[1] Rogerus de Ivri.   [2] See Vol. i. p. 442.   [3] Ibid.
[4] Launceston.

LANDRI, *Berks*, 61 b.

LANDRICUS, *Northampt.* 227 passim. *Yorksh.* 312. *Linc.* 348 b.

LANDRICUS homo Alani Comitis, *Yorksh.* 310 bis. 310 b. bis. *Linc.* 347.

LANGETOT, Radulfus de, *Bedf.* 211 b. passim.

LANGHETOT, Radulfus de,[1] *Suff.* 430 bis.

LANZELINUS, *Northampt.* 228 b. ter.

Lardarius, Oilardus, *Hunt.* 206.

LATIN', Robertus, *Kent*, 6 b. 8 bis. 8 b. bis. 11 b. 12.

Latinarius, Leuuinus, *Heref.* 180.

LATINUS, Rotbertus, *Kent*, 7 bis.

LAURENTIUS, *Staff.* 249 b.

LEDMANUS liber homo, *Suff.* 332 b.[2]

LEDMARUS, *Bedf.* 213 b.

LEFLET, *Berks*, 56 b.

LEFRIC, *Worc.* 174 b.

LEFSIUS, *Essex*, 49.

LEFSUNUS, *Essex*, 58 b.

LEFTANUS, *Essex*, 91.

LEMARUS, *Essex*, 102.

LEMEI, *Surr.* 34 b.

LEOFMINSTRE, Abbatia de, *Heref.* 180.[3]

---

[1] The Jermyn Collections for Suffolk say, "The town of Stow Langetot in Blackborn Hundred derived its name from this antient family, which was seated there *t.* Hen. I. and there continued very flourishing till the latter end of Hen. III., when Robert de Langetot left Matilda his sole daughter and heir, married to Sir Nicholas Peachey." Vol. xliv. fol. 154.

[2] He and Stauhart had held the land "in commendatione Regis et Reginæ, T. R. E."

[3] Although the Nunnery of Leominster forms no separate entry in the Domesday Survey, its existence and sup-

Lepsi, *Buck.* 146.

Lestanus presbyter, *Suff.* 290 b.

Letardus, *Wilts*, 69 b.

Lethelinus, *Wilts*, 70.

Letmarus prepositus, *Essex*, 103.

Leuecilt, *Essex*, 102.[1]

Leuegarus, *Bedf.* 217 b.[2]

Leuenot, *Sussex*, 26 b.[3] *Cornw.* 120, 124 b. bis.[4]
  Northampt. 224, 226 b. *Staff.* 247. *Norf.* 227.[5]

Leuenot presbyter, *Worc.* 174 b.

Leueua, *Berks*, 56 b. *Somers.* 87 b. *Oxf.* 154 bis.
  Warw. 241 b. *Linc.* 371 b. *Suff.* 446 b.

---

port are acknowledged. The manor of Leominster, belonging to the Crown, is expressly said to have been let out to farm for sixty pounds a year, exclusive of provision for the Nuns. " Hoc Manerium est ad firmam de LX. lib. *preter victum* Monialium." An Abbess, too, without the name of her monastery, but evidently of Leominster, follows in the second column of the same folio holding a hide of land at Fencote in capite.

There is a passage in the Saxon Chronicle, under the year 1046, relating either to this or a former Abbess of Leominster, which adds one to the many pictures of the lawless condition of those times. " This year went Earl Sweyne into Wales, and Griffin King of the northern men with him; and hostages were delivered to him. As he returned homeward, he ordered the Abbess of Leominster to be fetched to him; and he had her as long as he list, after which he let her go home."

[1] " In bebenhirs tenuit Leuicilt liber homo III. acras et adhuc tenet."

[2] " Iste qui nunc tenet tenuit. Homo Regis fuit, et vendere potuit."

[3] " Ipse tenuit de rege E."

[4] In one of these entries it is said, " Idem teneb. T.R.E."

[5] The Leuenot of this entry had held T. R. E.

LEUIET, *Hertf.* 137. *Bedf.* 213 b. *Warw.* 241.

LEUINC, *Derb.* 277.

LEUING, *Hants,* 41 b. *Warw.* 242 b.

LEUINGUS, *Cambr.* 198 b.

LEURIC, *Wilts,* 70 b. *Somers.* 90. *Dev.* 103 b. 118.[1]
    Oxf. 154. *Heref.* 184 b. 185. *Northampt.* 228 b.[2]
    Leic. 236 b. bis. *Warw.* 243.[3] *Shropsh.* 258.[3]
    Chesh. 267 b.

LEURIC presbyter, *Wilts,* 65.

LEURIC et EILEUA, *Warw.* 243.

LEURIC, Willielmus, *Wilts,* 72 b.

LEURICUS, *Essex,* 41, 58 b. *Suff.* 282, 352, 370, 397,
    446.

LEUSIN, *Yorksh.* 317 b.

LEUUARD, *Berks,* 61 b.

LEWES, S. Pancratius, *Sussex,* 26.

LEUUI, *Som.* 87 b.

LEUUINE, *Hunt.* 205 b. *Derb.* 278.

LEUUINUS, *Sussex,* 20. *Hants,* 50 b.[4] *Hertf.* 136 b.[5]
    Buck. 151 b. 153.[6] *Glouc.* 166. *Bedf.* 210 b.[7] *Leic.*
    237. *Derb.* 278 b. bis. *Essex,* 48, 58 b. 97, 102.
    Suff 397.

LEUUINUS OAURA, *Buck.* 153.[8]

LEUUINUS latinarius, *Heref.* 180.

---

[1] " Ipse tenebat T. R. E."

[2] " Idem Leuric tenuit T. R. E."

[3] " Ipse tenuit et liber homo fuit."

[4] " Ipse tenuit T. R. E."

[5] " Hanc terram tenuit isdem Leuinus de rege E. et vendere potuit. Modo tenet ad firmam de comite [de More-
taine]."

[6] " Istemet tenuit T. R. E. et vendere potuit."

[7] " Istemet tunc tenuit [T. R. E.] sed ab æcclesia [S. Bened. de Ramesy] separare non potuit."

[8] " Istemet tenuit T. R. E. et vendere potuit."

LEUURIC, *Suff.* 446 b.

LIBER homo unus, *Glouc.* 162 b. *Essex,* 31 b. 33 b.
    Suff. 446 bis.

LIBERI homines II. *Suff.* 367 b. 446 b. bis.

LIBERI homines III. *Suff.* 446.

LIBERI homines IIII. *Suff.* 446.

LIBERI homines VI. *Suff.* 446 b.

LIBERI homines Regis VII. *Essex,* 99.

LIBERI homines XXX. *Suff.* 446 b.

LIBORET, *Bedf.* 214.

LIGULFUS, *Yorksh.* 317 b.

LIMESEIO, Radulfus de, *Essex,* 90 b. ⎫

LIMESI, Radulfus de, *Hants,* 39. *Dors.* 80 b. *Somers.* ⎬ 1
    91. *Hertf.* 140. *Glouc.* 162 ter. 164, 166 b. bis. ⎭
    167. *Essex,* 90 b.

LINCOLE, Alured de, *Rutl.* 293 b. bis.

LINCOLIENSIS Episcopus, *Buck.* 143.

LIOFUS, *Hants,* 53 b. *Staff.* 250 b.

LIRA, abb. de,[2] *Hants,* 39 b. 52 bis. *Glouc.* 164. ⎫

LIRE, abb. de, *Hants,* 38 b. ⎬

LIRE, Monachi de, *Hants,* 52. ⎭

LISEMAN, *Wilts,* 74.[3]

LISIACENSIS Episcopus, *Kent,* 6 b. *Midd.* 127 b. ⎫
    Bucks, 144, 145 bis. ⎬

LISOIENSIS Episcopus, *Surr.* 30, 31 b. 32. *v.* GISLE- ⎭
    BERTUS.

LISOISUS, *Essex,* 49 b.

LIXOVIENSIS Episcopus, *Dors.* 76.

LOCELS, Willielmus de, *Bedf.* 213 bis.

LODERUS, *Suff.* 396 b.

LODOUUINUS, *Oxf.* 154.

---

[1] See Vol. i. p. 446.   [2] See Vol. i. p. 447.

[3] " Ipse tenuit T. R. E."

M.

---

[1] " Istemet tenuit T. R. E."
[2] " Ipse tenebat T. R. E."

MAIGNO, *Kent*, 13 ter.

MAINARDUS, *Linc.* 352, 352 b. *Essex*, 43.

MAINARDUS homo Rogeri Pictavensis, *Linc.* 352.

MAINFRIDUS, *Somers.* 95 b. 96. *Nottingh.* 291.

MAINFRIDUS homo Radulfi de Limesi, *Nottingh.* 289 b.

MAINO, *Oxf.* 160.

MAJORIS Monasterii Abbatia, *Dors.* 79.

MAIULF, *Northampt.* 226 b.

MALAUILL, Willielmus de, *Suff.* 306 b.

MALBEDENG, Willielmus, *Shropsh.* 257 b. passim. *Chesh.* 265 passim. 265 b. passim. 266 ter. 268, 268 b.

MALDOIT, Willielmus,[1] *Hants*, 46 b.

MALET, *Bedf.* 212 b.

MALET, Gislebertus de, *Suff.* 307 passim.

MALET, Robertus,[2] *Rutl.* 293 b. *Norf.* 155, 219 b. *Suff.* 332, 382 b. 384, 385, 385 b. 387 passim. 388, 388 b. 400, 447, 449 b.

MALET, W. de, *Suff.* 312 b. bis.

MALF, Filii Godrici, *Hants*, 51 b. passim.[3]

MALGER, *Dors.* 79 b. *Somers.* 92 passim. 92 b. bis. *Dev.* 105. *Yorksh.* 321 b. passim. *Linc.* 344, 344 b.

MALGERIUS, *Kent*, 4, 6 ter. 6 b. *Hants*, 40 b. 41. *Somers.* 86 b. 92.

MALGERUS, *Sussex*, 17, 17 b. *Hants*, 52 b. *Dors.* 79 b. *Somers.* 91 b. bis. 92 b. *Northampt.* 227. *Derb.* 277 b. *Yorksh.* 316. *Linc.* 344 b. *Essex*, 14 b. 24 b. bis. 31, 86. *Norf.* 189.

MALGERUS homo Episcopi Lincoliensis, *Linc.* 344 ter.

MALMESBERIA, Abb. de, *Glouc.* 164.

MALUS VICINUS, *Suff.* 447 b.

---

[1] See Vol. i. p. 449.   [2] Ibid. ut supr.

[3] " Pater eorum tenuit de rege E."

---

[1] See Vol. i. p. 450.   [2] Ibid. ut supr.

[3] See Vol. i. p. 451.

[4] On the last folio of Domesday, *Suff.* 450, is a head,
" De Calumpniis inter Episcopum Baiocensem et Matrem
Roberti Malet." It finishes, " modo est in pace Regis sicut
Rex præcepit inter Episcopum et Matrem Roberti."

Mattheus homo Colsuan, *Linc.* 357 bis. 357 b.

Mauricius Episcopus,[1] *Dors.* 76. *Somers.* 86 b. 87, 91.

Mechenta, *Leic.* 233 b.

Medicus, Aluricus, *Hants,* 51 b.

———— Nigellus, *Kent,* 1 b. *Hants,* 52. *Wilts,* 65. *Somers.* 91. *Glouc.* 162 b. *Worc.* 176 bis.

Meinardus homo abbatis de S. Bened. *Norf.* 117.

Meinardus vigil, *Norf.* 117.

Meinburgenses [Norwici], *Norf.* 117.

Meinfridus et Robertus, *Somers.* 96.

Meleburne, Burgenses in, *Somers.* 91. *v.* Mileburne.

Mellend, Comes de, *Warw.* 241 b.

Mellinges, Canonici de, *Sussex,* 16 b.

Merc, Adelolfus de, *Essex,* 27 b. 28 b.

Merde, Aluuardus de, *Hertf.* 142 b.[2]

Mereuinus, *Warw.* 240.

Merleberg, Aluredus, *Somers.* 91 b. *Worc.* 175. *Heref.* 180.

Michael, S. Canonici, *Sussex,* 16 b.

Michaelis, S. de Monte, Abbatia,[3] *Berks,* 57.

Mileburne, Burgenses in, *Somers.* 86 b. *v.* Meleburne.

Miles, v. Goisfridus. Heraldus. Louel. Oswar. Radus.

Miles unus, *Hants,* 41 b. 44 b. *Berks,* 62 b. *Wilts,* 67, 70. *Dors.* 77 b. 78. *Somers.* 88 b. 91. *Dev.* 109. *Oxf.* 156 b. *Glouc.* 169 b. *Worc.* 176 b. *Heref.* 182 b. bis. 186. *Hunt.* 205 b. *Leic.* 230 b. 231. *Shropsh.* 255 bis. 260 bis. *Yorksh.* 304, 304 bis. *Essex,* 35, 86 b.

Miles unus Comitis Rogerii, *Shropsh.* 253 b.

Miles unus Episcopi, *Essex,* 24 ter.

---

[1] Maurice bishop of London. See vol. i. p. 448.

[2] " Istemet tenuit T. R. E. et dare potuit cui voluit, et iii. den. per annum reddebat vicecomiti."

[3] See vol. i. p. 453.

MILES alter, *Glouc.* 169 b.

MILES quidam, *Berks,* 58 b. 61 bis. 62 b. *Glouc.* 165 b.
Yorksh. 304. *Essex,* 86.

MILES quidam Durandi de Glowec', *Glouc.* 168 b.

MILES quidam Gozelini filii Lanberti. *Linc.* 359.

MILES Ilberti de Laci, *Linc.* 353 b.

MILES jussu Regis, nepos Hermanni Episcopi, *Wilts,* 66.

MILES Radulfi, *Derb.* 277 b.

MILES I. et II. Angli, *Cambr.* 198 b.

MILITES, *Dors.* 77 b.

MILITES Willielmi f. Baderon, *Heref.* 180 b.

MILITES Episcopi London, *Hertf.* 134.

MILITES duo, *Dors.* 83 b. *Dev.* 111 bis. 113 bis. *Hertf.*
133 b. 137, 138 b. bis. 140 bis. *Buck.* 145, 152.
Glouc. 165 b. 166. *Worc.* 176 b. *Cambr.* 194 bis.
195 b. bis. 196, 197 b. 198 bis. 198 b. ter. 200,
200 b. bis. 201. *Hunt.* 206. *Bedf.* 212, 215 bis.
Northampt. 221 b. ter. *Shropsh.* 258. *Nottingh.* 283.
Yorksh. 302, 312 b. 319. *Essex,* 39 b.

MILITES archiepiscopi duo, *Kent,* 5.

MILITES duo Goisfridi Alselin, *Linc.* 369 b.

MILITES II. Drogonis de Bevrere, *Yorksh.* 324 b.

MILITES tres, *Kent,* 3. *Somers.* 89 bis. 95 b. bis. *Hertf.*
140 b. *Cambr.* 195. *Northampt.* 221 b. *Yorksh.*
312 b. 326 b.

MILITES tres Drogonis de Bevrere, *Yorksh.* 324, 325.

MILITES tres Abbatis S. Petri de Burgo, *Northampt.*
221 b. bis.

MILITES tres Episcopi, *Heref.* 182 b.

MILITES tres, et unus Anglicus, *Midd.* 129.

MILITES quatuor, *Som.* 97 b. *Dev.* 111. *Northampt.*
222. *Yorksh.* 312 b. *Essex,* 60, 86.

MILITES IIII. abbatis S. Petri de Burg. *Northampt.* 221 b.

MILITES V. *Northampt.* 221 b. bis.

MILITES V. Rogerii Comitis, *Shropsh.* 253 b.

MILITES sex, *Sussex*, 18.[1] *Nottingh.* 283.

MODBERTUS, *Dev.* 106, 106 b. *Essex*, 69 b.

MOION, W. de, *Dev.* 111 b. ⎫[2]
MOION, Willielmus, *Somers.* 87. ⎭

MOLEBEC, Hugo, *Buck.* 147.

MOLES, Rogerius de, *Dev.* 106.[3]

MONACHI Cantuar. *Kent*, 3 b.

MONACHI Episc. Sarisberiensis, *Dors.* 77.

MONACHI Episcopi (*vel* de Episcopatu) Winton', *Hants*,
41 b. bis. 43 ter. 50.

Monachus, v. ALNODUS. ALSI. COLUMBANUS. INGULFUS.

MONACHUS unus de S. Ebrulfo, *Sussex*, 23.

MONETARIUS, *Berks*, 56. *v.* SUETMAN.

MONFORT, Hugo de, *Kent*, 9. *Essex*, 6 b. *v.* MONTE-
FORTI. MONTFORD.

MONIALES in Civ. Cantuar. *Kent*, 12.

MONTE, S. Michael de, *Wilts*, 65. ⎫
MONTE, S. Michael, Monachi de, *Dev.* 107. ⎭

MONTEBURG, S. Maria de, *Wilts*, 73.

MONTE CANESITU, Hubertus de, *Suff.* 319 b. ⎫
MONTE CANISI, Hubertus de,[4] *Suff.* 325. ⎭

MONTEFORTI, Hugo de, *Essex*, 44 b. *Suff.* 281 b. bis.

MONTFORD, Hugo de, *Kent*, 4 b.

MONTFORT, Hugo de,[5] *Kent*, 4 b. 10 b. bis. 11 passim.
11 b. ter. *v.* MONFORT. MONTEFORTI. MONTFORT.

---

[1] " Unus eorum, Norman, tenuit T. R. E."

[2] He founded Dunster Monastery in the county of
Somerset, where he was buried. He left his name to
Ham Mohun in Dorsetshire. See Hutchins's Dissert. on
Domesd. for Dorset, p. 14.

[3] The Messrs. Lysons conjecture that this Roger de
Moles, or Miles, was brother or son to Baldwin de Moles,
vicecomes, under whom he held.

[4] See vol. i. p. 454.   [5] Ibid. ut supr.

---

[1] See vol. i. p. 455.   [2] Ibid. pp. 455, 456.

N.

N. [Normannus], *Suff.* 339 b. 340, 340 b. 341,[1] 341 b.
342 b. 343, 343 b. *v.* NORMANNUS.

NARDREDUS, *Suff.* 294 b.

NAUUEN, *Staff.* 247 b. bis.

NEMORE, Willielmus de, *Suff.* 344.

NEOTI, S. Monachi, *Bedf.* 216.

NEPOS Herberti, *Essex*, 24.

NEPOS Willielmi filii Azor, *Hants*, 53.

NEPTIS Episcopi Constantiensis, *Dev.* 103.

NICOL, *Cambr.* 196 b.

NICOLAI, S. Monachi, *Warw.* 243 b. ⎫
NICOLAO, S. Monachi de, *Buck.* 146. ⎭

NICOLAUS, *Berks*, 59. *Wilts*, 70 b. *Somers.* 97. *Warw.*
239 b.[2] *Staff.* 250 b. *Suff.* 398, 398 b.

NIGEL, *Hants*, 51. *Somers.* 88 bis. 88 b. passim. 96 bis.
Dev. 103 b. bis. 108 b. *Cornw.* 123 b. passim.
Yorksh. 305 passim. 305 b. passim. 306 passim.
306 b. passim. 307 passim. 307 b. passim. 308 ter.
308 b. *Linc.* 366 b.

NIGEL homo Episcopi Dunelmensis, *Linc.* 341.

NIGEL homo Episcopi Linc. *Nottingh.* 284.

NIGEL homo Ivonis Taillgebosc, *Linc.* 350 b.

NIGELLUS, *Kent*, 3 b. 13 b. *Sussex*, 23 b. 24, 26, 26 b.
27 b. bis. *Surr.* 32. *Hants*, 51 passim. 53, 53 b.
Berks, 56, 60 b. 63 b. *Wilts*, 64 b. bis. *Somers.* 88.
90 b. *Dev.* 109 b. *Cornw.* 123 bis. *Midd.* 130.
Buck. 150 bis. 150 b. 152 b. *Northampt.* 224, 229

---

[1] In these four entries Normannus, the sub-tenant, had
been the superior lord T. R. E.

[2] In this entry, " Nicolaus " held the lands of the Countess
Godiva " ad firmam, de Rege."

bis. *Leic.* 233, 233 b. ter. *Warw.* 242. *Staff.* 247 passim. 250 b. passim. *Shropsh.* 259 passim. *Chesh.* 267 b. ter. *Derb.* 274. 277. *Yorksh.* 304 b. bis. 305 passim. 305 b. passim. 306 passim. 306 b. passim. 307 passim. 307 b. passim. *Essex,* 53 b. 66, 67 b. 85, 85 b. *Norf.* 253 b. 259, 259 b. bis. *Suff.* 291.

NIGELLUS homo Episcopi Dunelmensis, *Linc.* 341 b.

NIGELLUS homo Juditæ Comitissæ, *Linc.* 366 b. bis.

NIGELLUS homo Episcopi Linc. *Nottingh.* 289.

NIGELLUS homo Ivonis Taillgebosc, *Linc.* 350, 350 b.

NIGELLUS medicus,[1] *Kent,* 1 b. *Hants,* 52. *Wilts,* 65. *Somers.* 91, *Glouc.* 162 b. *Worc.* 176 bis.

NIGELLUS miles, *Inter Rip. et Mersam,* 270.

NIGELLUS quidam serviens Rotberti Comitis de Moritania, *Suff.* 291.

NISTENESTOCH, Canonici de,[2] *Dev.* 117.

NOERS, Willielmus de, *Norf.* 194 b. 195 b. 196 b. 198, 199 b. *Suff.* 280 b.

NOIERS, Willielmus de, *Norf.* 116 b. 135 b. 136, 138, 192 b. 198 b. 199. 199 b. 200, 215 b.

NOIES, W. de, *Norf.* 117 b.

}*v.* DENUERS.

NOGIOLD, *Northampt.* 229.

NORGIOT, *Northampt.* 226 b. 227.

NORGOT, *Northampt.* 220 b.

NORMAN, *Berks,* 61 b. *Somers.* 86, 94 bis. 97 b. bis. *Devon,* 101 b. 111. *Leic.* 234. *Yorksh.* 310 b. *Suff.* 312.

NORMAN homo Willielmi de Perci, *Linc.* 353 b. ter.

NORMAN miles Com. de Ow. *Sussex,* 18 bis.

---

[1] See vol. i. p. 454.

[2] These canons, at the time of the Survey, held under Giroldus the chaplain. The place is unknown.

NORMAN presbyter, *Nottingh.* 284 b.

NORMANNUS, *Cambr.* 199 b. *Bedf.* 212 b.[1] *Northampt.*
225 b. *Leic.* 231 b. passim. 235 b. passim. *Shropsh.*
259 passim. *Suff.* 294 b. 316 b. bis. 325, 331 b.
332 bis. 338 b.[2] 339 b.[3] 343 b. 344, 344 b. passim.
345 b. 360 b. 377, 388 b. 406 b. 446 b. *v.* N.

NORMANNUS alias, *Suff.* 332.

NORMANUS, *Sussex*, 26. *Bedf.* 213 b.

NORMANUS Vicecomes, *Suff.* 327.

NORUN, Rad. de, *Norf.* 278.

NORWIC, Burgensis de, *Norf.* 117.

NOUI, *Heref.* 181.

NOUUERES, Willielmus de, *Cambr.* 189 b.

NOUUERS, Robertus de, *Buck.* 145 b.

NUBOLDUS, *Wilts*, 70.

O.

O. Episcopus, *Glouc.* 164.[4] *v.* OSBERNUS.

OBURUILLA, Rogerus de, *Suff.* 382 b.

---

[1] Normannus held several lands mentioned in this folio
T. R. E.

[2] Saxmondeham. He now held " sub Rogero," but he
had held the same land T. R. E. " pro manerio." The
record adds " Idem Normannus socam habet et tenet hoc
de Rogero. Hoc unum manerium de tribus quæ Rex reddidit Normanno et modo tenet de Rogero."

[3] " Waletuna tenuit Normannus T. R. E. et modo tenet
sub Rogero."

Harl. MS. 294. in an " Apparatus Genealogicus Anglicus
ex diversis in Archivis recordis compactus," one of Sir
Symond's D'Ewes's MSS. at fol. 17 b. is the Pedigree of
Norman of Suffolk.

[4] Frater W. Comitis. Compare vol. i. p. 460, note [1].

OFFRAN, *Linc.* 358 b.[1]

OGERIUS, *Dors.* 82 b. *Northampt.* 227. *Norf.* 167.

OGERUS filius Vngeman, *Rutl.* 293 b.

OGISUS, *Dors.* 82. *Somers.* 94 ter. 95 b.

OIDELARD, *Kent,* 12 b.

OIDELARDUS, *Kent,* 12 b. *Hants,* 47, 51. *Berks,* 62 b. bis. *Wilts,* 72. *Oxf.* 159. *Heref.* 183 b. *Shropsh.* 260 b.

OILARDUS, *Hunt.* 206.

OILARDUS lardarius, *Hunt.* 206.

OILGI, R. de, *Oxf.* 156 bis. 160 b.

OILGI, Radulfus de, *Oxf.* 154 b.

OILGI, Robertus de,[2] *Berks,* 57 b. *Oxf.* 155, 156 b. *Staff.* 248 b. *Nottingh.* 292. *v.* OLGI.

OISMELIN, *Sussex,* 16 b. 25. ⎫
OISMELINUS, *Sussex,* 25 b. ⎬

OLAF, *Sussex,* 18. *Midd.* 129.

OLBALDUS, *Northampt.* 227 b.

OLE, Robertus de, *Sussex,* 19 b.

OLF, *Suff.* 411 b.[3]

OLGI, R. de, *Warw.* 241 bis. 241 b. ter.

OLGI, Robertus de, *Berks,* 59 b. *Buck.* 144 b. *Glouc.* 163 b. *Worc.* 176 b. *Bedf.* 212. *Warw.* 238. *Nottingh.* 292. *v.* OILGI.

OLIUER, *Dev.* 115 b. passim.

OLNEI, Rogerius de, *Buck.* 152 b.

OLUU', *Dev.* 103.

ORBEC, Rogerus de, *Suff.* 447 b.

---

[1] In this entry he had held the land previous to Alured de Lincole. He had also held previously in another entry, but in the land there mentioned he did not continue as under-tenant.

[2] See vol. i. p. 458.

[3] " Tenuit T. R. E."

ORDMÆR, *Cambr.* 195 b. bis.[1]

ORDMER, *Shropsh.* 259 b.

ORDRIC, *Worc.* 173 b. bis. 241, 243.

ORDRIC tainus, *Somers.* 87. ⎫

ORDULF tainus, *Somers.* 87. ⎬[2]

ORDULFUS, *Somers.* 89 b.

ORDUUI, *Warw.* 242 b.

ORDUUI burgensis de Bedeford, *Bedf.* 218.

ORENET, Willielmus, *Hants,* 50 b.

ORENGE, W. de, *Buck.* 150 b.

ORGAR, *Berks,* 56 b. *Oxf.* 159 b. bis.

ORGARUS, *Cambr.* 194.

ORGARUS teinnus, *Essex,* 64.

ORGERUS prepositus abbatis [S. Edm. de Burgo], *Suff.* 371.

ORM, *Derb.* 275. *Yorksh.* 311 b.[3]

ORMARUS, *Northampt.* 224. *Suff.* 446 b.

ORME, *Derb.* 275 b.

ORNODUS, *Cambr.* 199 b.

OSBERNUS, *Kent,* 10 bis. 11, 11 b. *Sussex,* 17 b. bis. 18 passim. 18 b. 19 passim. 20 passim. 21 ter. *Surr.* 30. *Hants,* 40, 40 b. 41. *Berks,* 58 b. 60. *Wilts,* 67. *Dors.* 77 bis. *Somers.* 98. *Dev.* 103, 109, 112, 113 b. *Hertf.* 133 b. 134, 134 b. passim. *Glouc.* 163, 165, 168 b. *Heref.* 180, 184, 184 b. *Bedf.* 210 b. 217, 217 b. *Northampt.* 224 b. ter. 227, 227 b. *Leic.* 230 bis. 232 b. bis. 233 b. 236 b. *Warw.* 242. *Staff.* 249. *Shropsh.* 253, 256 b. 257 b.

---

[1] " Tenuit sub Eddeva pulchra."

[2] " Ipsi tenebant T. R. E. nec poterant a domino Manerii separari."

[3] " Ibi habet Orm manerium [Caldeber] nunc idem habet de Comite [Alano] et wast. est."

ter. *Chesh.* 268 bis. *Nottingh.* 282 b. *Yorksh.* 322 b.
Linc. 366 b. *Essex*, 23, 35, 42, 52 b. *Suff.* 295,
396, 403.

OSBERNUS clericus, *Sussex*, 17 b.

OSBERNUS clericus Episcopi Lincoliensis, *Linc.* 344 b.

OSBERNUS episcopus, *Wilts*, 64 b. 65 b. *Glouc.* 162 bis.

OSBERNUS filius Gosfridi, *Sussex*, 19 bis.

OSBERNUS filius Letard, *Kent*, 4 b. 9 b. bis. 11 b. bis.
12 b. *v.* OSBERTUS.

OSBERNUS f. Ricardi, *Worc.* 172 b. 173 b. *Heref.* 180.[1]
Staff. 247 b.

OSBERNUS f. Tezonis, *Chesh.* 268 b. bis.   ⎫
OSBERNUS filius Tezzonis, *Chesh.* 267 b. passim. ⎬

OSBERNUS homo Osberni de Arches, *Yorksh.* 329.

OSBERNUS homo archiepiscopi Eboracensis, *Linc.* 340.

OSBERNUS homo Comitis Hugonis, *Linc.* 349 b. ter.

OSBERNUS homo Willielmi de Perci, *Linc.* 353 b. 354.

OSBERNUS presbyter, *Wilts*, 65, 68 b. *Linc.* 338 b.

OSBERTUS, *Kent*, 10 b. 11 b. bis. *Wilts*, 66. *Hertf.* 140 b.
Buck. 149 b. 150. *Bedf.* 215 b. ter. *Essex*, 47 b.
59, 89 b. *Norf.* 190, 255 ter. 261 b.

OSBERTUS filius Letardi, *Kent*, 11, 11 b. *v.* OSBERNUS
f. Letard.

OSGOTUS, *Norf.* 202.

OSLACH, *Warw.* 241.

OSMUNDUS, *Wilts*, 68, 69, 69 b. 70 b. *Somers.* 89, 89 b.
Dev. 112 b. passim. *Oxf.* 160, 160 b. *Cambr.* 201 b.
Northampt. 220 b. 224. *Leic.* 234. *Warw.* 243.
Shropsh. 255. *Chesh.* 268 b. *Inter Rip. et Mersam*,
269 b. *Linc.* 344 b. bis. *Essex*, 84.

OSMUNDUS angevinus, *Essex*, 2 b.

OSMUNDUS canonicus S. Pauli de Bedeford, *Bedf.* 211.

---

[1] "Ipse tenuit T. R. E."

---

[1] Of whom see the former volume, pp. 461, 483.

[2] He had the same land previous to the Survey which he now held as an under-tenant to Ilbert de Laci.

[3] In this entry it is said " Rogerus de Otburuilla tenebat de Rege, modo de abbate " [*sc.* S. Ætheldredæ de Ely].

Otto aurifaber, *Essex*, 3 b. *v.* Otho.[1]

Oudchel, *Nottingh.* 284.

Ouethel, R. *Suff.* 440.

Outi, *Warw.* 239 bis.

Ow, Comes de, *Kent*, 4 bis.

Ow, Osbernus de, *Surr.* 30 b. 31.

Ow, Willielmus de, *Hants*, 48 b. *Wilts*, 67, 70. *Dev.* 100. *Glouc.* 162 bis. 164.

Ouus prepositus Regis, *Glouc.* 162.

Oxenef. Æcclesia S. Petri de, *Oxf.* 158 b.

Oxeneford, Burgenses de, *Buck.* 143 b.

Oxeneford, Saulf de, *Berks*, 56.

P.

Paganus, *Sussex*, 24. *Berks*, 62 bis. *Hertf.* 133 b. bis. 142. *Buck.* 148, 148 b. passim. 149 bis. 151 b. *Worc.* 177. *Cambr.* 198, 199 passim. *Essex*, 42 b. 45. *Suff.* 396 bis. 396 b.

Pagen, *Sussex*, 23. *Wilts*, 70 b. *Dors.* 75 b. *Oxf.* 159. *Northampt.* 226 passim. *Leic.* 235. *Staff.* 249 b. *Chesh.* 265, 266 ter.

Pagen et Sasfrid', homines Willielmi Peverel, *Nottingh.* 288.

Paisfor, Osbernus, *Kent*, 10 b. bis. ⎫
Paisforere, Osbernus, *Kent*, 9 b. ⎬ *v.* Pastforeire.
⎭

Pancratii S. [de Lewes], Clerici, *Suss.* 21.

Pancévold, Bernardus, *Wilts*, 72 b.

Pantul, Willielmus, *Staff.* 248.

Pantulf, Willielmus, *Shropsh.* 257 passim. 257 b. passim.

Papaldus, *Hants*, 48.

Parisiac̃, Fulcherus, *Bedf.* 211 b. ⎫
Parisiacensis, Fulcherus, *Bedf.* 214 b. ⎬
⎭

---

[1] See vol. i. p. 462.

Parler, Robertus, *Worc.* 175.

Passaq', Radulfus, *Bedf.* 214 b.

Pastforeire, Osbernus, *Kent,* 6. *v.* Paisfor. Paisforere.

Pauli, S. Canonici, *Surr.* 30 b. *Bedf.* 218 b.

Paupercula mulier, Kent, 9 b.

Peccatu', W. *Essex,* 39, 77. *Norf.* 175. *Suff.* 390 b.
396 b.

Perapund, Reinaldus de, *Norf.* 201 b.

Perci, Willielmus de,[1] *Yorksh.* 304 b. ter. 305 bis. *Linc.*
344, 357 b. 359.

Periton, Edwardus de, *Hertf.* 132 b.

Pertenai, W. de, *Norf.* 278 b.

Pesserara, *Suff.* 408 b.

Peteuinus, Rogerus, *Norf.* 117.

Petro ponte, Godefridus de, *Suff.* 399 b. 400.

Petro ponte, Rodbertus de, *Suff.* 399.

Petrus, *Surr.* 34 b. *Wilts,* 69 b. *Dev.* 111. *Hertf.* 134,
134 b. 138 b. bis. 141 b. *Oxf.* 158 bis. *Warw.* 243.
Essex, 65. *Norf.* 170. *Suff.* 360, 362, 363, 364,
366 b. 367 b.

Petrus clericus, *Suff.* 358, 358 b.

Petrus homo abbatis Sancti E. *Norf.* 117.

Petrus homo Ivonis Taillgebosc, *Linc.* 350.

Petrus, S. [Hereford], *Heref.* 184 b. ter. 185.

Petrus, S. Sciropesb. *Shropsh.* 252 b. 253 bis. 253 b,
254, 254 b.

Petrus Episcopus, *Berks,* 57. *Somers.* 98 b.

Petrus Vicecomes, *Hertf.* 133 bis. 135 b. 141 bis. *Essex,*
1 b. 2, 3, 4 b. 6, 6 b. 90 b.

Peverel, Rann. *Midd.* 128. *v.* Peurel.

Peverel, Willielmus, *Northampt.* 219 b. 229. *Derb.*
273.

Peverel quidam, *Hants,* 53.

---

[1] See vol. i. p. 465.

PEUREL, Rannulfus,[1] *Kent*, 9. *Shropsh.* 256 b. passim.
  Suff. 384 b. 397 b.

PEUREL, Willielmus, *Hants*, 40 b. *Northampt.* 220.
  Leic. 236. *Derb.* 273 b.

PHANEXON, *Norf.* 144.

PICOT, *Surr.* 35, 35 b. ter. 44 b. 50 b. 151 b. *Heref.*
  187. *Cambr.* 190,[2] 190 b. bis. 191, 194 b. bis. 195,
  197 ter. 200, 201 b. 202 passim. 202 b. *Northampt.*
  227. *Staff.* 247, 255 b. *Shropsh.* 258 passim. 258 b.
  ter. *Yorksh.* 309 b. passim. 310 b. 321 b. 322 b.
  328 b. *Essex*, 67, 68.

PICOT, homo Alani comitis, *Yorksh.* 310 b. *Linc.* 347
  ter.

PICOT, Rogerus, *Chesh.* 264 b.

PICOT Vicecom. de Exesse, *Cambr.* 201 b.

PICOTUS, *Sussex*, 25. *Cambr.* 190 passim. 193 b. *Essex*, 3 b.

PICTAVENSIS, Rogerus, *Suff.* 181 b.

PICTAVENSIS, Willelmus, *Kent*, 1 b.

PIERANO, S. Odo de, *Cornw.* 121.

PINCERNA, Ricardus, *Shropsh.* 253. *Chesh.* 265 ter.

———— Robertus, *Shropsh.* 256 passim.

PINCHENGI, Ansculfus de, *Buck.* 148 b.

PINCHENGI, Willielmus, *Wilts*, 69 b.

PINC'U'N', *Essex*, 76 b.

PINEL, Radulfus, *Suff.* 424.

PINELLUS, Radulfus, *Suff.* 424.

PIPE, *Somers.* 90.

PIPERELLUS, Ranulfus, *Essex*, 2, 4 b. 6, 18 b. 19, 31 b.
  64. *Norf.* 279 b. *Suff.* 393 b.

PIPIN, Radulfus, *Leic.* 234 b.

PIROT, *Essex*, 50. *Suff.* 403 b.

PIROTUS, *Cambr.* 197 b. ter. 212 b. bis. 214 b. ter.

---

[1] Of William, and Ralph Peverel, see Vol. i. pp. 466, 467.
[2] " Picot habet sub manu Regis I. hid."

Piscator reddens v. mil. Anguill. *Cambr.* 192.

Piscator habens I. sagenam in lacu Villæ de Saham, *Cambr.* 192.

Piscatores sex, Cambr. 196 b.

Piscatores octo in Wisbece, *Cambr.* 192 b.

PISTOR, Rainaldus, *Hants,* 52 b.

PLEINES, *Hunt.* 204 b.

POINGIANT, Ricardus, *Wilts,* 68.

POINTEL, *Essex,* 23, 23 b.

POINTEL, Tedricus, *Essex,* 2, 3, 4 b.

POINTELLUS, *Essex,* 69.

POLCEHARD, *Berks,* 60 b. 63 b.

POMEREI, Radulfus de, *Dev.* 105 b.[1]

PONT cardon, Robertus de, *Dev.* 100. *Hertf.* 138.

PONTHER, Walterus, *Worc.* 172 b. 173 b. passim. 174 bis. 174 b. 175, 175 b. *Glouc.* 166.

PONZ, *Berks,* 61.

PORT, Hugo de,[2] *Kent,* 2 b. bis. 6, 7 ter. 7 b. 9 ter. *Surr,* 32 bis. *Hants,* 39, 40 b. 41 b. 42 bis. 42 b. 43 bis. 43 b. 44 b. 46, 48, 48 b. 52. *Berks,* 59 b. *v.* PORTH.

Portarii duo de Montagud, *Somers.* 92.

PORTH, Hugo de, *Kent,* 6, 10 bis. 10 b. *Northampt.* 219. *v.* PORT.

PRATELLENSIS, S. Petrus, *Warw.* 240 b.

PRATELLIS, Abbatia de, *Berks,* 60.

Prebendarius quidam Regis, *Bedf.* 218.

Prepositus, v. ANSCHETELLUS. BALDUINUS. BLEIO. DURANDUS. ELMUI. IDHEL. LETMARUS. OUUS. SEOLF. VLMARUS.

---

[1] He occurs as under-tenant to Baldwin the Sheriff. His numerous estates, as a tenant in capite, in the same county, have been already referred to in the former volume, p. 468. In *Dev.* fol. 100, his payment of xxx d., from Smaurige to the paramount manor of Axeminster, is recorded.

[2] See Vol. i. p. 469.

PREPOSITUS Episcopi Baioc. *Surr.* 30.

PREPOSITUS Regis, *Hertf.* 141. *v.* ALMARUS.

PREPOSITUS unus Regis, *Dors.* 75 b.

Presbyter, *v.* ACARDUS. ÆLDRED. ÆLMER. ALRIC. ALUIET. ALURIC. ALURICUS. ALUUARDUS. ALUUINUS. ANCHITILLUS. ANSCHETIL. ANSFRIDUS. ANSGOT. ARNULF. ASCHIL. AZO. BERNARDUS. BOLLO. BORET. BRISTOALDUS. BRISTOARDUS. BRUN. EDRED. EDUIN. ELMER. ERNUINUS. GIRALDUS. GISLEBERTUS. GODEBOLDUS. LANBERTUS. LESTANUS. LEUENOT. LEURIC. RADFREDUS. RADULFUS. RAINBOLDUS. REINBALDUS. ROBERTUS. ROGERIUS. ROGERUS. RUMOLDUS. SALOMON. TASCELINUS. TOUI. TURCHIL. TUROLDUS. TURSTINUS. VITALIS. VLMERUS. VLUUARDUS. VLUUINUS.

PRESBYTER, *Heref.* 182 b.

PRESBYTER Goisfridi de Magne uile, *Berks*, 57.

PRESBYTER quidam, *Dors.* 76. *Hertf.* 140 b.

PRESBYTER alter, *Dors.* 76.

PRESBYTER manens in Tarente, *Dors.* 76.

PRESBYTER unus, *Somers.* 86 b. *Cambr.* 202. *Warw.* 241.

PRESBYTER et II. alii Angli, *Somers.* 89 b.

PRESBYTER manerii de Beiminstre, *Som.* 86 b.

PRESBYTER manerii de Hinetone, *Dors.* 76.

PRESBYTERI duo, *Berks*, 57.

PRESBYTERI trium Æcclesiarum in Arcenefeld, *Heref.* 179.

PUGNANT, Ricardus, *Hants*, 52.

PUNGIANT, Willielmus, *Berks*, 56 b.

Q.

QUINTINUS, *Wilts*, 66 bis. *Norf.* 233 b.

R.

bis. 106 bis. 106 b. passim. 107 b. bis. 108 bis.
108 b. 109 passim. 109 b. 110 passim. 110 b. passim. 111 bis. 114 b. 116 b. ter. 117, 117 b. ter.
Cornw. 125. *Midd.* 129 b. *Hertf.* 133 b. 134 b.
136 b. 137 bis. 138, 139, 139 b. 140 bis. *Buck.*
146 bis. 146 b. passim. 147 bis. 147 b. ter. 148 bis.
148 b. 149 b. ter. 150, 150 b. 151, 152, 152 b.
153. *Oxf.* 156 b. 157, 157 b. 158 b. 161. *Glouc.*
163 b. ter. 165, 166 b. 167, 167 b. bis. 168 b. bis.
Worc. 174, 176 b. *Heref.* 180, 183, 184 bis. 184 b.
185 b. 186, 186 b. *Cambr.* 191 b. 194, 194 b. 199,
200 bis. 200 b. passim. 201 b. *Bedf.* 213, 214 b.
217 b. *Shropsh.* 255 bis. 256. *Chesh.* 266 bis. 268 b.
Inter Rip. et Mersam, 269 b. 270. *Derb.* 274 b.
ter. 275 bis. 277 bis. 277 b. *Northampt.* 220 b.
223, 223 b. passim. 224 passim. 225, 226, 226 b.
Leic. 231 passim. 231 b. bis. 232 b. 235 b. 236 b.
ter. 237 passim. *Warw.* 239, 241, 241 b. bis. 242.
Staff. 247, 249 b. *Nottingh.* 284. *Yorksh.* 315,
316 bis. 318, 325 b. passim. *Linc.* 341, 370. *Essex*,
9 b. 11 b. 12, 45 b. 47, 55, 56, 58 b. 66 b. 67 b.
76 b. ter. 78 b. 79, 83 b. 88 b. 102. *Norf.* 159 b.
160 b. 169, 169 b. 183, 203 b. 226 b. 227, 231 b.
235, 239, 240, 257. *Suff.* 296, 318 b. 319, 345,
356 b. 360, 362, 396 b. 408 b. 423, 423 b.

Radulfus alter, *Sussex*, 22. *Dev.* 103 b.

Radulfus arbalistarius, *Norf.* 117.

Radulfus canonicus S. Pauli Lond. *Midd.* 127 b.

Radulfus cocus, *Shropsh.* 259.

Radulfus Comes,[1] *Hertf.* 140 b. *Glouc.* 169. *Essex*, 7 b.

Radulfus dapifer, *Northampt.* 224.

Radulfus filius Brien, *Essex*, 9 b. 12, 12 b. 74 b. 75,
99 b. *Suff.* 417.

---

[1] See Vol. i. p. 470.

RADULFUS venator, *Chesh.* 267, 268 b.

RAFRI, *Sussex*, 24 b.

RAIMAR clericus, *Somers.* 95 b.

RAIMUNDUS, *Essex*, 5.

RAINALDUS, *Sussex*, 25 b. *Surr.* 32 b. 36 b. *Berks,* 56,
57 b. 58 b. ter. 59 bis. 59 b. *Wilts,* 71 passim.
Somers. 92, 92 b. 98. *Dev.* 103 b. 104 b. passim.
105 passim. 108, 108 b. 111 bis. 115 passim. 116 b.
bis. *Cornw.* 120 b. 122 passim.[1] *Hertf.* 140 b. *Oxf.*
154 b. 155, 158, 158 b. bis. 159 bis. 159 b. ter. 161
passim. *Cambr.* 194 b. *Bedf.* 215. *Northampt.* 228.
Warw. 239 passim. *Staff.* 248 ter. *Shropsh.* 253 b.
259 b. *Chesh.* 267 b. 268 bis. *Yorksh.* 303 b. bis.
Essex, 57 b. *Norf.* 195. *Suff.* 440 b.

RAINALDUS capellanus, *Glouc.* 163 b.

RAINALDUS filius Iuonis, *Norf.* 110, 115, 116 b. 117 b.
214, 234 b. 275 b. 276.

RAINALDUS homo Rogeri Bigot, *Norf.* 116 b.

RAINALDUS homo Colsuan, *Linc.* 357.

RAINALDUS homo Goisfridi de Wirce, *Linc.* 369.

RAINALDUS pistor, *Hants,* 52 b.

RAINALDUS p̄r cum filia Pagani, *Norf.* 264.

---

[1] The Messrs. Lysons, in their Magna Britannia, explain
who the Rainaldus of this folio was. They say, " The
greatest landholder under the Earl of Moretaine, in this
county, was Rainaldus or Reginald, who held thirty (it
should be thirty-three) manors, including the manor and
castle of Trematon. This was Reginald de Valletort, who
is known to have possessed the honor of Trematon at a
period not much later. Dugdale mentions Reginald de
Valletort as witnessing a deed in the reign of William
Rufus, which he speaks of as the first mention he had found
of the family: he does not seem to have been aware, that
his property is described in the Domesday Survey." Mag.
Brit. *Cornw.* p. li.

RANNULFUS homo Ernegis de Burun, *Yorksh.* 328 b. *Linc.* 362.

RANNULFUS homo Widonis de Credun, *Linc.* 367 b. bis.

RANNULFUS homo Episcopi Lincoliensis, *Linc.* 344 bis. 344 b.

RANNULFUS homo Aluredi de Lincole, *Linc.* 358 bis.

RANNULFUS homo Goisfridi de Wirce, *Nottingh.* 291.

RANNULFUS Vicecomes, *Surr.* 30, 32.

RANULFUS, *Essex,* 36, 37, 38, 85 b. *Norf.* 152, 193, 231 bis. 232 b. bis. 234, 258 b. *Suff.* 307, 338 b.

RANULFUS f. G. *Norf.* 188 b.

RANULFUS filius Galteri, *Norf.* 173 b. 174, 175, 176, 176 b. 178 b.179, 180 b. 277. *v.* RANNULFUS filius Walteri.

RANULFUS frater Ilgeri, *Essex,* 1 b. 6 b. 15 b. *Suff.* 424, 425. *v.* RANNULFUS.

RANULFUS nepos, *Suff.* 400.

RARDULFUS, *Norf.* 157.

RASRIDUS, *Norf.* 212.

RATHO, *Norf.* 170 b.

RAUEMERUS homo Gisleberti de Gand. *Linc.* 355 b.

RAUEN, *Staff.* 247.

RAUENESORT et ARNEGRIM, *Nottingh.* 283 b.

RAUENGARIUS, *Essex,* 17 b. 23 bis. 23 b.

RAUENOT, *Essex,* 73, 75.

RAYNALD, *Bedf.* 213 b.

RAYNALDUS. *Glouc.* 165. *Bedf.* 215 b.

RAYNALDUS filius Croc,[1] *Hants,* 52.

RAYNALDUS homo Walterii de Aincurt, *Linc.* 361 bis.

RAYNALDUS Vicecomes, *Shropsh.* 254.

RAYNERUS, *Kent,* 8 b. *Berks,* 60 b. 61 b. *Worc.* 176. *Shropsh.* 254. *Yorksh.* 324 b.

---

[1] See Vol. i. p. 472.

RAYNERUS homo Drogonis de Bevrere, *Yorksh.* 324 b. *Linc.* 360.

RAYNERUS homo Gozelini filii Lanberti, *Linc.* 359, 359 b. bis.

RAYNOLDUS homo Walterii de Aincurt, *Nottingh.* 288 b.

RAYNOUUARDUS, *Derb.* 277.

REDUERS, Ricardus de, *Dors.* 83.

REGERUS, *Staff.* 248.

REIMUNDUS, Giraldus, *Essex*, 5.

REINALDUS, *Oxf.* 159. *Cambr.* 199 b. *Norf.* 200.

REINBALDI frater, *Glouc.* 165.

REINBALDUS, *Berks*, 58 b. *Glouc.* 162 b. 166.

REINBALDUS presbyter, *Berks*, 56 b.

REINBALDUS presbyter ecclesiæ S. Joh. de Froma, *Somers.* 86 b. bis.

REINBERTUS, *Sussex*, 17 b. 18 bis. 18 b. passim. 19, 19 b. passim. 20.

REINBUEDCURT, Ingelrannus filius Widonis de, *Linc.* 363 b.

REINERUS, *Norf.* 169 b.

REINFRIDUS, *Shropsh.* 255 b.

REINOLDUS filius Ivonis, *Norf.* 117.

RE'BUTCURT, Wido de, *Cambr.* 191 b.

REMIGIUS Episcopus Lincoliæ,[1] *Bedf.* 209 bis. 210 b. *Linc.* 366 b.

REMIRUS, *Sussex*, 20.

RENALDUS, *Essex*, 62 b. *Norf.* 233.

RENBALDUS, *Berks*, 58 b.

RENELMUS, *Essex*, 59 b.

RENEUUALDUS, *Somers.* 95 ter.

RENEUUARUS, *Somers.* 95.

RENOLDUS, *Norf.* 199 b.

---

[1] See Vol. i. p. 474.

Restaldus, *Surr.* 31 b. *Chesh.* 264.

Restoldus, *Surr.* 30 b.

Restolt, *Essex*, 83 b.

Ret, Aluuin, *Hants*, 50.

Ribald, *Yorksh.* 311 bis. 311 b. passim. 312, 313 bis.

Ribaldus, *Norf.* 144 b. bis. 145 b. 146 b. 148, 149 bis. 150.

Ricaiardus, *Norf.* 209 b.

Ricard, *Cornw.* 120. *Yorksh.* 307, 307 b.

Ricardus, *Kent*, 9 b. 10 b. *Sussex*, 16 b. 17 b. bis. 26, 28. *Surr.* 31 b. *Hants*, 49 b. 53. *Berks*, 61 b. bis. 62. *Wilts*, 72, 72 b. bis. *Dors.* 82 ter. 89, 89 b. 92 b. 94 b. 95 bis. 95 b. 96 b. 97 ter. *Somers.* 98 bis. *Dev.* 105 ter. 105 b. bis. 106 passim. 106 b. 108, 114. 117 b. *Cornw.* 120 b. 121, 122 bis. 122 b. passim.[1] *Midd.* 130. *Buck.* 147, 148. 150 bis. *Oxf.* 155 b. 158, 159 b. ter. *Worc.* 173. *Heref.* 180. 183 b. ter. 186 passim. *Cambr.* 197. *Bedf.* 213 b. *Northampt.* 220 b. bis. 222, 224 b. *Leic.* 234 b. bis. *Warw.* 241, 243. *Shropsh.* 254, 254 b. bis. 255, 256 b. 257, 258 b. bis. 259 b. 260 ter. 260 b. passim. *Chesh.* 265, 268, 268 b. *Nottingh.* 289 b. 291 b. *Yorksh.* 305 bis. 305 b. passim. 306, 306 b. bis. 307 b. passim. 308 passim. 308 b. passim. 323,

---

[1] Upon the Ricardus of Cornwall, the Messrs. Lysons say, " Ricardus held twenty-nine manors. Reginald, who was created Earl of Cornwall in 1140, married the daughter of William Fitz Richard of Cornwall, who is described as having ' Comitatus Cornubiensis amplissimum Principatum.' Gesta Stephani inter Hist. Normannorum Scriptores, p. 950. No doubt this was a son, and the Fitz Williams immediate descendants (through the Fitz Richards) of the Ricardus of Domesday. They were all possessors of the manor of Tywardreth, and benefactors to the Monastery of that place."

326 b. *Linc.* 361 b. *Essex,* 27, 31, 36 bis. 37 b.
38 bis. 38 b. bis. 39 b. 40, 40 b. 41 bis. 41 b. bis.
49, 49 b. 50, 50 b. 51 bis. 51 b. 55 b. 56, 56 b.
58 b. 61 b. 63 b. 64 b. 72 bis. 76, 80 bis. 81. *Norf.*
115 b. 191 b. 197, 226 b. 227 b. 228, 229 bis.
229 b. bis. 257 b. *Suff.* 393, 394, 394 b. 408 b.
436 b. 448.

RICARDUS [*i. e.* de Tonbridge], *Kent,* 56 b.

RICARDUS quidam juvenis, *Glouc.* 167.

RICARDUS filius Alann, *Norf.* 197.

RICARDUS filius Comitis Gisleberti,[1] *Essex,* 3 b. 6 b.
Suff. 385.

RICARDUS filius Willielmi, *Kent,* 9.

RICARDUS homo abbatis S. Petri de Burg, *Linc.* 345 b.

RICARDUS homo Rogerii de Busli, *Nottingh.* 285.

RICARDUS homo Archiepiscopi Cantuar. *Kent,* 4 bis.

RICARDUS homo Hamonis, *Essex,* 99.

RICARDUS homo Durandi Malet, *Linc.* 365.

RICARDUS homo Radulfi de Mortemer, *Linc.* 363.

RICARDUS homo Gisleberti Tison, *Yorksh.* 326 b.

RICARDUS pincerna, *Chesh.* 265 ter.

RICARDUS [Surd'v'], *Yorksh.* 305 passim. 305 b. passim.

RICARDUS Surd'v', *Yorksh.* 305.

RICARDUS soc' Ansgari, *Essex,* 62 b.

RICARDUS et HUGO milites Abbatis de Ramesyg, *Hunt.*
204.

RICARDUS et alii, *Berks,* 57.

RICARIUS, Sanctus, *Norf.* 167 b.

RICERUS, *Suff.* 414.

RICHARDUS, *Suff.* 354 b.

RICHERIUS, *Hants,* 40 b. bis. 41. *Wilts,* 65 b. *Heref.*
185 b.

RICHERIUS clericus, *Hants,* 41 b. bis.

---

[1] See Vol. i. p. 477.

RICHERUS, *Wilts*, 65 b.

RICOARDUS, *Sussex*, 26. *Hants*, 47.

RICOLF, *Leic.* 235.

RICTAN, *Suff.* 446 b.

RICUARD, *Suff.* 328.

RICUARDUS, *Norf.* 212.

RICULF, *Dev.* 112 b. bis.

RICULFUS, *Kent*, 11. *Hertf.* 134.

RIPPE, *Somers.* 97 b.

RISBOIL, Galt. de, *Suff.* 306, 306 b.

RISET de Wales, *Heref.* 179.

RIUOLDUS, *Norf.* 245 b. bis.

RIUUALO, *Bedf.* 213 b.

ROALDUS, *Leic.* 233.

ROBERTUS, RODBERTUS, *seu* ROTBERTUS, *Kent*, 13.
    Sussex, 17 b. 18 ter. 18 b. passim. 19 b. bis. 23 ter.
    23 b. passim. 24 bis. 24 b. 25 bis. 27 ter. 28 b.
    passim. 29 passim. *Surr.* 35 b. *Hants*, 40 bis. 46,
    48, 51, 52 b. bis. *Berks*, 57 bis. 60, 60 b. 61 b. 62.
    Wilts, 66 bis. 66 b. ter. 67, 69 b. ter. 70 passim.
    70 b. ter. 71, 72 bis. 72 b. 74 b. *Dors.* 75 b. 79
    passim. 79 b. passim. 80, 80 b. ter. 81 b. 82, 82 b.
    bis. 83 b. ter. 84 ter. *Som.* 87 b. 89, 90, 91 b.
    92 ter. 92 b. 93 passim. 93 b. passim. 94 passim.
    94 b. passim. 95 b. 96, 96 b. 97 b. bis. 98 b. *Dev.*
    103 b. ter. 104 b. 106, 106 b. passim. 107 passim.
    108, 109, 110 bis. 111 b. bis. 113 bis. 114 b. *Midd.*
    129. *Hertf.* 137 bis. 137 b. 140 b. *Buck.* 144 bis.
    144 b. ter. 145, 145 b. 146 b. 147, 147 b. 148,
    148 b. 149 b. 150, 151, 152. *Oxf.* 155 b. passim.
    156 b. 157, 157 b. bis. 158, 158 b. 159 b. 161
    passim. *Glouc.* 165 ter. 166 b. 168. *Worc.* 173 b.
    177 bis. 177 b. ter. *Heref.* 180, 184, 184 b. bis.
    185 bis. 187 b. *Cambr.* 190, 193 bis. 193 b. 194 b.

ter. 196 b. 200 b. 201, 201 b. 202. *Bedf.* 213 b.
214, 216 ter. 217 b. bis. *Northampt.* 220 b. ter.
221 bis. 222, 224 ter. 224 b. passim. 225 b. 226
passim. 227, 227 b. 228 b. 229 bis. *Leic.* 230 b.
231, 231 b. bis. 232 b. 233 b. passim. 234 passim.
234 b. bis. 235 ter. 235 b. bis. 236 b. bis. 237
passim. *Warw.* 240 ter. 241, 241 b. 242, 243,
243 b. *Staff.* 247 bis. 248, 249 bis. 249 b. ter. 250
passim. *Shropsh.* 253 b. 254, 254 b. 255 bis. 255 b.
256, 256 b. 259 bis. *Chesh.* 263 b. *Inter Rip. et
Mersam,* 269 b. 270. *Derb.* 273, 273 b. 274 b.
275, 275 b. 276 bis. 277 ter. *Nottingh.* 282 b. bis.
287 b. 304 b. bis. 312, 313, 316 ter. *Linc.* 346.
Essex, 29 b. 30 bis. 32 b. 39, 45, 45 b. bis. 47,
47 b. 48, 54, 64, 64 b. 65, 65 b. bis. 66 b. 67 b.
68, 75. *Norf.* 155 b. 179 b. 183, 183 b. *Suff.* 307 b.
358, 363 bis. 367 b. 399. 402 bis. 408 b. 427 b.

ROBERTUS alter, *Sussex,* 18. *Oxf.* 155 b.

ROBERTUS quidam, *Shropsh.* 253 b. *Yorksh.* 315 bis.

ROBERTUS arbalistarius, *Norf.* 118.

ROBERTUS calvus, *Cambr.* 198 b.

ROBERTUS (clericus), *Sussex,* 16 b.

ROBERTUS clericus, *Hants,* 40.

ROBERTUS cocus, *Kent,* 13 b. *Sussex,* 18 b.

ROBERTUS Comes, *Suff.* 281 b.

ROBERTUS dapifer Hugonis de Port, *Berks,* 59 b.

ROBERTUS dispensator, *Worc.* 172 b. 173, 173 b. bis.
174, 175.

ROBERTUS Episcopus, *Oxf.* 155.

ROBERTUS Episcopus Hereford, *Glouc.* 165.

ROBERTUS filius Corbet, *Shropsh.* 256 passim.

ROBERTUS filius Corbutionis,[1] *Essex,* 3 bis. *Norf.* 253 b.

---

[1] See Vol. i. p. 478.

Robertus f.Fasiton, *Hunt.* 207 bis.

Robertus filius Fulcheredi, *Suff.* 308.

Robertus filius Giroldi, *Somers.* 86 b.

Robertus f. Hugonis, *Chesh.* 263, 264 passim. 264 b. passim.

Robertus filius Nigelli, *Bedf.* 215.

Robertus filius Rozelini, *Hertf.* 137. *Bedf.* 211.

Robertus filius Tetbaldi, *Sussex*, 23. *Shropsh.* 256 b. passim.

Robertus filius W. hostiarii, *Leic.* 237.

Robertus filius Walterii, *Buck.* 149.

Robertus filius Wimarc, *Hertf.* 134, 137 b. *Essex*, 42.

Robertus flavus, *Wilts*, 73.

Robertus homo Normanni de Adreci, *Linc.* 361 b.

Robertus homo Comitis Alani, *Yorksh.* 312 b. 313. *Linc.* 347.

Robertus homo Drogonis de Bevrere, *Yorksh.* 324 b. 360 bis. 360 b.

Robertus homo Rogeri de Busli, *Nottingh.* 284 b. bis. 285 b.

Robertus homo Gisleberti de Gand, *Nottingh.* 290 b. 354 b. bis. 356.

Robertus homo Comitis Hugonis, *Nottingh.* 282 b.

Robertus homo Willielmi de Perci, *Linc.* 353 b. 354.

Robertus homo Willielmi Peverel, *Nottingh.* 287.

Robertus homo Goisfridi de Wirce, *Linc.* 369.

Robertus inuesiatus homo Roberti Grenonis, *Essex*, 15.

Robertus Latin', *Kent*, 6 b. 8, 8 b. bis. 11 b. 12.

Robertus Latinus, *Kent*, 7 bis.

Robertus lorimarius, *Norf.* 117.

Robertus [Malet], *Suff.* 379.

Robertus minister Regis, *Glouc.* 162.

Robertus niger, *Kent*, 1 b.

Robertus pincerna, *Shropsh.* 256 passim.

Robertus presbyter *Linc.* 345.[1]

Robertus venator, *Warw.* 242.

Robertus et ii.° Angli, *Cambr.* 194 b.

Robertus et Herbertus, *Somers.* 97.

Rodelend, Robertus de, *Chesh.* 262 b. bis. ⎫
Rodelent, Robertus de, *Chesh.* 264 b. passim. ⎭

Roderius, *Hertf.* 133 b. 134.

Rodulfus alter,[2] *Sussex*, 29.

Roelent, Robertus de, *Chesh.* 268 b. passim. 269 ter.

Rog'e, *Somers.* 88 b.

Rogerius, *Kent*, 13 bis. *Sussex*, 20 b. 22, 24 b. passim.
    Hants, 48 b. 53. *Wilts*, 66 ter. 66 b. 70 b. 71 b.
    passim. 72 b. *Dors.* 77 b. *Somers* 87, 88. 88 b. 90
    passim. 90 b. passim. 95 b. 96 passim. *Dev.* 102,
    105 b. 106 passim. 106 b. 114 passim. 108 bis.
    108 b. 114 b. passim. 115, 117. *Cornw.* 125 passim.
    Hertf. 134, 138, 140. *Buck.* 144 passim. 144 b.
    147, 149 b. 150 bis. 151 b. *Oxf.* 155, 155 b. bis.
    156 ter. 157 b. 158, 158 b. ter. 159 b. 161 ter.
    Glouc. 163, 168 passim. *Cambr.* 190 b. 197. *Bedf.*
    214, 218. *Northampt.* 221, 221 b. bis. *Leic.* 234 b.
    235, 237 bis. *Warw.* 241 b. *Staff.* 248, 248 b.
    250 bis. *Shropsh.* 253 b. ter. *Derb.* 274 bis. *Shropsh.*
    255 b.

Rogerius [*qu.* de Boscroard], *Buck.* 149.

Rogerius quidam, *Shropsh.* 255 b.

Rogerius Comes,[3] *Hants*, 38 b. 49 bis.

Rogerius filius Corbet, *Shropsh.* 255 b. passim.

Rogerius filius Teodrici, *Bedf.* 213 b.

Rogerius fr. Willielmi Comitis, *Glouc.* 164 b.

---

[1] " In hac villa [Hacam] ħɓ Robertus presbyter i. car.
terræ de Rege in elemosina, et modo cum eadem terra
effectus est monachus in S. Maria Stou. Sed non licet
terram alicui habere nisi Regis concessu."

[2] *sc.* Radulfus.   [3] See Vol. i. p. 479.

Rogerius presbyter, *Bedf.* 214.

Rogerius venator, *Shropsh.* 253, 259 passim.

Rogerius Vicecomes, *Midd.* 127. *Glouc.* 169.

Rogerus, *Sussex*, 20, 20 b. 21. *Surr.* 35. *Hants*, 48 b. *Berks*, 60, 63 bis. *Wilts*, 66 b. *Dors.* 82, 83 b. *Somers.* 88, 88 b. 89, 89 b. 96 passim. *Dev.* 111, 114, 114 b. passim. 115, 117, 117 b. *Hertf.* 137, 140 b. bis. 141 bis. *Buck.* 144 passim. 144 b. passim. 150, 152 b. bis. *Oxf.* 156, 156 b. bis. 161. *Glouc.* 164 b. 165, 169 bis. *Worc.* 176 b. 177. *Heref.* 185. *Cambr.* 197, 201 passim. 201 b. 202 b. ter. *Hunt.* 206 b. *Bedf.* 213 b. *Northampt.* 221 b. 222 bis. 225. *Leic.* 231, 232 b. 233 bis. 233 b. ter. 234 ter. 235 b. 237. *Warw.* 240 b. bis. 241, 242 bis. 243 passim. 243 b. *Staff.* 248, 249 b. *Shropsh.* 255, 257. *Chesh.* 267 b. 268 b. *Inter Ripam et Mersam*, 269 b. ter. 270. *Derb.* 274 b. 275, 276. *Yorksh.* 317 b. *Essex*, 9 b. 10, 11 b. 26 b. 34 bis. 40 b. 45 b. bis. 54, 70 b. 78 b. 80, 84, 84 b. ter. 91 bis. 101 b. *Norf.* 198, 209 b. 223, 230 b. 231 b. 234 b. ter. 238 b. 256 b. *Suff.* 282, 346, 394 b. 396 bis. 398 bis. 404 b. 427 b.

Rogerus alter, *Berks*, 63.

Rogerus clericus, *Sussex*, 18, 20 b. 22 bis.

Rogerus Comes, *Hants*, 38 b.

Rogerus filius Anschitil, *Kent*, 10 b. 11.

Rogerus filius Ernaldi, *Suff.* 346 b.

Rogerus filius Ernolf, *Suff.* 346 b.

Rogerus fil. W. Comitis, *Glouc.* 164.

Rogerus filius Rainart, *Norf.* 205 b.

Rogerus f. Seifridi, *Berks*, 56 b.

Rogerus homo Normanni de Adreci, *Linc.* 361 b.

Rogerus homo Drogonis de Bevrere, *Yorksh.* 325.

Rogerus homo Rainerii de Brimov, *Linc.* 364.

Rogerus homo abbatis S. Petri de Burg. *Linc.* 246.

ROGERUS homo Rogerii de Busli, *Nottingh.* 284 b. 285 b. 286 b. bis. 287.

ROGERUS homo Colsuan, *Linc.* 356 b.

ROGERUS homo Eustachii, *Hunt.* 206.

ROGERUS homo Gisleberti de Gand, *Linc.* 355, 355 b.

ROGERUS homo Episcopi Lincoliensis, *Linc.* 344 bis.

ROGERUS homo Episcopi Londoniensis, *Essex,* 6 b.

ROGERUS homo Rogeri Pictavensis, *Linc.* 352 passim.

ROGERUS homo Ivonis Taillgebosc, *Linc.* 350 b. bis.

ROGERUS homo Roberti de Todeni, *Linc.* 353.

ROGERUS minister Petri Valoniensis, *Hertf.* 138 b.

ROGERUS presbyter, *Berks,* 58.

ROGERUS Pictaviensis. *Essex,* 5. *Norf.* 140 b.

ROGERUS venator, *Worc.* 176. *Shropsh.* 254 b.

ROGERUS Vicecomes, *Suff.* 293.

ROGO, *Dev.* 107 bis.[1] 107 b. 108, 108 b. ⎫
ROGUS, *Dev.* 108.   ⎭

ROHARD, *Somers.* 89 b.

ROHARDUS, *Somers.* 89 b.

ROICUS, *Suff.* 365 b.

ROLD homo Colegrim, *Linc.* 370.

ROLF, *Dev.* 105 b. 111 b.

ROLLAND, *Northampt.* 227 bis.

ROLLANDUS, *Sussex,* 23 b. *Cornw.* 120 b. *Bedf.* 212 b.

ROMENEL, Rotbertus de, *Kent,* 4 b. 10 b. ter. 11 passim. *Buck.* 145.

RORICUS, *Suff.* 362 b.

Ros, Anschitil de, *Kent,* 8 b. 11 b.

Ros, Anschitillus de, *Kent,* 6 ter. 6 b. passim. *Surr.* ⎫
31 b. *Hertf.* 137.   ⎭

Ros, Ansgotus de, *Buck.* 144 b.

---

[1] Holcome, one of the manors entered to him in this folio, still bears the name of Holcombe Rogus, by which latter name Rogo is also called in fol. 108.

Ros, Goisfridus de, *Kent*, 6, 6 b. 8, 14 b.

Ros, Serlo de, *Bedf.* 213 b. bis. 214 b.

Rotroc, *Oxf.* 156 b. bis.

Rouecestra, Turoldus de, *Essex*, 25.

Rouecestre, Ansgotus de, *Kent*, 6, 7, 7 b. bis. 8 b. bis.
9. *Bedf.* 209 b. bis.

Rouecestre, Episcopus de,[1] *Kent*, 2 b. bis. *Cambr.* 190 b.[2]

Rozel', *Yorksh.* 321 b. passim.

Rozelinus, *Sussex*, 17. *Northampt.* 221 b. *Dev.* 114
bis. *Yorksh.* 321 b. passim.

Rozelinus homo Comitis Hugonis, *Linc.* 349.

Ruallon, *Bedf.* 215.

Ruallonus, *Bedf.* 214.

Rualon, *Bedf.* 213 b. bis.

Rufus, Hugo, *Linc.* 344 b.

Rumaldus, *Somers.* 98.

Rumbaldus, *Glouc.* 170 bis.

Rumoldus, *Hertf.* 137, 137 b.

Rumoldus presbyter, *Wilts*, 65.

Runeuile, Goisfr', *Hertf.* 140 b.

Ruuecestra, Turoldus de, *Essex*, 25 b.

S.

Sacerdos, *v.* Wal'a.

Sacheuilla, Ricardus de, *Essex*, 27.

Sæifridus, *Cambr.* 200 b.

Safridus homo Willielmi Peverel, *Nottingh.* 287 b.

Sagar unus sochemannus, *Cambr.* 190.

---

[1] See Vol. i. p. 482.

[2] The Bishop of Rochester stands in this folio as a
tenant in capite, probably from his station in the church:
but from the entry itself, it appears that he was under-
tenant for his land in this county to Archbishop Lanfranc.

---

[1] Blaculveslei. " Idem ipse tenuit T. R. E."

[2] Saintes, or Xaintes, was the capital of Haute-Saintonge, under the metropolitan See of Bordeaux. Rannulph, or Arnulph Facaudi, was Bishop of Saintes from 1083 to 1107. See Richard et Giraud, Bibliothéque Sacrée, tom. xxix. p. 150.

[3] The Benedictine Abbey of St. Martin, in the city of Seez, founded A. D. 1050, by Roger de Montgomery II. and Mabel his wife. Al. Pr. vol. i. p. 109. Neustr. Pia, p. 577.

[4] See Vol. i. p. 216.

Sauenie, Radulfus de, *Suff.* 373 b.

Sau'gno, Radulfus de, *Suff.* 373 b. bis.

Sauigneio, Rad. de, *Suff.* 417.

Sauigni, Radulfus de, *Suff.* 375 b. 376 b. 377, 378 b. 384 b. 417.

Sauigniaco, Radulfus de, *Suff.* 374.

Saulf, *Somers.* 90 b.

Sauuardus, *Hertf.* 139 b.

Sauuinus, *Hants,* 51 b. 53. *Cambr.* 201.

Sauuoldi filius, *Worc.* 176 b.

Sauuoldus, *Oxf.* 154, 155 b. bis.

Saxlef, *Suff.* 446 b.

Schelin, *Dors.* 83.

Schelinus, *Glouc.* 165.

Schelm, *Dors.* 84 bis.

Scireburn', Monachi de, *Dors.* 77.

Scohies, W. de, *Norf.* 213 b. 215 b.

Scoies, Willielmus de, *Norf.* 117. *Suff.* 383.

Scoies, W. de, *Suff.* 383 b.[1]

Scollandus, *Sussex,* 27 b.

Scoua, Leuuinus, *Hertf.* 134 b.

Scriba, Willielmus, *Glouc.* 162.

Scudet, Willielmus, *Wilts,* 65, 65 b.

Scutet, Willielmus, *Suff.* 310, 339.

Sedred, *Derb.* 278 b.

Segrim, *Oxf.* 154 bis.

Segrim alius, *Oxf.* 154 bis.

Seibertus, *Cornw.* 125.

Seifridus, *Cambr.* 200 b.

Semarus, *Hunt.* 204.

Semer, *Heref.* 180.

---

[1] " Hoc tenuit W. de Scoies de rege, modo de abbate " [S. Ætheldr. de Eli].

SENCLER, Richardus de, *Suff.* 354 b. }
SENT CLER, Ricardus de, *Norf.* 117 b. }

SENTEBOR, Richardus de, *Norf.* 117.

SEOLF quidam prepositus Willielmi Episcopi, *Norf.* 198 b.

SEPT MUELES, Willelmus de, *Sussex*, 18. }
SEPTMUELS, Willelmus de, *Sussex*, 19 b. }

SERIC, *Buck.* 150.

SERLO, *Wilts*, 66 b. *Dors.* 77. *Somers.* 89 b. 90, 90 b. passim. *Leic.* 232 b. bis. *Derb.* 276, 277. *Essex*, 55 ter. 71 b. bis. 72 bis. 73, 81 b.

SESSISBERT, *Glouc.* 162.

SEVERI, S. Monachi,[1] *Linc.* 349 b.

SEWARD, *Shropsh.* 259 b.[2] *Derb.* 276.

SEUUARDUS, *Shropsh.* 256 b.

SEUUARDUS venator, *Hants*, 42 b.

SEUUEN, canonicus S. Martini, *Kent*, 2.

SEUUI, *Oxf.* 154.

SIGAR, *Cambr.* 197 passim.[3]

SIGARUS, Edricus, *Suff.* 446 b.

SILUA, Willielmus de, *Suff.* 342 b.

SILUESTRIS, Hugo, *Dors.* 83.

SIMON, *Norf.* 164.

SIMOND', *Essex*, 37.

SIMUND homo Hepponis balistarii, *Linc.* 369 bis.

SINOD, *Dors.* 77 passim.

SIRED, *Kent*, 1 b. *Hants*, 44 b.[4]

---

[1] St. Sever, in the diocese of Avranches, founded by Hugh Earl of Chester about A. D. 1085. Al. Pr. vol. ii. p. 1.

[2] "Ipsemet tenuit."

[3] In several of the entries in this folio, Sigar appears to have held the same land under Asgar Stalre which he now held under Geoffrey de Mandeville.

[4] " Sired tenet de Comite [Rogerio] Nevtibrige. Ipsemet tenuit de Heraldo comite."

SIRED canonicus S. Martini, *Kent,* 2.

SIRED canonicus S. Pauli Lond. *Midd.* 130.

SIREDUS, *Midd.* 127.

SIREUUOLDUS, *Cornw.* 124 b.

SIRICUS, *Essex,* 42, 47 b. 48.

SIUERT, *Buck.* 149.

SIUUARD, *Northampt.* 222. *Shropsh.* 259 b.[1]

SIUUARD, *Linc.* 358.[2]

SIUUARDUS, *Sussex,* 25 b. *Surr.* 34 b. *Somers.* 90 b.
     Hertf. 139 b. 141 b. *Oxf.* 157. *Worc.* 173. *Shropsh.*
     260. *Norf.* 137.

SIUUARDUS tenus, *Wilts,* 71.

SIUUATE, *Nottingh.* 283 b.

SMALA VILL, Willielmus de, *Suff.* 307 bis.

SOCHEMANNI duo, *Hertf.* 141. *Cambr.* 190, 195,[3] 197.
     Bedf. 209 b. bis. 212.

SOCHEMANNI tres, *Hertf.* 133. *Buck.* 145 b. *Bedf.* 214, 218·

SOCHEMANNI homines III. Vlmari de Etone, *Bedf.* 212.

SOCHEMANNI IIII. *Bedf.* 210.

SOCHEMANNI v.[4] *Cambr.* 195.

SOCHEMANNI VI. *Cambr.* 197 b.[5] 198 b.

SOCHEMANNI VII. sub Abbate [de Elyg], *Cambr.* 192.

SOCHEMANNI VIII. *Cambr.* 197 b.

SOCHEMANNI XI. *Nottingh.* 284.

SOCHEMANNI Abbatis de Ramesy, *Hunt.* 204.[6]

---

[1] " Ipsemet tenuit "

[2] He had previously held the land of which he was now
under-tenant.

[3] " Istimet tenuerunt sub Eddeua et vendere potuerunt."

[4] " Ipsimet Sochemanni tenuerunt sub Eddeva, et potuerunt vendere cui voluerunt."

[5] " Istimet tenuerunt de Vlf et vendere potuerunt."

[6] " M̄. in Broctune. Ibi est terra sochemannorum. v.
hid. ad geld. Isti sochemanni dicunt se habuisse Legre-

---

uuitam et Blodeuuitam et Latrocinium suum usque IIII. den. et post IIII. denar. habeb' Abbas forisfacturam Latrocinii.''

[1] " Idem S. libere tenuit."

[2] He and Ledmanus had held the same manor of thirty acres T. R. E. " in commendatione Regis et Reginæ."

STEFANUS, *Berks*, 61 bis. *Somers.* 89 b. *Dev.* 107 b. bis. 108, 109 b. 110. *Heref.* 180, 185 b. *Bedf.* 214. *Northampt.* 220. *Warw.* 238 b. bis.

STEFANUS homo Comitis Alani, *Linc.* 348.

STEFANUS Stirman, *Hants*, 52.

STEFANUS f. Fulcheræ, *Worc.* 173.

STENULFUS, *Staff.* 249.

STIRMAN, Stefanus, *v.* STEFANUS.

STOCHES, Willielmus, *Buck.* 148.

STURM', Radulfus, *Norf.* 253.

STURMID, Ricardus, *Surr.* 32 b. *Hants*, 41. *Wilts*, 67 b.

STURSTANUS filius Widdonis,[1] *Suff.* 343 b.

SUNDUS, *Essex*, 77.

SUAIN, *Leic.* 232 b.

SUAN, *Derb.* 274.

SUARTING, *Buck.* 149 b.

SUARTRIC, *Suff.* 449 b.

SUAUESY, Monachi de, *Cambr.* 195.[2]

SUAUIS, *Leic.* 234.

SUENUS, *Essex*, 23 b. bis.

SUENUS Vicecomes, *Essex*, 6 b. 7.

SUERTIN, *Buck.* 148 b.

SUERTING, *Buck.* 149 b. 150 bis.

SUETING, *Oxf.* 156 b.

SUETINGUS, *Bedf.* 217 b.

SUETINUS, *Buck.* 151.

SUETMAN, *Northampt.* 227. *Oxf.* 154 bis.

SUETMAN alter, *Oxf.* 154.

---

[1] Probably the same person who is more frequently entered as Turstanus filius Widonis.

[2] The Priory of Swavesey was a Cell to the Abbey of St. Sergius and St. Bacchus in Normandy.

---

[1] In the Cabinet at the British Museum there is a Penny ascribed to Will. II. (No. 64.) bearing the King's head full-faced, crowned, which has on the reverse SPETMAN ON OXI. The P in the legend of this Coin is the usual Norman representation of the Saxon Ꝑ, *i. e.* W.

[2] " Unus tenebat dim. hid. et poterat abire sine licentia domini ipsius Mansionis."

[3] The lands which he here held of Ilbert de Laci had previously been his own.

TALEBOT, Goisfridus, *Essex*, 89 b.

TALEBOT, Ricardus, *Bedf.* 211, 211 b. bis.

TALGEBOSC, Radulfus, *Hertf.* ⎫ *v.* TAILGEBOSC.
    133.   ⎬   TALLEBOSC.
TALLB', Radulfus, *Bedf.* 213 b. ⎭ TALLIEBOSC.

TALLEBOSC, Iuo, *Bedf.* 209, 210.

TALLEBOSC, Radulfus, *Bedf.* 211, ⎫
    211 b. bis. 213.   ⎬ *v.* TAILGEBOSC.
TALLGEB', Radulfus, *Bedf.* 214.   ⎬ TALGEBOSC.
TALLGEBOSC, Radulfus, *Bedf.* 212 b. ⎬ TALLIEBOSC.
    bis. 213 b. 214, 218 b. ter. ⎭

TALLIEBOSC, Ivo, *Bedf.* 209.

TALLIEBOSC, Radulfus, *Bedf.* 209. *v.* TAILGEBOSC.
    TALGEBOSC. TALLEBOSC.

TAME, Alueredus de, *Buck.* 152 b.

TAMUUORDE, burgenses in, *Staff.* 246, 246 b.

TASCELINUS presbyter, *Essex*, 3 b.

TAURINI S. Æcclesia,[1] *Worc.* 176.

T'CHETEL, *Suff.* 446 b.

TEBALDUS, *Suff.* 358.

TEDALDUS, *Buck.* 144 b.

TEDBALDUS homo Drogonis de Bevrere, *Yorksh.* 324 b.

TEDBALDUS homo Juditæ Comitissæ, *Bedf.* 212.

TEDBERTUS, *Hertf.* 133 b. *Leic.* 235 b.

TEDRICUS, *Bedf.* 211 b.

TEHEL, *Buck.* 148.

TEHERUS, *Essex*, 23.

TEIGNI duo, *Buck.* 145 b.

TEIGNI tres, *Kent*, 3.

TEIGNI x. *Kent*, 11.

TEIGNUS unus, *Staff.* 247.

TEODBALD homo Abbatis [S. Trin. Norwic.], *Norf.* 117.

---

[1] A Benedictine Abbey in the city of Evreux. Al. Pr.
vol. i. p. 63.

TEODERICUS, *Sussex*, 17.

TEODERICUS frater Galteri diaconi, *Suff.* 427.

TETBALDUS, *Sussex*, 24 b. *Hants*, 38. *Wilts*, 69 b.
    Hertf. 141 b. passim. *Glouc.* 165. *Northampt.* 227 b.
    Leic. 235. *Inter Ripam et Mersam*, 269 b. bis.

TETBALDUS homo Drogonis de Bevrere, *Linc.* 360.

TETBALDUS presbyter, *Sussex*, 20.

TETBAUDUS, *Bedf.* 213 b.

TEODRICUS, *Berks*, 58, 60. *Wilts*, 67 bis. 69 b. *Oxf.*
    155 b.

TEODULFUS, *Shropsh.* 259 bis.

TERBERTUS, *Sussex*, 28 b.

TEZELINUS, *Sussex*, 26 b. *Surr.* 36. *Hants*, 45 b. bis.
    Dors. 77. *Heref.* 184 b. bis. *Chesh.* 267 b.

THAM, Robertus de, *Buck.* 145.

THEODRICUS, *Norf.* 257 b.

THOCHI, *Shropsh.* 259.

THOMAS archiepiscopus, *Glouc.* 164 b.

TIDBALDUS, *Essex*, 9 b.

TIGERUS, *Suff.* 315 b.

TINEL, Turstinus, et uxor ejus, *Kent*, 11.

TIRELDE, Walterus, *Essex*, 41.[1]

TIRUS, *Norf.* 257.

TOCHE, *Norf.* 160 b. 163.

TOCHI, *Shropsh.* 256 b. bis.

---

[1] At Langham in Essex: he held under Richard Fitz
Gilbert lord of Clare.

Morant says, " This was the famous Walter Tirel that
came over with William the Conqueror; and the same, as
some suppose, who afterwards shot King William Rufus by
mistake in the New Forest, at a place called Charingham.
However, it is more certain that the Walter mentioned in
the Record was the common ancestor of the very ancient
family of Tyrell, long seated in this county at East-Thorn-
don, and other parts." Hist. of Essex, vol. i. p. 244.

TOCHIL, *Shropsh.* 255.

TODENI, Berengerius de, *Oxf.* 159.

TODENI, Ilbertus de, *Heref.* 183.

TODENI, Radulfus de, *Hants,* 52. *v.* TOENI.

TODENI, Robertus de, *Leic.* 230 b.

TODENI, Willelmus de, *Heref.* 183.

TODENIENSIS, Robertus, *Hertf.* 138.

TOENI, Rad. de, *Norf.* 235 b. } *v.* TODENI.
TOENIO, Radulfus de, *Norf.* 245.

TOKA, *Norf.* 169.

TOLI, *Oxf.* 159 b. bis.[1] *Derb.* 278 b.[2]

TOLI homo Comitis Alani, *Linc.* 348, 348 b.

TONEBRIGE, Ricardus de, *Kent,* 3, 4 b. ter. 5 b. ter.
6 bis. 7 bis. 7 b. passim. 8 b. bis. 9. *Surr.* 30, 30 b.
36 b. *Hants,* 38.

TONEBRUGE, Ricardus de, *Kent,* 4.

TONNE, *Warw.* 241 b.

TOR, homo Episcopi Baiocensis, *Linc.* 343 b.

TORCHIL, *Hertf.* 139 b. *Bedf.* 217 b. *Yorksh.* 311 b.

TORCHILLUS, *Buck.* 152 b.

TORED, *Hunt.* 205 b.

TORET, *Shropsh.* 254 b. bis. 255 b. 259 b. *Suff.* 414.

TORGIS, *Dev.* 109 b. ter. 110.

TORNAI, Goisfridus, homo Comitis Alani, *Linc.* 348 b.

TOROLDUS, *Essex,* 11 b. 25 b. 26. *Suff.* 417 b.

TORSTINUS, *Buck.* 147 b.[3] *Norf.* 149 b.

TORSTINUS f. Wd. *Norf.* 185.

TORSTINUS [f. Widonis], *Norf.* 185.

TOSARDUS, *Sussex,* 26.

TOSTIUS, *Essex,* 84 b.

---

[1] In one entry it is said, " Idem Toli libere tenuit."

[2] " h'b'r," habebatur.

[3] " Isdem Torstinus ;" in the entry immediately previous
called Turstinus.

---

[1] See vol. i. p. 496.

[2] He was a sub-tenant to Roger Earl of Shrewsbury:
" Tuder quidam Walensis tenet de comite I. finem terræ
Walens' et inde reddit IIII. lib. 7 v. solid."

[3] " Ipse tenuit de Heraldo."

Turlauill', Radulfus de, *Suff.* 339.

Turius, *Suff.* 394 b.

Turmit, Radulfus, *Norf.* 252 b. bis.

Turnauilla, Radulfus de, *Norf.* 173 b.

Turold, *Shropsh.* 257 b. passim. 258 passim. *Norf.* 157 b. 177 b.

Turoldus, *Surr.* 34 b. *Berks,* 59 b. *Wilts,* 68 b. *Dors.* 83 b. *Hertf.* 139 b. *Worc.* 177 b. *Hunt.* 205 b. *Shropsh.* 253. *Essex,* 25, 42 b. bis. 57 b. 72 b. 73 b. 74 ter. 75 b. 99 b. *Norf.* 158, 158 b. 159, 172, 177 b. 178, 181 b. 182, 186, 228, 229 b. *Suff.* 408 b.

Turoldus abbas, *Linc.* 370 b.

Turoldus abbas S. Petri de Burgo, *Linc.* 345 b.

Turoldus homo Rogerii de Busli, *Nottingh.* 284 b. 285 bis. 285 b. bis. *Linc.* 352 b.

Turoldus nepos Wigot, *Glouc.* 166 b.

Turoldus presbyter, *Berks,* 60. *Linc.* 352 b. 356 b.

Turstanus filius Widoni, *Suff.* 343 b.

Turstanus filius Witdo, *Suff.* 343 b. *v.* Sturstanus.

Tursten, *Yorksh.* 315 b.

Tursten homo Ernegis de Burun, *Yorksh.* 328 b.

Turstinus, *Kent,* 11, 11 b. ter. *Hants,* 41 b. *Wilts,* 66, 66 b. 67 b. ter. 70 b. 71 b. 74 b. *Somers.* 86, 87, 90, 91 b. 92. *Dev.* 114 b. passim. *Cornw.* 120 ter. 122 b. passim. 123 bis. 125. *Hertf.* 134 b. *Buck.* 144 b. 145, 147, 147 b. 149 b. 151. *Oxf.* 158. *Glouc.* 169 b. *Heref.* 185, 185 b. 186 bis. *Cambr.* 196 b. *Hunt.* 203 b. bis. *Bedf.* 210, 218. *Northampt.* 221, 226 bis. *Leic.* 235 bis. 237 bis. *Warw.* 242. *Staff.* 250. *Shropsh.* 256 b. 260 bis. *Essex,* 84. *Suff.* 426 b.

Turstinus alter, *Heref.* 185 b.

Turstinus burgensis de Tedfort, *Norf.* 173.

Turstinus camerarius, *Hants,* 52.

V. & U.

(2)

---

[1] Robertus de Vallibus or Vals, otherwise De Vaux or
De Vaus.   Sir Robert de Vaus of Winham, Knt., occurs
5 Joh.   See the Jermyn Collections, vol. xlix. fol. 121.

[2] See Vol. i. p. 498.

VECI, Robertus, *Shropsh.* 256 b. *Linc.* 363 bis.

VENABLES, Gislebertus de, *Chesh.* 267 passim.

Venator, Gislebertus, *Chesh.* 267 passim.

———— Radulfus, *Chesh.* 267, 268 b.

———— Robertus, *Warw.* 242.

———— Rogerus, *Worc.* 176. *Shropsh.* 254 b.

———— Seuuardus, *Hants,* 42 b.

———— Waleran, *Hants,* 42 b.

———— Warmund, *Chesh.* 269.

VER, Alberic, *seu* Albericus de, *Midd.* 130 b.[1] *Cambr.* 190. *Hunt.* 204 b. 208. *Essex,* 35, 35 b. *Suff.* 287 b.

VER, Willielmus de, *Midd.* 127 b.

VERLEI, R. de, *Norf.* 262 b.[2]

VERLI, Hugo de, *Essex,* 63.

VERLI, Robertus de, *Essex,* 64 b. 67 b. 68.

VERLI, Willielmus de, *Yorksh.* 303 b. bis.

VERNON, Ricardus de, *Chesh.* 265 passim.

VERNON, Walterius de, *Chesh.* 265 passim.

VERNUN, Huardus de, *Suff.* 354.

VERNUN, Ricardus de, *Norf.* 152.

Vicecomes, v. B. BALDEUINUS. DURANDUS. EDUUARDUS. EUSTACHIUS. HAIMO. HAMO. HUGO.

VICTORIS S. Æcclesia, *Hants,* 46 b.

VIDUA quædam, *Dors.* 77 b. *Hertf.* 136 b.

---

[1] Although the entry in Middlesex, here referred to, ranges Alberic de Ver, and even numbers him as a tenant in capite, he appears really to have held in that county under the Bishop of Coutance. Kensington, the manor entered, was afterwards the absolute property of the Vere family, as parcel of their barony, by virtue of their office of high chamberlain. It continued in the family till John, the twelfth Earl, was beheaded, in 1461.

[2] "Modo tenet [Dallingam] dicens quod eam tenet pro mutuo de Rochinges, alterius terræ."

VIDUA quædam Femina Asgari, *Hertf.* 132 b.[1]

VIDUA una, *Dors.* 78 b.

Vigil, v. GERARDUS. GISBERTUS.

VILLANI v. *Cambr.* 198.

VILLANUS unus,[2] *Nottingh.* 281 b.

VILL'O, Robertus de, *Buck.* 148 b.[3]

VINITOR, Walterus, *Surr.* 36.

UISDE LEUU, Hunfridus, *Berks,* 56.

UISDELUPO, Hunfridus, *Berks,* 56. *Hants,* 50 b. } [4]

VISO LUPI, Radulfus, *Norf.* 118.

VITALIS, *Kent,* 3 b. 10 bis. 12 b. *Dors.* 80. *Somers.* 94, 94 b. 98. *Dev.* 107 b. *Staff.* 249. *Essex,* 55 b. 73 b.

VITALIS homo Widonis de Credun, *Linc.* 367 b. bis. 368.

VITALIS presbyter, *Hants,* 39. *Wilts,* 65 b.

VITARDUS, *Heref.* 180.

VLCHEL, *Nottingh.* 284 b. 285. *Yorksh.* 316, 317 b.

VLCHETEL, *Warw.* 241. *Staff.* 247.

VLCHETEL homo Hermeri, *Norf.* 213.

VLCHIL, *Nottingh.* 287.[5] *Yorksh.* 326 b.[6]

VLESTAN, *Suff.* 296.

VLF, *Sussex,* 17. *Northampt.* 228 b. *Leic.* 231, 232 b. bis. *Warw.* 241. *Shropsh.* 257.

VLFAC, *Staff.* 249.

---

[1] ⓣ Waldenei. " Eadem femina tenuit hoc ⓣ T. R. E. de Heraldo Comite."

[2] " In Sandebi tenet unus villanus I. ortum reddens salem in Bigredic ad piscem Regis."

[3] This seems an evident mistake for " Robertus de Will'o," Robert, under-tenant to William Fitz Ansculf.

[4] He occurs among the Tenants in capite, see Vol. i. p. 499, by the names of Vis de Lew.

[5] " ħƀ," he had been the previous possessor.

[6] He held under Gislebertus Tison, but had held the same land himself before the Survey.

VLFCHETEL, *Warw.* 240 b.

VLKETEL, *Norf.* 177 ter.

VLMAR, *Wilts,* 70 b.

VLMARUS, *Wilts,* 70 b. *Oxf.* 154. *Northampt.* 224 bis.[1]
   Essex, 53 b. *Suff.* 337, 390 b. 394, 395 b.

VLMARUS prepositus, *Suff.* 448 b.

VLMARUS burgensis de Bedeford, *Bedf.* 218.

VLMERUS, *Essex,* 89.

VLMERUS presbyter, *Sussex,* 19.

VLNOD, *Nottingh.* 287, 287 b.[2]

VLNODUS, *Leic.* 237.

VLOIUS, *Norf.* 222.

VLRIC, *Kent,* 1 b.

VLRIC de Oxeneford, *Kent,* 1 b.

VLRICUS homo Drogonis de Bevrere, *Linc.* 360 b.

VLRICUS homo Ernegis de Burun, *Linc.* 362 ter.

VLSI, *Surr.* 31 b. *Cornw.* 124 b. ter. *Warw.* 241. *Nottingh.* 290. *Essex,* 13. *Suff.* 288.

VLSIUS, *Suff.* 288 b.

VLSTAN f. Vluuin, *Kent,* 1 b.

VLTBERTUS, *Northampt.* 227.

VLTRESPONT, Abbatia de, *Sussex,* 18.

————— Monachi de, *Sussex,* 19 b.

VLUARDUS, *Suff.* 357 b.

VLUEUA, *Somers.* 88. *Suff.* 321 b.

VLUIET, ULUIET, *Wilts,* 70, 70 b. *Dors.* 77 b. *Buck.* 150 b. *Heref.* 180 b. *Staff.* 249, 249 bis. *Shropsh.* 259 b. *Chesh.* 267 b. *Norf.* 135.

VLUIET, *Nottingh.* 288. *Yorksh.* 304.

---

[1] In one of these instances it is said, " Idem ipse libere tenuit:" in the other, " Idem ipse tenuit."

[2] In this entry, respecting the manor of Lentune, it is said, " ħɓ *Vnlof,*" and then, " Ibi isd. *Vlnod* habet."

---

[1] Among the witnesses to a charter of Bishop Wlstan to the Church of Worcester, early in Rufus's reign, we have " Vrso vicecomes cum omnibus militibus vicecomitatus ejus." MS. Cotton. Tib. A. xiii. fol. 192 a.

[2] " Modo tenet eam [Ecleuuartunam] ad feudum Willielmi de Scohies, et revocat Regem ad tutorem."

UTTALIS, *Kent*, 7.

UUAL', Petrus de, *Suff.* 366.

UXOR quædam militis Rogeri de Ramis, *Essex*, 83 b.

UXOR Alberici, *Essex*, 24 bis.

UXOR Baduini, *Dev.* 107, 107 b.

UXOR Brien, *Midd.* 127.

UXOR Roberti Burdet, *Leic.* 234 b.

UXOR prepositi de Cainingham, *Wilts*, 66.

UXOR Edrici, *Wilts*, 70 bis.

UXOR Henrici, *Essex*, 83 b.

UXOR Hervei, *Dev.* 108.

UXOR Hugonis, *Wilts*, 66 b.

UXOR Hugonis [f. Grip], *Dors.* 77 bis. 77 b. bis. 78 bis. 78 b. bis. 84 b.

UXOR Ingelbaldi, *Dev.* 103 ter.

UXOR Walterii de Laci, *Glouc.* 165 b.

UXOR Manasse, *Somers.* 89.

UXOR Manasses coqui, *Somers.* 98 b.

UXOR prepositi de Ramesberie, *Wilts*, 66.

UXOR Roberti, *Leic.* 232 b.

UXOR Salie, *Surr.* 34 b. bis.

UXOR Willielmi de Wateuile, *Sussex*, 27.

UXOR fratris Vlurici, *Dors.* 84.

UXOR Vluuardi, *Somers.* 87.

W.

W. *Dev.* 108 b. 112 b. passim. *Essex*, 42 b. 44, 79 b. 81, 85.

W. Comes, *Glouc.* 169.

W. Episcopus, *Norf.* 115.

W. filius Grossæ, *Essex*, 100.

W. filius Sahuala, *Suff.* 412. *v.* WILLIELMUS.

WACHELINUS Episcopus, *Hants*, 38.

WADARD, *Oxf.* 156. *Warw.* 283 b.

WADARD, Rainaldus, *Oxf.* 155 b. bis.

WADARDUS, *Kent,* 2 b. 6 bis. 7 b. 10 b. bis. 12 b. bis.
Surr. 32. *Wilts,* 66. *Dors.* 77. *Oxf.* 155 b. 156
passim. 156 b. *Warw.* 239. *Linc.* 342, 343, 343 b.

WADARDUS homo Episcopi Baiocensis,[1] *Linc.* 342 bis.
342 b. passim. 343 bis.

---

[1] Wadard. Wadardus.   WADARD, TUROLD, and VITAL,
are three personages represented in the Baieux tapestry:
and it is remarkable that Wadard and Vitalis, with the son
of a person named Turold, should occur among the under-
tenants of Odo Bishop of Baieux in the Domesday Survey.

In the Baieux tapestry, as published by the Society of
Antiquaries, Plate III., the name of Turold stands above the
head of a bearded dwarf, who holds two horses.

In Plate X. of the tapestry, over the head of a mounted
warrior in armour, without his helmet, but with shield and
spear, are the words " Hic est Wadard." He stands between the soldiers who hasten to Hastings and the pre-
paration of refreshments.

In the lower compartment of Plate XII. are the words,
" Hic Willelm: Dux interrogat Vital: si vidisset exerci-
tum Haroldi." Vitalis is represented on horseback, in
armour, with sword, shield, and spear, his helmet on his
head, pointing backward, as if toward Harold's army, with
his left hand.

Wadard of the Survey, as the references above will show,
held property under the Bishop in no fewer than six
counties. In Oxfordshire alone he was the under-tenant
for six hides and a half.

His consequence is shewn in an entry in Surrey, fol. 32,
where he held the manor of Ditton under the Bishop, consisting of six hides, where it is said, " Ille qui tenet de
Wadardo reddit ei L. sol. et *servitium unius militis.*"

Vitalis held lands under Odo in Kent; and the son of
Turold, in Essex.

Filius Wadardi was an under-tenant of Roger de Ivri at
Trop (Thrup) in Oxfordshire, tom. i. fol. 159.

WAL', Petrus de, *Suff.* 366.

UUAL', Petrus de, *Suff.* 366.

WALA, *Norf.* 117.

WAL'A, sacerdos vicecomitis, *Norf.* 118.

WALANNUS, *Nottingh.* 287.

WALBERTUS, *Staff.* 249, 249 b. 250.

WALBERTUS homo Episcopi Dunelmensis, *Linc.* 341.

WALCHEL, *Nottingh.* 288 b.

WALCHEL' Episcopus, *Som.* 87, 90 b.

WALCHEL' homo archiepiscopi Eboracensis et II. filii Suuen, *Linc.* 340.

WALCHELIN homo archiepiscopi Eboracensis, *Linc.* 340 ter.

WALCHELINUS, *Northampt.* 220 b. passim. 225. *Linc.* 230 b. bis. *Shropsh.* 257 b. ter.

WALCHELINUS Episcopus, *Hants,* 38 b. *Wilts,* 65 b.

WALCHELINUS homo Walterii de Aincurt, *Nottingh.* 288 b.

WALCHELINUS miles, *Yorksh.* 303.

WALCHELINUS nepos Episcopi de Winton'. *Glouc.* 164 b.

WALCHERUS, *Dors.* 82. *Oxf.* 155.

WALCINUS, *Somers.* 90 b.

WALDIN, *Dev.* 108 b. 110.

WALDINUS, *Dev.* 109 b. 110.

WALDINUS homo Willielmi de Perci, *Linc.* 353 b.

WALENUS, Petrus de, *Suff.* 365 b.

WALIFRIDUS, homo Aluredi de Lincole, *Linc.* 358 b.

WALENSES, *Heref.* 179 b. 180 b.

WALER', *Wilts,* 72 bis. *Dors.* 82.

WALERAMUS, *Essex,* 6 b. 22.

WALERAN, *Hants,* 47, 50. *Dors.* 77. *Warw.* 239.

WALERAN venator, *Hants,* 42 b.

WALERANUS, *Wilts,* 65 b. 66 b. *Dors.* 77 b.

˙Walicherus, *Essex,* 69.

Wallef,[1] *Warw.* 240 bis. 240 b.[2]

Walo, *Sussex,* 18 b. 19.

Walo homo Gozelini filii Lanberti, *Linc.* 359 bis.

Walo homo Hugonis filii Baldrici, *Yorksh.* 327 b.

Walon', Petrus de,[3] *Suff.* 366.

Wals, Rotbertus de, *Norf.* 190. *v.* Vals. Duuals.

Waloniensis, Petrus,[3] *Norf.* 169.

Walscin, *Somers.* 95.

Walscinus, *Somers.* 95. *Dev.* 111 b.

Walterius, Walterus, *Kent,* 1 b. *Sussex,* 16, 17 b.
18 b. 19 b. passim. 20, 20 b. ter. 21, 21 b. ter. 22,
26 b. 28 passim. *Surr.* 36 b. *Hants,* 40, 40 b. 41,
44 b. 45 bis. 45 b. 50. *Wilts,* 66, 68, 69 bis. 72 bis.
Dors. 77 bis. 82 passim. 83 b. 84 bis. 87 b. 89 b. bis.
Somers. 90 bis. 95 bis. 97 bis. 97 b. ter. 98 bis.
Dev. 101 b. 103 b. 106, 106 b. bis. 107 b. 108, 112
passim. 112 b. passim. 114 b. bis. 115 bis. *Hertf.*
139,[4] 139 b. *Buck.* 144 passim. 146 b. bis. 148 b.
bis. *Buck.* 144 passim. *Glouc.* 168 b. passim. 170.
Worc. 172 b. bis. 176 bis. 177, 177 b. 180. *Heref.*
181 bis. 182 b. 184, 184 b. bis. 185. *Cambr.* 195,
199 b. 201. *Hunt.* 206. *Bedf.* 212, 213 b. 214,
214 b. bis. 218. *Northampt.* 221 bis. 221 b. 224 bis.
224 b. 225, 226, 227, 229. *Leic.* 232 b. 233 ter.
235 b. *Warw.* 239, 240, 242, 243 b. 244. *Staff.*
248, 249 b. *Shropsh.* 254, 256 b. 257, 258. *Inter*

---

[1] Under-tenant of the Earl of Mellent.

[2] At Scelftone. " Idem Wallef libere tenuit T. R. E."

[3] *sc.* Petrus Valongies, *seu* de Valoniis.

[4] The Walter of these entries, *Buck.* 144, is called by
Lysons, Walter de Deincourt : Bishops Wooburn, one of the
manors here held by him, remained in the Deincourt family
till 1422.

Ripam et Mersam, 270. *Yorksh.* 324 bis. *Essex*, 42, 58 b. *Norf.* 117, 154, 181 b. *Suff.* 316, 328 b. 329.

Walterius quidam, *Staff.* 248. *Yorksh.* 309 b.

Walterus [de Aincurt], *Linc.* 340.

Walterus filius Albrici, *Cambr.* 196 ter. *Suff.* 311 bis. 319, 319 b. 327 b.

Walterus arbalastarius, *Suff.* 324 bis.

Walter s abbas de Evesham, *Worc.* 175 b. 176.

Walterus balistarius, *Glouc.* 162 bis.

Walterus canonicus, *Midd.* 128.

Walterus diaconus, *Essex*, 6 b. *Norf.* 117 b.

Walterus filius Engelberti, *Kent*, 9 b.

Walterus f. Ercoldi, *Glouc.* 168.

Walterus filius Lamberti, *Sussex*, 18 b. 19 bis. 20 bis.

Walterus f. Other, *Hants*, 43 b. *Berks*, 56 b.

Walterus filius Otherii, *Surr.* 30.

Walterus filius Pontu, *Glouc.* 164 b.

Walterus filius Ponz, *Oxf.* 154 b.

Walterus f. Rog. *Glouc.* 164 b.

Walterus gener Gisleberti filius Turoldi, *Worc.* 177.

Walterus gener Hugonis fil. Baldrici, *Wilts*, 73.

Walterus homo Goisfridi Alselin, *Nottingh.* 289.

Walterus homo Drogonis de Bevrere, *Yorksh.* 324 b. *Linc.* 360 b.

Walterus homo Colsuan, *Linc.* 357.

Walterus homo Gozelini filii Lanberti, *Linc.* 359 b. bis.

Walterus homo Episcopi Lincoliensis, *Linc.* 344 b. bis.

Walterus homo Ivonis Taillgebosc, *Linc.* 351.

Walterus monachus, *Bedf.* 218.

Walterus nepos Durandi [de Glowec.], *Heref.* 186 b. bis.

Walterus vinitor, *Surr.* 36.

WALTHAM, Canonici de, *Hertf.* 140 b.

WALUILE, Willielmus de, *Dors.* 100 b. *Dev.* 102 b.

WANCEIO, Hugo de, *Suff.* 398 b.

WANCEIO, Osbernus de, *Suff.* 394.

WANDREGISILUS, S.[1] *Wilts,* 65, 65 b. *Northampt.* 229.

WANZ, Aluricus, *Suff.* 287 b.

WAR', Will. de, *Essex,* 15 b.

WARAS, Anschil de, *Hertf.* 138 b. 141. *v.* WARES.

WAREGERIUS, *Norf.* 188 b.

WAREGIUS, *Norf.* 263 bis.

WARENG', Rogerus, *Suff.* 374.

WARENGER, *Dors.* 82.

WARENGERUS, *Norf.* 263 b. *Suff.* 337 b. 338 b.

WAR', W. de, *Norf.* 115, 215 b.

WARENE, Willielmus de, *Susser,* 22 b. *Shropsh.* 257.

WARENNA, Will. de, *Essex,* 19. *Norf.* 109 b. 110 b.

WARES, Anschil de, *Hertf.* 141 b. *v.* WARAS.

WARHAM, Burgenses in, *Dors.* 75 b.

WARIBOLDUS, *Norf.* 274 b.

WARINBOLDUS, *Norf.* 207.

WARINCUS, *Norf.* 152, 254 b.

WARINUS, *Berks,* 58 b. 59 b. *Sussex,* 24, 24 b. 25, 25 b. *Dev.* 109, 110 b. passim. *Leic.* 234, 234 b. 235. *Warw.* 239, 240 b. 241 b. 242 b. *Staff.* 249 b. bis. *Shropsh.* 257 b. bis. *Inter Rip. et Mers.* 269 b. bis.

WARINUS filius Burn. *Suff.* 300 b.

WARINUS filius Burnini, *Suff.* 327 b.

WARINUS filius Burnnini, *Suff.* 301.

WARINUS homo Rogerii Comitis, *Sussex,* 17 b.

WARINUS miles, *Inter Rip. et Mersam,* 270.

---

[1] See Vol. i. p. 506.

Warinus alter miles, *Inter Rip. et Mersam*, 270.

Warmund, *Dors.* 77 b. *Somers.* 87, 90, 94 b.

Warmund venator, *Chesh.* 269.

Warmundus, *Somers.* 93, 96 b.

Warnarius, *Suff.* 441 b.

Warnerius, *Sussex*, 22 b. *Somers.* 96 b. *Heref.* 186.
Bedf. 213 b. *Derb.* 276.

Warnerus, *Wilts*, 71 b. *Derb.* 276. *Nottingh.* 290.

Warnerus homo Widonis de Credun, *Linc.* 367 bis.
367 b.

Warnerus homo Willielmi Peverel, *Nottingh.* 287 b.
bis.

Warr', W. de, *Norf.* 136 b. bis. 137 b.

Waruuelle, Abbatissa de, *Hants*, 52.

Waruuic, Ecclesia S. Mariæ de, *Warw.* 241 b.

Wast, Nigellus, *Buck.* 151 b. *Bedf.* 214 bis. 214 b. bis.

Wasuuic prepositus, *Glouc.* 162.

Wateuile, Ricardus de, *Surr.* 34 b. passim. 35 ter.

Wateuile, Robertus de, *Surr.* 30.

Wateuile, Willielmus de, *Surr.* 26 b. 27 bis. 27 b.
32 b. ter. 33.

Wateuill', W. de, *Essex*, 36 b.

Wazelinus, *Leic.* 233. *Warw.* 242 bis. *Derb.* 274 b.

Wazelinus homo Episcopi Baioc. *Nottingh.* 284.

Wazelinus homo Drogonis de Bevrere, *Yorksh.* 324 b.

Wazelinus homo Goisfridi de Wirce, *Linc.* 369.

Wazo, *Surr.* 31. *Berks*, 56 b.

Wenelincus, *Bedf.* 213 b.

Wenenc, *Sussex*, 18 bis.

Wenenc presbyter, *Sussex*, 18 b. bis.

Wennenc presbyter, *Sussex*, 18.

Wenricus, *Berks*, 59. *Oxf.* 156 b. ter.

Werelc, *Sussex*, 18.

Werenc, *Sussex*, 17 b. 18 b. bis.

---

[1] *sc.* Willielmus Gulafra. *v.* Gulafra.

WIGHEN, *Cambr.* 195.

WIGOT, *Hants*, 50 b. *Hertf.* 134 b. *Buck.* 146. *Shropsh.*
254. 252.

WIHANOC, *Glouc.* 167.

WIHOMARC, *Cambr.* 195 b. passim.

WIHOMARC homo Alani Comitis, *Yorksh.* 310 b. bis.
311 bis.

WIHTMARUS, *Suff.* 342 bis. 342 b.

WIHUENEC, *Dev.* 116. ⎫
WIHUENECH, *Dev.* 115 b. ⎬
                         ⎭

WIHUMAR, *Cornw.* 120, 125.

WIHVMARC, *Cornw.* 125.

WILARDUS, *Suff.* 396 b.

WILLAC, *Hants*, 51 b.

WILLELMUS, WILLIELMUS, *Kent*, 13 b. *Sussex*, 16 b. 18,
18 b. passim. 19 b. 20 ter. 20 b. passim. 21 passim.
21 b. ter. 22 passim. 22 b. passim. 23 b. 24 ter. 25
passim. 26 passim. *Surr.* 31, 32 b. *Hants*, 40 b. 41
ter. 44 b. bis. 46 ter. 51, 53, 53 b. *Berks*, 56 b.
58 b. ter. 60, 61 b. passim. 63. *Wilts*, 65 b. bis. 67
bis. 68, 68 b. 69 bis. 70, 71 b. 73, 74 b. *Dors.* 75 b.
77 bis. 77 b. 79, 79 b. bis. 80 passim. 80 b. passim.
83 b. passim. *Somers.* 87 b. bis. 88 passim. 88 b. bis.
89 bis. 89 b. 91 b. ter. 92 bis. 93, 93 b. passim. 94
passim. 94 b. passim. 95. *Dev.* 103 b. 105, 106 b.
bis. 107 passim. 108, 108 b. bis. 109 passim. 109 b.
passim. 110 ter. 113, 114 bis. 114 b. passim. 116
passim. *Cornw.* 124. *Hertf.* 133 b. bis. 134, 137 b.
passim. 138 passim. 138 b. bis. *Buck.* 145 bis.
145 b. 146, 147 bis. 147 b. 148 bis. 150 bis. 150 b.
Oxf. 154, 155 b. ter. 158 b. 159, 159 b. ter. *Glouc.*
167 b. bis. *Worc.* 172, 173, 177 b. passim. *Heref.*
181, 184 passim. 184 b. bis. 185, 186. *Cambr.*
196 b. bis. 197, 201. *Hunt.* 203 b. bis. *Northampt.*

220 b. 221, 221 b. 223 b. passim. 224 bis. 225 b.
bis. 227, 228 b. *Leic.* 232 b. 233 b. 234, 235 b.
ter. 237. *Warw.* 241, 241 b. bis. 242, 242 b. 243,
243 b. bis. 244 bis. *Staff.* 247, 248 passim. *Shropsh.*
256, 259. *Chesh.* 263 passim. 263 b. bis. 264 b.
passim. 268, 269. *Inter Rip. et Mers.* 269 b. bis.
Derb. 275 b. *Nottingh.* 282 b. *Yorksh.* 315, 315 b.
317, 321 b. bis. 322 passim. 322 b. bis. 323 passim.
Linc. 339 b. *Essex,* 9 b. bis. 11 b. 12 bis. 17 b. 19,
37, 37 b. ter. 38, 59 b. 61 b. bis. 62, 67, 79, 81 b.
Norf. 154, 155, 160, 161, 167 b. 180 b. 189 b.
205 b. 256, 258, 263 b. *Suff.* 300, 300 b. bis.
324 b. 380, 404 b. 434, 439.

WILLIELMUS alter, *Hants,* 53 b. *Heref.* 186 bis.

WILLIELMUS I. Anglicus, *Norf.* 117.

WILLIELMUS camerarius, *Surr.* 35 b. *Midd.* 127, 127 b.
Cambr. 190. *Bedf.* 209, 209 b. *Essex,* 15.

WILLIELMUS clericus, *Sussex,* 17. *Shropsh.* 252.

WILLIELMUS Comes, *Hants,* 38 b. 44 b. *Wilts,* 64 b.
65. *Glouc.* 163 ter. 163 b. bis. 164 ter.

WILLIELMUS d . . . fer,[1] *Bedf.* 210.

WILLIELMUS dapifer Episcopi Constantiensis, *Bedf.*
210.

WILLIELMUS diaconus, *Berks,* 57.

WILLIELMUS dispensator, *Kent,* 3.

WILLIELMUS Episcopus, *Norf.* 116 b.

WILLIELMUS Episcopus London, *Hertf.* 140. *Essex,* 10,
10 b. bis.

WILLIELMUS filius Ansculfi, *Surr.* 35 b. *Worc.* 172.

WILLIELMUS filius Azor, *Hants,* 52 bis.

WILLIELMUS filius Baderon, *Glouc.* 163, 166 bis. *Worc.*
174 b. *Heref.* 179 b. bis. 180 b.

---

[1] *sc.* dapifer.

WILLIELMUS filius Bonardi, *Sussex*, 29 bis.

WILLIELMUS [qu. de Boscroard], *Buck.* 149.

WILLIELMUS filius Boselini, *Northampt.* 219.

WILLIELMUS filius Brien, *Essex*, 11.

WILLELMUS filius Corbucion, *Staff.* 250.

WILLIELMUS filius Corbuz', *Worc.* 174 b.

WILLIELMUS filius Gaufridi, *Kent*, 1 b.

WILLELMUS filius Grosse, *Kent*, 13 b. *Essex*, 2, 19 b.
    52 b. *Suff.* 409 b.

WILLIELMUS f. Malger, *Northampt.* 226.

WILLIELMUS filius Manne, *Sussex*, 28.

WILLIELMUS filius Nigelli, *Buck.* 146. *Chesh.* 266
    passim. 268 b. *Linc.* 349.

WILLELMUS filius Normanni, *Sussex*, 28 b. ter. *Heref.*
    179 b. bis. 180, 181.

WILL. fil. Odonis, *Essex*, 43.

WILLIELMUS filius Ogeri, *Buck.* 144 b.   ⎫
WILLIELMUS filius Ogerii, *Kent*, 1 b. bis. 6 b. bis. ⎭

WILLIELMUS filius Osberni, *Worc.* 177.

WILLIELMUS filius Osmundi, *Berks*, 56 b.

WILLIELMUS filius Rainaldi, *Sussex*, 27 ter. 27 b. *Bedf.*
    214 b. *Suff.* 399 b. bis. 400 b.

WILLIELMUS filius Raineuuardi, *Bedf.* 215.

WILLIELMUS filius Rannulfi, *Sussex*, 28 b. passim. 29
    bis.

WILLIELMUS f. Ricardi, *Glouc.* 163.

WILLELMUS filius Roberti, *Kent*, 8.

WILLIELMUS filius Sahala, *Suff.* 413.

WILLIELMUS [filius Sahuala], *Suff.* 412 b.

WILLIELMUS filius Stur, *Hants*, 52 bis. 52 b.

WILLELMUS filius Tedaldi, *Kent*, 1 b.

WILLIELMUS filius Turoldi, *Surr.* 36 b.

WILLIELMUS forist. *Hants*, 53 b.

WILLIELMUS frater Gozelini, *Hants*, 52.

WIMERUS, *Dors.* 82. *Norf.* 118, 165, 165 b. *Suff.* 398 b.

WIMUNDUS, *Berks*, 59, 59 b. *Hertf.* 137 bis. *Oxf.* 156 b. *Bedf.* 213, 213 b. bis. *Linc.* 350. *Essex*, 56. *Norf.* 249 b.

WIMUNDUS homo Comitis Alani, *Linc.* 347 bis. 347 b.

WIMUNDUS homo Episcopi Baiocensis, *Linc.* 342 b.

WIMUNDUS homo Rogeri Pictavensis, *Linc.* 352.

WIMUNDUS homo Ivoris Taillgebosc, *Linc.* 350, 351 bis.

WINBVRNE, burgenses in, *Dors.* 76.

WINC', Odo de, *Hants*, 49.

WINDESORES, Odinus de, *Hants*, 41 b.

WINEMAN, *Sussex*, 25 b.

WINEMARUS, *Dev.* 111. *Northampt.* 220 b. 226 b. 227, 227 b. 229 b. passim.

WINEMERUS, *Norf.* 277.

WINTON, Ecclesia S. Mariæ, *Wilts*, 73.

WINTREHARDUS homo Walterii de Aincurt, *Linc.* 361.

WIRCE, Goisfridus de, *Warw.* 239 b.[1]

WIRECEST', II. burgenses ad, *Worc.* 176.

WISCAND, Gislebertus de, *Suff.* 316. ⎱
WISCANT, Gislebertus de, *Suff.* 306 b. ⎰

WISGAR, *Hertf.* 141 b.

WISGARUS, *Suff.* 448.

WISSAND, Gislebertus de, *Suff.* 327.

WITBERTUS, *Sussex*, 18.

WITBURGA, Sancta, *Shropsh.* 252 b.

WITG', *Suff.* 392.

WITSAND, Gislebertus de, *Suff.* 326 b.

---

[1] Custos of the lands of Earl Aubery.

WITSTHANT, Gislebertus de, *Suff.* 324.

WITUILE, Hugo de, *Leic.* 230.

WIZO homo Drogonis de Bevrere, *Linc.* 360 b.

WLB'TUS, *Essex*, 37 b.

WLSI, *Leic.* 236 b. *Warw.* 241 b.

WLUEUA, *Cambr.* 196 b. bis.

WLURIC, *Cornw.* 124 b. *Oxf.* 154.

WLUUARD, *Cornw.* 124 b.

WLUUARDUS, *Somers.* 87 b.

WLUUARDUS albus, *Wilts*, 86.

WLUUI, *Glouc.* 166.

WLUUIUS piscator, *Oxf.* 154.

WLUUOLDUS abb. *Surr.* 35.

WODEMAN, *Staff.* 249.

Y.

YMFRIDUS filius Roberti, *Suff.* 314 b. *v.* VMFRIDUS. HUMFRIDUS.

ABSTRACT

OF

THE POPULATION

OF

THE DIFFERENT COUNTIES OF ENGLAND,

AT THE CLOSE OF THE REIGN OF

WILLIAM THE CONQUEROR,

AS FAR AS THE SAME IS ACTUALLY RECORDED

IN

THE DOMESDAY SURVEY.

ABSTRACT OF POPULATION.

A CURSORY perusal of the Abstract here laid before the reader will convince him that it presents but an imperfect view of the total population of England in 1086. For the owners and occupiers of land, and for the agricultural population, it may probably be considered as a fair record.

Amongst its omissions, the state and population of the Cities and Towns cannot fail to be observed. The King's own burgesses, wherever they occurred, were carefully registered, as well as those who belonged to Tenants in capite; but further than these the Survey rarely goes; in fact, the information of the rent which was to be paid from the town, was more important for the receipt of the Exchequer; and we have some towns represented as paying rent, in which neither burgesses nor other residents are noticed.

In Middlesex pannage is returned for 16,535, in Hertfordshire for 30,705, and in Essex for 92,991 hogs, yet not a single swine-herd (a character so well known in the Saxon times) is entered in these Counties.

In the Norman period, as can be proved from records, the whole of Essex was, in a manner, one continued forest; yet once only in that county is a forester mentioned, in the entry concerning Writtle.

Salt-works, Works for the production of lead and iron, Mills, Vineyards, Fisheries, Trade, and the Manual Arts, must have given occupation to thousands who are unrecorded in the Survey; to say nothing of those who tended the flocks and herds, the returns of which so greatly enlarge the pages of the second Volume. In some counties we have no mention of a single priest, even where churches are found; and scarcely any inmate of a monastery is recorded beyond the abbat or abbess, who stands as a Tenant in capite.

These remarks might be extended, but they are sufficient for their purpose. They apprize the reader that, in this point of view, the Domesday Survey is but a partial Register. It was not intended to be a record of population further than was required for ascertaining the geld.

In the following Abstract the head of Tenants in Capite comprises the TAINI, MINISTRI, ELEMOSINARII, and all other persons who are entered as holding lands directly from the King.

The Under-tenants and minor Occupiers of land, beside all who are mentioned by name in the Record, include such MILITES, CLERICI, PRESBYTERI, and others, who occur as mesne lords, holding from those who held from the King.

The PRESBYTERI who occur in this enumeration under *their own title* are only those who are recorded with the mere church, or who stand alone without the occupation of land; in many instances they are classed in the Survey with the Villani, Servi, and Bordarii.[1] Many Milites also are put down in the Survey with the inferior cultivators; such have their own head in the Abstract.

In summing the total of the numbers together, due allowance has been made for the frequent recurrence of the same Tenant in capite in different Counties. Eudo Dapifer held lordships in twelve, Odo bishop of Baieux

---

[1] As in *Heref.* fol. 182. col. i, " Ibi xviii. villani et vi. bord. et presbyter."—" In dominio sunt ii. car. et xviii. villani et xi. bordarii, et ii. buri, et presbyter." So in *Northamptonshire*, fol. 219, col. ii. "xxiiii. uill. et v. bord. cum presbytero habentes xi. car,"—" Ibi sunt xii. soche-manni et xvi. bordarii cum presbytero habentes xii. car,"

in sixteen, the Earl of Moretaine in twenty, and Earl Hugh Lupus in twenty-one counties. The real number of the Tenants in capite will be very far exceeded, should the reader add together all who are set down in the tables for the distinct Counties.

A greater difficulty attends the establishment of the positive number of Under-tenants as mesne lords. There are so many Hughs, Ralphs, Rogers, and Walters entered upon the property of the same Baron, who, being without the distinction of surnames, may or may not be the same persons, and who sometimes likewise held land under a neighbouring lord.

In the present enumeration, where the name was continually repeated upon the property of the same superior lord, it has been counted but once. It is to be remembered, too, that many of the greater Barons were under-tenants to persons of their own rank, and that Corporate Bodies were also under-tenants.

The selection of the under and agricultural tenantry at the time of the Survey, from the second volume of Domesday, was more difficult than from the first. Throughout the entries in Essex, Norfolk, and Suffolk, the words *tenet* and *tenuit* are expressed but by one contraction; and even the word *tenet* is frequently used at length for *tenuit*.

The compiler of the present Abstract, in ascertaining the numbers of the inferior classes, wrote the numerical amount of each at the bottom of every page in his own copy of the Domesday Survey, and he believes that for them the numbers have been ascertained to minuteness.

For advice in the compilation, and for the use of some manuscript Collections on the Burghs, the editor stands much indebted to John Allen Esq.

E E 3

BEDFORDSHIRE.

―――

Tenants in capite, including the King - 104 [1]
Under-tenants as mesne lords, in-
cluding all occupiers of lands who had
agricultural tenantry under them - 229
Bordarii - - - - - 1,132
Servi - - - - - 474
Sochemanni - - - - 107
Villani - - - - 1,829

―――――

3,875

Of Bedford, the county town, no population is recorded. It paid geld, as for a half-hundred, " in expeditione et in navibus." The lands which were held by several of its burgesses individually[2] form a distinct title. The entry which relates to them has no concern with the town.

In fol. 214, col. 2, it is said, " In Meldone Johannes de Roches occupavit injuste xxv. acras super Homines *qui villam tenent.*"

―――――――――――――――――――――――――

[1] The titles of land in Bedfordshire are only fifty-six, but the individual burgesses of Bedford, and the Prefecti, Bedelli, and Elemosinarii Regis, extend the number of land-owners holding of the King to the above enumeration.

[2] Turner reckons nine burgesses of Bedford, in fol. 218; but of the five last persons under that title it is not said in the body of the Record that they were burgesses, though they are placed as if they were such.

BERKSHIRE.

Tenants in capite - - -	80 [1]
Under-tenants - - -	185
Aloarii - - - -	5 [2]
Bordarii - - - -	1,827
Burs - - - -	18 [3]
Coliberti - - - -	24
Cotarii - - - -	750
Mercatores - - - -	10 [4]
Milites - - - -	3 [5]
Miles anglicus - - -	1 [6]
Presbyteri - - -	5
Racheneste cum sua caruca -	1 [7]
Servi - - - -	792
Villani - - -	2,623
	6,324

[1] Sixty-three titles of land only appear at the head of the county, though sixty-five are in the Record itself; the last including lands of Thanes who held separately of the King, to the extent above enumerated. This method of calculating the real number of the Tenants in capite will be pursued in each succeeding county.

[2] Fol. 63 b. under Peleorde, " Ibi sunt v. alodiarii cum II. car. et bord. uno."

[3] They were on the King's demesne in Ledencumbe, now Letcombe, fol. 57 b., and occur in only this entry in Berkshire.

[4] At Bertone, now Barton in Abingdon, in the parish of St. Helen : " x. mercatores ante portam æcclesiæ manentes, red. XL. den." fol. 58 b.

[5] Fol. 57, classed with the lower tenantry, " Ibi IIII. servi, et æcclesia, et III. milites."

[6] " Unus miles anglicus, cum III. car." fol. 62. col. 2.

[7] Fol. 59.

In the time of King Edward the Confessor, the King had 276 hagæ in the burgh of WALINGFORD. These had been reduced at the time of the Survey to 263. Eight out of the thirteen which formed the deficiency had been removed, to make way for the buildings of the castle. Fifty-eight hagæ and ninety-three masuræ are enumerated in Walingford belonging to other persons, making a total of 414 in the folio in which Walingford is described. Forty-three hagæ in Walingford are enumerated in fol. 56 b.; and two priests of the name of Ælmer, and eight other persons, are said to have had the gable of their houses; increasing the number to 467. Houses in Walingford, beside these, appertaining to different manors in Oxfordshire, to Newington, Dorchester, Watlington, Ewelme, &c., are enumerated in other folios, to the number of 24; making a final total of 491. [1]

From folio 58 it appears that the King had twenty-eight hagæ in the town of READING. This town had been burnt by the Danes in 1006.

In WINDSOR, at the time of the Survey, there were 100 hagæ. This must have been the town of Old Windsor.

No burgesses of Walingford, Reading, or Windsor are recorded in the Survey.

---

[1] Brady, in the Appendix to his Historical Treatise of Cities and Burghs, fol. edit. 1690, p. 12, has printed the charter of King Henry the Second to Walingford, which mentions a Gilda Mercatorum in that town, with extensive privileges, in the time of King Edward the Confessor.

The expression " Burgenses testificantur" occurs in the Domesday account of Walingford.

BUCKINGHAMSHIRE.

Tenants in capite	- - -	70 [1]
Under-tenants	- - -	223
Angli	- - - -	2
Bordarii	- - - -	1,326
Burgenses in Bochingeham	-	26 [2]
Buri [3]	- - - -	4
Carried forward	- -	1,651

[1] The titles of land are fifty-seven only.

[2] The whole of these burgesses appear to have belonged to certain of the Barons, whose names, and the several numbers of burgesses which they held, are enumerated in a lower paragraph in the entry relating to the town. Tom. i. fol. 143.

[3] The Cottonian Manuscript, Titus, A. VIII. contains a sort of glossary upon ancient services, in which the following section occurs, " De GEBURI consuetudine." That this Glossary is of an early period may be inferred from the existence of a Saxon version of it in the library of Corpus Christi College, Cambridge. Till the pages of the former volume had been printed off, this curious Tract was unknown to the present editor.

" Geburi consuetudines inveniuntur multimode, et ubi sunt onorosæ, et ubi sunt leviores, aut mediæ. In quibusdam terris operatur opus septimanæ II. dies, sic opus sicut ei dicetur per anni spatium omni septimana. Et in Augusto III. dies pro septimanali operatione, et a festo Candelarum usque ad Pascha tres. Si averiat non cogitur operari quamdiu equus ejus foris moratur. Dare debet in festo Sancti Michaelis x^d. de gablo, et Sancti Martini die XXIII. et sextarium ordei et duas gallinas. Ad Pascha unam ovem in-

Brought forward	-	-	**1,651**
Cotarii	-	-	-	-	10
Faber	-	-	-	-	1
Francigena [1]	-	-	-	1

Carried forward   -   - **1,663**

venere vel II[d]. et jacebit a festo Sancti Martini usque ad
Pascha ad faldam domini sui quotiens ei pertinebit; et a ter-
mino quo primitus arabitur usque ad festum Sancti Martini
arabit unaquaque septimana I. acram et ipse parabit seminem
in hordeo domini sui.   Ad h' tres acras, pratum, et ovas de
herbagio.   Si plus indigeat herbagio arabit proinde sicut ei
permittetur.   De aratura gabli sui arabit III. acras et semi-
nabit de horreo suo, et dabit suum heorð penig et duo pas-
cant unum molosum.   Et omnis geburus det VI. panes porcario curiæ quando gregem suum minabit in pastinagium.
In ista terra ubi hæc consuetudo stat, moris est ut ad terram
assidendam dentur ei duo boves et una vacca et VII. boves
et VII. acræ seminatæ in sua virgata terra.   Post illum
annum faciat omnes rectitudines quæ ad eum attinent, et
committantur ei tela ad opus suum, et supellex ad domum
suam.   Si morte obeat, rehabeat dominus suus omnia.   Hæc
consuetudo stat in quibusdam locis, et alicubi est sicut præ-
diximus, gravior et alicubi levior, quia omnium terrarum
instituta non sunt equalia.   In quibusdam locis gebur dabit
hunigablum, in quibusdam metegablum, in quibusdam eala-
gablum.   Videat, qui scyram tenet, ut semper sciat quæ sit
antiqua terrarum institutio vel populi consuetudo."

[1] Kelham says, p. 216, from Rudder's Glouc. p. 80, that
this was a general name for all persons who could not prove
themselves to be English.

It was one of the Conqueror's constitutions, that such
foreigners as had been here in the time of King Edward
the Confessor should pay scot and lot with the natives of
the county.   See the former Volume, p. 197, note [1].

Brought forward	-	-	-	-	1,663
Homines	-	-	-	-	3
Loricati in custodia de Wende-					
sores	-	-	-	-	2
Milites	-	-	-	-	3
Salinarius	-	-	-	-	1
Servi	-	-	-	-	833
Sochemanni	-	-	-	-	20
Vavassores	-	-	-	-	2
Villani	-	-	-	-	2,893[1]

$$5,420$$

---

[1] In the glossary just quoted in illustration of the Buri, the following comment occurs upon the service of the VIL-LANUS. " Villani rectum est varium et multiplex, secundum quod in terra statutum est. In quibusdam terris debet dari landgablum et gerswin i. porcum herbagii, et equitare et avariare et summagium ducere, operari, et dominium suum firmare, metere, et falcare de orhege cedere, et stabilitam observare, edificare, et circumsepire, novam faram adducere, cyricsceatum dare, et elmesfeth i. pecuniam elemosinæ, heafodwardam custodire, et horswardam, in nuncium ire longe vel prope quocunque dicetur ei."

CAMBRIDGESHIRE.

Tenants in capite - - -	45
Under-tenants - - -	257
Bordarii - - - -	1,428
Cotarii - - -	736
Burgenses in Grentebrige -	29
Francigenæ - - -	6
Homines - - - -	2
Milites - - - -	11
Milites Francigenæ - -	3
Piscatores - - -	15
Presbyteri - - - -	4
Servi - - - -	548
Sochemanni - - -	213
Villani - - - -	1,902
Dimidii Villani - - -	5
	5,204

CAMBRIDGE, in the time of the Conqueror, as well as in that of Edward the Confessor, had 373 masuræ. Of these, 92 paid no customary rent. Some had been wasted, some were privileged, and 27 houses had been taken down to form a site for the Castle. Cambridge was rated at a whole Hundred, divided into ten wards; yet twenty-nine burgesses only are enumerated as belonging to the town, beside a priest, and three Francigenæ. The burgesses T. R. E. gave the sheriff the use of their " carrucæ," or carts, three times a year. The record says, they are now demanded nine times. The " harieta Lagemannorum" is mentioned in the account of Cambridge, but we have no enumeration of the Lagemanni. The heriot received for one of the Lagemanni (probably the last who died) was twenty shillings: this marks their rank and condition.

CHESHIRE,

Including the lands " inter Ripam et Mersam," which had been Roger of Poitou's, then in the Kiug's hands.[1]

Tenants in capite	-	-	-	-	2
Under-tenants	-	-	-	-	167
Ancillæ	-	-	-	-	8
Bordarii	-	-	-	-	635
	Carried forward		-	-	812

---

[1] It is remarkable that the name of Lancashire should not occur in the Domesday Survey, as well as that that part of it which lies between the Ribble and the Mersey should be surveyed in Cheshire, whilst the northern part of the county, including Amounderness and the hundred of Lonsdale, north and south of the Sands, is comprehended in Yorkshire.

Baines, in his History of Lancaster, p. 112, says, " The contrast between the nature of landed possessions in this district, in the time when the dane-geld tax was enforced in 1086, and the time when the property tax existed in 1814, is most striking ; in the former, all the lands between Mersey and Ribble were valued at £120 ; in the latter, at £2,569,761. Allowing for the difference in the value of money at the two periods, the statement will stand thus :

" Annual value in 1086, £120 × 110 = £13,200
In 1814 - - £2,569,761

Increased value - - £2,556,561"

When Domesday was formed, the district north of the Ribble seems to have been thinly peopled and imperfectly cultivated.

Brought forward - -	812
Bovarii - - - -	172
Burgenses in Civitate pertinentes ad manerium de Cleventune - -	8
Burgenses in civitate pertin. ad manerium Dodestune - - -	15
———— in civitate pertin. ad manerium Wivreham - - - -	10
———— in Roelent - - -	18
———— in Peneverdant - -	6
Drenghs - - - -	6
Fabri - - - - -	4
Francigenæ - - - -	41
Homines - - - -	27
Hospites - - - - -	3
Liberi Homines - - -	42
Molinarius - - - -	1
Piscatores - - - -	14
Prepositi Villarum - - -	6
Presbyteri - - -	29
Radmans - - -	145
Servi - - -	193
Villani - - - -	797
	2,349

Chester was rated at fifty hides, probably equivalent to a half-hundred. The houses in the city which paid geld in King Edward's time were in number 431, beside 56 which belonged to the Bishop; making a total of 487. When the city was given to Earl Hugh, as well as at the time of the Survey, the number was less by 205; "valde enim erat vastata," says the Record. The number of houses at the Survey was 282. The Church of St. John had eight houses in the City free from customary payment.   The Church of St. Werburgh had twelve houses.

In the time of King Edward the Confessor there were seven Moneyers and twelve " Judices Civitatis " in Chester.   Of the last, it is said, " hi erant de hominibus Regis, et Episcopi, et Comitis."   From the penalty which these Judices incurred when they neglected to attend the Hundred Court, it should seem that the attendance of these persons was necessary to enable that Court to transact the business brought before it, forming most probably the jury, as it was afterwards called, who heard and decided all complaints made on applications for redress.

CORNWALL.

Tenants in capite - - -	7
Under-tenants - - -	97
Bordarii - - -	2,355
Cervisarii - - - -	40
Coliberti - - -	49
Servi [1] - - - -	1,160
Villani - - - -	1,730
	5,438

DERBYSHIRE.

Tenants in capite - - -	25
Under-tenants - - -	75
Bordarii - - -	719
Burgenses in Burgo Derby -	100
———— alii Burgenses minores	40
Censarii - - -	42
Custos Molini - - -	1
Faber - - - -	1
Carried forward - -	1,003

[1] In Cornwall the Servi are ranked, or at least entered, before the Villani and Bordarii.

Brought forward	-	-	1,003
Homo	-	-	-	1
Presbyteri	-	-	-	49
Servi	-	-	-	20
Sochemanni	-	-	-	128
Villani	-	-	-	1,840

3,041

DERBY, in the time of King Edward the Confessor, had 243 burgesses : one church with seven clerks, and another church with six. There were fourteen mills in the town.

There are some circumstances mentioned with regard to the burgesses of Derby T. R. E. which seem worthy of notice as marking their condition. Forty-one burgesses held twelve carucates " ad geldum," and employed twelve ploughs in the cultivation of the land, though eight would have sufficed for that purpose. Also the Clerks of one of the two churches held two carucates " libere," and those of the other held four bovates " libere."

At the time of the Survey there were 100 greater and 40 lesser burgesses, 103 " mansiones wastæ," four churches, and ten mills: there were also 16 masuræ possessed of sac and soc, of which ten belonged to the King.

The account of Derby is found in Domesday, in the first page of Nottinghamshire, and follows that of Nottingham. It was probably so placed on account of the commercial connection between the two towns. King John, in his confirmation of the charter of Derby, in the 6th year of his reign, after referring to the privileges of the place n the time of Henry I., says,

" homines etiam de Derebisir et de Nottinghamsir
venire debent ad Burgum de Derebi die Jovis et die
Veneris cum quadrigiis et summagiis suis, nec aliquis
infra decem leucas in circuitu de Derebi tinctos pannos
operari debet, nisi in Burgo de Dereby, *salva libertate
Burgi de Nottingham.*"

DEVONSHIRE.

Tenants in capite - - -	77
Under-tenants - - -	402
Ancilla - - - -	1
Bordarii - - -	4,847
Burgenses in Barnstaple - -	67
———— in Lideford - -	69
———— in Luperige [1] - -	1
———— in Exonia - -	13
———— in Ochementone [2] -	4
———— in Totenais - -	110 [3]
Buri - - - -	4
Coliberti - - -	32
Coscez [4] - - - -	70
Carried forward - -	5,697

---

[1] Lupridge, now a village in the parish of North Huish. Fol. 112 b. " Ibi unus villanus cum i. burgensi habet i. car. et una acr. prati."

[2] Oakhampton. " Ibi iiii. burgenses et Mercat. redd. iiii. solid." *Dev.* fol. 105 b.

[3] " Judhel tenet de Rege Totenais burgum quod Rex Eduuardus in dominio tenebat. Ibi sunt intra burgum c. burgenses v. minus, et xv. extra burgum terram laborantes. Inter omnes redd. viii. lib. ad numerum pro geldo. Olim reddebat iii. lib. ad pensum et arsuram." *Dev.* fol. 108 b.

[4] In the MS. Glossary which has been already quoted from the Cottonian Collection, in illustration of the Buri and Villani, we have the following passage upon the duties required of the Cotscet:

" Cotsedæ rectum est juxta quod in terra constitutum est. Apud quosdam debet omni die Lunæ per anni spatium

Brought forward	-	-	-	5,697
Cotarii	-	-	-	19
Fabri	-	-	-	2
Ferrarii	-	-	-	4
Francigenæ	-	-	-	3
Homines	-	-	-	3
Porcarii	-	-	-	294
Salinarii	-	-	-	48
Servi	-	-	-	3,294
Villani	-	-	-	8,070

17,434

From different entries it will be seen that there were at least 411 houses in the city of EXETER at the time of the Survey, and 463 houses T. R. E.[1] Baldwin the

---

operari domino suo, et tribus diebus unaquaque septimana in Augusto, et apud quosdam operatur per totum Augustum omni die, et unam acram avenæ metit pro diurnali opere, et habet garbam suam, et de alia annona dimidiam acram, et habet garbam suam quam prepositus vel minister domini dabit ei. Non dabit landgablum. Debet habere v. acras ad perhabendum, plus si consuetudo sit ibi, et parum nimis est si minus sit quod deseruit, quia sepius est operi illius. Det super heorð penig in sancto die Jovis [a] sicut omnis liber facere debet, et adquietet inland domini sui. Submonitio fiat de sewearde i. de custodia maris, ut de Regis deðrhege, et cæteris rebus quæ suæ mensuræ sunt. Et unusquisque det suum scyrisceatum in festo Sancti Martini.''

[1] See the entries, *Dev.* fol. 100, col. 1. 101, col. 1. 101 b, col. 2. 102, col. 1. 103 b, col. 2. 104, col. 2. 104 b, col. 1. 105 b, col. 2. 108 b, col. 1. 110, col. 2. 112, col. 1. 113 b, col. 2. 114 b, col. 2. 115, col. 2. 115 b, col. 2. 116, col. 2. 117, coll. 1, 2.

---

[a] Holy Thursday.

sheriff is said to have 19 houses in Exeter, seven of which had belonged to King Edward the Confessor.[1] From a passage at the close of the short entry which relates to Exeter it would seem that the city was incorporated.[2] It never paid geld, except when London, York, and Winchester paid it. The geld seems, however, to have been trifling, only half a mark of silver " ad opus militum," or, as it is expressed in the Exon Domesday, fol. 89, ad *solidarios*. Upon any expedition by land or sea Exeter was rated as for five hides: Barnstaple, Lidford, and Totness were rated jointly at the same. This is confirmed by another passage, fol. 108 b.

At BARNSTAPLE it is said, " Ibi sunt XXIII. domus vastatæ postquam Rex venit in Angliam."[3] Fifteen other wasted houses occur in subsequent columns of the Survey.[4]

In LIDEFORDE forty houses are recorded to have been laid waste before William the Conqueror came to England.[5] The Messrs. Lysons say, " it is probable that this was in 997, when the town of Lidford was burned by the Danes." They add, " it is evident, from the Domesday account, (inferring from the words *intra* and *extra* burgum,) that Lidford was then a walled town."[6]

---

[1] *Dev.* fol. 105 b, col. 2.

[2] " Burgenses Exon. urbis habent extra Civitatem terram XII. caruc. quæ nullam consuetudinem redd. *nisi ad ipsam Civitatem.*"

[3] *Dev.* fol. 100, col. 2. The Exeter Domesday reads " postquam Willielmus habuit Angliam." Exon Domesd. p. 80.

[4] See *Dev.* foll. 102, col. 1. 105 b, col. 2. 113, col. 2. Two houses in Barnestaple yielding two shillings occur in fol. 106 b.

[5] Ibid. fol. 100, col. 2.   [6] Mag. Brit. *Dev.* p. 312.

DORSETSHIRE.

Tenants in capite - - -	146
Under-tenants - - -	195
Ancillæ - - - -	3
Angli - - - -	2
Bordarii - - - -	2,941
Burgenses in Dorecestre - -	1
———— in Sceptesberie -	151
———— in Warham - -	3
———— in Winburne - -	8
Censores - - -	11
Coliberti - - - -	33
Coscez - - - -	209
Cotarii - - - -	188
Faber - - - -	1
Homines - - - -	4
Piscatores - - - -	4
Piscatores in Lym - - -	—
Presbyteri - - -	5
Salinarii - - - -	56
Servi - - - -	1,231
Servientes Francigenæ - -	2
Villani - - - -	2,613
	7,807

The greater towns of Dorsetshire at the time of the formation of the Domesday Survey were Dorchester, Bridport, Wareham, and Shaftesbury.

One burgess only in DORCHESTER is mentioned in the Survey, and he was attached to the Bishop of Salisbury's manor of Cerminstre.[1] The number of houses in Dor-

---

[1] *Dors.* fol. 75 b, col. 2.

chester in King Edward's time had been a hundred and seventy-two. At the time of the Survey they amounted to eighty-eight only. A hundred houses had been destroyed between the time of Sheriff Hugh and the time of the Survey. This town had two moneyers, each of whom paid to the King a mark of silver, and twenty shillings " quando moneta vertebatur," probably meaning when the type of the coinage was changed.

Dorchester T. R. E. paid geld for ten hides, or double the geld of Exeter, *i. e.* a whole mark of silver *ad opus Huscarlium*. There seems to have been great variety in the rights and obligations of the Anglo-Saxon burghs.

In BRIDPORT a hundred and twenty houses had existed in King Edward's time : a hundred only remained at the time of the Survey. The other twenty were so far destroyed that their inhabitants were unable to pay geld. In King Edward's time Bridport had one moneyer, who made the same payment to the King as the moneyers of Dorchester.

At WAREHAM, in King Edward the Confessor's time, a hundred and forty-three houses had stood upon the King's demesne. At the Survey, seventy of these only remained : seventy-three had been destroyed from the time that Hugh was sheriff. In the division of St. Vandrille forty-five houses were standing, and seventeen ruined. Twenty houses on the portions belonging to different Barons were standing, and sixty destroyed. It is evident that Wareham contained two hundred and eighty-five inhabited houses in the time of the Confessor, which had been reduced, before the year 1086, to a hundred and thirty-five.

There were two moneyers in Wareham T. R. E., who paid the same rent to the King as the moneyers of Dochester and Bridport.

A hundred and fifty-one burgesses of SHAFTESBURY have already been included in the Abstract for Dorsetshire, who, with twenty empty manses and a garden, belonged to the Abbess of Shaftesbury, at the time of the Survey, in right of her Monastery. The 151 burgesses dwelling in 91 manses shows that the number of burgesses in a town might exceed the number of houses.

In the time of King Edward the Confessor, there were a hundred and four houses in Shaftesbury upon the King's demesne; but sixty-six only remained at the Survey. Thirty-eight had been destroyed since Hugh's time. In the part of the town belonging to the Abbess there had been a hundred and fifty-three houses T. R. E., which were reduced at the Survey to a hundred and eleven. Forty-two had been destroyed. Two hundred and fifty-seven inhabited houses, of which the town consisted in the time of the Confessor, had been reduced before the year 1086 to a hundred and seventy-seven.

ESSEX.

Tenants in capite	-	-	-	95
Under-tenants	-	-	-	520
Anglicus quidam	-	-	-	1
Bordarii	-	-	-	8,002
Burgenses in Colecestra	-	-	401 [1]
———— in Melduna	-	-	180
———— in Sudberia	-	-	20 [2]
Censarii	-	-	-	36
Custos Hundret	-	-	-	1
Faber	-	-	-	1
Famuli Regis	-	-	-	2
Femina	-	-	-	1
Franci homines	-	-	-	14
Homines	-	-	-	57
Homo dimidius	-	-	-	1
Liberi homines	-	-	-	314
Mercennarius	-	-	-	1
Piscatores	-	-	-	3
Porcarii	-	-	-	2
Presbyteri	-	-	-	33
Servi	-	-	-	1,768
Sochemanni	-	-	-	520
Villani	-	-	-	4,087

	16,060

---

[1] " Unus burgensis in Colecestr." occurs, *Essex*, fol. 27, belonging to Earl Eustace ; but he is no doubt included in the fifteen burgesses entered as belonging to Earl Eustace in the account of Colchester itself.

[2] Viz. *Essex*, fol. 40, upon the lands of Richard Fitz-Gilbert, " In Sudberia v. burgenses tenentes II. acras.

The account of COLCHESTER in the Survey is full.
One section of the entry relating to it begins, " Isti sunt
burgenses Regis qui reddunt consuetudinem." Then
follows a list of 294 names, of whom by far the greater
number had one house in the borough; some had two
houses; a few had four; and one person as many as
thirteen. To each of these houses a few acres seem to
have been attached, and after some of the names there
is no house, but only a small parcel of land. The
whole number of houses entered is 401, which has been
assumed in the preceding Abstract for the number of
the burgesses, or at least inhabitants. Most of the
names are of ordinary burgesses, but there are a few of
Barons who had estates elsewhere. Hamo Dapifer has
a house, a " curia," a whole hide of land, and fifteen
burgesses. In another part of the Survey the Bishop
of London holds fourteen houses in Colchester, " non
reddentes consuetudinem præter scotum," *Essex*, fol. 14.
These would increase the number of the burgesses to
415. The King had a demesne in Colchester of a hundred and two acres, on which were ten Bordarii. It was
the custom of Colchester for the King's burgesses to

Isti cum omnibus supradictis reddunt xv. lib. et vi. sol.
et vi. d. et totum est in dominio Ricardi." Sudberia, however, must be Sudbury in Suffolk. There is no place of
the name in Essex ; and the second entry, *Essex*, fol. 76 b.,
makes this matter clear, under Haingeham, " Huic manerio
jacent xv. burgenses in Sudberia et appretientur in illo."
In fact, the first of these entries, as the context of the
passage shows, belongs to the manor of Halsted, which
precedes it in the Record. Halsted in Essex is to this day
held of the honor of Clare in Suffolk, which lordship belonged at the time of the Survey, together with Halsted,
to Richard Fitz Gilbert.

pay two marks of silver " ad firmam regis," every year, a fortnight after Easter. Beside which every house paid sixpence a year, when the King had soldiers, or made an expedition.

Every thing marking the existence of communities in burghs deserves to be noticed. At Colchester, eighty acres of land, and eight perches round the wall, belonged to the *Commune Burgensium*, and produced sixty solidi a year, which, if not wanted for the King's service, was divided " in commune." [1]

In MALDON, the Record says, the King had one house, pasture for a hundred sheep, and one socheman; he had also 180 houses, which the burgesses held of him, and 18 wasted houses. Fifteen burgesses held half a hide and twenty-one acres; the others held nothing but their houses in the burgh.

---

[1] " In Commune Burgensium IIII. XX. acr. terræ; et circa murum VIII. percæ, de quo toto per annum habent burgenses LX. sol. ad servicium Regis si opus fuerit, sin autem in Commune Burgensium."

GLOUCESTERSHIRE.

Tenants in capite - - -	102
Under-tenants - - - -	166
Ancillæ - - - -	84
Bordarii - - -	1,792
Burgenses in Bristou (no number) [1] -	—
—— in Glouuecestre -	72 [2]
—— in Teodekesberie - -	13 [3]
—— in Wincelcumbe - -	18 [4]
Coliberti - - - -	103
Fabri - - - - -	2
Figuli, poters [5] - - -	5
Francigenæ - - - -	15
Homines - - - -	44
Homines manentes in foro de Berchelai [6]	17
Liberi Homines - - -	16
Milites - - - -	8
Prepositi - - - -	10
Presbyteri - - -	49 [7]

Carried forward   -   - 2,516

---

[1] See *Glouc.* fol. 163.

[2] They are found scattered, as appendant to different manors in the county, foll. 163, col. 2. 165, col. 1, 2. 166, col. 1, 2. 166 b, col. 1. 167 b, col. 2. 168, col. 2. 168 b, col. 1, 2. 169, col. 1.

[3] *Glouc.* fol. 163 b.

[4] They occur in *Glouc.* fol. 163 b, col. 1. 165, col. 1. 166, col. 1. 167, col. 2. 167 b, col. 2. 168, col. 1. 170 b.

[5] *Glouc.* fol. 168 b.   [6] *Glouc.* fol. 163.

[7] Presbyteri occur without any number added, in fol. 162 b.

	Brought forward	-	- 2,516
Radchenistri	-	-	- 137
Servi [1]	-	-	- 2,044
Sochemanni	-	-	- 6
Villani	-	-	- 3,627 [2]
Dimidii Villani	-	-	- 30
Uxores Villanorum defunctorum		-	4
Walenses	-	-	- 2

8,366

In GLOUCESTER, the rents which were paid to the King, with various mansions held in the city by tenants in capite and others, are enumerated; but the folio which contains them gives no account of the burgesses. Those mentioned in the above Abstract occur as appendant to different manors, scattered through the Survey of the County.[3] The passages are referred to in a note in the preceding page. In Worcestershire, folio 172 b,

---

[1] In fol. 165, col. 1, we have " VIII. servi et unus *afrus.*" And again, " Ibi xx. servi et III. *afri.*" Rudder, Hist. Glouc. p. 369, translates the Afri of these entries, *Moors;* and Kelham adopts this translation for the first entry. To the Afri of the last entry Kelham gives the interpretation of *cart-horses,* which is probably correct. Dufresne says, " AFFERI, Scriptoribus Anglis, jumenta, vel caballi colonici."

[2] In Berkeley, and its dependent lands, in the time of King Edward the Confessor, there had been 242 Villani and 142 Bordarii.

[3] The Cottonian Register of Evesham Abbey, marked Vespas. B. XXIV. foll. 53, 55. contains returns, possibly those which were made to the Commissioners who formed the Domesday Survey, and were afterwards abridged, in which GLOUCESTER appears to have had no fewer than 613 bur-

we have this entry: " In Wich est dimid. hida quæ
pertinet *ad aulam de* GLOUUECESTRE."

---

gesses, and WINCHCOMBE at least 116. These returns are
well deserving of the reader's attention.

GLOUCESTER, fol. 53.

" Tempore Regis Eadwardi erant in civitate Gloecestrie
ccc. burgenses in dominio reddentes XVIII. li. et x. sol. de
Gablo per annum. Ex his sunt c. III. minus residentes in
propria hereditate et c. III. minus manentes in emptis man-
sionibus, Francigenæ et Anglici, quæ valent x. li. per annum
et has tenuerunt per XII. annos hoc est sexcies xx. li.   Et
infra castellum manserunt de hiis ccc. XXIIII. et quater xx.
et II. mansiones sunt wastæ.   Archiepiscopus Eboracensis
habet in eadem civitate LX. burgenses.   Episcopus Samson
VI.   Abb. ejusdem civitatis LII. et exceptis iis Stanborc I.
mansionem habet.   Derherst XXXVI.   Abbas Evesham III.
Abbas Persore I.   Comes Hugo Cestriæ XIII.   Robertus
filius Haim' XXII.   Hugo de Laceio XXVIII.   Bertone regis
pertinent XXIII.   Berchelai III.   Walt. de Gloecestr' XV.
Hugo asinus II.   Walt. filius Ricardi II.   Rad. Bloiet VI.
Horseleia I.   Wlmarus I.   Ascelinus de Tateberia V.   W.
de Saio I.   Willielmus filius Badder' XVII.   Hamelinus de
Badelun I.   Henr. Com. I.   W. de Manauilla VI.   Patricus
de Cahorc' VI.   Gislebertus de Cenomann' I.   Et super
omnes istos habet Rex saccam et soccam et x. Ecclesiæ
sunt in socha Regis propriæ.   Tempore Rogeri vicecomitis
reddebant de firma XXXVIII. li. et IIII. sol.   Modo reddit'
XLVI. l' et Walterus vicecomes habuit LXIIII. sol. de rogatu,
et Prepositus XL.   Civitas vero pejorata est de LX. sol."

WINCHCOMBE, fol. 55.

" In WINCELCUMBE burgo.   In dominio R. E. erant LX.
burgenses reddentes XLI. sol. de Gablo per annum.   De hiis
sunt LII. in hereditate sua manentes et VIII. habent alii
burgenses quæ valent per annum xxx. sol. hoc est XXII. li.

The CASTLE of ESTRIGHOIEL is also mentioned, with lands between the Wye and Usk, and other lands in

---

et x. sol. per xv. ann. Preter hoc Abbas habet in eo xv. burgenses et Abbas Evesham ii. Episcopus Hereford. Derherst ii. Hugo asinus i. Langaberga iii. Ro. fil. Haim' v. Turst. de Cormeil ii. et i. molendin. Heroldus x. et ii. molendin. Rob. de Belhismo iii. Walt. de Walerico et Hugo de Laceio i. Rob. de Ferrer' ii. Hug. de Ham. i. Ric. de Solariis i. Rad. de Salceio iii. Will. Guiz in bod' iii. Rob. de Lacei i. W. Froisselupu' i. Et super omnes istos Rex habet suum geldum. Tempore Rogeri vicecomitis redd. x. li. et modo xxi. li. numero, et vicecomes habuit de rogatu xii. sol."

The abbat of Evesham, according to the statements just quoted, was the superior lord of three burgesses in Gloucester, and of two in Winchcombe. The Domesday Survey itself gives him four in Gloucester, and one in Winchcombe.

There is a short passage in the account of the Evesham property in Gloucestershire, in Domesday, fol. 166, relating to the manors of Stock and Hadecote, which must not be passed here without a comment. The Record says, " Has duo Villas habet Abbas *duobus militibus* suis commendatas." It is the only entry in which the " Milites Abbatis" occur: but the abbat must have had a greater number of " milites" upon his lands ready when called upon for service. The Cottonian Register already referred to, fol. 14 b., preserves what the Editor of the present Work believes to be the OLDEST WRIT of MILITARY SERVICE extant. It is from King William the Conqueror to Abbat Egelwin, and demands the service forthwith of five " milites." It must have been addressed to the Abbat in or before the year 1077, since the Saxon Chronicle places Egelwin's death in that year. The instrument is as follows :

" W. Rex Anglorum Agelwin abbati de Evesham salutem. Precipio tibi quod submoneas omnes illos qui sub ballia et

Wales, but no enumeration either of the occupiers or the agricultural population.

In WALES three Hardevices and sixty-seven Villæ are mentioned, but no notice whatever of inhabitants. Four Villæ are mentioned as " wastatæ per regem Caraduech." [1]

---

justitia tua sunt, quatinus omnes milites quos mihi debent paratos habeant ante me ad octaves Pentecostes apud Clarendon. Tu etiam illo die ad me venias, et illos quinque milites quos de Abbatia tua mihi debes tecum paratos adducas. Teste Eudone dapifero, apud Winton."

[1] See the former Volume, p. 321.

HAMPSHIRE,

exclusive of the New Forest and the Isle of Wight.

Tenants in capite - - -	128
Under-tenants - - - -	174
Bordarii - - - -	3,466
Burgenses in Bromelai - - -	3 [1]
————— in Hovston - -	3 [2]
————— in Sanburne - - -	9 [3]
————— in Thvinam - -	31 [4]
————— in Wincestre - - -	14 [5]
Coliberti - - - -	98
Francus homo - - - -	1
Forestarii [6] - - - -	—
Homines - - - - -	2
Homines quos Rex habet in dominio in Burgo de Hantune - - -	76
Francigenæ et Angligenæ hospitati in Hantone - - - -	96
Houses in Southampton, of which the consuetudo belonged to great persons of the court - - -	49 [7]
Carried forward - -	4,150

---

[1] *Hants,* fol. 45. " Silva de quater xx[ti] porc. et III. burgenses."

[2] Ibid. fol. 40 b. " III. burgenses de xxx. denar."

[3] Fol. 47. Kings-Somborne, " IX. mansiones burgensium."

[4] " In burgo de Thuinam xxxi. masuræ reddunt xvi. denar. de gablo." *Hants,* fol. 38 b.

[5] Fol. 43 b. col. 2.

[6] Fol. 38 b. col. 2. No number mentioned.

[7] Four masuræ in Hantone belonged to the manor of Strelei, fol. 46 b.

Brought forward	-	-	4,150
Presbyteri	-	-	-	3
Radchenistri	-	-	-	5
Servi	-	-	-	1,458
Villani	-	-	-	3,416
				9,032

NEW FOREST.

Tenants in capite	-	-	-	17
Under-tenants	-	-	-	17
Bordarii	-	-	-	87
Custos domus Regis [1]	-	-	1
Homines	-	-	-	7
Servi	-	-	-	22
Villani	-	-	-	66
				217

ISLE OF WIGHT.[2]

Tenants in capite	-	-	-	37
Under-tenants	-	-	-	45
Bordarii	-	-	-	441
Homines	-	-	-	8
Servi	-	-	-	232
Vavassorius quidam habens II. vaccas [3]	-	-	-	1
Villani	-	-	-	360
				1,124
Total of Hampshire	-	-	10,373

---

[1] *Hants*, fol. 51. col. 2.
[2] Ibid. foll. 39 b. and 52.   [3] Ibid. fol. 53.

Although no description of WINCHESTER occurs in the Survey, that City is repeatedly mentioned in the account of Hampshire, as will be seen in the references below,[1] in which, beside the Burgenses and Sub-urbani mentioned in the preceding Abstract, we have seven houses, thirty-nine hagæ, and thirty-two masuræ. The fourteen burgesses belonged to the Abbey of Rumsey; the sub-urbani to the Abbey of Wherwell.

The state of Winchester in the time of King Edward the Confessor, as well as in the reign of Henry the First, is fully detailed in the LIBER WINTON', published by order of His Majesty's Commissioners upon the public records, among the Additamenta to the Domesday Survey, in 1816.

---

[1] Foll. 38 b, col. 1. 2 hagæ. col. 2. 7 hagæ. 39, col. 2. 4 sub-urbani. 39 b. (in margin) 6 domus. 40 b, col. 1. 8 hagæ. 42. 1 haga. 43 b, col. 1. 1 haga. col. 2. 14 burgenses. 44, col. 1. 31 masuræ. 44 b, col. 1. 1 haga. 45, col. 2. 1 domus. 46, col. 2. 8 hagæ. 47 b, col. 2. 1 masura. 48, col. 2. 1 haga. 49 b, col. 1. 1 haga. col. 2. 5 hagæ. 3 hagæ 51 b, col. 2. 1 haga.

HEREFORDSHIRE.

Tenants in Capite - - -	37
Under-tenants - - -	282
Ancillæ - - - -	99
Anglicus - - - -	1
Bedelli - - - -	21
Bordarii - - - -	1,407 [1]
Bordarii pauperes - - -	10 [2]
Bovarii - - - -	104
Bovarii liberi - - -	12 [3]
Burgenses de Cliford - -	16 [4]
———— in Hanlie - -	1 [5]
———— in Hereford - -	10
Buri - - - -	16
Carpentarius - - -	1
Coliberti - - -	16
Cotarii - - - -	19
Carried forward - -	2,052

[1] Bordarii, without any number attached, occur *Heref.* fol. 182, col. 1.

[2] Upon the royal manor of Svchelie — "xxiiii. bord. cum xvii. car. Ibi alii x. bord. pauperes." fol. 180 b.

[3] "Unus liber Bovarius." fol. 183, col. 2. On the lands of Ralph de Mortemer, in Lenhale, "iiii. bovarii liberi." At Lintehale, "Ibi vi. bovarii liberi." At Canehop, "unus liber bovarius," fol. 183 b. col. 2.

[4] Fol. 183, col. 2. Ralph de Todeni held them in demesne, with 13 bordarii, in his castelry of Clifford.

[5] Under the manor of Hanlie, belonging to Drogo fitz Ponz, fol. 186 b. "Ibi i. servus et unus burgensis de iiii. denar."

Brought forward	-	-	2,052	
Custos Apium	-	-	-	1 [1]
Fabri	-	-	-	24
Carried forward		-	-	2,077

[1] Fol. 180, col. 1. The CUSTOS APUM is mentioned at considerable length in the Glossary of Services in the Cottonian MS. Titus A. xxvII. fol. 150: followed by the services of the PORCARIUS.

" BOCHERO, i. apum Custodi pertinet, si gafolheorde, i. gregem ad censum teneat, ut inde reddat sicut ibi mos erit. In quibusdam locis est institutum reddi vi. sextaria mellis ad censum, in quibusdam locis plus gabli redditur. Et aliquotiens etiam debet esse paratus ad multas operationes voluntatis domini sui, et ad benhyrðe i. arat'am parcum, et benripe i. ad partes metare et pratum falcare, et si bonam terram habeant quem ad summagium domini sui parare possit, vel ipse minare quocunque dicatur ei. Et hujusmodi plurima facienda sunt ei quæ modo nequiunt enarrari. Cum finis eum demediabitur hanc quod relinquit, nisi forte liberum aliquid intersit.

" GAFOLSPANE, i. ad censum Porcario pertinet ut suam occisionem det secundum quod in patria statutum est. In multis locis stat ut det singulis annis xv. porcos ad occisionem, x. veteres et v. juvenes. Ipse autem hanc super augmentum. In multis locis servilius rectum est porcari. Viderit etiam porcarius ut post occisam ipsam porcos occisos bene corrodiet et suspendat. Item habeatur dignus opera sua. Etiam erit sicut de Custode apum diximus, multis operibus frequentatus, et equum habeat in opus domini sui. Servus Porcarius, et servus Custos apum. Post obitum suum sint unius legis digni. 'Ahte spane i. servo porcario qui dominicum gregem Curiæ custodit pertinet habere stiparh i. porcellum de sude, et suum gepyrce quando bacones suos bene corrediaverit, et amplius eas rectitudines quæ servo jure pertinent."

Brought forward - -	2,077
Forestarii - - - -	2
Francigenæ - - -	22
Homines - - - -	204 [1]
Hospites - - - -	7 [2]
Liberi Homines - - -	15
Manentes - - - -	3 [3]
Milites - - - -	3
Molinarius - - - -	1
Porcarii - - - -	9
Prepositi - - - -	44
Presbyteri - - - -	43
Radchenistri - - - -	47
Radmans - - - -	24
Servi - - - -	691 [4]
Servientes Regis - - -	8 [5]
Vaccarii - - - -	2
Villani - - - -	2,124
Walenses - - - -	42
	5,368

In the time of King Edward the Confessor there
were 103 homagers in HEREFORD, within and without
the wall. [6] Six " fabri," or smiths, had each his forge in
the city. Earl Harold, it is added, had 27 burgesses,

---

[1] Homines are mentioned several times without the addition of any number, as in foll. 182, col. 1. 183, 184 b. col. 1.

[2] " Presbyter et VII. hospites," fol. 184 b.

[3] " Ibi manent III. habentes I. car." *Heref.* fol. 183 b.

[4] Servi et Ancillæ" occur several times in Herefordshire,
as well as in various other Counties, without any number
being expressed.

[5] On the manor of Maurdine, fol. 179, col. 2.

[6] *Heref.* fol. 179.

with the same privileges as others. In the Conqueror's time the burgesses were of two classes; the English, who enjoyed the privileges which they had been accustomed to in the reign of the Confessor; and foreigners, or " Francigenæ," who had some exemptions. No numbers, however, are specified. Roger de Laci had certain burgesses in Hereford [1]; Henry de Ferrars had one belonging to his manor of Frome [2]; and Alured de Merleberge had five appertaining to his manor of Burgelle. [3] Four belonged to the royal manor of Merchelai. [4] The burgesses of Hereford upon the three manors last mentioned are those which are counted in the Abstract above.

The payments and privileges of the moneyers of Hereford have been already detailed, vol. i. p. 176. All had sac and soc, and consequently had all their inmates under their own jurisdiction and frankpledge.

The Burgh of WIGMORE is mentioned as paying a rent of £7 to Ralph de Mortemer; but no burgesses are named in the entry. [5]

---

[1] " Burgenses quos habet in Hereford reddunt ei xx. solid." fol. 184.

[2] Fol. 185, col. 2. " Unus burgensis in Hereford redd. xii. denar."

[3] Fol. 186. " In Hereford v. burgenses reddunt huic Manerio lii. denar."

[4] Fol. 179 b. " Ad Hereford sunt iiii. burgenses huic Manerio reddentes xviii. socos carrucis.

[5] Fol. 183 b.

HERTFORDSHIRE.

Tenants in capite - - -	55
Under-tenants as mesne proprietors -	184
Anglici homines - - -	3
Bordarii - - - -	1,107
Burgenses in Villa S. Albani - -	46
——— in Berchamstede - -	52
——— in Escewelle [1] - - -	14
——— in Herteforde - -	18
——— in Stanestede [2] - -	7
Clericus - - - -	1
Cotarii - - - -	837
Fossarius quidam - - -	1
Francigena Elemosynarius Regis -	1
Carried forward - -	2,326

---

[1] Ashwell, near Baldock, on the borders of Cambridge-shire, once a market town. The Abbat of Westminster, to whom Ashwell belonged, in answer to an inquiry "de Quo Waranto," in the 15th Edw. I., stated that his predecessors had had both the manor and market of Ashwell granted to them by King Edward the Confessor: "Et quo ad præ-dictum Mercatum, dicit quod Sanctus Edwardus quondam Rex Angliæ contulit eis Manerium de Essewell cum præ-dicto Mercato, et quod ipse et omnes predecessores sui semper postea Mercatum illud habuerunt, et illo usi sunt huc usque." Plac. de Quo War., p. 288.

[2] Stansted Abbot, near Hoddesdon. Chauncy and Clut-terbuck, in their Histories of Hertfordshire, presume this village to have been formerly a place of trade; arising either from its proximity to the river Lea, or as of greater thoroughfare in early times.

Brought forward -	- 2,326
Francigenæ - - -	- 56
Homines - - -	- 37
Liberi homines - -	- 8
Mercatores [1] - - -	- 10
Milites [2] - - -	- 13
Prepositi Villarum - -	- 6
Presbyteri - - -	- 48
Servi - - - -	- 550
Serviens Comitis Moriton. -	- 1
Sochemanni - - -	- 41
Villani - . -	- 1,830
Dimidius Villanus - -	- 1

4,927

The Town of Hertford in Edward the Confessor's time had 146 burgesses under the protection of the King. It was rated at ten hides.

Eighteen burgesses only are noticed at the time of the Survey, who are comprised in the preceding Abstract: they were the King's, and are said previously to have been the homagers of the Earls Harold and Leuuin. Thirty-seven houses (including the mansion of Asgar stalre) are enumerated as held chiefly by the great Norman landholders of the County, which had previously belonged to burgesses.

Clutterbuck, in his History of Hertfordshire, states, that Hertford Castle was given by King William the Conqueror to Peter de Valoines; but the Charter to to which he refers, Cart. Antiq. K. 22, in Turre Lond., is from William Rufus, and no mention of Hertford Castle occurs in it.

---

[1] At Cheshunt, fol. 137. col. 1.
[2] Not mentioned as holding lands.

HUNTINGDONSHIRE.

Tenants in capite - - - -	35
Under-tenants ᵖ - -	85 [1]
Bordarii - - - -	490
Burgenses in Huntingdon " in duobus Ferlingis " - - -	116
————— " in aliis duobus Ferlingis "	140
————— Eustachii vicecomitis -	22
————— Gisleberti de Gant -	18
Faber - - - - -	1
Piscatores - - - -	5
Presbyteri - - - -	47
Sochemanni - - -	22
Villani - - - -	1,933
	2,914

The total number of the burgesses of HUNTINGDON at the time of the Survey, entered in the Record, was 296. The 116 burgesses, in the two quarters of the town which are mentioned first, had 100 Bordarii who assisted them in paying geld to the King. These are included, in the above Abstract, in their class. The Borough of Huntingdon paid geld for a fourth part of the hundred of Hyrstingstan, for fifty hides, but it is added, " Modo non geldat ita in illo Hundredo, postquam rex Willielmus geldum monetæ posuit in burgo." Previous to the time of the Survey there had been three Monetarii in Huntingdon, but they were employed there no longer.

The dues from Huntingdon were farmed; two thirds of the " firma burgi " were paid to the King, and one third to the Earl.

---

[1] All the Milites of Huntingdonshire, nineteen in number, as they held lands, are classed among the Under-tenants. So, also, the eight Homines.

KENT.

Tenants in capite	-	-	-	13
Under-tenants	-	-	-	212
Bordarii	-	-	-	3,118
Burgenses in Civitate Cantuar.		-		263 [1]

Carried forward	-	-	3,606

[1] The Burgesses in Canterbury T. R. E. are enumerated as follow:

" Reddentes gablum	-	-	51
Alii Burgenses	-	-	212
			263 "

The Burgesses at the time of the Survey:

" Reddentes gablum	-	-	19
Alii	-	-	32
Adhuc	-	-	212
			263 "

Under the title " Terra Archiepiscopi Cantuariensis " it is said, " In Civitate Cantuaria habet Archiepiscopus XII. burgenses et XXXII. mansuras quas tenent clerici de villa." Tom. i. fol. 3. Seven burgesses in Canterbury are recorded, fol. 4, as appertaining to the Archbishop's manor of Aldintone, and ninety-seven as belonging to the manor of Nordevde, fol. 5; seventy burgesses in Canterbury belonged to St. Augustine's manor of Lanport, fol. 12. It is presumed that all these are included in the 263 already enumerated.

Three masuræ in Canterbury belonged to the manor of Wicheham, fol. 9. Adam Fitz Hubert had four houses in Canterbury, fol. 9 b. Haimo the sheriff held lands under the Bishop of Baieux, in Latintone, which the Burgesses of Canterbury had held in the time of King Edward the Con-

Brought forward	-	- 3,606
Burgenses in Forewic	-	- 6 [1]
———— in Burgo Hedæ	-	231 [2]
———— in Romenel	-	- 156 [3]
Carried forward	-	- 3,999

fessor, and till the Bishop had taken them away; fol. 9 b. col. 1. Thirteen masuræ in Canterbury belonged to the manor of Cilleham; fol. 10, col. 1. One masura to the manor of Ernoltun; fol. 10. Five hagæ to the manor of Dodeham; fol. 10 b. Four hagæ in Canterbury belonged to the manor of Newetune; fol. 14 b.

T. R. E. the burgesses of Canterbury had 45 mansuræ without the city, of which they had the rent and customs, but the King had the sac and soc. They had also 33 acres of land " ad gildam suam;" and held 80 acres of the King " in allodio." In folio 9 b. we read that Haimo the sheriff held four carucates of land under the Bishop of Baieux, which the burgesses of Canterbury had held T. R. E., and of which they were afterwards deprived by the Bishop.

[1] " Ipse abbas (S. Augustini) tenet unum parvum burgum quod vocatur FOREWIC. Hujus burgi duas partes dedit rex Edwardus Sancto Augustino, tertiam vero partem, quæ fuerat Godwini Comitis, Episcopus Baiocensis concessit eidem sancto annuente Rege Willielmo. Ibi fuerunt c. masuræ terræ IIII. minus reddentes XIII. sol. Modo sunt LXXIII. masuræ. Ibidem sunt XXIIII. acr. terræ quas semper habuit Sanctus Augustinus ubi fuerunt et sunt VI. burgenses reddentes XXII. solid. In isto burgo tenet archiepiscopus Lanfr. VII. masuras terræ quæ T. R. E. serviebant S. Augustino." Fol. 12.

[2] These occur in the folios 4 and 4 b. " Burgenses in Hede VI. pertin. ad maner. Leminges." " Burgenses in burgo Hedæ pertin. ad maner. de Salteode Archiep. Cant. CCXXV."

[3] " Burgenses in Romenel LXXXV. pertin. ad Aldintone

Brought forward	-	- 3,999
Burgenses in Roucestre	- -	5 [1]
Cotarii	- - ..	- 364
Francigenæ	- - - -	4
Homines	- - - -	24
Milites	- - -	- 3
Moniales	- - - -	4 [2]
Mulier paupercula [3]	-	- 1
Presbyteri	- - -	- 12
Servi [4]	- - -	- 1,148
Sochemanni	- - -	- 44
Villani	- - -	- 6,597
		12,205

manerium Archiepiscopi;" fol. 4. " Burgenses in Romenel pertin. ad manerium Lamport Archiepiscopi Cant. xxi." fol. 4 b. " Robertus de Romenel habet L. burgenses in burgo de Romenel;" fol. 10 b.

[1] Fol. 3, col. 1. They were attached to the manor of Tarente. The Bishop of Baieux held four houses in Rochester appertaining to his manor of Ledesdune, fol. 7 b.; one house, by Anschitil his under-tenant, belonging to the manor of Ofeham, ibid.; and nine houses in Rochester appendant to his manor of Hov, fol. 8 b. Three hagæ in Rochester belonged to the Bishop of Baieux's manor of Celca, ibid. The Bishop of Rochester had eighty mansuræ in Rochester, appertaining to his manors of Frendesberie and Borestele, fol. 5, col. 2.

[2] " Juxta Civitatem Cantuar. habet S. Augustinus, &c. Ibidem sunt IIII. acr. terræ quas tenent IIII. moniales in elemosina de Abbate;" fol. 12.

[3] Fol. 9 b.

[4] It is observable, that in Kent the Servi are usually placed after the mention of a church, as in fol. 10, under Badlesmere; " Ibi æcclesia et II. servi." So again, in a reversed form, fol. 10 b., " Et III. servi et ecclesia."

DOVER had been burnt, we have therefore no enumeration of its burgesses or inhabitants. The burgesses,
however, must have been a powerful body in the time
of King Edward the Confessor, since they fitted out for
the King, once a year, twenty ships and four hundred
and twenty men for fifteen days. The " Gihalla Burgensium" at Dover has been noticed in the preceding
Volume. The King is said to have lost his custom upon
twenty-nine masuræ.

SANDWICH had T. R. E. 307 " masuræ hospitatæ;"
at the time of the Survey 383. These imply a considerable population, which is not otherwise recorded :
as well as that the town had increased.

LEICESTERSHIRE.

Tenants in capite	53
Under-tenants	196
Ancillæ	23
Bordarii	1,345
Burgenses in Ledecestre	65
Clericus	1
Diaconus	1
Francigenæ	43
Homines	11
Milites	13
Presbyteri	42
Servi	400
Sochemanni	1,914
Villani	2,665
	6,772

Sixty-five burgesses of LEICESTER, only, are actually mentioned in the Domesday Survey; but the number of inhabited houses belonging to different persons is 318, exclusive of four which are described as wastæ, and of 47 burgesses mentioned as appendant to the manors of Hanstigie, Siglesbie, Pontenei, and Erendesbi.[1] Allowing, therefore, only one burgess to a house, the real number must have been 365. Of the houses, seventy-one paid geld to the King.

---

[1] *Leic.* fol. 230. " xxiiii. burgenses pertinentes ad Hanstigie, et xiii. burgenses pertinentes ad Siglesbie." In Pontenei, fol. 231. " ix. burgenses in Civitate." Under Erendesbi, fol. 235. " In Ledecestre est unus burgensis pertinens ad hanc Villam."

The military service rendered by Leicester T. R. E. has been noticed in the former Volume. The Record says, " Modo habet Rex W. pro omnibus redditibus civitatis ejusdem et comitatus, XLII. lib. et x. solid. ad pondus. Pro uno accipitre, x. lib. ad numerum. Pro summario xx^{ti} sol. De monetariis xx. lib. per annum de xx. in Ora. De his xx. lib. habet Hugo de Grentemaisnil tercium denarium."

LINCOLNSHIRE.

Tenants in capite, including the Thains - - - -	92
Under-tenants - - -	414
Bordarii - - - -	4,024
Burgenses in Grantham - -	111 [1]
———— in Ludes - -	80 [2]
———— in Civitate Lincolia -	900
———— in Stanford - -	136 [3]
———— in Torchesey - -	102
Censarii - - - -	6
Censores, Censorii - -	8 [4]
Francigenæ - - -	7
Homines - - -	32
Homines non arantes - -	10
Lagemen in Lincolia - -	12
——— in Stanford - -	9
Presbyteri - - -	131
Sochemanni - - -	11,503 [5]
Sochemannus dimidius - -	1 [6]
Villani - - - -	7,723
	25,305

[1] The 72 Bordarii in Grantham, who are recorded beside the Burgenses, are enumerated in their class.

[2] Fol. 345.

[3] Nine burgesses in Stamford occur, *Linc.* fol. 358.

[4] Censores with no number attached are mentioned, fol. 360 b.

[5] In fol. 337 b. we have in Grantham also, beside the Burgenses and Bordarii, 77 Toftes Sochemannorum teignorum."

[6] Fol. 368 b.

In the first column of the folio of Domesday which relates to LINCOLN, the number of houses in that city in the time of King Edward the Confessor is calculated by six score to the hundred. They amounted consequently to 1,150.[1] The Record then gives a list of the twelve Lagemen as they existed in the time of the Confessor, [2] followed by the names of their successors as they stood at the time of the Survey. In the remainder of the column about 120 houses belonging to different persons are enumerated. Geoffrey Alselin held the hall or mansion which had belonged to Tochi the son of Outi, and Bishop Remigius held 30 mansiones which had belonged to the same person. From the names of Merlesuain, Morcar, Ulf, and Harold, as possessors of mansions here, it should seem that Lincoln had served for a resort to partisans opposed to the Conqueror at the beginning of his reign. Of the " mansiones hospitatæ " of the time of the Confessor, 240 lay waste at the time of the Survey; and 900 were inhabited. This last number has been adopted for the burgesses in the preceding Abstract.[3] Colsuen, it is said, had lately built 36 houses

---

[1] The passage of the original has been already quoted, Vol. i. p. 148.   [2] See Vol. i. p. 205.

[3] The three burgesses of Lincoln belonging to the Abbey of Peterborough's manor of Scotone, fol. 345 b., are, no doubt, included in the 900. It is to be remarked, however, that there might be more than one burgess in one house, and consequently that the number of houses is no certain indication of the number of burgesses. Where sac and soc was attached to a domus, it probably had inferior habitations annexed to the principal house, and probably in some cases patches of land. The churches and burgesses of Lincoln, for instance, had among them 36 crofts within the town. In Colchester, it has been already shown that some of the burgesses had more houses than one.

and two churches on a piece of waste ground outside the city, given to him by the King.   Of the 240 wasted houses within the city, 166 had been demolished in building the Castle, and 74 had fallen to ruin, not from the oppression of Sheriffs and other Officers of the Crown, but from misfortunes, poverty, and fire.

Nine burgesses of STAMFORD only are mentioned in the Survey[1] by title; but it is clear that there must have been a large population there.   In five out of the six wards into which it was divided there were 141 inhabited houses in the time of King Edward the Confessor, 136 of which remained at the Survey.   Five had been destroyed at the building of the Castle.   Stamford also had had 12 Lagemen in the time of the Confessor; but the number at the Survey was nine only.   The above number of 136 inhabitants, one for each house, has been adopted in the Abstract.

The lower part of the second column of *Linc.* folio 336 b., proceeds to enumerate 111 houses belonging to different persons, but whether exclusive of those contained in the general enumeration is difficult to say. They all existed T. R. E., but had changed their owners.   Seventy of these mansiones, which had belonged to Queen Editha, are said to be in Rutlandshire.

Stamford was rated T. R. E. for landfyrd, shipfyrd, and danegeld, as for Twelve Hundreds and a half.   The lagemen and burgesses held two hundred and seventy-two acres T. R. W. " sine consuetudine."

In TORKSEY, in the time of King Edward the Confessor, there were 213 burgesses; at the time of the Survey 102 ; one hundred and eleven " mansiones" lay waste.

---

[1] Appendant to one of the manors in Offintone, *Linc.* fol. 358, ut supr.

MIDDLESEX.

Tenants in capite - - -	30
Under-tenants as mesne lords -	62
Bordarii - - - -	343
Burgenses in Stanes [1] - -	46
Cotarii - - - -	464
Francigenæ - - -	8
Francus quidam [2] . -	1
Homines [3] - - - -	34
Presbyteri - - -	18
Servi - - - -	112
Villani - - - -	1,141
Villani et Bordarii - -	43
	2,302

[1] On the Abbat of Westminster's manor.

[2] Lands "inter Francos et Villanos" are twice mentioned in the first page of Middlesex, and again in fol. 128 b., but without any number of persons. Under Fulham, too, in fol. 127 b., we have "Inter francigen. et quosdam burgenses Lundon. xxiii. hid. de terra villanorum."

[3] In fol. 128. we have " xxv. domus Militum abbatis (Westmon.) et aliorum Hominum, qui reddunt viii. s. per annum ;" but no specification of the number of Milites.

NORFOLK.

Tenants in capite	- - -	63
Under-tenants	- - -	435
Anglicus quidam [1]	- - -	1
Bordarii	- - -	9,537
Bordarii in Norwic " qui propter pauperiem nullam reddunt consuetudinem"		480
Dimidii Bordarii	- - -	4 [2]
Burgenses Anglici in Norwic	-	665
————— in Novo Burgo de Norwic	-	124
————— in Gernemuta	- -	70
————— in Tetford	- -	725
Homines	- - - -	89
————— commendati Rogeri Bigot in burgo Tetford [3]	- -	33
————— consuetudinarii [4]	- -	8
Dimidii Homines integri [5]	- -	7
Liberæ feminæ	- - -	8
Liberi homines	- - -	4,277
————— homines faldæ	- - -	21 [6]
————— homines commendatione tantum [7]		117
Carried forward	- -	16,664

---

[1] *Norf.* fol. 209 b.

[2] " x. bord. et dim." fol. 197. " Habet dim. bord." fol. 198 b. " ii. bor. et dim." fol. 225.

[3] Fol. 173. [4] Fol. 215.

[5] Fol. 125. [6] Foll. 230, 250.

[7] See foll. 148 b. 149, 154, 154 b. 161 b. 167, 168, 188, 188 b. 193 b. 199, 205, 208 b. 216, 220, 275, 275 b. 277 b. 278 b. 279.

Brought forward - -	16,664
Dimidii liberi homines - -	63
Dimidius liber homo commendatione tantum - - - -	1 [1]
Piscatores - - - -	32
Presbyteri - - - -	8
Servi - - - -	995
Serviens Regis [2] - - -	1
Servientes - - -	4
Sochemanni - - -	4,571
Dimidii Sochemanni [3] - - -	17
Villani - - - -	4,656
Liberi Villani - - - -	73
Dimidii Villani - - -	2 [4]

27,087

In the time of King Edward the Confessor there were
1,320 burgesses in NORWICH. The King had soc, sac,
and customary rent of 1,230; Stigand had the soc, sac,
and " commendatio," or patronage, of 50; and Harold
of 32. Stigand held the two churches of St. Martin and
St. Michael in Norwich, which were together endowed
with a hundred and thirty acres of land: fifteen other
churches were held by the burgesses, to which there
belonged in alms 181 acres of land and meadow: and
twelve burgesses, in King Edward's time, held the
church of the Holy Trinity. The Abbat of St. Edmunds had one house, and a moiety of the church of

---

[1] Fol. 275.   [2] Fol. 258.
[3] See foll. 145, 229 b. 233, 259 b.
[4] Fol. 144.

St. Laurence. The church of All Saints in Norwich is also incidentally mentioned, and the church of St. Simon and St. Jude. So great was the consequence of Norwich at this period, that it was rated by itself as for a whole hundred.

At the formation of the Domesday Survey there were in Norwich no more than 665 English burgesses, beside 480 bordarii, who from poverty paid no custom.

On the land which Stigand had held T. R. E. there were 39 burgesses and 9 empty houses;[1] and on the land of which Harold had had the soc, 15 burgesses and 17 empty houses, then in the occupation of the Castle; and on the land which was in the soc of the King and Earl there were 190 empty houses; and 81 in the occupation of the Castle. There were besides 50 houses in the borough from which the King had no custom. The names of the owners of these houses follow in the Record.[2] Forty-three chapels, not mentioned in the Survey as existing in King Edward's time, are entered in the Conqueror's time as belonging to the burgesses.

The Record expressly states, that Norwich had suffered much. It had been deserted by part of its inhabitants, " partim propter forisfacturas Rogerii Comitis, partim propter arsuram, partim propter geltum Regis, partim propter Walerannum."

In spite, however, of this reduced ability, Norwich, which in King Edward's time had paid to the King

---

[1] Blomefield, Hist. Norfolk, vol. ii. p. 13, fol. edit., conjectures that ix. in the Record is a mistake for xi.: as 11 mansions void would fill up the 50 burgesses in Stigand's time.

[2] *Norf.* fol. 116 b. 117.

20*l.* and 10*l.* to the Earl,[1] at the time of the Survey, paid to the King 70*l.* by weight, and 100*s.* by tale " de gersuma," as a free gift to the Queen; a palfrey and twenty pounds of blanched silver to the Earl; and twenty shillings by tale to Godric, who is supposed to have been the Sheriff. Many of the inhabitants of Norwich had taken up their residence in other places. Domesday expressly states, that 22 burgesses had gone to Beccles, a town belonging to the Abbat of St. Edmundsbury; six had seated themselves in the hundred of Humbleyard;[2] one at King's Thorp; one on the land of Roger Bigot; one under William de Noiers; and one under Richard de Sent Cler.[3]

YARMOUTH remained in the same condition, nearly, in the Conqueror's time, as it had been in the time of King Edward the Confessor. " Semper LXX. Burgenses." The customary rent to the King and Earl was triflingly increased; and the burgesses gave 4*l.* to the sheriff, " gratis et amicitia."

THETFORD had had 943 burgesses in the time of King Edward. At the time of the Survey there were 720 burgesses only, and 224 empty houses. Twenty-one of these burgesses held of the King six carucates and sixty acres of land. The King had two thirds of the customs and rents of Thetford as belonging to his Crown, and one third in right of the Earldom

---

[1] See Vol. i. p. 206.

[2] The burgesses of Norwich were the owners of eighty acres of land in this hundred, for which they paid the customary rent of 13*s.* 4*d.* only. Whether this was the land upon which the six burgesses seated themselves is not said.

[3] *Norf.* fol. 117 b.

of Ralph Guader, which had come into his hands
by forfeiture. In the time of King Edward the Confessor, Thetford paid 20*l.* by tale to the King, and 10*l.*
to the Earl. At the time of the Survey it paid to
the Crown yearly no less than 50*l.* by weight, to the
Earldom 20*l.* blanch, and 6*l.* by tale, beside 40*l.* a year
to the King in coin, " de moneta," and 16*s.* for two
allowances of provender. The exaction here, on the
part of the Norman invaders, seems to have been
great.

NORTHAMPTONSHIRE.

Tenants in capite - - -	66
Under-tenants - - -	261
Ancillæ - - - -	59
Bordarii - - -	2,056
Burgenses in Northantone -	87
Fabri [1] - - - -	2
Francigenæ - - -	3
Homines - - - -	6
Liberi homines - - -	3
Milites - - - -	10 [2]
Prepositus - - -	1
Presbyteri - - - -	66 [3]
Servi - - - -	807
Sochemanni - - -	1,062
Villani - - -	3,952
	8,441

In the time of King Edward the Confessor the King
had in demesne 60 burgesses in NORTHAMPTON, who had

---

[1] Fabri are twice mentioned, *Northampt.* fol. 219 b. col. 1,
but without numbers. In one instance, fol. 227, col. 1, we
have bordarii, with no number attached.

[2] The Milites Abbatiæ S. Petri de Burgo, 33 in number,
foll. 221 b. 222, are counted as Under-tenants.

[3] It seems a peculiarity in the Survey of Northamptonshire, to class the priests with the villans and bordarii, as
in fol. 219, col. 2. " xxiiii. vill. et v. bord. cum presbytero
habentes xi. car." " Ibi sunt xxxiii. uillani et xxiii. bord.
cum presbytero." " xii. sochemanni et xvi. bord. cum
presbytero."

as many mansions.   At the Survey, King William had but 47 in demesne, with 40 " in Novo Burgo," which must mean a fresh extension of the place.   In this new Town 221 houses are enumerated as belonging, at the time of the Survey, to the Bishop of Coutance, the Abbies of St. Edmundsbury, Peterborough, Ramsey, Coventry, Evesham, and Selby, the Earl of Moretaine, Earl Hugh, the Countess Judith, and others, of which 21 lay waste; so that there were at least 287 houses inhabited in Northampton when Domesday was formed. The burgesses of Northampton, at the time of the Survey, paid 30*l*. 10*s*. as part of the Sheriff's farm of the county.

NOTTINGHAMSHIRE.

Tenants in capite - - -	50
Under-tenants - - -	138
Ancillæ - - - -	2
Bordarii - - - -	1,101
Burgenses in Newerche - -	56 [1]
Censores - - - -	2
Homines - - -	4
Homines manentes (*sc.* Burgenses in Burgo Snotingeham) -	120
Mercatores in Snotingham -	4
Presbyteri - - -	64
Servi - - - -	26
Sochemanni - - -	1,516
Villani - - - -	2,603
	5,686

In the time of King Edward the Confessor there were in NOTTINGHAM 173 burgesses, 19 villani, and two monetarii. In the Conqueror's time, when Hugh Fitz Baldric was sheriff, there were 136 resident burgesses, called "homines manentes;" there were 16 less in number, as the Abstract shows, at the time of the Survey.

Two hundred and fourteen houses are enumerated as belonging to different persons at the time of the Survey. Forty-eight of these, held by William Peverell, are called "domus Mercatorum," and twelve, held by the same person, "domus Equitum;" a title which is also given to thirteen houses held by Ralph de Burun. Sheriff Hugh, it is said, had built thirteen houses in the new burgh, on the land of Earl Tosti, and subjected them to the census of the New Burgh.

The burgesses of Nottingham held six carucates of land, twenty bordarii, and fourteen ploughs.

---

[1] These, with 42 villani and 4 bordarii, were upon the demesne of Remigius bishop of Lincoln in Newark.

OXFORDSHIRE.

Tenants in capite - - -	84
Under-tenants and occupiers -	207
Bordarii - - -	1,889
Burgensis in Wistelle - -	1
Buri - - - -	17
Francigenæ - - -	8
Homo - - - -	1
Homines Villæ de Banesberie -	
Homines hortulos habentes -	23
Liberi Homines - - -	26
Milites [1] - - -	6
Piscatores - - -	4
Presbyter - - - -	1
Servi - - - - -	963
Villani - - - - -	3,545
	6,775

No enumeration of the inhabitants of the city of OXFORD occurs in Domesday. [2] At the formation of the Survey there were 243 houses within and without the walls which paid geld; and 478 so dilapidated, from different causes, that they could not pay it.

The owners of 186 inhabited and of 126 waste houses are enumerated, most of whom are persons not residing in the town; but some appear to be resident burgesses.

---

[1] Numerous milites, of a higher class, are enumerated among the under-tenants.

[2] " Unus burgensis de Oxeneford " occurs in the Survey of Buckinghamshire, fol. 143 b. col. 1.

The greater part of these, however, are distinguished by the appellation of *Murales*. Robert de Oilgi occurs in this list as the owner of " XII. mansiones reddentes LXIV. denarios: ex his IIII. sunt vastæ." Robert de Oilgi's property in the city of Oxford is again mentioned, fol. 158, col. 2. " Idem Robertus habet XLII. domos hospitatas in Oxeneford, tam intra murum quam extra. Ex his XVI. reddunt geld et gablum. Aliæ neutrum reddunt quia præ paupertate non possunt, et VIII. mansiones habet vastas, et XXX. acras prati juxta murum, et molinum X. solid. Totum valet III. lib. et pro uno manerio tenet cum Beneficio Sancti Petri."

The customary rents and services of the burgesses of Oxford have been already enlarged upon, vol. i. pp. 193, 194.

RUTLANDSHIRE.

Tenants in capite	7
Under-tenants	4
Bordarii	109
Presbyteri	7
Sochemanni	5
Villani	730
	862

The churches mentioned in the last paragraph of Rutlandshire, fol. 294, had been first given by King William the Conqueror to the church of Westminster. The following is the passage relating to them in his earliest charter to that monastery : " Preterea quidem in Rotelande ei (*sc.* Cœnobio) subdidi duas matres Ecclesias, Ocham videlicet et Hameldonam et Ecclesiam S. Petri in Stanford ad prædictam Hameldonam pertinentem et quicquid ad eandem pertinet," &c. Chartul. Abb. Westmon. MS. Cotton. Faust A. III. fol. 40. This charter also gives to Westminster Abbey the churches of Yppingeham and Werlea in Rutlandshire. These are not specified in the Survey, unless they are two of the three churches mentioned under Redlinctune in fol. 293 b.

SHROPSHIRE.

Tenants in capite - - -	9
Under-tenants - - -	199
Ancillæ - - - -	52
Bordarii - - - -	1,157
Bovarii - - - -	384
Burgenses Francigenæ in Civitate[1] -	43
———— Abbatiæ de Sciropesb. in Civitate - - - -	39[2]
———— Episcopi Cestræ, in Civitate	6[3]
———— pertinentes ad Ecclesiam S. Aclmundi - - -	21[4]
———— pertinentes ad Ecclesiam S. Julianæ - - -	2[5]
———— pertinentes ad Manerium de Melam - - -	9
———— in Vdecote - -	1
Canonici in Sciropesb. - -	28
———— Ecclesiæ de Alnodestrev. -	8
Capellani Comitis Rogeri - -	
Coliberti - - - -	13
Cotarii - - - -	15
Cozets - - - -	9
Custos Apium - - -	1
Carried forward - -	1,996

---

[1] Linc. fol. 252. [2] Ibid. [3] Ibid. col. 2.
[4] Fol. 253. [5] Ibid. [6] Fol. 260 b.

Brought forward - -	1,996
Fabri - - - -	8
Feminæ cotar. - - - -	9
Franci Homines - - -	2
Francigenæ - - - -	33
Francigenæ servientes - - -	3
Homines - - - -	21
Homines arantes - - -	3
Hospites - - - -	7
Liber Bovarius - - -	1
Liberi Homines - - - -	14
Milites - - - -	6
Molinarius - - -	1
Prepositi - - - -	9
Presbyteri - - - -	50
Radchenistri - - - -	3
Radmans - - - -	167
Servi - - - -	871
Servientes - - - -	6
Viduæ feminæ - - - -	2
Villani - - -	1,788
Villani integri - - -	4
Villani dimidii - - -	9
Waleis, Walenses - - -	67
	5,080

In the time of King Edward the Confessor there were
252 houses in SHREWSBURY, inhabited by the same
number of burgesses, who paid gable.

At the time of the Survey the English burgesses com-
plained that they paid the whole geld which had been
paid in King Edward's time, although Earl Roger's
castle occupied fifty-one masures, and fifty more lay

waste. The geld was for a hundred hides. Forty-three foreign burgesses held masures which had paid T. R. E., but did not pay at the Survey; and 39 burgesses who did not pay, were given by the Earl to the Abbey. In the whole, 193 masures did not pay geld. The Bishop of Chester had sixteen masures, and as many burgesses, T. R. E. Of these ten had become waste; the remaining six still paid customary rent.

The penalties which King Edward the Confessor had in demesne in Shrewsbury have been already enlarged upon in vol. i. pp. 200, 201. The custom of the moneyers of Shrewsbury also, will be found vol. i. p. 176.

To the observations in the former pages here referred to, should be added, that from the circumstance of King Edward having penalties for breach of the peace, forestel, and heinfare, all over England, *extra firmas*, it is to be inferred that ferms of the revenue were not uncommon T. R. E.; although Mr. Hallam thought he found no instance in Domesday except that of Huntingdon.

SOMERSETSHIRE.

Tenants in capite	-	-	-	80
Under-tenants	-	-	-	368
Bordarii	-	-	-	4,770
Burgenses in Alsebruge [1]	-	-	32 [2]
—————— in Bada [3]	-	-	-	154
—————— in Briuuetone, Brumetone [4]			17
—————— in Givelcestre [5]	-	-	108 [6]
—————— in Lanporth [7]	-	-	39

Carried forward   -   -   **5,568**

---

[1] Axbridge.

[2] " In Alsebruge, xxxii. burgenses redd. xx. solid."
Somers. fol. 86, col. 1.

[3] Bath.

[4] Both these names mean the same place, Brewton, anciently a town of some consequence.   See Collinson's Somersetshire, vol. i. p. 40.   The entries relating to it are, fol. 86 b. col. 1, " Rex tenet Brometone.   Ibi v. burgenses et unus porcarius."   A single burgess occurs in another entry, fol. 95, col. 2, which will be quoted below.   Fol. 97 b. under Pidecome, " In Briuuetone xi. burgenses redd. xxiii. sol."

[5] Ilchester.

[6] Fol. 86 b. " In Givelcestre sunt cvii. burgenses redd. xx. solid."   On the Earl of Moretaine's tenanted lands under Cari, fol. 95, col. 2, it is said, " Et unus burgensis in Giuelecestre et alter in Briuueton redd. xvi. denar. et obolum."

[7] Langport. " Ibi Burgum quod vocatur Lanporth, in quo manent xxxiiii. Burgenses redd. xv. solid. et ii. piscariæ redd. x. sol. Reddit per annum lxxix. lib. et x.

Brought forward	-	-	5,568
Burgenses in Milebourne [1]	-	-	67
———— in Tantone [2]	-	-	64
Coliberti	-	-	218
Coscez	-	-	43
Cotarii	-	-	327
Fabri	-	-	8 [3]
Gablatores [4]	-	-	7
Homines	-	-	4
Piscatores	-	-	10 [5]
Porcarii	-	-	35
Presbyteri	-	-	5
Servi	-	-	2,110
Villani	-	-	5,298

13,764

BATH is said to have had, at the time of the Survey, 64 burgesses belonging to the King, and 90 belonging to other persons. The latter number probably includes the scattered burgesses who are recorded in different

---

solid. et VII. denar. de XX^ti. in Ora." fol. 86. " Rex tenet Nortcvri. Huic Manerio pertinent v. Burgenses in Langporth redd. XXXVIII. denar." fol. 86 b.

[1] Milbourn-Port. Under the manor of Combe, belonging to the Church of St. Edward : " In Meleburne VI. burgenses redd. L. denar." fol. 91, col. 2. Upon the Earl of Moretaine's tenanted lands, " Warmundus tenet de Comite in Meleburne I. hid. — et v. burgenses redd. III. solid."

[2] Taunton. " Episcopus Wintoniensis tenet Tantone. Ibi LXIIII. burgenses reddentes XXXII. solid." fol. 87 b. col. 1.

[3] All in the vill of Glastonbury, fol. 90.

[4] Payers of gable rent.

[5] All in the Isle of Mere at Glastonbury.

folios, and of whom 24 are entered as belonging to the Church of Bath.   The entries of these are given in a note below. [1]

BRISTOL occurs once; two houses in Bath, and ten in Bristol, are entered as appended to the manor of Bichevrde held under the Bishop of Coutance.   Bristol is chiefly accounted for in Gloucestershire,[2] where burgesses are mentioned, but without a specification of their number.

---

[1] Cainesham, fol. 87, col. 2.   " Huic Manerio pertinent VIII. burgenses in Bade reddentes v. sol. per annum." Under Ciwetune, " In Bade IIII. burgenses redd. XL. denar." On the land of the Bishop of Coutance at Liteltone, fol. 89, col. 1, " In Bada I. burgensis reddens xv. denar." Fol. 89 b.   " Ecclesia S. Petri de Bada habet in Burgo ipso XXIIII. burgenses reddentes xx. solid."

[2] See the Survey, *Glouc.* fol. 163, col. 2.   164 b.

STAFFORDSHIRE.

Tenants in capite - - -	32
Under-tenants - - -	138
Ancilla - - - -	1
Angli - - - -	10
Bordarii - - - -	912
Burgenses in Tamworde - -	12 [1]
———— in Burgo de Stadford -	36 [2]
Canonici Lecefelle - -	5
———— in Statford - -	18
Francigenæ - - -	6 [3]
Homines de Mercato de Tuteberie	42 [4]
Liberi Homines - -	13
Milites - - - -	5
Servi - - - -	212
Servientes - - -	2
Teini - - - -	6
Villani - - - -	1,728
	3,178

[1] Fol. 246, col. 2. 246 b. col. 2. Four burgesses in Wige-tone, and eight in Draitone. WIGGINGTON is a hamlet in the parish of Tamworth, situated about two miles north-east of Tamworth Church. Half of Tamworth, with the church, is in Staffordshire, which makes Tamworth always considered a parish of this county. The other half, that in which the castle is situated, is in Warwickshire: in which county, ten burgesses of Tamworth will hereafter be found enumerated.

[2] Fol. 246, col. 1. 248, col. 1.

[3] In one of the entries, fol. 247, " IIII. francig. et alii homines de eis."

[4] Fol. 248 b. col. 1.

King William had 18 burgesses in STAFFORD in demesne, beside 8 " manses," which are said to have been " wastæ." He had also 22 manses " de Honore Comitis," of which 17 only were inhabited. Eighteen more burgesses of Stafford were appendant to the manor of Mertone, held under Earl Roger by the Monastery of St. Evroul in Normandy.

The manses held in Stafford by tenants in capite of the County were 131 in number, of which 38 were " wastæ," and apparently unoccupied. The rents from the customary payments of the Town had diminished.

SUFFOLK.

Tenants in capite	-	-	-	-	74 [1]
Under-tenants	-	-	-	-	625
Abbatia S. Edmundi *sc.*					
Presbyteri, Diac. et Cler. S. E.	30				
Nonnæ et Pauperes	-	-	28		
Servientes Abbatiæ	-	-	75		
Manentes super terram Pre-					
positi	-	-	-	13	
Bordarii	.	-	-	27 [2]	
Milites S. E. inter Fr. et Angl.	34	——			207 [3]
Bordarii	-	-	-	-	6,205

Carried forward	-	- 7,111

---

[1] The Vavassores Regis, who form the 74th head of lands in capite, *Suff.* foll. 446, 446 b. 447, in the individual entries are called " Liberi Homines," without mention of their names; their total is 56, and is added to their class in the present Abstract.

[2] In *Suff.* fol. 439 b. we have, in Wica, " Semper II. bord. et sub eis II. *liberi homines* IIII. acr."

[3] This is the only account which occurs in the Domesday Survey of the number of retainers and servants belonging to a Monastery. The monks are not enumerated. The Record supplies a similar detail, but to a larger extent, of the retainers and servants of the monastery in the time of King Edward the Confessor. There were then 118 homagers living " ad victum monachorum," and under them 52 bordarii; 52 " liberi satis inopes;" and 43 elemosynarii who had 43 bordarii under them; making a total of 310.

The whole number of houses upon the Abbey demesne at the time of the Survey was 342.

Brought forward - - -	7,111
Dimidii Bordarii - - -	11
Bovarii - . - - -	4
Burgenses in Beccles - - - -	26 [1]
———— in Clare - - - -	43 [2]
———— in Dunewic - - -	316 [3]
———— in Eye - - - -	25 [4]
———— in Gipewiz - - -	210 [5]
———— in Sudberie - - -	118 [6]
Fabri - - - - -	2
Filii liberi hominis commendati - -	3 [7]
Franci Homines - - - -	29
Fratres tres et mater eorum - - -	4 [8]
Homines - - - -	103
Homines Bordarii - - - -	10 [9]
Homines Dimidii - - - -	3
Liberæ Feminæ - - - -	23
Liberæ Feminæ commendatæ - -	7
Libera Femina sub-commendata - -	1 [10]
Liberi Homines - - - -	5,344 [11]
Liberi Homines commendati - -	1,895
Liberi Homines commendatione tantum -	2 [12]
Carried forward - - -	15,290

---

[1] *Suff.* foll. 369 b. 370.   [2] Fol. 389 b.   [3] Fol. 311 b.
[4] " Modo unum mercatum et unus parcus, et in Mercato xxv. Burgenses." fol. 319 b.
[5] Fol. 290.   [6] Fol. 286 b.   [7] Fol. 319.
[8] Fol. 309.   [9] Fol. 290 b.   [10] Fol. 309 b.
[11] An entry occurs in Suffolk, fol. 318, where " liberi homines " are said to be under a " liber homo." " In Suttuna tenet idem W. de R. Malet ii. liberos homines commendatos Edrico LXI. acr. *et sub* i. *ex ipsis* v. *liberi homines.*"
[12] Fol. 374 b.

Brought forward - - - 15,290
Liberi Homines additi commendatione -   25 [1]
Liberi Homines commendati cuidam com-
mendato -   -   -   -   2 [2]
Dimidii Liberi Homines -   -   -   55 [3]
Dimidii Liberi Homines commendati -   78
Dimidii Liberi Homines sub-commendati -   28
Milites -   -   -   -   -   2 [4]
Monachi in Ecclesia de Wisseta -   -   12 [5]
Monetarii [6] -   -   -   -
Pauperes Homines -   -   -   -   178 [7]
Piscatores in Gernemutha -   -   24 [8]
Prepositi -   -   -   -   -   2
Presbyteri -   -   -   -   9
Presbyter sub-commendatus -   -   -   1 [9]
Dimidius Presbyter -   -   -   1 [10]
Servi -   -   -   -   -   909
Sochemanni -   -   -   -   -   998
Sochemanni commendati -   -   -   2 [11]
Sochemanni et Commendati S. E. -   -   60 [12]
Villani -   -   -   -   - 2,812
Dimidii Villani -   -   -   -   2
Uxor liberi hominis commendati -   -   1 [13]

20,491 [14]

---

[1] Fol. 306 b.   [2] Fol. 346 b.
[3] In one instance we have " III. dim. et quarta parte
I. liberi," in Bradefeld, fol. 318. Again, fol. 318 b. " In Mel-
tuna, II. liberi homines commend. Edrici, et I. lib. sub eo."
[4] Fol. 439.   [5] Fol. 293.
[6] No number, fol. 286 b.   [7] In Dunwich, fol. 311 b.
[8] Fol. 283.   [9] Fol. 330.   [10] Fol. 400.
[11] Foll. 326 b. 327.   [12] Fol. 371 b.   [13] Fol. 413 b.
[14] It is very clear that the numbers here enumerated do

In IPSWICH, in King Edward's time, there were 538 burgesses who paid customary rent to the King. At the Survey there were 110 who paid the rent, and 100 poor burgesses who paid a penny per head : 328 mansions which had paid geld, and made the total of 538 for the burgesses at the former period, were wasted. The Church of the Holy Trinity, two Churches dedicated to St. Mary, and the Churches of St. Michael, St. Botulph, St. Laurence, St. Peter, and St. Stephen, in this town, are mentioned in the same entry.[1] Three of these Churches belonged to priests, and others were in lay patronage. One of the Churches of St. Mary belonged to Culling, a burgess. Of the Church of St. Laurence it is said, " Hanc Ecclesiam tenebat Lefflet quædam libera femina T. R. E. quam reclamat Comes Alanus ad feudum Comitis Radulfi, et revocat Ivonem Tailebosc ad liberatorem." Roger de Ramis held a Church in Ipswich dedicated to St. George, with four burgesses and six wasted mansions.[2] Another Church, St. Julian's, belonging to Aluric the son of Rolf, a burgess of Ipswich, is mentioned among the lands of the Vavassors in Suffolk.[3]

In King Edward's time Earl Guert had the third penny of Ipswich.[4]

---

not comprise even all the agricultural tenantry of Suffolk. At the ends of very numerous entries, (see foll. 299, 315, 318, 336 b. 343, 353 b. 356 b. 358, 358 b. 359 b. 360, 363, 363 b. 364 b. 365 b. 366 b. 367, 368, 368 b. 369, 373 b. 380, 384 b. 385, 386, 390, 394 b. 413, 413 b. 428, 436 b. 439,) we read, " Alii ibi tenent :" in others, (foll. 358 b. 365, 366,) " Plures ibi tenent :" in one, (fol. 348 b.) " Alii habent ibi terram :" in another, (fol. 341,) " Alii tenent in istis maneriis."

[1] *Suff.* fol. 290 b.   [2] Fol. 421 b.
[3] Fol. 446.   [4] Foll. 294, 294 b.

One burgess in Ipswich belonged to Robert Malet's manor of Plegeforda.[1] Five burgesses belonged to the Church of St. Peter in Ipswich.[2] Richard son of Earl Gilbert had thirteen burgesses.[3] Forty-one in King Edward's time had belonged to Robert Fitz Wimarc, the commendatio of twenty-six of whom was still in his son Suein of Essex; the other fifteen were dead at the time of the Survey.[4] Ralph the brother of Ilger held " I. mansura vacua et altera hospitata " in Ipswich.[5] Walter the Deacon held five houses and three " mansuræ vacuæ" which had belonged to King Edward the Confessor's queen.[6] Norman the Sheriff had two burgesses.[7]

Two burgesses of Ipswich appertained to a grange near the burgh which in the Confessor's time had belonged to Queen Editha.[8] Two others, who had belonged to Stigand, were dead at the time of the Survey.[9]

BECCLES belonged to the Abbey of St. Edmundsbury. Beside the agricultural tenantry upon the manor, the Abbat had twenty-six burgesses and three parts of the market : the King the fourth. Thirty soc-men, with all customary payments, had twenty bordarii under them.[10]

---

[1] Fol. 314 b.   [2] Foll. 392 b. 393.   [3] Fol. 393.
[4] Fol. 402.   [5] Fol. 425.   [6] Fol. 427.
[7] Fol. 438. The passage has been quoted in a note in the former volume of this work, p. 208.
[8] Fol. 290.
[9] " Dimidium hundret de Gipesuuid. In burgo de Gipeuuid habuit Stigandus II. burgenses T. R. E. cum soca et saca, et Rex habebat consuetudinem. Modo mortui sunt, et Rex habet consuetudinem et socam et sacam;" fol. 289.
[10] Foll. 369 b. 370.

SUDBURY, which in the Confessor's time had belonged to the mother of Earl Morcar, at the time of the Survey belonged to the King. Sixty-three burgesses are described as " halle manentes," and fifty-five as in demesne. The Church of St. Gregory then possessed fifty acres of free land, and twenty-five of meadow. This town had a market, and moneyers, though it is not said how many.[1] The customary rent to the King had risen from £18 to £28.

DUNWICH was an improving place at the time of the Survey. Two bordarii and twenty-four foreigners, upon forty acres, paid rent to the manor. In the Confessor's time there had been 120 burgesses. At the Survey, when in Robert Malet's possession, there were 236, beside 178 " pauperes homines." Two churches out of three had been added. The sea had made an encroachment upon Dunwich, which has been alluded to in the former volume. The customary rent in the total was £50 and 60,000 herrings.[2] Eighty burgesses of Dunwich were attached to the manor of Alneterne, belonging to the Abbey of Ely.[3]

A market at CARAHALLA is recorded as " *de dono* REGIS."[4]

---

[1] " Ibi sunt Monetarii ;" fol. 286 b.

[2] Fol. 311 b.   [3] Fol. 385 b.   [4] Fol. 330 b.

SURREY.

Tenants in capite, including the King,	44
Under-tenants as mesne lords - -	108
Anglicus - - - -	1
Bordarii - - - - -	968
Cotarii - - - -	240
Forestarius - - - -	1
Homines de Gildeford - -	175
Homines de Sudwerca - - -	
Milites - - - -	5
Servi - - - - -	478
Villani - - - -	2,363
	4,383

Odo Bishop of Baieux held a monastery and water-course in SOUTHWARK, both of which had been King Edward's. Of the dues on shipping which lay there, King Edward had received two parts, and Earl Godwin the third. The church and watercourse were claimed for the King, but appear to have been exchanged away by the Bishop of Baieux. The rent from Southwark to the King amounted to 16*l.*

The " homines de Sudwercke " are twice mentioned, but it is not said of what condition they were, nor of what number. They had, however, obtained by legal process a haga and a toll which had been held by Earl Eustace.[1]

The Archbishop of Canterbury had four masures in Southwark,[2] Richard Fitz Gilbert had three hagæ,[3] and

---

[1] *Surr*. fol. 32.   [2] Fol. 30 b. col. 2.
[3] Fol. 34 b. col. 1.

Earl Roger four masures.[1] Sixteen masuræ belonged to the King's manor of Merton in Surrey.[2] St. Peter's, Westminster, had a bordarius in Southwark.[3]

In GUILDFORD, at the time of the Survey, the King had seventy-five hagæ, on which 175 homagers were resident. Of these, Ralph the clerk had three hagæ, upon which six homagers were resident. Some of the hagæ appear to have been surreptitiously obtained by the persons who possessed them at the Survey. Domesday makes no allusion to any corporate privileges in this place.[4]

Thirteen burgesses of London are recorded to have belonged to the manor of Bermondsey, T. R. E.;[5] and nineteen at the time of the Survey belonged to the Church of Lambeth.

---

[1] Fol. 36 b. col. 1.   [2] Fol. 30, col. 2.
[3] Fol. 32, col. 2.   [4] Fol. 30, col. 1.   [5] Ibid. col. 2.

SUSSEX.

Tenants in capite - - -	15
Under-tenants - - -	534
Berquarii - - -	10
Bordarii - - - -	2,497
Burgenses in Bolintun - -	20
———— in Cicestre - -	9
———— in Hastinges -	4
———— in Lewes - -	53
———— in Novo Burgo -	64 [1]
———— in Pevenesel - -	110
Clerici - - - -	7 [2]
Cotarii - - -	765
Molinarius - - - -	1
Presbyteri - - -	3
Servi - - - -	420
Villani - - - -	5,898
	10,410

At Chichester, in King Edward's time, ninety-eight "hagæ" are enumerated. These hagæ were inclosed plats of ground upon which houses stood. How many houses the total number contained cannot be conjectured. From the rent which one haga produced, it may be supposed that more than one house might stand upon a haga: [3] as is clearly shown at Guildford in

---

[1] *Suss.* fol. 17.

[2] The " Clerici Ecclesiæ de Bosgrave," fol. 26, are included in the enumeration of the Under-tenants.

[3] " Habet Rannulfus clericus III. hagas ubi manent VI. homines." Eleven " hagæ " in Chichester belonged to

Surrey, in page 495. At the time of the Survey, it is said, there were more houses than had been there in former time (probably King Edward's) by sixty. But here is no clue to the population of Chichester in 1086. Nine burgesses only, as above, are incidentally enumerated in the Survey. The city of Chichester is said to have been " in manu Roberti Comitis."

At LEWES, King Edward the Confessor had a hundred and thirty-seven burgesses in demesne; but the number of them at the time of the Survey, royal or other, is not mentioned. Fifty-three, like the nine burgesses of Chichester, occur incidentally in different pages. The inhabitants of Lewes had probably increased, as the annual value of the burgh, which in the Confessor's time had been rated at 26*l.*, had risen under the Conqueror to 34*l.* In subsequent entries to that which describes the town, it appears that William de Warene, at the time of the Survey, was the superior lord of a hundred and forty-seven " hagæ" and eleven " masuræ;" these are entered as part and parcel of distinct manors, held either by him or his under-tenants.

At CASTLE ARUNDEL, as it is called, we have the produce of the town, port, and dues from vessels, rated at 12*l.* a year; but the whole entry affords no materials whatever for estimating the number of inhabitants.

At PEVENSEY, in King Edward's time, there were twenty-four burgesses belonging to the King's demesne. The Bishop of Chichester had five; Edmer the priest two; Ormer the priest five; Doda the priest three. At the Survey, the Earl of Moretaine had sixty bur-

---

the royal manor of Boseham, *Suss.* fol. 16; three to the manor of Tangemere, ibid. fol. 16 b.; and six to the manor of Seleisie, ibid. fol. 17.

gesses,[1] the monks of Moretaine eight, and forty-two appertained to other individuals.

In the burgh of STEYNINGES, a hundred and twenty-four " masuræ " occur.   It is added, " ad curiam operantur sicut villani T. R. E."

---

[1] The Earl of Moretaine appears to have had a residence at Apedroc: " Ibi est una virgata ubi Comes habet aulam suam.   Similiter Heraldus Comes habuit, et abstulit S. Johanni."

WARWICKSHIRE.

Tenants in capite	-	-	-	55
Under-tenants	-	-	-	176
Ancillæ	-	-	-	34
Bordarii	-	-	-	1,775 [1]
Burgenses in Tameuorde	-	-	10 [2]
————— in Warwic	-	-	22 [3]
Coliberti	-	-	-	6
Fabri	-	-	-	2
Flandrenses	-	-	-	9 [4]
Francigenæ	-	-	-	12
Francones Homines	-	-	3 [5]
Homines	-	-	-	13

Carried forward   -   - 2,117

[1] Of these, one hundred were living in the suburbs of Warwick: " Extra burgum c. bord. cum hortulis suis redd. L. solidos." *Warw.* fol. 238, col. 2.

[2] " Rex tenet Coleshelle — in Tameuorde x. burgenses huic Manerio pertin." Ibid. fol. 238, col. 2. Other burgesses of Tamworth will be found in the Abstract of Staffordshire. See the present volume, p. 486.

[3] See foll. 238, col. 1, 242, col. 1, and 244, col. 2, under Haselove. The two burgesses mentioned in fol. 242 belonged to Hugh de Grentemaisnil's manor of Mersetone.

[4] Estone; on the lands of Osbern Fitz Richard. " Ibi sunt IX. Flandrenses et XVI. villani cum presbytero." fol. 244, col. 1.

[5] They were upon the same property at Berdingeberie in King Edward's time. " Ibi sunt III. francones homines cum IIII. villanis. Ipsi homines francones tenuerunt libere T. R. E." fol. 241, col. 2.

Brought forward	- -	2,117
Liberi Homines	- - -	19
Milites	- - - -	17
Milites Angli	- - -	5
Presbyteri	- - -	66
Servi	- - - -	845 [1]
Taini	- - , - -	5
Villani	- - -	3,500

6,574

The condition and customary services of WARWICK at the time of the Survey have been already stated vol. i. p. 198. The King had 113 houses in demesne. His barons, 112. Beside these, 19 burgesses had as many masures, with sac and soc. Houses in Warwick occur in several folios, belonging to different manors, some of which seem to be enumerated among the 112 already mentioned as belonging to the barons.[2]

---

[1] Lands "inter servos et ancillas" occur fol. 244, col. 2, but no number of either mentioned.

[2] See foll. 238 b, col. 1. 242 b, col. 1. 243, col. 1, 2.

WILTSHIRE.

Tenants in capite	- - -	156
Under-tenants	- - -	286
Angli	- - - -	4
Anglicus	- - - -	1 [1]
Bordarii	- - -	2,754
Burgenses in Bedvinde	- -	25 [2]
—————— in Bradeford	- -	33 [3]
—————— in Cauna, Calne	-	73 [4]
—————— in Crichelade	- -	33 [5]
—————— in Domnitone	- -	2 [6]
—————— in Draicote	- -	1 [7]
—————— in Gardone	- -	1 [8]
—————— in Guerminstre [9]	-	30
Carried forward	- -	3,399

---

[1] *Wilts,* fol. 69 b.   [2] Fol. 64 b, col. 2.

[3] Fol. 67 b, col. 1.

[4] Foll. 64 b, col. 2. 65. 66, col. 1. 70, col. 1.

[5] Foll. 65. 66, col. 1. 66 b, col. 1. 67, col. 2. 67 b, col. 2.
69, col. 2. 70 b, col. 2. 73 b, col. 1.

[6] Fol. 67 b, col. 2.   [7] Fol. 74 b, col. 1.

[8] Fol. 67, col. 2.

[9] Fol. 64 b, col. 2. Warminster: a royal manor. " Hoc
manerium reddit firmam unius noctis cum omnibus con-
suetudinibus suis." The obligation to find the King a
lodging, with his suite, for one night, was demanded, and
paid by the lord of the manor and baron of Warminster
to King George the Third, on Monday the 13th September
1786, the King, Queen, and Princesses being entertained at
Longleat by the Lord Viscount Weymouth.

Charles the Second was likewise entertained in the same
way in 1663, when Sir James Thynne possessed it. See

Brought forward - -	3,399
Burgenses in Malmesberie -	8 [1]
—————— in Smitecote - -	1 [2]
—————— in Sudtone - -	5 [3]
—————— in Theodulveside -	66 [4]
—————— in Wiltune - -	17 [5]
Coliberti - - -	260
Coscez - - - -	1,418
Cotarii - - -	279
Franci - - - -	2
Francigenæ - - -	3
Mellitarii - - - -	9
Milites - - - -	3
Porcarii - - - -	87
Potarii [6] - - - -	—
Presbyter - - - -	1
Rustici - - - -	4 [7]
Servi - - - - -	1,539 [8]
Villani - - - -	3,049 [9]
	10,150

Sir R. Hoare's Hist. of Modern Wiltshire, Hund. of Warminster, p. 1.

[1] Foll. 66 b, col. 1. 67, col. 1. 69 b, col. 2. 70 b, col. 2.
71. 72 b, col. 1.

[2] Fol. 70 b, col. 2.   [3] Fol. 72, col. 2.

[4] Fol. 65, col. 1.

[5] Foll. 65, col. 2. 66, col. 1. 69, col. 1. 70 b, col. 1. 72 b,
col. 2. 73 b, col. 1.

[6] No number enumerated. Fol. 65.

[7] Fol. 74, col. 1.

[8] In the western counties of Wilts, Dorset, Devon, and
Somerset, the Servi are usually ranked, or at least placed,
before the Villani and Bordarii.

[9] Villani occur under Newetone, fol. 67 b, col. 2, without
any number.

MALMESBURY, like Wallingford in Berkshire, fur-
nished soldiers for the army.   Sixty-five masures, seven
halves, and a quarter of a masure, are enumerated in
that town, with nine coscez " foris burgum," who paid
geld with the burgesses.   Walter Hosed, from two divi-
sions of the burgh of Malmesbury, paid 8*l.* to the
King.   The whole town paid the same sum in the time
of King Edward the Confessor.[1]   The military service
of the town consisted in either paying twenty shillings
to the King " ad pascendos suos buzecarl," or in fur-
nishing him with one man " pro honore v. hidarum;"
which shows that twenty shillings was the commutation
for the service of one man.

Only 17 burgesses of WILTON are mentioned; but
as the revenue to the Crown was 50*l.* the number of
burgesses must have been far greater.

We have no mention whatever of burgesses, or of the
borough of SALISBURY; but, fol. 64 b, col. 1, we have
" De tertio denario Sarisberie habet Rex VI. lib." and
fol. 66, col. 1, " Episcopus tenet Sarisberie.   Ibi xxv.
villani et L. bord."   Neither is MARLBOROUGH mentioned as a borough.

In different folios, as the references show, 33 burgesses of CREEKLADE are mentioned: exclusive of whom,
those which belonged to the Abbey of Westminster are
to be reckoned.   Under title IX. of this county, " QUOD
HABET SANCTUS PETRUS WESTMONASTERIENSIS," it is
said, " Ecclesia S. Petri Westmonast. tenet æcclesiam
de Crichelade, et habet ibi *plures burgenses,* et tertium
denarium ejusdem villæ.   Totum simul reddit IX. lib."

---

[1] It is then said, " et in hac firma erant placita Hundret
de Cicementone et Sutelesberg quæ Regi pertinebant,"
which shows that the revenues from Malmesbury were also
farmed before the Conquest.

WORCESTERSHIRE.

Tenants in capite	- -	28
Under-tenants	- - -	129
Ancillæ	- - -	101.[1]
Bedellus	- - -	1[2]
Bordarii	- - -	1,728
Bovarii	- - - -	73
Burgenses in Wiche	- -	113[3]
———— in Cochehi	- -	1[4]
———— in Mortune	- -	1[5]
———— in Persore	- -	28[6]
———— in Wircestre	- -	8
Buri	- - - -	3[7]

Carried forward   - - 2,214

---

[1] We have here the largest number of Ancillæ which occurs in any county. The Glossary upon ancient services, quoted in the present Volume, p. 453, has a sentence on the allowances to the Ancillæ. " Uni ANCILLÆ (contingunt) VII. pondia annonæ ad victum, unam ovem vel iii^d ad hyemale companagium, unum sester fabæ ad quadragesimale convictum. In æstate suum hpeiȝ, vel i^d."

[2] The same Glossary gives the reward of the Bedellus for his services. " BEDELLO pertinet ut pro servitio suo liberior sit ab operatione quam alii homines, quia sepius est impeditus, et etiam ei convenit ut aliquam terræ partiunculam habeat pro labore suo."

[3] See *Worc.* foll. 174, col. 2. 174 b, col. 2. 176, col. 1. 176 b, col. 1, 2. 177, col. 1. 177 b, col. 2.

[4] Fol. 177 b, col. 1.   [5] Fol. 176 b, col. 1.

[6] These belonged to the Abbey of Westminster.

[7] An interlineation above reads " Coliberti." See vol. i. p. 85.

Brought forward	- -	2,214
Coliberti	- - -	6
Cotarii	- - - -	41
Cotmanni	- - -	19
Custodes Silvæ [1]	- - -	
Fabri	- - - -	7
Francigenæ	- - -	24
Francigenæ Servientes	- -	2
Homo	- - - -	1
Liberi Homines	- - -	4
Molinarii	- - -	2
Monachus unus in Ecclesia de Evesham positus [2]	- -	1
Prepositi	- - - -	7
Presbyteri	- - -	59
Radchenistri	- - -	3
Carried forward	- -	2,388

[1] Fol. 172, col. 2.

[2] Fol. 176, col. 1. Although one monk of Evesham only is here mentioned, there can be little doubt but that the Monastery, at the time of the Domesday Survey, had at least one hundred inmates. The Evesham Register, which has been quoted under Gloucestershire, contains an entry, little if at all later than the time of Henry the First, from which we learn that this Abbey, half a century later than Domesday, contained a hundred and thirty-one inhabitants, exclusive of twelve monks who had been despatched by King William Rufus to Otheneseie in Denmark, a Cell to Evesham: *viz.* ¶. " LXVII. monachi fuerunt in Evesham et ex hiis fuerunt XII. in Denemarcia quos Rex Willielmus juvenis illuc transmisit; et v. Moniales, tres Pauperes ad mandatum, tres Clerici, qui omnes habent tantum quantum Monachi. LXV. Servientes fuerunt in Monasterio; scilicet v. in Ecclesia, duo in domo infirmorum, II. in cellario, v. in

Brought forward	-	-	-	2,388
Radmans	-	-	-	33
Rustici Porcarii		-	-	2
Salinarii	-	-	-	3 [1]
Servi	-	-	-	677
Venator		-	-	1
Vidua una	-	-	-	1
Villani	-	-	-	1,520

4,625

The account of the city of WORCESTER, in the first column of Worcestershire, refers to the rents, customs, and services of the place only: there is no enumeration of the burgesses; seven of whom, however, occur in other folios,[2] and one is mentioned in the Survey of Herefordshire as attached to the manor of Suchelei. [3]

Houses in Worcester are enumerated in various entries. Ninety are mentioned as appendant to the Bishop of Worcester's manor of Norwiche. Of these, the Bishop himself held forty-five in demesne; Urso held twenty-four; Osbern Fitz Richard, eight; Walter

---

coquina, VII. in pristino,[a] IIII. qui faciunt cervisiam, IIII. sertores,[b] II. in balneario, II. sutores, II. in pomerio, III. ortolani, I. ad hostium claustri, II. ad magnam portam, V. ad vineam, IIII. qui serviunt monachis quando pergunt foras, et IIII. piscatores; IIII. in cambra[c] abbatis, III. in aula, II. vigilantes."

[1] Under Bremesgrave, " Huic Manerio pertinent III. Salinæ in Wich, et III. salinarii reddentes de his Salinis CCC. mittas salis, quibus dabantur T. R. E. CCC. caretedes lignorum a custodibus silvæ." *Worc.* fol. 172, col. 2.

[2] See foll. 176, col. 2. 177 b, col. 1, 2. 178, col. 1.

[3] Fol. 180 b, col. 2.

---

[a] *Sc.* pistrino.   [b] sartores.   [c] camera.

Ponther, eleven; and Robert Dispenser, one. Vrso also held twenty-five houses of the Bishop in the market-place of Worcester, whioh paid 100s. per annum.[1] The Abbey of Evesham held twenty-eight masures in Worcester, five of which were wasted.[2] One house was appendant to Earl Roger's manor of Hala, and one to Urso d'Abetot's manor of Osmerlie.[3] One house belonged to the manor of Chideminstre.[4] Houses in Worcester were also attached to several manors in Herefordshire. Three belonged to the royal manor of Merlie in that county,[5] one to Halsede, two to Fecheham,[6] one to Buselie;[7] and three masures in Worcester, paying thirty pence yearly, belonged to the Church of Hereford, as appendant to its manor of Cotingtune.[8]

When Worcestershire paid geld, the City of Worcester was rated at fifteen hides.

Houses and Salinæ in WICH are numerously mentioned.

---

[1] *Worc.* fol. 173 b.
[2] Fol. 175 b, col. 2.
[3] Foll. 176, 177 b, col. 1.
[4] Fol. 172.
[5] *Heref.* fol. 180 b, col. 1.
[6] Ibid.
[7] Ibid. col. 2.
[8] Fol. 182, col. 2.

YORKSHIRE.

Tenants in capite	105[1]
Under-tenants	222[2]
Bordarii	1,819
Burgenses in Bretlinton	4[3]
———— in Dadesleia, Stantone, et	
Helgebi	31[4]
———— in Poclinton	15[5]
Burgenses minuti in Tateshale	60[6]
Censarii, Censores, Censorii	54
Clericus	1
Coteri, in Tateshale	16[7]
Ferrarii	6
Francus homo	1
Homines	30
Liberi homines	2
Milites	26
Carried forward	2,392

[1] Twenty-nine only of these were greater landholders. The rest were chiefly persons who are called the King's Thanes, who had once had large possessions, but now only held the ravaged remainder of them.

[2] The under-tenants in Yorkshire, compared with the extent of the lands, were few. · The whole of the Earl of Moretaine's lands in Yorkshire appear to have had but two under-tenants as mesne lords, Nigellus and Ricardus Sur Dive. There are no under-tenants recorded upon the Terra Regis.

[3] Fol. 299 b, col. 1.   [4] Fol. 319, col. 1.
[5] Fol. 299 b, col. 1.   [6] Fol. 316 b, col. 1.   [7] Ibid.

Brought forward	-	-	2,392
Prebendarius	-	-	-	1
Presbyteri	-	-	-	-	136
Sochemanni	-	-	-	447
Villani	-	-	-	-	5,079
				8,055

In the time of King Edward the Confessor there were six shires in YORK, beside the shire of the Archbishop. One of these shires, at the time of the Survey, had been demolished to make room for the castles. In the other five shires there were 1,418 " mansiones hospitatæ." In the shire of the Archbishop there were, T. R. E., 189 " mansiones hospitatæ ;" so that the full number of those " mansiones " was 1,597, beside the shire which was afterwards sacrificed to the castles. The whole number may be presumed to have been 1,800 or thereabout. The Curia of the Archbishop and the houses of the Canons not included in this estimate.

Of the houses within the King's shire, T. R. W., there were 391 which paid rent; 400 inhabited occasionally, which did not pay the ancient rents; 540 which were empty and paid nothing; and 145 held by Francigenæ. One hundred and fifty-four " mansiones" and an " hospitium" are next enumerated, possessed by different persons, which are probably included in the preceding enumeration. At the time of the Survey, 100 houses, great and small, were inhabited in the Archbishop's shire, exclusive of the Curia and houses of the Canons.

The whole number of " Domus hospitatæ " at the time of the Survey may be therefore reckoned at 1,036.

In one of the " mansiones" T. R. E. Gamel lived with four dingis.

There were four " Judices" in York T. R. E., but the privilege which they enjoyed by the King's writ is not clearly expressed.

Eighty-four carucates of land gelded with the city of York T. R. E., being probably the quantity of land within the bounds and jurisdiction of the city. The amount of the geld is not stated.

The ravage of the Conqueror's arms in YORKSHIRE in 1069 has already been detailed. It will account for the paucity of cultivators which marks this part of the Domesday Survey.[1] Upon four hundred and eleven manors, in folios 300, 300 b, 301, 301 b, and the first column of fol. 302, the only inhabitants enumerated are thirty-five villani and eight bordarii.

---

[1] The desolation extended to a portion of Lancashire.

TOTAL

OF

RECORDED POPULATION.

The Tenants in Capite, including Ecclesiastical
Corporations, amounted scarcely to - 1,400
Under-tenants - - - - 7,871
Aloarii - - - - 5
Ancillæ - - - - 467
Angli, Anglici - - - - 26
Bedelli - - - - - 22
Berquarii - - - - 10
Bordarii - - - - 82,119
Bordarii pauperes - - - - 490
Dimidii Bordarii - - - 15
Bovarii - - - - 749
Burgenses - - - - 7,968
Buri, Burs - - - - 62
Canonici - - - - 59
Capellani - - - - —
Carpentarius - - - - 1
Censarii, Censores, Censorii - - 159
Cervisarii - - - - 40
Clerici - - - - - 10
Coliberti - - - - 858
Coscets, Coscez - - - - 1,749
Cotarii - - - - 5,054
Coteri - - - - - 16

Carried forward - - 109,150

Brought forward   -   - 109,150
Custodes Apium   -   -   -   2
Custos Domus Regis   -   -   -   1
Custos Hundret   -   -   -   1
Custos Molini   -   -   -   1
Diaconus   -   -   -   -   1
Drenghs   -   -   -   -   6
Fabri   -   -   -   -   64
Famuli Regis   -   -   -   -   2
Femina   -   -   -   -   1
Feminæ cotar.   -   -   -   -   9
Ferrarii   -   -   -   -   10
Figuli, poters   -   -   -   -   5
Filii liberi hominis commendati   -   -   3
Flandrenses   -   -   -   -   9
Forestarii   -   -   -   -   3
Fossarius quidam   -   -   -   1
Franci   -   -   -   -   50
Francigenæ   -   -   -   -   296
Francigenæ servientes   -   -   -   5
Francones homines   -   -   -   3
Fratres tres et mater eorum   -   -   4
Gablatores   -   -   -   -   7
Homines   -   -   -   - 1,287
Homines arantes   -   -   -   3
Homines commendati   -   -   -   33
Homines consuetudinarii   -   -   8
Homines de Mercato de Tuteberie   -   42
Homines dimidii   -   -   -   -   11
Hospites   -   -   -   -   17
Lagemen   -   -   -   -   -   21
Liber Bovarius   -   -   -   -   1
_____
Carried forward   -   - 111,057

Brought forward - -	- 111,057
Libera femina sub-commendata - -	1
Liberæ feminæ - - - -	31
Liberæ feminæ commendatæ - -	7
Liberi homines - - -	10,097
Liberi homines commendati - -	2,041
Liberi homines faldæ - - -	21
Dimidii liberi homines - - -	224
Dimidius liber homo commendatione tantum - - - -	1
Loricati in custodia de Windesores -	2
Manentes - - - -	16
Manentes apud Abbatiam S. Edmundi -	207
Mellitarii - - - -	9
Mercatores - - - -	24
Mercennarius - - - -	1
Milites - - - - -	137
Milites Anglici - - -	2
Milites Francigenæ - - -	3
Molinarii - - - -	5
Monachi - - - -	13
Monetarii - - - -	—
Moniales - - - -	4
Mulier paupercula - - -	1
Pauperes Homines - - -	178
Piscatores - - - -	111
Porcarii - - - -	427
Prebendarius - - - -	1
Prepositi Villarum - - -	85
Presbyteri - - - -	994
Dimidius Presbyter - - -	1
Radchenistri - - - -	196
Carried forward -	- 125,897

Brought forward - -	125,897
Radmanni, Radmans - - -	369
Rustici - - - -	4
Rustici Porcarii - - - -	2
Salinarii - - - - -	108
Servi - - - - -	25,156
Serviens Comitis Moriton - -	1
Servientes - - - -	12
Servientes Francigenæ - - -	2
Servientes Regis - - -	9
Sochemanni - - - -	23,072
Sochemanni dimidii - - -	18
Teini - - - - -	11
Vaccarii - - - - -	2
Vavassores [1] - - - -	3
Venator - - - - -	1
Viduæ feminæ - - - -	3
Villani - - - - -	108,407
Dimidii Villani - - - -	49
Uxor liberi hominis commendati - -	1
Uxores Villanorum defunctorum - -	4
Waleis, Walenses - - -	111

283,242

[1] It has been already observed in Vol. i. p. 52, that, at the time of the Survey, the title of Vavassor had been sunk in the general name of " Liberi homines." See also the present Volume, p. 488.

GENERAL INDEX.

A.

ABBEY lands, discharge of from tithes, proved by Domesday, i. 358.

ABETOT, Vrso de, account of, i. 364. ii. 36, 402.

ABINGDON, possessions of the Monastery of, i. 363.

———— soldiers of the Abbey, how provided for, in the time of the Conqueror, ii. 196.

ABBOTSBURY Abbey, i. 363.

ABRINCIS, Hugh de, Earl of Chester, account of, i. 437.

ACCIPITRARII, or ANCIPITRARII, i. 91.

ACRE, definition of the term, i. 157.

———— the Normans have one, differing from that of the Saxons, ibid.

———— different proportions of, with the intermediate admensurations, settled in the "Statutum de admensuratione Terrarum" t. Edw. I. i. 158.

ADAM brother of Eudo dapifer, a commissioner for the compilation of Domesday Book, i. 18.

ADELIZA Countess of Albemarle, half-sister of the Conqueror, i. 366.

ADELIZA wife of Hugh de Grentemaisnil, notice of, i. 364.

ADRECI, Norman de, account of, i. 364.

" ADULTERIUM," i. 272.

" ÆCCLESIA sine terra," in the returns from Norfolk and Suffolk, i. 295.

" ÆCCLESIOLÆ" and " Capellæ" of the Survey, i. 297.

ÆLDRED archbishop of York, ii. 5.

ÆLFSTAN abbat of St. Augustine Canterbury, ii. 143.

ÆLVEVA, or ALVEVA, mother of Earl Morcar, i. 345.

ÆLVEVA, a sister of Harold, mentioned in the Survey, i. 309.

" ÆQUALITER et pariliter," a term explanatory of the tenure " in paragio," i. 243.

AERIES of Hawks, noticed, i. 340, 341.

ÆTHELRED, the father of King Edward the Confessor, once mentioned in the Survey, i. 303.

ÆTHELSIE, chamberlain to King Edgar, grant of land from, at Spersholt in Berkshire, to the Abbey of Abingdon, i. 333.

AINCURT, Walterius de, descendants of, i. 265.

AILRIC MARIETI SUNE, ii. 10.

AIULFUS the chamberlain, account of, i. 365.

ALAN Earl of Bretagne and Richmond, i. 226.

———— his castelry in Yorkshire, mentioned in the Survey, i. 221.

———— account of, and descent of his property, i. 366.

ALBAN'S, St., property of the Abbey of, T. R. E. ii. 12.

ALBERTUS Lothariensis, ii. 12.

ALBINGI, or ALBINI, Nigel de, i. 367.

———— account of, i. 368.

ALBRIC, or ALBERICUS, account of the Earl of that name, i. 367.

ALCMUND, St., Shrewsbury, Collegiate Church of, i. 369.

ALFRED, K., the existence of a Survey made by, similar to Domesday, doubted, i. 10, 11.

———— his Dom-Boc, the Code of Saxon Laws, i. 12.

ALGAR, Earl, i. 325.

L.

LACI, Ilbert de, i. 226, 442.

LACI, Roger de, i. 217, 226.

—— account of, i. 442.

—— his gift of land to the Abbey of Lira, i. 329.

LACI, Walter de, circumstances of his death, i. 431.

" LAGEMAN habens socam et sacam super homines suos," i. 225.

LAGEMANNI, LAGEMEN, i. 91, 205. ii. 428, 466, 467.

—————— heriot of the, at Cambridge, i. 269.

LAMBETH, co. Surrey, manor of, given by K. William Rufus to the church of Rochester, i. 307.

—————— possessions of the church of, at the time of the Survey, i. 441.

—————— ornaments belonging to Countess Goda found at, i. 307.

" LAMPRIDULÆ," rent of, at Petersham in Surrey, i. 141.

LANCASHIRE, in part described in Domesday, but not under its own name, i. 35. ii. 429.

LAND, measurement of, in the Survey, i. 145.

LAND-BOCS, or descriptions of the boundaries of lands, appended to Saxon charters, i. 11.

LANDRICUS carpentarius, i. 443.

LANDS, denominations of, i. 95.

LANFRANK, archbishop, his recovery of twenty-five manors from the Bishop of Baieux, i. 321.

—————— account of, and of the allotment of the revenues of his See, i. 394, 443.

LANGETOT, ancient family of, in Suffolk, ii. 346.

LANGPORT, ii. 483.

" LA QUIS, Castellum de," i. 213.

LATIMER, meaning of, i. 91.

LATINARIUS, i. 91.

" LATROCINIUM," i. 285.

LAVATORES, i. 93.

LEAD-WORKS mentioned in the Survey, i. 138.

" LEAD-WALLING," explanation of the term, i. 128.

LEFSTANUS abbat of St. Edmundsbury, ii. 157.

" LEGATI Regis," the King's Commissioners for the formation of Domesday, so stiled, i. 18.

LEGATUS, i. 91.

" LEGREWITA," or " LAIRWITA," i. 285.

LEICESTER, customs of, at the time of the Domesday Survey, i. 198. ii. 464.

LEICESTERSHIRE, Presbyteri in, enumerated in the Survey at no less than forty-one places, i. 290.

—————————— population of, at the Survey, ii. 463.

LEOFRIC, or LEURIC, last bishop of Crediton, ii. 163.

LEOFWINE bishop of Lichfield, ii. 166.

LEOMINSTER, Nunnery and abbess of, i. 363. ii. 1, 346, 347.

LEPELIE, co. Northampt., held by the church of Rheims, i. 324.

—————— Cell afterwards established there, i. 325.

LEST, LAST, or LATHE, the shire-division peculiar to Kent, i. 179.

LEUCA and QUARENTENA of the Survey, i. 159.

LEUCA or LEUGA Anglica, ibid.

LEUEUA abbess of a destroyed monastery at Reading, ii. 160.

LEUEUA abbess of Shaftsbury, ii. 160.

LEUFROY, St., Abbey of, i. 444.

—————— King William the Conqueror's gift of lands at Aissele to, i. 327.

LEUIET presbyter, ii. 161.

LEURIC abbat of Peterborough, ii. 162.

LEURIC cilt, ii. 162.

LEURICUS abbat of Burton, time of his death, i. 8.

Q.

"Quadraria," quarries or stone pits, i. 139.

Quarentena, measure of the, i. 160.

"Quia Emptores," statute of, i. 45.

R.

Rachenistres, or Radchenistres, i. 72, 73.

Rad-cniht, i. 74.

Rad-here, i. 74.

Radmanni, i. 72, 73.

Radulphus Comes, Ralph Guader or Waher, account of, i. 471.

Raleigh, castle of, in Essex, i. 222.

Rameslie, co. Sussex, held of King Edward by the Abbey of Fecamp, i. 324.

Rape, territorial division so called, peculiar to Sussex, i. 179.

—— a military district, i. 180.

"Raptum," i. 281.

Reading, co. Berks, town of, ii. 424.

Recommendati, i. 67.

"Rector," i. 299.

"Rector navis Regis," i. 92.

Reinbaldus or Rembaldus, chancellor to King Edward the Confessor, i. 345.

—————— account of, i. 398.

Reliefs, the Conqueror's law of, i. 269.

Remigius bishop of Lincoln, one of the Conqueror's commissioners for the midland counties at the formation of Domesday, i. 18.

—————— account of, i. 474, 475.

"Revelach," i. 281.

Reveland, explanation of, i. 231.

Revenue, ancient mode of paying in the, at the Exchequer, i. 163.

—————— the farming of, not unusual before the Conquest, ii. 482, 503.

Rheims, church of, its possessions in England, i. 324, 325.

—————— when founded, i. 475.

Ribble and Mersey, lands between the, surveyed in Domesday, part of Lancashire, ii. 429.

Ricardus of Cornwall, the Messrs. Lysons's account of the, ii. 377.

Ricardus venator, i. 111.

Richard, son of William the Conqueror, i. 322.

—————— death of, i. 106.

Richmond Castle in Yorkshire, i. 222.

Riding, territorial subdivision so called, i. 178.

—————— tridingmot, or court of the, i. 178, 179.

"Riehale" and "Belmestorp," lands so named, belonging to Peterborough Abbey, memorandum concerning, in the Black Book of Peterborough, ii. 263.

"Rispalia ad sepes," i. 100.

Robertus filius Wymarche, father of Suein of Essex, i. 489. ii. 206.

Rochester, bishop of, ii. 383.

Rochester, castle of, i. 211.

Rockingham, castle of, i. 218.

Roelent, castle of, in Cheshire, i. 219.

Roelent, Robert de, account of, i. 479.

Roncaria, or Runcaria, i. 101.

Rothais, wife of Richard Fitz Gilbert, account of, i. 481.

Rouen, penny of, i. 169.

Rouen, Abbey of St. Mary, i. 581.

Rouen, Will. the Conq. gift of land at Rovridge in Devonshire to, i. 327.

Rouen, Abbey of the Holy Trinity upon St. Catherine's hill at, i. 481.

—————— Abbey of St. Mary de Prè at, ibid.

Rufus, K. William, original grant from, of the church of Lambeth to Rochester, i. 307.

Rutlandshire, a part of, described in the counties of Northampton and Lincoln, i. 36.

—————— population of, upon the lands under its own title, in the Survey, ii. 479.

—————— churches in, given to Westminster Abbey by the Conqueror, ii. 479.

S.

" Saca," i. 273.
Sacerdos, i. 300.
" Sagena," i. 144.
Salictum parvum, i. 101.
" Salinæ," i. 127.
Salinarii, i. 93.
———— wallers, or boilers of salt, i. 128.
Salisbury, town of, ii. 503.
Salisbury, Edward of, ii. 311.
Salisbury, Osmund bishop of, i. 461.
Salmon fisheries and rents, i. 141.
Salt, rock or fossil, first pits of, discovered in Cheshire in 1670, on a spot where Domesday mentions brine springs, i. 126.
—— different measures for, noticed in the Survey, i. 133.
Salt-pans, conveyances of, in early times, still extant, i. 129.
Salt-works, i. 126.
———— the kinds of, mentioned in Domesday, ibid.
Sandwich, port of, anciently belonging to Christ Church Canterbury, ii. 143.
———— population of, at the Survey, ii. 462.
Saumur, church of St. Florentius at, i. 216.
Scalariis, Hardwinus de, account of, i. 484.
Scohies, William de, i. 217, 485.
Scutularius, i. 92, 93.
Seals of Edward the Confessor and King William, i. 40, 41.
—— of Odo bishop of Baieux, i. 41.
—— of Robert de Oilgi, i. 41.
Seisin, instances of the ancient method of giving, i. 338, 339.
Servi, i. 86, 264, 265.
—— form of emancipation of the, i. 87.
—— ranked, in the Survey of Cornwall, before the Villani and Bordarii, ii. 432.

Servi in Kent, placed after the mention of a church, ii. 461.
—— where ranked in the western counties in Domesday, ii. 502.
Servientes, i. 93.
" Servitium unius militis," i. 262.
Sewaldus, or Seuoldus, abbat of Bath, ii. 260.
" Sextarium," the measure of the, i. 133, 134.
———— for honey, of different capacities, i. 134.
Shaftsbury, Abbey of, i. 484.
———— population of the town of, at the Survey, ii. 440.
Sharnbrook, i. 468.
Shilling of the Domesday Survey, i. 166.
Shires, customs of the, enumerated, i. 189.
Shrewsbury, customs of, i. 200. ii. 482.
———— customs of the moneyers at, i. 176.
———— castle of, i. 219.
———— church of St. Mary at, i. 451.
———— churches of, generally, i. 485.
Shropshire, date of the Survey of that county ascertained, i. 8.
———— population of, at the Survey, ii. 480.
Sigar, ii. 307.
Sihricus, or Sihtricus, abbat of Tavistock, ii. 215.
" Silva alnorum," i. 101.
" Silva ad clausuram," i. 100.
" Silva in defenso," or "in defenso Regis," i. 100.
" Silva minuta or modica," i. 100.
Sites of places mentioned in Domesday, all memory of which is supposed to be lost, i. 41.
Siward, i. 320.
Siward, a rich Saxon of Shropshire, ii. 218.